A Handbook of Media and Communication Research

'This *Handbook* takes on a full range of communication research approaches with an intelligence, skill, and agility not found in methodology texts.'

Vincent Mosco, School of Journalism and Communication,
Carleton University, Canada

'*A Handbook of Media and Communication Research* presents an excellent overview of and introduction to the concepts and elements within major quantitative and qualitative research processes.'

Marit Bakke, Department of Media Studies, University of Bergen, Norway

'An authoritative, stimulating and rigorous survey of diverse research traditions in media and communications. The emphasis on identifying the potential for convergence across these traditions is both original and welcome.'

Sonia Livingstone, London School of Economics and Political Science

A Handbook of Media and Communication Research presents qualitative as well as quantitative approaches to the analysis and interpretation of media, covering perspectives from both the social sciences and the humanities. Combining practical approaches and theoretical concerns, the *Handbook* offers a comprehensive review of earlier research and a set of guidelines for how to think about, plan and carry out studies of media in different social and cultural contexts.

The *Handbook* comprises three main elements:

- a historical account of the development of key concepts and approaches
- a systematic section covering media production, texts and audience as well as the wider social, cultural and global contexts of media, and the changing role of computer-mediated communication
- a practical element taking readers through the stages of the research process as carried out in student projects.

Written by internationally acknowledged specialists in each area and supported throughout by keywords, up-to-date references and graphic models, the *Handbook* will be a standard reference work for students and researchers in the field of media, communication and cultural studies. Contributors include: Barrie Gunter, Stig Hjarvard, Klaus Bruhn Jensen, Peter Larsen, Amanda Lotz, Graham Murdock, Horace Newcomb, Paddy Scannell, Kim Christian Schroder, Gaye Tuchman.

Klaus Bruhn Jensen is Professor in the Department of Film and Media Studies, University of Copenhagen and Adjunct Professor at the University of Oslo. His previous publications include *A Handbook of Qualitative Methodologies for Mass Communication Research* (coeditor, Routledge, 1991) and *News of the World: World Cultures Look at Television News* (editor, Routledge, 1998).

A Handbook of Media and Communication Research

Qualitative and quantitative methodologies

Edited by
Klaus Bruhn Jensen

London and New York

First published 2002
by Routledge
11 New Fetter Lane, London EC4P 4EE

Simultaneously published in the USA and Canada
by Routledge
29 West 35th Street, New York, NY 10001

Routledge is an imprint of the Taylor & Francis Group

© 2002 Klaus Bruhn Jensen for selection and editorial;
individual chapters to their authors

Typeset in Sabon and Gill by
Florence Production Ltd, Stoodleigh, Devon.

Printed and bound in Great Britain by
Bell & Bain Ltd, Glasgow

British Library Cataloguing in Publication Data
A catalogue record for this book is available from the British Library

Library of Congress Cataloging in Publication Data
has been applied for

ISBN 0–415–22514–0 (hbk)
ISBN 0–415–22588–4 (pbk)

Contents

Illustrations

PLATES

TABLES

ANALYSIS BOXES

RESOURCE BOXES

Contributors

Barrie Gunter is Professor of Journalism Studies and Director of Research, Department of Journalism Studies, University of Sheffield. He is a chartered psychologist who has worked in the media sector as an audience researcher and has written 40 books and around 200 other publications on a range of media, marketing, and psychological topics.

Stig Hjarvard, Ph.D., Professor, Department of Film and Media Studies, University of Copenhagen. Head of the research program 'Global Media Cultures' (http://www.global. media.ku.dk). Recent books are *Internationale tv-nyheder* [International TV news] (1995), *Tv-nyheder i konkurrence* [TV news in competition] (1999), *Audiovisual Media in Transition* (co-edited with Thomas Tufte, Sekvens, 1998) and *News in a Globalized Society* (editor, 2001).

Klaus Bruhn Jensen is Professor in the Department of Film and Media Studies, University of Copenhagen, and Adjunct Professor at the University of Oslo. His work has addressed interdisciplinary theories and methodologies within media studies, with a special emphasis on reception analysis. Earlier publications include *A Handbook of Qualitative Methodologies for Mass Communication Research* (co-editor, 1991) and *News of the World: World Cultures Look at Television News* (editor, 1998). His current work focuses on computer-mediated communication, and its implications for the field of 'media' and 'communication' research.

Peter Larsen, Professor at the Department of Media Studies, University of Bergen, Norway. He is the author of books and articles on semiotics, rhetoric, music in the visual media, textual analysis, and text theory in connection with film, television, and other forms of visual communication.

Amanda D. Lotz (Ph.D., University of Texas at Austin) is a Mellon postdoctoral fellow and instructor in the Program in Film and Media Studies and Program in American Culture Studies at Washington University in St. Louis. Her research focuses on the representation of women and feminism on television, with attention to emerging feminist theories such as post-feminism and third-wave feminisms, and the U.S. institutional environment of the post-network era.

Graham Murdock graduated from the London School of Economics and went on to do research at the Centre for Mass Communications Research at Leicester University, before joining the interdisciplinary department of Social Sciences at Loughborough in 1990. He has been a visiting professor at the Universities of Bergen, Brussels, California, Mexico City, and Stockholm, and his work has been translated into thirteen languages. His most recent books include, as co-author, *Researching Communications* (1999), and as co-editor, *Television Across Europe* (2000).

Horace Newcomb is Lambdin Kay Distinguished Professor and Director of the Peabody Awards Program at the University of Georgia, and was, until recently, the F. J. Heyne Centennial Professor in Communication at the University of Texas at Austin. He is co-author, with Robert S. Alley, of *The Producer's Medium* (1983). He is also author of *TV: The Most Popular Art* (1974), editor of six editions of *Television: The Critical View* and editor of The Museum of Broadcast Communication *Encyclopedia of Television* (1997).

Paddy Scannell is Professor and Head of Research in the School of Communication and Creative Industries at the University of Westminster. He is a founding editor of *Media, Culture and Society*, author of *Radio, Television and Modern Life* (1996), and co-author, with David Cardiff, of *A Social History of British Broadcasting, 1922–1939* (1991).

Kim Christian Schrøder is Professor of Communication at Roskilde University, Denmark.

His research has dealt with discourse analysis and reception analysis of advertising and televised serial fiction. He has published widely on the theoretical and methodological aspects of qualitative audience research. His current research deals with political discourses and the media in a combined text/audience perspective.

Gaye Tuchman is Professor at the University of Connecticut, and has specialised in research within the Sociology of Culture, Gender, and Theory. She is the author of many publications in these areas, such as *Making News* (1978), *Edging Women Out: Victorian Novelists, Publishers, and Social Change* (1989, co-author) and a contribution to the first edition of *Handbook of Qualitative Research* (1994). Current research interests include special education and invisible differences in children.

Preface

This book covers the state of media and communication research – its development, present status, and future potential. It is addressed to students, researchers and media professionals seeking an in-depth treatment of the field.

In recent years, media studies have gone through a process of convergence between social sciences and humanities, quantitative and qualitative approaches. This book presents the diverse theoretical sources of current media studies and provides examples of different research techniques. It also outlines the profile of this academic field, as it relates to the rest of the academy and to contemporary society.

To serve as an accessible yet comprehensive handbook, the volume includes a number of features:

- *examples* of the main types of media *analysis*, including production research, textual analysis and audience studies;
- *reviews* and *comparisons* of the central traditions of theory and methodology;
- *resources* and extensive *references* for the planning of empirical research projects;
- *keywords* and *cross-references*;
- *abstracts*, as well as *figures and tables* summarizing the main points of each chapter.

In preparing the volume, I have had the privilege of cooperating with a number of competent and generous people. First of all, I am grateful to the contributors to the volume, who agreed to join me in the process of developing this reference work. Simultaneously, I have benefited from many discussions with, and suggestions from, colleagues at the University of Copenhagen and at the University of Oslo.

While drafting the text, I have drawn much inspiration as a member of two research programs: Global Media Cultures (1999 to 2001) at the University of Copenhagen (http://global.media.ku.dk) and DIWA (1999 to 2003) (Design and use of Interactive Web Applications – http://www.diwa.dk), a joint project of four Danish universities. Svein Østerud has been a continually constructive partner in debates on methodology for more than ten years. Special thanks are due to Peter Dahlgren and Søren Kjørup who both took the time to read and offer constructive criticisms on earlier drafts of several chapters.

My deepest thanks go to Ghita – my wife, my friend, and a real human being.

Klaus Bruhn Jensen
Copenhagen, April 2001

NOTE

Key concepts and discussions of key terms are indicated by a marginal note beside their first place of mention in the text.

The symbol ◄ in the text indicates a cross reference to the preceding text which can be found below.

The symbol ► at the foot of a column indicates the cross reference linked to its mention in the above column.

While the publishers have made every effort to contact copyright holders of material used, they would be grateful to hear from any they may have been unable to locate in order to rectify any omissions in subsequent printings of this volume.

Introduction

The state of convergence in media and communication research

Klaus Bruhn Jensen

- a reassessment of the field with reference to the three concepts of *media*, social *structure*, and human *agency*
- a distinction between *media of three degrees*: speech, technologically reproduced communication, and computer-mediated communication
- a comparison of *culture* in the narrow sense of aesthetic works and in the broad sense of a whole way of life
- a definition of modern media as *institutions-to-think-with*
- a presentation of a *communication model* which integrates traditional transmission and ritual models
- *outline* of the handbook, its elements, and interrelations.

MEDIA, STRUCTURE AND AGENCY

At least since the self-consciously titled 'Ferment in the Field' issue of the *Journal of Communication* (1983), there has been a recognition within media and communication research that the diverse theoretical and methodological sources of the field, in the social sciences and in the humanities, hold a significant potential for consolidation through integration. Toward this end, one comprehensive conceptual framework is available in the work of Giddens (1984), even if its particular relevance for media remains to be developed (for assessments, see Bryant and Jary 1991; Held and Thompson 1989). His structuration theory is, first and foremost, a meta-theory which seeks to move both empirical and theoretical studies beyond certain entrenched dualisms from more than a century of social and cultural research, including subjectivist *or* objectivist, interpretive *or* causal, hermeneutic *or* materialist, micro- *or* macro-approaches to society and culture.

The key to Giddens' integrative move is the notion of a 'duality of structure,' which defines human agency and social structure each as an enabling condition of the other. Human agency, accordingly, is not the manifestation of any free will, as exercised by individuals or collectivities, nor is social structure a set of external constraints on their action. Instead, social subjects and social systems must be seen as continually reproducing and, to a degree, reforming each other, and they interact, not as abstract principles, but in concrete practices and contexts: 'structure exists . . . only in its instantiations in such practices and as memory traces orienting the conduct of knowledgeable human agents' (Giddens 1984: 17). To exemplify, the press consists simultaneously of its structural properties – its economic, legal, technological, as well as cultural-conventional permanence – *and* of the myriad activities of journalists, advertisers, regulators, and audiences who both maintain and contest these properties. Like other social institutions, the press, and the media as

duality of structure

such, are not only reinterpreted, but re-enacted on a daily basis.

In order to explain how some measure of stability emerges from social flux, structuration theory places special emphasis on the concept *reflexivity* of reflexivity. (For additional discussions of reflexivity and the meaning–action nexus, see Beck 1999: 109–132; Bourdieu 1977.) Giddens describes reflexivity as a general interpretive faculty that enables humans to ascribe meaning to their transactions with others, both in one's most intimate relations and in encounters with institutions of political or religious authority. Importantly, this meaning may not be articulated in any explicit form, neither in discourse nor even in consciousness. '"Reflexivity" should be understood not merely as "self-consciousness" but as the monitored character of the ongoing flow of social life' (Giddens 1984: 3).

The point is that reflexivity orients people and allows them to act, to go on, and that it would be possible for them, as a rule, to justify their actions if they were challenged. In most cases, however, people will simply go about their business, and will be able to coordinate it with that of others to a remarkable degree, by relying on shared, implicit assumptions, what *practical* Giddens terms their practical consciousness. *consciousness* This is in contrast to discursive consciousness, *discursive* a focused form of intentionality, that can be *consciousness* mobilized in response to one's own doubts or to alternatives advanced by others. (The third element of Giddens' model of consciousness is *the uncon-* the unconscious, which is largely comparable *scious* to its original Freudian version.) Listening to the radio, for instance, often serves the practical purpose of monitoring a morning routine until it is time for members of the household to leave for work or school, but a particular news item about public transport or road conditions may shift the listeners' attention into a discursive key because this might require actions out of the ordinary.

The media play a special role, both as means of reflexivity and as sources of social structuration. Giddens recognizes this, in part, by one of his central distinctions between technologically mediated and non-mediated social interaction or, in his terminology, system inte-

gration and social integration. In contrast to social integration, which refers to local, face-to-face interaction, system integration is defined as 'reciprocity between actors or collectivities across extended time–space, outside conditions of co-presence' (Giddens 1984: 377). One outcome of such mediated interaction is a 'disembedding' of people from their traditional relations and environments, and a 're-embedding' into different social formations. The reference is primarily to the modern era, which is characterized by the coordination of economic, political, and cultural activity across great distances and time differences, what Giddens calls 'time–space distanciation,'◄ increasingly on a global and round-the-clock scale (see also Giddens 1990, 1991). While social integration is performed, above all, by oral communication, system integration has depended on shifting technologies and institutions of communication, from handwritten administrative and accounting systems to broadcasting and beyond.

Nevertheless, Giddens has paid surprisingly little attention to the media as a condition of modernity. 'Signification,' including its technologically mediated forms, is one of his three dimensions of social systems, the other two being domination, namely the exercise of power through political and economic institutions, and legitimation as exercised typically by legal institutions (Giddens 1984: 29). But the pervasive communicative aspects of each of these, and of practically any type of social action, have remained a blindspot in Giddens' work (see Jensen 1995; Silverstone 1999; Thompson 1995).

A meta-theoretical framework that treats communication not as incidental, but as a necessary constituent of social life, is relevant not just to the media field, but to theories of society and culture as such. In order to move beyond the lingering dualism of 'the duality of structure,' it is helpful to introduce a third category of *medium*, on a par with agency and structure. In a historical and anthropological perspective, media include spoken and body language, scratch notes and government administrations,

► time–space distanciation, disembedding, and re-embedding – Chapter 11, p. 182

RESOURCE BOX 1.1 GENERAL REFERENCE WORKS AND JOURNALS

The following texts provide general resources and overviews for the field of media and communication research. The titles cover different traditions, as indicated, and include qualitative as well as quantitative methodologies.

Encyclopedia
- Barnouw 1989 – a multi-volume comprehensive reference work on most aspects of communication, including mediated and interpersonal forms
- Watson and Hill 1999 – a concise reference work.

Abstracts
- *Communication abstracts* – a listing with abstracts and keywords of current research.

Handbooks and textbooks
- McQuail 2000 – a solid introduction to positions in the field, with a relative emphasis on social-scientific traditions
- Berger and Chaffee 1987 – a somewhat dated, but still useful overview summarizing work defining communication studies as a 'science'
- Jensen and Jankowski 1991 – an overview delineating the contributions of qualitative research, both social-scientific and humanistic, to the media field
- Lindlof 1995 – a reference work emphasizing the interpretive legacy in social science and its relevance for qualitative empirical studies.

Journals
- *Journal of Communication* – since the mid-1970s a central journal in the field, accommodating both quantitative and qualitative, administrative and critical work
- *Communication Theory* – a more recent addition to the field, covering interpersonal communication as well, and with important theoretical contributions to the media field
- *Critical Studies in Media and Communication* and *Media, Culture and Society* – two representatives of a primarily critical as well as interpretive strand of media research
- *Journal of Broadcasting and Electronic Media* and *Journalism and Mass Communication Quarterly* – two representatives primarily of the quantitative, American mainstream of media research
- *Screen* – one of the journals focusing on film (and television), which also includes contributions with implications for the wider field
- *New Media and Society* – one of several journals currently shaping the area of computer-mediated communication.

---

broadcasting and the Internet. Their common characteristic is that they serve to orient human agency as it enacts social structure, partly at the level of practical consciousness and everyday routines.

MEDIA OF THREE DEGREES

The growth of computer-supported communication has recently presented 'mass' media research with a need to reconsider its central objects of study. Computers can integrate previous media technologies in a single meta-medium (Kay and Goldberg 1999 [1977]: 112); to a degree, computers can also simulate embodied, interpersonal communication. To indicate the scope of this handbook, it is useful to distinguish three prototypes of media:

1 *Media of the first degree*. The biologically based, socially formed resources that enable humans to articulate an understanding of

reality, for a particular purpose, and to engage with others in communication about it. The central example is verbal language, or speech, but additional ones include song and other musical expression, dance, drama, painting, and creative arts generally. Such media depend on the presence of the human body, and operate in local time–space, often relying on comparatively simple, mechanical techniques such as musical instruments and artistic and writing utensils as constitutive elements. (Handwriting presents a special case, which has supported complex historical communication systems. However, its comparatively inefficient forms of reproduction and distribution arguably made this a transitional cultural form (Meyrowitz 1994: 54).)

2 *Media of the second degree.* The technically reproduced or enhanced forms of representation and interaction which support communication across space and time, irrespective of the presence and number of participants (Benjamin 1977 [1936]). Early modern examples included the standardized reproduction of religious and political texts through the printing press (Eisenstein 1979). In radio talkshows, conversation took on new forms, just as acting styles were adapted to cinema and television. Thus, media technologies have performed a 're-embedding,' both of the media of the first degree and of people in relation to distant others, issues, and arenas.◀

3 *Media of the third degree.* The digitally processed forms of representation and interaction which reproduce and recombine previous media on a single platform. The central current example is the networked personal computer.◀ This 'interface' is likely to change substantially as the technologies are adapted further to the human senses, and integrated into both common objects and social arrangements. In certain respects, humans are media; in certain respects, media can substitute the social roles of humans.

Agency
• *Discursive* consciousness • *Practical* consciousness • the *Unconscious*

Structure

• *Resources*
    – Allocative (Re: objects, goods, material phenomena)
    – Authoritative (Re: persons, actors)
 	
• *Rules* (Re: meaning and sanctioning of social conduct)

Media
• Media of the *first* degree • Media of the *second* degree • Media of the *third* degree

Figure 1.1 Media in the structuration of society

Figure 1.1 brings media into a revised conceptual table of structuration theory. Whereas Giddens (1984: 374) has linked discursive consciousness with verbal expressions only, it remains important to examine how the full range of media relate to different levels of consciousness and forms of culture. Moreover, particularly in contemporary society, media are among the central social 'resources' in Giddens' terms, just as they are vehicles of many of the 'rules' that inform social interaction. This handbook focuses on media of the second degree; reviews media of the third degree as a growing field of social activity and study; and includes discussion and references on media of the first degree, as they relate to the technological media. Each of these media types facilitates social structuration in specific ways, and they do so by participating in the production and circulation in society of meaning, which accumulates as culture.

THE DUALITY OF CULTURE

Like studies of society, research on culture has been divided by dualisms, with two dominant definitions criss-crossing the humanities and social sciences.◀ On the one hand, culture has

▶ history of media and communication – Chapter 12

▶ computer-mediated communication – Chapter 11, p. 182

▶ the concept of culture – Chapter 11, p. 172

culture as aesthetic representation

been conceived as representations of reality – texts and other artefacts – which express some privileged insight, often in an arena such as a museum that is separate in space and time from the rest of social life. This understanding of culture as entities of meaning and vehicles of tradition was captured in Matthew Arnold's definition (1869), 'the best which has been thought and said in the world.' On the other hand, culture has come to be understood as the totality of human expression, artefacts, and forms of interaction, what Raymond Williams (1975 [1958]: 18) summed up as 'a whole way of life.' The two definitions have been associated with a further set of dualisms, including a focus on either text *or* context, high *or* popular culture, a normative-critical *or* descriptive ideal of science, and the qualitative interpretation *or* quantitative measurement of culture.

culture as social practice

A next step beyond dualism is to recognize a duality not only of social structure, but of culture as well. Culture is both product and process, and both aspects enter into social structuration at large. To begin, the duality of culture may be illustrated through concepts from the world of sports: time-out and time-in. In basketball and (American) football, for example, coaches can call for an interval to discuss strategy with their teams. While temporarily suspending the game, the time-out occurs within and addresses the total time-in of the game. By analogy, an institutionalized cultural activity such as media use partly suspends other activities, but still takes place within the everyday and with reference to families, parliaments, and other well-known institutions. In different respects, news, soap operas, and talkshows offer a cultural forum for collective reflexivity (Newcomb and Hirsch 1984).

time-out culture

Time-out culture places reality on an explicit agenda, as an object of reflexivity, and provides an occasion for contemplating oneself in a social or existential perspective, perhaps suggesting new avenues for agency. In this regard, mediated communication joins other cultural forms, from religious rituals to fine arts. Time-in culture is continuous with, constitutive of, and orients everyday life, thus regenerating social structure. As such, it supplies the often implicit premises and procedures of social interaction. Time-out culture prefigures social action; time-in culture configures social action.

time-in culture

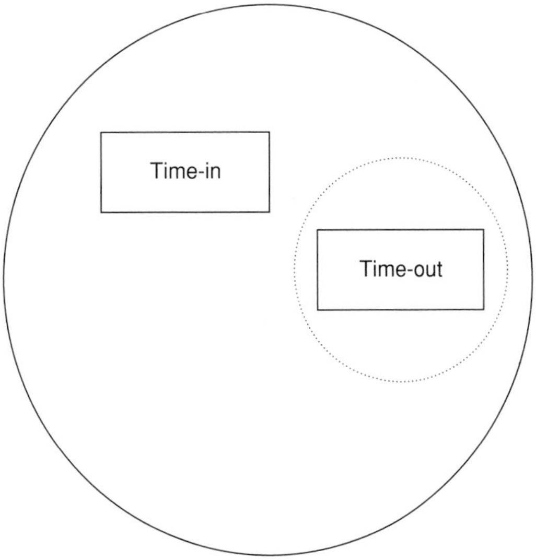

Figure 1.2 Time-in culture and time-out culture

Figure 1.2 illustrates the embedding of time-out within time-in culture and the permeable boundary between the two. Extending Giddens' (1984) terminology, one might say that various cultural practices enable their participants to commute between practical and discursive consciousness. Importantly, time-in culture and time-out culture are *not* separate activities or discourses, but simultaneous and complementary aspects of, for instance, media use. Going to the cinema can be an occasion to reflect on moral dilemmas in either marriage or business, not only in a generalized fictional universe, but equally in one's own life. Compared to reflexivity in psychotherapy, by which one may move from discursive and practical consciousness toward the unconscious, everybody thus moves back and forth between practical and discursive consciousness many times a day. While this recurring movement at the level of individual consciousness resembles the interchange between time-out and time-in culture at a systemic level, it is important to examine in detail how the two processes are intertwined under shifting historical circumstances. In social systems, reflexivity is commonly delegated to institutions of religion, science, and communication. In modern social systems, the practices of reflexivity are increasingly technologically mediated.

INSTITUTIONS-TO-THINK-WITH

The modern media are understood in this handbook, most basically, as technologies that enable reflexivity on a social scale, as they produce and circulate meaning in society. Beyond this meta-theoretical framework, one of the most applicable substantive theories of the media field has been provided in Jürgen Habermas' (1989 [1962]) early historical work, which is compatible with Giddens' systematic approach, despite differences of opinion and emphasis (e.g., Giddens 1984: 31).

Habermas' (1989 [1962]) main conclusion was that the social system of industrial capitalist democracies may be described as a set of interconnected, but relatively autonomous 'spheres' (Figure 1.3). The figure notes, to the right, the role of state agencies in providing a stable economic and legal frame for social life. To the left, industrial and other private enterprise or business unfolds in what is termed the social sphere, while the intimate sphere is the domain of family life. The mediating element of the system is the public sphere, comprising the major political and cultural institutions as well as the press as Fourth Estate.

the public sphere

Whereas, historically, the public sphere had a proactive function in asserting the economic and political rights of the individual, it can be said, more generally, to negotiate the terms of cooperation between social agents and the state. Most importantly, the public sphere is premised on the ideal of rational, democratic communication about the ends and means of social life. While Habermas emphasized the liberating, utopian potential of the public sphere, even while deploring its contemporary decline (see also Sennett 1974), later studies have continued to debate the status of the model as a historical, systematic, or normative theory of communication (see Calhoun 1992; Mortensen 1977; Negt and Kluge 1993 [1972]).

In this context, the model serves two purposes. First, it locates media on a conceptual map with the central institutions of contemporary society. Although Habermas (1989 [1962]) departed from early newspapers and literary clubs in Europe, the public sphere may be seen to include media of the first, second, as well as third degrees. What is commonly at issue, in both theoretical and normative approaches to media, is the nature of the interrelations between the spheres, especially their relative autonomy and the forces regulating conflicting interests. Evidently, the current media are governed as much by an economic logic as by a spirit of democratic dialogue, just as, in earlier periods, religious institutions and patrons of the arts set the conditions for cultural production. This handbook covers different theories of, and empirical findings about, the place of media in relation to the other spheres.

Second, the public sphere model offers an illustrative case of how the duality of structure, and of culture, operates. Rather than being a neutral organizational plan or an instance of 'false consciousness,' the model refers simultaneously to a *structure* of social institutions and to social *agents'* imagined relation to these institutions. In imagining this configuration, social agents reproduce, or contest, the institutional structure. Like the body (Johnson 1987), society is thus present in the human mind as a predisposition to act in particular ways. Because the public sphere model appears to inform the very organization of daily events, it is likely reproduced as common sense, as hegemony (Gramsci 1971) – 'a sense of absolute because experienced reality beyond which it is very difficult for most members of the society to move, in most areas of their lives' (Williams 1977: 110). Nevertheless, the public sphere institutions have introduced a potential for time-out reflexivity, as performed by individuals as well as collectivities.

To sum up, the modern technological media as social institutions are embedded in, but enable reflexivity about, the time-in of everyday life. They are institutions-to-think-with. The terminology derives from Claude Lévi-Strauss (1991 [1962]), who spoke of objects-to-think-with within anthropology (see also Douglas 1987). Especially animals, that can be

objects-to-think-with

	Society		State
	Private sphere	Public sphere	
	Intimate sphere	*Cultural public sphere*	The (agencies of the) state ensure(s) the material infrastructure, overall economic stability, law enforcement, and regulation of conflicts by economic, coercive, legal, and ideological means
Object	Religion, sexuality, emotion, friendship, etc.	Preaching, art, literature, music, etc.	
Institution	Family	Organizations, clubs	
	Social sphere	*Political public sphere*	
Object	Private economic activity, production and sale/purchase of commodities, including labor	'Politics' and 'the economy', including social issues	
Institution	Private enterprises and stores	Parliamentary organs, representing political parties, and the press	

Figure 1.3 A model of social spheres
Source: Adapted from Habermas 1989 [1962]; Mortensen 1977

eaten, become means of classifying and hence mastering reality. It is not so much that they are 'good to eat,' but that they are 'good to think (with)' (Lévi-Strauss 1991 [1962]: 89). In a different culture, the same object may mean something else, or may not be considered good to think with.

Compared to other objects-to-think-with, media technologies have material and structural features that designate them as specific cultural resources, the key feature being the 'programmability' also of pre-computer media. Unlike other artefacts, they serve as flexible, programmable vehicles of meaning in different cultures and historical periods. (In addition, media may function like other objects-to-think-with when, for example, a painting becomes a national symbol or a film genre is taken as symptomatic of cultural decline.) The most common way to link concretely the domain of media and com-munication research to wider cultural and social processes has probably been through models (McQuail and Windahl 1993; Meyrowitz 1993), being at once means of theoretical conceptualization and empirical operationalization.

THREE MODELS OF COMMUNICATION

In a 1975 benchmark article, James Carey (1989: 15) pinpointed the two communication models which arguably have been premises of most previous media research. (Several side- and substreams are documented in later chapters.) On the one hand, communication is the transmission of entities of meaning from a sender to a receiver via some contact. This model has typically informed social-scientific approaches to the field, and was given its classic formulation in Lasswell's (1966 [1948])

transmission model

questions, 'Who/Says What/In Which Channel/ To Whom/With What Effect?' A comparable formulation was the 'mathematical' theory of communication (Shannon and Weaver 1949), which, though initially addressing the transfer of messages in engineering terms as signals, became influential across the field, partly because Weaver's portion of the original text relied on metaphors that conflated notions of information and meaning (Jensen 1995: 8f.).

ritual model   On the other hand, Carey (1989) reasserted a ritual model of communication as the collective sharing of meaning and tradition and, hence, as a condition of community. The ritual model, with a particular emphasis on texts as the vehicles of shared meaning, can be traced in much humanistic research.

In a convergence perspective, both scholarly mainstreams can be seen to share two fundamental concerns about the *stages* and *levels* of communication in society, even if they have conceptualized and operationalized their concerns in distinctive ways. Although Lasswell's model has been widely criticized, both before and after Carey (1989), for compartmentalizing the stages in a topology of the communicative process, the humanities have joined the social sciences in recognizing that communication is stages of *also* a matter of message transmission in stages. communi- One of the most influential humanistic models cation   of communication (Figure 1.4) identified much the same elements as Lasswell (1966 [1948]), but conceptualized them as functions which, to varying degrees, manifest themselves *within* texts (Jakobson 1960). As a result, the text itself has been operationalized as the central object of analysis, leaving issues of production, reception, and context generally to be inferred from textual traces as well as supplementary evidence – much of which is available, not least, in organizational and audience studies from the social sciences.

Jakobson's (1960) model contributed two specific points to interdisciplinary research (italicized in Figure 1.4). First, communication depends on a *code*, i.e., a register of signs and symbols, beyond the physical contact or channel of Lasswell (1966 [1948]). Second, the *context* of communication should, for many analytical purposes, be conceived literally as

	Context	
Addresser	Message	Addressee
	Contact	
	Code	

Figure 1.4 The stages of communication
Source: Adapted from Jakobson 1960

discourse, as a con-text. Both of these points, in fact, have been taken to heart in much social science during its recent 'cultural turn' (Ray and Sayer 1999).

social levels   In addition, the several levels of communi- of communi- cation in society which maintain and transform cation   community, as emphasized in the humanistic-textual tradition, have been acknowledged in the 'dominant paradigm' of communication science (Gitlin 1978). A standard reference work such as Berger and Chaffee (1987) conceptualizes the field according to different social levels and contexts of communication, even if the individual acts of communication may tend to be operationalized as transmissions. The levels of interpersonal (for an overview see, e.g., interpersonal Knapp and Miller 1994) and organizational and organiza- (for an overview see, e.g., Goldhaber and tional com- Barnett 1988; Windahl *et al.* 1992) communi- munication cation are complementary to that of 'mass' communication.

Figure 1.5 illustrates the social levels of communication, each involving stages, agents, and differential forms of feedback, and each offering opportunities for both humanistic and social-scientific approaches, within and across levels. In addition, the figure reminds both traditions that mass-mediated communication is one of several types, and that, at least quantitatively, other forms of communication may be more important to the ongoing structuration of society.

Figure 1.6 proposes a way of integrating the ritual and transmission views in order to model the specific role of technological media. At the center of the model are the media (of the second and third degrees) operating in the public sphere. These media are the communicators – transmitters – of ideas and worldviews that feed into the processes of time-out as well as time-

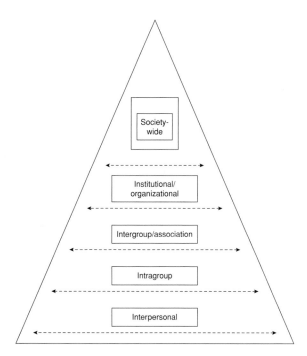

Figure 1.5 The levels of communication
Source: Adapted from McQuail 2000: 7

in the field – its identity – in a *methodological* sense. The fact that media are at once businesses, aesthetic forms, and cultural resources is of theoretical and empirical interest primarily to the extent that these features shape the mediated production of meaning. Precisely because of the complexity of the media as objects of analysis, the field must rely on a range of theoretical, disciplinary, as well as interdisciplinary approaches, taking into consideration a large periphery of explanatory factors that converge on its center.◀ The final section of this introduction explains how the theoretical, methodological, and empirical components of the handbook are prioritized and interrelated.

In review, Carey's (1989) account of the two disciplinary models indirectly recognized their integrative potential, when he quoted the pragmatist philosopher, John Dewey: 'Society exists not only by transmission, by communication, but it may fairly be said to exist in transmission, in communication' (p. 13f.). In a reconstructive formulation, society exists *both* by transmissions *and* in rituals. In structuration terms, communicative agency serves to both reproduce and contest social structure through transmission of, as well as ritual participation in, meaning.

Carey's 1975 definition of communication in public life as 'a symbolic process whereby reality is produced, maintained, repaired, and transformed' (Carey 1989: 23) seemed to anticipate Giddens' (1984) concept of 'the double hermeneutic.' Building on Winch (1963), and with special reference to how social science interprets an already interpreted reality, Giddens notes that such a double hermeneutic exchanges ideas back and forth between 'the meaningful social world as constituted by lay actors and the metalanguages invented by social scientists' (p. 384). Classic examples are the works of Freud and Marx, which have entered contemporary common sense. Opinion polls and policy studies similarly redirect the actions of both decision-makers and publics.

The modern media perform a continuous

the double hermeneutic

in culture, offering both a ritual sphere of reflexivity and practical means of coordinating everyday activities. The permeable boundaries indicate that the media themselves are part and parcel of social structuration. (The overlap between the media rectangle and the time-out circle is meant to suggest the distinctive role of media as institutions-to-think-with, not the degree of this overlap.)◀

The foundational question for the field, accordingly, is what difference the media make, not just in terms of their 'effects' on audiences, but for the rest of the social structure and for human agency, culture, and communication. This handbook takes the distinctive feature of media to be the production and circulation of meaning in modern societies, enabling collective reflexivity and coordinated action on an unprecedented scale. This implies that the media themselves occupy the center of interest

▶ models – and other forms of representations in research – Chapter 16, p. 275

▶ the media research institution as field or discipline? – Chapter 16, p. 279

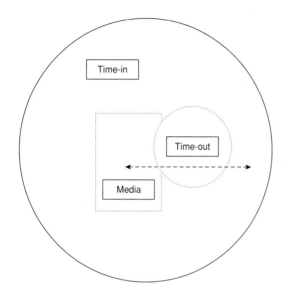

Figure 1.6 A model of media, communication and culture

and publicly accessible hermeneutic of social life. Media and communication research can contribute to a double hermeneutic by describing, interpreting, and explaining what difference the modern media make to different audiences and sectors of society.

OUTLINE OF THE HANDBOOK

This handbook is divided into three parts, covering the 'history' of media and communication studies in different disciplines and theoretical traditions; the 'systematics' of empirical research on different stages and contexts of communication; and the 'practice' of planning, conducting, and applying research. Figure 1.7 lays out this structure with reference to the scope and focus of each part, noting a key premise of each section; there can be no 'view from nowhere' in either communication (Epstein 1973) or science (Nagel 1986). Throughout this volume, methodologies are given special attention, because they encapsulate the analytical operations of the various traditions, along with their theoretical justifications, thus enabling concrete comparisons of the explanatory value of different forms of research.

- *Part 1 – History* traces the main explanatory concepts and approaches that have informed media and communication research. While noting the roots of the field in classical scholarship, such as rhetoric and poetics, and in early sociology, the two chapters, on the humanities and the social sciences, focus on contemporary conceptions of such key notions as culture and communication, interpretation and interaction. By way of introduction, Part I also delimits the media field from related cultural forms and areas of inquiry. One premise of the handbook, as outlined in this introduction, is that a convergence of social-scientific and humanistic perspectives has been taking place particularly since the 1980s. While this shift has arguably strengthened the overall quality and relevance of the field, the contributors also weigh the evidence regarding problems of convergence and integration.

convergence of social-scientific and humanistic perspectives

- *Part 2 – Systematics* turns from a diachronic to a synchronic view of different 'schools' of research. In a systematic perspective, the current schools represent distinctive conceptualizations of the stages, levels, and contexts of mediated communication. Whereas certain traditions are incompatible in their epistemological assumptions or research policies, they can be seen, in the systematic perspective, to complement and sometimes overlap each other in unrecognized ways. One divisive issue has been the degree to which technological, economic, and other conditioning factors could be said to determine either the structure or impact of media. Another premise of the handbook is that such factors exercise a determination in the first instance (Hall 1983), setting the limits of possible cultural forms, but not a determination in the final instance of either their social uses or aesthetics. This premise is in keeping with the dualities of structure and culture. The nature and degree of structuration in different aspects of mediated communication are empirical issues.

determination in the first instance

- *Part 3 – Practice* deals with various types of empirical research, and also addresses the social origins and applications of media studies. The orientation is to the future, to the extent that

	History	Systematics	Practice
Scope	Theoretical concepts and analytical procecures from: • Humanities • Social sciences	Empirical approaches to the stages and contexts of communication, as defined by different research traditions	Practices of conducting, justifying, and applying research
Focus	Past sources of ideas on media, culture, and communication	Present operationalizations and findings	Future uses of research in scientific and social institutions
Premise	Convergence	Determination in the first instance	Unification in the final instance

Figure 1.7 An anatomy of media and communication research

researchers and students are constantly re-enacting the field as part of a double hermeneutic that involves both the research institution and the rest of society. Special emphasis is placed on the methodological aspects of designing and conducting empirical studies, particularly the different procedures or 'logics' of qualitative and quantitative research – and the interfaces between them. Corresponding to the first premise concerning convergence, the last premise of the handbook is that a greater measure of unification is both possible and desirable for the field as such. Crucially, unification is more likely to succeed if it is developed not in the first instance, through a

standardization of the elementary research instruments, but in the final instance, through a comparative and meta-theoretical analysis of findings from different traditions, each with its distinctive explanatory value. Examining research as a social practice in itself, the final chapter returns to the political and historical contexts of media and communication studies, from the classic normative theories of the press, to contemporary media policy, and to instrumental uses in research and development. Like other sections of the handbook, Part III includes extensive references and boxed information with resources for further research.

unification in the final instance

History

SOURCES OF MEDIA AND COMMUNICATION RESEARCH

Media and communication research has developed from a long heritage of diverse scientific disciplines to address new conditions of communication in modern society. The two chapters in Part I present and assess the contributions of the humanities and the social sciences – the two 'faculties' or areas of inquiry which have been the main sources of theoretical concepts and analytical procedures.

As a preview, the following topics indicate the scope and focus of the field in its present configuration:

- *Media and communication.* The center of interest in the field are the technological media, but because they are examined as means of communication, they lend themselves to concepts and forms of analysis which have been derived from both oral and literate forms of communication down through history. And, because the media are studied in their social and cultural contexts, most of the research questions that have been developed by disciplines such as sociology and anthropology have proven their relevance for media studies, as well. 'Media' and 'communication,' in addition, are currently being redefined in the light of computer-mediated communication.

- *Humanities and social sciences.* The modern humanities can be traced from the early nineteenth century; the social sciences date from the late nineteenth and early twentieth centuries, when they separated institutionally from other 'human sciences.' During this entire period, the two areas of inquiry have been in contact, and frequently in dialogue. However, it was in the post-1945 period that specific components of each were brought together in the emerging field of media studies.

- *Field or discipline?* It remains an open question whether these contributions have merged sufficiently to constitute a traditional 'discipline,' as defined by its subject matter and consensual methods, as well as by its permanent institutional status. Several chapters in the volume address the question, and Chapter 16 elaborates on the current role of media studies in the wider society.

- *Convergence.* While leaving the question of disciplinary status open, this volume notes that a convergence between humanistic and social-scientific approaches has been ongoing in recent decades. The volume describes different elements and stages of this process, and indicates some possible lines of development for future research.

2 The humanities in media and communication research

Klaus Bruhn Jensen

- a *classical agenda*: the heritage of philosophy for communication theory
- *medium theory*: the implications of modern media technologies for classic issues of communication and culture
- four theoretical traditions originating in the humanities: *rhetoric, hermeneutics, phenomenology, semiotics*
- humanistic disciplines feeding into the interdisciplinary field of media studies: *art history, literary criticism, linguistics, film studies*
- current challenges to the humanities as well as to media and communication research: *postmodernism, feminism, cognitivism.*

A CLASSICAL AGENDA

Contrary to a widespread notion, the humanities are not direct descendants of classical Greek philosophy (Kristeller 1961: 3–23). In their recognizably modern form, the humanities date from the early nineteenth century, when universities were taking shape as institutions of research, as initially associated with the Humboldt tradition in Germany (Fallon 1980; Rudy 1984). The understanding of knowledge as a product of *research* had been preceded by at least two alternative conceptions of knowledge, either as *self-awareness* (summed up in the Delphi oracle's admonition to 'Know thyself!') or as traditional *learning*, administered and passed on by a class of learned people (Kjørup 1996: 31). While the latter two concepts are still encountered as subtexts, it is the development of analytical procedures and conceptual frameworks for research which has occupied humanistic scholars during the immediate 'prehistory' of media and communication research.

knowledge as
a product of
research

Much of the agenda for this development, to be sure, was inherited from the classics. They continue to be suggestive, less about what to think than which issues to think about, one example being conceptual problems shared across theories of knowledge and theories of communication. This chapter, accordingly, first retraces part of the classical agenda behind communication studies, before outlining the main traditions from the history of ideas that entered into the modern humanities – rhetoric, hermeneutics, phenomenology, and semiotics. These traditions, in turn, informed the disciplines – from linguistics and literary studies to art history and film studies – which ultimately fed into the field of media and communication. The chapter concludes with an assessment of how recent interdisciplinary challenges – postmodernism, feminism, and cognitivism – may redraw the map also of the media field.

A common denominator for the production of meaning in mediated communication and the production of knowledge in science is intersubjectivity:◄ How, by what means, is a shared understanding of certain phenomena in reality possible? Aristotle is sometimes credited with the first explicit formulation in Western philosophy, in *De Interpretatione* (*c.* 320 BCE), of the means by which a person can thus interact with other people about reality:

> Now spoken sounds are symbols of affections in the soul, and written marks symbols of spoken sounds. And just as written marks are not the same for all men, neither are spoken sounds. But what these are in the first place signs of – affections of the soul – are the same for all; and what these affections are likenesses of – actual things – are also the same.
>
> (Aristotle 1994: 43)

Things, *mental impressions*, and *communicative expressions* about each of these – those elements would be subscribed to by most theories of knowledge as well as of communication. But their interrelations, such as the assumption that the reality and the human experience to which communication bears witness, are in all circumstances 'the same,' have generated some of the most longstanding disputes across arts and sciences. Research has debated the existence of a unified reality, the social and cultural variability of experience, and the very relation between reality, the subject, and signs.

One particular implication of Aristotle's conception for communication theory was that signs serve as evidence of what is at least temporarily absent (Clarke 1990: 11) – in space, in time, from other people's purview, and from one's own immediate experience. Different media can represent phenomena that are not accessible through the senses (including the case of virtual or thought experiments). And certain durable media enable people to interact in each other's absence. Present signs allow for absent realities or communicators, or both.

If abstract thinking, self-awareness, and symbolic communication had provided the

minimal conditions for *humanitas*, for civilized   *humanitas*
social interaction (Megarry 1995: 48), writing and later technological media introduced a peculiar set of tools for human activity. They radically extended the potential for both social interaction and human transformation of the natural environment. That structural or conditioning 'effect' of media, for one thing, dwarfs any other effects the media may be shown to have on either individuals or institutions. For another thing, the understanding of such a 'medium effect' is one of the under-recognized contributions of historical and other humanistic research to media studies.

MEDIUM THEORY

In an overview and development of 'medium theory,' Meyrowitz (1994: 50) summed up its central question: 'What are the relatively fixed features of each means of communicating and how do these features make the medium physically, psychologically, and socially different from other media and from face-to-face interaction?' The last question in particular, suggesting a measure of technological determinism,◄ has given rise to a range of controversial answers.

The most well-known proponent of a strong position regarding the scope and depth of media impact on consciousness and culture, summed up in his dictum, 'the medium is the   'the medium
message,' remains Marshall McLuhan. One of   is the
his most influential books (McLuhan 1964)   message'
examined the media as extensions of the human senses with fundamental and permanent consequences for the awareness of self, others, and history. Among his polemical conclusions was that writing and, not least, print had constrained people within the linear logic of a typographic culture. In contrast, electronic media, and above all television, was said to signal a release of cultural creativity from 'the Gutenberg galaxy' (McLuhan 1962). This hope for a new polymorphous epoch is reminiscent of later utopian visions regarding cyberspace.

Being a literary scholar, McLuhan may have been tempted to map changes in the textual and

---

► intersubjectivity as a condition of communication and of research – Chapter 15, p. 267

► technological determinism – Chapter 12, p. 196

thematic structures of media rather directly onto the social and cultural context. His main source of inspiration, Harold A. Innis, another Canadian, but a political economist and historian, stated his arguments in a more traditional scholarly fashion (Innis 1964 [1951], 1972 [1950]). Applying principles from the study of economic monopolies to information monopolies, he identified some of the ways in which power can be exercised, and subverted, via media. Like other medium theorists, he pointed to the historical significance of media challenging religious authorities, when 'the medieval Church's monopoly over religious information, and thereby over salvation, was broken by the printing press' (Meyrowitz 1994: 51). Innis suggested, more grandly, that the structure of entire cultures and empires has a 'bias' toward either space or time, in the sense that the dominant media may favor either stability over time or extended territories.◄ Examples include stone tablets, whose inscriptions last a long time but do not travel well, as opposed to papyrus and paper, which will support the administration of distant provinces, but which are vulnerable to destruction and to being appropriated for purposes of social change.

Though less familiar in the media field, other researchers working from historical and anthropological angles have substantiated the relevance of medium theory. Like Innis, they seek to avoid any strong technological determinism, exploring the social and cultural forms in which technology is diffused and adapted. In a historical perspective, Havelock (1963) suggested how writing and literacy had paved the way for a novel category of social system, interpreting Plato's attack on the poets as announcing the passing of an oral culture. Poets could no longer be trusted in social matters, such as politics, the writing of history, and science, even if their poetry could still be appreciated as personal opinion or myth. Regarding the next categorical transition, Eisenstein (1979) showed how, initially, it was the scribal culture of elites centered in monasteries, not oral or popular culture, that was transformed by the printing press, leading into Renaissance and Reformation.

From an anthropological perspective, Goody and Watt (1963) questioned relativist positions regarding communication systems and the cultures they will support. One of their points was to reassert the understanding of literacy as a strategic resource and a necessary condition of, for example, political democracy (see also Goody 1987, 2000). The general point was documented empirically in a major study by Scribner and Cole (1981), who additionally showed that, within one culture, several different literacies and social uses may be associated with different languages (Vai, Arabic, and English). Also today, oral story-telling is a social movement in different cultural contexts as well as an active field of research (MacDonald 1998).◄

It seems an open question whether such different forms of communication and consciousness, as associated with different media technologies, should lead to categorizations or periodizations involving oral, scribal, print, electronic, and digital 'cultures.' Walter Ong (1982), for one, has described the distinctive experiential qualities of oral as opposed to literate culture, but has been tempted by his Jesuit frame of reference to privilege the quasi-religious authenticity of the Word. What the work of Ong and others does suggest, however, is the importance of studying the specificity of different media, as the technologies are given a particular social shape in historical and cultural context. As if to prove their point that ideas are shaped by contemporary media, several of the key studies cited here were published within the span of a few years (Goody and Watt 1963; Havelock 1963; McLuhan 1964). This happened at a time when television was contributing to a new agenda for research as well as public opinion about 'culture' and 'the media.'◄ In the academy as well as in the rest of society, television challenged taste cultures and social lines of division, as later studied by Meyrowitz (1985).

Medium theory has delineated a fertile area both for empirical research and for theoretical integration, occupying a middle ground

cultures: oral, scribal, print, electronic, digital

► the 'bias' of communication – Chapter 12, p. 195

► history of the media and of communication – Chapter 12, p. 194

– c. 25,000	cave paintings by prehistoric humans
– c. 3100	hieroglyphics and cuneiform writing
– c. 1800	Linear A writing
– c. 1600	first known alphabet (Palestine)
– c. 1450	Linear B writing
– c. 1200	Chinese ideographic writing
– c. 1000	Phoenician alphabet
– c. 730	phonetic alphabet (Greece)
1041	printing from movable type (China)
1241	metal type for printing (Korea)
1456	Gutenberg prints from movable metal type and hand press (Germany)
1609	regularly published newspaper (Germany)
1814	flatbed cylinder press
1839	photography
1844	telegraph
1846	double-cylinder rotary press
1867	typewriter
1876	telephone
1888	phonograph for public sale
1895	films shown to public
1895	radio transmission
1911	television transmission
1920	scheduled radio broadcasting
1936	scheduled television broadcasting
1945	programmable electronic computer
1947	transistor
1948	long-playing gramophone record
1956	videotape
1957	satellite (Sputnik)
1962	television transmission via satellite
1963	compact cassette audiotape
1969	ARPANET
1971	microprocessor
1976	VHS video cassette recorder
1976	teletext
1978	telefax (with international standard)
1979	Walkman
1980	Cable News Network (CNN)
1981	Music Television (MTV)
1981	IBM personal computer
1982	audio compact disk
1984	Apple Macintosh computer
1991	World Wide Web

Figure 2.1 A brief chronology of human communication

Source: Adapted from Rogers 1986: 25–26; see also Project 1996; Robinson 1995; Winston 1998

between the textual focus of the humanities and the institutional focus of the social sciences. Certainly, it lends itself to deterministic and hyperbolic formulations of the kind that made McLuhan a personality also *in* the media. Still, if applied carefully, medium theory can support a consolidation of media studies in a middle range (Merton 1968: 39),◀ steering empirical research between the Scylla of myopic methodologies and the Charybdis of grand theories. In the humanities, the main currents of ideas have themselves been shaped, in part, by their orientation toward a specific medium and its uses in social practice. The primary example, both historically and in terms of its continued influence on the study of communication, is the art, practice, and science of rhetoric, which revolves around spoken language.◀

▶ middle range theories – Chapter 3, p. 55

▶ speech as a medium of the first degree – Chapter 1, p. 3

FOUR TRADITIONS IN THE HISTORY OF IDEAS

Rhetoric

The rhetorical tradition is by far the oldest set of ideas informing humanistic research, and it remained centrally influential in both scholarship and education under different cultural and institutional circumstances from Antiquity into the nineteenth century (Kennedy 1980). Its legacy for contemporary research on communication and culture can be summarized briefly with reference to three sets of concepts. First, the rhetorical tradition refers to five stages in preparing a speech:

- *inventio* (the collection and conception of the subject matter)
- *dispositio* (structuring the speech)
- *elocutio* (its linguistic articulation)
- *memoria* (memorizing the resulting configuration of form and content)
- *actio* (performing the speech).

Of these five stages, *inventio* in particular recognizes an intimate relationship between knowing something and knowing how to communicate about it. Certain ways of speaking are appropriate in a political arena, others in a courtroom, others again on a festive occasion; each context has its own purpose and subject matter, which are given material shape in the speech. *Dispositio* and especially *elocutio*, next, supply the concrete means of shaping the speech. Rhetorical figures of speech and various symbolic forms have entered into both the study and practice of much literature and other arts.

Second, in addressing the audience through *actio*, a speaker draws on three means of persuasion:

- *ethos*
- *logos*
- *pathos*.

These focus, respectively, on the character of the speaker, the quality of his/her arguments, and the emotions which the speech is designed to evoke in the listeners. Importantly, the three means all appear in any act of communication, but in different measures and combinations, depending on the purpose and, hence, the genre of communication. Whereas the three aspects of addressing an audience have the most obvious relevance for such explicitly 'persuasive' genres as advertising and political communication, they lend themselves to the study of most types of mediated communication.

Third, the concept of *topos*, which classical rhetoric considered as one part of *inventio*, is of special interest, because it suggests a figure of thought that suffuses modern humanities as well. *Topos* means 'place,' and implies that commonplaces are, literally, common places in a known or imagined terrain which speakers share with their audience. This understanding of reality as a text and, conversely, of the text as a spatio-temporal universe that can be searched for traces and clues, has been a persistent metaphor in the humanities up until, and including, theories of postmodernity and cyberspace. A 'topical' form of argument can rely on one or a few concrete examples, rather than a great deal of inductive evidence, as long as the examples fit into the commonplaces which make up the working assumptions of people in their everyday affairs. Accordingly, Aristotle noted, rhetoric is the source of a kind of knowledge which is probable and reasonable. In this regard, rhetoric is complementary to logic, which addresses other aspects of reality about which certain or necessary knowledge can be achieved (Clarke 1990: 13).

The close link between communication and knowledge in classical rhetoric was gradually relaxed, as witnessed by the development of so many practical manuals of speaking well in public. This shift helps to account for the common pejorative reference to 'only rhetoric,' to communication as a superficial form and as misrepresentation and manipulation. Furthermore, rhetorical concepts were redeveloped from their oral sources and applied to literate forms of communication, for example, literary fiction and, later, to 'texts' in general. Nevertheless, the rhetorical tradition has remained an important source of ideas regarding the nature of both interpersonal and mediated communication. During the twentieth century, rhetoric enjoyed a renaissance, sometimes under the heading of a 'new rhetoric' (Perelman 1979), which, among other things, gave more specific

topos

the new rhetoric

attention to the interaction of communicators with their concrete audiences. A second inspiration for research on the social uses of communication came from analytic philosophy and its examination of the structure of informal argument (Toulmin 1958).

Although European scholarship may have been especially instrumental in feeding the rhetorical tradition into contemporary communication theory, also in this area there has been a vigorous American substream of humanistic research (Kennedy 1980). Among the most important influences has been the work of Kenneth Burke, who developed a view of language as action (Burke 1950), in addition to accounting for literature as a social, as well as an aesthetic, phenomenon (e.g., Burke 1957). His perspective was subsequently applied to the mass media, for example, in the case of political communication (e.g., Duncan 1968; Edelman 1971). In the media field, Carey (1989) has been a central figure advocating such a rhetorical as well as historical perspective on the interrelations between modern media and earlier cultural forms. As expressed in his ritual model,◄ also technologically mediated 'communication' serves to create and maintain 'community' – the common root of the two words suggests as much.

Saying something is doing something. One lesson of rhetoric for current media studies is the understanding of communication as a form of action. Throughout the history of the humanistic disciplines reviewed below, an important challenge has been to strike a balance between this pragmatic-processual conception of communication and a focus on the structure of linguistic and other textual vehicles. At different times, humanistic research has taken either linguistic◄ or pragmatic◄ turns, respectively emphasizing communication as structure or as action.

A similar balancing act has been performed by various literary as well as linguistic approaches to the contents or texts of media.

This has been especially important in the media field, since media texts are so evidently a part of social life. In comparison, literature and other fine arts have been studied, not least for their inherent structure and value. As a result, current media research has relied extensively on discourse analysis and other approaches to the social uses of language (for an overview see van Dijk 1997; Wetherell *et al.* 2001). A rhetorical-pragmatic concept of communication also furnishes one of the connections between humanistic research on media texts and social-scientific research on practices of communication.

The basic rhetorical insight, that language serves to configure knowledge, is borne out, finally, in the concrete analytical procedures of many humanistic media studies. Humanistic researchers tend to assume that ideas take on their final shape only when committed to language and paper. Just as children do not merely learn to read, but equally read to learn (Heath 1980: 130), so both researchers and other adults do not merely learn to write – they write to learn. Since the 1970s, a growing number of empirical studies have shown how the humanities as well as other scientific fields articulate themselves and their findings in distinctive rhetorical forms (e.g., Brodkey 1987; Gilbert and Mulkay 1984; Gross 1990; Hacking 1983; Latour 1987; Nelson *et al.* 1987; Simon 1989). The prototypical social-scientific journal article tends to assume that factual findings and a subsequent interpretive discussion can and should be placed in separate sections, and that the theoretical categories being examined can be stated succinctly from the outset. In contradistinction, humanistic articles or reports will move repeatedly among and across these several levels of analysis, in part to capture the many layers and contexts of their characteristic objects of analysis. These two formats of publication,◄ in fact, may be seen to mirror the two standard communication models: Social scientists 'transmit' their findings to readers, whereas humanistic scholars seek to join their readers in a form of rhetorical 'ritual.'

► ritual model of communication, see Chapter 1, p. 8

► the linguistic turn, p. 26

► the pragmatic turn, p. 38

► publication formats of different research traditions – Chapter 16, p. 274

Hermeneutics

While the point of departure for rhetoric was speech, particularly concerning matters of fact and how to argue about them, hermeneutics developed out of the practice of reading and understanding written texts,◄ not least narratives. Its general purpose has been to clarify the nature and conditions of interpretation, with reference both to the text and to the activity of the reader.

The texts at issue originally belonged to religion and law. Over time, the principles and procedures of hermeneutics came to be applied to the arts as well as to other kinds of texts, and indeed to human experience as such. In a historical overview, Ricoeur (1981: ch. 1), himself a central contributor to modern hermeneutic philosophy, identified a transition in the early nineteenth century from a 'regional' to a 'general' hermeneutics which now covered both secular and religious texts. The transition was advanced particularly in the work of the German theologian and philosopher, Friedrich Schleiermacher.

Hermeneutics thus participated in a long movement within the history of ideas, from a religious cosmology toward a historical, secular understanding of human existence.◄ The medieval analogy between The Book of Nature and other books as means of insight into 'the the great great chain of being' (Lovejoy 1936), in which chain of being everything has its divinely sanctioned place, was finally breaking down. Texts became a new focus of attention in themselves, as sources of scientific evidence and of aesthetic contemplation, rather than being primarily interfaces with the hereafter. At the inception of the modern humanities, then, the Text was taking center stage, together with the individual human being. Hermeneutics appeared to offer means of resolving interpretive conflicts, also beyond matters of faith and aesthetics.

The implications of hermeneutics for doing communication research are suggested by the the hermen- key concept of a 'hermeneutic circle' (Figure eutic circle

---

▶ writing as transitional form between media of the first and second degree – Chapter 1, p. 4

▶ secularization – Chapter 11, p. 174

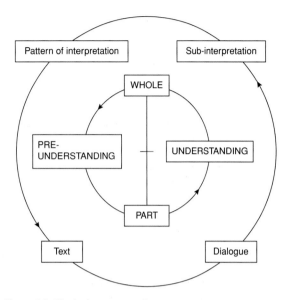

Figure 2.2 The hermeneutic circle

Source: Alvesson and Sköldberg 2000: 66. With permission of Sage Publications Ltd.

2.2). The most basic, ancient insight of hermeneutics is that the meaning of a textual part can only be understood in relation to the whole of the text. While perhaps commonsensical, this insight contradicts the equally common assumption that the meaning of a message is the sum of its parts, so that communication might be studied by breaking it down into its constituent elements. Hermeneutics suggests that the very process of both reading and analyzing a text is incremental and creative – readers gradually work out their categories of understanding in order to arrive at a coherent interpretation.

This dialectic at the level of the individual text, however, is only the first step in working out its meanings and implications. Next, the textual whole must itself be interpreted as part of larger totalities. For example, a novel may express the mindset of its author, who might be said to articulate the worldview of his epoch or culture. Such an understanding of the text–context nexus as one aspect of the part–whole dialectic dates from the period when a general hermeneutics, applying to all kinds of texts, was conceived.

A further development of the hermeneutic

circle which, more specifically, took into account the role of the reader, occurred during the twentieth century. The point appears from another set of twin concepts – pre-understanding and understanding – which was developed especially in the work of Gadamer (1975 [1960]). On the one hand, any understanding requires a pre-understanding – a 'prejudice' in the neutral sense. On the other hand, understanding serves to reproduce or contest the reader's pre-understanding. Throughout the activity of reading, people perform minimal or sub-interpretations, which may realign their frames of interpretation. In doing so, they enter into a 'dialogue' with the text and, by extension, with other minds, past as well as present. Most grandly, they partake of culture – the cultivation of tradition.

The hermeneutic circle may be understood as a model of communication, as it evolves not just in the here and now, but down through history and across cultures. In hermeneutic (and phenomenological) terminology, communica- **fusion of** tion involves a 'fusion of horizons' – a meeting **horizons** and merging of the expectations that communicators bring with them into the exchange. Especially recent contributors to hermeneutics have pointed to the dangers of fusion and of an immediate empathy with tradition. Referring to the works of Marx, Nietzsche, and Freud, Ricoeur (1981: 46) identified and developed **hermeneutics** a 'hermeneutics of suspicion.' Its particular **of suspicion** purpose is to discover hidden principles behind what other people as well as social institutions say and do, thus enabling a distinction between surface and 'reality.' Since the principles at work may equally be hidden to those persons and institutions, the social task of hermeneutics may be seen as a general one of reading between the lines of society and feeding its interpretations back into appropriate fora. In particular, the critical tradition in social science, and in media research, has taken on this task in studies both of texts and social practices.

The lasting influence of hermeneutics on media studies lies at two different levels. First, hermeneutics has been a source of specific inspirations, such as theoretical frameworks in reception studies of literature and media (for an overview see Holub 1984), and methodological

approaches to, for instance, source criticism in historiography (for an overview see Alvesson and Sköldberg 2000: ch. 3). Second, the hermeneutic tradition serves as a constant reminder that all social and cultural research is a hermeneutic, and doubly hermeneutic◄ (Giddens 1984), activity, interpreting the interpretations of others.

Phenomenology

Interrelated with hermeneutics in the history of ideas and as a methodological orientation in some current social research (e.g., Kvale 1996), phenomenology emerged as a distinctive school of philosophy around 1900. The date is significant, because phenomenology may be understood as a defensive reaction against the reductionism, in the form of either positivism◄ or 'psychologism,' which was then seen to threaten a humanistic understanding of consciousness as a lived and interpreted whole. In response, the phenomenological tradition insisted on the unique qualities and insights of ordinary human experience (for an overview see Schmitt 1972). In the social sciences, where its influence has arguably been at least as strong as in the humanities, phenomenology came to provide a philosophical legitimation for interpretive studies of social life, a minority position in the social sciences.◄ In the humanities, phenomenology entered into the mainstream, but proposed to redevelop key concepts of the humanistic heritage, such as interpretation and subjectivity.

Edmund Husserl, the originator of modern phenomenology, was also the author of its ambiguous motto, *Zu den Sachen selbst* (to the things themselves) (Alvesson and Sköldberg 2000: 36). These 'things' were not material objects, but those elements which constitute the core of human experience and existence, what Husserl referred to as the 'lifeworld.' In order **lifeworld** to gain a better understanding of one's lifeworld, one should perform 'reductions' of

▶ double hermeneutic – Chapter 1, p. 9

▶ positivism – Chapter 15, p. 260

▶ phenomenological social science – see Chapter 3, pp. 42, 56

various types in order to capture its qualitative essence. Far from breaking up experience into minimal units corresponding to, for instance, sense data, a phenomenological reduction *epoché* involves a 'bracketing' (*epoché*) of experience as a whole from its circumstances. Husserl's ambition was to reinvent philosophy as a science in the strict sense. Central to this ambition was an attempt to close the subject–object divide, which had been haunting Western philosophy at least since Descartes (Rorty 1979). Husserl argued that human consciousness, or intentionality, is always intentionality *of something*, not a mental category that is forever separated from external reality.

In order to explain more concretely how human subjects relate to objects in reality, *horizon* Husserl introduced the concept of a 'horizon' (as present also in hermeneutics). The concept refers to the configuration of a person's life-world at any given moment, pointing both forward and backward in time. A horizon comprises a set of interpretive categories available to the person from a long biography of socialization and acculturation. This horizon will change or be modified over time, as the person enters into new contexts, undertakes new projects, and interacts with other people. From this general philosophical category, other humanistic research derived a discursive conception of horizons, defined as historically and culturally specific frameworks of expectations that guide the interpretation of texts. A 'misunderstanding' of a text can result from an incompatibility between the horizon implicit in the text and the reader's horizon of expectations; a 'disagreement' about the meaning of a text can be the product of conflicting interpretive horizons.

Phenomenology has had less of an influence on media studies than either rhetoric or hermeneutics. This may be, in part, because its abstract conceptual analyses have seemed less applicable to the concrete textual vehicles and social practices of communication – phenomenology has no evident 'medium.' Nevertheless, some film studies in particular have taken their lead from the phenomenological bracketing of experience, and have gone on to bracket film texts in order to get at their essential experiential qualities that resemble the multimodal life-

world. More recently, Scannell (1996a) has suggested, with particular reference to broadcasting, that the radical hermeneutics (Ricoeur 1981: 45) and phenomenology of Martin Heidegger may capture the distinctive features of an increasingly mediatized modern existence.

Semiotics

Of the four humanistic traditions, semiotics exercised the most direct influence in the formation of media studies as a field, and thus calls for some elaboration. Defined most famously as a science that studies 'the life of signs within society' (Saussure 1959 [1916]: 16), semiotics became one of the most influential interdisciplinary approaches to the study of culture and communication generally from the 1960s onward. The tradition addresses all types of media,◀ and offers methodological procedures, theoretical models, as well as constituents of a theory of science. In its most ambitious formulations, semiotics proposed to examine languages, images, psyches, societies, even biology and cosmology as sign processes (Posner *et al.* 1997–98; Sebeok 1986). More commonly, the semiotic tradition has contributed analytical procedures and methodological frameworks, which have lent a new form of systematicity to humanistic research on texts.

Semiotics had two founding fathers in the late nineteenth and early twentieth centuries – the American philosopher and logician Charles Sanders Peirce and the Swiss linguist Ferdinand de Saussure. Their disciplinary backgrounds are key to their different conceptions of the study of signs. Recovering an undercurrent in the history of ideas, going back to Aristotle, Peirce developed a comprehensive philosophy of signs which he understood as a form of logic that would support inquiry into the nature of both knowledge and being (for key texts see Peirce 1992, 1998). In his definition, any sign has three aspects:

A sign, or *representamen*, is something   sign, object, which stands to somebody for something in   interpretant

---

▶ semiotics on media of the first, second, as well as third degrees – Chapter 1, p. 3

some respect or capacity. It addresses some-body, that is, creates in the mind of that person an equivalent sign, or perhaps a more developed sign. That sign which it creates I call the *interpretant* of the first sign. The sign stands for something, its *object*.

(Peirce 1931–58: vol. 2: 228)

Although signs are here said to mediate between objects (material and non-material) in reality and concepts in the mind, Peirce rejected any idealist, nominalist, or skepticist position. Peirce instead attempted to marry a classical, Aristotelian realism with the modern, Kantian insight that humans necessarily construct their understanding of reality in particular cognitive categories. Signs, then, are not *what* we know, but *how* we come to know what we can justify saying that we know, in science and in every-day life.

Peirce further suggested that human under-standing is a continuous process of interpreta-tion – semiosis – not a singular internalization of reality once and for all. In this perspective, examples of semiosis range from the ongoing coordination of everyday media use and other social life, to scientific discovery and aesthetic creativity. Figure 2.3 displays the process of semiosis, noting how any given interpretation (interpretant) itself serves as a sign in the next stage of interpretation. Even though Peirce's outlook was that of a logician and a natural scientist, the model may be taken to refer to the communicative processes by which cultures are maintained and societies reproduced.

Saussure (1959 [1916]), in comparison, focused almost entirely on verbal language. Even though it was he who coined the phrase anticipating a general science of signs (of which linguistics would be a subdivision), in practice Saussure and his followers took language as their model for the study of other sign types as well. Saussure's main achievement was to develop a framework for modern linguistics which, to a degree, proved applicable to other social and cultural phenomena.

In contrast to the emphasis of earlier phil-ology on the diachronic perspective of how lan-guages change over time, Saussure wanted to study language as a system in a synchronic

semiosis

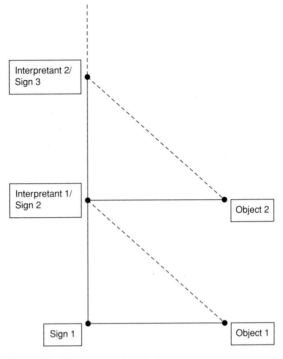

Figure 2.3 The process of semiosis

perspective. Language as an abstract system (*langue*) could be distinguished, at least for ana-lytical purposes, from its actual uses (*parole*), and this system could further be analyzed in two dimensions. Along the syntagmatic axis, letters, words, phrases, and so forth, are the units that combine to make up meaningful wholes; each of these units has been chosen as one of several possibilities along a paradigmatic axis, for example, one verb in preference to another. The resulting combinatory system accounts for the remarkable flexibility of lan-guage as a medium of social interaction.

In addition, the interchange between the paradigmatic and syntagmatic axes gives rise to two specific means of expression and represen-tation – metaphor and metonymy – which have been important in the understanding and analy-sis of media as textual messages. Metaphor may be defined as a paradigmatic choice which acti-vates an additional frame of reference (incor-porates it within the syntagm of the message as a whole). For example, in the 1980s, the

langue and *parole*

syntagms and *paradigms*

metaphor and *metonymy*

American politician and civil rights activist, Jesse Jackson, became the spokesperson for a 'rainbow coalition' which sought to bring together various ethnic and other disempowered groups as a new political force. This term is significantly different from the traditional reference to the U.S.A. as a 'melting pot.' Whereas the melting pot eliminates variety, the rainbow derives its essential quality and beauty from difference and contrast, so that speeches and campaigns can activate this sense for a particular political purpose (just as the melting-pot image serves a political purpose). Metonymy, in turn, is the process by which a single sign evokes the full syntagm to which it belongs. When 'the White House' was said to comment on the 'rainbow coalition,' the reference to the building would evoke both the American presidency and the political practices and vested interests associated with it (Drotner *et al.* 1996: 195).

arbitrariness of sign relations

An important contribution of Saussure was his account of the arbitrariness of the linguistic sign. The sign is said to have two sides: a

signified (signifié) and signifier (signifiant)

signified (conceptual content) and a signifier (the acoustic image or physical token associated with it). The relation between the two is arbitrary or conventional, as suggested by the wealth of terms in different languages for the same phenomenon. Saussure has sometimes been taken to suggest that also speakers of the same language are paradoxically free to choose their own meanings, and thus almost destined to remain divorced from any consensual reality. The point is rather that the linguistic system as a whole and its interrelations are arbitrary in principle, but fixed by social convention.

Much later research has extended the principle of arbitrariness to account for other social and cultural forms, for example, artworks, myths, and subcultures, all of which may be understood as 'languages' in the broad sense. The structural anthropology of Claude Lévi-Strauss (1958) was highly influential of such studies of culture as more or less arbitrary systems of signification. A similar perspective was developed within structuralist theories of social power (e.g., Althusser 1977 [1965]; Foucault 1972) and of the unconscious as a 'language' (e.g., Lacan 1977). A common argument in this work has been that the current organization of society, and of the human psyche, is a historical coincidence, and is open to challenge and change.

To be precise, Saussure referred to the science of signs, not as semiotics, but as semiology. The two terminologies point to the fact

semiology

that Peirce and Saussure, while contemporary, had no knowledge of each other's work. During its consolidation from the 1960s onwards, *semiotics* became the agreed term, as symbolized by the formation in 1969 of the International Association for Semiotic Studies. It was also during this period that the program for studying the life of signs in society, unfulfilled in Saussure's own work, began to be implemented in largely systemic, Saussurean approaches to culture and society. In recent decades, Peircean approaches have begun to inform a social semiotics, combining semiotic methodology with other social and communication theory (Hodge and Kress 1988; Jensen 1995).

Roland Barthes' widely influential model of two levels of signification (Figure 2.4) suggested an interface between Saussurean and Peircean semiotics, and a common agenda of the semiotic tradition: the analysis of concrete sign vehicles – texts and images – as vehicles of culture, ideology, or 'myth.' Barthes (1973 [1957]) showed how the combination of a signifier and a signified (expressive form and conceptual content) into one sign (e.g., a magazine cover with a picture of a black man in a French uniform saluting the flag) can become the expressive form of a further, ideological content (e.g., that French imperialism was not a discriminatory system). The two levels of meaning are normally referred to as denotation

denotation and connotation

and connotation, building on Hjelmslev (1963 [1943]). Barthes' critical point was that this two-layered semiotic mechanism serves to naturalize particular worldviews while silencing others, and should be deconstructed analytically. (Despite the predominantly critical orientation of semiotics, it has also been recruited for instrumental purposes, for example, in 'marketing semiotics' (Umiker-Sebeok 1987).)

It is only a relatively short step to the previous model of semiosis (Figure 2.3). The

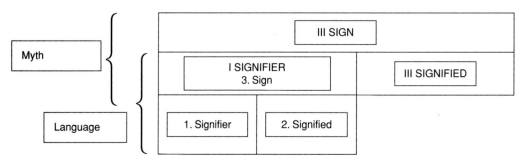

Figure 2.4 Two levels of signification
Source: Adapted from Barthes 1973 [1957]: 115. With permission, Farrar, Strauss & Giroux, and Random House.

Peircean model refers to a potentially infinite process, but recognizes that the process is always, in practice, arrested. Sooner or later, individual sign users must arrive at interpretations, and act, in particular social contexts (see further Barthes 1970). These questions, concerning meaning as process and as product, and concerning the relationship between interpretation and action, continued to occupy the humanities as such throughout the twentieth century, and became one of the key issues for the media field.

DISCURSIVE TURNS

In one sense, the humanities have always been preoccupied with language – as a means of persuasion, as testimony of the past, and as a model for other kinds of communication. Heim (1987) refers to 'the Logos tradition,' arising from classical Greek philosophy, as a long-lived worldview that has given priority to verbal language by assuming a 'transcendental intimacy of thought, words, and reality' (p. 42).

The twentieth century, however, witnessed an emphatic turn to the study of language and other signs in a number of disciplines, first and most explicitly in philosophy, and with a shared ambition of making the procedures for analyzing texts, artefacts, and events more explicit and systematic. In philosophy, 'the linguistic turn' (Rorty 1967) denotes the effort, particularly among Anglo-American analytic philosophers since the early 1900s, to examine the structures and functions of language as a primary way of knowing the structures of reality

the linguistic turn

as well as the conditions for knowing about them. Much ancient and premodern philosophy had been ontological (asking 'What does the world consist of?'); from the eighteenth century, philosophy came to address the same issues in epistemological terms ('What can we know about the world?'). It was these same issues which the twentieth century examined as a linguistic matter ('What do we mean by "know" and "world"?'). The linguistic turn, in effect, signaled a somewhat technical and reductionist conception of language as a modularized interface with reality.

The turn to the concrete and formal vehicles of knowledge posed problems as well as potentials. On the one hand, close analyses of language seemed to promise a new degree of precision, also in other humanistic research. On the other hand, language might end up being treated as a formalist universe unto itself, and as a fetish of science. Such an approach would be alien to the traditional cultural, historical, and aesthetic concerns of the humanities. On top of this, an overemphasis on verbal language would not do justice to the specific qualities of either nonverbal fine arts or popular audiovisual media. (From a different theoretical perspective, the analytical distinction between text and image was hotly debated also within semiotics.)◄ These dilemmas, which continue to affect media research today, can be laid out, first, with reference to their primary articulation in philosophy and, second, with reference

► semiotics of images as well as texts – Chapter 8, p. 120

to the solutions proposed in different humanistic disciplines.

The icon of twentieth-century philosophy was Ludwig Wittgenstein. In *Tractatus Logico-Philosophicus* (1921), the early Wittgenstein held that all knowledge must be founded on elementary propositions about minimal features of reality. Laws of nature as well as other types of inference and generalization should ultimately be reducible to direct observations of rudimentary phenomena. The ideal of both philosophy and science, accordingly, is to establish a correspondence between the structures of reality and the linguistic, logical, and other discursive structures expressing our understanding of it. In this way, Wittgenstein prepared arguments that were extended and applied also to the study of culture and society by logical positivism◄ of the 1920s to 1930s.

The later Wittgenstein himself rejected this formal and structural view of language. Instead, he came to define language as a complex set of discursive activities, so-called language games that are inseparable from the life form, or practice, which they serve to constitute. His dictum, that 'meaning is use' (Wittgenstein 1953: 20e), summed up the beginning of a larger shift from language as a medium of representation, to language as a means of action. It is no longer the form of language in itself, but its social uses which are the center of interest in much research. In the social sciences, a related shift has been noticeable – what is sometimes referred to as a 'cultural turn' (Ray and Sayer 1999) – which has entailed a renewed emphasis on the interpretive dimensions of social life, compared to its structural and institutional aspects.

It may be argued that these various discursive turns, promoting a precise focus on language and culture, have enabled the humanities to become 'harder' in methodological terms. In certain respects, the social sciences have grown 'softer.' Indeed, concepts of 'discourse' – the social uses of signs – have entered broadly into the convergence of the two scientific cultures. At the same time, several varieties of a discursive turn may be traced, also within humanistic disciplines.

──────────

► logical positivism – Chapter 15, p. 260

FOUR DISCIPLINES IN HUMANISTIC RESEARCH

Art history

In many respects, the modern media have taken over the social functions of both religious and secular fine arts – visual arts (painting, sculpture, architecture), music, and literature (including theater). The arts had taken shape as separate domains of social and aesthetic practice in the eighteenth century, as described by Habermas (1989 [1962]) under the heading of a *cultural* public sphere (see Figure 1.3). Defined programmatically by Kant in his *Critique of Judgment* (1790), the arts could be seen to establish a world apart, in which (initially only) the privileged classes were invited to engage in a disinterested contemplation of the beautiful, the true, and the good. Artworks could and should be appreciated for their immanent logic. In this perspective, art and culture have no ulterior purpose. *[fine arts: visual arts, music, literature]*

The classical understanding of the arts was challenged both from within and from without (for key texts see Harrison and Wood 1992). Internally, Romantic as well as avant-garde movements questioned the autonomous status of the artwork. Externally, the invention and diffusion of technological media increasingly undermined any understanding of art and culture as a realm apart, and one devoid of conflict. Quite evidently, the media were embedded in social institutions of power and in the daily lives of all classes. For one thing, culture was now manifestly a business – a source of capital. For another thing, the consumption of culture was a means of positioning oneself in society, being a symbol and a source of distinction (Bourdieu 1984 [1979]). *[distinction]*

Museums for the general public emerged alongside the press and other media as an institution of record, but also one of diversion (e.g., Bennett 1995). All the while, traditional forms of stage entertainment remained central carriers of the cultural heritage (e.g., Levine 1988). Nevertheless, the modern media became a categorically new form of cultural infrastructure – a continuous and conspicuous presence in the everyday, as well as an arena of social struggle. Over time, this common cultural infra- *[museums]*

structure served to blur many of the traditional distinctions of high and low cultural sectors. From a research perspective, this meant that any cultural expression or artefact could be studied for its inherent meaning – as 'texts.' It further meant that theories and approaches from the one sector might be transferred to account for the cultural practices of the other. Both art history and other disciplines have performed a very fruitful application of 'high' theory to 'low' culture (MacCabe 1986).

texts

One obvious point of contact has been between painting (and other visual arts) and photography (and other media images). (Sculpture and architecture have recently attained new relevance for studying the virtual worlds of digital media (see Rush 1999).) First, analytical models and methods, as derived, in part, from the psychology of perception and applied to different historical artforms (e.g., Arnheim 1974; Gombrich 1960), have provided some of the necessary tools for examining form, perspective, color, as well as iconographic conventions in film and television. Semiotics and structuralism were especially influential, in studies of both art and visual media, in applying linguistic models to visual phenomena. Building on Erwin Panofsky's iconology, Barthes (1984 [1964b]) contributed one of the most cited accounts of how image and text can relate to each other in different genres and media. Either the text 'anchors' or delimits the meanings of the image, or the reader's attention is allowed to wander back and forth between image and text as in a 'relay.'◄

Second, media studies took up and re-emphasized what has remained a more marginal interest within art history, namely the relationship between the arts and their social context. Art history itself has tended to reproduce elements both from a classic understanding of the artwork as autonomous, and from modern aestheticism, studying art for art's sake. Confronting this tradition from a materialist and psychoanalytic position, Hauser (1951), for example, began to rewrite the history of Western art, including new artforms such as cinema. Much media research went on to examine in detail the ways in which the selection of a particular visual subject matter as well as its composition may carry historically and socially specific messages, thus reading images as signs of their times. In an early exemplary study, Berger (1972) identified the many analogies between traditional oil paintings of the wealthy and powerful, and advertising which depicts role models that consumers are invited to identify with.

One implication of textual studies in this vein has been that visual media also carry a formal 'message,' in the sense that they frame and reinforce one particular perspective on the world. Another implication is that images address and attract viewers, who not only spend time and money, but 'invest' their subjectivity and identity in the discursive universe on offer. The general notion that the media serve to incorporate the human subject into a dominant view of society by textual means (and that subjects as well as social institutions can be understood as 'texts') has been central to much humanistic research since the 1960s (for an overview see Coward and Ellis 1977).

An issue which the ongoing cross-fertilization between elite art and popular culture has raised for future research is when the time may be ripe for an inclusive history of modern culture that bridges the high–low divide. Both media-oriented overviews (Pelfrey 1985; Walker 1994) and traditional art histories (Janson 1991) have, to varying degrees, recognized the interconnections – from the 'ready-mades' or everyday objects elevated as art by the Dada movement, through pop art, to installations and computer art. Presumably, the two fields of research must derive some form of integrative framework from related fields such as the history of ideas (e.g., Hughes 1991; Kern 1983; Peters 1999). The issue goes far beyond the question of whether the present is characterized, for instance, by a specifically visual culture (Evans and Hall 1999). Rather, the very category of 'art,' along with the distinction between 'text' and 'context,' has been complicated by about 100 years of technological and institutional shifts in the field of culture as a whole.

► anchorage and relay.– Chapter 7, p. 111

Literary criticism

Of the fine arts, literature, including theater, has often been ascribed a special role in modern culture, because it enables individuals to imagine radically different realities. Having imagined and reflected upon these, people will return to their everyday reality and practical concerns with a new awareness. This process of reflexivity is conducted within a range of traditional themes, forms, and genres, which educated readers are expected to master as part of their 'cultural literacy.' While authors might be expected to serve, to a degree, as the keepers of cultural tradition, a distinctive ambition of most modern high culture has been to transcend and constantly reinvent tradition. In the Romantic epoch, a new degree of autonomy was granted to the individual author. The genius which found expression in literature could be understood, in the words of the British poet William Wordsworth, as the 'spontaneous overflow of powerful feelings' (Abrams *et al.* 1962: 103). In modernism, authors came to be expected specifically to provide striking new insights for their readers, not least by formal, linguistic means. As a social institution, modern literature was called upon to 'make it new,' to present reality to its readers in new formats (Berman 1982; Huyssen 1986).

Literary research only gradually emerged as an area of specialized study, having been included as an element within historical and philological research in general. Moreover, literary research was, for a long time, founded on biographical studies of major authors and on historical approaches to the artworks and their place in a genealogy of styles, forms, and thematics (for an overview see Eagleton 1983; Wimsatt and Brooks 1957). The common term 'literary criticism' further suggests the affinity of this research to an appreciation of the 'canon' and a continuous evaluation of new artworks in this perspective. It was the rise of several formalist approaches during the twentieth century which promoted a more distantiated, disinterested study of literature and a sustained comparison with popular artforms.

The first internationally influential formalist 'school' was the New Criticism. From the 1940s, a group of scholars in the U.S.A. and the U.K. advocated studying literature as an objective, self-contained structure of textual paradoxes and ambivalences. Any interest in authorial intention or affective impact was labeled intentional and affective fallacies (see Wimsatt 1954). Although this position tended to isolate literature from its social circumstances, it helped to professionalize the analysis of literature and to gain academic legitimacy for the discipline. By performing close readings of 'the texts themselves' and bracketing readers, writers, as well as the literary institution, the New Criticism participated in the turn to an immanent analysis of texts.

Russian formalism, as developed from World War I and into the 1930s (Erlich 1955), prepared the main ingredients of structuralism, which gradually became the dominant position in literary theory from the 1960s. It was the formalists who noted that literature and other arts do not merely make reality new; rather their distinctive capacity is to defamiliarize reality, to make it 'strange.' An important ambition of structuralism was to account for such general features of literature, and of all texts and media.

Behind structuralism lies a 'generative' conception of language and meaning. The key idea is that any message amounts to a variation on a structural matrix of constants. The term 'generative' is sometimes associated with the transformational-generative grammar of Chomsky (1965), who described a 'deep' structure that produces the variable 'surface' structures of concrete sentences. However, the scope of the idea is much wider. Particular narratives also amount to variations on a few components, and a generative model is implicit, for instance, in the social-scientific concept of social roles, which in principle can be filled by anyone (e.g., Merton 1968). The most famous account of the modularity of narratives was the analysis by Propp (1958 [1928]) of the basic constituents in the Russian folktale and their recombination in any given tale. The model has been applied, for example, by Eco (1987 [1965]) in an analysis of the James Bond stories.◄

[margin notes:] historical–biographical approaches

the New Criticism

Russian formalism

defamiliarization

structuralism

generative model of language

► narratology – Chapter 8, p. 123

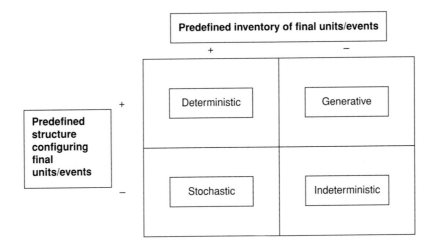

Figure 2.5 Four models of meaning

In Figure 2.5, the generative model is treated as a model of meaning generally, and is related to three other models in a typology. The typology arises from the combination of two dimensions, comprising the constituents and the combinatorial structures of meaning. In addition, the model refers to meaning in terms of units as well as events to allow for empirical research on both the systemic and the processual aspect of meaning production.

It may be argued that the main model of current humanistic media studies is generative, whereas the mainstream of social-scientific media research is stochastic. However, both deterministic and indeterministic conceptions of meaning easily creep into actual research, even while few researchers may align themselves explicitly with such models. For example, deterministic models continue to underlie assumptions about the direct impact of media on audiences (e.g., Postman 1985). In addition, postmodernist studies in particular tend to imply that both the textual content of media and its interpretation amount to free-floating, indeterministic processes (e.g., Fish 1979).

The concept of 'intertextuality' is another main contribution of structuralism to media and communication research.◄ The many

▶ intertextuality – Chapter 11, p. 186

interconnections across individual texts, series, and genres in the media suggest the particular importance of thinking of the units of content not as singular works, but as instances of 'textuality.' The idea was coined, again, by Russian linguists and literary scholars during the interwar years (Bakhtin 1981; Volosinov 1973 [1929]), and has been extended and reworked to apply to mediated communication. The concept has opened a terrain for a more focused analysis both of such classic issues as the relationship between 'text' and 'context,' and of current phenomena such as 'hypertextuality' in computer-mediated communication.

Linguistics

To recapitulate, modern linguistics was one of the main accomplishments of the semiotic tradition. It performed a shift from a diachronic philology that studied language in the broad context of history and culture, to a synchronic linguistics which examines language in systemic terms.

At first, much linguistics consisted in a relatively formal study of three main dimensions, namely grammar, semantics, and phonetics, often with reference to single, abstracted sentences. From the 1970s, however, there was a noticeable shift in the direction of also study-

from diachronic philology to synchronic, systemic linguistics

ing the social uses of language in context. In linguistic terminology, the shift involved a renewed emphasis on a fourth dimension of language study: pragmatics (for an overview see Coulthard 1985). In the wider perspective of social and cultural research, linguistics thus provided the basic ingredients of discourse analysis, ◄ as widely applied in interdisciplinary research. It was in this shape that linguistic concepts and procedures exercised most of their influence on the media field.

During the early stages in the development of humanistic media research, literary theory had been relatively more influential. This is likely explained, in part, by the initial understanding of media as sources of *mass* communication. The media could be seen, like traditional cultural forms, as one-way carriers of narratives, rather than as means of interaction comparable to conversation. (In the broader field of 'communication,' including interpersonal and organizational communication, linguistics has been a steady source of ideas (e.g., Knapp and Miller 1994).) Literary models might also seem more relevant for describing the relationship between media texts and ideological or psychological issues, compared to the more narrowly focused linguistic models.

In the past few decades, linguistics has gained somewhat of an equal standing with literary criticism in textual media studies. This may again be explained, in part, by developments in the media themselves. Ordinary conversation and informal modes of address have become pervasive in media, and have directed the attention of research toward spoken language as a constitutive feature of most mediated communication. Not least talkshows (e.g., Livingstone and Lunt 1994), but also other genres such as sportscasting (Kuiper 1996), have been studied. More generally, a rediscovery of the importance of interpersonal communication both in and around media has taken place (e.g., Gumpert and Cathcart 1986; Scannell 1991), and reception studies have noted the embedding of media in other everyday communication. Most recently, computer-

mediated communication has been studied for its hybrid genres, mixing interpersonal with mass communication.

The increased use of linguistic approaches in media studies has been facilitated by the redefinition of linguistics, incorporating more levels and contexts of language use among its objects of analysis. In addition to being a means of analyzing media texts, discourse analysis is also an instrument and a means of documentation *in research*. Media and communication researchers rely extensively on language for conceptualization, operationalization, data collection, data analysis, and reporting conclusions. Qualitative methodologies especially increasingly employ some form of language analysis for both discovery and documentation. ◄

Film studies

As in the case of art history and literary criticism, the social status as well as the nomenclature of 'film' or 'cinema' are contested. To begin, it may be perplexing that film studies are treated here as a source, rather than a variant, of media research. The fact that film was an early, and a specific type of medium – the first non-alphabetic form of communication with a mass audience – is only part of the explanation for the separate development of film studies. More important is the fact that academic research on film from the outset defined it primarily as an artform. It might have been defined from the outset as a medium of communication which, like books and other media, comprises high and low forms of expression and production.

film as artform

Growing out of literary studies in several national contexts, film studies have remained comparatively segregated from other media studies. This is witnessed in journals and conferences, and in separate film and media departments in universities. One consequence has been that the humanities account for the mainstream of film studies, compared to the social-scientific mainstream of international media

► pragmatics and discourse analysis – Chapter 7, p. 104

► linguistic analysis of research discourses – Chapter 14, p. 248

research. Film scholarship remains characterized by its aesthetic research questions, its 'textual' analyses, and its grand theory (for an overview see Andrew 1976) (for key texts see Mast *et al.* 1999).

Before the 1960s, film theory is normally divided into two traditions. The constructivist or formalist tradition emphasized the extent to which films literally produce and present one possible world for the spectators. The selection and recombination of elements, first, within the single shot and second, through the montage juxtaposing these elements, is a construction of reality (Berger and Luckmann 1966). The act of construction, moreover, is said to involve the spectators, who are invited to rediscover not only that world, but themselves in the process of viewing.

Despite different conceptions of film as 'language' or 'art,' and different interpretations of its psychological or political implications, key figures such as Sergei Eisenstein, Béla Balázs, and Rudolf Arnheim all centered on the productive moment of montage. For Eisenstein, a filmmaker as well as theorist, the constructivist position further entailed a special responsibility on the part of the filmmaker as well as a 'politics of film':

> the filmmaker must lead [the spectator to a confrontation with the theme] with his eyes open, exposing to the spectator his means, his mechanism, not merely because this style is preferable to the illusionary realism which is the hallmark of Hollywood but because the film derives its energy from the conscious mental leaps of the spectator.
>
> (Andrew 1976: 63)

Such an understanding of communication as a form of 'cognition through disruption' may be traced across different media and philosophies of art. Different articulations are found in the modernist aesthetics of 'making it new,' in the 'defamiliarization' of Russian formalism and in Bertolt Brecht's dramaturgical strategy of *Verfremdung*, as well as in recent poststructuralist notions of poetic language.◄

► poststructuralism – p. 33

the formalist tradition

montage

Realism was the second main tradition of classic film theory and, indeed, of much filmmaking. Siegfried Kracauer, who together with André Bazin (Bazin 1967–71) defined filmic realism, identified two tendencies in all film production until 1960, namely realism and formalism (Kracauer 1960). Whereas formalism seemed to characterize early and silent films, realism, with its longshots and longer-lasting shots, as well as its moving camera and unedited scenes, appeared to be dominant in many later works. As suggested by the subtitle of Kracauer's 1960 volume, 'the redemption of physical reality,' realism in the shape of a photographic offprint of reality may be the nature of film, manifesting itself after the medium has matured.

Up to this point, most film studies are best described as 'criticism,' developing theory through aesthetic and conceptual analyses of singular works, frequently in an essayistic form. From the 1960s onwards, film semiotics developed a much more elaborate and systematic set of analytical procedures and conceptual frameworks. Reacting against widespread and loose talk about the 'language' of film, the central figure of film semiotics, Christian Metz (1974 [1968]), set out to dismantle this mystifying metaphor. Metz concluded that although film, like television and other visual communication, shares certain categories with other sign systems, film is not a language system (*langue*) in Saussure's sense, consisting of minimal units with distinctive features that are recombined in speech (*parole*). Instead, Metz went on to apply semiotic concepts to selected aspects of the film medium, particularly the different types of syntagms (complex sequences of meaning) that structure a given film.◄

In some of his later work, Metz (1982) linked up with the psychoanalytic current in film theory, which became central to the discipline from the 1970s, as represented by the influential journal *Screen*. Taking its lead from Jacques Lacan's reinterpretation of Freud (e.g., Lacan 1977), a basic assumption of this research was that film is in a special position

the realist tradition

film semiotics

► semiotic analysis of film syntagms – Chapter 8, p. 121

to reactivate infantile forms of experience and identification in the spectator because of its apparent immediacy and sensuousness. An early text by Mulvey (1992 [1975]) elaborated on the gendered nature of the spectator's gaze, particularly the male scopophilia (pleasure of looking), which seemed to be anticipated by the narrative structure and mode of address in the classical Hollywood film.

psycho-semiotics: the gaze

Within the psychosemiotic current as well as in the great majority of other film studies, the main approach has been structuralist and other close analyses of film 'texts.' On this basis, researchers have made inferences, sometimes quite far-reaching, about the reception and impact of cinematic works, and about their political or psychoanalytic implications. Film history, by and large, still consists of the sum of scholarly interpretations, subject to ongoing revision, of the main genres and their masterpieces.

In comparison, research on film production and reception, or on institutional frameworks, has remained a minority interest. Nevertheless, the relatively few studies of this kind have indicated the importance of placing film in its social and cultural context. Among the contributions have been Gans' (1957) study of how filmmakers' views of their audience affect their films; and Bordwell *et al.*'s (1985) comprehensive analysis of the organizational as well as textual structures in Hollywood cinema. Recently, cognitivism has questioned the theoretical and methodological assumptions of much previous film research, being one of the current challengers to the humanistic mainstream. ◄

INTERDISCIPLINARY CHALLENGERS

Postmodernism

In order to assess the implications of one of the most controversial ideas in research as well as public debate in the past two decades, it is necessary to distinguish three different phenomena that are sometimes conflated in the term 'postmodernism' (for key texts see Foster 1985). Originally, the term was introduced into liter-

postmodernism as an aesthetic style

ary and cultural research to refer to an anti-modernist style in various arts. While the style may be found in the literary experiments of, for instance, Richard Brautigan and Thomas Pynchon, it has been associated particularly with architecture. In an influential volume, Robert Venturi and his co-authors suggested that architects should take their inspiration from popular culture, as epitomized by Las Vegas, in order to construct more imaginative buildings and environments around people's lives (Venturi *et al.* 1972). Precisely the questioning of traditional distinctions between high and low culture has been a position taken up by much postmodernist thinking.

Second, postmodernist styles have been taken by some theorists as one symptom of an entire epoch of 'postmodernity.' In more or less radical versions, researchers have claimed that modernity – specifically the Enlightenment project of achieving general social progress through rationalist science and politics – has ended, or is ending. Such projects have been labeled as 'grand' narratives, which could and should, according to Lyotard (1984 [1979]), be replaced by 'little' narratives. These latter narratives amount to open-ended and democratically accessible language games which, ideally, enable an unending dialogue between equal participants in communication. Beyond the level of narrative and discourse, Jameson (1991) has gone on to argue that postmodern culture has a concrete liberatory potential, and that postmodernism as such may be interpreted as 'the cultural logic of late capitalism.' The most radical view of postmodernity has been expressed by Baudrillard (1988), who suggests that the categorical distinction between discourse and reality has broken down, and who celebrates the resulting 'hyperreality.'

postmodernity as an epoch

Third, if postmodernism is a general current of ideas, 'poststructuralism' may be understood as its theoretical branch. (Another word, 'deconstructionism,' is associated with U.S. variants of the position, and is perhaps becoming the common term, but it derives from the same seminal texts, such as Derrida (1976 [1967]).) The analytical strategy is to expose internal contradictions in texts and to undermine their apparent intentions. The theoretical

poststructuralism as a theoretical position

deconstructionism

► cognitivism, see p. 36

premise is that no textual meaning is stable, nor is any genuine human insight into oneself or others a possibility.

Compared to some earlier philosophy and theory, the poststructuralist agenda is an emphatic skepticism and relativism. The aim is not merely to show that knowledge is uncertain, or to argue that it should be obtained by different means – knowledge as traditionally understood is said to be literally impossible. Yet much poststructuralism tends to conceive of itself as a critical and progressive position, implying alternative ideals. One argument is that any fixation of meaning and knowledge may be seen as a way of exercising definitional power, even of committing violence against the worldviews of others. In many ways, then, ideology critique poststructuralism reiterates the ideology critique of the 1960s–1970s, which sought to unmask texts as the carriers of bourgeois ideology (e.g., Barthes 1973 [1957]; Negt and Kluge 1993 [1972]; Williamson 1978).

The social and psychological consequences of texts, and the consequent need to 'deconstruct' them, have been emphasized within poststructuralism. Studies of discursive structures as means of oppression and suppression have taken their inspiration from the works of, among others, Foucault (1972) and Lacan (1977). Despite this orientation toward action and change, however, the practice of poststructuralist research has remained as centrally focused on the interpretation of texts as that of structuralism.

In media and communication research, poststructuralist studies have especially examined film, television, and other visual texts (for an overview see Brooker and Brooker 1997; Morse 1998). An underlying assumption is that images are relatively 'open,' and thus in principle allow viewers to take up shifting subject positions, but are stifled in current media forms. The psychosemiotic current above has explored how different visual genres may be said to fixate their audience in particular spectator positions. In addition, poststructuralism has lent itself to the study of emerging genres such as the music video (e.g., Kinder 1984) and of other media formats which are under commercial pressures to innovate; for example,

advertising or contemporary television (e.g., Caldwell 1995). Most recently, computer media and virtual realities have presented themselves as natural candidates for examining a phenomenon such as decentered identities (e.g., Stone 1991).

It should be added that references to 'postmodernism' in media studies sometimes do not express a particular theoretical or aesthetic commitment. Instead, they may articulate a general and unexamined sense of living in uncertain, 'postmodern times.' Particularly with reference to the assumption that the present period is an epoch of postmodernity, Harvey (1989), among others, has suggested that 'postmodern' culture is more appropriately thought of as a set of styles and practices which typify *modernity* at a particular historical juncture. These styles and practices – for example, an aestheticization of politics and a growing mediatization of everyday life – are perhaps best seen as the outcome of an intensified but continuous process of modernization. At least in this regard, no categorical shift may have occurred between the 'control society' (Beniger 1986) of the interwar period and the 'network society' (Castells 1996) of the new millennium.

Feminism

The study of gender has been central to anthropology and other social sciences from the outset about a century ago (Reinharz 1992), but it has been given a more explicitly critical inflection in recent decades, when feminism came to the fore also in the humanities (for key texts see Marks and de Courtivron 1981; Nicholson 1997).

Feminist media studies have been part of the 'second wave' of political as well as theoretical activity centering on women's liberation since the 1960s (the 'first' wave being associated with phases of securing political and other formal rights). Here, a notion of 'difference feminism' (Nicholson 1997: 3) has been influential. An important premise of difference feminism is that gender is not only a characteristic of individuals (a separate 'variable'), but a constitutive factor in all social interactions and gender: variable or constituent? institutions, including the research institution itself. Feminism has served as one reminder that science is shaped, in part, by its historical and ideological circumstances, and by the lives scientists live outside the academy. With reference to the 'double hermeneutic' of science (Giddens 1984), one may say that interpretive frames also feed *from* the historial and social context *into* the very activity of research from the outset of a study, not just vice versa at its conclusion.

Three aspects of feminist studies should be noted for their contribution to media and communication research (for an overview see also Press 2000; van Zoonen 1992). The three aspects correspond approximately to phases in the history of feminism, and to positions on a scale ranging from liberal to radical conceptions of gender and research.

images of women The earliest version of feminist media studies focused on 'images of women,' particularly stereotypical representations and their likely effect in socializing both female and male audiences (e.g., Tuchman *et al.* 1978). Such studies pre-date difference feminism, in the sense that they tended to assume equality between men and women as a neutral standard, and as an ideal that might be enforced by formal criteria. This premise is reminiscent of liberal feminism, whose activist struggles for equal political and economic rights go back, depending on the national context, to the early twentieth century and before.

In other humanistic disciplines such as literary studies, one concern of feminists has been to make visible, or to recover, female authors from the past, on the assumption that they would provide alternative images of women (see Moi 1985: 50–69). In media studies, it appears that the industrial organization of image production tends to cancel other differences between media professionals, including gender. Hence, more women employees may not result in a more balanced representation of gender (van Zoonen 1992: 43–65). A further argument may be (and has been) made that this state of affairs is due to an inherent 'masculine' logic of industrial production, also in the media.

difference feminism It is such a wider, cultural conception of gender which has informed the second formulation of (difference) feminism. Here, gender is conceived as a pervasive condition of all individual and social being, affecting the thinking and actions of both women and men. The notion of 'difference' also, to a degree, acknowledges that the category of 'woman' is not unified, but is traversed by, for example, class and ethnicity (Press 2000: 29). Referring to the phenomenological tradition, one might say that the purpose of a gender-specific analysis of, for instance, media use, becomes, not to isolate the gender element but to bracket it.◄ The aim is to capture its essential qualities and to understand how specific everyday uses of media arise from and feed back into gendered circumstances of social life.

By shifting the emphasis from formal political and economic institutions to cultural practices, feminism has joined cultural studies in the premise that culture is a site of social struggle in its own right. Nevertheless, certain conceptions of gender are likely to exercise hegemony (Gramsci 1971), because they are so pervasive and ingrained in cultural artefacts and practices. It is such hegemony that has especially been targeted for critical analysis by feminist media research. Studies range from examinations of the gendered gaze in visual communication (Mulvey 1992 [1975]) and ideology critiques of popular fiction (see studies in McRobbie 1991), to more recent attempts at legitimating the secret or ambivalent pleasures of popular culture aimed at women (e.g., Hobson 1982).

The third variety of feminism assumes a radical difference between women and men, not only regarding their cultural categories, but in epistemological terms of what men and women can and cannot know. Perhaps certain forms of knowledge are available only to women. An additional argument is sometimes made that this unique potential for insight originates in the specific psychology, or physiology, of the female body. With the ambiguous title, 'This Sex Which Is Not One,' Irigaray (1997 [1977]) has suggested several points – that there is no simple relationship between biological sex and cultural gender; that no man or woman has a homogeneous or unified gender; and that the

---

▶ phenomenological bracketing – p. 23

dual shape of the female genitals may be retraced in female forms of culture and discourse. Female culture might be said to privilege process and dialogue, inclusion and care. The main difficulty of assessing the merits of such arguments, however, is their shifting, metaphorical premises. The implication quickly becomes an untenable essentialism that conflates biology and epistemology.

essentialism: biological and epistemological

The dangers of essentialism for research have also been noted within feminism. Still, the notion that there may be separate or radically different orders of experience – a kind of gendered 'private languages' – has continued to hold an attraction for feminist research. One justification for exploring this form of theorizing has been the history of oppression which women have suffered, arguably in large measure because of a dominant 'masculine' epistemology. Some theorists, such as Gayatri Spivak, have advocated a 'strategic essentialism' (Nicholson 1997: 318) as a necessary and justified position from which research may counter oppression.

Essentialist feminism has had relatively little influence on media and communication research as such. It has, however, affected the field indirectly through the theory of science. In recent decades, this has been an interdisciplinary battleground regarding the interconnections between procedures of 'science' and social 'interests.' Advocates of 'standpoint epistemology,'◀ for instance, have argued that it is possible, indeed necessary, to conduct research from particular gendered and political standpoints.

Cognitivism

The latest challenge to textual and other humanistic research comes from cognitivism. Over the past decade or so, this tradition has proposed a major reconceptualization of humanistic, social, and cultural studies. Cognitivism derives its theoretical inspiration from 'hard' sciences – neuropsychology, cognitive psychology, medical science, and computer science. From the 1950s onwards, these disciplines joined forces in

the interdisciplinary field of cognitive science, in part around notions of artificial intelligence (for an overview see Gardner 1985). Recent developments in digital technologies have added to its perceived relevance for studies of communication and culture.

cognitive science

In media studies, cognitivism represents a 'third' academic culture, in addition to the two cultures of social sciences and humanities which, for the past few decades, have been converging.◀ Snow (1964) had identified a deep intellectual gap within the postwar academy between 'soft' arts and 'hard' sciences. This gap reproduced itself in the media field in the early stand-off between hard social science and soft, interpretive humanities. Cognitivism reactualizes issues from those debates, most basically about nature and nurture, as well as structure and agency, as explanatory factors in social and cultural research. If feminism has reminded media research, sometimes in metaphorical terms, that humans and their ways of communicating are gendered, cognitivism has insisted that both women and men are literally communicating animals.

Evolutionary and other biological perspectives on human communication, including its continuities with (other) animal communication, has long been a niche interest in the wider field of media studies (for an overview see Capella 1996). Studies of visual arts have also been influenced by cognitive science (Solso 1994). It was, however, film scholars who, during the 1980s, reintroduced cognitive theory into research on technologically mediated communication (for an overview see Zillmann and Vorderer 2000). A particular influential volume was David Bordwell's *Narration in the Fiction Film* (Bordwell 1985a), which sought to integrate an information-processing perspective with structuralist concepts of texts and their interpretation. Bordwell redeveloped aspects of literary theory, specifically Russian formalism, to account in detail for the interchange between the discursive structures of film and the viewer's cognitive activity.

natural evolution

The position of this approach in relation to earlier film theory was summed up in the title

---

▶ standpoint epistemology – Chapter 16, p. 286

▶ two cultures of research – Chapter 16, p. 279

of a stock-taking volume, co-edited by Bordwell with Noël Carroll and entitled *Post-Theory* (Bordwell and Carroll 1996). The Introduction notes that the title was not intended to signal 'the end of film theory,' but to question Theory, defined as 'that aggregate of doctrines derived from Lacanian psychoanalysis, Structuralist semiotics, Post-Structuralist literary theory, and variants of Althusserian Marxism' (p. xiii), which had hardened into an orthodoxy of 'grand theory' in film studies.◄ The stated aim of the editors, and of their contributors, was to promote pluralism in the choice of both theoretical frameworks and analytical procedures. Moreover, the articles advocated a return to middle-range and empirical work informed by concrete research questions, including economic and historical studies. In effect, however, the volume confronted cognitivism with the dominant psychoanalytic theories of film. The Introduction does recognize that the essays in *Post-Theory* converge on cognitivism, but argues that this stance allows for several articulations – by polemical contrast to a monolithic psychoanalysis (p. xvi).

Despite the natural-scientific inspirations of cognitivism, the center of interest has remained squarely on the film text and its appeals to the viewer. It is somewhat ironic that an approach which gains much of its legitimacy from an emphatically experimental tradition of science should still be practiced by solitary scholars scrutinizing texts. The 'findings' – or readings – within cognitive media studies are mostly the outcome of a methodological business-as-usual, relying extensively on hermeneutic and narratological procedures of analysis. This is especially controversial since cognitivism has given particular attention to audiences, and has proposed far-reaching inferences regarding the nature of media experience. In this respect, cognitive studies resemble semiotic textual studies, as performed before the advent of empirical reception studies.◄

This analytical practice may be due to the recency of cognitive media theory. It is also explained, in part, by the focus of cognitive science on universal, rather than the historically and culturally variable aspects of human cognition. Yet, for future media studies, an integration of cognitivism with the two other academic cultures of humanities and social sciences seems a necessary next step (see, e.g., Buckland 2000).

It should be mentioned that some cognitive media research has offered experimental as well as other non-textual evidence to substantiate its conclusions (e.g., Messaris 1994; Reeves and Nass 1996; Zillmann and Bryant 1994). The computer – originally the key metaphor for a general cognitive science about the human mind – has been promoting concrete research interest in more diverse forms of evidence. For one thing, the distributed forms of computer-mediated communication and interaction call for different analytical strategies from the matching of singular films with abstract cognitive schemata or frames.◄ For another, as a tool of analysis and documentation, the computer facilitates inquiries into the process of communication that are at once large scale and in depth.

Following an early cognitive conception of film viewing as puzzle-solving and other information processing, recent studies have addressed the emotional aspect of media reception. Grodal (1997), for example, has outlined a typology of genres in visual communication with reference to their different emotional and bodily affordances. Finally, while most of the recent interest in cognitivism has been directed toward the audiovisual media and their visual specificity, this literature remains to be integrated with earlier media research, for example, on audiences' recall of information, as presented also in print media.◄

It is inviting to speculate on the timing of cognitivism in the media field. It is likely that the abstract, contemplative, and occasionally idiosyncratic qualities of psychoanalytic Theory (Bordwell and Carroll 1996) contributed to swinging the pendulum in an opposite

---

► film studies – p. 33

► empirical reception studies – Chapter 10

► schemata and frames – Chapter 9, p. 149

► studies of media recall – Chapter 9, p. 144

direction. At the same time, it seems plausible that a focused interest in the biological, evolutionary aspects of culture and communication was delayed by discomfort at their essentialist, and potentially racist, implications – and by a related critical agenda in much early media research. If humans are assumed to have the capacity to emancipate, resocialize, and reculture themselves in radical ways, in part through the intervention of critical studies, then the unchanging conditions of communication will move out of focus in research.

In conclusion, cognitivism has restated classic issues in the history of ideas (for an overview see Lakoff and Johnson 1999). The biological and technological conditions of culture and communication, and their different historical forms and social variations, are research questions which are shared across the humanities and social sciences. In examining the human body as a medium of thinking, representing, and acting, cognitivism links up with parts of phenomenology which have suggested that bodies are not something humans 'have,' but something we 'are' (Merleau-Ponty 1962 [1945]: 174). However, cognitivist conceptions of technological media still appear preliminary. Johnson (1987) concluded that humans carry 'the body in the mind,' in the shape of metaphors and other basic-level concepts emerging from our bodily orientation in time and space. It remains equally necessary for media research to explore the ways in which we carry 'society and history in the mind,' as we interact with media and other humans.

A PRAGMATIC TURN

To sum up: the humanities have performed several discursive turns over the past two centuries. They are currently taking another, pragmatic turn as part of their engagement with both social and natural sciences. The omnipresence of mediated communication in social life may have contributed to a renewed understanding that language and texts are not merely, or even primarily, means of representation and sources of evidence about the past. Texts, genres, and media are cultural *resources* which are at once material and discursive.

As suggested by the trajectory of twentieth-century philosophy, there has been a noticeable interdisciplinary shift from an understanding of language (and media) as a formal structure, to an emphasis on its social uses. The emphasis on the pragmatic or performative aspect of communication was given a name in speech–act theory (Austin 1962; Searle 1969). As an epistemological position, speech–act theory entailed a recognition of the intimate relation between language, experience, and action. It also drove home a realization of the limitations of formal systems of representation in accounting for the structure of human experience. As a research program, the pragmatic turn is at present being implemented in empirical as well as theoretical research across and between the humanities and social sciences. In this process, media and communication research occupies a strategic position.

speech–act theory

In the long perspective of the humanities, the pragmatic turn may be summarized with reference to three characteristics, all of which involve the media:

1 *Performative concept of communication.* Retrieving aspects of classical rhetoric, and integrating elements of modern social theory, much current humanistic research examines the specific ways in which individuals and institutions co-construct society and culture. The modern technological media are significant sources of the frames of understanding that enter into such construction.

2 *General category of 'texts.'* The humanities have gradually come to include more audio-visual media and more everyday phenomena among its objects of analysis. Although the whole world is not a text, it may be studied as such.

3 *Secular notion of culture.* Related to the general conception of texts, culture is now commonly understood in the humanities as any vehicle or practice of meaning. Secularization, in this sense, goes beyond the denial of any divine origin and purpose of the world, and involves a questioning of any absolute standards in social meaning production.

cultural
studies

The most clearly delineated representative of the pragmatic turn in media and communication research has been the cultural studies tradition (for an overview see During 1999; Grossberg *et al.* 1992; Hartley and Pearson 2000; Striphas 1998). Although researchers in different national contexts have, predictably, cultivated different approaches,◄ the British variety of cultural studies, as associated with the Birmingham Centre for Contemporary Cultural Studies, has been particularly influential internationally (e.g., Hall *et al.* 1980). Since the 1970s, it has established itself as an identifiable 'school' alongside, for example, political economy (e.g., Murdock and Golding 1977) and cultivation research (e.g., Gerbner and Gross 1976). In certain respects, cultural studies represents a hybrid of humanistic and social-scientific perspectives. Within the media field as a whole, however, it has especially contributed a humanistic inflection of key concepts.

In a theoretical overview, Stuart Hall (1986), himself a seminal figure in the school (Morley and Chen 1996), argued that two paradigms came together in cultural studies (suggesting that 'paradigms,'◄ as introduced by Kuhn (1970), may not be as incommensurable as some later commentators have made them). On the one hand, 'structuralism,'◄ as noted above, tends to stress the determination of con-

sciousness and communication by economic, political, and other social frameworks. Hall traced this emphasis particularly to Althusser (1977 [1965]) and Lévi-Strauss (1958), in addition to Marx.

On the other hand, 'culturalism' insists on   culturalism   culture as a relatively autonomous practice and as a site on which some of the most important social struggles of the modern period have been conducted. The inspiration for cultural studies in this regard came, not least, from U.K. historians and literary scholars (Hoggart 1957; Thompson 1968 [1963]; Williams 1962, 1975 [1958]). This is one explanation for the special British connection in cultural studies. For Hall and others, the two paradigms were joined by Gramsci (1971), whose concept of hegemony◄ – a dominant range of worldviews that reinforce the social status quo – seemed to accommodate both cultural autonomy and relative determination.

The traditions and literatures that are reviewed in the chapters of this volume, in different ways, bear witness to influences and issues associated with the pragmatic turn. The pragmatic turn also manifests itself in the ongoing convergence of humanities and social sciences in the media field. The contribution of the social sciences to media and communication research is the subject of Chapter 3.

► national research traditions – Chapter 11, p. 190

►paradigms – Chapter 15, p. 255

►structuralism – p. 29

► hegemony – Chapter 1, p. 6

3 Media, culture and modern times

Social science investigations

Graham Murdock

- a description of media as central constituents of the *modern period*, and of the *social sciences* studying it
- a *recovery* of the different types of *research, analysis, and activism* which characterized early social science, and which fed into later media studies
- a review of work examining the relations between media and *democracy, social space,* and *public culture*
- a reassessment of *precursors of current social science,* e.g., regarding media effects and reception
- a summary of the transition *from structural functionalism to political economy and cultural studies* in contemporary media studies.

LINEAGES OF THE PRESENT

Many of the social institutions and patterns of everyday life with which we are now so familiar, assumed their present forms in the four decades between 1880 and 1920. Their development was inextricably tied up with the growth of modern media. The arrival of wireless telegraphy in 1895, and of automatic switchboards in telephone exchanges in 1892, allowed larger volumes of information and conversation to be transmitted instantly, over increasingly greater distances. The ability to reproduce photographs in newspapers and magazines for the first time (1880) transformed the popular press. And the launch of the gramophone, in 1887, and the arrival of cinema, in 1895, laid the basis for novel kinds of entertainment and experience.◄

This complex of new communications media played a central role in constructing the contemporary social order in four main ways. Firstly, they allowed both the large business enterprises that were coming to dominate the economy, and the new forms of state and government which were emerging in the political arena, to manage their proliferating activities more effectively. Modern business worked with ever more complex chains of supply, production, and distribution. Modern nation-states were assuming greater responsibility for social welfare in areas like pensions and education. With the age of total war ushered in by World War I, they faced the problem of managing military operations spread over a huge geographical area. Even in peacetime, the operations of many large corporations and western nation-states were global in scope. Empires, whether territorial or economic, posed formidable problems of command, coordination, and control.◄

Second, modern communications were central to the ways in which governments and

► chronological table of media and communication – Chapter 2, p. 18

► the control society – Chapter 16, p. 275

business corporations secured public support. Mature industrial capitalism was based on the mass production of standardised goods, typified by Henry Ford's Model T motor car (first introduced in 1909). To maximise profits in this new system, mass production had to be matched by mass consumption. Consequently, the development of modern assembly line manufacture and of mass offices using the new typewriters (introduced in 1873) was accompanied by the rise of department stores and mail order catalogues that were designed to engineer consumer desire and to translate wishes and wants into purchases.

advertising and public relations
At the centre of this selling system stood the new advertising agencies and public relations firms dedicated to promoting their clients' brands, massaging their company images, and combating criticisms and attacks. Modern governments too were in the business of selling. With the development of representative democracy and the extension of the vote, political parties who wished to form a government had to compete aggressively for public support and try to ensure that 'public opinion' reflected their priorities and constructions of events. The public media, particularly the popular press and later commercial broadcasting, rapidly became the main arenas where these competitions for sales and votes were played out. As we shall see below, many commentators saw the private ownership of key news media, and the ever-present possibility of self-interested interventions by owners and advertisers, as a fundamental problem for democracies based on the ideal of open debate in the pursuit of the public interest.

Third, these concerns were part of a wider debate about the state of public culture. More and more of the language and imagery through which people understood and interpreted the world was manufactured by professionals working in media industries that were dedicated mainly to making a profit. This situation generated fierce debates over whether art and thought which challenged dominant assumptions could survive in the factory-like conditions of the modern newspaper office, film studio, or popular song-writing system. Another question was whether manufactured meanings could ever

be an 'authentic' expression of popular feelings and opinions.

Fourth, questions about the central tendencies of mediated public culture led easily on to concerns about their impact on 'ordinary' people. How did popular media influence beliefs and behaviour? How were they changing everyday patterns of activity and sociability? How did people manage the relations between mediated meanings and meanings grounded in everyday experience?

When these issues first emerged, they attracted the attention of a variety of analysts and commentators – from cultural critics to investigative journalists and social activists. But a number of the most important contributions came from people who thought of themselves in one way or another as social scientists.◄ There are good reasons why we should reread their pioneering interventions. For one thing, the issues they grappled with remain central to contemporary debates, and many of their definitions of core problems remain highly pertinent to present-day debate. For another, their attempts to develop systematic techniques of investigation have essential lessons to teach us about the potentials and limits of different methods and how they might be productively combined. To ignore this legacy is to condemn media research to perpetually rediscovering old methods, having forgotten their previous history. We develop intellectually by climbing on other people's shoulders so that we can see further and more clearly. We have no choice, but, as a field of research, we should at least acknowledge our debt to them and call them by name.

RESEARCHERS, REPORTERS, ANALYSTS AND ACTIVISTS

The social sciences were relatively late additions to the intellectual field. Their emergence as the university-based disciplines we now know coincided exactly with the development of contemporary social and media systems. Up until then, thinking about individual consciousness, social action and the good society had been over-

---

▶ types of theory and analysis – Chapter 16, p. 274

whelmingly concentrated in departments of philosophy, with history and law making minor contributions. Consequently, as John Watson, one of the founders of modern psychology, put it, establishing the social sciences meant breaking philosophy's 'stranglehold' over social inquiry (1924: xi).

This assault on intellectual monopoly began in earnest in the late 1880s. In 1887, Émile Durkheim was appointed to the first named professorial chair of sociology in France, at Bordeaux. In 1890, Alfred Marshall published his *Principles of Economics*, deliberately rejecting the established tradition of political economy with its strong links to moral philosophy and its concern with the relations between economic activity and 'the good society.' Instead, he argued for a new discipline that would analyse 'the economy' as a bounded sphere of action. In 1892, William James (brother of the novelist Henry James) invited the German scholar, Hugo Münsterberg, to Harvard to take charge of the pioneering psychology laboratory he had established there. And in 1898, two English anthropologists, Haddon and Rivers, set off for the Torres Straits, intent on replacing the impressions of missionaries and adventurers with a study of tribal life based on firsthand observation.

Underpinning many of these initiatives was the idea that the social sciences were continuous with the natural sciences and should adopt the same basic aims and techniques of inquiry.◄ That conception privileged systematic experimentation and testing, objective observation purged of all personal values, and the translation of 'results' into statistics wherever possible. The aim was to identify the stable patterns governing social life and to formulate the connections binding them together as relations of cause and effect. The result was knowledge that could be used to manage existing institutions more effectively.

This positivist conception of 'science' was strongly opposed from the outset by those who insisted that the study of social life remained an interpretive activity dedicated to understanding what life looks and feels like to other people.

One of the founding texts for this approach was Alfred Schütz's 1932 book, *The Phenomenology of the Social World*, in which he argued that social-scientific inquiry must always begin with 'the already constituted meanings of active participants in the social world' (Schütz 1956: 10).◄ This argument – that social 'reality' is being continually built and rebuilt by 'ordinary' people as they struggle to make sense of their situation and devise strategies for action – has proved massively influential. It underpins the broad tradition of work that is now often called 'constructionism' (a term deliberately chosen for its strong associations with building work) as well as much recent work on 'active audiences.'◄ By highlighting the range of skills required by everyday social practices and exploring the logics underpinning unfamiliar beliefs, early contributors to this tradition hoped to deconstruct prevailing stereotypes and demonstrate the creativity with which 'ordinary' people negotiated the circumstances in which they found themselves.

construc-
tionism

The impetus to illuminate the connections between biography and history was shared by critical researchers aiming to expose the gaps between official promises and everyday realities, ideals, and performance. They rejected what they saw as the phenomenologists' 'radically individualistic and subjective' approach to the social (Outhwaite 1975: 92), insisting that people's lives and worldviews were shaped in fundamental ways by structural forces which they may misunderstand, or not even be aware of. This argument laid the basis for what has come to be called the critical realist tradition of social analysis (see Sayer 2000).◄ Its supporters saw themselves less as celebrants of the complexities of lived reality and more as critics of the processes which had produced these experiences and meanings and of the prevailing patterns of power that blocked alternatives.

These three positions entailed different roles for the professional social analyst:

► natural and social sciences – Chapter 15, p. 255

► phenomenology and social science – Chapter 2, p. 22

► active audiences – Chapter 10

► critical realism – Chapter 15, p. 268

- management
- interpretation
- critique.◀

All these roles found a niche within the emerging social science disciplines, but their practice was not monopolised by university departments. Important contributions were made by writers working outside the academy, and the lines separating the academy from the wider worlds of letters and political action were fluid rather than fixed.

Upton Sinclair, who produced one of the best early critiques of press performance (Sinclair 1920), had already achieved early fame with his novel, *The Jungle* (1906), an exposé of conditions in the Chicago slaughterhouses and meat-packing plants, and later went on to run (unsuccessfully) for the governorship of California on a radical ticket. Robert Park had been a journalist as well as the secretary to a well-known black activist before taking a position in the Sociology Department at the University of Chicago, where he played a central role in developing the tradition of urban ethnography, including studies of the media in everyday life, for which the department is best known. The influential cultural analyst, Siegfried Kracauer, moved from the department of sociology at Berlin to become a journalist, and later a cultural critic, for the leading German daily newspaper, the *Frankfurter Zeitung*.

There was traffic, too, across the border between universities and business. When John Watson was dismissed from his chair of psychology at Johns Hopkins University for moral impropriety, he went to work for the country's biggest advertising agency, J. Walter Thompson, where he eventually rose to become Vice-President. Similarly, when Ernest Dichter, who had worked with Paul Lazarsfeld, one of the leading academic figures in early communications research, in Vienna, moved to the U.S.A., he set up his own commercial research consultancy where he developed his ideas on the motivations behind consumer choices and became one of the central figures in postwar market research (e.g., Dichter 1947).

the Chicago School of Sociology

The traffic across institutional borders had several important consequences. First, it meant that research agendas were often shaped by issues originally raised in political debate, and that leading academics frequently wrote for major magazines and newspapers as well as for professional journals. Many thought of themselves primarily as public intellectuals◀ contributing to national and international debate, and only secondarily as researchers pursuing academic careers.

Second, because media and communications were new areas of inquiry without an established tradition of methodology, researchers were more open to improvisation. Sometimes the choice of methods was the result of pure chance, as in the case of the pioneering Chicago sociologist, W. I. Thomas (see Janowitz 1966: xxiv). One morning, while walking down a back alley in the Polish community on the West Side, he had to sidestep quickly to avoid some garbage just thrown out of an upstairs window. It contained several packets of letters arranged in chronological order. Since he read Polish, he started to read one of the bundles and decided to use letters as the basic data for his monumental study of migrant experience, later published as *The Polish Peasant in Europe and America* (Thomas and Znaniecki 1927).

Early analysts were also more willing to work with a range of methods. True, some favoured rigorous experimentation, sample surveys, and structured questionnaires, while others preferred to work with depth interviewing, personal documents, and ethnographic observation. However, the separation between quantitative and qualitative methods was often less rigid than it later became. Paul Lazarsfeld, for example, is remembered today as one of the pioneers of statistical methods, and is often dismissed as a crude empiricist. In fact, he was a pioneer of multi-method research. His choices were always dictated by the issue to be addressed, and there was no question of one method being suitable for all questions (Morrison 1998: 140).

A third consequence of this movement across intellectual check-points is that the story

▶ three knowledge interests – Chapter 16, p. 279

▶ intelligentsia – Chapter 16, p. 278

of the social-scientific contribution to media and communication research is as much a history of commercial research and critical inquiry as of academic projects. Lazarsfeld, whose early work was often funded from commercial sources, argued that because of the way he formulated problems he always 'got results which were interesting for the theoretical psychologists and worth the money to the business man' (1934: 71). His critics disagreed, insisting that intellectual inquiry must remain independent of pressure from both government and business, and must define its own terms of inquiry.

In reply, Lazarsfeld could point to *Personal Influence* (Katz and Lazarsfeld 1955), which identified the ways people drew on the opinions and recommendations of friends and people they admired when making everyday choices. The research was funded by two commercial sponsors, the magazine publisher Mcfadden and the Roper polling organisation, and examined people's choice of consumer goods and fashions as well as their political choices. However, Lazarsfeld and his co-author, Elihu Katz, used the opportunity to refine the 'two-step flow' model of communications which had emerged (serendipitously) in Lazarsfeld *et al.*'s (1944) earlier work on an election campaign. The model immediately attracted enormous interest and was widely used in later academic studies of media audiences.◀ Ironically, however, new ideas and methods that were pioneered within the academy were often more enthusiastically adopted by commercial researchers than by academics. As we shall see below, focus groups are a case in point.

Retrieving the history of the social-scientific work on media and reassessing the contemporary relevance of key studies is a mammoth task, and will have to wait for another occasion (see Murdock and Pickering forthcoming). Here, I simply want to indicate how some of the most interesting early contributors set about tackling central issues which we still face, and I will suggest how their pioneering work illuminates contemporary debates. Important contributions have come from across the range of

social science disciplines – from sociology, anthropology, and psychology, to economics, political economy, and political science (for an overview and references see Alexander *et al.* 1997; Boudon *et al.* 1997). It was primarily political scientists and other concerned observers who raised the central question of the role of media in modern democracies.

MEDIA AND DEMOCRACY

Liberal democratic models of mass democracy presupposed universal access to certain basic informational and cultural resources:

• Citizens required comprehensive and disinterested *information* on developments that affected their personal and political choices, particularly where changes were being promoted by agencies – whether governmental or business – with significant power over their lives.

• Citizens were entitled to see their own experiences, opinions, and aspirations given a fair *representation* in the major media of public culture.

• Citizens had a right to *participation* in open debates over the relative merits of competing explanations of prevailing conditions and rival proposals for change.◀

Surveying the state of public media at the turn of the twentieth century, particularly the popular press which was the main forum for information and debate, many commentators detected a substantial gap between democratic ideals and press performance. As America's leading political philosopher of the time, John Dewey, noted in his influential book of 1926, *The Public and its Problems*, the popular media had signally failed to convert a people into a public fully involved in the political process. Their failure to provide adequate communicative resources for citizenship had, he lamented, left 'the public ... formless ... seizing and holding its shadow rather than its substance,' a

▶ two-step flow model – Chapter 10, p. 159

▶ information, representation, and participation as democratic resources – Chapter 16, p. 276

social science disciplines

political science

phantom, glimpsed occasionally only to disappear again (Dewey 1926: 141). Dewey's criticism focused on the eclipse of political news and debate by coverage of 'crime, accident, family rows, personal clashes and conflicts' (p. 180). As we shall see below, his alarm at this 'sensationalist' turn was widely shared.

More radical critics, however, offered another explanation of the press's democratic failure, focusing on journalism's role in providing what Upton Sinclair in his savagely critical book, *The Brass Check* (1920), called the 'day-to-day, between-elections propaganda' which allows the 'Empire of Business' to maintain its effective 'control over political democracy' and to ensure that its agendas and priorities prevail (p. 222). In Sinclair's view, this eclipse of the public interest by private interests had two origins. First, newspapers were privately owned and therefore open to abuses of power by proprietors pursuing their opinions or those of their allies and associates. Second, they were funded primarily by advertising, leaving them open to pressure from companies wanting to promote their corporate interests.

'What,' asked another prominent critic, Will Irwin, 'does the advertiser ask as a bonus in return for his business favour ? . . . suppression of . . . disasters injurious to his business' (Irwin 1969 [1911]: 15). He supports his argument by pointing to the substantial publicity given to the relatively trivial sums which some train conductors had 'fiddled' from their employer, compared with the lack of coverage given to a case of wrongful arrest for shoplifting brought against a department store by a woman who had almost died of shock when apprehended. He gleefully notes that in both cases the companies involved were major advertisers. The argument that money talks and also buys silence had been made even more forcefully by Edward Ross, a sociology professor at the University of Chicago. In one of America's leading journals of opinion, *The Atlantic Monthly*, a year before, he wrote a piece provocatively entitled, 'The Suppression of Important News' (1910). His major concrete examples concerned the press coverage of labour relations and strikes, which could be considered the touchstone of a corporation's treatment of its employees.

Other commentators at the time analysed the news management activities of government, focusing particularly on the mismanagement of information flows in times of national crisis. This second major 'filter' of news (alongside the filters operating within the media themselves) was starkly illuminated by the prominent political scientist, Walter Lippmann, and his associate, Charles Merz, in their case study of the *New York Times*'s coverage of the Russian Revolution, entitled 'A Test of the News' and published in 1920. Their detailed textual analysis revealed that, at every stage of the Revolution and the ensuing Civil War (in which the U.S.A. had intervened to support the Communists' main opponents), some of America's leading journalists had been seriously misled by 'the official purveyors of information' offering opinions dictated by vested political interests rather than 'trustworthy news' (Lippmann and Merz 1920: 41). As a result, 'a great people in a supreme crisis could not secure the minimum necessary information on a supremely important event' (p. 3).

Still other critics of press performance focused on ways in which the press amplified incidents of social deviance and helped provoke a public and, subsequently, an official reaction which was out of proportion to the scale of the original threat and may well have added to the problem rather than alleviating it. In 1922, for example, Roscoe Pound and his colleagues undertook a detailed quantitative study of crime reporting in Cleveland newspapers for the month of January 1919, using column inch counts.◄ They found that whereas, in the first half of the month, the total amount of space given over to crime was 925 inches, in the second half it leapt to 6642 inches. This was in spite of the fact that the number of crimes reported to the police had only increased from 345 to 363. They concluded that although the city's much publicised 'crime wave' was largely fictitious and manufactured by the press, the coverage had very real consequences for the administration of criminal justice. Because the public believed they were in the middle of a crime epidemic, they demanded an immediate

► quantitative content analysis – Chapter 13, p. 219

response from the police and the city authorities. These agencies, wishing to retain public support, complied, caring 'more to satisfy popular demands than to be observant of the tried processes of law' (Pound and Frankfurter 1922: 546). The result was a greatly increased likelihood of miscarriages of justice and sentences more severe than the offences warranted.

This vigorous tradition of news critique in the context of political democracy, although largely unacknowledged now, paved the way for four major currents of work that have been very influential in media research in recent years:

1 Work within the *political economy* of communications which explores the corporate control of public communications. It is typified by Robert McChesney's recent volume, *Rich Media, Poor Democracy* (1999).

2 An account of the various filters blocking and directing news flows on behalf of the powerful has been outlined in the influential *'propaganda model'* of news production which was developed by Edward Herman and Noam Chomsky in their book *Manufacturing Consent* (1988). The model is pursued in detail in their successive case studies of reporting in the American press in times of war and crisis.

3 A substantial body of work has analysed *systematic biases* in news reporting of social conflict, including labour disputes. The Glasgow Media Group's *Bad News* study (1976) has played a particularly prominent role.

4 Analyses of moral panics and media amplification generally have played a major role in studies of public responses to youth subcultures (see Thompson 1998) and to environmental and other risks (see Douglas 1997; Renn 1991).

MEDIA, NETWORKS AND EMPIRES

As commentators recognised at the time, the rapid growth of the telegraph in the 1830s and 1840s was a truly revolutionary development in human communications. By separating communication from transportation for the first time in history and translating messages of all kinds into patterned electrical pulses – travelling over wires, through undersea cables and, later, through the atmosphere – it dismantled the material barriers that are presented by washed-out roads and storms at sea. The effect was to create new communicative spaces released from the confines of geographical place. These spaces inhabited a no-man's land between the point of transmission and the point of arrival.◀

The importance of this development was forcefully put by Charles Cooley in a long essay on 'The Theory of Transportation,' published in the official journal of the American Economic Association in 1894. He had been a senior civil servant in the transport division, and he went on to become a significant figure in early American sociology. At the time of writing, however, he was working as a political economy teacher at the University of Michigan. He argued that any 'study of communication from the point of view of place relations ... cannot penetrate more than skin-deep into the social meaning of communication' because 'in communication, place relations, as such, are of diminishing importance, and since the introduction of the telegraph it may almost be said that there are no place relations' (Cooley 1894: 293). Or, as a poem of 1872, written in honour of Samuel Morse, whose code of dots and dashes had become the global language of telegraphy, put it: 'And science proclaimed, from shore to shore, / That Time and Space ruled man no more' (quoted in Standage 1998: 23).

At the time, this vivid perception that communicative spaces were displacing geographical places as the key organising nodes of social activity was not pursued particularly vigorously by social analysts. Most saw 'society' as more or less synonymous with the nation-state.◀ The Canadian political economist, Harold Innis, was a notable exception. His early work, *The Fur Trade in Canada* (1930), had explained the choices facing Canada with reference to its place within the centre–periphery systems which characterised relations between empires

---

▶ space and social organization – Chapter 11, p. 182

▶ the nation-state – Chapter 11, p. 173

and their colonies more generally. His later work, *Empire and Communications* (1950) and *The Bias of Communication* (1951) focused more concertedly on the relations between communications and empire, arguing that all communication systems exhibited a 'bias' that favoured either control over time or control over space. By facilitating coordination over increasingly greater distances, the development of portable and mobile media had facilitated both the extension of modern imperial systems and the corporate concentration of control over key communications facilities.◄ Innis's dense writing style and the fact that much of his empirical material was historical discouraged many social scientists from pursuing his ideas. But the perception that communications was central to contemporary forms of imperialism was gathering momentum elsewhere.

By the mid-1920s, it was clear that American popular culture was rapidly becoming a global lingua franca, led by Hollywood's ascendancy in the international film market. As one observer put it, 'Language varies, manners vary, money varies, even railway gauges vary. The one universal unit in the world to-day is that slender ribbon [of film] which can carry hocus-pocus, growing pains and dreams' (Merz 1926: 165). Countries at the other end of this cultural chain were rapidly coming to see America's cultural ascendancy as a new form of imperialism, based on the annexation not of territory but of imagination. Commentators in Britain were particularly alarmed, viewing the language they shared with America as a Trojan horse. In 1937, the radical art historian, F. D. Klingender, collaborated with the activist, Stuart Legg, to produce *The Money Behind the Screen*, detailing the parlous state of Britain's national film industry and the extent of American dominance. It was one of the first studies of its kind and set an important precedent for future work on the organisation of the media industries. However, because it focused mainly on the economic and financial aspects of film-making and distribution, it had little to say about the social and cultural impact of imported movies. It was left to an American,

Charles Merz (Lippmann's collaborator on the 'Test of the News' study), to put these issues on the table.

Merz saw the sale of movies in overseas markets as the heavy artillery in a trade war which was designed to make the American way of life the model for popular aspirations across the globe. This assault was organised around the ideology of consumerism – the promise that consumer goods can deliver both happiness and freedom – as dramatised in the lives of the stars and the lush settings of popular films. It was exactly this incorporation of film into the culture of selling that had so angered Hugo Münsterberg when he set out to defend American movies from their critics and to demonstrate their potential to become a new artform, in his influential book, *The Photoplay*, the original title of his 1916 work (Münsterberg 1970).◄ In his view, whenever spectators were encouraged to think of themselves as consumers, any possibility of true art was annihilated. 'The interior decoration of the rooms is not exhibited as a display for a department store . . . A good [film] is not an advertisement for the newest fashions' (Munsterberg 1970: 81). Writing less than a decade later, Merz was in no doubt that the battering ram of seductive consumer style was breaking down resistance to 'the American Way' around the world. He observed that

> Automobiles manufactured here are ordered abroad after screen shadows have been observed to ride in them . . . rich Peruvians buy piano-players; orders come to Grand Rapids from Japanese who have admired mission armchairs in the films . . . Yorkshire manufacturers of boots and clothing have been obliged to alter their plants because the near east now wishes to dress like Rudolph Valentino.
>
> (Merz 1926: 162)

Later writers have returned to these economic and imaginative flows by way of the notion of 'cultural imperialism,'◄ as outlined in its

consumerism

► 'medium theory' and history – Chapter 2, p. 16

► film studies – Chapter 2, p. 31
► cultural imperialism – Chapter 11, p. 177

most forceful form in Herbert Schiller's book, *Mass Communications and American Empire* (1969).

The tangled connection between modernisation◄ and Americanisation was also a major theme in studies of the waves of economic and political migrants who had moved from Europe to the U.S.A. in the two decades on either side of 1900. The shifting relations between place and space were at the heart of the immigrant experience. They were simultaneously living in the United States and being members of global diasporic cultures◄ which linked their new homes to their original homelands through multiple ties of kinship, memory, travel, and economic remittance.

As one of the major destinations for inward migration to the U.S.A., Chicago offered a rich locale for investigating these issues, and a number of sociologists took up the challenge. In these studies, the role of mediated communications in sustaining old allegiances and identities, as well as in building new ones, emerges as a major theme. The letters collected in Thomas and Znaniecki's (1927) study of the Polish migrants contain multiple references, for example, to the importance of family photographs in cementing memories and marking change. Robert Park, with his background in journalism, undertook a major study of *The Immigrant Press and its Control* (1922). One of the Chicago department's graduate students, Paul Cressey, went on to make young people's movement through the imaginative landscapes of American consumerism, as offered in the movies, one of the major themes in his unpublished (1936) ethnography of juvenile delinquency in the Italian quarter of New York (see Jowett *et al.* 1996).

In a situation where migration and diaspora are increasingly characteristic of people's everyday experience around the world (the major focus, then and now, of anthropological research) and where American brands and cultural productions have achieved global currency, these pioneering attempts to explore how

anthropology

place and space intersect to organise memories, identities, and desires are more pertinent than ever. Similarly, as Manuel Castells has argued in his influential analysis of transnational networks (1996), the role of electronic communications in shifting the relations between space and place is central to understanding the structural organisation of social and economic life in the era of globalisation.◄ Other commentators, like John Urry, go further, arguing that, faced with these challenges, sociology needs to focus not on 'societies,' but on global mobilities and flows – of images, information, peoples, and goods (Urry 2000: 2–3).

This new agenda places issues of communications at the heart of social inquiry. The point can be oversold, however. People still have to live somewhere, and many aspects of their lives are still structured in fundamental ways by institutions and processes operating at local and national level. As a consequence, national and local media remain crucial resources for people's understanding of themselves and their situation.

TRAVELS CLOSER TO HOME

Although the impact of the shifting relations between physical locations and communicative spaces was felt most acutely by migrants, it was also an integral feature of the way everyday life was being restructured everywhere, even in the most conservative-looking towns. In 1921, Robert Lynd and his wife, Helen, set off for the modest-sized city of Muncie in Indiana to assess the effects of social and cultural change on everyday life. Muncie was the archetypal small town, middle-of-the-road politically and in the mid-West geographically, qualities the Lynds captured perfectly in their fictitious name, Middletown. The study was funded by a religious foundation which was particularly interested in shifts in religious behaviour, but from the outset, the Lynds decided to look at life in Muncie in the round.

The researchers were immediately struck by how comprehensively and rapidly a town sixty miles away from the nearest sizeable city and

▶ modernization – Chapter 11, p. 193

▶ diaspora – Chapter 11, p. 180

▶ globalisation – Chapter 11, p. 181

half a day's train ride from the nearest large city was being transformed by change. They were particularly impressed by the way that 'increasingly frequent and strong culture waves sweep over us from without, drenching us with the material and non-material habits of other centres' (Lynd and Lynd 1929: 5) They saw this process as centrally driven by the increasing diffusion of two technologies – cars and radios – the first offering physical release from the confines of the town, the second imaginative mobility. They pictured the radio 'rolling back the horizons of Middletown for the bank clerk or the mechanic sitting at home and listening to a Philharmonic concert ... or to President Coolidge bidding his father good night on the eve of election' (p. 269). And they were adamant that it was impossible to study 'Middletown as a self-contained, self-starting community ... when one watches these space-binding leisure-time inventions imported from without ... reshaping the city' (p. 271).

The fact that Muncie had a population of only 35,000 made it possible for the Lynds to study it relatively intensively, using a range of methods from documentary research to personal observations and interviews. Larger towns and cities, however, posed formidable logistical problems for this intensive style of 'community study' (as it came to be called). Consequently, urban ethnographies of everyday media activity have tended to focus on particular neighbourhoods or locales within a city.◄

The Lynds' central focus on the role of communication technologies in restructuring everyday life gave added impetus to longstanding concerns about the range of cultural and informational resources which the popular media offered for meaning-making.

MEDIA AND PUBLIC CULTURE

Looking at the popular press – the major forum for information and debate before the launch of radio broadcasting in the 1920s – earlier commentators had seen the discussion of political affairs and public policy being steadily edged out by crime, scandal, and human interest stories. They lamented this movement towards the appeals and styles of entertainment and theatre because it seemed a move away from the rational public debate which democracy required, and to mark an eclipse of active citizenship by spectatorship.

In the ensuing debate on 'sensationalism' (as this new journalistic style came to be called), many contributors were content to rely on illustrative examples selected for their rhetorical effect. Within the emerging social sciences, however, there was a desire to calibrate this shift more precisely. Addressing the first meeting of the German Sociological Association in 1910, the country's leading sociologist, Max Weber, urged his audience to pick up 'scissors and compass to measure the quantitative changes of newspaper contents during the last generation.' Interestingly, however, he was careful to emphasise that these initial counts should be seen as the first stage of a wider research programme that 'will proceed to qualitative [analyses]' (quoted in Hardt 1979: 181–182).

In the USA, however, Weber's programme was already well underway. In 1900, for example, Delos Wilcox had published an extensive study of the differences between 'serious' and 'yellow' (or 'tabloid') newspapers in one of America's most prestigious scholarly publications, the *Annals of the Academy of Political and Social Science*. His painstaking 'column by column' count of the space occupied by various categories of content demonstrated that critics of the popular press were right (Wilcox 1900: 65). 'Yellow' newspapers carried more news of crime and vice, whereas 'serious' (or 'conservative' papers as he calls them) carried more of the political and business news as well as letters and exchanges, as required by classical democratic models of the press as a public sphere (Habermas 1989 [1962]). This argument is also encountered today in discussions over the 'tabloidisation'◄ of contemporary news and accusations of 'dumbing down' (see, e.g., Sparks and Tulloch 2000). Quantitative content analysis continues to play a central role in furnishing empirical evidence for these debates.

sensationalism

▶ ethnography – Chapter 10, p. 164

▶ tabloidisation – Chapter 7, p. 107

By no means all commentators saw the popular press as the enemy of democratic ideals, however. In a seminal paper on the human interest story, the Chicago sociologist, Helen Hughes, argued strongly that by incorporating the stories of ordinary people into the news, the popular press was rebuilding the empathy for strangers which modern life had eroded, and which a democracy that is based on equal respect and attention to plural voices required. In her view, 'moral speculations are not evoked by news of court procedure; they take form on the reading of an intimate story that shows what the impact of law and convention means as a private experience' (Hughes 1937: 81). Again, analysts have recently returned to these relations between personal testimony and democratic sensibilities in detailed studies of both tabloid news (e.g., Langer 1998) and a new wave of confessional television talkshows (e.g., Murdock 2000).

While some early social scientists were mapping popular representations using content analysis, others were addressing the second part of Weber's programme, namely the development of detailed case studies◄ of particular texts. Critical analysts were particularly interested in how the themes and styles of popular media constructed the world in ways that supported prevailing relations of power. Siegfried Kracauer's (1927) essay, 'The Little Shopgirls Go to the Movies,' is a particularly good example of this tradition of ideology critique◄ in action. Movies, he argues, 'are babbling a rude secret, without really wanting to. In the endless sequence of films, a limited number of typical themes recur again and again [revealing] the sum of the society's ideologies, whose spell is broken by ... interpretation' (Kracauer 1995: 295). This characterisation of the critic as a guerrilla fighter in the war of signs, revealing the power behind the pleasures, has been central to much subsequent work in textual analysis. However, proponents of this model of strong media have too often assumed that audiences are vulnerable or, at the very least, not

properly equipped to see through the disguises of power without the help of a professional analyst.◄

Kracauer emphatically sees the 'little shopgirls' watching the films that he deconstructs as open to suggestion. After sitting absorbed in a film that reveals the soft heart concealed within the iron chest of a Berlin businessman, for example, he imagines them learning to forget their exploitative and unequal working conditions and coming 'to understand that their brilliant boss is made of gold on the inside as well' (p. 300). Interestingly, Roland Barthes employed almost exactly the same metaphor thirty years later in his (1957) book, *Mythologies*. He argued that it is only once 'a typist earning twenty pound a month *recognizes herself* in the big wedding of the bourgeoisie' that ideology can be said to be fully effective (Barthes 1973: 154).

Barthes's semiotic approach to critiquing popular media went on to exert an enormous influence on later work in media and cultural studies. However, it was also subjected to fierce criticism from commentators who argued that it did scant justice to the complexities of women's relations to the media they consumed. This argument was later pursued in a range of detailed empirical work which fed into a more general celebration of the 'active audience.' Once again, however, far from marking a decisive break with the past, as some commentators have claimed, this general perspective has long roots in social science inquiry.

In 1913, Emilie Altenloh, a graduate student at the University of Heidelberg, published the doctoral thesis in sociology which she had conducted under the supervision of Alfred Weber (Max Weber's brother). Entitled *The Sociology of Cinema*, it was based on replies to over a thousand questionnaires given out to cinemagoers, supplemented by personal observations and interviews. In contrast to Kracauer, she sees the women at the centre of her study not as dupes of prevailing ideology, but as self-reflexive actors in the new social and imaginative spaces opened up by the cinema and the

► case study – Chapter 14, p. 239

► ideology critique – Chapter 2, p. 34

► audience as semiotic guerilla fighters – Chapter 10, p. 167

modern city. Their choices are crucially determined by the dynamics and pressures of a mature capitalist economy (see Hansen 1990). However, this sociological approach to audiences as actively negotiating mediated meanings and experiences, but embedded in wider social contexts that structured their responses in complex ways, had an uphill struggle. It was faced with the growing enthusiasm for the stimulus–response models being developed within psychology | individual psychology.

QUESTIONS OF INFLUENCE AND EFFECTS

behaviourism: stimulus and response | One of the leading proponents of this psychological model was John Watson. His 'behaviourist' approach saw all human action, from 'jumping at a sound' to 'writing books' as responses to environmental stimuli (1930: 6). He further insisted that only records of behaviour that was observed directly in the laboratory counted as relevant data in social inquiries wishing to claim the mantle of 'science.'

As he conceded, however, 'the social problems which psychology sometimes has to study' could 'probably never be brought under laboratory control' (Watson 1924: 28). He had discovered this for himself when he set out in the summer of 1919 to evaluate the impact on the sexual behaviour of young people of a government-sponsored film which warned that promiscuity could lead to venereal disease. After a monumental research effort involving over a thousand questionnaires, nearly a hundred personal interviews, and a number of observations of film screenings, he reluctantly concluded that his evidence suggested that 'there is no indication that behaviour is modified significantly' (Lashley and Watson 1922: 216). A powerful stimulus, expressly designed to persuade, appeared to have had no discernible effect that could be detected by his measuring instruments. Unfortunately, this cautionary tale did not dissuade subsequent psychological researchers from pursuing the Holy Grail of direct media 'effects,' both in and out of the laboratory.

Had later researchers looked closely at Watson's own description of his research, they would have come across a brief account of an incident that pointed to an alternative strategy of inquiry. Watson was disturbed to find that far from instilling the fear and disgust that the producers had hoped for, the film frequently provoked ribald and risqué comments. After one screening, members of the research team decided to talk 'with a number of young men, loafers about the hotel lobby, and the like.' They told the researchers that when 'boys and girls who had seen the picture talked about it afterward . . . flippancy and innuendo prevailed in their talk' (Lashley and Watson 1922: 204). Watson saw this 'talk' simply as an interesting supplement to his main data. For other researchers, however, listening attentively to casual talk and loafing around hotel lobbies and other places where people socialised spontaneously provided the basis for an entirely different approach to investigating the role of media in everyday life.

LIVING WITH MEDIA: ACTIVE AUDIENCES

When Paul Cressey set out to study the place of movies in the lives of young men living in the predominantly Italian area of East Harlem in New York in the early 1930s, he declared his wish to 'avoid the "social vacuum fallacy" so prevalent in much . . . psychological research' and to 'see the motion picture' in 'relationship to all the other forces and influences which bear in upon the delinquent boy in these areas' and in the motion picture theatre (quoted in Jowett *et al.* 1996: 160). Cressey had already undertaken an acclaimed ethnography of a dance-hall (later published as *Taxi Hall Dance)* for his Master's degree in sociology at Chicago. He decided to approach this new study as an ethnography of an urban neighbourhood, drawing on systematic observation and open-ended interviews to construct a thick description◄ of the cinema's role in the social and imaginative lives of the boys he was asked to study.

Cressey produced a path-breaking manuscript which suggested fertile links between the movies' equation of success and happiness with money and consumption, his subjects' sense of

---

► thick description – Chapter 14, p. 242

themselves, and the careers actually open to them. Crime, he argued, was not a simple 'effect' of crime films, but was produced in the cracks between consumer aspirations and blocked social opportunities. 'For boys who have been restricted on all sides by poverty, the appeal of [the] expensive apartments, costly automobiles, and "flashy" clothes' enjoyed by the gangsters in the films they watched is 'in itself an invitation towards that type of activity and aspiration' (ibid.: 209).

Unfortunately, the study was never published, and the unfinished draft lay unread in the archives and was rediscovered only recently. However, if we look at other enthographies of young people undertaken in the same period, such as Frederick Thrasher's *The Gang* (1927), we see the same drive to anchor accounts of deviance in everyday experiences and to present young people as actively creating their own meanings. Some of these meanings (as Thrasher argued) might form the basis for a distinctive subculture with its own rituals and emblems of identity.

Again, these early studies of youth subcultures, together with the preference for ethnographic modes of inquiry and the insistence on placing everyday media activity in its wider contexts, have all been enormously influential within academic studies of audiences and consumption over the past two decades or so. This has been the case particularly within cultural studies.◄ Prompted by the early ethnographic work of the Birmingham Centre, researchers have returned to the tradition of inquiry pioneered by Cressey, Thrasher, and others. Now as then, however, there have been relatively few full ethnographies based on contact and observation sustained over several years. For practical reasons, most researchers have had to settle for qualitative studies compressed into much shorter time periods, using open-ended interviews, focus groups, or personal documents to access grounded interpretations and everyday experiences. Given Lazarsfeld's reputation as an arch number-cruncher, it is ironic that three of the most important efforts to develop qualitative methods and apply them to the study of

audience activity should have come either from researchers working on projects he helped to set up, or from his close collaborators.

The value of conducting detailed interviews with respondents had been amply demonstrated in a study of public reaction to Orson Welles's 1938 radio dramatisation of H. G. Wells's *The War of the Worlds*. Welles, who already had a reputation for breaking established generic rules, decided to present this story of a Martian invasion of Earth in a form that was as close as possible to the conventions of radio news reporting. Some listeners believed it was a newscast and panicked. Although the leader of the research project, Hadley Cantril, was a psychologist, he saw very clearly that personal differences could not explain the complex variations in responses to the programme, as described by the 138 people his research team interviewed. Instead, he sought to account for differences in terms of inequalities in the amounts and types of social and cultural capital◄ people possessed, such as how familiar they were with contemporary artistic conventions, and whether they had someone they trusted whom they could ask for advice.

Read in this way, Cantril's explanatory framework is closer to the account that the French sociologist, Pierre Bourdieu, gives of the social basis of cultural taste in his highly influential book *Distinction* (published in English in 1984). To characterise it as simply another exercise in 'selective influence,' as one widely read American textbook on media research does (Lowery and DeFleur 1983: 83), is to ignore how thoroughly the study emphasises the 'social' in social psychology.

Cantril's *Invasion From Mars*, published in 1940, was the first book produced by the Radio Research Project, directed by Paul Lazarsfeld. The following year, Herta Herzog, one of Cantril's co-authors and a member of Lazarsfeld's project team, published a path-breaking study of women's relations with daytime radio soap operas. The study was based primarily on personal interviews with a hundred women living in the Greater New York area, initially open-ended, but later using a prepared ques-

► cultural studies – p. 57

► social and cultural capital – Chapter 9, p. 154

tionnaire. This work is often presented as an early example of 'uses and gratifications' research.◄ Herzog certainly uses these words, but again, to see it simply in these terms is to miss its more radical implications. Like Emilie Altenloh almost thirty years before, what emerges if we read the data carefully is an account of women's strategies for coming to terms with the expectations, inequalities, and buried resentments of domesticity, and of how the imaginary worlds of the soaps intersect with the mundane realities of everyday life. As such, it stands as an early precursor of the very influential qualitative work on women as audiences for romantic fiction and television soaps that followed the emergence of feminist scholarship in the 1970s.◄

Another of Lazarsfeld's intellectual colleagues, Robert Merton, also used personal interviews to good effect in a study of news magazine readership in a small town (Merton 1949). After preliminary work, he was intrigued to find that influential people in the community approached the magazine with very different purposes. 'Local' influentials, who had grown up in the town and owed their position to their local social connections, showed very little interest in stories dealing with national of international affairs. In comparison, 'cosmopolitan' influentials, who had come from elsewhere and owed their reputation to nationally recognised qualifications, tended to gravitate to these items first.

Interestingly, it was exactly this last group that Edward Ross had had in mind when in 1910 he called for the establishment of a newspaper endowed by public subscription to promote serious news and debate. He admitted that it was unlikely to attract a general readership, but he hoped that 'it would inform the teachers, preachers, lecturers and public men, who speak to the people eye to eye' (Ross 1910: 311). This describes exactly the 'two-step flow' model of communications that Merton and Lazarsfeld developed in their work. However, to see Merton's work on 'locals' and 'cos-

local and cosmopolitan social types

mopolitans' simply in these terms is once again to miss its full implications. Merton's emphasis on variations in cultural and social capital, and on differences in the strategies of distinction and advantage pursued by different social segments, prefigures Bourdieu's work. In this regard, Merton may be seen as one of the pioneers in establishing a distinctively sociological approach to differences in media consumption and cultural tastes.

Merton also played a major role in pioneering a method that has been central to recent work on active audiences: focus group research.◄ He developed the technique which he called 'the focused interview' during his involvement in wartime studies of military motivation and morale. Just after World War II, he published a paper outlining its uses and rationales in one of the major professional journals of sociology (Merton and Kendall 1946). At the time, however, the growing ascendancy of quantitative methods tended to discourage academic researchers from pursuing its possibilities. It was taken up within market research (see Morrison 1998), but it has only recently re-emerged as a major technique in social-scientific studies of audiences.

Sometimes, however, direct interviewing proved impossible because of shortage of time, limited resources, or difficulties of access. In these instances, researchers wishing to work with qualitative materials fell back on the 'frozen speech' embodied in personal documents. We have already noted how W.I. Thomas built his study of Polish migrants to America around collections of existing family letters. Where there were no existing documents, researchers set out to create them.◄ Herbert Blumer, another leading figure in the Chicago Sociology Department, collected 'a number of autobiographical accounts dealing with motion-picture experiences' (Blumer and Hauser 1933: 20). He then used these as the basis for a study eventually published as *Motion Pictures and Youth*. As with Cressey's study (which formed part of the same Payne

---

▶ uses and gratifications research – Chapter 9, p. 142

▶ qualitative studies of women as audiences – Chapter 10, p. 163

▶ focus group research – Chapter 14, p. 241

▶ autobiographies and other documents – Chapter 14, p. 243

Fund research programme),◄ Blumer's materials, with their strong emphasis on situated experience, led him to emphasise the importance of 'social milieu' and 'social background' in forming film preferences and organising responses (ibid.: 202).

At the same time, the scope of Blumer's study was limited by the project's focus on the possible links between the cinema and juvenile crime. A more open account of the relations between cinema-going, everyday life, and aspirations was offered by J.P. Mayer in his 1948 study, *British Cinemas and Their Audiences*. Mayer had hit on the bright idea of collecting cinema autobiographies by placing an advertisement in *Picturegoer*, one of the major magazines for film fans, asking people to write to him. Ien Ang was later to use the same technique to collect Dutch women's accounts of their experiences of watching the American television soap, *Dallas*, for her very influential study, *Watching Dallas* (Ang 1985).

Mayer freely acknowledges his debt to Blumer's pioneering efforts, but uses his own material to explore a range of themes not tackled in Blumer's work. These include the central role of films, particularly American films and their stars, in offering models for personal style and consumption. As one of the women who wrote to Mayer explained,

> When I was 17 I saw a star (I forget her name) about whom the boy I was with said: 'She has the most lovely feet and her shoes are always beautiful.' I had nice feet and made a vow that the same should be said of me. I don't know whether it ever was, but I always bought the nicest shoes and stockings I could afford and shoes are still my pet luxury.
>
> (quoted in Mayer 1948: 25)

Mayer claimed in the Introduction to the study that, despite the self-selecting nature of his sample, his 'anonymous contributors speak for twenty million or more' addressing us, the readers, directly in their own words, rather than 'through the mouth of the "superior" intellectual who by chance or choice went to a

► Payne Fund studies – Chapter 10, p. 158

better school, to university' (p. 11). This celebration of the authenticity of everyday talk and its ability to offer the analyst direct, unmediated access to 'real' experiences and feelings is a blindspot comparable to the wholesale rejection of such evidence by some quantitative researchers. This inclination to romanticise 'ordinary' lives runs through much later work on everyday life and media consumption within cultural studies and qualitative sociology like a goodwill message embedded in a stick of seaside rock. Its impetus is generous and democratic in spirit, but by playing down the researcher's responsibility to reinterpret people's own accounts and to tease out the hidden threads that bind biographies to histories, strategies to structures, it blunts the critical edge of social investigation.

REACTIONS, RUPTURES AND REDISCOVERIES

The account offered here has deliberately concentrated on work conducted in the first half of the twentieth century in order to show that current research in media and communications continually draws on traditions of social science inquiry which are longer, richer, and more varied than many contemporary writers imagine. However, there is no doubt that the majority of research in the field has been conducted since 1950.

Along with other specialisms, media and communication research benefited enormously from the rapid growth in social scientific research both inside and outside the universities in the postwar years.◄ But it was also profoundly shaped by the political climate created by the onset of the Cold War between the USA and the Soviet Union. This ideological conflict dominated the intellectual landscape. In the USA, the obsessive hunt for communist 'subversives' in cultural and intellectual life, spearheaded by Senator McCarthy's investigations into 'un-American' activities, had a profoundly chilling effect on scholarship, and it comprehensively discouraged the pursuit of critical inquiry.

► development of media research institution – Chapter 16, p. 278

ontoauv

noilmbef

structural functionalism

The dominant model of the social order during that period, structural functionalism, fitted this climate of caution perfectly. The principal architect of the position was the American sociologist, Talcott Parsons, whose key book, *The Social System*, published in 1951 (in the early years of the Cold War), saw every social institution as having a particular role or 'function' in maintaining social stability and cementing consensus. Media and communications systems were assigned a central role in this gluing-together process.

This model of society as a smoothly functioning, self-correcting organism was itself highly functional politically. It presented postwar America as a society that had successfully transcended the class conflicts that the Soviets (following Marx) saw as the major driving force of historical change. It was also a useful intellectual weapon in the fierce global-wide struggle for the hearts and minds of citizens in the former colonial territories that had achieved political independence after the war. It allowed the USA to present the 'American way' of doing things as a self-evidently superior path to 'modernisation,' both materially and morally, one that would deliver social integration as well as economic improvement. In line with this view, degrees of 'modernisation' came to be measured in terms of how closely a country approximated to the USA in terms of the relative distribution of selected consumer goods, including communications goods.

Although the long shadow cast by the ideological and military struggle between the world's two great superpowers silenced or deflected many sceptical voices within the American academy, there were exceptions, most notably C. Wright Mills. Mills had studied sociology at the University of Wisconsin under Edward Ross (whose blistering attack on the press we looked at earlier). He shared his mentor's radical populist perception that the democratic rights of 'ordinary' people were continually blocked by entrenched centres of power intent on retaining their privileges and extending their influence. This led him to argue that, far from being agents of organic unity and voluntary consensus as Parsons supposed, mediated communications were central to the

play of power. We cannot, he argued, 'merely assume that some set of values, or legitimations, *must* prevail lest a social structure come apart' (Mills 1970: 46). On the contrary, if there is

> a unified symbol sphere, one monopolised by certain master symbols, [it] is more likely to be the result of a monopoly of channels of communications, and of forceful tabooing of certain countersymbols, than the result of any harmonious institutional basis. It is more likely to be imposed than to grow.
> (Gerth and Mills 1954: 297)

Mills went on to develop this point five years later, in his most influential book, *The Power Elite* (1959). In it, he presented America, not as the ideal democracy of official Cold War rhetoric, but as 'a naked and arbitrary power,' controlled by the interlocking interests of industry, the military, and government, in which 'the second-rate mind is in command of the ponderously spoken platitude' and 'its men of decision enforce their often crackpot ideas on world reality' (Mills 1959: 360–361). Measured against the scale of this perceived threat to democratic ideals, it is not surprising that Mills found that most work by his colleagues in the social sciences fell some way short of the challenge.

the sociological imagination

In his manifesto for engaged inquiry, *The Sociological Imagination* (1959), he argued that the social sciences are distinguished from other forms of commentary precisely by their 'capacity to range from the most impersonal and remote transformations to the most intimate features of the human self – and to see the relations between the two' (Mills 1970: 14). This required all aspects of social life to be placed squarely in their full historical and structural context. Their failure to do this was his principal complaint against Merton and Lazarsfeld, his colleagues at Columbia, where he was working at the time.

theories of the middle range

If Parsons' bland, empty categories represented the betrayal of 'grand theory,' Mills saw Lazarsfeld and Merton's concentration on 'theories of the middle range' (working concepts and models like the 'two-step' flow

abstracted
empiricism

model of communications) as prime examples of the derelictions of what he called 'abstracted empiricism.' How, he asked, could Lazarsfeld, in his well-known study of the 1940 election campaign in Erie County, Ohio, *The People's Choice* (1944), focus so enthusiastically on voting behaviour and still make 'no reference to the party machinery for "getting out the vote," or indeed to any political institutions' (Mills 1970: 63)?

As noted above, though, this characterisation of Lazarsfeld as an essentially conservative figure does him less than justice. In a speech he made soon after arriving in America from Vienna (where he had been active in the socialist movement), Lazarsfeld described himself as 'a Marxist on leave.' Mills clearly felt that this leave had become permanent. However, a careful reading of Lazarsfeld's writings reveals strong continuities with his radical youth. In an essay written jointly with Merton, published in the same year as *The People's Choice*, he had presented a strong critique of corporate control over communications, arguing that 'increasingly, the chief power groups, among which organised business occupies the most spectacular place [seem] to have reduced direct exploitation, and turned to a subtler type of exploitation, achieved largely by disseminating propaganda through the mass media of communication' (Lazarsfeld and Merton 1960: 493).

Mills died in 1962, before one of the other major challenges to structural functionalism, the revival of phenomenology, had got fully into its stride. Had he lived to comment, his observations would have been highly critical, since the leaders of this movement signally failed to take account of 'the historical structures in which the milieux of everyday life are organised,' or to relate biographies to histories as he had advocated (Mills 1970: 175). The attempt to build on the phenomenological approach to everyday life, as pioneered by Alfred Schütz, was led by Harold Garfinkel,

ethno-
methodology

who called his work ethnomethodology because it was based on closely observed accounts of the 'methods' that people ('ethnos') use in everyday encounters. In many ways, the research collected in his best-known book, *Studies in Ethnomethodology* (1967), may be

read as an attempt to radicalise Parsons by interrogating the tacit agreements that his model of social consensus depends on, but which he had taken for granted (see Sharrock and Anderson 1986: ch. 3). By exposing the provisionality of the rules and schemas governing personal interaction, and detailing how they were continually recreated and reaffirmed in everyday social encounters, Garfinkel presents 'ordinary' people as the true architects of social order and social change. In this conception, 'social structure cannot refer to anything more than members' everyday sense [of it] since it has no identity which is independent of that sense' (Filmer *et al.* 1972: 54).

This radically reductionist account of social structure, with its exclusive focus on the micropolitics of everyday life, could not offer a concerted challenge to structural functionalism, because it refused to examine the structural sedimentation of institutional power. Such challenges were beginning to gather momentum elsewhere, however. When the political consensus was finally broken open in the 1960s – by the Civil Rights movement, the opposition to the American war in Vietnam, and the international student movements – critical traditions of inquiry began to gain increasing currency and support. Two intellectual movements, in particular, have had a major impact on contemporary work in media and communications: the revival of critical political economy and the development of cultural studies.

Although some of the key figures in the return to political economy, such as Dallas Smythe and Herbert Schiller, had trained as economists, their political allegiances were always to the older tradition of inquiry with its deep roots in longstanding debates about the relations between economic organisation, cultural life and the common good. From the mid-1960s onwards, writers like Herbert Schiller returned to this central focus on the relations between the production and circulation of material goods and the constitution of the good life and the good society. Borrowing from Marx and from earlier radical commentators like Upton Sinclair, they developed a powerful critique of the role of the American media and communications indus-

critical
political
economy

tries in supporting prevailing inequalities of power and benefit, both at home and overseas.

At the same time, the emerging field of cultural studies◄ was exploring how the general dynamics of capitalist cultural production worked themselves out in styles and representations which were carried by everyday artefacts, and in the strategies devised by audiences and consumers in constructing their own meanings and uses. From the outset, cultural studies was a point of intersection between two intellectual traditions – ideology critique and ethnographies of everyday cultural practice. Consequently, within the corpus of literature it has produced, accounts of powerful media have continually rubbed up against celebrations of audience refusal and resistance. Analyses of the unequal distribution of vernacular and radical discourses and meaning systems (as in David Morley's influential work on *The 'Nationwide' Audience* (1980)) attempted to mediate between the two traditions.

ON NOT REINVENTING THE WHEEL

For many analysts, including myself, illuminating the exercise of power and structural constraints and exploring the possibilities for change remain the central aims of a critical social-scientific approach to media and communication. As I have tried to indicate, in pursuing this task, we have a rich stock of concepts and methods to draw upon. Their originators are not distant figures to be consigned to dusty back rooms in the museum of ideas. They remain our contemporaries. We still confront the central questions they grappled with, and their search for answers still has much to teach us. We are part of a continuing conversation about the structure and meaning of modern times and the ways they are changing. They stand at our shoulder, advising, carping, urging us on. To refuse their invitation to debate is to condemn ourselves to regularly reinventing the wheel.

► cultural studies – also Chapter 2, p. 39

II Systematics

PROCESSES OF MEDIATED COMMUNICATION

An implicit model of communication

The bulk of previous media studies are premised on a basic and sometimes implicit model of communication which centers attention on senders, messages and recipients. That is in spite of the fact that most current research recognizes problems in thus segmenting the process of communication, and in divorcing mediated communication from its social and cultural contexts.

The chapters of Part II follow this model of communication as a structuring device that facilitates a review of earlier empirical as well as theoretical contributions. Each chapter, in various ways, also considers how evidence about, and conceptions of, one stage of communication reflect on the process as a whole. In particular, Chapter 9 returns to the issue in an analysis of the several stages of media uses and effects. Furthermore, Chapters 11 and 12 examine research on media as they enter different cultural and historical contexts.

The different traditions of research which are covered in the following chapters are often characterized by a focus, for instance, on particular types of media organizations, or on specific genres. Similarly, the traditions are distinguished, in part, by their reliance on particular methodologies.

Media organizations

The three chapters on media organizations address both fiction and fact, entertainment and news, which have given rise to different forms of production. The presentations also draw attention to differences between media types, and between the national and international levels of media organization. Finally, the chapters include both reassessment and critique of classic studies, and a concrete illustration of field research on media production.

- *Ficton production* (Chapter 4). The chapter reviews the several interrelated levels of determination which shape the final media product, including the international economy, technological developments, and professional work routines. The importance of each level is exemplified with reference to a case study of production for cable television.
- *News production* (Chapter 5). An analysis of news studies over the last five decades identifies three main traditions, and goes on to suggest their compatibility, in the light also of changes within the media themselves. As such, the chapter addresses the various levels of determination in media production (presented in Chapter 4) from the perspective of different research traditions.

- *International news* (Chapter 6). The area of news, and of political communication generally, has particular implications for international relations, which have been an important concern in media studies. The last chapter on media production reviews studies of the flow of news in the world as a fourth tradition of news research, alongside the three traditions identified in Chapter 5.

Media texts

The messages of mediated communication have been studied as 'texts' and as 'contents' by different theoretical and methodological traditions. Fiction has primarily lent itself to qualitative approaches, as derived from the study of literature and other arts, whereas factual genres have been examined by a mixture of quantitative and qualitative approaches. In addition, the modern technological media have posed research questions concerning the specificity of audiovisual 'texts,' and concerning the interrelations between media texts in 'intertextual' networks.

- *Media fact* (Chapter 7). The first chapter addresses both quantitative content analysis and qualitative discourse analysis of media texts. The chapter reviews developments within content analysis in recent decades, and compares different varieties of discourse studies. One of the example analyses takes up still images and their interrelations with verbal texts.
- *Media fiction* (Chapter 8). Following a brief account of quantitative studies of fiction, the second chapter gives special attention to semiotic, structuralist, and narratological approaches to media texts. Referring to the classic feature movie, *The Big Sleep*, as its recurring example, the chapter shows how various models of analysis may be applied to different media, including moving images and sound.

Media audiences

From the beginnings of the field, audiences have been a central object of analysis, and have been studied especially by quantitative social science through experimental and survey methodologies. More recently, research with a textual and qualitative orientation has begun to examine audiences empirically. Indeed, 'reception' and 'effects' have been a key area of convergence in recent decades.

- *Media effects* (Chapter 9). After a brief history of the notion of 'effects,' the chapter summarizes the multiple traditions of inquiry which have developed since the 1930s. Their various contributions are systematized with reference to stages of communication and influence, and to short-term and long-term effects.
- *Media reception* (Chapter 10). This chapter begins by conferring the recognized 'milestones' of the effects tradition with important contributions to reception studies. Next, the chapter reviews varieties of reception analysis, and considers the potentials and problems of 'ethnography' as currently practiced in media studies.

Media contexts

The last two chapters under the heading of systematics take up the interconnections of media with their social, historical and cultural contexts, thus emphasizing the *communication* aspect of media and communication research. The purpose is to present relevant adjoining fields of research, some of which have already been incorporated into the media field, while others may hold an untapped potential. Specifically, computer-mediated communication is redefining the distinctions between media, text, and context, and calls, not least, for theory development in further research.

- *Space – culture* (Chapter 11). On the one hand, media are embedded in social and cultural spaces – from the local to the global level. The chapter gives special attention to research on the cultural formations that are associated with geographical areas, but also considers, for example, the subcultural formations which the media help to maintain. In addition, the chapter provides an overview of research so far on computer media.
- *Time – history* (Chapter 12). On the other hand, the technological media are embedded in, and emerge from, the long history of human communication. Perhaps surprisingly, 'the media' is a recent notion, dating from the 1960s. The chapter covers the history both of 'communication' and of particular 'media,' and presents concepts and methodologies for understanding the modern media in historical perspective.

Determination in the first instance

Each chapter examines a number of factors that affect processes of mediated communication, both within the media and in their social contexts. A shared premise of the chapters is that each individual factor – whether technological, economic, political, or cultural – may exercise a determination in the first instance (Hall 1983: 58), but not a determination in the final instance. Neither the concrete products nor the actual practices of communication are the outcome of any simple causality. Different traditions of research have identified, and tried to explain, empirical variations of mediated communication. Here, the traditions are brought together and compared as part of a systematics of media and communication studies.

4 The production of media fiction

Horace Newcomb and Amanda Lotz

- an outline of the main *levels of analysis* in production research – from *political economy* to *professional routines*
- a description of the diverse *sources of evidence* and of relevant *methods of analysis*
- a *case study*: the production of a *cable television series*
- a review of findings from the *case study in relation to the levels of analysis*.

Since the mid-1980s, the most intensively researched topics in media studies have been audiences, their reception and uses of mediated texts. Following the preponderance of prior research that made claims about the meanings of such texts, their ideological significance and their social effectivities, the emphasis on audiences seems both predictable and warranted. One result of this focus, however, is that during the same period far less work has focused on production processes. This also follows, in part, from the presumption that mass-mediated fiction remains, in many cases, a 'factory product,' standardized content emerging from routinized production processes. We suggest, however, that the situation is more complicated than this. Variations within routines, the points of tension engaged in contests between standardization and differentiation, are of equal significance and equally instructive in exploring the significance of media fictions. It is necessary, then, to provide a more thorough and detailed analysis of production practices than the usual generalizations about 'media factories' allow.

One approach is outlined in David Bordwell's concept of 'historical poetics' (Bordwell 1989). Under that category, he suggests that it is necessary to explore options open to media-makers at given points in time and in specific social contexts, attending to industrial, economic, and regulatory factors. While Bordwell tends to focus on those options generating the standardized elements found in much mass-mediated material, we believe it is possible to discover important manipulations of production processes that indicate the 'relative autonomy' of individuals, groups, even organizations within media industries. What this suggests most importantly is that any study of the production of media fiction must recognize multiple types of influence. Factors ranging from policy formation to the application of new technologies may affect the production of any particular media fiction. While research taking account of multiple causal elements usually provides stronger explanations, it often remains the case that specific instances of production studies privilege particular aspects over others. In some cases, this results in reductive assertions about causation or influence, although in most instances it simply means that one factor is taken as dominant, overdetermining all others. These factors and the relations among them may be described as 'levels of analysis.'

relative autonomy

We emphasize that this term should not imply a universally effective hierarchy of influence or determination, but it is the case that such a categorization of influence works from more general to more specific sites and applications. The most effective production research will seek to identify the interdependence of the influences, while demonstrating their variations in different cases, settings, and systems.

LEVELS OF ANALYSIS

National and international political economy and policy

commercial and state-supported media

The production of particular media artefacts within specific industrial systems obviously takes place within more general contexts. Among the most influential works at this level are those exploring differences between commercial broadcasting or film industries and media reliant on various forms of state support (e.g., Blumler 1992; Katz and Wedell 1977; Schiller 1969). Although analyses of production practices generally acknowledge such differences, broad assumptions rather than detailed analysis commonly guide the study of the relations between policy and production. This is so, in part, because descriptive and source material related to media policy often focuses on generalizations rather than cases, while detailed case studies take the constraints of political economy for granted. Overlooked in both models is the fact that individual productions are enabled as well as constrained by general conditions. Varied responses to those conditions illuminate the complexity of the larger structures, reminding us that while media production is indeed a modern, factory product, the differences among the products are as telling as their similarities. Nevertheless, a number of policy works provide useful contextual information for production research. Among them, Alexander *et al.* (1998), Hoskins *et al.* (1997), and Moran (1996) offer extensive overviews of contemporary media industry policies that can be applied analytically.

Some studies do, in fact, bring together the macro-levels of policy and economic structure with analyses of cases. They include explo-rations of the ways in which media products are affected by social problems, such as 'censorship' or 'violence.' Doherty (1999) and Gardner (1987) provide examples of the first topic, showing how particular American films were produced before and during periods of heavy social control. Cowan (1979) focuses on engagements with policy by individuals (e.g., Norman Lear) and institutions (e.g., The Writers Guild of America) with regard to sex and violence on television, and shows how production strategies were affected by congressional actions mandating a 'family hour' for commercial television.

As these publications suggest, a major approach to studying the relationship between policy and production has been historical.◄ Boddy (1990), for example, explores relations among television executives, the U.S. Congress, and television critics in the 1950s. He carefully establishes how, in the struggle among these groups, industry executives managed to secure their economic interests through legislative and judicial decision-making. The outcome of these battles led to major industry developments, such as the shift from 'live' television production in New York to filmed programming from Hollywood, resulting in fundamental changes in aesthetics, altered production practices, and ultimately the distinctive place of television fiction in U.S. culture.

Methodologically, all these works have depended on the analysis of archival data.◄ While public policy records are usually freely available, corporate papers have sometimes been deposited in reference archives, making access for researchers relatively simple. In other cases, such materials may be proprietary and access severely restricted. These records are essential for production research, because the documents contain evidence both of conflicting points of view and of concrete decision-making related to particular media artefacts.

▶ historical studies of media – Chapter 12
▶ archival data – Chapter 12, p. 203

Specific industrial contexts

Historical approaches have also been prominent in research examining the institutional
configuration of media industries, but here
analysis is focused more precisely on specific
industrial practices. Among the strongest examples is *The Classical Hollywood Cinema*
(Bordwell *et al.* 1985), which examined the
development of the Hollywood film industry
and the resulting reliance on a particular narrative style, as indicated in the title.◄ The study
tracks the establishment of regularized industrial strategies, consequent divisions of labor,
instrumental applications of new technologies,
and other features of the Hollywood film factories. It suggests that, after a period of experimentation, the U.S. film industry narrowed
into certain industrial operations that were
developed in the service of particular narrative
conventions. The analysis also demonstrates
how this general pattern of regularization was
realized in particular films. The central argument points to the reduction of possible narrative strategies and, ultimately, of the styles,
genres, and meanings within an industry that
was increasingly successful on its own terms.
The ideological result was the establishment of
a particular cultural meaning of 'cinema' to the
exclusion or marginalization of alternative
forms.

Here again, researchers rely heavily on primary historical records – contracts, inter-office
memoranda, extant interviews, handbooks,
production manuals, instructional pamphlets,
variously revised scripts, and story conference
memoranda recording decision-making processes. These are explored in order to describe,
analyze, and contextualize the actual production
practices involved in film- and television-
making. Because sustained archival research is
needed to uncover more evidence, and because
the study of media fiction, in particular, is of
relatively recent development, new histories
continue to refine our knowledge of much-
needed background and circumstances. Hilmes
(1997), for example, provided new information
regarding the shifting arrangements among

► Hollywood cinema – also Chapter 8, pp. 119, 121

media industries, including the radio industry,
which have altered the cultural definition of
'film' and 'television' in the U.S.A.

A contemporary example illustrates how
this level of analysis takes research beyond
more generalized descriptions. Montgomery
(1989) focused on the different ways in which
interest groups engage television networks in
order to gain a more favorable representation.
Using interview and ethnographic methods, as
well as analysis of records and contracts, she
also examined individual television texts to
show how these groups variously succeeded or
failed in their attempts to alter detailed television production practices. A similar case is
in progress, and invites study, as we write. In
the U.S.A., the National Association for the
Advancement of Colored People has recently
secured contractual arrangements with major
television networks that will lead to the
employment of more people of color in television's executive and creative communities
(Jensen *et al.* 2000). In this case, as in cases
studied by Montgomery, interest groups have
used strategies, such as boycotts or threats of
boycotts, which recognize the role played by
political economy and government policies in
media production.

interest groups

Particular organizations: studios, production companies, networks

Studies of institutional relations often rely on
the next more specific level of analysis, exploring the connection between an organization
and the industrial configuration in which it
operates. Textual analysis of individual works
or collections of films and television programs
is much more prominent at this level, frequently
with an emphasis on genre and format as
indicative of an organizational 'style.' An outstanding example of this type of analysis is
Schatz (1988), who focused on regularized and
systemic aspects of the film industry, using
sources and approaches similar to other histories of cinema. In using archival sources, however, his primary method was the case study,
and by focusing on several studio organizations, the production of particular films, and
the roles of powerful individual studio heads,

he placed greater emphasis on human agency and documented important variations. The findings, again, indicate greater diversity within 'the studio system' than is sometimes assumed in studies of the general institutional arrangements.

the studio system of film

For television, a primary example is Feuer *et al.* (1984), a study of the MTM production company, which argues for the existence of a 'signature style' associated with a number of its productions. The identification of that style enabled the authors to describe variations within the general structures of both genre (the situation/domestic/workplace comedy) and the U.S. television industry as such. Cunningham (1988) provided a similar example of house style from Australian television. Such studies must rely heavily on company histories and production case studies in order to support the textual analyses that identify particular elements as a distinctive 'style.' In addition, they may make use of interviews and observations when access to individuals and ongoing productions can be arranged.

house style in television – also Ellis (1982)

Individual productions

A yet more specific level of analysis focuses on individual artefacts – films or television programs or series. Here, for example, we would include works exploring 'the making of' particular films and television programs such as Carringer's *The Making of Citizen Kane* (1996). Often, such works are designed to be more popular in appeal, providing behind-the-scenes information for fans or interested observers. Their popularity, however, does not necessarily diminish their usefulness for more complex research, and they may be cited as evidence in any of the other types of analysis described above. And, when such cases are examined within a more generalized theoretical framework, they can result in production studies of great analytical power. Indeed, scholarly works often offer similar information, making them informative for general readers as well as for researchers. A primary example for television is Gitlin (1983), who explored various fiction productions in order to show both variation and similarity within the process

the making of

and in the resulting product. Relying on interview and observation methods, combined with close analysis of both production techniques and narrative strategies, Gitlin used his cases to support more far-reaching inferences regarding the role of television in American culture.

One of the most significant recent examples of work focused on an individual television production is Julie D'Acci's *Defining Women: The Case of Cagney and Lacey* (1994). In this book, D'Acci traces the development of the program, explaining the roles of individual writer-producers, actors, studio executives, network heads, programmers, publicity teams, and other participants. She also examines the responses of critics, viewers, and organized interest groups, showing how their commentary contributed to keeping the series on air, in addition to continuing the debate on television portrayals of women. By combining this wealth of background material with her own detailed textual analysis, D'Acci presents one of the most complete pictures of the production of a fictional television program to date.

social roles in production units

Individual agents

Closely related to case studies of projects are those focusing on the 'makers' of fictional content, on their enactment as well as manipulation of all these structural factors. Many works at this level, among them most studies dependent on 'auteurist' theories of creative control, grant extraordinary freedom to individuals and their 'genius' (e.g., Bogdanovich 1967; Sarris 1968). Equally as significant, however, are contributions critiquing such notions. One of the most influential studies of the television industry, for example, is Cantor (1971). Using surveys and interviews in which producers remain anonymous, her work highlights the systemic constraints on 'true' notions of creativity as it might have been exercised by producers. In Cantor's analysis, the fundamental structure of American media industries – rooted in capitalism, supported by advertising, organized as oligopoly, and structured as factory labor – prevents their creative potential from being realized.

auteur theory

Other approaches have worked from a different assumption: that personnel involved

in creating media fiction are in fact aware, to varying degrees, of the constraints and opportunities implied in the 'levels' of influence, as reviewed here, which affect their work. The final emergence of any fiction film or television program is seen as the result of intensely collaborative processes – something frequently acknowledged within the industries as well as in theory. Thus, the work of individuals is viewed as tightly woven into such collaboration, which, further, is embedded in the more general levels of influence. In another study of American television producers, Newcomb and Alley (1983) emphasized the potential for
creativity and systemic constraints creative manipulation of the very same systemic constraints cited by Cantor. Their analysis also depended on interviews with producers self-reporting their decision-making processes, and was amplified with textual analyses designed to check those reports.

Primary data for studying the work of individuals need not always be gathered by interview or survey, however. For example, our library lists eighty-five works related to Alfred Hitchcock, and while many, perhaps most, of these are textual analyses of aspects of Hitchcock's films, a number provide original commentary on the production process. Gottlieb (1995) collected, in the director's own words, explanations, theories, and accounts regarding the production of 'his' works. In a related cross-reference, Behlmer (1981), by gathering David O. Selznick's memos relating to numerous productions, offered another, the producer's, perspective on some of Hitchcock, the director's, projects. A complete analysis of the specific projects on which they collaborated, and of their respective individual contributions, may be developed only in the production contexts embedding their sometimes conflicted relationship.

To sum up, these examples support the general recommendation of this essay: to account fully for the production of media fiction, it is necessary, at some point and in some measure, to acknowledge the extraordinary range of levels of influence, from the broadest structural arrangements to the most particular creative or administrative decisions made. It is the interdependence of these factors which, above all, defines media production practices.

SOURCES AND METHODS

In order to develop an accordingly complex study of media production, it is necessary to apply a wide range of analytical approaches to an equal range of sources. Research on current fiction production may usefully begin by describing the historical development of the contemporary situation. As already indicated, newer histories continue to provide substantial additional detail, hence elaborating a more precise understanding of how media industries came to their current status. A project would next require a description of the general regulatory and economic context at the level of the media system (commercial, public service, mixed, etc.). In addition to legislative sources concerning such industrial formations, macro-level information is usually available in national statistical abstracts. These latter national statistics sources provide details of import and export, viewer ratings and other statistics for television, gross numbers of completed productions for various media industries, distribution and attendance figures for films, the contribution of specific industries to the Gross Domestic Product, and so on. The significance of this information is often best recognized in comparative studies, as in Sinclair et al. (1996), where shifts in national policies and support systems are linked to changes in production practices. Comparative data may also be found in publications of organizations such as the European Audiovisual Observatory or the European Broadcasting Union.

For the study of individual corporations or production companies, some limited information may often be found in public corporate corporate records records, annual reports, and similar documents. More general information such as size of companies, principal officers, location and address, and recent projects is provided in sources such as the annually published *International Television and Video Almanac* and the *International Motion Picture Almanac*. It is far more difficult to obtain access to current corporate records concerning specific projects or corporate strategies. As alternatives, or complements, both original interviews and trade press reportage are valuable on this topic, but researchers must be aware that much of the information may be designed for public relations purposes.

Even more difficult to obtain is information related to the costs and other financial arrangements of particular productions. Still, general- production budgets ized budgets are widely acknowledged. It is well known, for example, that the average cost of a one-hour episode of a U.S. fictional television series was between $1.5 and $2 million in 1999. With this factor in mind, it is possible to assess the significance of the decision by the NBC network to pay $13 million per episode for its top program, *ER*. Similarly, high film budgets, such as those reported for *Titanic*, or low expenditures, such as those for *The Blair Witch Project*, are discussed in the trade and general press as directly related to aesthetic choices, creative decision-making, and resulting works.

But financial matters are only part of the complex negotiations leading to the production of fiction. It is more difficult still to account for the exercise of power that is involved in bringing a film to the screen or a television program to distribution, because the process involves complicated interactions involving many complex organizations. It is perhaps for this reason that historical production studies, with some benefit of hindsight, have been among the most informative in recent years. Works such as Schatz (1988) are based on archival records which, somewhat surprisingly, maintain detailed accounts of some of the most complicated, acrimonious, and revealing exchanges in the production of particular films. The account of struggles within the creative process are extremely instructive, as long as one remembers that each case is likely to work variations on standard industry practices.

Comparable contemporary 'behind the scenes' information, while often among the most important sources in these matters, may be the least available. Most of it must be gath- trade press ered from the 'trade press,' newspaper and magazine publications focused on the media industries. In the U.S.A., the daily and weekly editions of *Variety* provide extensive coverage of the financial arrangements within the film, television, cable, news media, music, and legitimate (stage) theater industries. Moreover, these papers present detailed information about individual productions, publish running records of box-office receipts, provide extensive coverage of countries other than the U.S.A., and frequently offer interpretive analysis of industry changes. Many other trade journals are equally useful, for instance, *Broadcasting and Cable*, *Advertising Age*, and *Electronic Media*.

Ultimately, in order to develop a broad understanding of any fiction production, it is necessary to supplement such background information with field research. This entails field research observation of production practices and interviewing of the personnel involved, often supplemented by published interviews and other library sources. Perhaps surprisingly, it is often rather easy for academic researchers to gain access to media production sites, where creative personnel working on a project are likely to be rather open regarding the choices they make, though less likely to provide details related to individual power struggles.

Thus, preparations addressing the various contextual levels should precede the analysis of a specific set of creative practices. The more thorough the preparation, the more precise and efficient the observations and interviews conducted in the case study. Demonstrating full preparation also makes it more likely that access to the production site will be granted by self-conscious professionals. To illustrate these points, and to elaborate the various levels of analysis in production research, the following section explores a specific research project.

ANY DAY NOW: A CASE STUDY

Preparing the project

The case study◀ was designed as part of dissertation research, conducted by Amanda Lotz for a project focusing on the representation of feminist discourses◀ in contemporary U.S. television. The larger study examines three television series on three different networks in some detail – *Ally McBeal* (FOX), *Sex in the*

▶ case study – Chapter 14, p. 239

▶ feminism – Chapter 2, p. 34

City (HBO), and *Any Day Now*, an original production for the Lifetime cable network. On-site production research was conducted only for this last series, and is supplemented with detailed institutional, textual, and audience analyses. The last program was selected, in part, because Lifetime promoted itself as 'television for women,' but also because of the richness of its textual representations. The series is, in addition, distinctive by being produced originally for cable distribution, rather than purchased from a studio following broadcast on network television, which was the common practice in earlier periods of cable television programming, and still more common than the production of original programs.

Any Day Now is an hour-long dramatic series focusing on the friendship between two women living in Birmingham, Alabama: Rene, an African-American, financially successful, single lawyer, and Mary Elizabeth, a white, working-class housewife. Set both in the present and in the 1960s childhood of the two women, the series dramatizes the different forces that make their friendship challenging. The series uses an innovative narrative structure, alternating representations of the present with those of the past, including scenes in which the two friends are played by child actors. This linking of past and present carries over into the portrayal of long-term family relationships (relatives appear in both time frames), and of social issues: the primary narrative consistently focuses on issues of race in American society, specifically in the deep South. Nancy Miller, Gary Randall, and Sheldon Pinchuk are the executive producers of the series, which is shot on set and on location in Santa Clarita, California, forty minutes north of Los Angeles.

Box 4.1 describes the steps involved in arranging and carrying out interviews with key personnel as well as observations of the series while it was in production in the summer of 1999. Not described in this chapter are additional preparations which included development of a thorough working knowledge of the production history of the program, textual analysis of previously aired episodes, and examination of published critical responses to the show.

As an hour-long dramatic series, *Any Day Now* is produced on a schedule that has become standardized in U.S. television production. Following extensive writing and pre-production, each episode is filmed in about eight days, and the actual production schedule for an episode is not available until a few days before shooting for the episode begins. (Post-production, including editing, dubbing, and preparation of the sound-track, occurs in a brief period following production, and was not observed for this project. But since decisions made during these processes may be significant for the final product, researchers may attempt to observe and discuss these aspects of the production process as well.) A production schedule dictates whether the crew is filming on the standing set or on location each day of the 'episode shoot.' Because it was necessary, as is commonly the case, to arrange the research visit in advance, the hope was to make arrangements so that the production would be filming primarily on set during the observation period in Los Angeles. Filming on set would provide more opportunities for interviews with key creative personnel and for observing various production activities that might not occur on location. Chances were good that this would be the case, since the budget for this series allowed only two days of shooting on location for each episode, with the bulk of filming done on standing interior sets.

It is important to add that the access afforded in this instance may be atypical of television production in general. *Any Day Now* was beginning its second season on Lifetime Television. Although in no danger of cancellation, the executive producers were on a campaign to increase the visibility of the series, and were focusing especially on the program's attention to racism and the ethnic diversity of the cast. Because of the series' history – Nancy Miller, one of the executive producers, spent eight years trying to get the series produced, and personally viewed it as a vehicle for social change rather than financial profit – our expression of interest in the series, and the limited exposure the research could provide, were important to the producers. In addition, because it did not draw an audience as large as a network series, our request was less common

pre-production

post-production

than might be the case for a network program deigned 'significant' by some academic researchers and journalists for whom cable television programs, with their smaller audiences, remain less important.

Preparing the field visit

Before making extensive plans for this case study, or for making the overall project design exclusively dependent on the single case, preliminary telephone calls were made to the *Any Day Now* production office to discuss the possibility of a visit. The calls were made a few months before the intended visit, allowing the project to be reconfigured if the producers were not open to a visit to their production site. (On the importance of this type of preliminary planning, see 'A counter-example,' below.) The first contact was made with Executive Producer Miller's assistant in April 1999. The assistant responded positively to the research interests, and suggested that the visit be made later in the summer, when the writers returned from their hiatus, the break between periods of production. At this point, it was clear that Lotz had established a personal relationship with a person who was aware of the research interest in the series, and who had tentatively approved a visit.

Before granting permission◄ for the visit, the executive producers requested information regarding the purpose of the research, the general topics of study, lists of individuals who might be involved in interviews, and details of an official university affiliation. Such requests are common and natural, and researchers should be prepared to respond in detail. The information was provided in a succinct two-page letter which described the research in general terms, and explained the significance of this series for the larger project.

The letter also outlined the aspects of production that Lotz wished to observe. These included being present at writers' meetings, observing production in progress, and interviewing writers, producers, and actors. At this

► permission of access – research ethics, Chapter 16, p. 289

stage, no interviews were firmly scheduled. It is often difficult to pre-plan which aspects of the process will be most beneficial for the larger project, or which appointments might have to be canceled later. Because the production of media fiction is affected by anything from an actor's illness to bad weather, researchers must be prepared to respond quickly to changes in schedules, and to seize occasions for gathering information in unexpected and unplanned ways.

A counter-example

Although, as noted above, access to television productions can often be readily obtained, this is not always the case, as suggested by a less successful endeavor within the same project. An attempt was made to arrange an interview with David E. Kelley, the writer and Executive Producer of *Ally McBeal*. As a 'top' series in U.S. network television at that time, this program received much more popular and critical attention, and has become something of a touchstone in contemporary discussions of feminism.

A letter was sent to Kelley's offices requesting an interview during the Los Angeles visit arranged for *Any Day Now*. The letter also requested a telephone interview if a visit was not possible. The letter was sent via express mail to make it stand out from the volumes of correspondence received at Kelley's production company, and a telephone message was left with Kelley's assistant. In that conversation, Lotz described the project, and the assistant was informed of the forthcoming letter. A few weeks later, Lotz received a message from the assistant explaining that Mr Kelley was too busy for an interview. While the popularity of Kelley's series may have made an interview impossible, it was still feasible to gather a range of interviews from trade publications, popular magazines, and other media which would be valuable in the larger project. This information, however, would not allow firsthand knowledge of the negotiating process that is part of any production. Given Kelley's extremely unusual position in the television industry and on this series (he has written or co-written every

ANALYSIS BOX 4.1 FIELD VISIT TO THE PRODUCTION SET OF *ANY DAY NOW* (1999)

Once the agreements had been confirmed, the visit was scheduled, and over the next few months the practical arrangements were completed through several telephone calls. The last call before the visit secured logistical information such as directions to the studio and where to park. Because many production sites have security guards at entrance gates, it is important to know such details, as well as whose name to give the guard upon arrival.

logistics

Other information on logistics made it clear that the daily schedule was often quite unpredictable. Writers tend to work fairly stable eight-hour days from about 10 a.m. to 6 p.m., but individual writers are also variously involved in general production meetings, depending on whether their script is currently in production, or if they are writing an upcoming episode. A production crew works twelve-hour days, with each morning's call-time dependent on when work was finished the previous night. Typically, shooting concludes between 9 and 10 p.m., and production resumes the following day around noon, although many members of the crew are on hand and preparing earlier. Securing this information early on made some aspects of production at least partially predictable, but, as we indicate below, hardly controllable.

the production crew

The first entry on the set of *Any Day Now* came at mid-afternoon on a Tuesday, following arrival in Los Angeles that morning, securing a rental car, and driving to the studios north of the city. Production had started for the day, and the writers were at lunch. The assistant who had been the main contact provided a tour of the site, including the studios and the offices. She introduced Lotz around the office and to the production staff as 'Amanda from the University of Texas who is doing her dissertation on representations of ethnicity and feminism on television. So she's looking at *Any Day Now*'. Once people were aware of the general purpose of the visit, they were eager to answer questions and discuss the show.

Three and a half days were spent visiting the series, a duration largely dictated by the time available to Lotz for this portion of her project. Despite the relatively brief length of the visit, it was sufficient for the purpose of the inquiry, and, because such visits are granted out of professional courtesy, it is unlikely that a longer stay could be arranged except under exceptional circumstances. By the end of the second day, the components of the production company and the general rhythm of production were clear. The final day and a half was helpful in securing interviews – which were repeatedly rescheduled, but which also, unexpectedly, made it possible to observe a promotions meeting. Many events and meetings were scheduled, canceled, and rescheduled in just these few days, making it difficult to plan ahead for every event, and, because a limited amount of time had been allotted for the studio visit, much of what actually took place had to be left to chance. However, even if the visit was thus completed without securing some important interviews, a relationship had been established, assuring that additional or follow-up interviews could easily be arranged at a later date.

On the set of *Any Day Now*, Lotz was largely free to do as she wished. If the writers were meeting, she generally sat with them, and when they were out, or working independently, she visited the set. Here, the observations were, in part, determined by the concrete production process in film and television, which is very slow going, indeed quite tedious. Production of *Any Day Now* followed standard television industry practices and protocols. For each scene, the actors come on the set first, rehearse their lines and the 'blocking,' the process in which they learn their 'marks,' their positions and movements during the scene. Next, the actors move out, and the 'second team' comes on: doubles for the actors take their places while the production crew sets the lighting, camera, and audio equipment. The full process may take as much as an hour for a scene of less than five minutes. Once the stage is set, the actors return and perform the scene, which is repeated until the director is satisfied with the 'take.' Being present on the set afforded particular opportunities to observe the dynamics among the writer, director, and actors.

the production set

the director

cont.

For this particular project, however, observing the writing process and the roles of the executive producers was more important. In their meetings, the central decisions regarding the series concept, the contribution of individual episodes to that concept, and the general social and political goals of the executive producers became increasingly clear. During the visit, the writers were working on scripts for the final episodes of the season, planned to air about six episodes after the one in production. The writers used Nancy Miller's office, a comfortable space lined with overstuffed couches and chairs and decorated with memorabilia from *Any Day Now* and Miller's other series. Here, it was possible to observe meetings on each step of the writing process, which followed a well-known and relatively routine procedure. writers and the writing process

The process began with outlining script ideas, and proceeded to the presentation of ideas to Executive Producer Miller, followed by Miller's discussion of the ideas with the Lifetime executives assigned to work with the show. After securing approval from Miller and Lifetime, the writers would continue to develop the story, and the individual writer assigned to an episode would spend a few days writing alone. In the meetings, Lotz was able to watch the group dynamic of developing and polishing scripts that were in the later draft stages. In other meetings, writers brainstormed ideas for many other possible episodes and discussed the future trajectory of the series with Miller. network executives

One fortunate aspect of this visit was that it occurred during 'pilot season,' when the company was in the process of presenting ('pitching') ideas for new series to various networks. The environment was constantly chaotic, and it was actually being present within this activity that allowed the best understanding of the overall production process. A significant amount of research time was spent merely sitting in the production company office observing the assistants to each of the executive producers. Lotz developed a relationship with the assistants, and gained a great deal of information about the series through talking with them. Their tasks provided additional insight into the ways in which the series was being developed. They also agreed to maintain contact after the visit, making themselves available for inquiries about developments, ratings information, and for addressing questions that would inevitably arise during the analysis and writing related to the series. pilot season

assistants to executive producers

During the visit, it also became clear that there was much to be learned by looking around, listening, and asking simple questions. For example, on the wall in the writers' office was a list of criteria – a reminder to the writers – of the vision the executive producers were aiming for in each episode. Similarly, by being present in the office during the daily telephone calls between the studio and Lifetime, it was possible to develop an understanding of the intricate relationship between the producers and the network airing the series.

Because of developments in production, interviews with the executive producers were repeatedly postponed. In some ways this was beneficial, for as the week progressed, other personnel answered some questions, while new questions arose. It was necessary to be flexible, but also persistent, in order to get some of the important interviews, for example, finally being granted 'a few minutes' during a smoke break – that ended almost an hour later.

Although only some interviews were taped, the recorder was also valuable for reviewing each day's events during the hour-long commute back to the city. While it would probably have been possible to tape the entire writers' meetings, these were often long, rambling discussions about characters and current events which went on for hours, and which might have been inhibited by recording. Instead, it was possible to create notes about specific discussions and to gather information important to the larger study. note-taking vs. tape-recording

Staying close to Miller during the week led to attendance at some meetings discussing topics not previously defined in the production research literature. For example, a 'tone meeting' was held as part of planning the production of the next episode. Here, the writer, director, and first assistant director met with Miller, and went through the script to make sure all the participants agreed on how the episode should be acted and shot in terms of tone and attitude. While the *cont.*

term 'tone meeting' may be specific to this production company, it is likely that others engage in similar activities, but may not have been observed in the process. In another instance, by sheer chance, a promotions meeting was held during the visit, and proved an excellent opportunity for gaining information on competing visions of the show held by various participants in the production process. The meeting included representatives from two promotions companies, one hired by Lifetime Television, one hired by Miller and Randall (two of the three executive producers), co-star Annie Potts's publicist (by telephone), and (also by telephone) a representative from Spelling Entertainment, the parent production company.

Much of the information gathered during this field visit confirmed earlier conceptions and ideas related to the program, and to the topics of feminism and racism embedded within it, but other information amplified and refined those ideas, and provided details that would not otherwise have been available. The observations and interviews further enabled later stages of the analysis to draw on the multiple perspectives of those involved in the creative and production process.

episode to date), the lack of an interview as well as of observational sources is unfortunate, but not decisive for the total project.

THE LEVELS OF ANALYSIS REVISITED

We begin this analysis by emphasizing that the case is not intended as the only model of qualitative production research. Moreover, it is most emphatically not an ethnographic study.◄ That term implies much more extensive involvement, more detailed encounters with informants, and closer engagement with the entire 'culture' of the production process (e.g., Alvarado and Buscombe 1978; Elliott 1972). The present field visit was intended as observational and informational. It provided knowledge that could not be obtained in other ways, but the primary purpose was to gather material with which to supplement textual analysis and library research. It was therefore more open-ended, more opportunistic than a systematic ethnographic project would be.

This sort of project, often more available to researchers, thus reiterates the main point regarding research on the production of fictional entertainment. The practices observed and the information obtained in this project – or in any other – must be examined from several perspectives, from macro- to micro-contexts, all of which affect the final form of the television program.

At the general level of *political economy*,◄ the television series *Any Day Now* is produced within the U.S. commercial television system. Its key purpose is to attract audiences and make them available to advertisers. Producer-writers, actors, and the entire production staff and crew are well aware of this goal, and scripts, production practices, and post-production decisions are made in ways which acknowledge that the fictional narrative will be broken into sections, or acts, between which commercial advertisements will be shown. Creative personnel may or may not know what specific products will be advertised, but they are aware of the general range of items likely to be included in a program targeted to particular demographic groups. In the U.S.A., and increasingly throughout the world, both producers and other creative personnel are regularly informed of their audience. On the one hand, the fictions they create must serve as relatively comfortable settings for those products. On the other hand, the fictions serve as forms of expression for stories the producers wish to tell for personal, ideological reasons. In addition, each fiction is presented on a network with its own strategic goals within the changing context of U.S. broadcasting.

The *specific industrial context* of U.S. television has been fundamentally reconfigured in recent years by changes in both technology and

► ethnography – Chapter 10, p. 164

► political economy: audience as product – Chapter 9, p. 143

policy. Any current exploration of media production is therefore undertaken at one of the most fluid moments in media history. As a result, identifying the general commercial goal of television programming, as we did above, tells us even less than in the past about a complex process. While the commercial goal still implies particular economic as well as ideological configurations of organizations and contents, the industrial relations that are established to accomplish those goals have changed in a dramatic fashion. The recent (2000) merger of an internet service provider, America Online (AOL), and a media production and distribution company, Time-Warner, illustrates not only the merging of massive capital accumulations, but also the media's increasing dependence on *integration: vertical and horizontal* both vertical and horizontal integration (in order to control all stages of production and distribution, or to expand one's reach within one stage). AOL, the distribution site, can now depend on Time-Warner, the content provider (and, with its cable holdings, also a distributor) for extensive influence throughout multiple media industries and multiple audiences.

more distribution technologies Fundamental to these changes has been the diversification of distribution outlets, which has modified existing production practices in the U.S.A. and around the world. Cable television, along with home video, has placed pressure on both commercial and public service networks in different national contexts, partly intensified by satellite transmission and digital streaming for computer delivery. As a result, both television and film industries are now required to produce more, more cheaply, and to vary the appearance of their products to attract audiences who can choose from a variety of content and playback options.

Describing this context, Caldwell (1995) argues that 'television' has shifted into an age of 'televisuality,' in which 'style' has become the primary content of the medium. Television producers work within the conditions of 'post-network' television, in which every program must strive for some sort of distinction that might catch viewers, made 'mobile' with their remote control device. Curtin (1996, 1999) makes a similar point when defining an age of 'neo-network' television in which a distinctive

'edginess' is the norm for the medium, rather than any generalized, consensual narratives. It is within this context that cable networks and their programming strategies take on primary significance.

The *particular organization*, Lifetime Television, serves as an example of the descriptions offered by Caldwell and Curtin. It is certainly more carefully 'targeted,' more precisely defined than traditional broadcast networks. It is a twenty-four-hour cable network, included in the 'basic,' non-subscription offering of cable systems. Launched in February 1984, it is jointly owned by the Walt Disney Co. (50 percent) and Hearst Communications (50 percent). The network reaches approximately 78 million potential viewers, placing it eleventh among basic cable offerings, but it is viewed in an average 1,319,000 homes in prime time, ranking it sixth in viewership among cable channels. A more useful description of viewership emerges when we look at the response to a special two-hour movie version of *Any Day Now* which aired in October 1999. That screening received a 2.3 rating in the overall television viewing population (2.3 percent of all U.S. homes with television, namely about 2.3 million homes). Within its cable 'universe' (around 78 million homes with access to Lifetime), the program received a 3.1 rating, or *ratings and revenues* 2.25 million homes. Revenues for 1998, combining advertising and license fees, totaled $523 million, almost double that of the average basic cable channel, and were projected at $550 million for 2000 (McAvoy 2000). Expenditures for programming reached $196.4 million, more than twice the average among cable channels (McAdams 1999). Included in this figure are funds for *Any Day Now*, Lifetime Original Movies, and other, non-fiction programming.

In 1994, Lifetime began promoting itself as 'Television for Women.' In 1998, the network averaged 208,000 women viewers in the 18 to 34 age group during prime time. In the 18 to 49 age group, Lifetime's 'target' demographic group, the network averaged 523,000 women viewers, and in the 25 to 54 age group, the average was 594,000 viewers (McAdams 1999). It is within this context that *Any Day Now* is produced.

At this *individual production*, the network's goals and successes are among the conditions enabling Miller to produce her show. Previously considered too specific, and perhaps too controversial in its treatment of race, the series was repeatedly rejected by the major U.S. television networks that still attempt to reach the largest and most widely defined audience in demographic terms, and plan much of their programming accordingly. For Lifetime's more precisely targeted audience, *Any Day Now* was an 'appropriate vehicle' – which is not, of course, the same as a 'safe bet.' The show could have failed to attract audiences, in which case Lifetime would have canceled it. But Lifetime's expectations of 'acceptable numbers' are substantially different from those of conventional network television, and the show is considered a success.

This is not to say that the program would never have been developed for another distribution system. Indeed, recently, many major network programs have been far more narrowly targeted than previously, precisely because cable television has been successful with this type of edgier, potentially more controversial programming. Broadcast networks must compete for audiences which are increasingly accustomed to such choice, which, in turn, means that those networks are willing to accept smaller audiences. The numbers required to keep a television program on air have dropped significantly in the past ten years. Put another way, *Any Day Now* would probably have a better chance of being programmed on a major network today than when it was first bought by Lifetime. These changes have benefitted producers, such as Miller, who not only have more outlets for their work, but can present material more clearly defined by their own vision and personal goals.

network policies The network maintains strong ongoing involvement with all aspects of the production through making suggestions and decisions. Like most television networks, Lifetime assigns executives to be responsible for 'Current Programming.' The 'Current' office and staff are paralleled by another organizational division responsible for the 'Development' of new programming. Executives from these offices express their views in the form of 'notes,' or suggestions, presented to producers, writers, and sometimes actors.

As is typical of series–network relations, Executive Producer Miller cleared script ideas with Lifetime, first when the writers originated general plot ideas, and again once episode outlines were firmly in place. Miller expressed satisfaction with the network's willingness to air more controversial themes and more explicit dialogue than a broadcast network might accept. Still, the network exerted its influence in other ways. One writer commented that the network often expressed concern that the content was not 'dramatic' enough, and sought for the writers to incorporate more melodrama. The network's influence was also evident when a writer suggested a story about aging. Miller dismissed this idea before it was developed, because the network did not want to acknowledge the fact that the characters would be in their forties, perhaps near their fifties, if a real timeline were applied to their fictional world – Lifetime attempts to appeal to a younger demographic segment.

As with scripts, casting decisions are carefully discussed with the network. Notes from the network are, of course, always backed with the authority of financial support, which could be withdrawn. Such executive commentary from positions of considerable power is often resented by the creative personnel, and may lead into a negotiating game, in which some suggestions are implemented while others are ignored. Sometimes, however, the notes are appreciated and important adjustments made to the program. In either case, the more successful a program becomes, the more it wins autonomy for the producers, and a higher degree of creative freedom.

Other participants in the creative process are also given varying degrees of responsibility and involvement. It is not coincidental, for example, that a representative of one of the two principal actors was present at the *Any Day Now* promotion meeting. The role of Annie Potts's publicist was to put the views of his client into play as part of the advertising process. Star performers can be exceptionally **stars** powerful in determining the shape of a production. Although this tends to be even more the case in film than in television, the concerns of 'talent,' like those of all powerful participants, enter into an interactive process. While the contributions of stars and their representatives could be considered at the next, individual level of analysis, we treat them here as expressions of roles within the production context and of particular types of organizational power.

the executive producer

To analyze the roles of *individual agents* in fiction production, it is necessary to place all the previous 'levels' in relation to the final product. We emphasize the role of the executive producer, who has primary authority in the day-to-day, 'on the ground' creative process. While Executive Producer Nancy Miller is fully aware of the commercial role of television in American culture, of the network's goals and its power, and of the influence of the star performers, she is equally aware of her own authority. Indeed, one of her key creative activities is negotiating the concerns of all those involved parties while maintaining her own goals for *Any Day Now*, which she has created to express her views and those of her collaborators.

Miller and co-creator Deborah Joy Levine sold the original conception for *Any Day Now* to CBS in 1990. This early version of the series, about the interracial friendship of two girls in 1960s Birmingham, was designed as a half-hour production combining comedy and drama in what is sometimes referred to as a 'dramedy.' Miller based the series on a childhood relationship of her own, but changed the ethnicity of one character to make it more interesting. The series was to be produced by the Orion production company, then headed by Gary Randall. Days before the series was to go into production, Randall stopped it, feeling the time was not right for a series about children. Next, Miller spent eight years trying to find an outlet, and became partners with Randall before she was contacted by Lifetime. Lifetime was preparing to launch their first drama, and wanted Miller's series if she could add a contemporary dimension to the show by depicting the girls as adults. Miller and Randall reshaped the series, focusing the genre more precisely and adding the adult characters.

During the field visit, Miller expressed her aim of having the discussion of racial politics carry over from the series to become 'watercooler conversation' for the country. She grew up in Oklahoma, often visiting relatives in the deep South, and feels she understands southerners, but not the bigotry she saw daily in the shape of separate water fountains and other practices excluding blacks. Still, Miller said she understands how people can be racist yet have a good heart, a contradiction she explores in the series. She also feels the country's struggle to understand ethnic difference and racism is a part of U.S. cultural history largely ignored in storytelling, and another gap she seeks to fill.◄

In addition, Miller recognized a dearth of multi-dimensional female characters on television, or even the presence of many women's stories. She recounted that, after writing for police shows, she was sick of writing about female rape victims and wives who functioned only to service their husbands. Miller said she seeks to disprove conventional industry wisdom that if women are 'not twelve and weigh eight pounds and have 38D breasts, they don't want to see you.' Instead, she argued, 'if you make people laugh and you're telling compelling stories,' you will draw an audience.

Miller designed this fictional world for U.S., commercially sponsored television, knowing its limitations and restrictions, but recognizing cable television as a less constrained environment in which executives would be willing to support her somewhat riskier project. Because *Any Day Now* has been successful in cable television terms, as noted above, she has been able to determine many of the decisions regarding content, direction, and 'tone.' Her power to continue creative control over the program results from its success, and from her ability to draw on the related commitments of the network and others who hold degrees of power to shape 'her' show. But she must still work to maintain that trust, with all these factors in mind, by making dozens of decisions, small and large, on a daily basis.

So, too, must those on her staff who occupy positions of creative involvement. Although

---

► ethnicity – Chapter 11, p. 179

they do not hold the same level of responsibility for the overall success and vision of the program, many of them hope to achieve just that authority at some point in their careers. For some of them, working as staff writers, or holding the title of producer, is part of the training process leading toward a time when they will create programs of their own. Just as Miller negotiates with the executives of Lifetime, then, other producer-writers and staff members negotiate with her. These efforts may be described as a balance between short-term narrative stakes and long-term narrative intentions. In the observed meetings of writers, discussion focused on how the particular narrative goals of an episode would suit the larger goals of the series. And while the Executive Producer maintains primary control over the long-term narrative, she is also immediately concerned with each episode, even with a particular scene or a single line of dialogue. In fact, executive producers may, and often do, rewrite the efforts of other writers in order to maintain focus. The fact that writers for *Any Day Now* specifically noted that Miller does little rewriting of their material indicates a clarity regarding narrative goals, characterizations, and overall content. This is borne out by the list of 'tone' suggestions, posted in Miller's office, which were always visible to other writers as a material indication of the collective creative process.

Following completion of the writing process and the production of an episode, Miller, her production staff, and numerous technical personnel will work to add music, special sound, visual, and other enhancements, all within very tight time constraints. In this final phase, as well, the negotiation rarely ceases, and if the program remains successful the process will begin once again, when production for the next season goes into operation during the following July.

CONCLUSION

We conclude by emphasizing that whereas the types of social interaction observed in this study of *Any Day Now*, and common to most media fiction production, have been repeatedly characterized as 'struggles' and addressed in terms

of 'power relations,' they may also be defined in terms of 'collaboration.' Disputes and disagreements, sometimes severe, are inevitable, but it would be wrong to suggest that unequal power relations always reflect fundamentally opposed perspectives, or that 'winners' exercise power in order to obliterate the ideas and contributions of 'losers.'

This is not to say that the outcome should be studied, much less explained, in terms of individual agency, at least if individuals are understood only as 'autonomous,' 'coherent,' 'free' subjects. Individuals often express and enact internalized institutional goals as well as restraints, rather than any uniquely personal perspectives, as part of an ongoing structuration of media and society (Giddens 1984). Of course, collaborations occur within accepted ideological ranges – from single lines and scenes, to episodes, the series as a whole, and even the media system in which it appears. Such constraints and restrictions are recognized, worked within, battled against, and acknowledged by the various agents as forces that shape, but do not totally determine the final production. While the collaborative process does work to shut out some perspectives, the emerging fictions can themselves be critical of systemic aspects of the social structure. Certainly, this is the case with *Any Day Now* and its critique of persistent racism in the U.S.A. Our point has been to illustrate the complexity of fiction production as a socially interactive process, carried out by individuals, within institutional, organizational, technological, and other structural contexts.

The discussion of the roles of individuals also serves as a reminder that the analytical process should move back 'up' the levels of analysis. For instance, we have noted the transitional role of writers in television, where writers move into the producer role and assume creative control of a series. In the film industry, creative control is primarily assumed by directors, while writers are relegated to a lower status and involvement. They are not under contract, but make professional arrangements, through agents and lawyers, to work on individual projects. And, unlike television producers, who are most often directly involved in

film production vs. television production

the creative process, the role of the film producer is generally focused on arranging finance for specific productions. In the context of the more general economic arrangements for fiction production, still other differences emerge. Film financing is based on income from the box-office and home rentals, both nationally and internationally. Television financing comes from either advertising or nationally regulated license fees and other support, or a combination of the two. These differences in political-economic contexts, which will tend to shape institutional structures, organizational practices, and the consequent roles of individuals, should be taken into account in concrete production studies.

Partly for these reasons, many of the most significant current questions within production research involve corporate mergers, technological interconnections, and the cultural and other social implications of new industrial configurations. When a book may become a movie that becomes a television series that becomes a theme park ride that becomes a video game that becomes a line of toys, production researchers find themselves involved with new sets of issues.◀ The research process may start with any one of these media products, studying the distinctive work processes at a given production site. But it should ultimately address not only the goals of creative individuals, but also the configuration of media organizations with particular industrial strategies which are embedded in, and responding to, large-scale political-economic conditions.

The current state of television in the U.S.A., and increasingly elsewhere, as defined in part by technological developments leading to more, and more differentiated, distribution outlets, may favor those who, like Nancy Miller, work to place their visions on screens, even if viewed by comparatively smaller numbers. Within the commercial political economy, the creative process of producing media fiction remains complex, dense, and variously inflected by those involved. Particularly at a time when media systems throughout the world are in a process of vital change, resulting from economic, regulatory, and technological developments, it is important that comparative studies of production processes be undertaken, including different national and regional contexts. Analyzing these processes in more detail will complement the studies of audiences in relation to media products, and will help explain the equally complicated responses recorded in reception studies. In this way, our understanding of the social roles of mediated fiction will be enriched and more precisely understood.

▶ integrated production and intertextuality – also
Chapter 11, p. 186

5 The production of news

Gaye Tuchman

- a description of *early functionalist* production research
- a comparison of *three separate traditions* in subsequent studies of news production
- a review of recent *developments within U.S. news media*
- an assessment of the ability of the *three research traditions in combination* to account for current developments of news media.

Contemporary approaches to research on the production of news can be read as a reaction to those functionalist models of the mass media which were dominant in the mid-twentieth century, particularly in the U.S.A., but also in other societies that were then embracing aspects of a dominant American culture (Lemert 1993). Some current research has drawn its theories from political economy, others from symbolic interactionism – two traditions focusing respectively on the entire social system and on the interactions among and between individuals and institutions, what sociologists refer to as macro- and micro-theories.◄ Still others have examined news as a cultural form with particular ideological implications. Despite their common rejection of structural functionalism,◄ however, these traditions have yet to be integrated in a satisfactory fashion. There is some irony in this, because the functional models at least claimed to have integrated micro- and macro-analysis. This chapter takes stock of news production studies with reference

to ongoing changes within the media system itself. These changes may once again force research to reconsider its premises and procedures (see also Cottle 2000), and to explore ways of integrating the several traditions in the area in future empirical practice.

Following a characterization of the early functionalist models, this chapter reviews some of the main contributions to news production research since the 1950s. A key point of later studies has been that journalists and other newsworkers do not merely select and combine information; rather they can be seen to literally 'produce' the news in the context of organizational and other social frameworks. Three traditions have emerged which, in distinctive ways, study the social origins and consequences of news. With shifting technological and economic frameworks, moreover, have come a different set of circumstances for the production and circulation of news in society. Current changes in the social system of news are exemplified next, with special reference to the U.S.A. The final section revisits the three research traditions and reassesses their explanatory value with regard to these changes, exploring to what degree they may ultimately be 'complementary.'

► macro- and micro-theories of production – Chapter 6, p. 91

► structural functionalism – Chapter 3, p. 55

FROM GATEKEEPING TO NEWS PRODUCTION

Media sociology in the mid-twentieth century

One common feature of various functionalist models during the 1950s was that they described media as components of a larger social system in which media organizations and their audiences were equal and parallel entities. Drawing their inspiration as students of Robert K. Merton (e.g., Merton 1968), Riley and Riley (1965) proposed one of the best known and influential of these (see also DeFleur 1975; Wright 1959). Applying Merton's middle-range approach,◄ Riley and Riley implied that mass communications are a balanced set of social structures which contribute to the stability of the social system. On the one hand, employees, managers, and other 'members' of media institutions respond to the interests of such reference groups as co-workers and competitors. On the other hand, individuals receive messages from media institutions, and respond in turn, according to their orientation toward their own reference groups, who represent a parallel structure within the social system. In a well-functioning system, the reactions and subsequent actions of individuals in relation to media amount to a (rudimentary) feedback, which prompts the media to either reiterate or modify their output, so as to ensure the continued operation and stability of the social system as such.

To be sure, not all sociologists agreed with the full model, as suggested by alternative graphic depictions (e.g., DeFleur 1975; McQuail 1976). Rather than drawing parallel boxes, other models placed the media above the recipients of messages, suggesting a hierarchical system of communication and social interaction. The media thus seemed to be more powerful, in both institutional and discursive terms, than those ordinary social agents who read newspapers, go to the movies, listen to the radio, or watch television. Nevertheless, the underlying metaphor of communication remained that of the transmission of an information flow, which might be used selectively or even cut off, but which relayed full-fledged messages about a pre-existing reality to media audiences.◄

Like much social science, early research on news had often been qualitative, exploring the place of this strategic genre in political and other social life. Max Weber (1958a [1918]) had found that the press was a set of political organizations rather than being neutral relayers of information or scandal, and that journalists were 'professional politicians.' Robert E. Park (1922) had examined the role of newspapers in building social cohesion in the heterogeneous American nation. By the 1950s, however, news studies were joining the emerging social-scientific orthodoxy of quantitative methodologies coupled with functionalist theories. Although some research combined qualitative and quantitative approaches (e.g., Janowitz 1967), most studies involved content analysis◄ or the quantitative examination of the editorial and other journalistic decisions of individuals termed 'gatekeepers'◄ (White 1950). When, for instance, participant observation was employed, it was either placed in a functionalist framework (Breed 1955), or it was largely dismissed as 'unscientific,' only to be recovered in later news studies (Lang and Lang 1953).

An alternative, preliminary model is displayed in Figure 5.1, focusing on the news organization amidst a field of often conflicting social forces (see also Curran 2000). These forces comprise at least four types:

1 *Economic agents.* Owners and investors will, in the nature of the matter, aim for news policies and procedures that ensure a profit, in the short or long term. In doing so, they respond to both audience and advertiser interests. At the same time, each news organization must orient itself toward its competitors, which operate in the same or a related force field.

► social theories of the middle range – Chapter 3, p. 55

► transmission model of communication – Chapter 1, p. 7

► quantitative content analysis – Chapter 13, p. 219

► gatekeeping studies – Chapter 6, p. 91

2 *Political agents*. Political, legal, and other regulatory entities establish the general framework in which news organizations operate. At least in the European setting, moreover, public funding of broadcasting represents an alternative or a substantial supplement to advertising.

3 *Source agents*. Sources, on the one hand, represent necessary lines of information feeding into news, and hence are cultivated to ensure continuous coverage of key social sectors. On the other hand, both official political sources and *ad hoc* interest organizations amount to pressure groups seeking a voice in the news.

4 *Audience agents*. In addition to being a market of consumers whose interests any news medium must continually try to fathom, in a wider sense the 'audiences' of a news organization comprise a heterogeneous set of constituencies, from other professional journalists evaluating it as peers, to the general public who will label and rank news media in relation to each other.

In responding to and accommodating such external forces, a news organization devises practices and procedures internally for accomplishing its daily news work. Because these forces have so many diverse origins and exercise their impact on the news at different moments, current news research has come to employ a range of methodologies.

Making news

During the late 1960s and throughout the 1970s, many media sociologists discarded the functionalist legacy. Despite their different sources of theoretical inspiration and their more or less explicit ambitions of opposing the powers that be in news and politics, the alternative positions all emphasized a notion of 'production' – news is made, not found. Further, it is not the attitude or 'bias' of individual journalists, but their social and organizational context which primarily determines how news is made. This common denominator

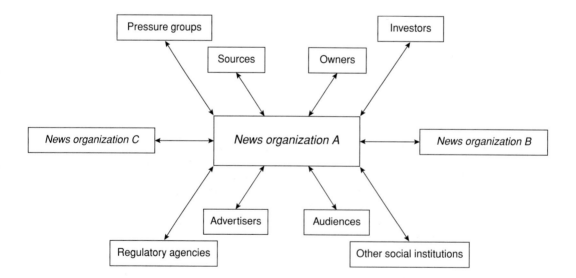

Figure 5.1 The news organization in a field of social forces

Source: Adapted from McQuail and Windahl 1993: 61

was signaled in the titles of a whole list of influential studies on 'making,' 'creating,' 'manufacturing,' and 'deciding' what is news. (A further shift toward research on audiences 'making sense' of news began during the 1980s (e.g., Jensen 1986).) While some comparative production studies included different regions of the world (e.g., Golding and Elliott 1979), most of this work centered on the American and British media (e.g., Altheide 1976; Fishman 1980; Gans 1979; Schlesinger 1978; Tuchman 1978).

The notion of production, however, was given several inflections. Whereas some critical and Marxist approaches proposed to subsume news and media as such under general political-economic categories, examining their specific contribution to the production and reproduction of the social status quo, other work relied on a phenomenological framework to explore how (news) media necessarily contribute to producing and maintaining society as a shared symbolic environment. In addition, textual studies analyzed the ways in which news texts produce particular perspectives on social reality, while blurring or obscuring others. In an overview, Schudson (1991) thus identified three traditions in recent research on the social production of news, superseding functionalism:

1 *Political economy.* Building upon classic Marxist ideas, the political economy tradition has argued that both functionalist and other models of mediated communication tend to ignore issues of class and power generally (e.g., Golding and Middleton 1982; Herman and Chomsky 1988; Murdock 1982; Murdock and Golding 1977). One relatively separate strand, drawing on Gramsci (1971) and French neo-Marxism (e.g., Althusser 1977 [1965]), has recognized the semi-autonomous status of media, but has suggested that the media nevertheless exercise hegemony by limiting both the specific agendas of the political process and the cultural universes made available through media representations (e.g., Sallach 1974).

2 *Phenomenology and ethnomethodology.* A second group of studies has emphasized the meaningful nature of social life, and have examined the role of news media in constituting and disseminating meaning (e.g., Molotch and Lester 1974; Tuchman 1978). While the inspirations range from traditional phenomenology◄ to symbolic interactionism and ethnomethodology,◄ a common premise of this tradition is that individual journalists, single news outlets, as well as the media institution as such, collectively accomplish the social construction of reality (Berger and Luckmann 1966). (For recent studies see, e.g., Chomsky 1999; Sumpter 2000.)

3 *Textual studies.* The third type of news research has argued for a closer reading of news as narratives that are replete with symbols of the society which shaped them, and which they, in turn, reshape and reassert.◄ Whereas such studies typically do not examine the production process in an empirical sense, news texts evidently bear witness to this process; constitute the media-audience nexus in the further dissemination of news; and can be seen as necessary objects of analysis also in production research.

The different empirical foci of the three traditions are explained, in part, by their theoretical assumptions. Similarly, their characteristic purposes of inquiry have entailed different methodological choices. Political economy has accounted for the economic, legislative, and, to a degree, technological conditions of mediated news, and for inequalities and inadequacies in the resulting infrastructure, often by relying on quantitative analyses of available statistical evidence as well as of original datasets. Social constructionism has uncovered the routinized, yet finely nuanced practices of daily news work, primarily through observational and interview techniques. In addition, textual studies have typologized and interpreted the formats of news, their historical roots, and current transformations, especially in qualitative discourse studies and, to a more limited extent, in quantitative content analyses.

► phenomenology – Chapter 2, p. 22

► symbolic interactionism and ethnomethodology – Chapter 3, p. 56

► news as texts – Chapter 7

'All three approaches ... have greatly advanced our understanding of the media by focusing on the specific institutions and the specific processes in those institutions responsible for creating the cultural product we call news' (Schudson 1991: 150). However, both Schudson and others sometimes appear to assume that these traditions have not been informed by one another. In fact, they have, more often than not, defined themselves through competition or conflict, first with the functionalist heritage and second with each other (e.g., Ferguson and Golding 1997). Schudson (1991), moreover, chastised all three traditions for being 'indifferent to comparative as well as historical studies' (p. 156). Partially in response, this chapter begins to show how, jointly, the three approaches may help us to understand ongoing changes in news as a social institution and as a political genre over the past three decades.

The next section accordingly reviews recent changes in the American media system, as revealed by content analysis, participant observation, as well as structural evidence. The U.S. media serve as an example of more general issues, in media research as well as in media politics, partly because of their international dissemination, partly because of their status as role models also in professional education and news organizations around the world. Furthermore, the process of 'conglomeration,' so evident in U.S. media, is also advancing in other countries (Croteau and Hoynes 2001: 72–145). Writing well over twenty years ago about the British communications industry, Murdock and Golding (1977: 31) noted 'the overall concentration of ownership,' 'the network of interlocking shareholdings,' and the resulting 'high degree of connectedness and communality of interests between the various sectors of industrial and financial capital.' All these factors frame the more localized processes through which media professionals produce both news and entertainment on a daily basis. Indeed, the main trend of media conglomeration at present may not be Americanization (Tunstall 1977), but transnationalization.◀

▶ transnational concentration and conglomeration – Chapter 4, p. 73

These transformations are explained, to a large degree, by the simple but far from trivial fact that news *is* a product – manufactured, sold, and consumed daily. To paraphrase a comment that Max Weber made at the end of the *Protestant Ethic* (1904), however much participants in an institution, or the institution itself, may claim that the 'maw' of capitalism is irrelevant to its existence, no news medium or news audience is untouched by the economic conditions of their communication (Weber 1958b: 181–182). For empirical media studies, one central question is how changing economic conditions affect both the process of news production and the final news product.

WHAT'S NEW – IN THE NEWS MEDIA

In hindsight, it is easy to forget a general development in news media since the 1970s: the dramatic growth in the total number of sources that consumers have available and combine in their daily use. To briefly list the newcomers in their order of appearance, they included cable television, additional television networks, cable news networks, the Internet, and linkages between cable news stations and the Internet. This general expansion has resulted in increased competition, not only within but between media.

competition between more types of news media

A daily newspaper and a national nightly network news show compete with other similar products, but also with all media distributing news. On a local level, in southern Connecticut, for example, the *New Haven Register* vies for circulation with the *New York Times*. On a national level, what used to be the three major American networks in the mid-1970s held about 90 percent of the total television audience at any given time, whereas the four largest networks currently attain about 50 percent of the total (Croteau and Hoynes 2001: 124). In this context, network news has faced a crisis which is comparable to that experienced by newspapers and other print media after the coming of electronic media, as the classic networks have been challenged by new networks in general, and by cable news networks in particular (Croteau and Hoynes 2001: 46–68; Hyuhn 2000).

In order to unravel this increasingly integrated news system, it is helpful to identify some specific challenges experienced by two classic news media – newspapers and television – and their attempted solutions in terms of both product development and new production processes.

Newspapers

afternoon newspapers

Once upon a time in the U.S.A., afternoon newspapers both presented fresh stories and updated the morning newspaper (Emery and Emery 1988). Because of their competition particularly with television from the 1950s, afternoon editions typically devoted more space to analysis. When that practice, too, failed to maintain their circulation, most afternoon dailies folded (Kaniss 1991: 35). To survive, newspapers sometimes entered into a 'joint operating agreement,' in which they shared advertising and production costs but were responsible for their own reporting and editorial content, as currently done by the *Denver Post* and *Rocky Mountain News*. But even such cooperative arrangements could not prevent failure for some afternoon newspapers. Thus, in 1998 the afternoon *Nashville Banner* folded after having a 'joint operating agreement' with the *Nashville Tennessean* for about twenty years.

Alongside competition, a second reason for the demise of the afternoon daily in most U.S. cities has been the changed nature of metropolitan areas. As more workers moved to the suburbs, their need for a daily paper became less self-evident. For one thing, more people commuted to work in the city by car than by public transport, which would have facilitated reading during the ride. For another thing, many suburbanites no longer identified with the city (Kaniss 1991).

By the late 1960s, many morning newspapers had succumbed to the competition from radio and television (Emery and Emery 1988; Kaniss 1991). The newspapers' response was multi-pronged. One strategy for maintaining, or even broadening, circulation was to invoke the central position of the city in all of metropolitan life as well as to present specific activities as matters of concern to suburban residents. Such 'metropolitanism' entailed coverage of entertainment, but also of the urban political process, which affected the living conditions of suburban readers both within and outside the city itself. An additional, highly practical motivation for newspapers to promote metropolitanism was that the city as a political center is much easier to cover than its many satellites. During the 1980s, such newspapers as the *New York Times* and the *Los Angeles Times* tried to make the best of both urban worlds when they began to issue special editions for selected locations, featuring regional news, but also representing the city as a pivot in the lives of people in each suburb or region.

A second set of strategies in the fight for newspaper circulation in the U.S. went beyond special content, and affected the format of the individual article (Benhurst and Mutz 1997). Whereas some newspapers now carried shorter articles, and others aimed for longer ones, both patterns may be related to the presentation of news on television. As is frequently pointed out, also in self-reflective articles in other newspapers, the format of *USA Today* (launched in 1984) mimics television: short articles, eye-catching typography ('blips'), and 'factoids' (precise but decontextualized items of information) that reproduce features of national television news. In addition to the attempt to create a product for readers throughout the country (the U.S. press has traditionally been entirely local and regional), *USA Today* especially seeks to appeal to those who have neither the inclination nor the time to seek out more in-depth coverage.

In an opposite strategy, other newspapers have reacted against television, and have found alternative ideals for their news formats in the magazine press. By presenting fewer and longer stories, this group of papers announces an insistence that print media are capable of more depth and nuance than the 'headline service' of television. Indeed, some research has found that American newspapers today tend to offer more analysis than they did thirty years ago (Benhurst and Mutz 1997). In covering elections, for instance, newspapers devote relatively more space to the issues, and less to the

Margin notes: afternoon newspapers; joint operating agreements; suburbs; morning newspapers; metropolitanism; article formats

candidates' 'horse race.' Compared to the spread of 'sound bite' news in television during the same period (Hallin 1992), this newspaper strategy is one more indication of how each news medium has sought to achieve 'product differentiation' within an increasingly integrated news system.

Within this last group of newspapers, a third strategy of differentiation has been in evidence, which involves a redefinition of the professional status of news workers. In contrast to 'editors' papers' or 'reporters' papers,' some presses have come to be termed 'writers' papers' (Manzella 1997). The implication is that managements permit their writers greater latitude or creativity in developing stories outside of the most familiar protocols or conventions of news writing (see also Becker 1982). For example, one reporter for the *Hartford Courant* wrote a multi-week series of articles in 1997 about his experiences as he paddled a canoe from the source of the Connecticut River through the Long Island Sound to Manhattan Island. A prize-winning series, these stories were not premised on getting and reporting 'the facts,' but on telling a real story. Another change of protocol at such newspapers has been that they no longer require stories appearing on the front page to be structured in a classic inverted pyramid, proceeding from the basic elements of who, what, when, and where, to how and, perhaps, why, and to other elaboration, exemplification, and background (Manzella 1997).While these journalistic formats recall the 'new journalism' originating in the 1960s as part of a political as well as aesthetic counterculture (Wolfe 1973), current developments are probably best seen in market terms – in the context of such new media as the Internet and all-news cable networks that deliver updated, basic information in a speedier fashion than any newspaper could.

Margin notes: product differentiation · writers' papers · inverted pyramid · new journalism

Television

If the newspaper was the main vehicle of a modern political public, in the U.S. (Schiller 1981; Schudson 1978) as in Europe (Habermas 1989 [1962]), television took over central aspects of that role in the post-1945 period, especially at the national or network level. It is also at this level that the most important transformations have occurred, as increased competition from new networks, such as FOX, and news networks, such as CNN, has spelled a decrease in profits for the three classic networks (ABC, CBS, NBC) (Croteau and Hoynes 2001). Whereas in the 1950s network executives were charmed to realize that the nightly news could make a profit (e.g., Epstein 1973), today's executives are beset by smaller audience shares and by the demand from the media conglomerates which now own these once powerful networks that they make a profit in themselves (although the audience for any one news show is comparatively small). Of course, a smaller audience share means a smaller budget also for news operations. As a result, the individual network news divisions have decreased their number of correspondents both within the U.S.A. and around the world (Remnick 1998). At the same time, the news divisions as a group have become more explicitly interdependent, even sharing information, as done, for instance, for exit polls in the 2000 U.S. presidential election, and buying materials from competitors, especially if they can be rebroadcast in a different format.

Admittedly, network news reporters were always interdependent, covering the same story for different companies, and routinely chatting with one another, which could result in group and sometimes 'pack' journalism (Crouse 1973). Reporters received the same news releases, interviewed the same people, and used the same techniques to transform film and sound into stories; but through what reporters still like to call 'enterprise,' they might put different spins on their stories. Today, both the more limited number of correspondents and the standardization of the available image and sound, and of press conferences and interviews, have decreased the possibility of differentiation at the level of the individual story.

And yet news channels must differentiate themselves, their 'brand,' to audiences. One strategy has been to develop a distinctive mix of stories. Hyuhn (2000), for instance, found greater diversity in the news stories offered on broadcast networks than on cable stations.

Margin notes: more television networks · newscasts as brands sound bites Another and perhaps more prominent strategy has been to profile the anchorperson in at least two different ways. First, the well-documented prevalence of shorter sound bites (Hallin 1992) has meant that news anchors (and reporters) are on screen for a larger proportion of the program. On the one hand, the identification of their statements as 'analysis' represents a step away from a previous practice of introducing and summing up politicians and other news-makers, and thus insisting that the 'facts' speak for themselves. On the other hand, the news team's increased time-on-screen brings them to center stage. Some audience members have probably always been motivated to watch, for instance, ABC nightly news because they preferred Peter Jennings to Dan Rather of CBS or Tom Brokaw of NBC, but the greater prominence of news-readers and, to a lesser extent, of reporters, might suggest that the staff or team, not the news, is the product.

A second, related development has placed the anchor more centrally not only in the news message itself, but in its 'mode of address' to viewers.◄ From the advent of television news-casts in the 1950s, anchors had sat behind a desk and read the news, switching their glance from hard copy on the desk to teleprompters to the audience, a tradition which the new-comer, CNN, still maintains. However, in 2000, the nightly news shows of CBS and NBC opened with shots of standing anchorpersons, seemingly active and ready to enter the viewer's home, and symbolically different from the classic anchormen sitting authoritatively behind a desk and waiting for the camera to slowly pan toward them. (In February 2001, Dan Rather of CBS was back behind his desk, whereas Tom Brokaw of NBC continued to stand.) While still wearing stylish suits and ties and speaking in their convincing announcers' voices, these anchorpersons have come to seem less like a doctor or lawyer pronouncing judgment, and more like a messenger reaching out to the viewer.

The presentation of news-readers on CNN and local television news appears to support the perception of news teams which the viewer is

▶ personalized address to viewers – Chapter 7, p. 106

invited to join, symbolically, in dialogue. Here, news-readers sit behind long desks and interact continuously, a practice introduced by U.S. local news stations in the 1960s. At CNN, news-readers are frequently paired by gender (one man, one woman), and joined at the desk by on-staff commentators or outside experts. On local news, anchors share their desk with a sports reporter or even a weatherperson, who then moves to stand before maps and diagrams in order to present the forecast.

In sum, while these modified forms of representation and modes of address in television news, in one sense, merely bring out certain potentials of the audiovisual medium, they are recruited for specific economic and cultural purposes in a particular historical context. Communicative immediacy, involving news workers and audiences in what Thompson (1995: 82) has called 'mediated quasi-inter-action' may be a unique selling proposition (Schudson 1984: 50) for television at a time when many more print and electronic outlets have become available; when audiences have lost part of their faith in the immediacy of news images as representations of reality; and when computer media do not yet offer the sensory richness of television. It is such a complex interchange of economic and cultural factors which empirical production research is called upon to address in future studies, and it is this complexity which may be engaged by combining several complementary research traditions.

THREE TRADITIONS OF NEWS PRODUCTION RESEARCH IN REVIEW

The three main traditions in news production research, delineated by Schudson (1991), might initially seem to lead in different directions. The political economy position would, in one sense or another, return research to Marx's dictum in *The German Ideology* (1845–46) that the ideas of the dominant class are the ideas of an age. Hence, it would encourage examination of how the technological media participate in a wider ideological 'mediation' – the transformation of ideas into forms of social domination. The classic issues have been re-emphasized at the momentous and still contested transition to a global 'network society' (Castells 1996), whose seminal ideas and slogans, again, may serve powerful minority interests. Next, a focus on the social organization and production of news might raise questions, for instance, of how news workers' use of the Internet affects the sorts of information they obtain and report as news (e.g., Borden and Harvey 1998; Garrison 2000). In addition, within textual media studies, historical and comparative research on how myths of individualism and of the 'team' coexist in the wider culture, suggests itself as a means of accounting for the forms of representation and the modes of address noted above in current television news, but also for the novel forms of community arising within computer-mediated communication (e.g., Jones 1998).

To indicate the extent to which the three traditions address some of the same research questions, I start from within the tradition that I know best, the social construction of news, or what Schudson (1991) called the social organization of news, and consider three U.S. studies (Fishman 1980; Gitlin 1980; Tuchman 1978). To begin, all three books take up both the social organization of newswork and what Murdock and Golding (1977) had identified as the problem of 'mediation' – how the ideas of a dominant class become the ideas of an epoch. Of the three books, Gitlin's work on media coverage of the U.S. student movement relied the least on formal participant observation or a theoretical framework of phenomenology. His empirical data were derived partly from his own records of participation in Students for a Democratic Society (SDS), partly from interviews with news workers and friends who had been involved in the news stories being analyzed. Nonetheless, one basis for his larger argument that journalists and editors 'put reality together' was concepts from symbolic interactionism, such as Goffman's (1974) notion of a frame◄ which brings some aspects of reality into view, while excluding others. One of the most interesting portions of Gitlin's (1980) data concerns those cases where personnel at news headquarters in New York City told their team how *not* to cover a story, and

**'mediation':
dominant
classes and
ideas**

where, in addition, these instructions had a chilling effect on other network teams covering other stories which they perceived as similar. In a next step, then, organizational and policy deliberations could be read off at the level of textual structures as well, even if this was not the empirical focus of Gitlin's study.

Compared to such a clear-cut intervention of powerful interests into concrete news decisions, the books by Tuchman (1978) and Fishman (1980) also included examples of the *routine* imposition of what might be called 'an ideological imperative' on the selection and structure of news. Tuchman's study of a local television station described, among other things, how the business office of the station intervened to obtain newspaper coverage of stories that involved its advertisers; how the order of stories in the late evening newscast was rearranged to please advertisers (an airline sponsoring the news had an agreement that an air crash would not be the first story when it was the lead sponsor); and how women reporters complained that they were ordered specifically to cover certain stories because they involved women. (The wall between news and advertising departments has since been breaking down (Croteau and Hoynes 2001: 163–181; Underwood 1993).) Fishman showed, for example, how reporters tended to accept and reproduce the presumed distinction between policy-making and policy implementation within municipal government, and hence how news stories would hide conflicts, compromises, and processes of undue influence in local politics. What both Fishman and Tuchman shared with Gitlin, nevertheless, is the assumption that a detailed empirical accounting of the daily routines and *practices* of news production is required in order to explain how social infrastructures, *institutions*, and their interests are translated into concrete news *texts*.

**practices and
routines of
news
production**

In addition to their different empirical foci, the three studies also relied, in part, on separate theoretical frameworks regarding the determination of news by its social contexts, and regarding the agency of journalists as a source of indeterminacy. Gitlin (1980), for one, argued that, in structural terms, the ideas and actions of news workers articulate and serve the

► frames – Chapter 9, p. 149

interests of a dominant class to which they themselves belong. However, rather than accepting an understanding of ideology as a simple and, perhaps, intentional misrepresentation, the volume resonated with both of the author's classic articles on media sociology, hegemony, and ideology (Gitlin 1978, 1979), suggesting that news systematically prefers certain worldviews.

Fishman (1980) and Tuchman (1978), in their turn, elaborated the concept of ideology from Smith (1974), and argued that news media are ideological in the sense that news work 'is an interested procedure'◄ and 'a means *not* to know.' Their point was not the (real) lack of analysis in many news stories, nor did these authors suggest that the ultimately class-based 'interested procedure' was the result of owners or managers interfering with news procedures. Instead, like Smith, they proposed to see all methods of knowing, including news gathering, as 'embedded' in a particular social and historical context (Garfinkel 1967; Giddens 1984). As concluded also by Gitlin (1980), news workers do not intend to frame the news so as to support either private economic or state interests, but, because of their institutional position and organizational practices, they are likely to serve those interests, and to reproduce their structural and power bases.

Any 'ideological' impact takes effect through concrete news stories – as focused by the textual studies tradition, but recognized in production research traditions as well. Admittedly, news texts vary a great deal, for example, in their precise cognitive and narrative frames, which are used to tell particular stories, and which, further, are capable of multiple interpretations, some of which may oppose a dominant ideological message (Gamson 1992). However, in most mainstream media, such frames as well as other formal features of news are the product of protocols or conventions which transmit at least two additional, implicit messages. First, news still tends to present itself to audiences in a few standard formats that can be taken as evidence of professionalism in

general and objectivity in particular, a notion that remains central to the self-understanding of news workers, and has been referred to by Hallin (1986) as one of the myths of the profession. Second, the selection and combination of information in familiar news formats normally take place with reference to a relatively small set of institutional agendas,◄ which tend to be reinforced as reporters interact with their institutional sources. To exemplify, the U.S. media only came to question the Vietnam War when their elite sources no longer had one agenda, but became willing to disclose their intensifying disagreements with one another as to whether the U.S.A. could win the war (Hallin 1986).

When, from to time, the protocols of writing the news change, it is relevant for research to ask how this discursive change relates to possible changes in professional routines and in the political economy of news. The section above on changing conventions of newspaper journalism noted the spread of 'magazine-like' lead paragraphs in news articles. In political-economic terms, such paragraphs may be interpreted as a response to competition, specifically the ability of the Internet and of all-news cable networks to deliver information in a much speedier fashion than newspapers. In terms of organizational routines and professional ideals, the actual shift is presumably the result of both management deliberations and contestations among professionals about the relatively prestigious 'product' which they co-sign. Product development may occur simultaneously within several organizations, as news workers migrate, and as journalistic associations and publications debate the identity of the genre and of the profession. As a textual form, the 'magazine structure' seems to announce to readers: 'We may not be the first to bring you the news, but you will learn it in a form which allows for identification and interaction with the people in the news.' Significantly, the core definition of news as the presentation of facts remains untouched by this joint commercial, professional, and discursive strategy.

objectivity

product development

► interested procedures – knowledge interests, Chapter 16, p. 279

► agenda-setting – Chapter 9, p. 145

The analysis of news texts thus provides a supplementary approach to the study of news in its social and cultural contexts. Like news events, societies and cultures become meaningful and interpretable when they are considered in their textual or symbolic forms. As noted by Schudson (1991: 151), quoting Marshall Sahlins (1985), 'an event is not just a happening in the world; it is a *relation* between a certain happening and a given symbolic system.' In this perspective, what Gans (1979) uncovered in his analysis of the basic values held by journalists in television network news and major news magazines were the elements of a symbolic system, for example, an idealization of small-town life, which resonates with much of American culture. From a reception perspective, Gamson (1992) similarly identified specific frames of understanding news, involving elements of, for instance, justice and identity, and referring to common symbolic dimensions of technology and nationalism that Americans associate with political issues.

Indeed, it may be argued that a concern not only with political life, but with culture broadly, permeated U.S. news research from the outset. When Park (1922) examined how the immigrant press helped newly arrived Americans to assimilate, he necessarily addressed some of the main symbols of cultural consonance and participation in public life: how to dress, how to eat in a mannerly fashion, how to fill out a job application. Equally, when Hughes (1940) identified the criteria of a suitable human interest story, she necessarily uncovered symbols of what it meant to be a private individual in the American context. Although both Park and Hughes merely claimed to be analyzing news, they simultaneously provided a description of the culture in which the news was embedded and refracted.◀ Also in other cultural contexts, variations in the news form, and in its social and cultural uses, have been subject to structural, organizational, as well as textual study (for an overview see Jensen 1998).

CONCLUSION

The parallel lives of political economy, social phenomenology, and textual studies in news research since the 1960s may have been due to the shared ambition of these three traditions of staying out of, and moving against, the functionalist mainstream of a field which, at the time, was being institutionalized, not only in the U.S.A., but in much of the world.◀ According to the theoretical and political agendas of the period, integration might entail cooptation and neutralization. In the currently consolidated as well as diversified field, an argument may be made for reconsidering the complementarity of the three traditions as well as their interfaces with any remaining mainstream. This chapter has reviewed the traditions, and has exemplified some of their theoretical and empirical points of contact.

A common premise of the three traditions is that news cannot be accounted for in terms of either liberal-leftist 'bias' or establishment 'propaganda.' Instead, it is necessary to examine empirically the several moments of its 'production' – its political-economic preconditions, its organizational enactment, and its textual articulation. Whereas some research, like some public debate, still invokes metaphors of 'selectivity filters' to explain media 'propaganda' (Herman and Chomsky 1988), the political economy tradition from the outset has argued against 'presenting the mass media as a simple relay system for the direct tranmission of a ruling ideology to subordinate groups' (Murdock and Golding 1977: 34). The same researchers have continued to formulate research questions concerning 'the ways in which the representations present in media products are related to the material realities of their production' (Golding and Murdock 1991: 22). Textual studies of news, in their turn, have recognized the diverse institutional purposes of media discourses, as evidenced in their modes of address as well as their concrete linguistic selections.◀

Whichever configuration of the research traditions will be the outcome in future

---

▶ acculturation and socialization via media – Chapter 9, p. 151

▶ media research institution – Chapter 16, p. 279
▶ language of news – Chapter 7

research, they must address classic issues of political philosophy and of the normative theories of media,◄ including:

• the *relative autonomy* of individual news workers, particular news organizations, and the media institution as such within the social system;

• the differences, similarities, and interconnections (via the same market) between *commercial and public service media*, as they produce and circulate meaning in society.

Figure 5.1 indicated the range of social agents that exercise an influence on news production, whereas the different research traditions provide methodologies and theoretical frameworks for studying the nature of these agents' interchange. One important issue for further studies is the relationship between 'pull' and 'push' in the news market – between journalists pulling together information from various sources, and sources pushing their agendas and frames of understanding into the media.

pull and push in news markets

'Push' activities are increasingly important, as planned media coverage has become integral to the conduct of both business and politics (e.g., Glenn *et al.* 1997; Manheim 1998; Shoemaker and Reese 1991; Windahl *et al.* 1992).

Figure 5.2 summarizes key elements of the push–pull nexus. Whereas 'source organizations' – typically political bodies and corporations – have different aims and procedures from news organizations, they equally process 'occurrences' at the interface between the organization and its social context, which certain strategically placed (source) persons can present to reporters as 'events,' hoping that these will be further processed within news organizations and disseminated to a wider public as news. At the juncture between sources and reporters, 'source media' (press releases, government reports, telephone interviews, etc.) provide important and still under-researched raw material for what ends up as news texts. At the same juncture, it also remains important to ask to what degree journalists in different media and cultural contexts perceive their role,

journalistic self-conceptions

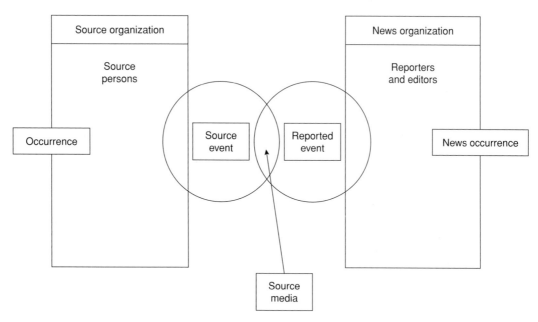

Figure 5.2 Sources and news media as interconnected organizations

Source: Adapted from Ericson *et al.* 1987: 41; see also McQuail and Windahl 1993: 178

► normative theories – Chapter 16, p. 276

for example, as information dissemination, interpretation and investigation, or an adversarial relation to institutions of power (Patterson 1998; Weaver and Wilhoit 1996; Wu *et al.* 1996), despite the overdetermining influence of organizational practices and professional protocols.

The areas of agreement between the three traditions of news research cannot now be summarized in one elegant model, such as that of Riley and Riley (1965). Instead, it will be important to take another, meta-theoretical look at the traditions, asking where and how they may complement one another in further empirical studies. The constitution of news, like the constitution of society itself, is perhaps best described as a complex and continuous structuration (Giddens 1984), involving infrastructural, organizational, as well as discursive components. News is both a permanent social structure and a means of social reflexivity and contestation; a product as well as a productive process. For now, the realization that seemingly disparate research traditions represent complementary perspectives on the same object of analysis will be a significant step forward in studies of news production.

6 The study of international news

Stig Hjarvard

- a distinction between *four types of research* on news
- a review of previous studies of *international news flow*
- a *critique of Galtung and Ruge's* (1965) classic study
- a research agenda on news and *globalization.*

FOUR APPROACHES TO NEWS RESEARCH

When providing an overview of the field of international news research, it is useful to specify the level of analysis (i.e., micro or macro), and the kind of perspective applied to the news process (i.e., how the social phenomenon of news is conceptualized). Two perspectives on the news process have dominated research on international news: those of selection and construction. Research using a selection perspective traditionally focuses on the news 'event.' Events in the world are the independent variables determining the structure of foreign news. Here, social institutions (the press, the journalistic profession, the news market, etc.) are said to play a secondary, intermediate role as a 'selector' or gatekeeper; they perform such functions as selection, rejection, re-editing, etc.

The construction perspective takes the opposite view: news is seen as a social artefact. Social conventions and practices, specific values, and the allocation of material resources work together to produce a particular outcome: the news. Here, social institutions constitute the primary variable; the form, content, and volume of foreign news are all products of the social practices of news institutions. In Figure

selection vs. construction of news

6.1, these two perspectives are paired with the micro–macro distinction, thus producing a matrix of four approaches to the analysis of international news.

1 In the first approach – *micro-level and selection perspective* – we find the oldest tradition: gatekeeper analysis. This began with the seminal study by White (1950), and was further developed by McNelly (1959) to include the whole chain of gatekeepers, from the initial reporting of the event in a foreign location, to the editor of a local newspaper in another part of the world. Even though, during the past two decades, severe criticism of the gatekeeper approach has been raised, it has not completely lost its place in the field (Shoemaker 1991). The concept of gatekeeping intuitively corresponds to certain basic empirical observations at the micro level: foreign news is brought into the newsroom, some of it is selected, rewritten, and so on.

gatekeeping research

2 In the second approach – *macro-level and selection perspective* – we find the news flow analyses. These studies have so far dominated research on international news; examples are, among many others, UNESCO (1953),

	Selection perspective	Construction perspective
Micro-level analysis	Gatekeeper analysis	Ideology critique of foreign news content Analysis of news media organizations
Macro-level analysis	News flow analysis	Media imperialism Political economy of news media

Figure 6.1 Four approaches to the study of international news

Nnaemeka and Richstad (1980), Stevenson and Shaw (1984), UNESCO (1985), and Varis and Jokelin (1976). Although news flow analysis entails detailed counting of individual news items, it has been conducted at the macro level. The general idea has been that the more data one collects and summarizes, the more general propositions one can make as to the structure of international news.

3 In the third approach – *micro-level and construction perspective* – we find empirical studies of news content, often comparative case studies focusing, for instance, on the different U.S. TV networks' coverage of events in the Third World (see, e.g., Adams 1982). We also find a few detailed studies of news agency organizations (see, e.g., Boyd-Barrett 1980; Boyd-Barrett and Thussu, 1992; Fenby 1986; Höhne 1984), and studies of foreign correspondents (see, e.g., Batscha 1975). In both cases, the underlying assumption is that social institutions heavily influence the form, content, and volume of foreign news. However, the analysis is, in practice, concerned with micro-level phenomena: the content of individual news stories or the particulars of an individual news agency.

4 In the fourth approach – *macro-level and construction perspective* – we generally find more theoretical contributions, which are concerned with international news in the context of broader questions of media or cultural imperialism, or of the political economy of the media (see, e.g., Galtung 1971; Mosco 1996; Mowlana 1997; Schiller 1976; Tunstall 1977; Tunstall and Machin 1999).

TV NEWS FLOW STUDIES

In this chapter, I will focus on studies of the international flow of television news. ◀ What is

surprising here is that the bulk of research that has been carried out within the news flow tradition fails to examine, in any real detail, the actual flow or exchange of TV news between news organizations (news agencies, broadcasters, etc.) and across countries. In fact, news flow research does not take the 'flow' metaphor very seriously. Most studies consist only of comparative analyses of the output of national broadcast news. As a consequence, the actual process of news flow is left unexplained. This may be likened to trying to understand the ecological system of the sea by counting the number of fish one can catch from the shore.

A few studies have tried to analyze the content and volume of television news items that are actually exchanged between actors at the wholesale level, and between wholesale and retail levels. In the case of Europe, there is a handful of studies (Golding and Elliot 1979; Gurevitch 1992; Hjarvard 1995, 1999; Melnik 1981; Ruby 1965; Varis and Jokelin 1976). In the case of the so-called Third World continents, there are only one or two studies per continent (see, e.g., Turkistani (1988), which covers news flow in the Arab region). Taken together, these few studies also reveal that few – if any – general conclusions may be drawn about the character (volume, direction, content, etc.) of TV news flow at the global level. The studies seem to indicate that stable or uniform patterns of news flow may instead be identified at a lower level, namely as a function of the region, the historical period, and the specific actors involved (kind of wholesale agencies, kind of broadcasters, etc.). For instance, the idea that international TV news flow could be characterized as 'one-way traffic,' as suggested by Nordenstreng and Varis (1974) and by

wholesale and retail news exchange

▶ three other traditions of news research – Chapter 5

UNESCO (1989: 145), receives support in only some of these studies, and is actually contradicted by more recent findings.

There are at least two major problems with how news flow data have been interpreted in earlier research. First, key concepts are frequently changed when analyses move from the stage of empirical analysis to that of interpretation and theoretical explanation – a shift commonly occurs from a selection to a construction perspective. News flow patterns are often explained using concepts from theories of media and cultural imperialism or from dependency theory.◄ But little work has been done to mediate between the construction perspective of these theoretical explanations and the selection perspective implied by the empirical flow studies. There are very few attempts to explain how macro-social structures actually determine or influence news flow patterns. For instance, how does media imperialism work at the level of social actors (e.g., in TV news agency newsrooms) – actors whose combined actions at the micro level result in the observable news flow patterns? What is missing is a theoretical framework that could create a common ground accommodating both the general social structure and the social actors involved in micro-social actions.

Second, data interpretation has been guided by a theoretical and/or political position where international news flow is considered to be structured by a rather limited set of factors. Both the realm of foreign news and the social world have often been assumed to be much simpler and more homogeneous than is actually the case. In particular, the connection between the operations of the news media and broader social forces (such as cultural imperialism, economic dependency, etc.) has been portrayed as a rather simple one. Studies of news flow patterns have seldom dealt with the more specific, and relatively autonomous, features of media institutions: editorial practices, journalistic education, technology, conventions of expression, and so on. Foreign news is both a discursive-symbolic and a social-economic practice, and both dimensions must be taken into account in

research. Thus, it is necessary to bridge the gap between social-scientific and humanistic traditions in order to provide a comprehensive analysis also of international news.

GALTUNG AND RUGE REVISITED

Some of the problems characterizing the study of international news in the 1960s, 1970s and into the 1980s may be illuminated through a critical discussion of the most important theoretical contribution to the field during this period: Johan Galtung and Mari Holmboe Ruge's article 'The Structure of Foreign News' (1965). The article has been required reading at many schools of journalism and media departments. Galtung and Ruge's hypotheses and methodology also became paradigmatic for much of the research on international news. Two decades after its publication, the Finnish media scholar, Kaarle Nordenstreng, noted that much of the research and critical advocacy of a New World Information and Communication Order (NWICO)◄ could be traced to Galtung and Ruge: 'Most of the criticism, analytical conceptualization, and guidelines for change voiced over the past few years were articulated in the 1960s by Johan Galtung and Mari Holmboe Ruge' (Nordenstreng 1984: 29).

The key propositions of Galtung and Ruge are stated as hypotheses involving twelve factors (such as lack of ambiguity, reference to elite nations, etc.), which together are said to determine the structure of foreign news. They test the importance of these factors through a quantitative content analysis◄ of four Norwegian newspapers with different political leanings. Concretely, the analysis deals with the coverage of three international crises: Congo in 1960, Cuba in 1960, and Cyprus in 1964. They find partial confirmation of their hypotheses and of the relevance of the twelve factors, but also state that there is much empirical testing to be done, and that 'much remains to be done in terms of refinement of the hypothesis' (Galtung and Ruge 1965: 70). Later attempts at verifying the various hypotheses have been

---

► cultural imperialism – Chapter 11, p. 177

► NWICO – Chapter 11, p. 178

► quantitative content analysis – Chapter 13, p. 219

mixed. A major review of the research literature in English caused Hur to conclude that:
'the generality of the proposed hypotheses
remains questionable because one hypothesis
has been supported in some studies and rejected
in others' (Hur 1984: 367). Large German
research projects, Schulz (1976) and Wilke
(1984), reached similarly mixed conclusions.

In spite of the uncertainty surrounding the
empirical validity◄ of both hypotheses and
factors, they have continued to inform the
theoretical and methodological framework of
research on international news. The theoretical
standing of the position was further strengthened by the publication of Johan Galtung's
influential article, 'A Structural Theory of
Imperialism' (1971), in which he incorporated
the field of international news into what he
labeled 'communication and cultural imperialism.' However, Galtung and Ruge's theoretical
and methodological framework contains a
series of problems that make it untenable as a
starting point for empirical analysis.

The first problem concerns their conception
of the news production process. The proposed
news 'factors' constitute an *abstract synthesis*
of a whole series of different social structures
and processes which enter into the production
and circulation of foreign news. These include
the correspondent network, editorial structure
and policy, the different, distinctive news media
(TV, radio, newspapers, etc.), audience characteristics, and so on.

The research literature, furthermore, reveals
diverging interpretations of the proposed news
factors. In some cases they are considered as
the imaginary list of news criteria according to
which individual gatekeepers make their
choices (e.g., Ahern 1984). In other cases they
are considered as psychological determinants of
the news process as a whole (e.g., Rosengren
1974). Others again see the factors as an expression of macro-social determinants (e.g.,
Nnaemeka and Richstad 1980; Pollock and
Guidette 1980). In other words, Galtung and
Ruge's theoretical construction of the empirical
object was inadequate, since it is not at all clear
what kind of social process in the real world is

being uncovered by the analytical use of the
news factors. It may be processes at the micro,
meso, or macro level, and it may be social phenomena as different as economic, journalistic,
political, ideological, or psychological aspects
of the news production process.

Moreover, the proposed methodology is
flawed. A heuristic model – a 'radio' metaphor
– informs the development of hypotheses and
factors. According to Galtung and Ruge, the
news factors are 'nothing but common-sense
perception psychology translated into radio-
scanning and event-scanning activities' (Galtung and Ruge 1965: 66). It follows from this
that the factors should be understood as selection criteria regarding the characteristics of
events. However, the method employed is concerned neither with the selection process nor
with the characteristics of the events. Instead,
a quantitative analysis of the final news product
is used to test the hypotheses.

Rosengren (1970, 1974) drew attention to
the fact that a valid test of the hypotheses
must include a comparison of extra-media data
(the universe of events from which the news is
selected) and intra-media data (the selected
news items). Rosengren admits that, in practice,
it may be difficult to demarcate such an extra-
media dataset. However, the problems involved
in the construction of an extra-media data set
should not justify the application of a 'faulty
Ersatz methodology' (Rosengren 1974: 146).
If the factors address the social and symbolic
transformation of events into news, hypotheses
about them cannot be confirmed solely through
an analysis of the resulting news. For instance,
it is impossible to know whether a predominance of elite persons as actors in the news is
due to a bias in the selection and presentation of news, or to the fact that elite persons
actually play a greater role in the events
reported.

A third problem is the notion that it would
be possible, once and for all, to isolate a definite number of factors that determine the way
foreign news is structured in the (Western)
world. Galtung's and Ruge's ambition was to
propose some very general hypotheses about
the characteristics of (foreign) news in general,
or as Johan Galtung himself expressed it: 'It is

extra-media
and intra-
media data

► validity – Chapter 15, p. 266

a theory concerning what kinds of things are referred to as news. "The theory of news"' (Galtung 1973). As such, their hypotheses as well as the news factors are based on the assumption that, in news from and about the Western world, there is a high degree of uniformity across countries, types of media, political and cultural traditions, and so on.

Consequently, according to Galtung and Ruge, the perspective for further research on international news was to test and refine such factors and hypotheses, which would allow scholars to predict with increased accuracy the likely content and, hence, the fundamental structure of foreign news. Their ambition was not to look for specificities or differences. The logic justifying their own analysis of four different newspapers was that the more newspapers the hypotheses turned out to be valid for, the more support the hypotheses would receive.

Their own empirical analysis can, in fact, validate a quite different – indeed contradictory – relationship, namely that the editorial policy of the specific newspapers in question may account for a high degree of variation in the news. A report from 1962 (published only in Norwegian) by Johan Galtung and Mari Holmboe Ruge used the same empirical materials as the 1965 article (not the 1964 Cyprus crisis, for obvious reasons). It presented a conclusion which is rather surprising, compared to that of the 1965 article: 'What we have found is simply that even if newspapers receive exactly the same agency material via the teleprinter, the changes made by the editorial staff will nevertheless be enough to produce a completely different type of news product' (Galtung and Ruge 1962: 74; my translation).

It is, of course, perfectly legitimate to use the same empirical data to test different hypotheses, but in this case the hypotheses contradict each other. If the hypotheses from the 1965 articles are unable to capture differences which, according to the 1962 report, are prominent in the news, this is perhaps because the 1965 hypotheses operate at a level of abstraction where one is able, for example, to separate news from non-news. However, such hypotheses and their constituent factors are unsuited for guiding research that aims at understanding the differences, variations, and historical developments in international news.

GLOBALIZATION – A NEW AGENDA

The research paradigm established by Galtung and Ruge (1965) was influenced by the rather stable structure of international society at the time: the East–West division between communist and capitalist states, and the North–South division between the affluent and poor countries. The critical debates about inequalities of news flows, uneven communication resources, and the dominance of Western actors – followed by the call for a New World Information and Communication Order – were strongly articulated within the Cold War framework of international relations.◄

Since the mid-1980s, this structure has gradually been eroded, which has given rise to a new research agenda that cuts across previous distinctions between micro and macro levels, and between selection versus construction perspectives. The collapse of communism in the Soviet Union and Eastern Europe, the demise of the apartheid regime in South Africa, and the Gulf War were important events which signaled both the emergence of new power structures in international politics, and the rise of news media to a new prominence. Increasingly, the news media were important not only for their reporting of these events, but seemed to play a role in the very course of events. It became clear that news media were not only part of a distinct political geography (typically within the national political framework), but that they also play a role in creating and rearticulating boundaries of the spaces in which social communities are organized (Morley and Robins 1995).

The Gulf War has been the subject of a great number of studies, which, taken as a whole, reflect a more diverse methodological palette than earlier news research. Some studies of Gulf War coverage focused on the media as tools of political communication (Denton 1993); other studies dealt with the audience reception of war news coverage (Morrison 1992); and still

the Gulf War

▶ the (end of the) Cold War – Chapter 11, p. 178

others used different forms of textual analysis to uncover differences and similarities in the coverage of the war in various media and nations (Nohrstedt and Ottosen 2000). Other major regional events, such as the Balkan wars, were also subjected to detailed analysis (Thompson 1999).

The new conditions in Europe were examined in studies of changes in the institutional and market structures of the wholesale news business. Boyd-Barrett and Rantanen (1999) analyzed, among other things, developments in new Eastern European states, and Hjarvard (1995) examined the impact of deregulation◄ on the Eurovision News Exchange and commercial TV news agencies. The Europeanization of news and journalism was examined in light of the increasingly important role of the European Union (Hjarvard 1993; Meinhof and Richardson 1999; Slaatta 1999). The emergence of transnational TV news channels was dealt with in several studies; in particular, CNN International was analyzed with regard to both organization and content (Flourney and Stewart 1997; Volkmer 1999). The previously quite dominant tradition of news flow analysis was also renewed in the 1990s, in particular through the 'Cooperative Study of Foreign News and International News in the 1990s' (Sreberny and Stevenson in preparation). The study of international news in the 1990s was also influenced by new trends in reception analysis. Reception studies began – albeit slowly – to gain ground, and a few comparative studies of the reception of foreign news were published (Biltereyst 2001; Cohen *et al.* 1996; Jensen 1998).

During the 1990s, the different contributions to the field seemed to share several characteristics. Compared to research in the 1960s, 1970s, and 1980s, there was now less of a focus on discerning grand macro-social relationships (such as the 'one-way flow' hypothesis). At the same time, the simple counting of news items at the micro level was considered insufficient and in need of supplementation or combination with other methods. Increasingly, research on international news found its focus at a middle-range

(margin) CNN International

level.◄ Working somewhere between the macro and micro levels seemed to increase the likelihood of making valid generalizations. Stable patterns of interaction could be discerned at a regional level (e.g., Western Europe), within a specific medium or sector (e.g., foreign news on television or the news agencies), or at a particular stage in the communication sequence (e.g., the reception of foreign news). Research in the 1990s also tried to combine methodologies from the humanities and the social sciences. Ginneken's (1998) introduction to the field, for one, clearly demonstrated the advantage of using a broader methodological palette (e.g., organizational studies and discourse analysis) in order to understand global news.

Similarly, recent research has abandoned the dichotomy of construction vs. selection. Instead, social interaction is interpreted as a dual relationship involving both action and structure (Giddens 1984).◄ International news may be understood neither as the mere product of willful gatekeepers selecting from world events with a heavy hand, nor as the sole outcome of overarching social structures, such as media and cultural imperialism. Social actors in the field of foreign news are knowledgeable agents, whose actions at times may make a specific difference. Simultaneously, however, they are informed by, and to some extent subordinated to, the social structures that govern the journalistic profession, the particular media organization, the political and cultural framework of the country in question, and so on.

Research on international news in the 1990s has demonstrated that both actors and structures are subject to considerable change. A series of new actors have entered the field, among them dedicated news channels with regional and global reach. Newspapers, news broadcasters, and Internet news services have been taken over by large media conglomerates, and this organizational and economic concentration has created new conditions for the production and distribution of foreign news.◄

(margin) dedicated, monogeneric news channels

▶ deregulation – Chapter 16, p. 278

▶ theories of the middle range – Chapter 3, p. 55

▶ duality of structure – Chapter 1, p. 1

▶ conglomeration – in fiction production, Chapter 4, p. 73

Another very important structural change is the rise of the Internet as a news medium.◄ Internet news services may entail a further blurring of the distinction between wholesale and retail news providers, and may bring new actors with no journalistic background into the business (Paterson 2001). Finally, the very notions of 'international news' or 'foreign news' are no longer self-evident in a globalized world with more open boundaries and overlaps between the local, regional, national, and global levels. For instance, in some countries in the European Union, news about the EU is no longer considered foreign news, but a kind of quasi-national news.◄

The agenda of globalization constitutes a challenge for future research. An important task will be to analyze how globalization both changes the content and structure of international news, and influences the political and other social processes that depend on this public communication. A parallel task will be to understand how globalization itself is furthered by changes in the field of international news media.

► the Internet – Chapter 11, p. 188

7 Discourses of fact

Kim Christian Schrøder

- an overview of the *development of quantitative content analysis*
- an *example* of content analysis in practice
- a comparison of three forms of *qualitative discourse analysis*
- a review of studies of *visual media content*
- an example of the analysis of *still images* and texts in advertising.

TEXTS TO REMEMBER: INTRODUCTION

Every time a year comes to an end, we may use the chronological threshold to think back on events of the past year and their significance for ourselves and for the many social formations to which we happen to belong. Within the private circles of life, our personal memory is perhaps supported by letters and diaries, photographs or home video recordings. The further we move into the history of our local community or region, via ethnic and national collectivities, toward events on a global scale that have affected us despite their geographical distance, the more we have to rely on mediated memories, as recorded and disseminated by others, to understand what happened.◄ This chapter deals with the ways in which the media select, combine, and present events in the real world in verbal and visual form, thus constructing versions of reality which shape the meanings and values that inform our attitudes and behaviors, primarily as citizens and consumers.

At the end of 1998, the BBC broadcast its annual *Review of the Year* program, offering

a selective, collective memory of a year whose events included the Bill Clinton–Monica Lewinsky case, the Football World Cup in France, British Northern Ireland Minister Mo Mowlam's exploits at the negotiating table as well as her trials as a cancer patient, South African President Nelson Mandela's eightieth birthday, pop singer George Michael being arrested for lewd conduct in a public lavatory, *Titanic* – the most expensive movie ever made (so far), and many other events from the domestic and international scene. In just over an hour, this retrospective provided one particular answer to the question, 'What happened in 1998?', at the same time implicitly labeling numerous other events as not worth remembering. In addition to omissions and absences, however, textual analysis should be curious about the 'lenses,' both literal and metaphorical, through which events are to be viewed.

This is how anchorwoman Sue Lawley introduces the program as she is walking around a huge, dark television editing room with dozens of tiny screens behind her:

Welcome to *Review of the Year 1998*, the year Britain went digital, or a tiny bit of it

► memory: immediate and mediated – Chapter 2, p. 16

did anyway. Very soon, we're told, we'll all be able to watch hundreds, possibly thousands of channels, so this year we thought we'd embrace the future as we review the past. Tonight on *Review of the Year* we launch a few channels ourselves. Their content, of course: the events of the past year streamed and themed as they might be for the digital age. The Sports Channel dominated by World Cup 1998, The Medical Channel including a brief history of Viagra, The Women's Channel featuring Mo Mowlam, Gerri Spice and more. But we begin with The Men's Channel, not *for* men, you understand, but *about* them, their triumphs and their follies: some did well, others behaved badly. . . .

The visual environment, first of all, locates viewers in a multi-channel, digital universe. The screens in the editing room function as a 'metonymic' visual sign, being 'part of' and thereby signifying the 'whole of' the digital age.◄ In the verbal part of the message, viewers may respond to the jocular style of the anchorwoman; to the rhetorically balanced phrase, 'embrace the future/review the past'; to the rhyming neologism 'themed and streamed'; and to the definite article in the phrase '*the* events of the past year,' which presupposes that the events chosen by the program are the events worth remembering.

A recurring structural feature is Sue Lawley aligning herself with viewers through pronouns.◄ The 'inclusive we' of 'we're told, we'll all' differs from the 'exclusive we' of 'we thought' and 'we begin', as she claims membership of the production team. All in all, the anchor relies on the viewers' complicity in pretending, for the sake of this program's format, that Britain did 'go digital' in 1998. In fact, the rest of its content is structured in accordance with the narrative framework of an imagined multi-channel universe, including several channels not mentioned in the opening, such as The Disaster Channel, The Crime Channel, and

The Goodbye Channel, the last commemorating people who died in 1998. Lawley's reference to some who 'behaved badly' prefigures the first item on The Men's Channel:

> 1998 was the year in which one man found himself starring in his own real-life soap opera. Presenting Bill Clinton, the most powerful man in the world, and a womanizer. Monica Lewinsky, the woman whose lips could destroy a president.

The musical, visual, and verbal sequence, comprising a familiar fanfare, an aerial shot of a massive white building with a helicopter hovering in the air, and a split screen with three different pictures of President Bill Clinton, is a sustained pastiche of the internationally successful 1980s soap opera *Dallas*. Having introduced the main characters and the plot line, the soap-style title sequence carries into an imitation of 'Last week on *Dallas*' that brings the viewer up to date on the Clinton–Lewinsky real-life soap. Beyond this selection (paradigmatically) and combination (syntagmatically) of elements,◄ as with other media, television brings to the configuration a repertoire of genres and styles that are themselves a media creation. This self-referentiality◄ is particularly evident here, because the generic lens for describing political events is taken from fiction, and may question not only conventional divisions between news and soaps, the serious and the trivial, but between fact and fiction, and between the public and private spheres of social life.

Whereas this brief, informal analysis has not pursued political or moral implications, it is the public's dependency on media representations to keep track of events, and years, in order to make politically or morally informed decisions which has often led media researchers to focus attention on the precise manner in which pictures of social reality are constructed for us by the media through topical structures and expressive forms.

► metonymy – Chapter 2, p. 24

► pronouns – p. 106

► paradigms and syntagms – Chapter 2, p. 24

► self-referentiality – intertextuality, Chapter 11, p. 186

While complaints about 'bias' in the media are legion across the spectrum of public debate, academic research has usually been driven by a 'critical' interest◄ in exposing the differential *news* treatment of social groups in conformity with entrenched hierarchies of power and privilege, for example, in the strategic area of industrial conflict (Glasgow Media Group 1976; Hall *et al.* 1976). Similarly, studies of *advertising* have taken on stereotypical gender roles (e.g., Andrén *et al.* 1978; Goffman 1979 [1976]; Millum 1975), and the promotion of consumption as a solution to complex social or personal problems (e.g., Leiss *et al.* 1986; Vestergaard and Schrøder 1985; Williamson 1978). A third body of research has examined the realities implied in media fiction – particularly *television series* – from the 1960s (e.g., DeFleur 1964), via U.S. commission reports on television as a social issue (Comstock *et al.* 1971), to cultivation research.◄ Over several decades, cultivation studies have identified a discrepancy between crime statistics and the amounts and kinds of violence depicted on television, as well as the possible impact of TV violence especially on heavy viewers and its potential political support for conservative law-and-order policies (Gerbner and Gross 1976; for critiques see Hirsch 1980; Newcomb 1978).

The critical orientation is commonly found on both sides of the quantitative–qualitative divide, even though the readiness to accept a conception of discursive representations as a 'construction' has varied in the development of textual and content studies. In a first phase, a number of studies tended to assume that the media could be studied as a phenomenon separate from the rest of society, asking how 'faithfully' media represented social reality.◄ This has been the rationale of most quantitative content studies, but also of 'critical linguistics,' reviewed below. A second phase has emphasized the mutual constitution of media and modern societies, so that it may not be feasible, methodologically or epistemologically, to compare 'media realities' with any independent indicators. 'Critical discourse analysis' as well as 'discursive psychology', but also certain approaches to content measurement, increasingly take as their premise that media content is not so much a secondary reflection as an artefact and a practice in which society is both reproduced and contested.

QUANTITATIVE CONTENT ANALYSIS

Questions that audiences – and researchers – ask

Having watched a program like *Review of the Year 1998*, the audience, being instinctively analytical, or semiotic, creatures, is left with certain general impressions of what the program was 'about,' and how this 'content' is likely to affect both viewers like themselves and the larger society represented. Predictably, there will be critical comments about women being depicted as secondary in political and economic matters, about a supposedly serious news review spending too much time on the trifles of the entertainment world, or about Third World events being all but ignored in an increasingly global society. In interpersonal everyday discussions, people will next try to substantiate their claims by referring to specific program elements, but because lay discussion is rarely sustained beyond impressions or speculations, it is difficult to determine who is right and who is wrong. One task of media and communication research, in the garb of 'content analysis,' is to address such issues, supposedly on behalf of a democratic society as an input to, and influence on, political and public debates about how its citizens and their concerns should collectively be portrayed by the media.

In order to interpret the implications of findings regarding both gender and other categories, content analysts need a standard of comparison. If one subscribes to the first-phase focus on media as separate from other social structuration, one may refer to 'reality itself,' as documented typically with official statistics regarding, for instance, the proportion of women and men in parliaments or occupational roles. If, instead, one relies on the second-phase

---

► critical knowledge interest – Chapter 16, p. 281

► cultivation research – Chapter 9, p. 150

► selection vs. construction of news – Chapter 6, p. 79

ANALYSIS BOX 7.1 CONTENT ANALYSIS OF *REVIEW OF THE YEAR 1998*, BBC1 1998

Table 7.1 Representation of protagonists on *Review of the Year 1998*

	Men	%	Women	%	Total	%
Geographical belonging						
British	39	56	15	65	54	58
American	8	11	4	17	12	13
European	8	11	2	9	10	11
Rest of the world	14	20	1	4	15	16
Unidentifiable	1	1	0	0	1	1
Total characters	70	100	23	100	93	100
Social arena						
Politics	38	54	7	30	45	48
Showbiz	22	31	12	52	34	37
Sports	16	23	4	17	20	22
Entertainment	6	9	8	35	14	15
Science	2	3	0	0	2	2
Everyday life	8	11	4	17	12	13
Total characters	70	100	23	100	93	100
Gender	70	75	23	25	93	100

Table 7.1 displays a basic quantitative content analysis◄ of the 1998 *Review of the Year*. Among several potential categories, the analysis singled out the human individual, specifically characteristics of the program's personalities. It was decided to consider only the protagonists, defined as individuals at the center of attention by virtue of their being both mentioned verbally by name (in spoken or written form) and appearing visually on screen. Thus, Rupert Murdoch, mentioned in the voice-over but not shown, and Leonardo DiCaprio, shown but not named, were excluded from the counts. This criterion is controversial, and led to the inclusion of perhaps less-prominent individuals like Russian Premier Primakov who had been the premier for only a few months. The point is that such criteria must be justified theoretically through the operationalization of 'protagonist,' and then applied consistently across all cases. A particular theoretical motivation for analyzing individual protagonists is that they are the vehicles of particular social and cultural characteristics which together delineate a particular possible world. Three types of characteristics were studied for present purposes:

1   *geographical origin* (perhaps suggesting a view of the world from a particular perspective);
2   *gender* (considering claims about male dominance in the world of television);
3   *social arenas of activity* (exploring the prominence of four different sectors with which protagonists may commonly be associated: politics, showbiz (subdivided into sports and entertainment/media), science, and everyday life).

It should be noted that categorization and subsequent quantification (lasting approximately four hours for this seventy-five-minute program, including calculation of percentages with a pocket

► content analysis, sampling, coding, and statistical procedures – Chapter 13, p. 219

cont.

calculator) is by no means an automatic process. Almost every instance requires the discriminating ability of the analyst before assigning, for example, Princess Diana to the entertainment category, Monica Lewinsky to politics, former astronaut and U.S. senator John Glenn as a contributor to science (rather than a politician or media celebrity), Boris Yeltsin (and Russia) to Europe. In one interesting case, the Israeli singer Dana International was categorized as female (before a sex change, 'she' was a man) and European (appearing because she won the *European Song Contest*). Any discussion about findings and their validity must begin by thus explicitly noting the criteria, procedures, and decisions of the analysis as conditions of intersubjectivity, disagreement, and research dialogue.

The findings regarding *geographical origin*, indicating three British out of every five protagonists, are hardly surprising in a national program, whereas the minor role of European protagonists might raise eyebrows among EU observers at an insular British outlook. (A further breakdown would reveal that four of the ten Europeans are sports stars, four are Russian presidents or premiers, leaving German Chancellor Helmuth Kohl and Serbian President Slobodan Milosevic as the sole representatives of non-Russian Europe.) In comparison, the rest-of-the-world figures might seem high, but includes protagonists from Africa (three), Asia (six), the Middle East (three), and Latin America (three). Moreover, a preliminary, qualitative assessment suggests that most of the events dealt with in this rag-bag category are economic or political crises and natural disasters.

Regarding *social arenas*, citizens might welcome the fact that almost half the protagonists belong to the realm of politics, and might worry about the fact that showbiz accounts for no less than one-third (mainly sports personalities) of the program's main characters, while science, site of both revolutionary discoveries and ethical concerns, reaches a low of 2 percent. Again, a qualitative look behind the numbers suggests that politics is seen repeatedly through a lens of ridicule, in the case of the American presidency, parliamentary struggles in the Russian Duma, and the sexual politics of male British Members of Parliament. In addition, the apparently astonishing fact that people from everyday life are almost as prominent as entertainment personalities is placed in perspective when it turns out that no less than eleven of the twelve instances represent either victims or perpetrators of sensational crime.

Finally, regarding *gender*, across the board three-quarters of the protagonists in this particular program are men, a quarter women. The variations, however, suggest that women are relatively more prominent in the British than in the rest-of-the-world category, less so in politics and science, more so in showbiz, and even outnumbering men in entertainment.

---

premise regarding the mutual constitution of societies and their symbolic forms, an internal standard suggests itself, such as previous 'reviews of the year' going back five, ten, or twenty years, perhaps conferring, as well, with other genres.◄ Additional sources of comparison arise from the distinction between public-service and commercial channels, and between print media and this broadcast medium.

It remains to emphasize that the analysis in Box 7.1 provides an illustration of, and reflec-

tion on, basic principles and applications of content analysis, not a full-fledged methodology of representative sampling, dual coding, and hypothesis testing. A main advantage of quantitative content studies is that they can serve to confirm or disconfirm intuitive impressions by performing a systematic description of a large set of media discourses through numbers that express the frequency and prominence of particular textual properties. A drawback, or trade-off, is the inevitable reduction of complexity that follows from the decontextualization of meaningful elements. While qualitative researchers have sometimes been blunt in their critique of what appeared to be a

---

► extra-media or intra-media standards of evaluation – Chapter 6, p. 94

scientistic attempt 'to eliminate, as far as possible, any human element or bias' from the research process (Fiske 1990: 135), content analysts have also engaged in a critical redevelopment of their premises and procedures.

Revising categories

So far, this chapter has used the cumbersome term 'quantitative content analysis,' but the literature normally refers simply to 'content analysis,' while the qualitative study of media texts is variously called 'textual analysis' or, more recently, 'discourse analysis.' In a sense, quantitative social sciences have monopolized the generic term, as suggested by classic titles like *Content Analysis in Communication Research* (Berelson 1952), *Content Analysis: An Introduction to its Methodology* (Krippendorff 1980), or *Content Analysis for the Social Sciences and Humanities* (Holsti 1969). In the early decades of the twentieth century, quantitative newspaper analysis measured the column inches devoted by newspapers to particular subject matters, seeking to reveal 'the truth about newspapers' and possibly criticize journalistic practice (Street (1909), quoted in Krippendorff 1980: 14). Other studies used content-analytical procedures not just to learn about media, but to monitor topics in press content in continuous surveys so as 'to establish a system of bookkeeping of the "social weather" comparable in principle to the statistics of the U.S. Weather Bureau' (Krippendorff 1980: 14), and comparable, in certain respects, to agenda-setting research half a century later.◀ A third ancestor of modern content analysis were the propaganda studies◀ of enemy media during World War II, when American researchers monitored 'domestic enemy broadcasts to understand and predict events within Nazi Germany and its allies and to estimate the effects of military actions on war mood' (Krippendorff 1980: 16).

Around 1950, following developments in survey and other analytical techniques since

the 1930s, content analysis was approaching maturity. In his famous and henceforth authoritative definition, Bernard Berelson (1952) synthesized earlier methodological reflections on the approach: 'Content analysis is a research technique for the objective, systematic, and quantitative description of the manifest content of communication' (p. 18). The fundamental distinction in the analytical process, according to Berelson, is between 'knowledge' and 'interpretation' of media content ('inferences' to Berelson). While he recognized that the end goal of research is to make interpretations of the media, and of their relationship with either the intentions of senders or the consequences for the attitudes and behaviors of recipients, Berelson stipulated that such interpretation must not be mixed into the analytical process proper. The distinction appears from the statement that 'knowledge of the content can legitimately support inferences about non-content events' (p. 18), and is clarified in a discussion of the difference between qualitative and quantitative approaches:

> In 'qualitative' analysis the interpretations (i.e. inferences about intent or effect) are more often made as *part* of the analytical process whereas in quantitative analysis the interpretations are more often likely to *follow* the analytic procedure. . . . The tendency of the qualitative analyst is to make his interpretations as he goes through the material – whenever a piece of material cues him in some way. The tendency of the 'quantitative' analyst is to base his interpretation upon the total completed analysis in order to see particular pieces of content in perspective.
>
> (pp. 122–123)

The quantitative analyst, then, can hope to avoid 'interpreting' his data only if he concerns himself entirely with 'manifest,' or denotative, meanings and excludes latent, or connotative,◀ meanings, since manifest meanings are defined as those which everybody (both senders and recipients of messages) will spontaneously agree

---

▶ agenda-setting research – Chapter 9, p. 145
▶ propaganda studies – Chapter 9, p. 147

▶ denotation and connotation – Chapter 2, p. 25

on. Berelson does acknowledge that, in a strict sense, 'manifest content' is merely that end of a continuum of meaning where 'understanding is simple and direct' (p. 20), or where meanings are more likely to be shared than at the other, radically polysemic◄ extreme. In hermeneutic terminology,◄ Berelson still assumed that one can, after all, examine understanding without a pre-understanding or horizon of expectations.

What amounted to a suppression in research practice of the role of interpretation in any human activity, has been at the heart of controversies in the theory of science since Berelson (see the early critique of Berelson by Kracauer (1953: 693). More recent definitions, also within content analysis, have involved a marked departure from Berelson's model. Thirty years on, Krippendorff (1980) advanced an alternative and influential definition: 'Content analysis is a research technique for making replicable and valid inferences from data to their context' (p. 21). In developing his definition, Krippendorff was explicitly critical of Berelson's position, which he found unnecessarily restrictive. Krippendorff did agree that content analysis must be replicable, and therefore systematic, but he saw no reason why content analysis must be quantitative, and also dismissed the exclusion of latent meanings from the researcher's legitimate horizon of interests. Although his book remained focused on the mechanics and accreditation of content quantification, his conceptualization of interpretation differed fundamentally from Berelson's, despite relatively subtle differences of wording. Crucially, Krippendorff identified inferential processes in all stages of the research process, 'from data to their context.' In the establishment of analytical categories, the ascription of textual units to these categories, as well as the correlation of findings with theoretical conceptions of society and culture, the content analyst is inevitably an interpreter. In Krippendorff's (1980) words, the analyst is a reader of the meanings of a text, someone who is not merely engaged in '"extracting" content from the data

as if it was objectively "contained" in them. . . . meanings are always relative to a communicator' (p. 22).

With a cautious interpretation, one might suggest that this definition of 'content analysis' implies a constructivist reconceptualization of quantitative measurement. As such, Krippendorff's (1980) intervention represents one specification of the sometimes rather abstract acknowledgment that quantitative and qualitative approaches, also to media texts, are complementary in that they produce different analytical versions of reality, as an input to public debate about social reality and its mediation. In the qualitative literature on media texts, both the constructionist and critical points of departure have been in evidence from the beginning.

QUALITATIVE DISCOURSE ANALYSIS

Critical linguistics

In the conclusion to a now classic qualitative analysis of a newspaper report about racial conflict in Southern Africa, Tony Trew, one of the founders of 'critical linguistics,' stated that the text 'is so far from the truth that only a powerful grip on the press and information and the diligence of the media in resolving the flood of anomalies which they report are adequate to preserve the pretence that the press is truthful' (Trew 1979: 106). The quotation might give the impression that critical linguistics simplistically checks whether a verbal account of political and other events is 'true' or not. While this is not the case, analyses in the 'critical linguistic' tradition will often lapse into direct contradiction of the media's picture of reality, fueled by a strong political and educational commitment.

Critical linguistics developed in the 1970s as an influential early school of discourse analysis. The approach was able to document a close relationship between the linguistic details of media texts and the production of ideology and, by implication, to substantiate that media ideology contributes to the reproduction of a social order founded on inequality and oppression. Its epistemology was a somewhat heavy-handed linguistic constructivism according to

---

▶ polysemy – Chapter 10, p. 167

▶ hermeneutics – Chapter 2, p. 21

which words construct a mental grid. Words are conventional, but constitutive of the reality they designate, so that, for instance, newspapers inevitably construct the social states and events they describe.

Critical linguistics went on to claim that not just lexical, but also syntactic choices have semantic and hence ideological implications, as exemplified below. Relying on Saussure's notion of the arbitrary sign,◄ the point is not that linguistic choices can be made by journalists at will, but instead that these choices articulate and enact social power in practice. Since the formation of public opinion in capitalist societies is controlled by those with economic and organizational power over the mass media, who will see to it that representations do not jeopardize their interests and privileges, public communication has a pervasive ideological thrust that renders current social arrangements natural, even inevitable, while discrediting alternatives as contrary to common sense. As summed up by Fowler (1985), the task of critical linguists is to expose such ideology in the best interest of the majority: 'Of course from my point of view this has to be regarded as an undesirable situation and one that a critical linguist ought to expose' (p. 67).

Dissolving seemingly innocent linguistic features, critical textual analyses can debunk 'warped versions of reality' (p. 68). Building on Halliday's functional grammar and social semiotic (Halliday 1973, 1978), numerous publications from the late 1970s and into the 1980s (e.g., Fowler *et al.* 1979; Hodge and Kress 1988) identified linguistic features that 'will probably repay close examination,' according to Fowler (1985: 68). He offered the following 'checklist' (with examples in parentheses referring to the opening extract of *Review of the Year 1998*):

1 *Lexical processes* arise from the particular vocabulary, including metaphors, which a media text mobilizes concerning a given area of experience, such as scientific vocabulary in a cosmetics ad, or management jargon in political coverage (the 'launch' of digital channels in the BBC program refers simultaneously to actual, future channels and to the program's own format).

2 *Transitivity*, a relation obtaining between verbs and nouns, adds up to a construction and configuration of the participants and processes in a text (the review not only 'launches' new channels, but it 'embraces' the future, and anticipates what, very soon, 'we'll all be able to watch').

3 *Syntactic transformations*, particularly those labeled 'passivization' and 'nominalization,' can be considered ideologically problematic because they may obscure agency – who did what to whom – or change the participants' relative prominence ('we're told' that a digital cornucopia will soon be available, but not who tells us, or with what justification).

4 *Modality*, in the form especially of modal verbs and adverbs, serves to express speakers' and other senders' assessments of, and attitudes towards, the events rendered by the sentences constituting the text (the reference to 'possibly' thousands of channels is partly a qualification of the prediction itself, but also partly an expression of skepticism toward everything 'we're told').

5 *Speech acts*◄ and turn-taking refer to the fact that speech is a coordinated form of action, in which speakers take turns in complex ways. One insight of discourse analysis generally is that there is no one-to-one relation between sentence types and communicative functions. Instead, analysts should ask which speech act is accomplished by the utterance of a sentence, and how both the single act and the structure of turn-taking may build positions of power into the communicative context (e.g., a classroom or a medical consultation). (While the news review is not dialogic in the sense of talk or discussion programs, already the opening 'Welcome,' itself a conventional act of greeting, invites the viewer to attend to the 'turn' of this program).

6 *Implicature*, comprising a variety of communicative features, is perhaps best explained

► arbitrariness of signs – Chapter 2, p. 25

► speech acts – Chapter 2, p. 38

as the ability of most language users to 'read between the lines,' to infer what is 'really' meant. It is this ability which is made systematic and procedural in (critical) linguistics, particularly in attempts to recover 'latent' meanings through a 'hermeneutics of suspicion'◄ (the reference to The Men's Channel as being not *for*, but *about*, men implies the existence of monogeneric pornographic channels, and relies on viewers' knowledge of this to poke gentle fun at men's 'follies').

7 *Address and personal reference*, finally, allow linguistic analysis to consider how stylistic choices anticipate an audience with a particular social or educational status; how naming conventions affect the degree of formality; and how personal pronouns assert a particular 'interpersonal' relationship with an audience (in addition to the inclusive and exclusive *we*, 'you understand' is an explicit appeal to both female and male viewers to accept the terminological joke about The Men's Channel).

Although this checklist has found its way into later discourse studies of media, it is not always evident that its elements represent productive analytical categories. Transitivity, for example, requires a very time-consuming scrutiny of textual detail to establish an ideological pattern (e.g., Fowler 1985), which might be predictable from a more cursory examination. Furthermore, it is doubtful whether claims about the 'mystifying' effects of syntactic transformations are warranted, being based on assumptions about the 'non-recoverability' of the deleted linguistic component (Trew 1979). It seems equally probable that average media-users will have no difficulty inferring who did what to whom, despite passive sentences or nominalizations, on the basis of their background knowledge of the world, their familiarity with a current news agenda, and their general communicative competence. Interestingly, an empirical study of readers' reception of the newspaper articles previously analyzed by Trew found that the readers' views of the

events reported in the articles were determined less by their 'syntactically constructed' ideology than by the readers' social identities and life histories (Sigman and Fry 1985).

In sum, critical linguistics made an important departure, both beyond content analyses of manifest meaning, and beyond formal and poetic traditions of textual analysis, but remained closely focused on linguistic indicators. Other forms of discourse analysis have gone some way toward placing such indicators in their communicative and social contexts.

Critical discourse analysis

Although intellectually rooted in critical linguistics, critical discourse analysis (CDA), as developed mainly by Norman Fairclough since the late 1980s, represents a significant theoretical as well as methodological contribution to the interdisciplinary study of media discourse (Fairclough 1992, 1995). Its theoretical framework, relating textual features, first, to the concrete social situations in which texts are produced and consumed, and second, to social processes at large, is usually displayed as a model of three embedded boxes (Figure 7.1). 'Texts' stand at the core of the model, and are explored largely through the categories of critical linguistics. The second dimension of analysis concerns 'discourse practices,' for instance, the processes through which specific media texts are produced in media organizations and consumed, or 'decoded,' by audiences in the context of their everyday lives. These discourse practices are understood as mediators between certain delimited texts and much wider 'sociocultural practices,' which constitute the third dimension of analysis. At this third, macro-social level, the discursive phenomena brought to light at the first two levels are adduced in claims about, and interpretations of, the prevailing 'order of discourse' at a given historical time. Thus, CDA has sought to join a linguistic, analytical approach to discourses, in the plural, with a critical, theoretical conception of one dominant discourse, in the singular, following Foucault (1972).

In addition to its sources in critical linguistics, and in critical social theory, the model of

two definitions of discourse – as concrete uses of language and other signs, and as a dominant worldview

---

◄ hermeneutics of suspicion – Chapter 2, p. 22

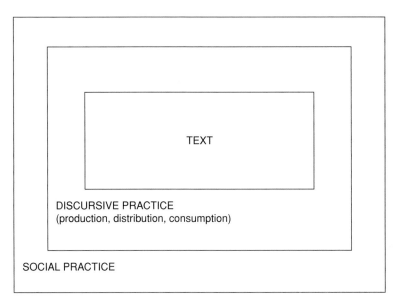

Figure 7.1 Dimensions of critical discourse analysis
Source: Fairclough 1995: 59

CDA is inscribed in current debates about 'structure' and 'agency' (e.g., Beck 1994; Giddens 1984, 1994), as suggested by its constructivist position, specifically the dual role of media as constituted by, as well as constituting, the social formation. The media clearly operate within a set of economic and political frameworks, representing the prevailing social order, but its diversity as well as its internal representational struggles, as articulated by the media, serve also to poise the media uneasily between convention and innovation, reproduction and change. In order to account for such social and discursive processes, 'intertextuality' has been imported as a key analytical concept into CDA.◄ Concretely, any text is indebted to innumerable source texts, and may itself become the source of an infinite number of future texts. In the case of news and other factual coverage, CDA analyses will examine various media genres (news reports, interviews, commentaries, etc.) as 'discourse types,' which, in their turn, draw on different political discourse types (government reports, parliamen-

tary speeches, press conferences, etc.) that grow out of related, but different discourse practices.

The intertextual perspective also attains relevance at the level of the 'orders of discourse,' where conventional political discourse may be intermingled with the discourses of science and technology, of grass-roots politics, or of the everyday. It is at this macro-social level that, ultimately, the 'meaning' of discourses and practices may be evaluated. One example is what Fairclough terms the 'conversationalization'◄ of public discourse in the media: the spread of informal speech and colloquial expressions. On the one hand, this might trivialize complex social issues and relations; on the other hand, by making key problems accessible it might be a source of cultural democratization: 'The communicative style of broadcasting lies at the intersection of . . . democratizing, legitimizing and marketing pressures, and its ambivalence follows from that' (Fairclough 1995: 149). Similarly, Fairclough has referred to a colonization of

───────────

▶ intertextuality – Chapter 11, p. 186

▶ conversationalization and tabloidization – Chapter 3, p. 49

public speech by commercial discourses as 'marketization,' while he has been less aware of the complementary process of the 'politicization' of market discourses, as ecological and ethical considerations gain attention in the business world.

The main limitation of critical discourse analysis is that no empirical attention is given to the middle range of the discourse practices. Fairclough has deliberately excluded this aspect from his own analyses, stating that 'my emphasis will be upon linguistic analysis of texts . . . I am not concerned . . . with direct analysis of production or consumption of texts' (Fairclough 1995: 62). Certainly so far, few researchers overall have undertaken holistic, empirical studies of media and their circulation of discourses between senders and recipients, some exceptions being Swales and Rogers' (1995) study of corporate mission statements and Deacon *et al.* (1999) on the news circuit. As a research program, however, Fairclough's rejection of empirically studying audiences and other social agents of discourse tends to limit the applicability and explanatory value of the approach.

Conversation analysis and discursive psychology

In his important overview and redevelopment of discourse analysis, Potter (1996) discusses an extract from a news report about a bomb attack in Cape Town in which 'the attack *was believed to be* the work of the UPLAR' (National Public Radio, December 12, 1993; emphasis added). Potter uses the sentence to illustrate a main difference between critical discourse analysis and his own 'discursive psychology.' Critical discourse analysis (and linguistics) would take issue with the 'agent deletion' of the sentence, the missing 'believer,' which might covertly support the powers that be against a political liberation movement without adequate evidence. Without denying the potential ideological implication, Potter adopts an interaction perspective, asking what pragmatic function the agent deletion may fulfill for a journalist working under certain institutional pressures and professional norms,

which make it inappropriate for himself to be the origin of any such belief. Further, Potter hypothesizes that other available sources, such as the police, were not perceived as credible in context. Potter's (1996) conclusion is that the agent-less construction may serve as 'a specific design solution to a range of fact construction and warranting problems' (p. 157) which face a news report intent on establishing its objectivity and accountability. At the end of the day the journalist needed sources, did not have any credible ones, and resorted to making them discursively present and absent at the same time.

Among the heterogeneous ancestry of discursive psychology, the most formative influence has come from the tradition of ethnomethodology◀ and conversation analysis, particularly when it comes to its analytical procedures. For four decades, the aim of conversation analysis has been to explore the situational micro-mechanics of verbal interaction. Many studies have probed, for example, speakers' turn-taking through so-called adjacency pairs, the role of silences and interruptions in the flow of interaction, the management of topic development and topic change, and several other structuring features (for overviews see Have 1999; Nofsinger 1991).   turn-taking

Like conversation analysis, discursive psychology takes its point of departure in the situational contexts of language use. Its purpose, however, is to go on to account for the ways in which the communicative micro-mechanics enter into everyday as well as institutional processes of social life, for instance, in the case of nationalism or racism (Billig 1995; Wetherell and Potter 1992). In thoroughly 'discursifying' categories like attitudes and memory, discursive psychology thus departs both from critical discourse analysis, with its distinctions between discursive and other social processes, and from much traditional psychology and social psychology (Edwards and Potter 1992; Potter and Wetherell 1987).

Discursive psychology is particularly concerned with speakers' fact construction and their own positioning in co-constructing social

▶ ethnomethodology – Chapter 3, p. 56

reality; that is, their attempts to establish their own 'versions' or accounts of social events as true and factual, and to undermine the factuality and truth of their interlocutors' versions. Familiar examples are television news interviews and debate programs, but the strategies may be found across many genres of talk and text. When staking a claim to their own version, communicators will draw on 'interpretive repertoires,'◀ which amount to frameworks of understanding that are reminiscent of Fairclough's orders of discourse, even if the notion of repertoires conceives discourse as a practical resource, rather than an end-product:

> By interpretative repertoires we mean broadly discernible clusters of terms, descriptions and figures of speech often assembled around metaphors or vivid images. In more structuralist language we can talk of these things as systems of signification and as the building blocks used for manufacturing versions of actions, self and social structures in talk.
>
> (Potter and Wetherell 1996: 89)

In an interview-based study of discourse and racism in New Zealand, the authors found that white New Zealanders would draw on two different interpretive repertoires regarding the position of Maori culture in contemporary society, which they called culture-as-heritage and culture-as-therapy. The former repertoire frames culture, almost in biological terms, as an endangered species, something to be preserved and treasured; the latter conceives culture in psychological terms as a need, particularly for young Maoris, who 'need to rediscover their cultural "roots" to become "whole" again' (p. 90). An important analytical point is that the repertoires are not mutually exclusive, but may coexist also in a given individual's discourse about race, serving different rhetorical purposes in different situational circumstances. Most importantly, interpretive repertoires are neither personal nor socially specific 'attitudes' as in much social psychology and survey research, but the concrete linguistic manifesta-

tion and exercise of social practices of discrimination, and thus of social power.

Although the mass media have not been central to discursive psychology – a recent introduction does not even mention its applicability to media studies (Potter and Wetherell 1996) – it seems clear that the approach has much to offer, theoretically as well as analytically, especially as the electronic media have become increasingly dominated by formats that borrow from or replicate everyday verbal interaction (as also suggested by Fairclough's 'conversationalization'), and as verbal exchange through computer media serves to establish new forms of 'virtual' community. Researchers in the tradition suggest as much in their choice of empirical materials. For example, Potter's (1996) analyses of the situational construction of facticity are full of single examples from media discourses, as he demonstrates how speakers in news programs take great pains verbally to demonstrate that they do not 'have an axe to grind'; to confess voluntarily to having a stake in some matter in order to create an impression of honesty and trustworthiness; to claim that 'the facts show' something to be the case; or to bolster their own credibility by adducing testimony from sources with an uncertain identity (e.g., quoting 'community sources' for information about gang warfare).

So far, however, perhaps the most systematic and directly applicable work on media discourses has come from scholars who see themselves as conversation analysts, rather than discursive psychologists (or critical discourse analysts) (e.g., Drew and Heritage 1992; Greatbatch 1998; Heritage and Greatbatch 1991; see also Scannell 1991). One growing body of work has analyzed the inherently interactive genre of the news interview. In such studies, attention is focused not on the possible ideological meanings of a sequence of utterances, but on the social as well as the discursive dynamics of the exchange – on communication as a form of action that is embedded in several contexts at once. These contexts of interaction can be specified, in part, through comparison of turn-taking patterns within media genres with those of ordinary conversation, but also by comparing the conditions of discourse

---

▶ interpretive repertoires – Chapter 10, p. 167

production in, for example, public service and other professional news organizations. Noting that news interviews deviate systematically from ordinary conversation in replacing the latter's question–answer–receipt pattern with a question–answer–question sequence, Heritage (1985) explains this difference with reference to 'the overhearing audience' of the interview. By avoiding the evaluation inherent in the 'receipt' turn of normal conversational sequences, the interviewer declines the role of being the (only) recipient of the answer, while maintaining his/her role as the elicitor of ever more answers, in both cases on the part of the overhearing audience.

the overhearing audience

An additional consequence of 'the overhearing audience' for the interactional dynamics of the news interview are the frequent so-called 'formulating' questions (e.g., 'So you're suggesting that . . . '), by which an interviewer may make explicit the potentially controversial implications of an answer while appearing to merely rephrase what the interviewee had just said. Within the institutional framework of professional journalism, then, discursive formulations can serve to both signal and reaffirm the impartiality and balance of news in controversial matters. By contrast, the overhearing audience is offered an entirely different discursive position in the case of a U.S. television phone-in program, analyzed by Crow (1986), in which a sexologist host gives advice about sexual problems, a genre which toes the line between private confession and public talk, explicitly designed for an overhearing (and overseeing) audience. Montgomery (1986) throws light on broadcast monologues as he demonstrates how radio DJ talk, in contrast to the monologue of

radio news to abstracted third-person citizens, operates along the more intimate axis of first- and second-person pronouns. The DJ constructs a particular kind of 'imagined community' (Anderson 1991) with his listeners in a simulated dialogue, in which he does not display any sign of awkwardness when his directive speech acts, such as greetings and questions, are not responded to by anybody.

Figure 7.2 summarizes the relative emphases of the three main qualitative approaches to media texts. (The parentheses indicate that the element is recognized in principle, but not developed in analytical practice.) A challenge for future research is the integration and redevelopment of these several dimensions, both theoretically and analytically, in interdisciplinary studies of the media–society nexus. In that process, theories and analyses of visual media remain a special challenge.

VISUAL MEDIA DISCOURSES

In all the above approaches, including quantitative content analysis, the visual aspect of news and other factual genres in newspapers, magazines, television, and computer media is at best given secondary attention, in spite of the conventional wisdom of research that the media environment is increasingly dominated by still and moving pictures. While one early exception in the case of individual TV news stories was Fiske and Hartley (1978: ch. 6), it is next to impossible to locate full-scale visual analyses of entire news bulletins. Content analysis may be relatively ill suited for the analysis of visual communication beyond the identification of, for instance, types of protagonists or formal

	Critical linguistics	Critical discourse analysis	Discursive psychology
Sociocultural practices	(+)	+	(+)
Discourse practices	–	(+)	++
Textual analysis	++	++	+

Figure 7.2 Comparison of different approaches to qualitative discourse analysis

features, given its categorical conception of meaning, as mentioned, *vis-à-vis* the frequently context-dependent and continuous features of visuals.

Qualitative discourse analysis has greater promise in this regard, and has been given several different formulations, usually with recourse to one of two theoretical sources: Roland Barthes and Charles Sanders Peirce (for a detailed analysis of news photographs, see Fiske 1990: 104ff.; Hall 1973a; Deacon *et al.* (1999: chs 9–10) carry the analysis from still photographs to moving images; see also Hansen *et al.* 1998: chs 6–8).

Barthes (1964b) suggested that the denotative and connotative 'levels of meaning' apply also to the analysis of visual signs. In a photograph, for instance, we may distinguish between the denotative level, which carries the innocent, factual meanings available to any observer irrespective of cultural background, and the connotative level, which carries the visual meanings that a specific culture assigns to the denotative message.

In his 1964 article, moreover, Barthes theorizes the possible relationships between different sign systems within the same message, specifically 'the linking of text and image,' asking 'what are the functions of the linguistic message with regard to the (twofold) iconic message?' (Barthes 1964: 38). Barthes discusses two such functions: anchorage and relay, which **anchorage and** may coexist in a message and which share the **relay** function of 'fix[ing] the floating chain of signifieds' of the inherently polysemic image (p. 39).

Anchorage, which may appear in the form of a title, a caption, or an accompanying press article, may be subdivided into *identifying anchorage*, where 'the text helps to identify purely and simply the elements of the scene' as a 'denoted description of the image' (p. 39), and *interpreting anchorage*, which guides the interpretation of the connoted meaning away from too personal associations or ideologically undesirable meanings. In a formulation that is reminiscent of contemporary critical linguistics, Barthes claimed that the anchoring text has 'a *repressive* value' which is able to 'remote-control [the reader] towards a meaning chosen in advance' (p. 40).

Relay, which may appear via comic strip balloons or film dialogue, is established through snatches of text that may be perceived as an utterance spoken by a character in the image. Here, text and image stand in a 'complementary relationship' to each other, the text 'setting out ... meanings that are not to be found in the image itself,' and the joint meaning of image and text being 'realized at a higher level, that of the story, the anecdote, the diegesis' (p. 41).

While analytically useful, this conceptualization of the text–image relationship can nevertheless be criticized, echoing a famous chiasmus from the history of communication research, for being mainly interested in what the text does to the picture, to the relative neglect of what the picture does to the text – an issue taken up in the analysis in Box 7.2.

In the case of Peircean semiotics, it is particularly one set of analytical concepts that has been selectively applied to arrive at a typology of three possible relations between (visual) signs and objects in reality (Peirce 1985). First, a 'symbol' is a sign whose relation with its object **symbol, icon,** is a matter of convention, with verbal language, **index** such as the words 'oil company' in the BP advertisement examined in Box 7.2, as the prototypical example. Second, an 'icon' is related to its referent through similarity; a photograph entering into a news article or an advertisement (e.g., of the speakers and listeners in the BP ad) is an iconic sign resembling certain real-world phenomena. Third, an 'index' signifies its object through some existential or physical connection with it. While classical examples include smoke as an index of fire, in media and other cultural forms an index may operate at a more inferential level, so that the people appearing in the BP ad may be understood as indices of the age group, gender, or ethnicity, or the personnel profile of the oil company, which they appear to represent. In this specific respect, indexicality is comparable to metonymy in the Saussurean tradition.◄

The typology is immediately complicated by the fact that, for example, an (iconic) photograph is also an index of a segment of reality

---

► metonymy – Chapter 2, p. 24

ANALYSIS BOX 7.2 DISCOURSE ANALYSIS OF ADVERTISEMENT FOR BP (*THE GREEN MAGAZINE*, DECEMBER 1991, INSIDE FRONT COVER)

Plate 7.1 BP advertisement

cont.

The BP advertisement, 'Oil companies tend to invite criticism. At BP, we actively encourage it,' appeared in *The Green Magazine*, a publication whose readership has a greater-than-average interest in the environment.

In the reading situation, as the readers turn the front page of the magazine, they encounter a page which presents itself at first glance as a polysemic visual and verbal puzzle. The graphic layout of the page with its distribution of iconic and symbolic signs, and the BP logo in the bottom right-hand corner, identifies it as an advertisement. The headline functions as a caption of the picture, and as an attention-catching device – many readers read no further! It provides no 'identifying anchorage' for the composite picture, merely an aid to interpretation ('interpreting anchorage'), assisting the readers' inferential processes about who the people in the picture are and what they are doing.

As the caption headline associates 'oil companies' with 'BP' and a pronominal 'we' who 'encourage criticism,' the inferential process of interpretation may perceive the iconic representation of the eleven individuals around the periphery similarly as an indexical representation of BP employees. They also indexically represent several social backgrounds: men and women, age groups between the twenties and fifties, and different ethnic groups (one black man, one Asian woman, the remainder white). Their common gesture of placing an open palm behind an ear is an iconic-symbolic sign conventionally used to indicate a listening attitude. The headline may therefore also be seen as a collective utterance by the eleven employees on behalf of the company, i.e., text as 'relay.'

The headline's choice of the nominalization 'criticism' begs the question of the agency behind the criticizing activity, which may, however, be inferred, from the situational context now established, to be environmental activists, thus filling in the identity of the central picture element. The speaker depicted in the middle wears a suit but no tie, which may connote that he belongs neither to the establishment nor to a counterculture – he is a decent person, someone to be taken seriously, his visible teeth perhaps an index of a certain insistence. A first reading thus suggests that not only are the diverse employees of BP responsive to criticism, so that there might be no need to shout, but the company is responsive precisely because it is made up of a cross-section of the society it serves.

In addition to the paradigmatic choices mentioned above, the syntagmatic ensemble of the ad also springs from the choice to use black and white only, as opposed to color. This is just one of a number of 'absences' in the semiotic composition of this ad as opposed to consumer advertising, which distance this ad from any glamorous impression or visual 'hype,' instead suggesting soberness.

The language of the copy is straightforward, fairly colloquial, with no difficult or specialist terminology. It uses declarative sentence structures only, apart from a few cases of independent sentence fragments, one example being the adverb 'loudly,' punctuating the rhetorical authority of the critics and establishing an intratextual link of recognition to the pictorial representation of the megaphone. The absence of imperatives and interrogatives, compared with consumer ads, comes to represent the absence of any direct attempt to actively involve the reader (Myers 1994: ch. 4). Again this adds to the impression of soberness, of the company simply putting its case forward, leaving it up to the reader to pass the verdict of relevance or irrelevance, acceptance or rejection.

This feature of the sentence structure is supplemented by a complete absence of the second-person pronoun 'you.' The ad thus, without any sense of intrusion, merely invites the reader to witness an account of a relationship between the company ('we') and different representatives of third parties, i.e., community and environmental groups ('they'). The 'we' used is an 'exclusive we' (because it excludes the readers) through most of the text; however, it slides imperceptibly into an 'inclusive we' in the last sentence of the copy, which is repeated in the slogan 'For all our

cont.

tomorrows.' This may be seen as an attempt to involve the reader in BP's objectives by instilling a logic which may run something like this: 'If BP is doing all of this for our (shared) tomorrows, BP is worthy of my respect.'

The text has two instances of word play. The headline plays on two meanings of the phrase 'invite criticism,' one to attract *unwanted* criticism, the other to welcome criticism, to even help create it. The effect may be one of surprise at the fact that BP faces myths about ruthless oil companies head-on, and appreciation of the copy-writer's ingenuity. The other instance of word play concerns BP's 'patronizing' the environmental groups, so that they may all the better supply advice to BP. Again BP faces a common myth about multinational companies, i.e., that they 'show inappropriate superiority,' then turns the myth around by exploiting the other meaning of 'patronize': 'to enable someone to develop their full potential.'

These instances of word play may also be seen as a kind of absence *vis-à-vis* consumer ads. What is absent in the BP ad's word plays is the frivolousness of the typical advertising pun, the cheap joke impression. In the BP ad, word play is used as an intelligent, even sober, way of anticipating the reader's objection to the claims of harmony between the oil company and environmental activists.

This unflawed impression of cooperation and dialogue is made possible, in part, by the absence of the past in the ad's universe. There is no mention of 'yesterday,' the time when oil companies *did* ruthlessly exploit the environment and when there *was* antagonism between oil companies and environmentalists. The absence of a lexicalized 'yesterday' is supported by the absence of past tense verbs.

The verbal and visual signs of the BP ad thus appear to create a universe of meaning in which all conflicts between oil companies and environmental activists have been harmonized away, in a spirit of sympathy and mutuality. Whether this universe, as mapped here through a mixture of descriptive discovery and hypothetical interpretation, corresponds to the respective meaning universes of the corporate communicators and the magazine readers is for the empirical study of encoding and decoding processes to discover (for the reception of corporate advertising, see Schrøder 1997; for a holistic analysis of the news process, see Deacon *et al.* 1999).

imprinting itself on film. The complication arises, in part, from Peirce's epistemology, which emphasized that signs are not entities, but relations or functions mediating knowledge of objects in reality. One interpretation is to understand the three sign relations as properties of any sign, whose combination helps to account for the cognitive status and experiential qualities of a given sign (Johansen 1993: 95). To exemplify, a news photo of the White House can be, at one and the same time, an iconic representation of a particular building located in Washington, D.C.; an indexical representation of the government of the U.S.A., housing and standing for its chief executive officer; and a symbolic representation, depending on the context, of values conventionally associated with the U.S.A. or its president, from global capitalism to liberal democracy.

The semiotic characterization of visual signs

may be taken one step further to suggest why visual communication is intuitively ascribed a high measure of naturalism, potentially with important ideological implications. On the one hand, the visual sign appears to provide some natural, iconic connection with reality, as reinforced by common knowledge of how photography, film, and video is produced. On the other hand, it follows from the indexical, inferential aspect of the visual sign that the issue of what, exactly, is being 'indicated' is inherently controversial. First, one part of a scene or event being covered is selected and reproduced by a (news) photographer, depending on both practical circumstances and aesthetic priorities. Next, a sequence of editors will make additional choices regarding both editing of the visuals themselves and of their placement in a larger discursive whole, which serves as a complex index for specific scenes, events, or issues. Further steps in the indexical chain may involve a widening context of interpretation, from the rest of the newspaper and its genre conventions, to the contemporary social setting and readers' horizon of expectations.◄ All these factors contradict any assumption of naturalism, and instead call for intertextual, reception, and other forms of analysis to establish the status of a particular visual index in the larger communicative process.

The two sources of semiotic concepts – Barthes and Peirce – have been drawn on, liberally and in combination, by numerous analysts, and have had considerable heuristic value for illustrative analyses of how media images communicate (Hall 1973a; Williamson 1978). At the same time, it should be acknowledged that there have been few systematic, large-scale, or cumulative studies of the specificity of visual media. One complaint is that analyses may seem commonsensical, perhaps because of the saturation of current society by news and advertising genres, as well as the critical attitude toward them that has been promoted by a double hermeneutic (Giddens 1984) operating in both education and public debate.

Other, more specific complaints target key theoretical premises of visual analysis so far. Despite Barthes' (1970) redevelopment of the distinction between denotation and connotation, as well as other critiques of the implicit threshold between 'natural' and culturally invested meaning (Eco 1976), studies have in practice often performed a heavy-handed operationalization of the dyad, just as icon, index, and symbol have been approached as separate sign types, rather than complementary functions of one sign complex. Equally, anchorage and relay would seem far from exhaustive as categorizations of image–text relations in different genres and media. In the further development of visual studies, the under-recognized area of comics (e.g., McCloud 1994; Sabin 1993) and the hypertextual formats of computer media (e.g., Bolter and Grusin 1999), in addition to film theory and art history, can be sources of theoretical concepts and analytical procedures. Recently, two distinct programs for such re-

comics (margin note)

► horizon of expectations – Chapter 10, p. 167

development have been outlined, drawing respectively on semiotics and cognitive theory.

With a background in critical linguistics, Gunther Kress and Theo van Leeuwen (1996) have proposed to go beyond a mere extension of discourse analysis from linguistic to visual signs. They emphasize that the modern media, from school textbooks to the World Wide Web, increasingly feature texts which are 'multi-modal,' comprising a range of representational and communicative forms within the limits of one text, such as, in addition to verbal language, sound, graphics, and images (including gestures and proxemics). To these may be added the tactile, olfactory, and gustatory modes of communicating which may seem rather peripheral, but which may become more widespread in computer-simulated form. All these means of human communication are said to require an inclusive 'discourse semiotics' on one theoretical platform:

multi-modal communication (margin note)

> Discourse analysis has, on the whole, focused on the linguistically realized text. In the multi-modal approach the attempt is to understand all the representational modes which are in play in the text, in the same degree of detail and with the same methodological precision as discourse analysis is able to do with linguistic text.
>
> (Kress *et al.* 1997: 258)

The theoretical platform of their discourse semiotics strongly resembles Fairclough's (1992) three-dimensional model, whereas their analytical practice is inspired eclectically by linguistics, visual semiotics, film theory, art criticism, as well as media research on advertising in particular. In its present form, however, it is not evident that this multi-modal approach represents a genuine, or completed, innovation of either discourse or visual media analysis. Irrespective of the authors' protestations to the contrary, their indebtedness to Halliday's (1978) social semiotics implies a linguistic bias toward other modes of representation. Moreover, like some earlier applications of the denotation–connotation distinction, this preliminary integration of diverse 'visual' and other modes into a discourse semiotics may appear commonsensical, a limitation which is exacerbated by occasionally simplistic assumptions regarding the resulting discursive transfer of ideology to audiences.

The other program for visual media analysis deviates more radically from linguistic discourse analysis and semiotics. Cognitive media theory◄ takes as its premise that visual stimuli from the media activate the same mental processes as other perception and cognition. Contrary to much semiotics, cognitivism finds that images have no explicit syntax of minimal elements, communicating instead through iconicity and indexicality. In one of the relatively few cognitivist analyses of still media images so far (see also Solso 1994), Messaris (1997: 182–203) suggested a more general typology of 'propositions' or principles in visual communication, involving causality, contrast, analogy, and generalization. In this regard, cognitive image analysis joins attempts in other communication theory at integrating the analysis of 'texts' with an understanding of its place in human cognition and action.

CONCLUSION

This chapter has outlined the main approaches to the analysis of media texts, recognizing the division into quantitative and qualitative studies, as well as identifying variations within each tradition, some of which suggest shared concerns across the traditions regarding both the definition of discursive or content 'entities' and the development of context-sensitive analytical procedures. An important, if implicit ambition of many discourse and content studies has been to infer from the properties of media texts to their probable 'effects' on or, in more modest but also more complex terms, their relative contribution to social and cultural processes at large, with special reference to public opinion or the reproduction of ideology. Despite the ambition of thus informing either policy or public debate on media reception (or media institutions), content studies have conformed to the traditional focus of media research on distinct 'moments' of the commu-

nicative process, and have, most commonly, not related the 'textual moment' methodologically to the moments of encoding and decoding, production and use. This is in spite of the fact that 'discourses' equally enter into, and are analytical points of access to, both media production and reception.◄

Since neither the intentions of communicators nor the meanings created by audiences can be 'read off' media by means of discourse or content analysis, a more complete understanding of the production and circulation of meaning in society requires a differentiated analytical attention to media texts as vehicles which are necessary but not sufficient conditions of communication; to their specific moment in the communicative process; and to their interrelations with other moments. This requirement has been underscored by the development of 'interactive' media, in which users navigate an enhanced intertextual and intermedial supply of meaning – selecting, combining, and interpreting what is, to a degree, their customized text and one which, in both work and leisure, blends into the context of use. The challenge for discourse and content studies under changing technological and historical circumstances remains one of clarifying its particular domain of analysis and explanatory value, in particular to distinguish the descriptive discovery of a text's verbal and visual characteristics from the hypothetical interpretation of its potential meanings for different audience-users, and from studies of its actualized meanings in social processes of production and reception. Both in analytical descriptions and in the generation of hypothetical interpretations, the relative relevance of the available, qualitative as well as quantitative approaches must be assessed with reference to the purpose of analysis and the particular object of analysis. Irrespective of their theoretical and methodological origins, all these approaches are faced with socially constructed textual objects, and are themselves socially constructing whatever insights they provide.

descriptive discovery

hypothetical interpretation

► cognitivism – Chapter 2, p. 36

► discourses as general elements in research – Chapter 15, p. 251

8 Mediated fiction

Peter Larsen

- a description of *quantitative studies of representation* in media fiction
- *formal* studies in the semiotic tradition, including *shot-to-shot* analyses of film
- *narrative* studies and models, applied *across media* types
- a presentation of *genre* analysis as a middle range, connecting text and context
- a discussion of *sound* as an under-researched aspects of media 'texts'
- *The Big Sleep* (1946) as the main analytical example.

INTRODUCTION

The word 'text' is derived from the Latin verb *texo*, meaning to weave or twine together, and to construct or build something. The Latin noun *textum* means woven cloth or fabric, but was also used to denote speech and writing. A written or spoken text, then, is like a woven cloth – a construction of meaning made out of words.

Since the 1960s, 'text'◄ has been used as a general term covering diverse phenomena such as music, still images, films, and so on, in addition to written and spoken language. The underlying argument is that all these means of expression are semantic constructions – 'fabrics' of signs – and most of them are meant to be 'read' in linear, temporal sequences. Such constructions may be described and analyzed by analogy to a verbal text, drawing on concepts, models, and procedures that were developed within disciplines and fields like linguistics, semiotics, and literary studies. Analyses of 'texts' in this broad sense form a central part

of media studies. Whether such analyses are carried out as studies of single texts or important textual genres, or as part of projects studying media reception and media institutions, the central concern is with questions of meaning and interpretation. The point of departure is the texts themselves – their structure and their content.

Like any other form of analysis, textual analysis examines a given object – a text or a group of texts – as closely and as systematically as possible in order to answer specific research questions. These questions can lead to two basic types of textual analysis: one focused on *generalities*, the other on *particulars*. The first describes recurrent, typical features in order to establish textual models or prototypes. The second examines the texts in question as isolated occurrences with reference to their specificities.◄ Obviously, there are both transitional variants and logical connections between the two types. In practice, generalities are always established through the study of particulars,

---

► texts as a general category – Chapter 2, p. 28

► generalities and particulars – theory of science, Chapter 15, p. 256

and the analysis of particulars presupposes some knowledge about generalities. Importantly, qualitative and quantitative methodologies both lend themselves, in specific ways, to the study of generalities as well as particulars.

This chapter presents a number of content-analytical and text-analytical traditions in media studies. Many of the relevant procedures and principles are not specific to particular media or genres. However, this chapter focuses mainly on fiction in film and television, which accounts for the bulk of mediated fiction, and which has also been the point of departure for the most significant developments in research. Throughout the chapter, examples from Howard Hawks's film *The Big Sleep* (1946) will be used to illustrate the various theoretical positions and analytical procedures.

QUANTITATIVE CONTENT ANALYSIS

Content studies of media representations

Some questions about *generalities* can be answered in relatively precise terms by measuring or counting certain textual features. Since the 1940s, such quantitative analyses have played an important role in several forms of media research. In the first general account of this type of analysis, Bernard Berelson (1952) used the term 'content analysis,' defining it as a research technique 'for the objective, systematic, and quantitative description of the manifest content of communication' (p. 18).◄

As this definition suggests, content analysis is basically descriptive. Certain well-defined textual elements or characteristics are measured in various ways; for example, the amount of newspaper coverage of certain issues, the topics of television news programs, the occurrence of particular symbols in fictional genres, and so on. Such quantitative descriptions of the features of a group of texts are then typically used as a basis for more general inferences about the meaning of these texts and their implications regarding various social phenomena.

One early example of this approach was Leo

▶ content analysis – Chapter 13, p. 219; example analysis, Chapter 7, p. 101

Lowenthal's study of 'mass idols' from 1941. In a quantitative analysis of biographical articles in popular U.S. magazines, he showed that while political leaders, businessmen, and scientists were portrayed in 46 percent of the cases at the beginning of the twentieth century, this percentage had dropped to 25 by 1940, and the interest was now focused, instead, on film actors, entertainers, and athletes. This shift had begun in the 1920s, and was accompanied by an additional shift of focus from the public life and achievements of the people in question, to their love life, their ways of dressing, and other private matters. Lowenthal interpreted this change of emphasis from 'idols of production' to 'idols of consumption,' and from the public to the private sphere, as a textual expression of general changes in social values during the period.

Since the early days of content analysis, then, this quantitative methodology has been used in a variety of research contexts, often in combination with other methodologies. The main varieties have included (for a more detailed overview see Wimmer and Dominick 1994):

- studies of patterns and trends in media *representations as such*;
- studies of the relationship between textual representations and '*the real world*';
- studies concerning media *effects*.

In some studies, the overall content of a specific media genre (e.g., television news) has been analyzed by the Glasgow University Media Group (1976 and 1980). Other studies have undertaken analyses of how the media handle specific events, such as political demonstrations (e.g., Halloran *et al.* 1970) and wars (e.g., Morrison and Tumber (1988) on the Falklands conflict, and Morrison (1992) on the Gulf War).

The depiction of violence, particularly in television fiction, has been a favorite topic. In such studies, researchers commonly start by defining how 'violence' should be understood, and in which specific discursive contexts it should be measured. Next, coders watch samples of television programs and count the incidents which match the definition. The longest running and most well known of these studies was started in the late 1960s by George Gerbner. In the initial research design, he defined violence as 'the overt expression of physical force (with or without a weapon) against self or other, compelling action against one's will on pain of being hurt or killed, or actually hurting or killing' (Gerbner 1972: 31). From this definition, Gerbner further established a series of guidelines regarding the types of events to be included in studies with reference to their place in the fictional universe and their relation to the overall plot (see Gerbner and Gross 1976; Gerbner *et al.* 1977). Continued during the 1990s by Gerbner and his team, this series of studies is an example of research projects in which content analysis is used to compare media representations with actual occurrences in society. These studies have repeatedly shown that the world of U.S. prime-time television fiction is a far more violent place than the real world, and that the portrayal of certain social groups as frequent victims of crime is inconsistent with social statistics. The same set of studies has also addressed media effects. Comparing content analyses with survey data, Gerbner and his team have argued that television fiction 'cultivates' or shapes people's perceptions of social reality, so that heavy viewers tend to have misconceptions of the role of violence in everyday life.◄

A quantitative analysis of classical Hollywood cinema

Many content analyses thus form part of larger projects concerning media effects or the relationship between media representations and real life. Other quantitative analyses, however, have focused on intratextual research questions. A well-known example of the use of content analysis for describing and interpreting particular textual genres is a study by David Bordwell (1985b) of the style of classical Hollywood cinema.

The point of departure for that study was a list of the approximately fifteen thousand

feature films produced in the U.S.A. in the period 1915 to 1960. Bordwell and his co-authors used a table of random numbers to select 841 films from this list. Of these, 100 could be located in various collections and archives. As the authors emphasize, this was not, strictly speaking, a random sample, since each film did not have an equal chance of being selected, because not every film on the original list had survived. The point, however, is that the actual choices of films 'were not biased by personal preferences or conceptions of influential or masterful films' (Bordwell 1985b: 388). In fact, four-fifths of the resulting sample were fairly obscure productions.

The authors studied each film in the sample on a viewing machine, recording stylistic details of each shot and summarizing actions scene by scene. On the basis of these descriptions, they constructed a model of the 'typical film' of the period, with special attention to style and narration, and went on to test this generalization by analyzing almost two hundred other Hollywood films from the same period. Although many of the films in this second sample were chosen precisely for their quality or historical influence, the analyses confirmed the general model (Bordwell 1985b: 10). The study stands as an impressive account of typical aspects of the classical Hollywood film in terms of features such as story construction, narrational strategies, the construction of time and space, etc. Moreover, this description of invariables and stabilities provides an important framework for further research on the equally obvious stylistic changes during the classical Hollywood period.

QUALITATIVE TEXTUAL ANALYSIS AND SEMIOTICS

While quantitative content analyses are descriptive in nature, aiming at 'the manifest content of communication' (Berelson 1952: 18), textual analyses in the tradition of literary criticism and art history are usually interpretive, aiming at what is sometimes termed latent meaning. The basic questions, consequently, are 'qualitative': What does the text *really* mean, and how are its meanings organized? Still, analyses may be

manifest vs. latent meaning

► cultivation research – Chapter 9, p. 150

concerned with either particulars or generalities. While focusing on features that are characteristic of a single work or a small group of works, studies also examine how the given works differ from all other works in structural and thematic terms.

The sources of this analytical practice include the attentive 'close reading' practiced by the Anglo-American school of New Criticism◀ and its French counterpart, the *explication du texte*. In both of these traditions, it is the singular or *particular* analytical object, its parts and its whole, which is at the center of interest. The underlying assumption, and the very reason for giving particular attention to the works in question, is that they are thought to be significant carriers of cultural values and insights, or that they provide important and valuable aesthetic experiences. This type of textual analysis has been transferred successfully to film studies – an area of media studies that deals with textual objects which are, in some ways, comparable to the unique works analyzed by literary critics and art historians (see, e.g., Robin Wood on Hitchcock (1965) and on Hawks (1968)). However, the basic aim of most other media research has been to study prototypes, regularities, repeated patterns, and features which are shared by masses of texts. Accordingly, textual analyses of media have usually taken their inspiration from humanistic traditions which are oriented toward the study of *generalities*, particularly structural linguistics and general semiotics.◀

Applied to media studies, Ferdinand de Saussure's (1916) linguistic dichotomy of *langue* and *parole*◀ has proven to be an effective conceptual tool: concrete media texts may be regarded as instances of *parole*, as generated from one or more *langues*. Even though the various instances of *parole* are carried by different types of signifiers (images, written or spoken language, combinations of these, etc.); are transmitted through different media; and are produced according to specific rules, it may

be argued that all sign production is based on certain general principles. Whether the analytical intention is to reconstruct the *langue* behind a group of texts, or to study a single text as *parole*, knowledge of such general textual principles is useful. The underlying *langue* is usually understood as a 'code'◀ that consists of signs, on the one hand, and of series of syntactic rules, on the other. Meaning production is thus thought of as a process by which signs are selected from latent groups of possibilities (paradigms) and combined according to the relevant syntactic rules into strings of text (syntagms).◀

Saussure (1916) defined the sign as a material object – a signifier – evoking a certain mental representation – a signified.◀ Corresponding to these two aspects, there are two main types of semiotic media analysis: a formal and material study of signs in the media, and an analysis of media contents as representations with an inherent meaning. However, since the two aspects of the sign are interdependent, there can be no absolute distinction between the two types of textual analysis.

FORMAL ANALYSIS

Formal analyses (of signifiers) highlight the material specificity of the medium in question. What are its particular properties, and how do these properties translate into communicative possibilities? In the case of visual media, key theoretical questions have been: What is an image? Are images signs? (Barthes 1964b; Eco 1968, 1976; Sonesson 1989). How do photographic images differ from other types of signs? (Barthes 1980). Concrete analyses in the area have dealt with questions concerning pictorial representation, composition, and style, in some cases relying on concepts and analytical procedures from the study of traditional arts (for a brief overview see Bryson 1991).◀

▶ New Criticism – Chapter 2, p. 29

▶ semiotics – Chapter 2, p, 23

▶ *langue* and *parole* – Chapter 2, p. 24

▶ code – Chapter 1, p. 8

▶ paradigms and syntagms – Chapter 2, p. 24

▶ signifier and signified – Chapter 2, p. 25

▶ art history – Chapter 2, p. 27

Moving images: syntagm analyses

The ways in which moving images are produced and structured raise special theoretical and analytical problems.◄ One of the first researchers to address these problems from a semiotic perspective was the French linguist, Christian Metz. In an influential study of how cinematic signifiers are organized, he showed that the majority of films are based on seven **seven types of** types of 'syntagms,' or seven basic series of **syntagms** shots (Metz 1968). Two of the most central types are exemplified in Plate 8.1.

Four *narrative* syntagms indicate temporal relations between narrative events:

1 The *scene* is the most widely used of these – a series of shots presenting an event in continuous time and space.

2 In the *alternating syntagm*, there is crosscutting between several narrative spaces (for example, in a 'chase') as well as indications of temporal simultaneity between the shots.

3 In *sequences*, the shots indicate discontinuous time: the *ordinary* sequence is an elliptical construction in which unimportant events and other details are left out.

4 The *episodic* sequence, in comparison, organizes the shots so that the omissions suggest a compressed chronological development.

In addition to the four narrative syntagms there are three *a-chronological* ones:

1 The *descriptive* syntagm is a series of shots suggesting spatial co-presence of people or objects.

2 The *bracket* syntagm depicts typical aspects of a phenomenon or a concept ('poverty,' 'morning in the city,' etc.).

3 The *parallel* syntagm organizes two series of contrasting motifs ('rich and poor,' 'town and country,' etc.).

Metz' intention was to describe cinema as a general *langue*, or at least one of its main com-

► analysis of still images – Chapter 7, p. 110

ponent structures. His framework has also proven useful, however, for the analysis of individual films. Knowledge of the basic syntagm system can serve as an 'attention-focusing device' for the analyst (Stam *et al.* 1992: 48), and is also helpful when one aims at defining fundamental formal characteristics of specific genres or films (see, e.g., Ellis (1975) on Ealing comedies; Flitterman-Lewis (1983) on soap operas; Heath (1975) on Orson Welles's *Touch of Evil*).

A brief example from *The Big Sleep* illustrates this point. The story concerns old General Sternwood, who hires the private detective Marlowe to solve a mystery. The case involves the General's youngest daughter, Carmen, who is being blackmailed. As Marlowe is working on the case, additional mysteries are introduced: a former employee of the General has disappeared; the blackmailer is found murdered; a powerful gangster plays an obscure role in all of these events. Along the way, Marlowe also falls in love with the General's oldest daughter, Vivian. At the end of the film, Marlowe solves the mysteries, and the gangster, who is the main culprit, is shot by his own men.

During the first few minutes of the film, we see Marlowe visiting the General. First, he meets Carmen in the hall of the Sternwood mansion; he then meets the general himself in a winter garden; and finally he meets Vivian in her room. A butler leads him from room to room and finally back to the entrance. From these encounters, Marlowe – and we, the audience – learn a lot about the Sternwoods and the case. Next follows a shot of a sign saying 'Hollywood Public Library,' a close-up of books and documents, and a series of shots of Marlowe sitting in the library, reading and taking notes.

On the level of signifieds or content, the introduction provides Marlowe (and the audience) with necessary background information. On the level of signifiers or form, this information is organized in three distinct 'scenes' (Marlowe's three encounters in the Sternwood mansion, each of them presented in spatio-temporal continuity). When he starts working on the case, a summarizing 'ordinary sequence' follows (Marlowe is seen in the library study-

Plate 8.1 The introduction to *The Big Sleep*: Marlowe's encounters with Carmen Sternwood, General Sternwood, Vivian Sternwood, and his visit to the public library

ing, but unimportant details are skipped). (See Plate 8.1.)

Most of the rest of the film is constructed along these lines. The narrative is presented mainly in the form of scenes and ordinary sequences, in addition to the occasional alternating syntagm. This is a familiar pattern, the pattern of classical Hollywood cinema. Most films from this period use a very limited part of the general syntagm system, as described by Metz. Indeed, Bordwell (1985a: 158), analyzing classical Hollywood films from a cognitivist perspective,◀ arrived at a similar conclusion. The majority of films in this period are based on only two syntagms or 'segments' as he calls them – the 'scene' and the 'montage sequence' – corresponding roughly to Metz's 'scene' and 'sequence.'

▶ cognitivism – Chapter 2, p. 36

The correspondence between a semiotic and a cognitivist description of the classical Hollywood film is no coincidence. When Metz worked out his system, he followed the general semiotic and linguistic principle of describing his materials according to the distinctions that a 'native speaker' – in his case, an experienced film spectator – would make. Each of his syntagms are defined with reference to the characteristic spatio-temporal effect which any member of a cinema audience would immediately recognize. There is an evident connection between this approach and cognitivist studies of the various 'schemata' (organized clusters of knowledge) which people apply in their everyday life. In both cases, the intention is to describe and systematize what 'everybody' intuitively 'knows' about the world (for a discussion of the relation between semiotics and cognitive science in film studies see Buckland 2000).

Compared to other types of films, classical Hollywood films constitute a class of their own in terms of both formal and narrative strategy. The so-called montage films that were produced in the USSR during the 1920s are obvious counter-examples to this norm. They are overtly 'rhetorical,' constantly presenting political arguments by visual means. While, for instance, the 'parallel syntagm' is very rare in classical Hollywood cinema, it is a central device in these Soviet films, where it was used to suggest all kinds of rhetorical analogies or contrasts (Bordwell 1985a: 239).

montage films [margin note, left]

Shot-to-shot analyses

While Metz's concerns were theoretical, his account of the basic syntagm system provides a useful, if rather broad framework for the analysis of particular films. Raymond Bellour is an example of a film semiotician whose works are not theoretical in a strict sense, but primarily concerned with practical, analytical questions and, as such, more closely related to traditional literary analysis. During the 1970s, Bellour presented a series of 'close readings' of well-known Hollywood films (see the collection in Bellour 1979). By means of meticulous shot-to-shot analyses, primarily of formal features and often of very short fragments, he described the films in question, established their individual cinematic systems, as it were, and used these characterizations as a basis for conclusions about formal aspects of the classical Hollywood system in general.

shot: continuous visual sequence, filmed by one camera, without cuts, wipes, dissolves, or other editing [margin note, left]

One example of this procedure is his analysis of a short segment from *The Big Sleep* (Bellour 1973). Consisting of twelve shots, the segment, inconspicuous, almost trivial, marks a transition between two action-packed, narrative climaxes. After a shoot-out at a gas station in the country, Marlowe and Vivian drive away in a car; on the road toward the final shoot-out, they declare their love for each other. (The twelve shots are rendered in Plate 8.2.)

Bellour describes the twelve shots with regard to framing, camera movement, camera angles, absence or presence of characters in shots, absence or presence of speech during shots, and relative length of shots. His results

may be summarized as follows. Although nothing much happens, the number of shots is relatively high – a fact which Bellour explains as a strategy of discontinuity, of introducing variations into the filmic space within the given time frame. At the same time, these variations appear against a background of similarities. After the location of the scene is established by a shot showing the car driving along seen from the outside, there follows:

- a medium-close shot of Marlowe and Vivian side by side;
- a close-up of Marlowe;
- a close-up of Vivian;
- the remainder of the scene is made up of almost identical medium-close shots and close-ups of Marlowe and Vivian.

This repetition of formal qualities produces a sense of constraint around the actual variation in the actors' dialogue and comportment, making the variations stand out as differences which ensure the forward movement and continuity of the narrative. Bellour finds this formal arrangement to be characteristic not only of *The Big Sleep*, but of classical Hollywood cinema as such.

NARRATIVE ANALYSIS

Narrative semiotics or narratology – the study of basic narrative patterns and procedures – has been one of the most fertile interdisciplinary fields of study during recent decades, and has proven particularly effective and valuable for analytical purposes. By way of introduction, it should be noted that narrative is both a mental structure and a specific type of text. As a mental 'tool,' it functions as a fundamental interpretive frame: humans make narratives in order to organize their experiences and to make their world intelligible (on the relations between narrative thought and narrative discourse see Branigan 1992; Bruner 1986, 1994; Labov and Waletzky 1967).

narratology [margin note, right]

narrative: textual as well as mental structure [margin note, right]

Narrative texts appear in all kinds of discursive forms and in all kinds of media (Barthes 1966). As a textual type, however, the narrative is defined solely by its *content*: a narrative

Plate 8.2 Bellour's (1973) shot-to-shot analysis of a segment from *The Big Sleep*

is a representation of *events* in time and space. These events are organized in series of *causes and effects*, and viewed in relation to *human projects* which they either further or impede (for detailed definitions of narrative see Bal 1985 [1977]; Branigan 1992; Bremond 1966; Rimmon-Kenan 1983; Todorov 1971).

Narratives as sequences of events

The causal organization of events leads to characteristic narrative patterns. In 1928, the Russian formalist Vladimir Propp showed that virtually all narratives within a large selection of folk-tales were based on identical events and, further, that these events were presented in identical order (Propp 1958). Some of these recurrences could be explained as the result of genre conventions, but later studies have confirmed that there is a more general and systematic regularity at work in the ordering of narrative events. At a basic level, not only these

Russian folk-tales but all narratives are series of variations on a simple pattern, consisting of an initial state which is transformed by a dynamic event into a new state (Bremond 1966; Todorov 1971).

No matter what a narrative is about, it will always be constructed from such modules or 'elementary sequences.' The same characteristic pattern may also be observed at the narrative macro level. A narrative will usually start with the presentation of a situation, a setting, the principal characters, the general state of affairs, and so on. This initial situation is then gradually transformed by a series of events and actions, until a new situation has been established and the story ends. According to story-comprehension psychologists, this macro pattern is also the mental schema that people mobilize when they recognize and try to structure unfamiliar narratives (see Bower and Cirilo 1985; Gulich and Quasthoff 1985; Van Dijk and Kintsch 1983; also Branigan 1992).

elementary sequences

At the macro level, the narrative sequence from beginning to end usually involves a movement between central thematic positions or 'values' – from an initial, problematic, and unstable situation, through successive actions, to a final, stable, and acceptable situation. In analyses of concrete narratives, it is therefore helpful to begin by describing how the string of elementary sequences is organized at the macro level. This procedure provides not only a rough outline, but a way of gaining important insights into the underlying value system.

The what and how of narratives

Any narrative may be viewed from two different points of view. On the one hand, there is the series of events; on the other hand, there is the actual text by means of which these events are represented. These two aspects may be defined in terms of the general sign model: the *what* of the narrative (the series of events) is the narrative signified, while the *how* (the actual text) is the signifier. This distinction is usually referred to in narratology by the terms *story and discourse* (Genette 1980 [1972]; see also Chatman 1989).

The Russian formalists◀ employed a similar distinction, but emphasized the audience's active participation in the construction of narrative coherence. David Bordwell has reintroduced the formalists' term *syuzhet* to cover the series of events which is presented explicitly in the narrative text, while *fabula* refers to the spectator's construction of connections between these events. No narrative discourse presents the full story – there will always be indeterminacies and vaguenesses. To understand a narrative is precisely to interpret the available information (syuzhet), and to construct textual coherence (fabula) (Bordwell 1985a).

The construction of the fabula by the audience, then, is dependent on the syuzhet, but the specific syuzhet, in its turn, is also only one among many possible implementations of the fabula. Moreover, the particular way in which crucial narrative information from the fabula is organized and presented in the syuzhet has

story and discourse

syuzhet and fabula

▶ Russian formalism – Chapter 2, p. 29

important consequences for the audience's expectations and comprehension. The fabula–syuzhet relationship may even be a decisive element in the definition of a particular narrative genre. Mystery and other suspense stories are well-known examples of this. Their narrative strategy is to generate suspense by breaking the chronological order of events, so that crucial fabula information about the original cause of the mystery is presented very late in the syuzhet.

Just as one fabula may give rise to a multitude of syuzhets, it may also be implemented in many discursive forms and media types. Consequently, the fabula–syuzhet distinction is very useful for analyzing adaptations of narratives across different media, as illustrated by *The Big Sleep*. The film is based on Raymond Chandler's debut novel of the same name from 1939. A textual analysis of fabula and syuzhet shows that most of the novel's events (fabula) as well as their presentation (syuzhet) have been transferred to the film relatively faithfully by the scriptwriters. Nevertheless, the film differs from the novel in several respects because of two types of changes. First, several minor events and minor characters have simply been cut during the adaptation process. This was, and is, standard procedure in adaptations: 'unnecessary' details and narrative intricacies are pruned away for the sake of comprehensibility, but also to make long stories fit the relatively short feature film format (on adaptation practices see Lothe 2000; Naremore 2000).

Second, and more interestingly, the constellation of the central characters has been changed rather dramatically. In the novel, a scheming Vivian tries to seduce Marlowe in order to obstruct his detection work, while he for his part firmly refuses her advances; in the film, she saves his life, helps him solve the mystery, and they end up being lovers. Giving a traditional happy ending to the original melancholy story of a lonely, disillusioned detective is quite a radical rewrite, which calls for contextual explanations over and above the textual, narrative economy. Film historians usually suggest that Hawks's previous movie, *To Have And Have Not* (1944), had established Humphrey Bogart and Lauren

adaptations across media

textual and contextual evidence

Bacall as Hollywood's new romantic couple, and that the rewriting of Chandler's story was done in order to support this constellation (Clark 1983).

Characters and actants

Narrative series of events, then, are structured according to certain basic patterns. Similar regularities apply to the individual characters or agents who are involved in and affected by the events. On the face of it, there is a multitude of characters, each of them endowed with specific, individual traits and qualities. However, these characters have rather limited spheres of action. As demonstrated by A.J. Greimas, there are six 'basic positions' that characters can assume in relation to the central project of the narrative. The multitude of narrative characters can thus be viewed as surface manifestations of six underlying narrative roles, the so-called 'actants' (Greimas 1966). The actant model is presented in Figure 8.1.

agents and actants

The moment a narrative *project* is stated, two actants are established: a *Subject* who desires an *Object*. In addition, all narrative projects have to do with *communication* in the sense of 'transport': the Object has to be 'moved' between two positions. Therefore, the statement of a project also establishes two further actants: the potential *Sender* who 'has' the Object, and the potential *Receiver* who 'lacks' it. The transport of the Object is usually complicated by a *conflict* between competing projects within the narrative universe. In such cases, the Subject is faced with an *Opponent* who will try to prevent the transport. Furthermore, there will often be a *Helper*, i.e., an actant who supports the project and works to facilitate the transport of the Object.

The actant model is a simple and effective analytical tool. Its strength is that it accounts for all actions and characters from the same point of view. Focusing on how characters are positioned in relation to the core project of the narrative, the model makes it possible to provide a description of the most basic relations and conflicts in a narrative.

In *The Big Sleep,* old General Sternwood hires Marlowe to solve the mystery. The basic

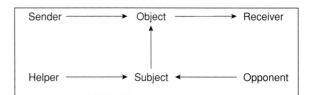

Figure 8.1 The actant model

project for Marlowe (*Subject*) is to obtain information (*Object*) for his client, the General (*Receiver*). But who has the necessary information, i.e., who is the *Sender*? Trying to find the answer to this question, Marlowe meets the two daughters, assorted gangsters, and several other people who all try to prevent him from looking deeper into the matter. All these characters fill the *Opponent* position. Late in the story, Vivian decides to side with Marlowe. She becomes his *Helper,* and it turns out that she is also a *Sender,* one of the many people who have tried to hide important information from him. After a series of dramatic events, Marlowe ultimately solves the mystery.

As this summary analysis shows, there is no one-to-one relation between characters and actants. For one thing, one actant position may be filled by many different characters. In this case, both the *Opponent* and the *Sender* positions are filled by large groups of characters. For another thing, the same character can have several functions in the narrative, and may therefore fill several actant positions. Most *Opponents* in *The Big Sleep* are also *Senders* – quite a common constellation. Another common constellation is identity between the characters filling the *Subject* and *Receiver* actants. In many narratives, the 'hero' undertakes the narrative project for his or her own sake. There are, however, also many examples of *Subjects* working selflessly for others, or – as in detective narratives like *The Big Sleep* – a *Receiver* hiring somebody else to do the *Subject*'s job.

A final observation is that the actant model may be used in two different ways. It is most commonly applied to the fabula as a whole – after the fact, so to speak. However, as the example of Vivian suggests, characters can – and often do – change actant position in the course of a narrative. Thus, the model may also usefully be applied to shorter narrative sequences as a means of getting an overview of 'local' or individual projects and their configuration within the unfolding presentation of the syuzhet.

local and global narrative projects

The canonical story

A textual presentation of a coherent series of events centered around a human project – this is a broad definition aimed at covering all narratives. Some narratives, however, are obviously more well suited for a given purpose than others. Story-comprehension researchers have argued that the main narrative forms of Western culture represent a special variant of the basic pattern.◀ This 'canonical story' is the foundation, for example, of the classical Hollywood film, which, according to David Bordwell,

> presents psychologically defined individuals who struggle to solve a clear-cut problem or to attain specific goals. In the course of this struggle, the characters enter into conflict with others or with external circumstances. The story ends with a decisive victory or defeat, a resolution of the problem and a clear achievement or nonachievement of the goals. The principal causal agency is thus the character, a discriminated individual endowed with a consistent batch of evident traits, qualities, and behaviors.
> (Bordwell 1985a: 157)

Compared to the general definition of narrative, this description of the canonical story is far more detailed. All narratives involve human projects, but in the canonical story, the series of events appears totally controlled by individuals. The resulting clarity is the most general feature of this mode of narration. The central characters are clearly defined in terms of their psychological make-up; their problems and goals are clear; the story ends with a clear resolution, and so on.

▶ Western and non-Western narratives – Chapter 11, p. 179

The canonical story is even predefined at the level of actants. The main narrative project and the Object is clearly stated from the outset, and the other actant positions are filled with individuals. There is always a conflict in this narrative universe, i.e., conflicting projects and hence a clearly defined Opponent. In addition, there are also parallel projects. The canonical story commonly presents two storylines with the same Subject. One part of the story is 'private' and deals with the (usually male) Subject's project of getting the Object-woman he loves; the other part is more 'public,' in that it deals with 'another sphere – work, war, a mission or quest, other personal relationships' (Bordwell 1985a: 157). These two projects are usually interwoven – 'textually' – in such a way that the success of the 'public' project is a precondition for the completion of the 'personal' project.

parallel projects: private and public

The Big Sleep meets most of the requirements of the canonical story. The narrative is character-driven, the project is clear, there is conflict, and the story ends with a decisive victory for Marlowe. The film is also a good example of parallel projects. During Marlowe's quest for information, he and Vivian fall in love, and since she is deeply involved in the case he is working on, he is faced with two intertwined problems in the last portion of the film. Not only must he solve the General's mystery, but he must also save Vivian from gangsters and from the police.

Narration and narrators

Some narratives are told face-to-face with an actual narrator addressing an actual audience 'live.' In technologically mediated narratives, narrators and their audiences are separated in time and space. And yet a novel, a film, and an episode in a television series all seem to 'address' their audiences, and give the impression of being 'told' by someone. Most studies of such textual signs of 'narration' assume that the structure of the actual communicative encounter is repeated, as it were, within the textual object itself. This view was originally put forward by Jakobson (1960), who argued that most texts contain elements whose prime

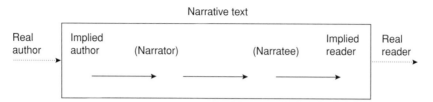

Figure 8.2 A model of narrative communication

function is to refer to the 'sender,' the 'receiver,' and to the 'message' or the textual object itself.◄

In an influential study of narration in literature and film, Chatman (1989) adopted this view, and went on to suggest some additional conceptual distinctions (Figure 8.2). In the empirical communication situation, a *Real author* presents a *Narrative text* to a *Real reader;* within the Narrative text, there are traces of an *Implied author* and an *Implied reader.*

implied author
and reader

The term 'implied author' was coined by Wayne Booth to indicate 'the picture a reader gets' of an author by reading a novel (Booth 1961: 70–71). Chatman expanded the term to denote the 'principle . . . that stacked the cards in this particular way, had these things happen to these characters, in these words or images. . . . It instructs us silently, through the design of the whole, with all the voices, by all the means it has chosen to let us learn' (Chatman 1989: 148). The implied author is shorthand for the norms and values that a text suggests to its reader by the way in which it is organized. Similarly, the term 'implied reader' refers to 'the audience presupposed by the narrative itself' (p. 150). Chatman's distinction between the 'real reader' and the 'implied reader' further corresponds to a distinction in reception analysis: the empirical readers, or the actual media audience, as opposed to the reader-in-the-text, i.e., the various roles or positions which a text offers its reader by means of its organization (see Eco 1987; Iser 1972, 1976).◄

The implied author and reader are structures present in any text. In addition, some

texts explicitly mark themselves as being told by 'someone,' a narrator, usually a character speaking in the first person, an 'I.' The narrator may be a character acting inside the narrative universe, or an observer reporting from an external position. Sometimes, the narrator has a counterpart in a narratee, when the narrator explicitly addresses 'someone,' a 'you,' a 'Dear Reader,' etc. narrator and
narratee

Chatman's simple narration model (Figure 8.2) has been criticized by film scholars. This is partly because it is so obviously based on literature and written language, but also because it implies the traditional communication sequence of a message being transported from a clearly delimited sender to a receiver. Terms like 'author' and 'narrator' inevitably suggest a type of individual artistic production which is very rare in modern cultural industries. Arguing against Chatman, David Bordwell has suggested that one should avoid thinking of narration as a process driven by narrators, as modeled on the 'author' of a novel. Narration

> is better understood as the organization of a set of cues for the construction of a story. This presupposes a perceiver, but not any sender, of a message. This scheme allows for the possibility that the *narrational process may sometimes mimic the communication situation more or less fully.* A text's narration may emit cues that suggest a narrator, or a 'narratee,' or it may not.
>
> (Bordwell 1985a: 62)

In fact, Bordwell's view of narration is not radically different from that of Chatman. Both agree that identifiable narrators and narratees are special cases, and both are primarily concerned with narration, which both regard as a

---

► three models of communication – Chapter 1, p. 8

► empirical reception analysis – Chapter 10

special type of textual organization (see Chatman 1990; for an overview of the discussion, see Lothe 2000). However, for an analysis of the means of the narration in actual texts, one needs a more differentiated description of the area than the ones suggested by either Bordwell or Chatman.

Levels of narration

In a helpful discussion of the possible ways of providing narrative information in a film, Edward Branigan argues that there are eight levels of narration, all of which derive from the traditional communication structure – 'someone tells something to someone' (Branigan 1992: 86f.). Figure 8.3 is a simplified version of his overview.

The point of departure for Branigan, as for Chatman, is a *historical author* and a historical artefact, a *text*, presented to a *historical audience*. Inside this text, the communication structure is repeated on seven levels:

1   The *extra-fictional narrator* appears in the text, but is not part of its *fiction*, and is therefore capable of referring to it precisely as fiction. The title sequence of a film is a typical example of information provided by this type of narrator ('Warner Bros. Pictures Inc. | Jack L. Warner, executive producer | Presents | Humphrey Bogart | Lauren Bacall | 'The Big Sleep' | A Howard Hawks Production . . .'). The extra-fictional narrator may be marked explicitly in the text, as in this title sequence. He/she may also work like Chatman's 'implied author,' i.e., as an implicit presence suggested to the audience by the arrangement of certain elements in the fiction. Early in *The Big Sleep*, there is an example of an extra-fictional narrator 'stacking the cards' in order to control the reading of the narrative. Marlowe is waiting outside the house of the blackmailer, when he hears gunshots and a scream. As he runs toward the entrance door, someone is running away on the other side of the house. The audience actually sees the person in the following shot, but this is cropped in such a way that it shows only the running feet. Clearly, this is not Marlowe's vision of the scene. Being on the

Historical author	: Text
Extra-fictional narrator	: Fiction
Nondiegetic narrator	: Story World
Diegetic narrator	: Events
Character	: Action
External focalization	: Speech
Internal focalization, surface	: Perception
Internal focalization, depth	: Thought

Figure 8.3 Eight levels of narration
Source: Adapted from Branigan 1992

wrong side of the house, he hears only the sound of footsteps. The shot of the feet must be attributed, instead, to 'someone' who, from a position outside the fiction, is creating suspense. This is accomplished by organizing the audience view of events in such a way that we are allowed to see the running person, but are denied full knowledge of his identity.

2   A *non-diegetic narrator* is present inside the text as well as inside the fiction, but is outside the 'diegesis,' or the *story world*. This type of   diegesis
narrator observes the story world, but does not act in it. Well-known cinematic examples are the titles that help spectators orient themselves in the story world, ranging from simple statements of time or place ('San Francisco') to more elaborate presentations of necessary information, such as the one opening John Houston's *The Maltese Falcon* (1941): 'In 1539 the Knights Templar of Malta paid tribute to Charles V of Spain by sending him a Golden Falcon encrusted from beak to claw with rarest jewels. But pirates seized the galley carrying this priceless token, and the fate of the Maltese Falcon remains a mystery to this day.'

3   The *diegetic narrator* is inside the story world and can address *events* in which he or she has participated. Narrators of this type manifest themselves whenever characters in the story world tell each other about their experi-

ences. In addition, entire narratives may be told by diegetic narrators. A novel like Joseph Conrad's *Heart of Darkness* (1899, revised 1902) is an example. Here, the complex story of a fateful journey to Africa is told in retrospect in the first person by one of the characters. When Francis Ford Coppola made *Apocalypse Now* (1979), a film adaptation of Conrad's novel, he chose the cinematic counterpart to diegetic narration by letting the main character report and comment on narrative events on the sound-track in voice-over (see Lothe 2000; for a discussion of voice-over narration, see Kozloff 1988).

voice-over narration

The term 'narrator' suggests the presence of a 'voice.' Beyond this, characters within the story world may provide us with information about this world in other ways than by simply 'telling' it:

- *Characters* enable us to learn about them as we observe their *actions*, what is also known as 'character narration'.
- *External focalization* is one way of learning about the story world by sharing a character's experiences. Here, the character is presented from the outside, but we understand that we are in his or her world – that it is this particular character who is the source of our knowledge.
- *Internal focalizations* allow us to see the story world more literally from a character's perspective. In the first type, *surface focalization*, we share a character's subjective experience, for example, by seeing what the character sees by means of a point-of-view-shot.
- In a *deep focalization*, finally, we – the audience – share a character's thoughts, dreams, hallucinations, etc.

character narration

point-of-view shot

Narrative analysis is always centrally concerned with how a given narrative applies these several modes of narration. A narrative derives its distinctive character not only from its presentation of various events and characters to the audience, but also from the specific ways in which information about these events and characters is organized, and how the audience is addressed. Some narratives belong to genres which adhere to relatively fixed narrational systems. A brief account of how Western television news is presented illustrates this point. The example also serves to emphasize that, as textual form, the narrative cuts across traditional boundaries between fact and fiction.

fictional as well as factual narratives

A typical news program is made up of various stories from real life. These stories are told primarily by anchorpersons and journalists in the studio, and by journalists reporting from the field. In Branigan's (1992) terminology, the anchorpersons and journalists in the studio are non-diegetic narrators who observe the story world and talk about it from the outside. Journalists in the field, on the scene where the events are taking or have taken place, are diegetic narrators. Reporting from inside the story world, these journalists may interview people who are directly involved in events. When talking about their experiences, these people equally become diegetic narrators, as do people who are interviewed by journalists in the studio.

The relations between these narrators are usually indicated by a simple visual code (Larsen 1974). The most important elements of this code are, first, the presence or absence of eye contact with the viewers, and second, the distinction between being present in the studio or in the field (Figure 8.4).

The anchorpersons and journalists in the studio as well as the journalists in the field are allowed to address the audience directly, thus

	Studio	Field
Eye contact	Anchorpersons, journalists	Journalists
No eye contact	Interviewees	Interviewees

Figure 8.4 The visual code of television news

simulating face-to-face communication. In contrast, the interviewees both in the studio and in the field have to address the interviewer. These distinctions – direct/non-direct address; studio/field – thus form a simple system which helps the audience to distinguish between the various types of narrators, and to understand their relative authority within the narrative hierarchy. The most important feature of each narrative sequence is decided by the eye contact, which shows, in a very concrete and visually explicit way, who has the right to address the viewers, and to interpret the world for them.

In a mainstream feature film, the relations between the various levels of narration are considerably more complex, and not marked as clearly as in a news program. The characters in a film address each other – they talk and act 'inwards' into the story world, seemingly unaware of the audience outside the text. In certain cases, the narration becomes rather conspicuous – for example, when the audience is allowed to share a character's perceptions and thoughts by means of internal focalization – but mostly the story seems to tell itself in an almost imperceptible manner. This general impression of 'invisible narration' in the mainstream film is the result of a subtle narrational system that is based primarily on non-diegetic narration via the camera and various forms of external focalization (on editing see, e.g., Bordwell and Thompson 1997).

GENRE ANALYSIS

Genre is the French translation of the Latin *genus*, a word originally referring to phenomena which resemble each other due to their common source or other close, mutual relations. *Genus* means *origin*, but also *family*, biological *genus*, grammatical *gender*, and, more generally, *kind*, *sort*, or *class*. Its French counterpart is similarly used in reference to groups of texts or works of art that are connected by a number of common features. The underlying assumption is that a unique text is quite a rare phenomenon. Most texts belong to larger classes of texts, and these classes, in turn, are defined by the features shared by the individual texts.

Classical writings on textual genres dealt with a relatively manageable field. The classes were few and defined by a limited number of textual features, as witnessed by the traditional partitioning of the field into drama, epic, and poetry. Contemporary theorists of genre who deal with media texts face a more complex situation. Throughout the media system, and particularly in the area of film and television fiction, there is a multitude of genre categories, and a constant proliferation of new genres and subgenres (on film genres see Altman 1999; Grant 1986, 1995; Kaminsky and Mahan 1985; Neale 1980, 2000; on television genres see Newcomb 1974; Rose 1985).

The media industry itself uses genres as convenient labels in production planning and in the marketing of new products. From the audience's point of view, references to genre function as appetizers that suggest the type of interpretive frame which should be applied to a particular text. Genre references, then, create certain expectations which are based on the audience's prior experience with similar media products. As such, a genre may be regarded as a kind of 'contract' between the media industry and its audience. More specifically, it amounts to an agreement between sender and receiver about some basic features of a certain type of textual product which is designed to perform a particular cultural task.

In sum, a genre is a system of textual conventions, or – to use semiotic terminology – a kind of latent *langue* governing the production of individual instances of *parole*. Because of the contractual nature of the relation between sender and receiver, it can also be regarded as a kind of mental tool, provided by the media and feeding into cultural processes. Media audiences use such tools to interpret the world and to address certain recurring sociocultural issues within familiar formats.

Practical and theoretical genres

In some cases, a 'genre' refers to a group of texts which is classified differently by the media industry and by portions of the audience. The prime example is the term *film noir*, which was introduced by French film critics after World

Margin notes:
narrative hierarchy

invisible narration

camera narration

drama, epic, poetry

genre as contract between sender and receiver

War II to refer to a group of Hollywood films that the industry was marketing as crime stories or melodramas (Borde and Chaumeton 1955). By using the term *film noir*, the film critics suggested that the films in question were somehow united across the established industrial genre categories (the history of the *film noir* concept is discussed in Cook 1999).

film noir
Film noir has been called a 'theoretical' genre as opposed to the 'practical' genres employed by the producers and consumers of media texts. The distinction calls attention to the fact that any given genre term usually covers two different phenomena. On the one hand, a genre is part of the practical, almost unconscious knowledge◄ about textual features and classes which members of the audience draw upon in their everyday lives. On the other hand, it is also a theoretical and analytical object, or rather it becomes such an object the moment people start discussing which textual features define a particular group of texts, or how this group differs from other groups (see Todorov 1978). *Film noir* is one of the relatively rare examples of a classification which started out as a theoretical genre, was accepted by the industry and the audience, and ended up being a practical genre.◄

The theoretical definition of genres is no easy task. The history of genre theory shows that it is, in fact, quite impossible to classify texts on the basis of simple, well-defined features, or to make genres form a clear-cut, unambiguous system. One solution is to rely on
family resemblances
the concept of 'family resemblances,' as defined by Wittgenstein (1953). While it is quite rare for a few common features to constitute an entire genre, a group of texts may nevertheless be closely related because of the partial and incremental overlaps between its various subgroups – just as individual children within a family may have features in common with both their father and their mother without resembling each other. Genres are, indeed, defined with reference to a common pool of textual features, but these features may not all be shared

---

▶ practical consciousness – Chapter 1, p. 2
▶ practical and other 'theory' – Chapter 16, p. 274

by all members of the group. In this view, a genre amounts to a series of transitions or displacements between texts, an aspect which makes the concept particularly useful for the description and analysis of the historical development of textual forms. The individual genre may be regarded as a mobile textual field in which new subcategories or branches are constantly being developed.

When texts are used recurrently to perform more or less similar cultural and social functions, prototypical forms develop almost automatically. And, as these recurrent discursive features are institutionalized and codified, individual texts will eventually be produced and received in accordance with the codified norms. According to Todorov (1978), a genre is precisely such a codification of discursive characteristics, i.e., a group of texts that serve a common purpose, and which therefore have certain discursive qualities in common. Still, as implied by the concept of family resemblances, these characteristics may be associated with many different textual levels and aspects.

Textual characteristics of genres

The genre label suggests an interpretive frame to the audience as well as to the analyst. To analyze a particular film *as* a western or *as* a *film noir* is to regard it as an example of a general type. It is also to identify a series of textual features which this particular film has in common with other films, and which may be relevant for the analysis. Another reference to *The Big Sleep* illustrates how, and further suggests the basic textual aspects at work in genre definitions (on these aspects see further Todorov 1978).

In reference works as well as in popular movie guides, *The Big Sleep* is usually labeled a *mystery movie* (but also sometimes a thriller, a gangster film, or a crime film (see, e.g., Cook 1999; Halliwell 1999). The genre label points out that this particular film belongs to a larger group of films which, despite other differences, have a common core: they present a mystery, there is a crime which is to be solved – usually, but not always, by a private investigator or a police officer. This kind of genre definition focuses on 'content,' or what linguists might call 'semantic' aspects of the texts in question.

Semantic definitions focus on signifieds (What is the text about? What kind of 'themes' or 'motifs' does it deal with?, etc.). In addition, they may raise questions of referentiality (Is the textual universe presented as fictional or factual? What kind of sociohistorical context does the text refer to?, etc.).

The Big Sleep has the semantic features necessary for being labeled a *mystery*, but it is also a mystery *movie*. The 'movie' part of the label refers to what Todorov (1978) calls the 'verbal'

aspect of the text, its 'material' form. First of all, there are the basic material conditions of communication: What kind of discursive substance are we dealing with? In the case of *The Big Sleep*, the mystery is not presented in any simple, homogeneous discourse (as, for example, in Chandler's original detective novel), but in a complex sequence of moving images, dialogue, written texts, music, and so on. Second, and more importantly, the material

aspect concerns questions of 'style' or '*mise-en-scène*' – the way in which events are staged for the camera in terms of setting, lighting, costumes, and character behavior (see Bordwell and Thompson 1997). To say that a Hollywood film from the 1940s is a mystery movie almost automatically suggests a fixed stylistic pattern: images in black and white, usually an urban setting, a certain type of lighting with a preference for night scenes, rainy streets and dramatic shadows, and so on.

Finally, there is the 'syntactic' aspect – the actual structuration of the text, its sequential organization or composition. In the case of mystery movies like *The Big Sleep*, the central characteristics follow from the relation between *syuzhet* and *fabula*, as already described: fabula events are presented in reverse chronological order in the syuzhet; the film presents murders and mysteries, but withholds information about their causes until the very last moment.

To sum up, analyzing *The Big Sleep* as a mystery movie implies that special attention will be paid to the narrative construction (semantically: What type of mystery is presented here? syntactically: How is it solved? What kind of ideological values are involved?,

etc.) as well as to its material aspect, or the stylistic presentation of the narrative. It remains to emphasize again, however, that genres are not fixed classes with precise borderlines. *The Big Sleep* is an example that one film may very well belong to several genres at once. It shares decisive textual features with a number of other mystery films, but it is also one of those films which can be, and usually is, labeled *film noir*. If one were to analyze it as a *film noir* one would cover much of the same ground, but the analysis would focus more on the 'dark' aspects of the story, the violence, the cynical and disillusioned detective, the dangerous *femme fatale*, and so on – aspects which all play an important role in the definition of the *film noir*.

The configuration of semantic, material, and syntactical aspects, noted above, highlights a number of textual features. Moreover, since genres are established and institutionalized according to the functions of texts in fixed, recurring situations, they also always have a 'pragmatic' aspect. What are the demands

of the situation on the discursive characteristics of a given genre? What is the intention governing the production of the texts? What is their purpose? Even though this fourth aspect of a definition of genre primarily concerns the social context, the pragmatic functions which a text has to fulfill within a given context obviously affect the details of its discursive construction. In this regard, one particularly important issue is the way in which the text addresses its audience. As indicated by the brief

analysis of television news, this is one textual genre in which a central pragmatic question – the interpretive authority of different narrators – is solved by means of a fixed narrational system.

HETEROGENEOUS TEXTS

A film is not only a sequence of moving images, but an organized mixture of images, words, texts, music, and noises. Most media texts are like this: *montages*, or heterogeneous constructions that are characterized by a constant displacement and circulation of meaning. In film and television, in newspapers and magazines, information is doubled or tripled, presented through several channels, discourses, and senses at once.

This complexity raises a series of theoretical and analytical issues which are often neglected in media studies. Like much earlier film theory, Christian Metz's semiotic works in the 1960s were primarily concerned with sequences of shots. The focus of many current film studies is primarily on the fabula – the narrative as constructed by a spectator after the fact. Journalism studies frequently describe newspaper stories and even television news as merely verbal phenomena.

Similarities and differences

Although the need for studies of the heterogeneity of the modern media was acknowledged by the semioticians of the 1960s, the problem proved difficult to handle within a theoretical framework which takes the homogeneous verbal text as its model. In his authoritative introduction to semiotics, Barthes (1964a) simply stated that semioticians, like linguists, must work primarily with homogeneous materials. Even if he saw the need for descriptions of, for example, films or fashion magazines as complex structural totalities, he wanted to postpone the analysis of such heterogeneous materials and to concentrate on studies of individual, homogeneous substances.

Nevertheless, in his influential essay on 'the rhetoric of the image,' Barthes did suggest some basic relations between two such substances, namely image and text. According to Barthes, a text can function as an 'anchorage' of visual signifieds, either by identifying the objects represented by the image (e.g., a caption for a news photo), or by suggesting and authorizing how the image should be interpreted (e.g., the title of a painting). The 'anchorage' relation is based on redundancy: the text repeats or explains the information given by the image. In contrast, the other basic relation, 'relay,' operates on differences. In this relation, text and image are complementary, and the unity of the message is realized at a higher level. Barthes's own example was the relation between dialogue and images in a film. Here, text and image carry different signifieds; the text adds meanings to

the narrative which are not found in the sequence of images (Barthes 1964b).◄

With this simple outline, particularly the concept of relay, Barthes hinted at ways of analyzing not only text–image relationships, but the total mix of substances which are characteristic of films and television programs. In various versions, this notion of complementarity has been a key issue since the 1980s in studies trying to account for the heterogeneity of media materials.

Studies of sound

Most of these discussions have focused on the status of sound and its functions in film. In 1980, in a seminal issue of *Yale French Studies* on cinema and sound, Rick Altman (1980) criticized traditional film theory as well as contemporary film semiotics for their focus on the cinematic image and their corresponding neglect of sound. Here and in later writings, he argued that sound is just as important as – and in certain respects perhaps even more important than – images for the total cinematic experience (e.g., Altman 1992). From a similar position, French sound theorist Michel Chion has argued in a series of books that most film theory is characterized by 'vococentrism.' In so far as film sound is acknowledged at all, it is usually the human voice of the dialogue, or the voiceover, which is privileged analytically in favor of, for instance, music or noise. Chion presents detailed analyses of the importance of sound in film and television with particular emphasis on the 'point-of-hearing,' i.e., the effect which is obtained by the positioning of the sound source in relation to the point of view of the camera (Chion 1999 [1982], 1985, 1988, 1998).

point-of-hearing

In their justified criticism of the dominant focus on visuality in previous film and media studies, Altman and Chion sometimes place themselves at the opposite extreme, claiming the superiority of sound in relation to images. Most later works in this area emphasize the complementarity of sound and image. This, for example, is the position of Sarah Kozloff in her

► anchorage and relay, with example analysis – Chapter 7, p. 111

studies of the various ways in which voice-over and dialogue are used in film (Kozloff 1988, 2000). It is also the dominant position at present in studies of music and its functions in film.

The role of music

Traditional film studies tended to distinguish between two types of music, one supporting the image, the other working contrapuntal to the image (e.g., Eisler and Adorno 1947). Arguing that music should be described more directly for its relations with the narrative and its events, Chion (1985, 1994 [1990], 1995) suggests three basic categories:

1 *empathetic* music, which supports and expresses the emotions of the characters;
2 *a-empathetic* music, which is independent of the actions on the screen;
3 *didactic* music, which is employed as a distanciating, often ironical commentary on the action.

In concrete studies of music in film and television, a more differentiated analytical framework is needed. As in narrative studies and genre studies, classical Hollywood cinema has also been the central case in studies of film music. One example is Claudia Gorbman (1987), who takes the practice of classical Hollywood as the basis for a general description of narrative film music. Drawing on analyses of, among others, Bernard Herrmann's score for *Hangover Square* (John Brahm, 1944) and Max Steiner's score for *Mildred Pierce* (Michael Curtiz, 1945), she argues that most film music performs one of four basic functions:

1 a *signifier of emotion,* i.e., the music sets specific moods and emphasizes particular emotions suggested by the images;
2 formal and rhythmic *continuity* between shots and in transitions between scenes;
3 *narrative cues* or interpretations of narrative events;
4 formal and narrative *unity* may be constructed by means of the repetition and variation of musical material and instrumentation.

Most of these functions are examples of what Barthes called anchorage: the music supports the meaning of the images (for a further discussion of musical anchorage see Larsen 2000). There are, however, also examples of film music functioning as relay, i.e., working complementary to the images and to the dialogue, and adding qualities of its own to the narrative. This aspect has been underlined by Kathryn Kalinak (1992), who, in a study similar to that by Gorbman, analyzes Max Steiner's score for *The Informer* (John Ford, 1935) and David Raksin's score for *Laura* (Otto Preminger, 1944) as examples of the classic Hollywood style. She emphasizes the central composers' reworking of the musical practices of late Romanticism, in particular their use of *leitmotifs* – short musical themes *leitmotifs* functioning as kinds of signposts announcing the arrival of characters, or referring to prior events or central narrative issues. In an analysis of John Williams's score for *The Empire Strikes Back* (Irvin Kershner, 1980), Kalinak further shows that this classic Hollywood practice has been continued in later productions.

Sound in television

The turn toward sound in film studies during the 1980s was, if not prompted, at least reinforced by the remarkable technological developments of the period. The introduction of the Dolby noise reduction system in 1977, the successive generations of Dolby stereo and surround sound, the new multitrack recording systems, and so on greatly improved the quality of cinema sound, and also led to a series of experiments with sound by both avant-garde and mainstream directors. Although television has gone through almost identical technological developments during the same period, resulting in a similarly increased emphasis on sound communication in the medium as a whole as well as in individual programs and genres, there has been no corresponding focus on sound in television studies.

The role of music is sometimes discussed in studies of major television genres (see, e.g., on music in soap operas, Gripsrud 1995: 183f.). The establishment of international promotional channels like MTV during the 1980s prompted some studies of the music–image relationship in music videos (e.g., Kaplan 1988; Larsen 1989). In recent years, there have been additional studies of music in relation to multimedia presentations. One example is musicologist Nicholas Cook's (1998) analyses of the ways in which music, words, moving pictures, and dance work together in television commercials and music videos.

On the whole, however, there have been remarkably few contributions in this area. Regarding television sound in general, the only major work is a short article from the mid-1980s in which Rick Altman discussed the function of sound in relation to the domestic viewing situation (Altman 1986). Obviously, this is an area of media studies in which further research is greatly needed, not only because of the centrality of sound in the media, but because such research may contribute to a better understanding of sound as 'text,' in its own right and in conjunction with other media texts.

9 Media effects
Quantitative traditions

Klaus Bruhn Jensen

- a brief *history of research* on media effects
- a review of the main traditions of audience research, focusing on different *stages of the process* of mediated communication
- a presentation of additional studies on how media serve to *socialize* individuals and to *institutionalize* society
- an example of the study of *lifestyles* as they relate to media use.

'effects' – traditionally defined as cognitive and behavioral impacts on individuals in the short term

If any one issue can be said to have motivated media studies, it is the question of 'effects.' From the perspective of policy-makers and the general public, the field has been expected to supply evidence of what the media may do to people and to society. From within the academic perspective, the field has justified itself by examining what specific difference the modern media make, compared to other cultural forms and social institutions. The question of effects has largely been stated in terms of the relatively short-term cognitive and behavioral impacts of different media and their contents on mass audiences, which have been studied by quantitative social-scientific methodologies. Especially in this area, it is still appropriate to speak of a *dominant paradigm* or model (Gitlin 1978; Webster and Phalen 1997), even if the quantitative mainstream is quite differentiated and currently in dialogue with a qualitative substream (Chapter 10).

the dominant paradigm

This chapter reviews the main varieties of audience studies with reference to their foci on particular stages of the communicative process. While contemporary research commonly dis-

tanciates itself from a chain-like model of the process, it is the case that each tradition is defined, in part, by its orientation toward a particular moment of the interchange between media and audiences, whether in the short or the long term. In addition to being an intuitively helpful configuration of the empirical field, this implicit model holds the potential both for specifying the scope of each tradition, and for indicating areas of contact between them. To anticipate one argument of the chapter, each tradition may be said to identify a social 'context' of interaction between media and audiences. For example, an 'early' context of interaction is examined in terms of national and international television ratings and other measures of media exposure; a 'late' context has been studied with reference to the question of whether media contribute over time to closing or deepening so-called knowledge gaps in society (Tichenor *et al.* 1970). In each of these two examples, an interchange occurs between audience and medium which has implications for audience members' actions in other social contexts: the act of television viewing is

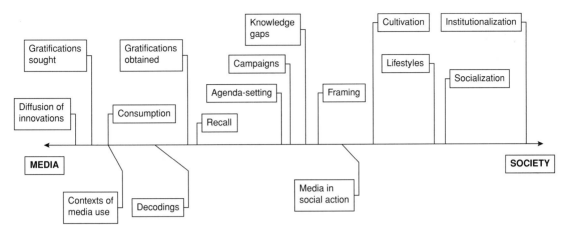

Figure 9.1 The 'stages' of mediated communication, as defined by audience research traditions

Note: The qualitative traditions, indicated below the line, are reviewed in Chapter 10, this volume

a way of giving priority to one form of cultural activity over others; the command of certain forms of public knowledge is one necessary condition for political participation.

Figure 9.1 lays out the main stages as defined by different research traditions. Before examining these several moments of mediated communication in society, this chapter briefly notes the controversial history of effects research. The following sections describe and exemplify each research tradition, with special reference to its theoretical assumptions and preferred methodologies. A more detailed account is given of research on lifestyles, which has recently attracted attention in media studies, and which is one of the links between the quantitative mainstream and the qualitative substream.

HISTORIES OF EFFECTS RESEARCH

Because of the sustained social and scientific interest in effects, this area has more of an identifiable, if contested history than most other subspecialties. As summarized by McQuail (2000: 417–22), four phases may be singled out:

• *Phase 1: All-powerful media.* From about 1900, when an identifiable research specialization was emerging (e.g., Bryce 1966 [1900]), to 1940, the media were widely thought to be able

to shape both opinion and behavior through propaganda (e.g., Lasswell 1938). However, 'this view was based not on scientific investigation but on observation of the enormous popularity of the press and of the new media of film and radio' (McQuail 2000: 417).

• *Phase 2: Theory of powerful media put to the test.* From the beginnings of academic media research in the 1930s, studies began to suggest that at least no direct link could be established between media stimulus and audience response. Klapper (1960) provided an influential digest of findings which seemed to support this position.

• *Phase 3: Powerful media rediscovered.* In part through a reassessment of the same evidence (see Chaffee and Hochheimer 1985; Delia 1987), the 1960s witnessed a return to hypotheses about media power. Such hypotheses were also fueled partly by the arrival of television, partly by research on various cognitive and structural impacts, over and above effects on individuals' attitudes, and partly by the rediscovery of critical social theory.

• *Phase 4: Negotiated media influence.* Since around 1980, a turn to understanding media as necessarily constructing meanings, with implications for social structure as well as individual agency, has been in evidence. While partly associated with qualitative reception studies, the shift can also be traced in several of the quantitative traditions reviewed below.

As the periodization suggests, the development of research, and the definition of 'effects,' has been intimately related to contemporary concerns, including two world wars and the rise of television as a vehicle of popular culture. In the process, researchers themselves have also held changing notions of their own social and intellectual role. Moreover, it should be noted that both this periodization and the definition of 'milestone' studies (Lowery and DeFleur 1995) enter into a received history of the field, which is as informative of current ideas about the mission of media effects research as it is of past findings (see Figure 10.1).

One of the abiding issues has been the social level at which effects should be conceptualized and studied. Overwhelmingly, previous research has focused on the individual user's level, despite exceptions such as studies on the structural dependency of different social groups on media (Ball-Rokeach 1985). This chapter, while retracing the individualist mainstream, returns whenever relevant to technologies, institutions, and genres as preparatory conditions of mediated communication and its impact.◀ In this respect, the empirical domain of effects research shades into the domains of both 'medium theory' (Chapter 2) and of research on the historical and cultural contexts of communication (Chapters 11–12).

MOMENTS OF IMPACT: FROM DIFFUSION TO CULTIVATION

Diffusion of innovations

One necessary condition of mediated communication on any social scale is the availability and accessibility of media as cultural resources for a significant portion of the population. On *material availability* the one hand, the material availability of a technology presupposes its invention, development, distribution, and relative affordability in the

historical context. On the other hand, its discursive accessibility requires both that its potential social uses are perceived as relevant or attractive, and that audiences have the corresponding cognitive and cultural competences. This complex social dynamic, in certain respects reiterating the development and spread of literacy, has been studied in the media field under the heading of 'diffusion of innovations.' *discursive accessibility*

It is important to note that this research tradition has been quite inclusive in studying not only the diffusion of new media technologies, but perhaps more typically the diffusion of information via media. An important background was postwar attempts by Western nations at modernizing health, education, and other social sectors in developing countries (e.g., Lerner 1958). The central theoretical model was advanced by Rogers (1962), who described a rather linear and hierarchical process of information diffusion, concerning ideas as well as products. In this process, the media were found to be important especially in the first stage of information and awareness (followed by stages of persuasion, decision or adoption, and confirmation). Importantly, personal contacts and concrete experience could be shown to replace technological media as the main vehicles of diffusion in later stages.◀ In addition, studies of news diffusion suggested that the higher the proportion of a population that knows about some event or issue, the higher the proportion that learned about these from an interpersonal source (Greenberg 1964).

Later work on development communication◀ as well as on the introduction of new media has moved away from a paternalist and logistical conception of cultural change, and toward a recognition of cultural specificity as a condition of how technologies may be implemented (Rogers 1986, 2000). A wider implication for communication theory has been that technological media are more than engineering solutions, and always come with a 'message' whose interpretation will depend on historical and social circumstances. With this revised

▶ structures and conditions as sources of 'effects' – Chapter 2, p. 16

▶ interpersonal communication – Chapter 1, p. 8

▶ development communication – Chapter 11, p. 179

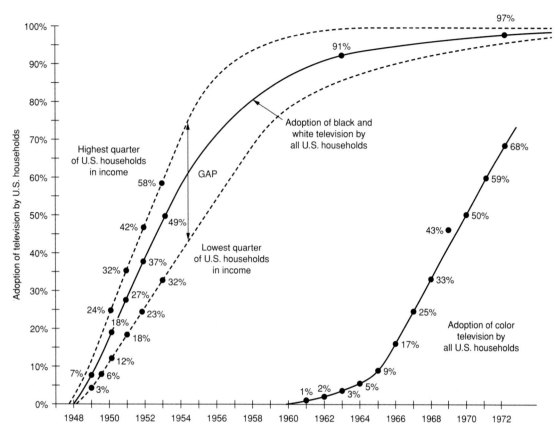

Figure 9.2 Examples of differential rates of the diffusion of innovations, in percent over time
Source: Rogers 1986: 171. Reprinted with permission of The Free Press, a division of Simon & Schuster, Inc., © 1986 The Free Press.

agenda, diffusion research has remained relevant for studies on how media are adopted in various cultural settings, and on which segments of a community or society are likely to be 'early' or 'late' adopters (see Figure 9.2). For each new medium, a recurring concern has been the extent to which media can reinforce, rather than counteract, social inequalities. This may be either because the 'ideal' S-curve (from a slow and unequal start, via an accelerated diffusion, to a plateau where the medium is materially available to practically everybody) does not occur, or because some audiences with limited cognitive or cultural competences find the media less accessible. Both conditions may result in 'knowledge gaps,' as addressed below.

The most common approach to diffusion studies has been survey methodologies, which make it possible to compare and contrast the basic availability and accessibility of either media or information in different social groups and contexts. National statistical abstracts as well as continuous market studies are among the sources of evidence, which also lend themselves to 'secondary analyses' that extract additional patterns of diffusion and use from existing datasets. Perhaps partly for this methodological reason, diffusion research has given less attention to the interpretive aspect of such social processes, or what has been called symbolic diffusion (Jensen 1993a). Similarly, questions of material availability have been given priority over discursive accessibility, in the sense that generic and other cultural conventions as well as audiences' pre-understandings – their 'literacy' in a broad sense (Messaris 1994)

symbolic diffusion

– remain under-researched, yet important conditions of how new forms of communication are diffused.

Gratifications sought

Audiences' orientation toward media has been the main focus of the second tradition, 'uses and gratifications' research, so much so that its position is frequently summarized by asking,

what audiences do with media

not what media do to audiences, but what audiences do with media (e.g., Halloran 1970). Following pioneering studies in the 1940s (Berelson 1949; Herzog 1944), the tradition was rediscovered and redeveloped from the 1960s, partly in response to the contemporary conclusion concerning 'limited effects.' The resulting research program articulated an ambition of relating the impact of media to both psychological needs and social conditions, including the alternatives to media use. That program may be read as a restatement of the chain of communication, referring to '(1) the social and psychological origins of (2) needs which generate (3) expectations of (4) the mass media or other sources which lead to (5) differential exposure (or engaging in other activities), resulting in (6) need gratification and (7) other consequences' (Katz et al. 1974: 20).

Uses and gratifications research became widely influential, at least into the 1980s (Rosengren et al. 1985), on several counts. For one thing, studies began to outline general typologies of the media–audience nexus. The

functions of media use

concept of 'functions,' familiar in sociology from Durkheim to Parsons, lent itself to accounts of the relationship between human needs, media provisions, and the gratifications generated at their interface. A number of studies converged on three main functions of media, namely information-seeking, diversion, and the maintenance of personal identity (see Blumler 1979; McQuail et al. 1972). In addition, research addressed the complicated, yet crucial question of whether and how the public perceives different media and genres as providers of distinctive gratifications (see Katz et al. 1973). In certain respects, such studies are comparable to opinion polls, conducted regularly in many

countries, on public perceptions of various media.

The gratifications tradition soon came in for theoretical criticism from at least two different quarters. On the one hand, critical theorists argued that the approach was compromised by its functionalist premises, specifically the presumption that audience uses of media might be examined in relation to a 'common interest' and an actual or emerging social consensus (e.g., Elliott 1974). Despite references in the literature to 'dysfunctions' of media (Lazarsfeld and Merton 1960 [1948]; Wright 1959), these tended to be conceived as deviations from a norm rather than indicators of any structural conflict. On the other hand, scholars of a culturalist bent noted that the entire processual and participatory aspect of communication seemed to fall outside this framework (e.g., Carey and Kreiling 1974). In addition, empirical research questioned the status and explanatory value of the key notion of gratifications. Lichtenstein and Rosenfeld (1983), for instance, found that heavy and light viewers, as well as fans and non-fans, tended to agree on their gratifications, and concluded that audiences at large may reproduce a generally accepted image of both content formats and specific media.

Later work has responded to some of these criticisms, and has elaborated the uses and gratifications tradition in several respects. One response has been attempts to integrate gratifications into more general models of communication and media choice (McQuail 2000: 393). Another response has been to explore links between personality and media gratifications (Conway and Rubin 1991). Others again have differentiated theoretically between studies of audience activity before, during, and after media exposure, which may substantiate rather different conclusions about the nature of media use, and which may require different methodologies (Levy and Windahl 1985). However, despite the occasional experimental or qualitative study, the tradition has relied primarily on survey techniques to examine the audience experience of media as a whole. Thus, while gratifications research has documented and systematized public perceptions of various media

public perceptions of media and genres

and genres in general categories, partly in comparison with other cultural forms, it has proven less applicable to studying specific audience responses or contextual uses of media and their contents. (One attempt in this last regard is taken up below in the section that distinguishes between gratifications sought and obtained.)

Consumption

The bread and butter of media research as a modern institution of social surveillance and control (Beniger 1986) have always been measurements which answer questions of who attends to which media, and to what portion of their contents, when, and for how long. In addition to the commercial value of such measurements, they document the moment of exposure 'exposure,' or the concrete interaction between *a* medium and *an* audience, without which there would be no communication, interpretation, or effects. While the term 'consumption' might suggest either an applied, marketing approach or a critique of the economic functions of media, here it refers inclusively to the fact that audiences do spend time and, directly or indirectly, money on media.

The time and money spent, by various sociodemographic groups, on different media, genres, and texts, are of interest as necessary baseline information, even while both the categories of measurement and the social uses of findings will be subject to epistemological as well as political controversy. For example, Smythe (1977) has argued that the primary audience as product of media organizations is not contents, product but audiences – media deliver audience attention to advertisers, or they construct an apparently attractive role of 'being an audience,' for which people are willing to pay money.

Just as the conceptualization of 'audiences' has remained controversial, the definition of their 'attention' to media has proven a stumbling-block to research, in very practical terms. For one thing, audience attention to media is typically discontinuous, either because events in the immediate context disrupt attention, or because the media themselves fail to hold the audience's attention, for instance, through a commercial break or a full newspaper article.

For another thing, media use, such as television viewing, is often a secondary activity in relation to some primary activity in the household (e.g., Robinson and Converse 1972). Indeed, these activities may be so thoroughly integrated that it is difficult to distinguish and rank them, for both researchers and respondents.

secondary media use

Partly because of such methodological difficulties, audience research has gone through several 'generations' of techniques (for an overview see Gunter 2000). In addition to the increasing reliance on computers, not just in data analysis, but also in the process of collecting and organizing data (e.g., Computer Assisted Telephone Interviewing (CATI)), the movement has been from in-person techniques such as diaries (and interviews), toward semi-automatic techniques (or a combination of techniques), particularly for television. From the mid-1980s, 'peoplemeters'◀ have been used to go beyond measures of whether the television set is turned on (and to which channel it is tuned), and have relied on respondents to push a button to identify their presence as 'viewers' and, in some systems, to indicate their level of appreciation of the program. On a smaller scale, studies have videotaped audiences in front of the set to assess their presence and attention (see Bechtel *et al.* 1972; Borzekowski and Robinson 1999). Other studies have employed eye-tracking techniques to determine what readers look at, and in what sequence (e.g., Thorson 1994) – techniques which are also applied to computer media. Also, the use of remote control devices has been examined by electronic monitoring (Kaye and Sapolsky 1997). For all the techniques mentioned, however, there are trade-offs that depend on the purpose of study, between, for example, the comprehensiveness and potential intrusiveness of peoplemeter methodologies.

viewing the viewers

eye-tracking

Because of the focus on individuals' exposure to media, particularly in commercial research, less emphasis has been placed on questions of 'where' and especially 'with whom' media are used. Whereas qualitative studies have highlighted the social contexts of media use (Chapter 10), some quantitative research

---

▶ TV- and peoplemeters – Chapter 13, p. 228

has also addressed related questions. For example, studies of television have traced its impact on family life, and concluded already in the 1970s that 'multiple sets disrupt the established pattern of family interaction' (Comstock 1978: 158). Another characteristic of quantitative audience research more generally is that comparatively little empirical attention has been given to the 'what' of communication – the cultural and discursive forms which give rise to the adoption, gratifications, and effects of media. While this helps to explain a frequent complaint, also within media industries, that audience measurements fall short of being audience research (Wober 1981: 410), still, exposure is the *sine qua non* of communication and one inevitable focus of media research.

consumption of what, with whom

Gratifications obtained

As noted above gratifications research has been criticized for a functionalist notion of communication, but also on its own terms, because 'it has not provided much successful prediction or causal explanation of media choice and use' (McQuail 2000: 389). That may be due, first, to the contextual, even accidental nature of much media use, which is difficult to account for in terms of motivations and plans. Second, the comparative failure of gratifications research has entailed a questioning of the preferred survey methodologies of the tradition, which are especially appropriate for examining conscious, unambiguous, and relatively uncontroversial aspects of media use.

Nevertheless, in order to capture the evident gratifications of media – pleasurable experiences and valued information – gratifications researchers have proposed to distinguish expectations of what will be provided (gratifications sought – GS) from the resulting satisfactions (gratifications obtained – GO). Importantly, GS is, in part, the outcome of past experiences with particular media (genres, texts), and GO amounts to a feedback concerning which gratifications to seek in the future, and from which media. This processual perspective on gratifications has been summed up in an 'expectancy value' model (Palmgreen and Rayburn 1985).

In one study, Palmgreen *et al.* (1980) solicited responses to two sets of statements, presented in telephone interviews immediately after each other. GS was operationalized as, 'I watch television news to keep up with current issues and events.' GO, next, was restated with reference to the program that the respondent would ordinarily watch, thus 'CBS News helps me to keep up with current issues and events' (p. 171). Whatever the correlations between the two sets of measures, however, the empirical design does not warrant conclusions about the viewer's satisfactions or experiences in any specific sense. The GO and GS statements were presented in the same interview session, in equally abstract formulations, and, most important, there was no concrete point of reference in an actual program or context of viewing. Instead, the findings may support a public-opinion profile of the particular news program or organization in question. In addition, such conceptual and methodological difficulties have made the gratifications tradition less influential since the 1980s.

An alternative approach – the 'experience sampling method' – has been applied by Kubey and Csikszentmihalyi (1990) to television. The basic idea is that respondents are contacted with a paging device at random times, and are asked each time to complete self-reports on what they are doing, and how they feel. These data may then be used to explore, for instance, the relationship between types of media use, simultaneous activities, and the respondent's moods and other mental states. While the approach requires considerable resources, it offers one means of securing immediate feedback from media-users about their experiences in relatively naturalistic circumstances.

experience sampling method

Recall

Parallel to respondents' statements about their conscious motivations for, and benefits from, media use, a favorite measure of audience research has been recall, i.e., respondents' ability to reproduce items of information within a relatively short time span after media exposure. This aspect of media use has been examined especially through experiments and surveys (for overviews see Gunter 2000: 215–225; Robinson and Levy 1986).

Basic recall is of interest as a preparatory condition of other forms of impact, from factual learning and education to informed political participation. Studies have normally found that recall is positively correlated with prior the recipients' level of prior knowledge (and knowledge hence their social status), in addition to the perceived concrete relevance of the information. Furthermore, recall studies have offered an opportunity to probe the specificity and 'efficiency' of different media, including multimodal communication, not least the visual component of television news. Research in print and this area tends to suggest that print and audioaudiovisual visual media do not in themselves constitute a media hierarchy of more or less efficient vehicles of communication, but rather that narrative and message structure in general, and the meaningful integration of verbal and visual elements in particular, will determine recall and potential learning by audiences.

Within the recall stage of communication and impact, it is possible to identify at least two different strands of research. First, some studies have departed from the premise that media have a significant potential as sources of enlightenment for the general public. Not surprisingly, much of this work has been associated with European public-service traditions of broadcasting, and was, to a degree, conceived as a means of product development in the public interest (e.g., Findahl 1985; Gunter 1987b). Partly for this reason, studies would commonly analyze programs closely in conjunction with the audience response, thus anticipating and complementing qualitative reception studies.

The second body of research has been motivated by commercial aims of establishing whether consumers recall or recognize particular commodities or brands. As such, it enters into the wider applied field of marketing research (e.g., Shimp and Gresham 1983; Thorson 1990). From a more general perspective of theory development, this research has reiterated some key difficulties in determining how different stages of communication and impact are interrelated. In an influential elaboration of the basic stimulus–response model, McGuire (1973) indicated six stages of a sequence: presentation, attention, comprehension, yielding, retention, and overt behavior.◀ In fact, this seemingly logical order is not necessarily borne out by empirical research (see Windahl *et al.* 1992). For example, consumers may have no explicit recall of a product, and yet may buy it on sight.

Once again, the preconscious and practical (Giddens 1984) aspects of much media-related behavior present a central methodological challenge, and one which calls for further research on the nature of the 'stages' reviewed in this chapter. The difficulties of ascertaining effects have repeatedly led to the postulation of additional stages, competing theories, or a reinterpretation of findings in alternative frameworks. In one early assessment of the finding that people seem to want news, as indicated by their habitual consumption, yet recall little or nothing, Nordenstreng (1972) concluded that 'the main thing retained from the news is that nothing special has happened' (p. 390). Recall and other measures of media impact might thus be reinterpreted, in part, with reference to various institutionalized, social uses of media, as audiences deliberate on public issues and make personal decisions.

Agenda-setting

The research tradition which emphasizes that the media set an agenda for public debate and decision-making, especially within politics, has focused not on discrete units of information, as transmitted and recalled, but on 'issues' – those configurations of information that are associated with the activities of particular social institutions, such as parties and parliaments. At the same time, the agenda-setting tradition has helped to shift the focus of much audience research. The general move has been away from what used to be the foundational question at least into the 1960s, namely how the media may shape and change, for example, people's attitudes or voting – and toward more general issues of how people process

▶ 'stages' of stimulus and response – Chapter 3, p. 51

information as part, for instance, of their political participation (for an overview see Kraus and Davis 1976).

This shift is summed up in the conclusion that the media do not tell people what to think, **what to think about** but what to think *about*. In American research, this formulation is normally credited to Cohen (1963), but, before him, Trenaman and McQuail (1961: 178) concluded, 'The evidence strongly suggests that people think *about* what they are told but at no level do they think *what* they are told.' In addition, an early classic such as Lazarsfeld *et al.* (1944) had noted that media, among other things, serve to structure political issues. It is also worth noting that such earlier suggestions in the literature were given new attention from the 1960s, following the conclusion that the media had little or no effect. In this regard, agenda-setting joined gratifications research in the attempt to differentiate the concept of effects, asking what people do with media and what, consequently, they think about.

Agenda-setting was given its name and its foundational work by McCombs and Shaw (1972). In brief, their study in a small North Carolina community during the 1968 presidential campaign found that although different news media would represent political life differently, there was a significant correlation between issues that were defined as important by the media and by the voters: 'voters tend to share the media's *composite* definition of what is important' (p. 184).◄

Subsequent research has debated and re-examined the approach, both methodologically and theoretically. One methodological concern is that both the media and audience sides of the equation are often examined in the aggregate, through surveys and content analysis, but with little empirical attention to, for example, variations in the public's media use or in the foci of news coverage over time. Accordingly, one **parallel content analysis** ambitious program of 'parallel content analysis' has been outlined by Neuman (1989). Its purpose would be to examine the 'content' of both media and public opinion, their thematic

foci and formal articulation, including variations over time. In addition, Lang and Lang (1981) called for more empirical attention not only to agenda-setting on the audience side, but to 'agenda-building' in the interplay between media and various political agents.

An alternative theoretical explanation for the correlations identified in agenda-setting research follows if one reverses the causality, i.e., if one assumes that issues and priorities flow from the public to the media and/or to politicians in an ideal democratic system. More recent work has sought to address the complexity of the entire process by distinguishing three kinds of agendas – those of the media, of **three agendas: media, public, policy** the public, and of policy (Dearing and Rogers 1996). The majority of studies appear to confirm the impact of media on the public agenda, whereas the evidence concerning the policy agenda is more uncertain (p. 87).

While some reviews conclude that the agenda-setting hypothesis is 'a plausible but unproven idea' (McQuail 2000: 456), it remains a fertile area for further studies. At the theoretical level, it has affinities with Newcomb and Hirsch's (1984) proposal that media be studied not as distribution systems, but as a 'cultural **media as cultural forum** forum' to which matters of public interest may be brought, articulated, and contested. Research topics include the short-term management of agendas and sources by different interest groups, and the more long-term adaptation of institutional agendas and logics to shifting social circumstances. Dearing and Rogers (1996: 98) also note that the approach lends itself to research on other genres than news and political communication.

Despite its distinctive terminology, agenda-setting research can thus be seen to converge with other work on the role of media in the social construction of reality (Berger and Luckmann 1966), and on the media's 'framing' of reality, as addressed below. This convergence has been supported by experimental research on how the media may perform a 'priming' of **priming** the audience-public as to which issues are the decisive ones in assessing political candidates (Iyengar and Kinder 1987). A similar direction for research is indicated by recent survey **second-level agenda-setting** studies of so-called second-level agenda-setting,

► hypothetico-deductive methodology of agenda-setting research – Chapter 15, p. 262

which affects the audience perception of various detailed attributes of issues, candidates, and so forth (McCombs *et al.* 2000).

Campaigns

Given the embedding of modern media in complex and distributed social systems, it is hardly surprising that they should be employed, and studied, as planned means of communication and coordination. In this capacity, media are vehicles of 'campaigns' to inform, persuade, or mobilize a mass public. Especially in view of the market-driven nature of most contemporary economies, it is equally unsurprising that most communication campaigns are of a commercial nature, and have been theorized accordingly (for an overview see Windahl *et al.* 1992) – following early influential work on media as propaganda means of propaganda during wartime (Hov-

land *et al.* 1953). Recently, ethical and social accountability have become more important ethical and social accountability ingredients of how corporations and other organizations present themselves in public. Campaign studies thus have more general implications for the understanding of social communication processes. As conducted in several media and over time, campaigns may also be understood in discursive terms as instances of 'intertextuality.'

In their overview, Rogers and Storey (1987: 821) noted four common features of campaigns: '(1) a campaign intends to generate specific outcomes or effects (2) in a relatively large number of individuals, (3) usually within a specified period of time and (4) through an organized set of communication activities.' From this definition, the authors go on to elaborate several dimensions of a campaign. Figure 9.3 summarizes three main dimensions,

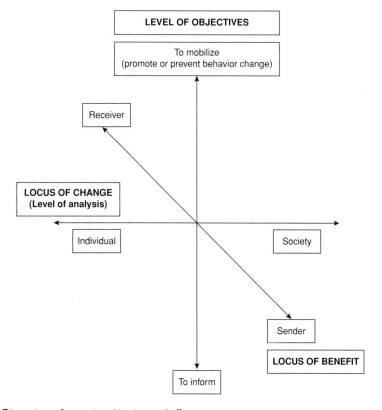

Figure 9.3 Dimensions of campaign objectives and effects
Source: Rogers and Storey 1987: 823. With permission of Sage Publications Ltd.

each of which are continua, not dichotomous categories.

First, the objectives of a campaign may be more or less ambitious, from informing or persuading, to mobilizing the audience to act in a particular way. Importantly, the aim may be either to promote or to prevent a change of behavior, in the latter case, for example, maintaining the audience's preference for a commercial brand. Media planners need to differentiate, then, between communications which are designed to introduce, maintain, or reposition a product or an idea.

promoting or
preventing
change

Second, the campaign may be designed to effect changes at the individual, organizational, institutional, or social levels. Although the concrete recipients of information will be individuals, the communication effort may be focused on whole segments of a population, such as smokers or car owners (by tobacco and car manufacturers, environmental interest groups, or health authorities). Partly for this reason, communication campaigns – and research about them – also need to take into account the place of interpersonal communication among these individuals' sources of information. The dimension of change is also where the empirical focus of a campaign study is specified.

Third, campaigns may be distinguished in terms of their primary beneficiary. The prototypical campaign may be the one illustrated in Figure 9.3, with an individual receiver and an institutional sender, who is likely to benefit. It is important, however, to note varieties also of this prototype. While commercial advertising is on behalf of the advertiser, the communication is also, arguably, of some informational and economic value to consumers. And, whereas a health campaign is designed to prevent, for instance, employees or the general public from suffering as patients, at the systemic level it is likely to save money for corporations and healthcare systems.

Because of their diversity and complexity, campaigns have been studied by means of various methodologies – surveys, experiments, focus groups, and so on. These approaches can each tap different moments of impact, which do not always constitute a logical sequence but which may complement each other in assessing

a particular campaign. An additional consideration, for media planners as well as researchers, is what might happen in the absence of a campaign – a question which normally cannot be addressed in any clear-cut, experimental design, but calls for indirect evidence. Advertising professionals and researchers tend to recognize that it is 'almost always impossible to estimate the impact of advertising on sales volume' (cited in Schudson 1984: 17). Even though it can be difficult, then, to document the marginal value of both advertising and public-service campaigns, it still may be necessary for an advertiser, interest group, or government agency to maintain a presence in the social field of attention that is made up by the media.

Campaign research shares its focus on the several media and moments of communication with studies of intertextuality,◄ even if their theories and methodologies differ substantially. A point of convergence is the sort of 'planned intertextuality' that is characteristic of much current media marketing, from the merchandising of fictional characters across several media, artefacts, and theme parks, to the rediscovery and recirculation of figures such as the Batman (Pearson and Uricchio 1990). One exemplary intertextual study, which also addressed the economic aspects of the James Bond figure since the 1950s, is Bennett and Woollacott (1987).

Knowledge gaps

Compared to diffusion research, which, to a degree, has examined inequalities in the availability of different media, research on 'knowledge gaps' has stressed the extent to which such inequalities may be cumulated, over time and in conjunction with other forms of social inequality. Furthermore, this tradition has emphasized that the point may not be the material availability of the technologies, but their discursive accessibility – their perceived relevance as resources for civic life and daily living.◄ An implicit premise of much public

► intertextuality – Chapter 11, p. 186

► availability vs. accessibility – see p. 140

debate on the media, and of many media practitioners, is that information and communication technologies make information and
aesthetic experience much more accessible than
at any earlier point in history. In response to
that premise, the knowledge-gap hypothesis
asserts that the flow of information in society
via the media tends to widen, rather than close,
the gaps between the information-rich and
information-poor (Tichenor *et al.* 1970).

Like other research on cumulative and long-
term effects, knowledge-gap surveys tend to
produce suggestive rather than conclusive evidence. This is due, in part, to pre-existing
inequalities in the distribution of informational
and cultural resources between different social
segments, of which the media are only one
source. However, by examining public knowledge of specific issues and events which
received extensive media coverage during a
particular period, the original group of
researchers concluded that better-educated
people were better able to the assimilate the
information (Tichenor *et al.* 1970; Donohue
et al. 1987; for experimental evidence see
Grabe *et al.* 2000).

The same researchers did note that the
media may work to close gaps under conditions
of social conflict, when public information
becomes more urgent, relevant, and hence
learnable (Donohue *et al.* 1975). Other studies
have gone on to counter the general hypothesis, suggesting that audiences' levels of interest
may be more important for their recall than
their level of prior knowledge (Genova and
Greenberg 1979). It has also been argued that
each medium works in specific ways, so that,
for instance, television, which reaches a higher
proportion of the population than print media,
and whose formats do not privilege the well
educated, might work as a leveler of knowledge
(Neuman 1976). Of course, any further assessment of such knowledge-leveling would have to
take into account the types of television systems
and presses being compared.

In view of previous studies, also of recall of
media content in the shorter term, the contribution of the media to knowledge gaps in
society remains a plausible hypothesis. More
recent work has suggested links between know-

ledge gaps and other aspects of audiences' cognitive orientations, such as a disaffection with
politcs (Fredin *et al.* 1994). Overviews of the
literature conclude that media appear not to be
closing or narrowing gaps (Gaziano 1997;
Viswanath and Finnegan 1996). Returning to
the widespread assumption that media can
serve as vehicles of democracy, at least in the
formal sense of making information universally
available, one can note that knowledge gaps do
seem to persist in diverse areas of economic,
political, and cultural activity. To be sure, such
conclusions are themselves premised on an
'educated' definition of information and knowledge, which may depreciate other forms of
cognition and competence. Nevertheless, explicit and operational knowledge regarding
politics and economy must be considered central social resources, as suggested most recently
by debates addressing a 'digital divide' in an   **digital divide**
information or network society.

Framing

The concept of 'frame' suggests that an item of
information, whether arising from media, from
other sources, or from direct perception, is
invested with meaning only once it is placed in
a context of other information. In framing
certain items of information, we simultaneously
bracket these from potentially endless masses
of information. Compared to studies of recall
and knowledge gaps, the focus is shifted away
from information as discrete entities, and
toward the complex and socially specific worldviews that audiences hold. Compared to
'agendas,' which may be understood as a temporary set of priorities, 'frames' amount to
more permanent dispositions of a social or   **social and**
mental variety. As such, frames are of special   **mental frames**
interest for understanding the media–society
nexus, but correspondingly difficult to operationalize in empirical research.

Perhaps for this reason, studies of framing
have rather diverse sources, and have produced
some strange bedfellows. In an overview of
previous research, Scheufele (1999) noted the
contributions of both experimental social psychology, particularly Heider's (1958) classic
attribution theory, and of qualitative micro-

levels of
interest and
knowledge

sociology in the form of Goffman's (1974) frame analysis. In certain respects, work relying on concepts of framing has begun to bridge both such theories and the qualitative–quantitative divide. In one exemplary study that employed depth interviewing, surveys, content analysis, as well as experiments, Neuman *et al.* (1992) showed how audiences would rely on frames which were derived largely from personal experience in order to make sense of the news – interpretive frames that differed from those offered by the news media. This is consistent with qualitative reception studies which **super-themes** have found that audiences employ 'super-themes' in order to establish meaningful links between the worlds of news and of everyday life (Jensen 1988, 1998).

One further potential of the concept of frames (and of agenda-setting) is that it enables **production and reception as framing** a more detailed comparison of media production and reception. On the one hand, journalists and other media professionals are constantly engaged in framing content, and in anticipating how they may be interpreted (e.g., Ettema and Whitney 1994; Gans 1957). On the other hand, media audiences necessarily employ interpretive frames that are generated and reformulated over time, with reference to media as well as other sources (Gamson 1992; Graber 1984). Presumably, audiences in their turn are also aware that both news professionals and other sources have a stake in the dissemination of particular perspectives, which can be resisted. In this regard, framing research has theoretical affinities with Hall's (1973b) seminal work on processes of encoding and decoding, including oppositional frames of interpretation.◄

Scheufele (1999) makes the additional point that agenda-setting and framing may represent different, but interrelated phenomenal aspects of media impact. 'While the process of issue selection or agenda-setting by mass media . . . needs to be a conscious one, framing is based on subtle nuances in wording and syntax and therefore . . . most likely [has] unintentional effects, or at least effects that are hard to predict and control by journalists' (p. 19).

▶ oppositional frames – Chapter 10, p. 162

Extending this line of argument, it is natural to conclude that processes of agenda-setting and of framing will be interdependent, and that such more or less conscious and planned aspects of the audience response will require complementary methodologies. In a comparative perspective, framing has introduced another important differentiation in the notion of effects, since 'framing influences *how* audiences think about issues' (p. 19), just as agenda-setting influences *what* issues to think about. **how to think about issues**

Cultivation theory

This section begins to enter 'an area where there is much theory and speculation but little firm evidence of confirmed relationships between the mass media and matters of values, beliefs, opinions and social attitudes' (McQuail 2000: 459). Whereas both findings and theoretical models from the research traditions reviewed so far have certainly been contested, the possibility of empirically studying the relatively more short-term effects of media is rarely challenged. When it comes to the contributions of media to long-term and unplanned social change (or stability), it has proven considerably more difficult to conceptualize and operationalize 'effects.'

The difficulties are of at least two different kinds. On the one hand, media evidently contribute to the socialization of individuals – but in exceedingly complex ways. On the other hand, media enter into an interchange also with all other social institutions, with current events, and with the cultural practices of the public at large. The final sections of this chapter review issues regarding the study of 'socialization' and 'institutionalization' via the media. First, this section examines one of the most extensively studied theories of how media may cultivate people's worldviews – an approach which is situated in the borderlands between individual and systemic effects of media. It is the cradle-to-grave socialization of everybody (Americans) through media (television) which has been the focus of cultivation research.

The key assumption of the cultivation **cultivation** hypothesis is that television has taken on such **hypothesis** a central place in modern American culture that it constitutes a 'symbolic environment' in and of itself. As such, it competes with, distorts, and, to a degree, substitutes the reality of personal experience, as informed by other media and interpersonal sources as well (e.g., Gerbner and Gross 1976). The methodology designed to test the hypothesis has been a combination of survey and content analysis, comparing the representation of social reality on television (not least violence, crime, and other 'risks') with viewers' awareness of and attitudes towards such concerns. The conclusion of the original group of researchers, with George Gerbner as the seminal figure, is that such a cultivation of knowledge and attitudes does occur. Consequently, 'heavy' viewers are more likely to produce 'the television answer' to questions, for example, about risks to them personally, but also about issues such as ethnicity, gender, or poverty. While debated, the approach has continued to attract interest, and to recruit researchers to study diverse aspects of cultivation, but documenting rather mixed evidence (Shanahan and Morgan 1999).

In certain respects comparable to agenda-setting research, cultivation research goes beyond any simple stimulus–response model, both by noting the cumulative nature of the impact, and by studying it within a carefully articulated theoretical and methodological framework. Moreover, the cultivation studies were originally conceived as part of a holistic 'cultural indicators' research program. The purpose was, from a critical position, to document how the media, being the central modern means of cultural expression, maintain and reinforce the social status quo. The research program also included analyses of television as a social institution, although most efforts have gone into the combined audience-content studies.

cultural indicators

Criticism, especially of the more specific cultivation hypothesis, has been severe, and has taken two forms. First, cultivation researchers have been attacked on their own turf through a re-analysis of the original datasets. In brief, critics have argued that, if sufficiently stringent statistical controls are introduced, the cultivation hypothesis cannot be upheld (Hirsch 1980, 1981). In addition, humanistic researchers have questioned the entire theoretical rationale

behind the datasets, arguing that the approach neglects television as 'texts' and their variable interpretation by viewers (Newcomb 1978). Second, a number of studies in countries other than the U.S.A. have not found support for the hypothesis.◄ Beyond surveys, some of this research has included a component of experimental methodologies, which came to be applied to cultivation studies during the 1990s (Shrum 1996).

A third issue is whether the focus of cultivation research on television has been misguided, theoretically and historically. Not only are the media institutionally and discursively interconnected, as suggested by, for instance, campaign and intertextual studies, but 'the age of television' is probably coming to an end, at least in the present technological and institutional definition of 'television.' If the theory of aggregate cultivation stands and falls with one medium, it is not sufficiently general to guide media research. If, in addition, one takes into account the ongoing extension and redefinition of the field of media and *communication* research, it may be an appropriate occasion to reconsider the status and explanatory value of categories such as 'cultivation,' 'socialization,' and 'effects.'

SOCIALIZATION BY MEDIA

One response to the difficulty of ascertaining the long-term effects of media on humans and their societies in empirical studies has been a return, for at least a decade, to more 'grand' theories of culture and society. This reorientation has entailed a return, as well, to the disciplinary sources of the interdisciplinary field of media studies. For example, history has come to the fore in the shape of 'medium theory' (Meyrowitz 1994), and sociology has been the source of theories of modernity, as increasingly applied to media (e.g., Thompson 1995). A common aim has been to relocate media on a more inclusive and, hence, more illuminating conceptual map, as witnessed also by the convergence of different research traditions.

▶ cultivation research in non-U.S. contexts – see Chapter 13, p. 229

lifestyle and
life forms

Grand theory, however, does not preclude empirical testing. An example is research on 'lifestyle' and, more broadly, the 'life forms' of different social classes. Here, the seminal work of Bourdieu (1977; 1984 [1979]) on 'habitus,' 'cultural capital,' and their role in different social fields of practice has been especially influential. In addition, however, lifestyle research has become a somewhat surprising meeting-place of critical social theorists and marketing professionals. The two groups are brought together by an ambition of understanding cultural forms, values, and styles, not just as individual expressions but as the manifestation of embodied, persistent, yet contested social structures. This perspective follows, in part, from the 'rediscovery' of agency and reflexivity in current social theory, including Bourdieu and Giddens, following the conflicted coexistence of structural functionalism and Marxism in the post-1945 period. During this same period, marketing practitioners have been challenged to refine their tools of prediction and planning, so as to gain a marginal advantage in the market. The means to this end, increasingly, has become a better understanding of how consumers make sense of products, and of themselves.

Box 9.1 presents an example of lifestyle research as it relates to media issues. Figure 9.4 further illustrates the methodology of the study in question and its way of displaying findings, both of which are characteristic of lifestyle studies.

Research on living conditions, lifestyles, and media uses offer one indication that any inclusive terminology referring to 'effects' in general may be a misnomer. Instead, 'socialization' via the technological media is an inescapable condition of modernity – just as the medieval church and early modern technologies (e.g., the printing press) were constitutive elements of the social order of *their* epochs.

An issue currently facing media and communication research is how to specify the elements and processes of socialization, including the distinction between primary and secondary socialization. Most basically perhaps, secondary socialization, as associated with other social institutions than the family (schools, interest organizations, media), has arguably

primary and
secondary
socialization

taken on greater importance overall, and has become more formative of the individual over time. This appears to be the case, both in quantitative terms of the time spent on formal education as well as mediated leisure, and in qualitative terms of where decisive social standards and knowledges come from (e.g., Beck *et al.* 1994). Moreover, the line between primary and secondary socialization has become blurred, if it was ever clear. The fact that the primary socialization of children and youth, as traditionally performed in the family, is increasingly interdependent with media, has been suggested in a wide variety of earlier research – from the Payne Fund studies of the the 1930s (Jowett *et al.* 1996), via Himmelweit *et al.* (1958) and Schramm *et al.* (1961), to Livingstone and Bovill (2001), and Rosengren and Windahl (1989). For centuries, print media have been agents of socialization that originate in the public sphere, and take effect in the private sphere (e.g., Drotner 1988), whereas the electronic media have come to redefine the very meaning of 'private' and 'public' (e.g., Meyrowitz 1985).

At the level of individual socialization, then, the modern media are bound to inform how people think and act, even if the evidence will normally be indirect or circumstantial. At the level of social institutions as well, the media are one of the inevitable structural conditions under which social interaction takes place.

INSTITUTIONALIZATION BY MEDIA

In view of the comparative recency of 'the media,' research on their structural or systemic interdependence with other social institutions may be premature, and might be left for future historical studies. However, the field of media and communication research has had an ambition both of explaining current institutional arrangements and of projecting the future of media. This has been due, in part, to the strategic placement of the media sector from the perspective of commercial and political interests.

While each of the traditions reviewed in this chapter have produced some evidence for infer-

▶ Payne Fund studies – Chapter 10, p. 158

ANALYSIS BOX 9.1 CORRESPONDENCE ANALYSIS OF LIVING CONDITIONS, LIFESTYLES AND MEDIA USE

A common method of relating people's material living conditions with their interpretation of those conditions, as informed partly by the media, is, first, to ask them a complex set of survey questions regarding fundamental values (in addition to sociodemographic information). Next, both the value statements and other items of information are analyzed and compared through a multivariate technique of 'correspondence analysis' (Greenacre 1993).◄ In essence, the analysis is able to establish the degree to which different answers are correlated, and the pattern of these correlations, as they apply to both single respondents and entire samples. The analysis thus results in a set of interrelated values, which may be understood in terms of a 'worldview' that affects people's political and cultural orientations and actions. Because the approach normally relies on large samples, lifestyle research can produce robust findings. And, because it is longitudinal, tracking shifts and trends◄ in the public's tastes and preferences, it might be said to offer an approximation of the *Zeitgeist* – the cultural universe of an age.

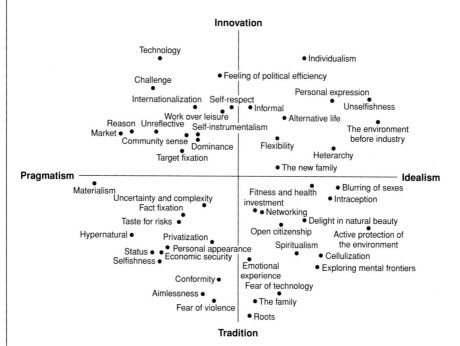

Figure 9.4 Chart of values among Danish respondents according to Research Institute on Social Change principles (1995)

Source: Schrøder 1999: 57. Reprinted with permission of Sage Publications, Ltd.

In technical terms, the different values constitute points in a multidimensional mathematical space, but are normally represented in a two-dimensional model, as in Figure 9.4. The two

► correspondence analysis and multivariate statistics – Chapter 13, p. 232

► trend studies – Chapter 13, p. 218

cont.

cont.

dimensions of this model correspond to those two underlying principles which are found, in the given analysis, to be the most important in accounting for the particular pattern. Figure 9.4 exemplifies a configuration of values with reference to a study of everyday life and political participation in Denmark, conducted in 1994 to 1995 (Schrøder 1999). The two dimensions (which recur in comparable studies) indicate different degrees of orientation toward a 'modern' (innovative) or a 'traditional' life form, and toward an idealist or a pragmatic view of life. Furthermore, these patterns are more or less analogous to a differential distribution in society of what Bourdieu (1984 [1979]) terms economic and cultural capital (typically operationalized as money and education).

economic and cultural capital

Specific configurations suggest different conceptions of self and society, and will vary across cultural contexts as well as historical time. At issue along these dimensions are classic questions of economy, politics, technology, and ethics. In the present context, the social field of media use may be broken down along similar dimensions, so that media preferences correlate with fundamental values as well as sociodemographics. One example from the European context arises from the different types of broadcasters. While the original public service monopoly in the Danish study has its stronghold in the upper, 'northern' part of the chart, especially its 'eastern' segment, a preference for the commercial broadcasters in the past ten to fifteen years is associated with the values clustered in the lower, 'southern' part, especially its 'western' segment.

It should be noted that details of both the theory and operationalization of 'lifestyle' vary. Compared to Bourdieu's (1984 [1979]: 128–129) social-systemic chart of values, other studies have taken a more individualist conception of lifestyles (e.g., Inglehart 1990; Inglehart et al. 1996), or have adapted the concept for marketing purposes. (For a philosophical elaboration of the category of 'taste,' see Douglas 1996.) In addition to the U.S.A., the general approach has been employed in several European countries, in part as an instrument of planning television programming in the face-off between commercial and public service broadcasters. However, comparable studies have also suggested that the explanatory principles may hold, in a modified form, in a cross-cultural perspective for studying both modern and modernizing cultures (e.g., Schwartz and Bilsky 1990).

taste

ences about the long-term significance of media, four additional types of research have focused more specifically on the long term. In each case, a late 'stage' of the interaction between media and audiences in a social context is taken up in order to examine and typologize changes in how people go about their business, in public or in private, as a result of the presence of media.

• *Natural experiments on the introduction of media.* Particularly in the case of television (which developed after the formation of media research as a field), the first introduction of the medium into a community or culture has provided opportunities to assess any changes in, for example, time use and the role of different media as reference points, for instance, for play or conversation. Because of the explicit before-after situation, such issues have lent themselves to study in natural experiments.◄

• *Public events.* A distinctive role of modern media is to present events and issues to the public for some form of collective consideration. In doing so, they necessarily shape the content and form of the available coverage, but they may also influence the course and final outcome of events in other social institutions and sectors. Whereas agenda-setting research has focused on the part played by media in articulating political issues, studies have also examined how other types of social activity unfold and are resolved, in part, through media intervention. In contrast to the common lament that media create 'pseudo-events' (Boorstin 1961), several important qualitative studies have shown how media both frame and enable public participation in major social events – such as national ceremonies, political scandals,

► natural experiments – Chapter 13, p. 226

and international sports – by making them into 'media events' (e.g., Dayan and Katz 1992; G. E. Lang and Lang 1981; K. Lang and Lang 1953).

media events

- *Institutional practices.* Media occupy a special position among other modern institutions because they constitute a common arena – a cultural forum (Newcomb and Hirsch 1984) – in which the standards, priorities, and instruments of other institutions may be negotiated and coordinated. Again, this is especially evident in political life, which is subject to a specific public accountability, and which, further, is increasingly carried on *in* the media. (In comparison, private *economic* enterprise is, to a large extent, exempt from detailed public control; and high forms of *culture* are still commonly conducted and covered in separate arenas or media.) Accordingly, much research has examined how the media may be changing the practices of political democracy, and has worried, not least, that the actual participation and influence of the audience-public is being diminished (for an overview see Blumler and Gurevitch 1995). In addition to structural and normative-theoretical analyses,◀ research in this area has often relied on either content or discourse analysis to identify the shortening of political dialogue into 'sound bites' (Hallin 1992) or historical shifts in how prime ministers communicate via television (Seymour-Ure 1989).

cultural forum

- *Cultural formations.* In the most general sense, the technological media can contribute to making certain cultural practices and worldviews dominant. On the one hand, a critical strand of research has, for example, made the general argument that a 'media logic' (Altheide

and Snow 1979) has been invading other social contexts. Other critical studies have employed content studies to document systematic omissions in news coverage, which might fragment public understanding and legitimate the social status quo (Group 1976, 1980). On the other hand, more recent work has argued for the democratizing potential of popular culture, as carried by the media. As is suggested, for instance, by Hobson's (1982) study of television fans demanding 'their' soap back on the screen, the media may encourage audiences to insist on their cultural preferences and pleasures. In addition, 'medium theory'◀ is among current attempts in research to capture the specificity of modern culture. Much further research is needed, not only on each 'stage' of communicative impact, but perhaps even more on the nature of their interrelations.

In conclusion, this chapter has reviewed the main traditions of quantitative audience research, with special reference to their theoretical premises and methodological procedures. The review has suggested, first, the complementarity of the several stages and levels investigated in previous studies. Second, it has indicated that quantitative audience research has been particularly successful in accounting for the 'early' stages of mediated communication, such as the diffusion and consumption of each medium, and for 'mid-term' effects, such as recall and agenda-setting. Qualitative reception studies, as reviewed in the next chapter, have proven able to supplement quantitative research by focusing on other stages of the communicative process, including the everyday contexts of media use and some of the long-term cultural implications of media.

▶ normative media theories – Chapter 16, p. 276   ▶ medium theory – Chapter 2, p. 16

10 Media reception

Qualitative traditions

Klaus Bruhn Jensen

- a presentation of the *established 'milestones'* of quantitative audience research together with *seminal qualitative contributions*
- a *review* of the main forms of *reception analysis*
- an assessment of recent work in *'media ethnography'*
- a discussion of the place of *media discourses* and other relevant forms of evidence in further reception studies.

MILESTONES REVISITED

One way of encapsulating the field of study has been through systematics and models, such as Figure 9.1, which identified some main stages of the communicative process and the traditions of audience research associated with each. Another means of taking stock has been to identify historical 'milestone' studies which, arguably, defined appropriate ways of conceptualizing and examining the various stages of communication empirically. By way of introduction, and of joining qualitative and quantitative traditions, this chapter revisits some of the milestones of audience studies, as received – and sometimes overlooked – in later research.

Figure 10.1 lays out fourteen milestones, as defined by Lowery and DeFleur (1995) through three editions of their widely circulated text-book, and adds a number of candidates from outside the dominant paradigm (Webster and Phalen 1997). While any such listing is essentially contestable, the aim is to consider a broader range of defining contributions to the field in order to explain, and promote, the process of convergence between research traditions.

In the case of the established 'Milestones I,' it may be especially apparent that several contributions were shaped by their historical and social context – from war to political or public demand for evidence on media effects.◄ At the same time, it is appropriate to note also that the primarily European, qualitative, and critical perspectives under 'Milestones II' bear witness to the impact both of war and of the cultural revolution of the 1960s on scientific ideas and practice. In both cases, these circumstances do not disqualify either findings or approaches, but serve as a necessary context for assessing the specific explanatory value of the entries and for considering their commensurability in future theory development.

To begin a review of the milestones, a few caveats are in order. First, the listing considers only publications post-1900. As indicated in Chapter 2, before the earliest origins of 'media' research, most thinking on communication and its effects had been conducted in rhetorical and aesthetic traditions of inquiry,◄ from

---

► social origins of media research – Chapter 16

► rhetorical and aesthetic effects – Chapter 2

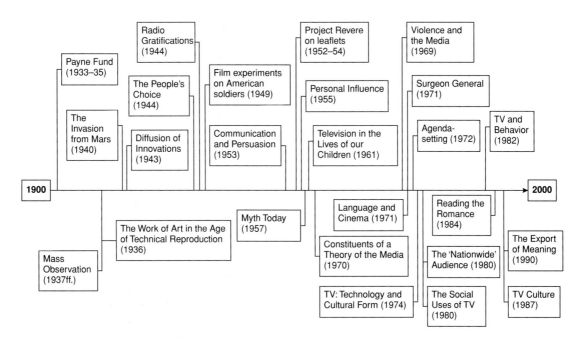

Figure 10.1 Milestones of media and communication research

Aristotle's rhetoric, via Kantian aesthetics and nineteenth-century hermeneutics, to semiotics – all of which continue to inform contemporary communication theory. Second, the revised set of milestones remains limited by the fact that so much of the field's activities – as currently institutionalized internationally through journals, conferences, and translation – originates in either the U.S.A. or Europe. Third, a particular difficulty in selecting additional candidates for 'milestones' is that much previous research, while bearing on reception and effects, has not always examined audiences empirically. The difficult dividing line between 'text' and 'audience' is a product both of the rudimentary theorization of content that has characterized quantitative research traditions, and of the quite recent turn to empirical audience studies among humanistic scholars.

The two groups of 'milestone' studies are noted here for the record, and as a point of departure for theory development and empirical collaboration. Having largely developed in separate spheres of research, much of their potential for convergence simply remains to be

assessed. In addition to the affinities between the Payne Fund and Mass Observation research programs, the diffusion of innovations, for example, and medium theory, as anticipated by Walter Benjamin, would seem to share a number of research questions regarding the social consequences of new technological resources for communication. Further, agenda-setting studies overlap conceptually with much qualitative research on the socially and culturally specific frames of decoding media texts (e.g., Gamson 1992; Liebes and Katz 1990). Cantril *et al.*'s (1940) contribution, employing a liberal mix of qualitative and quantitative methodologies, was an early indication of what may be gained if research programs as well as individual scholars reconsider their theoretical and methodological predilections.

The rest of this chapter reviews the contribution of qualitative research traditions. While being late starters in terms of empirical studies, these traditions have produced new insight into at least three different moments of the process of mediated communication. Reviewed in the following section, the three foci of reception

MILESTONES I

- *Payne Fund.* This first substantial media research program in the U.S.A. examined the effects of movies on children and youth through a variety of content, survey, experimental, and other methodologies, arising from and feeding into contemporary concerns and debates (for an overview see Jowett *et al.* 1996).
- *The Invasion from Mars.* Cantril *et al.*'s (1940) multimethod study of how the American public responded to Orson Welles's radio dramatization of *War of the Worlds* suggested, among other things, how to combine qualitative and quantitative methodologies for a concrete research purpose. (For a critical reassessment, see Rosengren *et al.* 1978).
- *Diffusion of Innovations.* Following 1940s studies on the adoption of agricultural techniques, diffusion research expanded to address other kinds of innovations and their place in processes of social change, including media and their dissemination of information (for an overview see Rogers 1962).
- *The People's Choice.* In certain respects the inaugural work of U.S. communication research, this study focused on the place of media in political democracy, relying on panels and other state-of-the-art survey methodology (Lazarsfeld *et al.* 1944). At least in its reception history, the study has often been taken to suggest that media reinforce rather than change people's positions, and that, overall, media serve democracy (for a classic critique see Gitlin 1978).
- *Radio Gratifications.* Among the contributions of the first generation of U.S. researchers were some of the seminal ideas which were later developed as uses- and-gratifications research. Apart from its inherent quality, the work by Herzog (1944) was unusual in considering the 'feminine' genre of daytime radio serials.

MILESTONES II

- *Mass Observation.* The mass observation studies in the U.K., from the 1930s onward, documented various aspects of social life, including cinema-going and other media use (for an overview see Richards and Sheridan 1987). Comparable in certain respects to the American Payne Fund studies, the studies represent an early proposal for ways of examining the place of media in an increasingly urbanized and modernized everyday, providing valuable insights into processes of media consumption and reception.
- *The Work of Art in the Age of Technical Reproduction.* This title (sometimes translated as 'mechanical' reproduction) covers Walter Benjamin's (1977 [1936]) early attempt to capture what was distinctively new about the cultural forms being disseminated by the technological media. Taking 'medium theory' (see Chapter 2) to the level of concrete textual analysis, this work identified the loss of 'aura' in media, compared to traditional artworks, as a key factor which may be said to overdetermine the interpretations and effects of specific media items. Like other critical social theory of the 1930s to 1940s (e.g., Adorno and Horkheimer 1977 [1944]), Benjamin's work was, in part, an intellectual response to the conditions of fascism – a response that was different in kind from the U.S. milestones participating in the war effort, but which engaged related social circumstances.
- *Myth Today.* Following the rebuilding of postwar Europe, new societies (and research institutions) were taking shape, in which the definition of 'culture' was again at issue, not only in debates over 'Americanization' (see Webster 1988), but with reference to popular culture as such. One of the undoubted, early influences on research in this area was Barthes's (1973 [1957]) work on the modern 'mythologies' disseminated in large part by the media.

cont.

cont.

MILESTONES I

- *Film experiments on American soldiers.* As part of U.S. involvement in World War II, a series of experimental studies were conducted of Frank Capra's *Why We Fight* films, asking to what extent they might not only provide information, but also shape attitudes (Hovland *et al.* 1949).
- *Communication and Persuasion.* Departing from this and other earlier experimental research, and from theories of the selective influence of media on individuals, the Yale Program of Research on Communication and Attitude Change proposed to generalize the perspective, but were able to document especially short-term changes (Hovland *et al.* 1953).
- *Personal Influence.* Elaborating, in part, the (serendipitous) finding of Lazarsfeld *et al.* (1944), that technological media work, not least, by being mediated further in interpersonal communication by opinion leaders, Katz and Lazarsfeld (1955) helped to establish the two-step flow of communication as a generally influential model.
- *Project Revere.* At the height of the Cold War, and with the Korean War still being fought, this project (1952–1954) was funded by the U.S. military to explore the use of airborne leaflets to replace, or circumvent, other channels (for an overview see DeFleur and Larsen 1987).
- *Television in the Lives of our Children.* This first major study of TV's effects on children in the U.S.A. was characterized partly by the diversity of issues (and methodologies) included, such as social differences, partly by a renewed uses-and-gratifications perspective (Schramm *et al.* 1961). A close (and earlier) European cousin, not recognized among the 'milestones' of Lowery and DeFleur (1995) (but duly noted in the preface to Schramm *et al.*), is Himmelweit *et al.* (1958).
- *Mass Media and Violence.* Growing out of U.S. government and public concern over

MILESTONES II

Particularly his essay, 'Myth Today,' introducing the distinction between denotation and connotation into analyses of how meanings are offered by media, and taken by audiences, has shaped the understanding among the first generation of European media researchers of how media come to take effect on both individuals and societies.

- *Constituents of a Theory of the Media.* Enzensberger's (1972 [1970]) article returned to Bertolt Brecht's point regarding radio in the 1930s, that the equipment for receiving could as well be used for sending messages and participating in a society-wide dialogue, thus suggesting the critical potential of media (as well as the generally constitutive role of media in social systems). In addition to the period-specific ideological message, Enzensberger's theoretical message anticipated, to a degree, later work on the 'active' audience and on computer media.
- *Language and Cinema.* The title of one of the film theorist, Christian Metz's (1974 [1968]), main publications suggests the 'milestone' nature of theoretical work during the 1960s to 1970s on the specific verbal and visual vehicles of communication, and on their mode of address to the audience. While other contributors to semiotics and discourse analysis could have been singled out (see Chapter 2), the key question of whether cinema and other non-alphabetic communication might be studied as 'languages' (and if not, then how), has been given perhaps its most elaborate articulation in Metz and other European semiotics and structuralism.
- *TV: Technology and Cultural Form.* Williams's (1974) definition of broadcasting (radio and TV) as a 'flow,' rather than autonomous works, identified a key aspect of much mediated communication, and anticipated certain features of computer media (see also Ellis 1982).

cont.

cont.

MILESTONES I

social unrest during the 1960s, this report (Lange *et al.* 1969) summarized earlier research, and presented new evidence and conclusions, particularly on the impact of violence in entertainment programs, relying on approaches which have been extended in cultivation research (see Chapter 9).

Surgeon General. Traditionally referred to as the 'Surgeon General's Report on Television and Social Behavior,' the relevant work (Comstock *et al.* 1971) is, in fact, a large collection of studies which informed such a report. In one sense following up on the previous 'milestone' on a grand scale, the issues and findings of this publication were, again, oriented toward specific policy issues.

Agenda-setting. Since the 1970s, agenda-setting research has been influential in restating one key question of audience research as that of setting (political) agendas, rather than changing attitudes and voting preferences (McCombs and Shaw 1972).

Television and Behavior. Explicitly following up on the 'Surgeon General's Report,' this last 'milestone' took stock of research ten years later, but included a wider range of issues than televised violence (Pearl *et al.* 1982). While no new research was commissioned, the integrative reviews of the massive research output since 1971 provided an authoritative overview, with special reference to television.

MILESTONES II

• *The 'Nationwide' Audience.* Drawing on both discourse analysis and gratifications research, Morley's (1980) was the first major publication to bring together social-scientific and humanistic perspectives on the audience in a qualitative empirical design regarding television news reception, and is reviewed below, together with the following entries.

• *The Social Uses of Television.* In the same year, Lull (1980) went beyond the individual focus of gratifications research to study the social uses of television in the family, also relying on qualitative methodology and re-emphasizing the explanatory value of microsociological traditions.

• *Reading the Romance.* At the same juncture, Radway (1984) provided an integrated study of the institutions, texts, and audiences of the print romance genre, of which especially the audience portion and its fieldwork established a model for further research.

• *Television Culture.* As part of a textbook on television studies, Fiske (1987) presented an operational approach to intertextuality that went beyond immanent analyses of either the narrative structures or modes of address in media texts (see Chapter 11).

• *The Export of Meaning.* Finally, this qualitative study of the experience of the *Dallas* television series among different cultural and ethnic groups (Liebes and Katz 1990) was one of the first attempts to conduct comparative reception research (see also Jensen 1998).

studies so far have been the everyday contexts of media use; the decodings or textual interpretations of media content; and audience uses of this content as a resource in other social contexts. The following section discusses recent proposals for a more inclusive research position of 'media ethnography.' Finally, the chapter returns to the importance of 'texts' or 'discourses' for the study of reception, and of mediated communication as such, and describes the relevance of various discourses and other types of evidence for future reception studies.

MOMENTS OF INTERPRETATION

Contexts of media use

As previewed in Figure 9.1, one focus of qualitative audience studies has been the context of use, particularly in the household. Whereas

media use in the household

predecessors included, for instance, the British mass observation studies (Richards and Sheridan 1987) and innovative techniques for videotaping television viewers (Bechtel *et al.* 1972), the seminal recent study was by Lull (1980). Referring to the social-scientific undercurrents of symbolic interactionism, ethnomethodology, and other 'microsociology,'◄ and relying on prolonged observation of television viewing in American households, the study developed a typology of the 'social' uses of television. On the one hand, it went beyond the individual focus of uses and gratifications research; on the other, it restricted the definition of 'social' uses to the private family setting, and did not address the uses of media for political, economic, or cultural purposes in the public

structural and relational uses of television

domain. The typology noted, first, the 'structural' uses of television in generating an environment or atmosphere, and in regulating, for instance, bedtime. Second, the study documented several 'relational' or interactional uses of television, for example, for facilitating or avoiding contact between parents and children, or between spouses.

A number of later studies have examined how media are integrated with and, to a degree, modify other everyday activities (for overviews see Alasuutari 1999; Moores 1993). Despite

media use in public places

research considering media use in public places (Lemish 1982), in quasi-public settings such as a prison (Lindlof 1987), or in peer groups (Buckingham 1993), the focus has remained on households and the dynamics of family life, with some reference to other social contexts (e.g., Gauntlett and Hill 1999). This is explained, in part, by the simultaneous focus of reception studies on the television medium, which has lent itself as a convenient reference point in exploring the family as a natural social and cultural unit.

Radio, while generally under-researched (presumably in part because its heyday came before the institutionalization of media research, which coincided with the rise of television), has received less attention, but has been studied, for instance, in a historical perspective (e.g., Moores 1988; Scannell 1988). Similarly,

print media, from newspapers and magazines to books, which are eminently transportable and adaptable to different social circumstances, apparently have rarely been studied on site. Although this may be due to the seemingly solitary experience of reading, print media have a range of social uses, from seeking to ward off contact, and for individual readers to establish a separate social sphere in which they can be 'absent' though present (see Radway 1984). The film medium, again, has been studied more as an artform than as a social practice, although recent work has begun to cover the decoding of films as well as the social acts of going to movies, and sharing the experience with others (e.g., Barker and Brooks 1998; Gomery 1992; Stacey 1994; Stokes and Maltby 1999a,b). The reception literature also includes studies of how several media enter into the everyday lives of individuals and families (e.g., Barnhurst and Wartella 1998; Jordan 1992).

As with work by Lull (1988b, 1991), some studies have employed participating observation to produce a fine-grained analysis of media in a particular locale (e.g., Gillespie 1995). However, in a number of cases, the main method of data collection has, in fact, been qualitative interviewing, whether individually or in groups (e.g., Gray 1992; Hobson 1980; Morley 1986). While relevant, interview methodologies depend on the respondents' introspection, retrospection, and verbal recollection of their actions, which necessarily reproduce events from a current perspective. Particularly in research on the concrete contexts of media use, a weighing of the strengths of observation and interviewing, depending on the purpose of study, is thus of the essence.

Observational studies, in their turn, have rarely been able to capture audience members' response to particular narratives and other content elements. Indeed, Lull (1980) did not explicitly relate the different social uses of television, and their relative prominence, to different genres. One tendency of reception studies so far, then, has been for observational studies to detail the everyday lives of people around media, and for interview studies to probe their interpretations of specific media discourses.

► microsociology – Chapter 3, p. 56

It should be added that computer media pose new challenges as well as opportunities for research on the contexts of media use. Over and above the various physical locales in which new media are used – households, cybercafés, peer settings – the computer tends to blur the distinction between medium and context◀ (Jensen 2000a). Compared to, for instance, television, where social interaction occurs around, and with reference to, the medium as a distinct technological and cultural artefact, social interaction is itself constitutive of many genres of computer media, from chat to online gaming. If the interaction ends, the medium simply becomes inoperative. In this regard, interactivity is not merely an offer, but a requirement and a condition of computer-mediated communication. This condition entails a different conceptualization and operationalization of 'media' and 'contexts,' and may lead research to explore, in more concrete terms, the performative aspects of media use.

Decodings

Research on 'decodings' – audience interpretations of specific media discourses – accounts for the bulk of previous qualitative reception studies (for an overview see Livingstone 1998). Much of the tradition originates from a culturalist and, in part, literary interest in how meaning is produced and shared.◀ This interest led to a dual strategy of including the actual media 'works' in the empirical research designs, but also of insisting that cultural artefacts can have several meanings, and may have no one core meaning.

On the one hand, then, decoding studies have retained a number of concepts and analytical procedures from literary and other cultural theory. On the other hand, these empirical audience-cum-content studies◀ have recuperated and redeveloped those parts of the literary tradition which have underscored the rela-

tive indeterminacy of meaning, particularly the work of reception aesthetics (for an overview see Eco 1987; Holub 1984). Other important sources of inspiration have been critical social theory noting the volatility of the dominant ideology, as presented also in media (Parkin 1971). Uses and gratifications studies served, simultaneously, as a main object of criticism because of their preference for functionalism and quantification as a source of ideas.

This somewhat eclectic mixture of social-scientific and humanistic notions was brought together in the cultural studies tradition.◀ Taking his lead from the work of Hall (1973b) on the less than perfect correspondence between media practitioners' encoding of texts and the audience decodings, Morley (1980) presented the seminal study on socially specific forms of decoding news. Employing a focus-group methodology, Morley documented a range of decodings of what was assumed to be the (ideologically) 'preferred' meaning of the news discourse – from an accepting or 'dominant' reading, via a 'negotiated,' to an 'oppositional' reading. Across the focus groups in the study, these readings appeared correlated with the social positions and organizational involvement of the participants. For example, the combination of low social status with shop-floor union involvement seemed to produce some of the most explicitly oppositional readings (p. 141). In this regard, audiences themselves could be said to perform a 'hermeneutics of suspicion.'◀

In retrospect, it was perhaps the general perspective, of linking the social-systemic and the discursive-interpretive attributes of the respondents, which most influenced later work in the area. Morley (1981) himself was among the first to criticize the somewhat undifferentiated conception of decoding as the (degree of) reproduction of a dominant ideology. He also called for the study of, for example, basic comprehension and derived pleasure as aspects of news reception (see also Lewis 1983, 1985). Later studies have noted several varieties of opposi-

dominant, negotiated, and oppositional readings of a textually 'preferred' meaning

---

▶ context as locale and as virtual space – Chapter 11, p. 189

▶ culturalist or ritual model of communication – Chapter 1, p. 8

▶ audience-cum-content studies – p. 167

▶ cultural studies – Chapter 2, p. 39

▶ hermeneutics of suspicion – Chapter 2, p. 22

tional decodings, and have uncovered the difficulties that even comparatively sophisticated
audiences may have in deconstructing the
implied message of a media text (Hacker *et al.*
1991).

class, gender, ethnicity, age

   In keeping with its critical-political agenda,
Morley's (1980) study paid special attention to
the class status of the different respondent
groups. Later studies have examined gender
and class on a more or less equal footing, and
have sometimes explored the interrelation
between these factors in concrete media experience (e.g., Press 1991; Schlesinger *et al.* 1992).
In comparison, ethnicity and cultural difference, for a time, received relatively less attention as backgrounds to decoding and media
use, but figure more prominently in recent
studies (e.g., Duke 2000; J. Lewis 1991;
Parameswaran 1999). Age has rarely been at
the center of reception and audience studies (or
of theory development in other media research)
(but see, e.g., Jensen 1990; Press 1991; Tulloch
1989). This is in spite of the familiar concern
especially with the potentially adverse effects of
media on children and youth, which has
informed, and helped to fund, many audience
studies.

   Television, again, has been the preferred
medium of decoding studies. The centrality of
the medium in the field as such may have been
reinforced in research on decoding by two
developments in the social context of research.
For one thing, deregulation, which made more,
especially commercial, formats available, particularly in the European setting, raised questions concerning the international 'cultivation'
of local cultures and audiences, which might be
addressed by in-depth audience studies. For
another thing, almost simultaneously, research
seemed to rediscover 'pleasure' as a legitimate
topic of research – with television seemingly
offering the bulk of pleasurable experience for
the public at large. (At the same time, research
on television audiences – whether qualitative or
quantitative – has been limited, in part, by its
reliance primarily on verbal methodologies to
study both pleasure and knowledge arising
from an audiovisual medium.)

   While the news genre has remained central
in reception studies (for an overview see Jensen

1998), it was joined, not least, by melodrama,
including daytime as well as prime-time soaps,
as a favorite area of analysis. The cross-cultural
work of Liebes and Katz (1990) was one influential contribution, and was complemented by
several other theoretical and methodological
perspectives (e.g., Brown 1994; Livingstone
1990; Seiter *et al.* 1989). Despite their focus on
television, previous reception studies have also
taken up a variety of other media and genres,
for example:

television, news, melodrama: main areas of reception analysis

- *books* (e.g., Parameswaran 1999; Radway 1984)
- *films* (e.g., Cooper 1999; Stacey 1994)
- *magazines* (e.g., Hermes 1995; Lutz and Collins 1993)
- *advertising* (e.g., Mick and Buhl 1992; Schrøder 1997).

Media in social contexts of action

The third moment or stage of reception – the
embedding and use of media in other social
contexts of action – has produced a smaller and
more heterogeneous body of research. This may
be due partly to the difficulty of operationalizing a vast empirical domain, partly to a widespread tendency to conceptualize media as
means of representation, rather than as resources for action.

media as representation or resource

   At issue in this third group of reception
studies is how, concretely, media are integrated
into both everyday life and various institutionalized practices. In this regard, reception
studies have a significant overlap with the issues
addressed as 'agenda-setting' and 'framing,'◄
and, to a degree, 'lifestyles.' Moreover, qualitative methodologies enable reception studies to
address the stages of 'socialization' and 'institutionalization' in ways which complement the
more common survey approaches in those
areas.◄ When it comes to documenting the
contextual processes of interpreting, adapting,
and integrating media into social life, a qualitative, case-based approach may be preferable

► agenda-setting and framing – Chapter 9

► socialization and institutionalization – Chapter 9

to a variable-based approach in this 'late' stage of media impact.◄

Three examples may indicate the nature of this third form of reception research:

1 In her study of *print romances*, Radway (1984) showed not only that readers produce a variety of textual interpretations, but also that they conceive of romances as a resource for living. Romances could be seen to provide indirect advice on married life, and to allow their women readers to insist on their 'own' time for reading. Compared to decoding studies, the focus here is shifted away from the text, even
the act of   its interpretation, toward the act of reading and
reading   its place in a wider field of social action.

2 In a study of American *television news*, I examined news stories from the viewers' perspective, less as accounts than as resources for both political participation and daily living (Jensen 1986). The findings suggested that viewers may approach the news genre with a divided, ambiguous consciousness. While arguing for the dutiful importance of the daily act of news-viewing, the respondents bore witness to the limited instrumental value of the information for voting or any other practical purpose.

3 Studies of *fan cultures* have shown how the 'foundational' texts of fandom (a feature film, the music of a band) become the object of – a resource for – a range of cultural practices (see Jenkins 1992; L. Lewis 1991). In addition to giving rise to active and creative decodings, partly within groups of readers, the texts are processed and redeveloped by fans in their own writing, music, or audiovisual production.

What unites these previous studies is their emphasis on the contextual and socially interested nature of all (media) interpretation. Media reception is embedded in a historical and cultural context, as well as in the immediate context of media use; audiences' interpretations, equally, are prefigured by their 'interests,' their frames, lifestyles, and trajectories of

socialization. Whereas most reception (and other media) studies have left behind any Kantian notion of the disinterested contemplation of reality through aesthetic artefacts,◄ the text is often given theoretical priority. One contribution of qualitative reception studies has been to elucidate how media are recruited by audiences as resources to inform and enhance their actions in a variety of social contexts. Media use is a specific, reflexive form of social action (Jensen 1995).

MEDIA 'ETHNOGRAPHY'?

A recent development, designed in part to re-emphasize the status of media use as a form of social action, has taken place under the heading of 'ethnography,' particularly since the mid-1980s. Most generally, the widespread invocation of ethnography may be understood as one way of coming to terms with the convergence between social-scientific and humanistic inspirations – a development that has been especially noticeable in audience studies. It may be necessary to carve out a specific research position, or niche, which would recognize that media use is simultaneously a discursive and a performative phenomenon. It may also be necessary still to oppose this position, as a camp, to the dominant paradigm (Webster and Phalen 1997). In fact, an earlier edition of Lowery and DeFleur (1995) had credited the coming of a 'meaning paradigm,' which, curiously, was remarginalized in the third edition of the 'milestones' (for discussion see Jensen 2000b).

Radway (1988: 363), early on, pinpointed the underlying problem, and suggested a cure for both textual reification and the decontextualized study of audiences:

> Audiences . . . are set in relation to a single set of isolated texts which qualify already as categorically distinct objects. No matter how extensive the effort to dissolve the boundaries of the textual object or the audience, most recent studies of reception, including my own, continue to begin with the 'factual' existence of a particular kind of

► case-based and variable-based research – Chapter 15, p. 256

► aesthetic contemplation – Chapter 2, p. 27

text which is understood to be received by some set of individuals. Such studies perpetuate, then, the notion of a circuit neatly bounded and therefore identifiable, locatable, and open to observation.

Her less reifying alternative was classic ethnographic fieldwork about all the cultural as well as other social practices of an entire community, covering work and leisure:

> a collaborative project that would begin within the already defined boundaries of a politically constituted municipality and attempt to map there the complex, collective production of 'popular culture' across the terrain of everyday life . . . a project that would take as its object of study the range of practices engaged in by individuals within a single heterogeneous community as they elaborate their own form of popular culture through the realms of leisure and then articulate those practices to others engaged in during their working lives.
>
> (Radway 1988: 368)

Ang went several steps further in assuming that an ethnographic methodology represents a radically different epistemology from both qualitative reception studies and quantitative forms of audience research. Indeed, she discredited both positions, since, to Ang, the scientific act of categorization is, in itself, an act of violence committed against the public and the everyday:

> From this [ethnographic] perspective, 'television audience' is a nonsensical category, for there is only the dispersed, indefinitely proliferating chain of situations in which television audiencehood is practised and experienced – together making up the diffuse and fragmentary social world of actual audiences.
>
> (Ang 1991: 164)

It seems difficult to specify how then, concretely, empirical studies should proceed. Nevertheless, as a theoretical point, this line of argument became influential. Also Radway's (1988) less

radical position implied a considerable complication of the task at hand – of the relevant objects of analysis, of the collaborative research activity, and of the eventual interpretation of 'findings,' if that term is appropriate.

The record suggests that media studies have rarely delivered the sort of projects outlined by Radway (1988). Instead, there has been a tendency, in some publications, to describe assorted qualitative methodologies, including interviewing, as the equivalent of 'ethnography.' This, in turn, has provoked severe criticism, particularly of the standards of data collection, analysis, and reporting, summed up in the conclusion that ' "ethnography" has become an abused buzz-word in our field' (Lull 1988a: 242).

In response, some researchers (e.g., Drotner 1994, 1996) have attempted to reclaim the 'ethnographic' terminology, not only by acknowledging the technical requirements of the approach (e.g., Schensul and LeCompte 1999), but by suggesting that it has its own methodological, and perhaps epistemological, specificity. Accordingly, 'ethnography' might imply a focus, not on media, but on the social practices and gendered identities which media help to constitute across contexts. Still, it remains unclear how this approach would differ from the qualitative methodologies and constructivist epistemologies of most other reception studies. More seriously, perhaps, 'media ethnography' appears to be a contradiction in terms – it assumes that an inclusive and holistic study of a social group or context could, nevertheless, legitimately predefine media use as its empirical focus. If, in addition, 'media ethnography' would propose to cover all moments of the communicative process, not just audiences, it would become a misnomer for a whole variety of multimethod approaches◄ to the practice of mediated communication as such, already in the literature (e.g., Aron 1998; Gay *et al.* 1997).

One problem with media studies with an 'ethnographic' ambition is that they tend to confuse the inevitably limited field of empirical

---

► multimethod research – Chapter 15, p. 272

inquiry with the more inclusive domain of theoretical interest. Hence, it becomes hard to justify *what not to study* – a dilemma that may lead either to 'data death' or unwarranted claims about doing 'ethnography.'

A more pertinent alternative is to describe reception analysis and so-called 'ethnographic' approaches as complementary varieties of multimethod, as well as multidisciplinary, approaches to the audience experience and use of media. Figure 10.2 indicates two such prototypical varieties. Both varieties take the media as their methodological focus, but emphasize either the distinctive uses of a medium or genre by several audience groups in different contexts, or the uses of several media and genres by one specific social group across contexts, who thus define their culture and lifestyle, in part, with reference to media. In both cases, the reception and social uses of media are, to varying degrees, analyzed and interpreted with reference to the wider historical and social context embedding both media and audiences. The methodological orientation of media research must be toward the specific difference media make in society, even while its theoretical frame of reference is the entire social system which shapes, and is shaped by, media. In methodological terms, meaning flows from media to society; in theoretical terms, it flows from society to media.

The upshot of debates since the 1980s on 'ethnography' is that anthropology still has much to offer to the media field in the way of theory and methodology. The abiding relevance of the anthropological tradition has been indicated, as well, by studies of media audiences originating outside the media field as such (e.g., Dickey 1993; Lutz and Collins 1993). However, the comprehensive, classic technique of ethnography, as applied to research in both premodern and modern settings, seems less suited for the specific purposes of media and communication research. Other recent contributions to media and cultural research have suggested additional, alternative ways of conceptualizing audiences with reference to their exercise of agency in different social and historical contexts (e.g., Abercrombie and Longhurst 1998; Butsch 2000; Lembo 2000).

MEDIA DISCOURSES AS RECEIVED

A recurring issue – in 'ethnographic' studies, in reception analysis, but also in quantitative

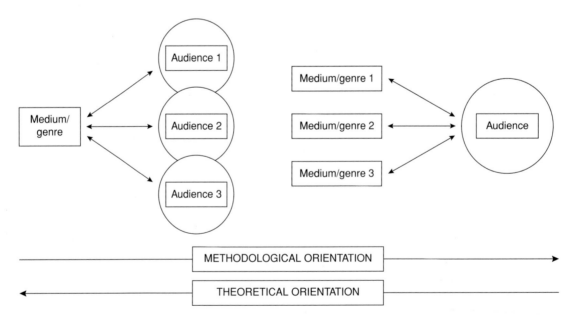

Figure 10.2 Two varieties of reception study

research traditions – has been the status of the text in audience studies. A specific aim of qualitative audience research has been to develop a conceptual understanding of the media–audience nexus that would not privilege one or the other side. From the outset, reception analysis was motivated by a concern that, in humanistic textual studies, the media text was being reified, or at least privileged as a source of evidence. In response, some researchers have worried that reception studies would themselves lose sight altogether of the texts which are, in fact, received and interpreted (e.g., Brunsdon 1989). In this regard, reception studies might repeat the mistakes of some quantitative audience research that has neglected the specific cultural forms in which 'content' is communicated. Such worries were reinforced by influential theoretical contributions which asserted that (media) texts are 'empty,' waiting only to be filled with meaning by audiences acting as 'interpretive communities' (Fish 1979). Other interventions seemed to over-

polysemy   emphasize, in semiotic terms, the 'polysemy' of media texts – the variability and indeterminacy of the meanings which audiences might attribute to them (Fiske 1987). Eco (1976: 150) even suggested the possibility of 'semiotic guerilla warfare,' as performed by media audiences as well as analysts.

The challenge for reception analysis has been, and remains, to perform *audience-cum-content analysis* – comparative studies of media discourses and their interpretation and uses by specific audiences. This section presents some of the key concepts which have been developed for this purpose, before describing the several types of 'texts' which are relevant for empirical reception studies.

The audience in the text

An important legacy of literary theory for empirical reception analysis has been the notion of the reader, or 'audience in the text.' While resembling earlier notions of 'point of view' in literary genres, the argument is that texts literally anticipate and 'inscribe' readers into their structures. The idea was developed into analytical tools within several research traditions –

by 1960s structuralism and semiotics on how texts 'enunciate' their message to readers,◀ and perhaps most influentially by German reception aesthetics. Jauss (1982) advanced the concept of a 'horizon of expectations'◀ within which a reader encounters a text; Iser (1976) identified the structural 'blanks' of a text as an invitation for the reader to complete it, and later outlined a more inclusive 'literary anthropology' (Iser 1989). Eco (1987), further, contributed a distinction between texts which, respectively, are 'open' or 'closed' in terms of their range of potential decodings. Eco also distinguished between 'interpreting' a text along the lines suggested by its structural attributes, and 'using' a text for the reader's more or less idiosyncratic purposes – perhaps reading it against the grain.

reception aesthetics

textual blanks

open and closed texts

interpretations or uses of texts

Whereas literary reception studies have remained largely preoccupied with the texts themselves, a number of its concepts have thus proven applicable to the study of media audiences. Here, the concept of 'interpretive communities' has been particularly influential. A helpful redevelopment for empirical purposes has been Potter and Wetherell's (1987) more operational notion of 'interpretive repertoires.' Rather than assuming that individuals 'belong' to delimited communities, the latter notion suggests that they rely on a range of repertoires, depending on their own background, the text at hand, as well as the particular context of media use. Accordingly, data analysis can trace the semantic relations, metaphors, and other interpretive procedures that different respondents employ (e.g., Jensen 1990). As such, 'interpretive repertoires' avoid the implication either that 'interpretive communities' are monolithic formations, or that they are constituted entirely *ad hoc*, for each text and reading, or by analogy to fan groups. One promising perspective for audience research, and for media studies generally, is that such interpretive categories may be mapped onto sociodemographic categories, thus enabling research to explore both discursively and socially specific aspects of mediated communication.

interpretive communities and repertoires

interpretive and socio-demographic categories

▶ enunciation and semiotic analysis – Chapter 8, p. 128

▶ horizon of expectations – Chapter 2, p. 22

The texts in front of the audience

Compared to literary theory which, by tradition, has centered on the singular artwork, studies of the technological media must address a broader variety of content structures and formats. Moreover, some of these formats emerge from the activity of the audience – most notably in 'interactive' media, but also, for example, in the case of radio and television flow whose elements are selected and combined by audiences. While Chapters 7 and 8 cover the analysis of various types of media contents, it is appropriate to review the full range of media discourses in the present context of reception studies.

Decoding studies in particular, as noted above, have often examined television programs and other delimited media texts. In addition, one may identify the following discursive types:

• *Discursive elements.* Although reception analysis has most commonly involved entire narratives or news stories, some studies have traced the presence of particular themes or images in the media and their reproduction by audiences (e.g., Philo 1990). In this regard, reception research was preceded, and influenced, by studies of recall and comprehension◀ (e.g., Findahl 1985).

• *Singular texts.* Media content is perhaps best understood generally as 'discourse'◀ – the social uses of language and other signs. Still, individual texts may call for a sustained reception analysis, because of their presumed impact on the public (e.g., Cantril *et al.* 1940), or, for instance, because of their prolonged presence as part of 'international' media culture (e.g., Gripsrud 1995).

• *Genres.* A central aim of qualitative reception studies so far has been to explore the audience response to generic attributes across individual media texts. The purpose is to describe in depth what may be certain general interpretive procedures that audiences apply to major genres. The ambition is found in much decoding research, and has been developed explicitly in studies of media as social resources (e.g., Jensen 1986; Radway 1984). Another reason for focusing on genres is that their mode of address, in addition to their form and content, anticipates particular uses of media in social contexts.

• *Media.* Compared to their 'contents,' other aspects of media – as means of structuring daily routines, or as physical artefacts – have received relatively less attention. Recently, such aspects have been addressed, for example, in work on the place of media within everyday life (for an overview see Silverstone 1994).

• *Flow.* Like genre, flow (Williams 1974) in television, radio, and some other media, presents itself as a strategically important level of analysis. Flow captures a distinctive feature of an important portion of all mediated communication. Yet studies so far have been comparatively few in qualitative research. One reason presumably is the difficulty of operationalizing the audience experience across several content elements, across channels, and over time. Jensen (1994) outlined an approach to documenting the concrete movements of viewers across the several channel flows of a television universe, what could be described as a super flow. This record lent itself to an analysis of the resulting viewer flow with reference, for example, to (narrative) structure and recurring themes. A model of the several types of flow involved in media use is given in Figure 10.3.

• *Hypertexts.* The discursive structures of computer media are comparable, in certain respects, to the flow of broadcasting. A challenge for current reception studies is to move beyond the manifest structures and narratives of virtual environments, to the experiences and uses by their 'audiences.'

• *Media environments.* At the most general level of analysis, the media constitute a cultural environment of sorts. Its complexity may seem forbidding, but its interrelations remain a central topic for further research. One option is studies of the 'life history' of a news item (Deacon *et al.* 1999) (or fictional event, or

▶ recall studies – Chapter 9, p. 144

▶ two definitions of discourse – Chapter 7, p. 106

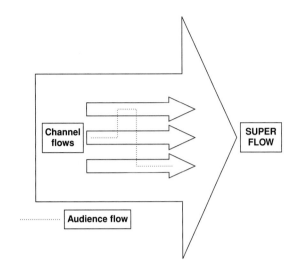

Figure 10.3 Three flows of media use

resonant metaphor) with reference to the contexts in which it is interpreted and appropriated by audiences. So far, intertextual studies have gone some way toward defining issues and relevant approaches (Bennett and Woollacott 1987; Gay *et al.* 1997; Pearson and Uricchio 1990).◄ At the same time, the blurring of the divisions between 'text' and 'context' in virtual environments is adding to the complexity and challenge.

THE MEDIA–AUDIENCE–SOCIETY NEXUS

The trajectory of reception analysis may be summarized with reference to the concrete empirical materials being examined within different varieties of audience research. What distinguishes reception studies, perhaps most of all, in comparison with the majority of the quantitative milestones, is their focus simultaneously on media discourses and 'audience discourses,' i.e., the statements and actions of audiences which serve as evidence about their experiences and uses of media. The conceptualization and operationalization of these various discourses call for specification in further qualitative empirical research.

► intertextuality and hypertext – Chapter 11, p. 187

In an overview of different varieties of communication theory, Meyrowitz (1993) distinguished between conceptions of media as either conduits, languages, or environments. The dual status of media as channels and texts – within transmission and ritual models of communication – is increasingly recognized as part of the convergence between social-scientific and humanistic communication studies. A better understanding of media, in addition, as a cultural environment is one of the next challenges also for reception studies. In meeting this challenge, research will have to consider at least three types of analytical objects:

1   This chapter has referred to the contents of media as *discourses* – vehicles of potential meaning which are actualized and enacted by audiences in various everyday circumstances. The interpretive actualization of media content has also been approached in reception studies as discourses, as analyzed through various qualitative methodologies.

2   Media are *material artefacts* – they have a very concrete presence in the space, time, and interpersonal relations of everyday life. Chapter 1 noted that the modern media may be defined as institutions-to-think-with. However, in their local and distributed settings, they are also objects-to-think-with (Lévi-Strauss 1991 [1962]). Relatively little attention has been given so far to this aspect of reception, even though some studies have examined the place of television sets in the family context in different cultural settings (Lull 1988b) and the representation of television as a new element of social space during its introduction (Spigel 1992). The Walkman (Gay *et al.* 1997) and mobile computing devices also suggest themselves as objects of research in this perspective.

3   Media, finally, serve to constitute *practices*. Not only are media received and applied within particular social and cultural environments, but they help to constitute those environments, as also suggested by 'medium theory' (Chapter 2). The media enter into specific forms of interaction, association, and community – in variable contexts from the local to the global level. At this point, media research blends into other forms of social and cultural research.

In conclusion, audiences, broadly speaking, constitute a strategic nexus between media and their social contexts. It is for this reason, in part, that audience research has been a central ingredient of media and communication studies, both its quantitative and, more recently, its qualitative variants. Other types of research have gone on to address the wider cultural and historical contexts of mediated communication. These research traditions are the topics of the next two chapters.

Contexts, cultures and computers
The cultural contexts of mediated communication

Klaus Bruhn Jensen

- a definition of key concepts relating media to the rest of society: *context* and *culture*
- a review of studies concerning different levels of the cultural contexts of media: *national, local, intercultural,* and *global*
- an examination of research on *subcultures, cultural imperialism,* and *postcolonialism*
- a special section on *computer media* and *virtual cultures.*

FROM MEDIA, TO COMMUNICATION, TO CULTURES

Contextualization and recontextualization

An important characteristic of 'media' research around 2000 has been a renewed emphasis on the practices of 'communication.' Information and communication technologies support multiple forms of interaction at many levels of the social structure. Neither theoretically nor empirically can the media be understood as separate entities – add-ons or plug-ins. Instead, the technological media are necessary infrastructural resources in maintaining and structuring modern societies (Giddens 1984; Thompson 1995).

contexts as nexus between media, cultures, and societies The moments of mutual constitution, concrete interchange, and structuration may be examined as 'contexts.' These contexts extend far beyond the stages of impact of media on particular audiences.

This chapter reviews selected research traditions which examine the geographical, technological, institutional, and discursive contexts of media – linkages between media and the rest of the social structure (even while not all of

these traditions may subscribe to the metatheoretical perspective of 'contexts'). The logic of the presentation proceeds from subcultures and communities, via the nation-state as an essentially modern context that has depended upon print and broadcast technologies, to issues of transnationalism and postcolonialism. The final section examines the (still unresolved) status of those social 'contexts' which are established in and of computer media networks. While frequently at odds with each other in their theoretical and political assumptions, each tradition has been important in addressing questions of media impact and determination, not at the level of individual response or socialization, but at the institutional and cultural levels of social structuration.

From the classic question regarding the relative determination of social life by either economic, political, or cultural factors, follows the question of how the media, in particular, affect and respond to their various social contexts. The distinctive, reflexive function of media may be summed up, first, as 'contextualization.' The media relate issues and events in the world to each other, and allow audiences to contemplate and, perhaps, act upon such relations – with reference to a specific level or domain of social reality. Second, the media can serve to 'recontextualize' those events and issues, indicating a range of alternative perspectives and interpretations.◀ With reference to science and politics, Rorty (1991: 94) has suggested that these institutions perform recontextualizations which range 'from instinctive revision of intentions through routine calculation toward revolutionary science and politics.' Although Rorty's position tends to go overboard in its postmodernist textualization of social issues (for a critique, see Jensen 1995: 180–185), the concept of recontextualization is helpful if understood as a concrete activity which both media practitioners and audiences perform. By contextualizing and recontextualizing the world, the media participate centrally in maintaining society, and they do so across a variety of settings where culture is constructed and contested.

Culture and cultures

In order to anticipate some familiar problems in defining 'culture,' a few conceptual distinctions are in order. Kroeber and Kluckhohn (1952), by the 1950s, noted as many as 164 definitions of culture. Similar problems affect communication studies, where Anderson (1996) has recently identified 249 definitions or theories of communication.

   An inclusive, modern definition of culture dates from the Romantic age, specifically the work of Johann Gottfried Herder (*Ideas for a Philosophy of the History of Mankind*, 1784). Culture is that which simultaneously unites and differentiates human beings (for an overview see Williams 1983). On the one hand, all human beings share culture – the ability to experience, reproduce, and communicate meaning. On the other hand, humans can be distinguished according to the specific meanings with which they align themselves – the cultural formations to which they 'belong' or 'owe' their identity and solidarity. While cultures, in the plural, have traditionally been coupled with

164 definitions of culture; 249 definitions of communication

culture unites and differentiates all humans

particular social groups in a geographical location, cultures have increasingly come to extend across space and time with the advent of writing, print, and later communication technologies. It is this extension, not least, which requires a careful account of the several cultural contexts in which media are embedded.

   An additional complication for media studies arises from the distinction between culture as product and culture as process (e.g., Jensen 1986: ch. 5). Culture has been understood, on the one hand, as specific 'products' of human creativity, as 'containers' of culture, and often as privileged means of insight for social elites. With industrialization came a wider range of cultural products which addressed a mass public, as well. On the other hand, culture has been examined as a 'process' which pervades all of mental and social life. This process was traditionally understood literally as the cultivation of the human spirit either in a secular or a religious sense. Increasingly, reference has also been made to the mundane and lived reality of the everyday.

   This last reorientation has itself been associated with the industrialization of culture during the modern period. Industrialization has entailed a recognition – for commercial as well as ideal purposes – of popular, informal, and emergent cultural practices alongside the long-established and institutionalized arts. In academia, the reorientation has entailed a relativization, in part, of both classical learning and Western civilization. The relativization has been performed over the past century most notably by anthropology and, more recently, by research fields on (mass) communication and (popular) culture. The distinction between culture as product and as process has nevertheless been persistent, and has challenged research to conceptualize and operationalize communication in ways that capture both sides of the cultural coin of exchange.

   One implication for media and communication research has been a call, increasingly, to study not only *cultures* – in the plural – but cultural contexts of multiple kinds. These contexts lend themselves to empirical studies as moments of interchange between media and other social and cultural circumstances, broadly speaking. Accordingly, in the following reviews,

culture as product and process

▶ (re)contextualization and mediated reflexivity – time-in and time-out culture, Chapter 1, p. 5

both media production and reception are taken up as sites of the production of culture. Key issues in research as well as public debate – concerning cultural identity or authenticity, and concerning economic and political power – have frequently revolved around the production–reception nexus. What is the relative determining influence of, for example, transnational economic infrastructures, national political regulation, and local cultural formations in the experience and use of mediated communication? For each of the contexts below, a broad working definition of culture is adopted: culture has been studied as reproduced, cumulated, and sedimented structures of meaning. The empirical questions have centered on the specific contributions the media make to cultural production and social interaction.

NATIONS AS MODERN CULTURES

The rise of the technological media coincides historically with the rise of the nation-state. Far from one being a singular determinant of the other, both developments entered into a third, long-term shift toward the modernization◄ of social relations in most areas of human activity. Whereas the scope and current status of modernization remain debated, its main ingredients are fairly well established (for an overview see Thompson 1995):

- *industrialization and capitalization* of the material economy, along with a growing division and rationalization of labor, leading into variable phases of market competition, incorporation, imperialism, and conglomeration;
- *democratization and bureaucratization* of the institutions and practices of political representation and government;
- *secularization* of the cultural forms of expression, including the securing of niches for non- or anti-religious reflexivity, and the recognition of popular alternatives or complements to the fine arts.

From the outset, the modern nation-state was a contested entity. It developed, moreover,

in conjunction with other nations as part of a new world economic system, centered in Western Europe. Wallerstein (1974: 348) has made the point that, in contrast to previous such systems – for example, in the Middle East or China – this international system of capitalist production and trade did not grow into an empire in any traditional sense. The modern world system, taking shape from the sixteenth century to *c.* 1900, developed as an economic, not a political entity. Hence, it allowed for, and supported, not only a global division of labor, but the formation of political structures at the level of the nation-state (see also Wallerstein 1980, 1989).

In the domain of culture, nation-building was supported by arguments and narratives concerning the legitimacy of such arrangements, as widely disseminated by print media. The process of dissemination, in turn, was facilitated by the fact that these cultural artefacts could be distributed as commodities. More people – developing into a mass public – moved above the level of subsistence, and became able and willing to pay for mediated experiences.

culture as commodities

Anderson (1991) has offered the helpful notion of 'imagined communities' to characterize nations not only in terms of geography and constitutions, but as cultural and discursive formations. In one sense, all communities, from face-to-face to virtual interaction, are, to a degree, imagined (Jensen 2001). Anderson (1991), however, described in further detail the many forms of mediated communication which came to serve as means of symbolic control and repair within nations – from newspapers and novels, to museums, maps, and the census. Moreover, he noted the role of print technologies in stabilizing and enforcing national languages, over and above the sacred languages of scripture, and as means of collective self-definition.

imagined communities

The media did not only help to replace religious frames of reference with national ones, and to question the status of 'divine' rulers. The media also became unprecedented resources for redefining the future – for oneself and for society. If historical time and its subjects were no longer subordinated to a divine cosmology, then the future presented itself as an open field

► modernization – Chapter 3, p. 48

of action, both for individuals and for social interest groups. The future had to be made. It is this inherent openness which some theorists have identified as the essence of modernity (Berman 1982; Giddens 1991; Huyssen 1986), recognizing, as well, that openness is a source of existential uncertainty and perhaps ambivalence. It is this same openness which media have been called upon as institutions to interpret, with the nation as the new center of an imagined universe.

The history of the modern nation-state is, in large measure, a history of expansionism and warfare, as supported, in part, by media propaganda.◄ Also internally, the definition of what is a nation, and what should be the political and economic rights of citizens, has been subject to continuous controversy, carried on partly through media. In the European setting, Habermas (1989 [1962]) described the development of the classic public sphere.◄ The eighteenth-century press was instrumental in defining both citizenship and nationhood. (Habermas, interestingly, also noted the complementary role of interpersonal communication in clubs and coffee-houses.) Regarding the early history of the press, moreover, studies from both the U.S.A. and the U.K. have suggested that left-radical papers lost out in the economic competition and political conflicts that accompanied the establishment of the press (Curran and Seaton 1997; Schiller 1981). These conditions, arguably, resulted in less diverse national media systems also in a longer and current perspective.

Since the early 1990s, the formation of a renewed public sphere has been in progress, following the transition of Eastern European nations, and of nations within the former Soviet Union, to various liberal press systems. At this historical juncture, media, legislators, as well as audiences face many more technologies and a range of policy choices regarding public service and market-driven organizations (see, e.g., Kelly and Shepherd 1998; Sparks 1997). One consequence of the transition has been a heightened awareness, also in research, regarding sub-

merged national and cultural sentiments (which social science had largely failed to predict as forces behind 1989 and its aftermath (K.B. Jensen 1999: 427)). Another consequence has been publications which aim to document and recuperate earlier periods of these cultures, for example, of the Baltic nations before Soviet supremacy (Høyer et al. 1993).

During the twentieth century, broadcasting became a central reference point in the construction and maintenance of national culture. Radio, and later television, have depicted especially the official life of the nation. Broadcast schedules have also served, more instrumentally, to maintain cycles and rhythms of social life, from the twenty-four-hour cycle of the family to the seasonal ceremonies of the nation (sometimes understood as a 'family') (Scannell 1988; Scannell and Cardiff 1991).

In developing countries, nation-building has been a special concern for policy-makers as well as media practitioners. The diffusion of communication technologies◄ has commonly been perceived as a necessary condition for material progress and, more generally, modern life forms. A prototypical example was the 1975 to 1976 SITE experiment in India, where community television sets were introduced into 2330 largely rural villages. The purpose was to transmit especially educational and informational programs on agriculture, health, and family planning (for an overview see *Journal of Communication*, 29(4), 1979: 89–144). Beyond the concrete goals of enlightenment, an important structural effect of such projects has been to promote particular understandings of nationhood and citizenship.

It bears repeating that nation-states have developed in conjunction, as part of a transnational system. While later sections detail research traditions that have focused on transnational issues, it is useful here to distinguish the several flows of communication that reach audiences in their national context. Indeed, by far the majority of all mediated communication is still transmitted by national senders to national audiences. Figure 11.1 indicates three flows:

▶ propaganda studies – Chapter 10, p. 159

▶ public-sphere model – Chapter 1, p. 7

▶ diffusion of innovations – Chapter 9, p. 140

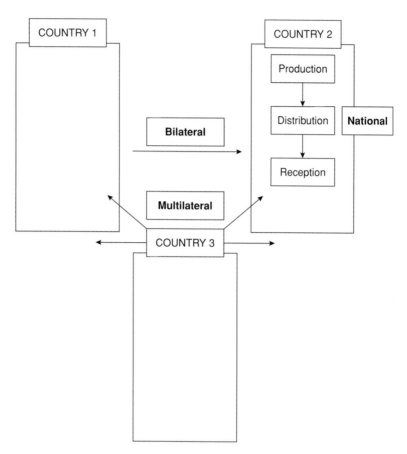

Figure 11.1 Three media flows in and between countries
Source: Sepstrup 1989; see also McQuail and Windahl 1993: 225

1 *National flow*, which refers to foreign or imported (over and above home-produced) contents that are adapted by distributors to the tastes and cultural background of the national market. Importantly, such adaptation includes not merely translation, but the recontextualization or 'domestication' of news items (Cohen *et al.* 1996), and the redevelopment of formats for fiction series and other entertainment (e.g., O'Donnell 1999; Silj 1988). In this respect, national media, from early newspapers and popular literature onwards, have always been transnational.

2 *Bilateral flow*, which covers direct, regular, and 'accidental' transmission to audiences in a neighboring and often culturally affiliated country.

3 *Multilateral flow*, which refers to explicitly international forms of communication, such as CNN and MTV, as well as many Internet services.

SUBCULTURES AND LOCALITIES

Below the national level of social organization, media studies have specifically addressed two types of 'communities of interest' – local or regional forms of culture and communication, and subcultures. In both cases, the implicit point of reference has tended to be the nation-

center and
periphery

state. The nation could be defined as a (metropolitan) center with an under-recognized periphery of self-reliant cultural formations. This center could also be understood as a historical form of social organization that has grown out of touch with its constituencies in terms of age, class, gender, and ethnicity. The nation might even be considered an obstacle to the full cultural realization of such local communities and lived constituencies.

Research interest in communities and subcultures dates back at least to early sociology. Tönnies (1974 [1887]) presented a distinction which has remained influential:

- *Gemeinschaft* – homogeneous, communitarian, and non-contractually governed social formations;
- *Gesellschaft* – heterogeneous, individualist, and contractual arrangements.

The two terms do not refer to distinct types of society, but to forms of social organization which, to varying degrees, characterize particular historical cases. In addition, the Chicago school sociological tradition◄ has been an important source of ideas for research on 'communities' since the early twentieth century.

The two prototypes also represent imagined forms of social organization. Since the Romantic age, modern societies and cultures have, from time to time, entertained the notion of returning to, or reintroducing elements of, *Gemeinschaft* in the modern context. The potentials and implications of local agency have continued to occupy social theory. In media studies, various community media, especially local radio and television, attracted renewed attention from the 1960s. This was due partly to new technological possibilities of production and distribution. However, research also seemed to be attracted by the democratizing and locally empowering potential of such communication (for an overview see Jankowski *et al.* 1992). In some cases, studies sought to develop this potential further through action research.◄

► Chicago School sociology – Chapter 3, p. 43

► action research – Chapter 16, p. 287

Studies of local and community media have primarily served to document what remains a significant level of social communication. In comparison, research on subcultures has been the more theoretically innovative tradition. Subcultural studies developed particularly from the 1970s, and examined primarily youth groups which had manifested themselves, through their cultural practices, from the 1950s (for an overview see Gelder and Thornton 1997). As the term suggests, these cultural formations could be seen as somehow subordinated to a national culture of sorts. In response, subcultures might express and gratify particular cultural preferences and lifestyles alongside the national provision. Alternatively, subcultures might, in a stronger sense, represent fullfledged social and cultural universes. As such, they would be separate from, and largely in opposition to, a perceived mainstream national culture, in part with reference to the political and economic interests underpinning the mainstream.

It is especially this last conception which subcultural research has defended and explored. A central object of analyis has been subcultural universes that are simultaneously local and transnational, being practiced in several different geographical locations and generating a sense of community and solidarity across national borders. Concretely, variants of rock-'n'roll have been a center-piece, not only of fan groups, but of international social movements of some scope, from anti-Vietnam War protests to Live Aid concerts. The actual cultural artefacts have generally come out of American or multinational media industries, but the common perception of members of these subcultures (and of many researchers) has been that the media are thus redefined and reappropriated for alternative purposes.

A particularly influential approach to subcultures has been associated with 'the Birmingham School' (Hall *et al.* 1980).◄ Beyond its fruitful combination of humanistic and social-scientific inspirations, the cultural studies tradition has been premised on the definition of culture as a constitutive ingredient of social

---

► Birmingham cultural studies – Chapter 2, p. 39

conflict and change. Rather than being secondary to, or derived from, economic or political matters, subcultural practices are an example of culture becoming a site of social struggle in its own right. To cite the title of an influential volume, the members of subcultures exercise 'resistance through rituals' (Hall and Jefferson 1975).

Certainly, resistant cultural practices can be more or less self-consciously and proactively social in their orientation. At least in some respects, membership of a subculture may not be categorically different from fandom. Critics such as Gitlin (1997) have described cultural studies researchers more broadly as disappointed revolutionaries who find it 'reassuring to detect "resistance" saturating the pores of everyday life' (p. 30). Furthermore, subcultural research has not been without its romantic and self-righteous streaks, re-emphasizing the authenticity and legitimacy of specific subcultures. Consequently, there has been a relative neglect of their position within the wider social structure. As noted by Middleton (1990: 161) with reference to music-oriented youth subcultures, studies have given less attention to 'the subcultures' relationships with their parent cultures, with the dominant culture and with other youth cultures.' Nevertheless, subcultural studies have been successful in conceptualizing and interpreting culture as a multiply contextual practice, thus extending Williams's (1975 [1958]) agenda for studying culture as 'a whole way of life.'

A special focus of subcultural research, not surprisingly, has been popular music. Postwar subcultures emerged as part of anti-authoritarian turns within the family as well as in educational, cultural, and other social institutions. The generalized revolt was symbolized and articulated in innovative rhythms and lyrics. One difficulty, however, has been to accommodate the analysis of music as – music. Middleton (1990), for one, argues that subcultural theory has tended to rely excessively and abstractly on the identification of homologies – structural similarities between the organization of, for instance, musical materials and the social interactions around the music, as in references to rock 'n' roll as 'screw and smash music' (p. 158).

analysis
through
homology

In fairness, music is one of the most underresearched aspects of mediated communication across the entire field. The resulting gap in theory and evidence is presumably due, at least in part, to the neglect of popular music by traditional disciplinary musicology. Compared to, for instance, literature departments, popular culture only very slowly seems to be making inroads into most departments of music. However, it is incumbent on the media field to develop more comprehensive theories of communication which incorporate the different vehicles and modalities of communication – verbal, visual, auditive – also in view of the massive presence of music in the current media environment as a whole.◄

BETWEEN CULTURES

Cultural imperialism

Given the role of culture, often in the guise of religion, throughout centuries of warfare and international conflict, it is hardly surprising that the modern media have been recruited for similar ends. Media research has been alert to the potential consequences, and to the possible role of research in documenting and counteracting abuses. To reformulate the military historian, Karl von Clausewitz, who concluded that war is a continuation of politics by different means, many communication studies have been motivated by a concern that the media might continue both politics and war by cultural means. Specifically, the media might serve to subordinate non-Western cultures in an extension of colonialism, which was officially being dismantled after 1945, and particularly from the 1960s.

Much work in this area of the media field may be summed up as a critique of 'cultural imperialism.' While the nuances of the research and debate are many (for an early overview see Tunstall 1977), the main thesis can be stated briefly. The Western media industries serve as the agents of a continued imperialism, as exercised most noticeably by the U.S.A. over developing nations, and made possible by the

► research on media and music – Chapter 8, p. 135

principles of an international capitalist economy. For one thing, the relevant technologies and professional competences have not been diffused sufficiently to allow for indigenous media production in most world settings. For another, comparatively cheap news and fiction which have already made a profit in their primary, Western markets can be marketed massively and cheaply to secondary markets in the developing world.

Two aspects of the historical context of cultural imperialism research should be noted. First, the general setting was a divided world in which two superpowers, the U.S.A. and the U.S.S.R., were engaged in a 'Cold War.' Against *the Third* this background, the 'Third World' could be *World in the* considered a residual to be enlisted, also by *Cold War* cultural means, against the opposing side. The several different philosophies of the press which representatives of all three worlds invoked were thus clearly informed by additional and conflicting conceptions of both culture and imperialism, markets and governments. The different positions emerged most pointedly in the debates and reports which grew out of attempts, sponsored by the United Nations and conducted within UNESCO, to outline a New World Information and Communication Order (NWICO) (see MacBride 1980).◄

A second background to assessing the cultural imperialism thesis is the ambiguous response which American and other popular media had evoked in various national settings, including Europe (see Webster 1988). At times, advocates of the thesis seemed to resent this challenge to national cultural establishments, or they resisted modernization as such, as symbolized by contemporary American popular culture. In the European setting, much research was conducted which questioned the actual cultural diversity especially of television programming (for overviews see Richardson and Meinhof 1999; Wieten *et al.* 2000).

Being part of the revitalization of critical social theory from the 1960s, research on cultural imperialism derived much of its theoretical impetus from the 'political economy'◄

tradition which was then taking shape in media research (e.g., Murdock and Golding 1977). Whereas Schiller (1969) became an inspiration to a generation of critical U.S. researchers, a characteristic feature of studies in this area was the alliances fostered among researchers on several continents, including both Latin and North America (see Roach 1997). A classic study of the ideological implications of Donald Duck comics (Dorfman and Mattelart 1975 [1971]) is representative of one variety of research which performed 'ideology critique'◄ of media texts. Perhaps more important was research which documented the technological, knowledge, and other gaps affecting international communication and cooperation (e.g., Nordenstreng and Schiller 1979), and the specific studies of imbalances in the international flow of news that informed the NWICO debates (e.g., Sreberny *et al.* 1985).◄

Recent publications have come to question some earlier positions regarding cultural imperialism (for an overview see Golding and Harris 1997). Again, this has happened alongside changes in the world orders of politics and economy, including the dissolution of the Soviet Union. Media research has largely rejected the more determinist assumptions of the tradition, and has identified, for example, the substantial role of regional media organizations (e.g., Boyd-Barrett and Thussu 1992). In addition, studies have documented how local cultures and communities can both accommodate and counteract transnational media. Besides reception studies (e.g., Biltereyst 1991; Liebes and Katz 1990), textual and production studies have also found that 'local' contents (albeit sometimes in 'Americanized' formats) may have the greatest audience appeal (e.g., O'Donnell 1999; Silj 1988). Faced with more recent research, the cultural imperialism tradition has been hampered by the generality of its argument and by its (paradoxically) limited research interest in the specific cultures at issue.

▶ NWICO – Chapter 16, p. 277

▶ political economy – Chapter 3, p. 56

▶ ideology critique – Chapter 2, p. 34

▶ news flow – Chapter 6, p. 92

Intercultural communication

Several other approaches to differences between cultures and their ways of communicating are sometimes gathered under a heading of 'intercultural communication' (for overviews see Martin and Nakayama 1999; Park 1998). Whereas much of this work emphasizes interpersonal or organizational communication, this section briefly notes some key points applying to mediated communication.

The term 'intercultural communication' is normally associated with the 'codes' of communication, in the broadest sense, as conceptualized within interpersonal communication studies (Gudykunst and Kim 1997; Jandt 2001). A common premise is that these codes may inhibit understanding between people of different national or ethnic origins. Nonverbal behavior is an important topic of analysis, as is the question of how different communicative behaviors may aid in 'uncertainty reduction.' Invoking educational and other proactive means of avoiding or managing conflict, the tradition operates with such ideals as 'the intercultural person as a model for human development' (Gudykunst and Kim 1992: 253). Some reference works in the area do cover technological media (Asante and Gudykunst 1989), but these contributions rarely have a distinctive theoretical focus, or they attempt to extrapolate from the interpersonal to the macro-social level of communication.

The discipline of anthropology,◄ traditionally the home of comparative studies of cultures, has been less of a direct influence on the media field than, for instance, sociology or psychology. It is worth noting that, despite the potential of the media field in this respect, comprehensive comparative studies of media and their uses in cultural context are still relatively few (see Blumler *et al.* 1992). Instead, the impact of anthropology has been more piecemeal, for example, methodologically in the case of debates on 'ethnography'◄ as well as in specific theoretical inspirations (e.g., Dayan and Katz 1992).

► anthropology – Chapter 3, p. 48
► ethnography – Chapter 10, p. 164

Perhaps partly for these reasons, intercultural and cross-cultural issues have sometimes been examined in an *ad hoc* or 'applied' fashion. The classic example is the (largely failed) attempt in 'development communication' to employ information and communication technologies to advance economic and political life in the developing world (Lerner 1958; Schramm 1964; for an assessment and discussion see Schramm and Lerner 1976). In addition, the cultural imperialism tradition, operating from a different point of the political spectrum, could be said to represent an *ad hoc* effort, since little theory development has addressed the 'cultures' at stake.

development communi-cation

Common to the conceptions of culture and communication considered in this volume is that they grow out of Western models of science and scholarship, for historical and institutional reasons. However, a number of publications have explored the potential links of communication theory with other ontologies, including the world's religions (see Christians and Traber 1997; Dissanayake 1988b; Kincaid 1987). In some cases, interventions have been thinly veiled attempts at promoting and applying religious axioms to contemporary policy issues (Mowlana 1993; see also Mowlana and Wilson 1990). In other cases, publications have suggested relevant conceptual family resemblances between East and West with a view to theory development and meta-theory. If, as noted by Dissanayake (1988a: 1), 'a preoccupation with metatheory is a clear sign that a given discipline has attained a certain level of maturity,' more intercultural approaches to theorizing 'culture' and 'communication' may contribute to maturity and consolidation in the future.

non-Western ontologies and (meta)theories

Postcolonial theory

A recent approach to intercultural relations is postcolonial theory, which has re-emphasized the implications of the colonial past for present social interaction and cultural forms. The issues have been addressed from a variety of perspectives by intellectuals in the former colonies as well as by literary and historical researchers (for an overview see Ashcroft *et al.* 1995). The most distinctive position, however, has its theoretical background in poststructuralist theories of discourse.◄ Compared, for example, to a historical definition of postcolonialism, which might focus on economic and political mechanisms of oppression, a discursive definition shifts the attention toward narratives and worldviews as cultural means of oppression. In particular, postcolonial theory has been informed by a Foucauldian notion of discursive formations which privilege certain worldviews over others (Foucault 1972). The position has been influenced, in addition, by the psychoanalytic theory of Lacan (1977). He has contributed the notion that language (and other cultural forms) creates a 'speaking position,' from which a dominant group differentiates

the other   itself from – excommunicates – their 'others.'

The classic statement on cultural 'othering,' which tends to label other cultural formations

orientalism   as inferior, is Saïd's (1978) work on 'orientalism.' From a wide variety of sources and genres, his volume documents a deep-seated tension in how Western 'authors,' in a broad sense, have expressed their understanding of non-Western cultures. These 'others' are, on the one hand, appealing, and, on the other, repelling. This ambivalent experience, next, leads to the perception that the 'others' must be mastered, and may more or less legitimately be controlled for ulterior purposes. While the mechanism of 'othering' becomes more controversial and urgent in periods and in settings where several cultural formations are brought together by migration, disaster, or conflict, it may be taken as pervasive, and as an obstacle to intercultural communication.

More recently, influential contributions to the area have shifted the emphasis further toward a discursive conception of oppression and power generally (Bhabha 1994; Spivak 1988). Despite nuances regarding the extent to which these authors recognize a potential for alternative viewpoints, resistance, or liberation under present sociocultural circumstances, Bhabha and Spivak have both concentrated their analytical efforts on developing abstract and rather stipulative theories of discourse. A central question has been how – through what

► poststructuralism – Chapter 2, p. 33

discursive forms – an autonomous and genuinely postcolonial subject might finally articulate itself. As a result, these authors could be said to neglect both the material contexts of discourse and the variable interpretations of discourse by actual, embodied human beings. These factors would seem to be necessary conditions in any explanation of how colonialism is reproduced and perpetuated. The discursive focus has, in turn, evoked complaints from other researchers in the area, who suggest that postcolonial theory may end up as an introverted 'academic glass-bead game' (Slemon 1995: 52).

In the context of media studies, postcolonial theory might serve as a corrective to the infrastructural and institutional focus of research traditions ranging from development communication to cultural imperialism. So far, however, its influence has been relatively limited, and has manifested itself particularly in the cultural studies tradition (e.g., Morley 2000). A key concept whose relevance for the media field as such is becoming apparent is that of 'diaspora'   diaspora
– the dispersion and diversification of previously more homogeneous cultures across locales. Another question suggesting itself to the field as a whole is how the term 'postcolonial' should be applied: to the relatively short period since the postwar independence of many developing nations, to the longer period since the original colonization, or broadly to social and cultural affairs in a world affected by diverse and only partially recognized forms of colonialism (Ashcroft *et al.* 1995: xv)? This question may take on new relevance at a time when digital means of communication are again redefining the terms of international interaction.

AMONG CULTURES

The lines of division between intercultural, transnational, and global communications can be difficult to draw, both in practice and conceptually. Nevertheless, the 1990s witnessed a marked, renewed research interest in the global level of mediated communication. This happened partly in response to the wider diffusion of computer and satellite technologies. Indeed, these developments within communications were key to a commonly perceived trend toward the globalization of economy and politics generally. Thus, changes in the social context of media and communication have once again offered the field new opportunities in addressing contemporary issues.

globalization

To some degree, studies of media and globalization have extended earlier work on the technologies and institutions of modernity (for overviews see Morley and Robins 1995; Thompson 1995). In addition, recent work on globalization has taken some of its inspiration from inclusive theoretical frameworks regarding either culture (e.g., Appadurai 1996; Hannerz 1996) or economy and society (e.g., Castells 1996; Harvey 1989; Held *et al.* 2000). The difficulties of grasping the nature and scope of ongoing social transformations may account for the somewhat 'grand' nature of some of these theories. Symbolized by the networked computer, with its potential for 'interactivity' across space and time, and its radically dispersed 'virtual' cultures, current developments have, in particular, made the area of computer-mediated communication a strategic subspecialty of research, examined in the next section.

Despite technological and economic change, it is important to bear in mind that 'globalization' is not unique to the present age. One outcome of modernization was the economic 'world system' (Wallerstein 1974) that developed from the sixteenth century. This system never took the shape of any full-fledged political structure, is comprised of independent nation-states, and is likely to remain that way for the foreseeable future. This is in spite of the fact that a variety of supranational treaties and entities have emerged over time, and may be currently on the rise, as exemplified by the European Union.

the modern world system

In present circumstances, the media continue to occupy a dual position. Media are:

- *commodities* in a transnational economy
- national and local *political institutions*.

This duality helps to identify some of the conflicts which enter into processes of globalization – conflicts previously addressed in research

under headings of cultural imperialism and postcolonialism. It is in the field of culture that many of these conflicts are articulated and addressed, and it is this cultural aspect of globalization which has brought media to the fore of current research on globalization (for overviews see Robertson 1992; Tomlinson 1999).

In order to describe the place of media in globalization, it is helpful to distinguish between the world as a context of action and as a frame of reference (Tomlinson 1999: 11). As a *context of action* – including business investments, transborder political mobilization, and tourism – the material world has undoubtedly become more interconnected in recent decades. In the media sector, this has perhaps been especially clear on the production side through the formation of large conglomerates in a process of intensified concentration.◄ The news and popular music industries are among the foremost examples of this development (even though cultural industries, including the press and cinema, have long been large international enterprises) (for an overview see Sreberny 2000).

the world as context of action

One countervailing tendency in a complicated field is that, in terms of distribution and consumption, local media systems may be holding their own. For example, the *relative* proportion of home-produced content (and its consumption) in the culturally central television medium appears to have grown at least in some regions of the world. This may be attributed to 'the enormous expansion of television production and transmission outside the United States since the 1970s' (McQuail 2000: 232).

It is, however, as a *frame of reference* that globalization applies most directly to media. For most people most of the time, the rest of the world is an imagined entity, occasionally an imagined community (Anderson 1991) they encounter through media. What I do to other people and institutions elsewhere in either material or discursive terms – and what they do to me – only affects us in the most indirect and cumulative of ways. This condition does not render the world less real, nor does it make the

the world as frame of reference

► concentration, integration, conglomeration – Chapter 4, p. 73

individual less of an agent – it is a general condition of social interaction under modernity, and it is this condition that is accentuated as well as modified by globalization.

time–space distanciation, disembedding, and re-embedding

The modern condition has been characterized by, among others, Giddens (1990) as 'time-space distanciation.' The term refers to the fact that media and other types of modern institutions allow for larger and more complex social entities. Interaction in the literal sense of 'acting together' within a shared frame of reference does not equal being present in the same space and time. One result of interaction at a distance is a 'disembedding' (Giddens) or 'deterritorialization' (Tomlinson 1999: 106) of much of actual social life from co-presence in familiar arenas. Presumably, such interaction results in a measure of disorientation for the individual. A central means of reorienting oneself – of being 're-embedded' in various contexts of action – is the technological media. From the individual's perspective, then, the media are ambivalent resources under conditions of modernity and globalization. The media help support a social system that is not only complex but opaque; they also provide means of making that system more transparent.

It is through such a multidimensional conception of globalization that references to 'the local in the global,' and vice versa, can be specified and justified. For media conglomerates, the entire globe is a context of action. However, for purposes of product development, conglomerates also need to consider the globe as an imagined entity. In order to attract audiences, who are always localized, producers and distributors of media commodities must take into account the several frames of reference – national, regional, transnational – which enter into 'local' cultures. One lesson from monogeneric transnational television channels, such as MTV and CNN, appears to be that, when faced with national competition, they can be forced to regionalize or customize their product (Roe and De Meyer 2000; see also Volkmer 1999). In theories of globalization, this process has been referred to as 'glocalization' (Robertson 1995).

glocalization

In sum, it is important to distinguish between several sectors or levels of globalization:

- *economic* – which has been ongoing for centuries;
- *political* – which remains limited, at least in institutional terms;
- *cultural* – which has been intensifying in recent decades.

It is these several aspects of globalization which come together in the case of media. Further, they have different implications for different moments of the process of mediated communication:

- *Media production.* The impact of transnational conglomeration in different media and genres, while significant, is tempered by the concurrent expansion of national and local production and transmission.

- *Media discourses.* The export of meaning (Liebes and Katz 1990) from the U.S.A. and other global media centers may be reinforced by national adaptations of similar formats. But homogenization is counteracted by the special and continued popularity of local product in the local language.

- *Media audiences.* The reception of 'foreign' media and genres further serves to mediate their cultural impact. The modes of reception have been shaped, in part, by the cultural practices and conventions of local contexts. A case in point is sports (e.g., Coakley 2000; Whannel 1992) – a ritualized form of play and international combat which nevertheless remains anchored in the nation-state. International sports is an ingrained part of national schedules and seasons. It also lends itself both to local, collective participation on site and to vicarious, mediated forms of experience. sports

COMPUTER-MEDIATED CULTURES

Building on the seminal theories of Alan Turing about the computer as a universal machine, and about its social uses from visionaries such as Vannevar Bush, Ted Nelson, and Alan Kay (for key texts see Mayer 1999), the computer became recognizable as a medium particularly during the 1980s. This followed the diffusion of personal computers, as suggested by advertising introducing it to the general public (Jensen 1993a). It was not until the 1990s, however, that the computer seemed to be recognized, not as a mass medium, but as a new category of medium for a mass public. This happened following the introduction of the World Wide Web and of many more network connections in the industrialized world.

Studies of the computer as a medium are currently being conceptualized in relation to other forms of communication and culture. Research is simultaneously being institutionalized in relation to a variety of disciplines and fields across the social, natural, and human sciences. The purpose of this section is to outline the place of the computer on the current map of the field of media and communication research, and to review some of the main contributions to conceptualizing and studying the computer as a medium (for overviews see Benedikt 1991; Jones 1998; Porter 1997).

Methodological preface

Introductory textbooks in the emerging subspecialty of computer media studies rightly note the importance of technological integration or convergence between previously separate media (Slevin 2000; van Dijk 1999). This feature, however, facilitates social divergence: media devices enable more diverse, and more dispersed, forms of interaction.

The dual process of convergence and divergence poses a methodological challenge for research. For example, 'audience' or, better, 'user' studies must gain access to and document more, and more differentiated, contexts of media use. The methodological complexity is only underscored by phenomena such as 'mobile' and 'ubiquitous' computing. With a growing miniaturization of input–output devices and an increased transmission capacity, the mobility of media and the time–space distanciation of communication (Giddens 1990) are accentuated. Further, with the embedding of computers into more everyday objects, the definition of computer 'media' is brought more radically into question.

Standard reference works are in the making

(Jankowski and van Selm in press; Jones 1999; Lievrouw and Livingstone 2002; Mann and Stewart 2000), transferring theories, empirical designs, and methods to digital settings and, in part, devising new ones. In overview, at least three different sets of issues and concerns which are specific to computer media may be identified:

1 *Online data collection.* Computer networks offer an accessible, economical, and efficient instrument of data collection (for example, online surveys (Witmer *et al.* 1999) or focus groups (Mann and Stewart 2000)). However, their potential is limited in several respects. First, a comparatively large percentage of most populations of interest will not be connected to a network. Second, there are difficulties of verifying the nature of a sample contacted in 'cyberspace.' So far, then, online data collection is most appropriate for studying online interaction or online communities as such. In addition, traditional methodologies such as observation and interviewing take on a new meaning in a news group or chat room, and blend into content or discourse analysis (of log files) (e.g., Baym 2000; Downey 1998; Hine 2000; Miller and Slater 2000).

2 *Validity of findings.* A particular aspect of interaction via the Internet is that people can, and do, present and explore multiple identities or *personae* (e.g., Turkle 1995). This clearly limits the explanatory value both of the basic information provided and of any inferences about the respondents. Furthermore, compared to census or postal information, computer 'addresses' may be less precise in identifying the source of a response. Online findings also tend to focus attention on the mediated interaction in itself, rather than on its social contexts, as focused by recent media studies.

3 *Research ethics.* Whatever evidence becomes available online raises a number of ethical issues. This is, in part, because the status of computer-mediated communication as a social context – on a scale from public to private – is unresolved. As professional guidelines and some form of a cultural consensus are still being negotiated, research projects need to consider

technological convergence

social divergence

ubiquitous computing

log files

multiple personae

carefully issues of anonymity, confidentiality, and 'informed consent.'

Interactivities

A key characteristic of computer media is the extent to which they are becoming integrated with, and constitutive of, other social contexts. The dividing lines between 'medium,' 'text,' and 'context' pose a host of theoretical and analytical questions. The relationship between media as means of representing reality, and as resources for intervening in reality, has thus been re-emphasized as a research question by developments in digital technology.

textual representation and contextual action

While the term 'interactivity' has been widely employed to refer to *the* defining characteristic of computer media, it has been used in a variety of senses (for an overview see J. F. Jensen 1999). Indeed, it may be argued that the term refers to several distinct phenomena, and should be studied in the plural.

Figure 11.2 lays out three types of interactivity with reference to key concepts of media and communication theory, as introduced in Chapter 1.

• *Interactivity 1* refers to the medium-user relation of communication. In computer science, this relation has been examined, for instance, by the influential human–computer interaction (HCI) tradition. Its research issues include both technological design and ergonomics (Preece 1994). Compared to print as well as electronic media, computer users anticipate and redirect later stages of the interactive sequence. This affords greater flexibility and dynamism, with computer games as the prototypical example, but also in, for instance, interactive fictions (e.g., Murray 1997). Most concretely, this type of interactivity may be defined as selectivity – selections by the user are required for the interaction to proceed at all. As a communicative sequence, moreover, the interchange may be described as a structured turn-taking,◄ in certain respects corresponding to

the turns of a conversation (Sacks *et al.* 1974). Compared to, for instance, film directors and their crews, system developers and programmers play a specific role in facilitating turn-taking – over and above content providers – and are, in one sense, 'communicating' with users. Users, in turn, may customize their interface. Together, these various communicative options raise to a new degree the question of who – how many, in what capacity – is the 'author'◄ of media discourses.

• *Interactivity 2* refers to a broader relation between media and the rest of the social structure. The research questions are familiar to the media field – media have been said to function as a watchdog, a Fourth Estate (Cater 1959), a public sphere (Habermas 1989 [1962]), or an institution-to-think-with (Chapter 1). At issue are classic questions of how computer-mediated communication shapes, and is shaped by, the political and economic infrastructures of social life. A helpful attempt at modeling this link has been the typology of Bordewijk and Kaam (1986) (Figure 11.3). The conceptual matrix distinguishes between central and distributed control over an available information base, and between central or distributed control over the retrieval of particular items at a particular time, resulting in four ideal types of communication. The more familar ones are 'conversation,' as in face-to-face or real-time online dialogue (e.g., chat or conferencing), and 'allocution,' which corresponds to traditional mass communication. Next, 'consultation' is a variant especially associated with computers, for instance, in the use of databases or online gaming. Finally, 'registration' refers to the more or less automated documentation of users' trajectories on the Internet and other systems. This 'communication' raises a host of issues regarding data security, confidentiality, as well as commercial (ab)uses of information. One important implication of the model is that all four (as well as other) communicative forms can be brought together on a single platform, making the computer a 'metamedium' (Kay and Goldberg 1999 [1977]).

computer as metamedium

▶ research ethics – Chapter 16, p. 289

▶ turn-taking – Chapter 7, p. 108

▶ authorship – media production, Chapter 4, p. 65

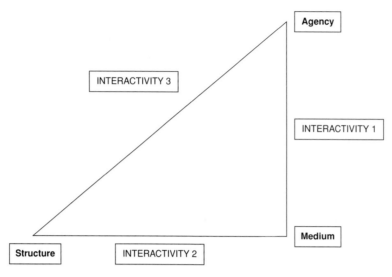

Figure 11.2 Three types of interactivity
Source: Jensen 2000a

	CONTROL OF INFORMATION BASE	
CONTROL OF TIME AND ITEMS SELECTED	**Central**	**Distributed**
Central	allocution	registration
Distributed	consultation	conversation

Figure 11.3 Four modes of communication
Source: Bordewijk and Kaam 1986; see also McQuail and Windahl 1993: 209

• *Interactivity 3* refers to the individual–society nexus, as mediated by computer media. Social agents participate continuously and locally in the structuration of society, through reference to a medium. The potential for localized action via computer media has been highlighted by some utopian visions regarding citizen involvement in society (e.g., Negroponte 1995) (the dystopian counterparts have noted the capacity of computers for surveillance of citizens by state and other social agencies). In more general theoretical terms, computer media users perform a range of actions – the (re)production of physical objects, of personal relationships, organizations, communities, and of entire societies. To exemplify, the material pro-

duction of commodities increasingly involves computer-aided design and manufacture (CAD/CAM). A second example is organizations, such as banks, insurance companies, and grass-roots movements, which cohere and operate, in part, through computer media (see Hauben and Hauben 1997; Rheingold 1994). If communities and societies can be understood as systems of communication, computer-mediated communication is one preparatory condition for new social formations. Finally, political democracy is one specific example of a radically distributed form of social interaction. With news services on the Internet and elsewhere as an increasingly strategic center-piece, media-users participate in, and reproduce, political

societies as systems of communication

institutions. Like other institutions, politics has no unified appearance or locale. This does not make that political participation via (digital) media less than real, or necessarily inferior to conversation. Mediated communication is a necessary condition of political democracy in modernity.

Intertextualities

The spread of digital and distributed forms of communication has given the theoretical concept of intertextuality renewed importance, also for empirical studies of media. To clarify the present relevance of the concept, its genealogy must be briefly retraced.

The seminal contributions were made by Mikhail Bakhtin and the circle around him in the early decades of the twentieth century (see Bakhtin 1981; also Bell and Gardiner 1998). Bakhtin's most basic concept, 'dialogism' (which was translated by Kristeva (1984) as 'intertextuality') underscores 'the necessary relation of any utterance to other utterances' (Stam *et al.* 1992: 203). 'Utterances' are here understood in a broad semiotic◄ sense as vehicles of meaning, including conversations, plays, novels, newspapers, or hypertext systems. The constituent signs of each of these communications may be said to acquire their meaning in relation to other signs, past as well as present. Given this abstract definition, the reference to a 'necessary' relation between utterances may be puzzling. In addition to the trivial observation that a set of utterances is related in time and space, and by the communicators, the point is that they enter into a particular configuration, and that this structure will follow certain social and cultural patterns. A culture might even be considered an (almost infinitely complex) instance of intertextuality.

In contrast to some later appropriations of his idea, Bakhtin (1981) recognized the social determination of texts and communications. The more difficult question is how society makes its presence felt in language. A preliminary and almost poetic answer was offered by the Bakhtin circle, in a central statement attributed to

Volosinov (1985: 53): 'The immediate social situation and the broader social milieu wholly determine – and determine from within, so to speak – the structure of an utterance.' The phrase 'determine from within' suggests the theoretical ambition in the Bakhtin circle of transcending a classic Marxist position that would see the ideological or cultural superstructure as more or less directly determined by, and secondary to, the material basis of society. The distinction between 'immediate social situation' and 'the broader social milieu,' moreover, pointed to the several moments of social determination. It is such a weaker, processual notion of determination, or hegemony,◄ as developed also by other social theorists such as Gramsci (1971), which has informed much work about intertextuality.

The methodological question, however, of how to examine intertextual structures and the social processes shaping them has tended to divide researchers. The majority of intertextual studies, as exemplified by Genette (1997 [1982]), have centered on texts as relatively self-contained entities. This research has made little or no reference to complementary sources of evidence about literary and media institutions, or about the audiences who respond to intertextuality.

An alternative approach was outlined by Fiske (1987), who distinguished different types of intertextuality according to their social functions. 'Horizontal' intertextuality concerns the transfer and accumulation of particular meanings over historical time, as preserved in metaphors, themes, characters, and genres. 'Vertical' intertextuality operates during a more delimited time period, but across several media and social contexts. To clarify this synchronic perspective, Fiske referred to three types of texts: 'Primary' texts are comparable to traditional artworks, being vehicles of central meanings or insights. (In a historical or horizontal perspective, the primary texts are the center of attention.) If the primary text, for instance, is a feature movie, the 'secondary' texts will consist of studio publicity, reviews, and criticism. The 'tertiary' texts are contributed by audiences in conversations and other interaction around media. Together, the two axes of

horizontal and vertical intertextuality

primary, secondary, and tertiary texts

► semiotics – Chapter 2, p. 23

► hegemony – Chapter 2, p. 39

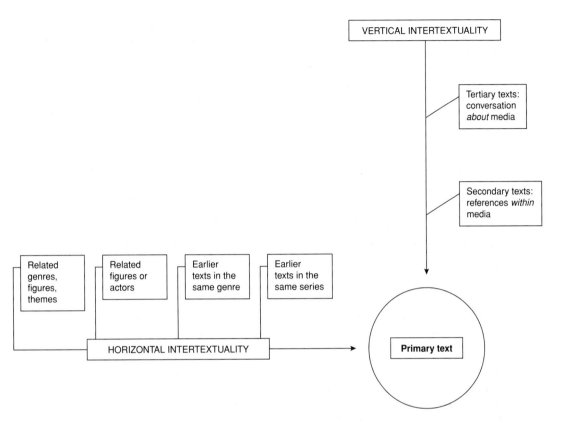

Figure 11.4 Horizontal and vertical intertextuality

intertextuality may be understood as a model of how textual meaning is produced and circulated in society (Figure 11.4).

It should be added that Fiske's (1987) terminology still privileges media texts as the primary sources of meaning, apparently in contradiction of the logic of his argument (see Jensen 1995: 61–62). Surely, media are not the main sources of meaning in social life. Instead, as suggested in Figure 10.2, meaning rather flows from society to the media. This is in spite of the fact that the methodologies of media research must be designed to account for the specific difference media make in society.

A natural candidate for intertextual analysis in previous research has been (radio and) television flow◄ (for an overview see Jensen 1994). The several channels in the television universe

▶ flow – Chapter 10, p. 168

of most countries allow viewers to select and combine discursive elements into an intertextual configuration. Flow thus anticipates aspects of computer-mediated communication.

'Hypertext' and 'hypermedia' serve to link message elements in computer-mediated communication (see Aarseth 1997; Bolter 1991; Landow 1997). 'Texts' (or parts of texts) can be linked, for example, for easy access or for purposes of indexing. 'Media' can be connected, for instance, in the form of verbal explanations of video sequences in 'multimedia' discourses. In each case, the 'hyperlink' may be understood as a form of instrumental or operationalized intertextuality – a means of making explicit, retrievable, modifiable, and communicable what might have remained a more or less random association. This discursive structure has been one practical key to the development, for example, of the World Wide Web.

hypertext and hypermedia

For theory development and further research, it may prove helpful to conceptualize the computer as a multiply semiotic machine, which processes and communicates information through several links and levels of 'code' (e.g., Finnemann 1999). A generative model of meaning,◄ which focuses on the different levels at which 'information' and 'meaning' are coded (and which was originally inspired by computing), suggests itself for this purpose. Media and communication theory still has to arrive at a basic typology of computer media discourses, noting how particular types of hardware and software allow for different forms of navigation and interaction.

Toward this end, one can return to the basic vehicles or units of meaning – verbal, visual, and other signs. What distinguishes verbal language from images, above all, is 'double articulation' (Martinet 1964 [1960]). A verbal statement and a photograph both have a first level of articulation, in the sense that they each communicate a meaning, but they do so in distinctive ways. Only verbal language has a second level of articulation, i.e., a fixed repertoire of minimal units – sounds or letters. The formal constituents of an image cannot be graded or parsed in any similar way.

Hyperstructures, being a key organizing principle of digital media, may be understood as a third level of articulation. Both the meanings of ordinary delimited media messages (first articulation) and their constituents (second articulation) have normally been ascertained 'internally,' with reference to an immanent structure of discourse. Compared to such a structure, a hyperlink may be said to articulate an 'external' meaning, joining one text (verbal, visual, other) with another and suggesting a whole that is not inherent in the parts. This discursive whole, to be sure, may still be studied in its own right or with reference to decodings and uses. The point is that hyperlinks and other features of digital media may be different in kind from most other media texts, including the links between image and text which◄ have been at the center of visual communication studies since Barthes (1984 [1964b]). Hyperstructures give rise to different types of

double articulation (margin note)

interpretation as well as intervention, because the entire system of communication is both more flexible in itself and modifiable by users.

Figure 11.5 illustrates the three levels of articulation. The solid vertical lines indicate the connection between first- and second-level articulation in texts; the horizontal lines indicate connections between text and image at the first level of articulation; and the dotted lines suggest links across the third level of articulation. Here, texts and their verbal elements – letters, words, sentences, sections, etc. – as well as images (or fields within them) can serve as 'nodes.' When joined at the third level, these links produce meanings of a different order and complexity. It is the nature of these links and meanings that further research must account for – a task that is complicated, but also made potentially rewarding, by the dynamic nature of the full discursive system.

Intermedialities

With computer-mediated communication, research on 'media' has come full circle in two respects. First, the individual media are increasingly interrelated – technologically, in marketing terms, and as cultural forms (for an overview see Bolter and Grusin 1999). As noted in Chapter 1, it is helpful to conceptualize the computer as a third degree of medium,◄ which incorporates several previous technological media, and which re-emphasizes features otherwise associated with face-to-face interaction. Compared to some earlier notions of an 'information society' (e.g., Nora and Minc 1980; Porat 1977), which pointed to a growing information sector and its consequences for culture and society, it may be the integral 'informatization' of work, leisure, and most major social institutions which will distinguish a 'network society' (Castells 1996).

the information society (margin note)

At present, research is beginning to explore the several 'intermedialities' and social forms through which computers take effect. Computers enter into the social infrastructure; they also provide imagined partners in interaction, from avatars and intelligent agents to cus-

the network society (margin note)

► generative model of meaning – Chapter 2, p. 30

► media of the third degree – Chapter 1, p. 4

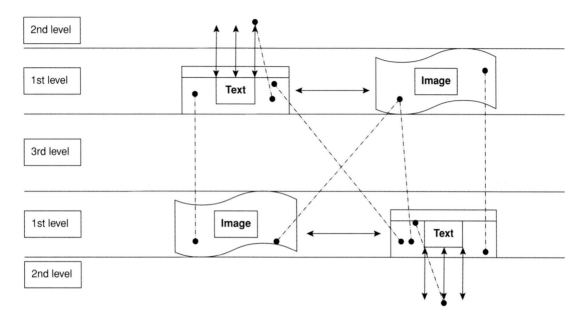

Figure 11.5 Three levels of articulation

tomized communication systems. For the time being, research in this strategic and much publicized area must proceed amidst hyperbolic projections. Utopian proclamations note the democratic and intercultural potential of the Internet, while dystopian statements anticipate cyborgs the demise of humans and the rise of cyborgs (cybernetic organisms). Such visions should come as no surprise after two centuries of ambivalently embracing modern technologies, from Shelley's *Frankenstein* (1818), via 1950s cyberspace artificial intelligence, to the cyberspace of Gibson's *Neuromancer* (1984).

Besides the convergence of previously separate media, a second implication of computer-mediated communication is sometimes taken to be a questioning of any absolute dividing line, not only between 'media' and 'context,' but also between 'reality' and 'virtuality.' In fact, far from the collapsing material and virtual realms, computer media may simply offer one more prosaic resource for human cultural activity (see further Jensen 2001). Referring to Anderson's (1991) notion of national (and other) cultures as 'imagined communities,'◀ one may argue that, in premodern as well as modern settings,

media have been instruments for imagining other people, projects, and solutions – for getting jobs done. Certainly, virtuality can and virtual reality must be examined as a matter of degree in phenomenal terms, since different modes of communication give rise to different experiences of sociality. However, it is an important premise for research that the differentiation and distanciation of communicative interaction via computers do not make either the interaction or the social context less real. By imagining other people, in face-to-face as well as technologically mediated communication, we become virtual partners in real social activity.

To sum up, several traditions of research, each with a more or less explicit model of communication, have informed the attempt so far to conceptualize computer media:

• the computer as yet another *channel* of social communication, for example, in the interdisciplinary tradition of computer-mediated communication (CMC) (for an overview, see Jones 1998);

▶ imagined communities – p. 173

• the computer as an augmentation of the human intellect, not least as a *tool* for reorganizing work and education, as represented by human–computer interaction (HCI), but dating back to early conceptions of computing as communication (e.g., Licklider and Taylor 1999 [1968]);

• the computer as a *substitution* of humans altogether, as evidenced in artificial-intelligence research (for an overview see Gardner 1985), and as radicalized in current notions of the cyborg (e.g., Haraway 1997);

• the computer as one resource in the *constitution* of contemporary societies, mediating between agency and structure – a position elaborated in Chapter 1.

In conclusion, computer media have contributed new issues to the agenda of media and communication research, and have highlighted other issues, such as the global level of communications and the relationship between representation and (inter-)action. At the same time, research is well advised to keep in mind the specific local and national circumstances in which media continue to be produced and received. A lesson of media studies has been that the social consequences of media depend, to an important degree, on the concrete contexts and cultures in which they are introduced and applied. This lesson is brought home by historical studies of media, which are the topic of the next chapter.

RESOURCE BOX 11.1 NATIONAL AND INTERNATIONAL VARIETIES OF MEDIA STUDIES

Different national and cultural contexts, not surprisingly, have developed different traditions of research. Whereas the volume focuses on the English-speaking cultures that have been central in institutionalizing the media field internationally in recent decades, this box indicates additional references to other literatures. In fact, much of this literature is available in English translation or in excerpts, as reviewed in these titles. Moreover, the section in this chapter entitled 'Between cultures' references contributions which have sought to overcome East–West as well as North–South divides, also within media and communication research.

Russia
• Kelly and Shepherd 1998 – a broad, non-sectarian collection addressing Russian cultural research, including the Soviet period and the 1991 transition, with many references.

Japan
• Ito and Tanaka 1992 – an overview of institutions of media research and education in Japan.

Latin America and Spain
• Martin-Barbero 1993 – an original contribution to social and cultural theory, as well as an overview of Latin research traditions;
• Graham and Labanyi 1995 – a broad collection covering developments in both Latin America and Spain.

Germany
• Burns 1995 – a broad collection, including historical overviews of the place of Germany in international and intellectual history;
• Schulz 1997 – a review focusing on political communication, and on the 1990s, but with coverage of the development of the field.

France
• *Reseaux* – a journal presenting translations in English of selected research;
• Forbes and Kelly 1995 – a broad collection, including historical overviews of the place of France in international and intellectual history;
• Cayrol and Mercier 1998 – a review focusing on political communication, but with extensive contextualization and coverage of the development of the field.

12 History, media and communication

Paddy Scannell

- an overview of the *history of history* as a field of research
- a discussion of '*media history*' as an inclusive phenomenon
- a presentation of histories of *oral and written communication*
- a review of histories of different technological media, including the *press and broadcasting*
- an example of *archival research* on historical data.

INTRODUCTION

In this chapter, I review developments in historical studies of communication and media. In order to contextualize these developments it is necessary to consider, historically, the formation of history as an academic discipline. Throughout the chapter, I attend to theoretical and methodological issues concerning historiography (the practice of writing history) in order to illuminate some of the more specific problems in writing histories of media and communication. What is not dealt with in this chapter, since to do so would turn a chapter into a book, are questions concerning the nature of history itself. The given facticity of history as an academic field of inquiry is taken as the starting point, but it is obvious that history itself – whatever it may be – is not something invented by historians; that is, the emergence of history as an academic domain is itself a reflection of the historical process. It is precisely a question for historians as to why it should be – at a particular time and in particular places – that a new kind of historical consciousness should emerge, one of whose manifestations is academic historiography.

historiography

A historical sensibility comes fully into being in nineteenth-century Europe and North America, and is undoubtedly connected with the unprecedented speeding up of technological innovation, economic, political, and other social change – in short, the phenomenon of modernity.◀ Transformations in communication and the continuing development of 'new' media (radio in the 1920s was as much a matter of wonder for the contemporary world as the Internet is today) have contributed to the heightened sense of social change – the sharp awareness of the difference between past and present, then and now – which is the mark of historical consciousness. Recent social theory (e.g., Giddens 1990; Harvey 1989) has also shown a renewed interest in time and space, and especially in the consequences of their shrinkage to the point of disappearing as obstacles to be overcome in the circulation of information and commodities. At this point in time, however, the Internet has no history to speak of, but only a future. The work of historians – unlike that of social theorists – begins only as the past emerges as distinct from the

---

▶ modernity – Chapter 11, p. 173

present. That this has begun to happen in respect of modern media and communication technologies is what gives the possibility of the substantive concerns of this chapter.

THE HISTORY OF HISTORY

The professionalization of history began in the nineteenth century. A chair in history at the University of Oxford was first established in 1848. In his inaugural lecture, the first Regius Professor of History, H. H. Vaughan, defined the job of the historian as the 'disclosure of the critical changes in the conditions of a society' (Stone 1987: 4). From the late nineteenth century, history developed into an independent academic discipline. Separate history departments were established with Ph.D. programs for the training of future historians. Professional associations were created, taught programs at the undergraduate and graduate levels were established, and a curriculum (an 'agenda') for the study of history as a distinctive academic subject was put in place within the emerging fields of the humanities and social sciences (Stone 1987: 5).

There were two aspects to this development: first, a definition of the right way of 'doing' history (the professionalization of methods), and, second, a specification of the subject matter of historical inquiry (what history is properly 'about'). Both aspects came to the fore in Germany, where there was pioneering concern with the establishment of history as an academic discipline on a 'scientific' basis. What this meant, above all, was a renewed concern about the 'objectivity' of historical research whose scientific truth claims were underpinned by rigorous research methods linked to temporal distance on the part of the historian from the field of inquiry, and careful scholarly interpretation and evaluation of the evidence. The doyen of German 'historicism' (see Bambach 1995) was Leopold von Ranke, whose name is particularly associated with a revolution in sources and methods – a shift away from earlier histories or 'chronicles' to the use of the official records of governments. Historians now began to work regularly in archives, and they elaborated an increasingly sophisticated set of techniques for assessing the reliability of documents. They claimed that their own histories were therefore more objective and more 'scientific' than those of their predecessors (Burke 1992: 7).

The primary subject matter of these inquiries was the nation-state◄ and, in particular, its administrative and constitutional development, as linked to its diplomatic and military relations with other nation-states. National record offices were opened up to academic historians, and the basic political documents relating to these matters were indexed and made publicly available for research free of charge. Thus, by the beginning of the twentieth century, the academic profession of history was in place. Its agenda consisted of narrative histories – firmly supported by archival research into primary documentary source material – whose subject matter was the activities of those political and military elites who created, defined, and maintained the modern nation-state. Historians no longer wrote for an educated general public (Stone 1987: 3–7). They wrote for each other or for their students, and talked among themselves as a self-legitimating subset of a new historical genus – *homo academicus* (Bourdieu 1988).

Not unnaturally, these foundational developments, set in place between the 1870s and the 1930s, were subject to critique in the course of the twentieth century. On the one hand, a set of methodological objections was raised against the privileging of 'narrative' as the definitive mode of historiography (history writing). On the other hand, the narrowly elitist base of the subject matter of history as the actions of 'great men' came under increasing critical scrutiny. The issue of history as narrative is fundamental to it as an academic discipline, since it raises crucial questions concerning the nature and status of historical *events* and of historical *agents*. In short, the problems are: What is history about, who are historical agents, and what is historiography (the writing of history)?

Political history, history of events, and narrative history – these are almost interchangeable terms, as Paul Ricoeur points out in his review

Margin notes: history as an academic discipline; German historicism and scientific objectivity; narrative history

---

► the nation-state – Chapter 10, p. 173

of 'the eclipse of narrative' (Ricoeur 1983: 95–120). They were treated as such by the French historian, Fernand Braudel, a leading the Annales School member of the *Annales* School, so called after the journal of that name founded in 1929 by Marcel Bloch and Lucien Febvre, who, along with Braudel, were the leading critics of traditional history and vigorous opponents of what they called *histoire evenementielle* (Burke 1991: 7–8). They argued that it was naive to think of historical events as being 'made' by historical actors, because what determines or structures events has no level of explanation, in traditional historical narratives, beyond the deeds of significant individuals themselves. Their structuralist◀ critique of history-as-events (or the 'great man' view of history) draws attention to all those shaping factors, ignored in narrative histories, that determine the character and behaviour of historical actors and the scope of their actions. The objectivity claimed by political histories is at the expense of underlying economic, social, political, cultural, and religious factors which all, in different ways, combine to predetermine the form and content of historical events. Moreover, and this was the crucial point of Braudel and others, the nature of historical time remains under-theorized in narrative histories, since they presuppose, without any critical reflection on the matter, first, that the time of events is somehow self-evident, and second, that it is essentially the same as the time(s) of history.

If history is the sum of all that has ever happened in the past, then a basic methodological and theoretical issue for historians is how they establish manageable time spans for their activities. As Braudel points out, 'All historical work is concerned with the breaking down of time past, choosing among its chronological realities according to more or less conscious preferences and exclusions.' He is highly critical of 'traditional' history's concern with the short time span and 'the headlong, dramatic, breathless rush of its narratives' which are tied to 'the individual and the event' (Braudel 1980: 27–28). He points to new kinds of economic and social history whose concern is not with particular individuals, moments, or events, but

with the larger economic and social forces that structure their terrain, that shape the ground upon which events are enacted. Such macro (large-scale) histories necessarily take a more long-term view of the processes of historical change. They are concerned with, for instance, the mapping of the cyclical rise and fall of prices, which calls for complex, large-scale data-gathering of quantitative information about prices, wages, money, rent, output per capita, capital investment, overseas trade, and other key economic variables (Stone 1987: 13–14) compared to the qualitative methodologies most prevalent in historical research.◀ The focus of macro histories is not on individuals and their actions, but on underlying factors that mould the processes of social change through time. These 'conjunctural' histories attempt to analyse the ways in which a range of economic variables combine in a particular historical conjuncture to precipitate crises that play themselves out at the level of events and actions. The intermediate time span of such histories is measured in decades; ten, twenty, fifty years; but beyond this lies the long-term – the *longue durée* – which stretches over centuries. It is a kind of 'motionless history' which tries to establish the most fundamental constraints upon the shape and scope of human actions: the impact of climate and geography, for example, upon the historical life of a region such as the Mediterranean, the subject of Braudel's most famous work (Braudel 1972, 1974).

macro and long-term history

the *longue durée*

The critique of narrative history as privileging elites came to the fore in the 1950s and 1960s. New kinds of social history were developed which insisted, as the historical novel had done (Lukacs 1989 [1916]), on the significance of the apparently insignificant – ordinary men and women, and the character of everyday life (Burke 1991). These 'histories from below'◀ (Sharpe 1991) – as opposed to history from above (political history) – rediscovered

---

▶ structuralism – Chapter 2, p. 29

▶ quantitative methodologies – Chapter 13. See also the diffusion of innovations, Chapter 9, p. 140, and the spread of literacy (Vincent 2000)

▶ histories from below and oral history – Chapter 14, p. 241

such 'hidden' or 'invisible' histories as those of the English working class (Thompson 1968), or of women (Rowbottom 1974; Scott 1991), of the family (Stone 1979), or the body (Porter 1991). Thus, in the second half of the twentieth century, academic history began to broaden out and diversify. It was in this context of expanding areas of research and inquiry that historical attention began to focus on, among other things, the media.

MEDIA HISTORY?

What would a history of the media be about? We must first determine what the word refers to. Note that it is a plural noun: a 'medium', *the* media. This plurality is usually taken to include the press and broadcasting (radio and television), and cinema too, perhaps. One useful way of reconstructing how terms gather certain meanings is to look at their historical usage. When did they begin to be used in a particular way, and why? What we can say of 'the media' is that the sense in which it is commonly used today – and by now it is a commonsense term and part of everyone's ordinary usage – is no older than the early 1960s. Earlier usage of the word 'medium' was associated with the late nineteenth-century vogue for spiritualism which, as John D. Peters (1999) has cogently shown, was linked with the impact of new communication technologies: the telegraph and telephone. The idea of a 'media society' shows up for the first time in the 1960s, and coincides with the rapid rise of television as the dominant 'medium' of daily life in Europe. In everyday usage, the term now recognizes that, in our kind of society, the press and broadcasting are central social institutions and a taken-for-granted part of everyone's ordinary, everyday life, but the 'media society' as we know it came into being only in the second half of the twentieth century.

To put it like this invites the question, 'What was there before that?' The Norwegian historian, Hans Fredrik Dahl (1994), has pointed out that before the 'media society' there was 'mass society', and terms such as 'mass culture' and 'mass communication' referred to the impact and effect of new technologies of commu-

'the media' from the 1960s

nication on early twentieth-century society. Thus, in the 1930s, we find a whole series of debates (in Britain, Europe and the USA) about the effect on social values, the beliefs and tastes of new kinds of 'mass' journalism, Hollywood cinema, commercial radio, and an emerging 'popular' music industry. The issue Dahl raises is as follows: first, do we try and study historically the development of 'the media', or do we go back and try and trace the development of particular 'mediums'? Second and relatedly, what is the difference between studying 'the media' and studying 'communication'?

In this chapter, I will treat this difference as essentially one of historical scale. Communication is as old as mankind, insofar as language is constitutive of human being. Modern media of communication – daily newspapers, radio and television services – stand in a long temporal continuum that reaches back through written systems of communication (often taken as the point of entry into history) to spoken language and the beginnings of human social life. Thus histories of communication are anterior to, and distinct from, media histories. Moreover, 'the media' is a synthetic descriptor and as such misleading when used in respect of something called 'media history', for the different mediums that make up 'the media' have thus far only been studied historically as discrete phenomena, and not as the relational totality which the term itself implies. Accordingly, I begin with histories of communication and proceed thence to more recent histories of different mediums which make up the known and understood 'media society', familiar as such to all of us today. I will then briefly review some issues that arise when trying to 'do' historical work on aspects of 'the media'.

writing as beginning of history

THE HISTORY OF COMMUNICATION

The fundamental, universal form of communication in all human societies is language, or, more precisely, spoken language, or speech.◄ We know that systems of writing, as devices for representing spoken language, developed much later – on current evidence around 7000 years

----

► speech – Chapter 2, p. 19

ago. There are, of course, different systems of writing, but today two systems prevail: alphabetic systems – the Roman alphabet is massively dominant, but there are others (Greek, Cyrillic) – and ideographic systems (Chinese, Japanese). We can take these two modes of communication – speech and writing – as intimately connected, but there is no doubt that spoken language is ontologically (as well as historically) prior. That is, speech is constitutive of our (human) way of being: some would say it is *the* species-defining characteristic. It is the very essence of our human, social life. All human societies have a spoken language. Far fewer have developed systems of writing. Thus a primary question is: If both are systems of communication, what are the differences between them? What is it that we can and cannot do with speech as our only available means of communication? What does writing do for us (and what do we do with it)? And what is it that later means of communication (print, radio, television) do for us, and what do we do with them? Such questions have a positive and negative side to them: What does any particular means (medium) of communication enable us to do, and what are the limits to what we can do with it?

To put this slightly differently, a fundamental constraint on the scope of human actions is imposed by the temporal and spatial characteristics of our available resources, including our resources for communicating with each other. The question, first clearly put by the Canadian economic historian, Harold Innis, is: What are the implications of the available means of communication for the character of a particular human society (Innis 1972 [1950])? What is a society like that has only speech as its available means of communication? Innis's answer was that such societies are necessarily spatially (geographically) small in scale. They may be nomadic or pastoral (they may move about or remain in one place) but, since their shared spoken language is what makes them what they are and holds them together, the size of their community is restricted by its face-to-face character. The group's social memory – its knowledge in the present of 'how and what and when' to do things, as derived from past prac-

tices – is orally transmitted in a spoken tradition that is passed on from one generation to the next.

Systems of writing, Innis argued, developed as means of coordinating and controlling human activities across extended time and space. Writing is a system of record: a way of putting things down, so that information may be transmitted through space over great distances and be preserved through time as a record of what was said and done. Innis drew special attention to the different materials used for writing, and the ways they affect the scope, character, and purposes of the messages they record. Messages carved with a chisel on heavy, durable materials – such as slate, granite or marble – have a monumental character that endures through deep, or slow, time. Messages written on lightweight materials such as papyrus or paper (invented in China and available in Europe, via the Moors, from the thirteenth century) are portable and easily carried over great distances.

More generally, Innis argued that different media, using different materials, had different consequences for the human, social control of time and space: he called this 'the bias of communication' (Innis 1964 [1951]). He noted the importance of written technologies for the establishment and maintenance of empires – the creation of power blocs spread over great distances and preserved through many generations. He observed that the complex task of administering, coordinating, and policing a vast imperium, such as the Roman empire, required written systems both as means of recording decisions, laws and so on, *and* of communicating them throughout the empire. Writing was one essential underpinning of the whole colossal enterprise. Innis's analysis of written systems of communication shows clearly that writing, in its primary functions, has always been linked to political and economic power. Wherever writing has established itself, it has immediately produced a fundamental distinction between the lettered and the unlettered, the educated and the uneducated. To have the skills of reading and writing is a passport to individual self-advancement. Literacy gives rise to educated elites (in the past they were called priests;

alphabetic and ideographic systems of writing

time and space as aspects of communication systems

writing materials

the bias of communication

writing as record and communication

literacy and social difference

today they are called academics) that gravitate to the centres of power.

Innis's major work focused on the character of communication in ancient societies. It was Marshall McLuhan who picked up on Innis's ideas and applied them to modern societies. McLuhan, following Innis, made a fundamental distinction between 'oral' and 'written' cultures. He focused particularly on the impact of the new technology of printing in the late fifteenth century on the older 'manuscript culture' of the Middle Ages. McLuhan argued that Europe's take-off into the modern world was powerfully supported by the new culture of the book, which rapidly spread through Europe in the sixteenth century, creating new 'knowledge communities' based on print (McLuhan 1962). He went on, in *Understanding Media* (1964), to compare print cultures with the newer electronic cultures of modern media, especially radio and television, arguing that they had the effect of rescuing oral forms of communication from the dominance of printed and written forms. McLuhan was one of the first real analysts of modern media as communication technologies. It is in his writings that 'the media' are first examined as interrelated technologies that come together to create media societies. It is from McLuhan that we learned to think of 'the media'.

Perhaps his most striking and important perception of the impact of electronic media was that it could no longer be thought of as particular to this or that society. What was new about electronic media was their *global* impact: they created, for the first time in history, the possibility of point-to-point, instant, live communication between any two points on the globe – 'the global village,'◄ in his famous phrase (McLuhan 1964). Electronic media have powerful transforming effects on the character of social time and space. In effect, they help to create and sustain the 'world-historical' character of modern life (Giddens 1990). It is increasingly difficult *not* to know what is going on elsewhere in the world today. Time and space have drastically shrunk. Each one of us

► the global village and globalization – Chapter 11, p. 180

has the world in our living room. Global television is a very real phenomenon when millions and millions of people, scattered all over the world, have simultaneous access to an event such as the Olympics (Dayan and Katz 1992). Television today is intimately linked to the character of national and international politics, business and war. Through television, cultural narratives, images, songs and jokes circulate around the world. When a programme like *Dallas* is watched in over a hundred different countries it is clear that electronic media contribute to the formation of a global culture – a culture of consumption, many have argued, underpinned by global capitalism – which has serious implications for national and local cultures. A key aspect of the 'gap' between North and South, the so-called developed and developing regions of the world, is a communications divide – the unequal flow of information and entertainment between first and third worlds.

Innis and McLuhan provide a fascinating way of identifying the impact and effect of media of communication on human societies by focusing on them as technologies that extend the scope and scale of human, social activity. Their emphasis on the 'bias of communication' implicit in different media technologies draws attention to their effect on the social organization of time and space. Their approach has an intrinsically historical thrust and, indeed, conceives of history in terms of time periods dominated or characterized by different media: from small-scale oral societies, to empires underpinned by writing, to the early modern European culture of the book, to today's electronic global culture. It is valuable to emphasize that the media are not simply 'neutral' carriers of information, but have a determinate effect on the character and scope of what they convey.

We should, however, note some of the limitations of this approach and, in particular, the charge of 'technological determinism' which is often made against it. As Raymond Williams (1974: 13) succinctly put it:

> New technologies are discovered, by an essentially internal process of research and

technological determinism

development, which then sets the conditions for social change and progress. Progress, in particular, is the history of these inventions, which 'created the modern world.' The effects of these technologies, whether direct or indirect, foreseen or unforeseen, are as it were, the rest of history. The steam engine, the automobile, television, the atom bomb, have *made* modern man and the modern condition.

The kind of argument advanced by Innis and McLuhan has the effect of making technologies of communication into instruments that appear, somehow, outside and beyond the control of their makers. It is another subtle kind of historicism: a 'grand narrative' of progress in which the hero is technology. The media shape human societies in their own likeness. The effect of such an argument is to remove the very stuff of history – the actions of human beings, politics, war, culture, entertainment – from the analysis. Do we use media or do they use us? For McLuhan, as he famously put it, 'the medium *is* the message.' Its content is irrelevant. But what is missing in this kind of approach is any attention to how media are caught up in the histories of human societies, and are used in various ways and for various purposes.

the medium is the message

Nevertheless, these pioneering historical studies of human communication, as determined by media technologies which shape and constrain human action, have become increasingly influential after a period in the 1970s when McLuhan fell out of favour, particularly with the Left, whose theories were then in fashion (Winthrop-Young and Wutz 1999: xi–xvi). Anthropologists took up the basic distinction between 'oral' societies and those with written or print-based cultures (Goody 1968; Ong 1982). McLuhan's thesis about the transition from manuscript to print cultures in Europe was explored by Elizabeth Eisenstein (1979). More recent work, such as Friedrich Kittler's historical study, first published in 1986, of *Gramophone, Film, Typewriter* took up the basic insights of Innis and McLuhan, and reworked them in a postmodern, antihumanist reading of the ways in which 'media determine our situation' (Kittler 1999: xxxix).

Kittler's work, in turn, has been an important source for John Durham Peters's remarkable historical study of the *idea* of communication (Peters 1999). There is a history not just of technologies of communication, but also of how we *think* about communication (our changing understanding of what it means). The connections between the two are explored by Peters in a highly original way. Kittler's work showed how new communication technologies – the gramophone, for instance – change the ways in which we think of ourselves. Today we are all familiar with the *idea* that human brains are rather like computers. This seems a natural idea to us. A hundred years ago, it seemed natural to think of the brain as rather like Edison's phonograph (Kittler 1999: 38–45), an idea that to us now seems bizarre.

history of the idea of communication

Peters, following Kittler, shows in fascinating detail some of the ways in which new communication technologies have shaped how we think about ourselves and others. He traces the *idea* of communication as occurring not only between human beings, but also with the dead, with angels, with aliens, with animals, and with machines. If this sounds odd, consider the huge investment, since the 1950s, in 'scientific' efforts to communicate with 'the rest of the universe' on the assumption that somewhere – out there in infinite time–space – there are intelligent alien beings to receive the messages that we are beaming out into the void. Peters's brilliant description and analysis of the SETI project (the Search for Extra-Terrestrial Intelligence), an international scientific programme that began in the USA after World War II and which still continues, is indicative of a theme that is central to his book, namely that an increasing awareness of communication generates increasing anxiety about it (Peters 1999: 246–261).

It is only in the modern era, with the huge proliferation of technologies of communication, that communication has become an issue for us. Today we are highly aware of the fragility of 'successful' communication, and of the endless possibilities of communicative failure or breakdown both as technical problems *and* as social problems of our relations and interactions with others. To think about how we think about communication as such in relation to new means of communicating is the distinctive contribution Peters makes to the historical study of communication.

MEDIA HISTORIES

The historical study of communication tends, as the brief review above indicates, to exhibit the following characteristics. Especially in Innis and McLuhan, a synoptic approach is taken which operates within large, epochal time spans, which embraces a 'total' or global view of history transcending national boundaries, and which deploys an analysis of the historical process whereby the emphasis is not on human beings as historical agents (i.e. as 'makers' of history) but on external (technological) factors which determine the scale and scope of human agency. In all these ways, the history of communication is part of the 'new history' that reacted against the ways in which the academic discipline and field of study was originally established. Histories of communication mobilise a deterministic (or structuralist) approach to their field of study and are strongly anti-humanist, notably so in Kittler's (1999) work, which throughout writes mockingly of 'so-called Man'.

Histories of media tend, by comparison, to be old-fashioned, humanist narratives which focus on the histories of particular media institutions or of particular historic 'moments'. They eschew synthetic, synoptic accounts. These differences should not, of course, be thought of in terms of the preferences of individual historians. It is rather that these two different historical 'topics' – communication and media – call for different methods and accounts. Written histories are, of necessity, about the past, but how much time must pass before histories can begin to be written? The history of print goes back centuries. The history of television goes back fifty years. The history of the Internet goes back ten years, if that. In order for History to appear, there must be some distance between the present time (in which history is written) and the past time (which is to be written about). In other words, it may not yet be possible to write histories of 'the

media', since this presupposes a synthesis so recent that its historical lineaments are scarcely visible at this time. What we find instead, as Dahl (1994) pointed out, are institutional histories of particular media: newspapers, radio and television.

institutional histories of single media

But even this is problematic. What are the grounds for taking newspapers, radio and television as 'the media'? Different taxonomies show up in media and communication departments in European and North American universities, where radio, film and television are often studied together along with 'journalism'. The common tendency to bracket film and television together because they are thought of as 'visual media', and the tendency to neglect the study of radio (often called 'the Cinderella' of media studies) are the results of another 'hidden history', namely, the history of the development of the academic field of study itself. ◄ This too, like its object domain of inquiry, is as yet so recent as to be barely visible.

The legitimacy of any academic field of study takes time to become established. At the beginning of the twentieth century, the study of modern literatures did not exist as an academic discipline, and, within a university culture that privileged the study of ancient literatures (Greek and Roman), the study of things like the modern novel seemed trivial and irrelevant (Doyle 1989; Mathieson 1975). The first undergraduate degree in media studies in the UK was established at the then Polytechnic of Central London (now University of Westminster) in 1975. Time has yet to work its alchemy on the academic study of the media, transforming it from its present lowly status (in Britain at least) into a respectable field of study such as modern literature. Meanwhile, it should be noted that the emergence and definition of the field has been fitful and uneven, and has often been the outcome of internal institutional reorganization and the rationalization of existing resources. Film studies developed earlier than media studies, and usually within modern literature departments, from which they sometimes broke away. Film histories, however, continued to

---

► history of media research institutions – Chapter 16, p. 278

privilege the cinematic texts.◄ As film studies developed, it extended its interests to what it regarded as cognate fields of inquiry, namely photography and television. There is no necessary correspondence between the structure of the media in 'the real world' and the ways in which 'the media' are studied in universities. Historically and 'as a matter of fact', radio and television are very closely linked in terms of their technological, economic, political and institutional formation. Yet they are seldom studied or researched by academics as related to each other under the rubric of 'broadcasting'. It is thus necessary to argue the case for treating 'the media' as, in essence, the interconnections between newspapers (the press), radio and television (broadcasting). I have made this case elsewhere, arguing that the shared structural characteristic of all three is 'dailiness'; a specific temporality that is articulated and given substance in the contemporary world by the interplay of daily newspaper, radio and television services (Scannell 1988, 1996c, 2000).

dailiness

PRESS HISTORIES

The time spans of the development of newspapers, radio and television are quite different. Newspapers as we now know them in North America and Europe can be traced back to the seventeenth century. The technology of wireless telephony was worked out in the late nineteenth century, and its widespread social application as radio begins after World War I. The technology of television dates from the early twentieth century, and the history of its social usage begins properly after World War II (for an overview see Winston 1998).◄ Not surprisingly, historical work on these developments has a different time span in each case.

In the UK, histories of newspapers go back at least to the mid-nineteenth century, and there is a large body of literature on particular newspapers (a five-volume history of *The Times* being the outstanding example (Anon 1935–1958)), journalists and newspaper owners,

nearly all of which was written by people in the business, rather than by professional historians. As such they are largely anecdotal, concerned with significant individuals (there is a subgenre of journalism biographies about outstanding newspaper editors and outrageous newspaper proprietors) and the politics of their day. However, as James Curran has argued in an influential synoptic account of British press history (Curran and Seaton 1997), a distinctive consensus emerges as to the meaning and significance of its historical formation. It is yet another variant of the 'Whig interpretation of British history' (Butterworth 1965), in which the emergence of a 'free' political press is seen as a victory over government censorship and control (Curran and Seaton 1997: 5–113). The key moment is the mid-nineteenth century, when newspapers were freed from punitive forms of taxation imposed by government to prevent 'unlicensed' radical newspapers from criticizing those in power and fomenting civil unrest. In this account, 'the market' appears as the hero; the guarantor of civil liberties and the protector of the political independence of newspapers which no longer function as the mouthpiece of various political factions. In Curran's view, the most authoritative academic history of the British press (Koss 1981, 1984) simply extends this 'myth' through to the present (Curran and Seaton 1997: 28–31). Curran, however, has his own 'alternative' account of this history, in which the hero is the ultimately suppressed radical press of the early nineteenth century, and the villain is the market, which, he argues, has destroyed the possibility of a properly political press. Thus, his account reverses the terms of the Whig teleology, but retains its premises. The terms in which press history is thought in Curran's account remain within the traditional concerns of political historiography. The past is interrogated and criticized in the light of a set of unexamined political concerns in the present.

The most influential history of the US press starts from rather different premises. It is a social, rather than a political history, and began as a Ph.D. dissertation in the Sociology Department of Harvard University. Its author, Michael Schudson, was interested in the history of ideals

British press

Whig interpretation of history

► film studies – Chapter 2, p. 31

► chronological table of media and communication – Chapter 2, p. 18

and the sociology of values. He combined both in a historical study of the American press, which began as 'a case study in the history of professions and in the genesis of professional ideology'. As such, its main concern was with the relationship between the institutionalization of modern journalism and general currents in economic, political, social and cultural life (Schudson 1978: 10–11). The issue that brings into focus all these concerns is the question of 'objectivity' as an ideology or norm for practising journalists:◄ it is the history of the rise and fall of this idea that is traced in *Discovering the News*. Schudson's account, though a chronological narrative, avoids the pitfalls of a teleology. 'Objectivity' is neither the triumph of value-free journalism, nor the hidden, self-deceiving bias of a dominant, market-driven press. What is shown, rather, is that 'objectivity' as a social value is intrinsically historical. The early American press had no concept of 'objectivity', which arose only as the press was industrialized and journalism became fully professional in the twentieth century. The separation of 'facts' and 'opinion', information and comment was the complex outcome of the commercial pressures of mass production and the extension of democracy. Objectivity became the lodestone of professional journalism in the early nineteenth century, not out of a naive empiricism and faith in 'facts', but rather the reverse. It was a bulwark, Schudson argues, against scepticism and anxieties about the corrosive relativism, the arbitrariness of values, and the subjectivity of belief in a world where one man's opinion was as good as another's and neither had any special claim to truth. Journalistic objectivity was one response to 'the hollow silence of modernity' (Schudson 1978: 158). Yet even as it was articulated as a professional value in the 1930s, the criticism of 'the myth' of objectivity was enunciated, and this criticism became routine in the adversarial Left culture of the 1960s (from which Curran attacks the dominant interpretation of British press history).

► journalistic objectivity – Chapter 5, p. 87

HISTORIES OF BROADCASTING

Radio and television are products of the twentieth century, and their historical significance as well as their histories have only recently begun to emerge. The oldest, and longest running, history of broadcasting is by the British historian, Asa Briggs, who began working on the institutional history of the British Broadcasting Corporation (BBC) in the 1950s. The fifth volume in this massive history was published in 1995 (at which point Briggs laid down his pen), and a sixth volume (to be written by Jean Seaton) has just been commissioned. When Briggs began, he was operating, as he noted, in uncharted waters. There were no general histories of broadcasting in any country to serve as models. The three-volume history of American broadcasting by Erik Barnouw (1966–1970) had not yet appeared. Neither communication nor media studies had yet appeared as academic fields of study.

BBC: institutional history

Briggs therefore found himself in the position of 'inventing' broadcasting history, and his reflections on the methodological and other problems he faced are thus of particular interest. He wanted to write a 'total history' that covered all aspects of the activities of the BBC. This was a truly monumental undertaking since, by the time he got up to World War II, the BBC's activities were on a global scale; in 1942 it was broadcasting in the short-wave radio band to all parts of the world. There were real difficulties of narrative organization and coherence as his history moved forward slowly on all fronts: home broadcasting, overseas broadcasting, radio, and, later, television. There were difficulties of writing an institutional history, which might result in a 'history from above' (reproducing the management view of the BBC and underplaying the attitudes of insubordinate dissidents in the ranks). There was the danger of not being able to see the wood for the trees: it was hard to find room for a historical account of the history of output – the programmes themselves – and their impact and effect on contemporary society. There was, finally, the issue of perspective. Briggs was anxious to avoid 'reading back into the past current fashions of description and explanation.' He wanted his history to be, above all else, definitive: 'to be as accurate and as well backed up (in footnotes) by *all* available evidence as possible.' He elected to quote at length from original sources – even though this was not then fashionable among historians – partly to capture lost modes of expression and mood, but also to enable readers who might draw different conclusions from his own assessments to have the necessary amount of published evidence before them (Briggs 1980: 8).

BBC: social history

Briggs's work is, above all, a historian's history, which allows subsequent researchers to pursue in greater detail the study of, say, programme making without having to reconstruct yet again the house that Briggs built. The social history of the beginnings of broadcasting in the UK that I wrote with David Cardiff (Scannell and Cardiff 1991) could not have been written without the prior existence of a definitive 'total' history of the BBC. Historians of public service broadcasting in other European countries have also acknowledged their debt to Briggs's history (e.g., Dahl 1976).

historical archives

It is a truism that histories are as good as the archives on which they depend. Historians of British broadcasting are lucky to have such a remarkable resource as the BBC Written Archives at Caversham (near Reading), whose holdings currently cover all aspects of the BBC's activities from the earliest days through to the end of the 1970s. Historians of the beginnings of broadcasting in other countries have had a more difficult task, since radio almost everywhere began on a local, commercial basis, and data about the very first radio stations have all but vanished. The perishable character of the spoken word shows up in stark contrast with the permanent trace of writing. Leslie Johnson, historian of early Australian broadcasting, notes what a difficult and disheartening task it was to gather information about the radio stations of the 1920s and 1930s (Johnson 1988: viii–ix). Susan Smulyan, in the absence of data from the stations themselves, draws heavily on early popular radio magazines for her history of the commercialization of American radio in the 1920s (Smulyan 1994). C Cecile Meadel faced similar difficulties when writing the history of the beginnings of French radio. When she did find data on some of the many radio stations of the period, they were invariably scanty, poorly kept and unclassified (Meadel 1994: 16–17).

histories of genres

In spite of such difficulties, in North America and in many European countries there are now in place histories of the beginnings and development of national broadcasting systems, starting with radio and continuing with television. These institutional histories have been complemented by more detailed 'genre' studies of particular aspects of broadcast output; news, drama, and documentary, for instance, having received considerable attention. Alongside these are social histories of audiences and of the place of radio and television in everyday life (e.g., Lacey 1994; Moores 1988; O'Sullivan 1991; van Zoonen and Wieten 1994).

'DOING' HISTORY

The past in its fullness is beyond recall. Only its traces remain today, and the task of piecing together the fragments, interpreting and reworking them into coherent narrative accounts and other formats, is, of necessity, a cumulative and collaborative process. There is no one 'correct' way of doing this. Historical work is partly determined by the available data (or lack of it), and partly by the predispositions and attitudes brought to bear upon the past by historians in their present. The literature referenced above is characterized by the diversity of its approaches and attitudes to history, but those attitudes are only partly determined by the concerns and prejudices of the historian. They are also shaped by the nature of the topic and the extent to which it is, or is not, established as an object of historical inquiry. In this respect, the problems of 'doing' broadcasting history are instructive.

Why should it be that *in the first place* broadcasting histories tend to be accounts of particular institutions? We may note that the first 'period' of broadcasting (a historiographical construct, of course) is the history of radio and its institutionalization within the context of particular nation-states. For although radio began, almost everywhere, on a small-scale local basis, technical, distributional and economic pressures rapidly led to the consolidation of the production and distribution of programmes into centralized, large-scale, national institutions, funded either by advertising revenues or by some form of hypothecated tax (a 'licence fee'). The history of broadcasting thus begins with accounts of that process. When that is in place, other historians can engage with what might be called 'second-generation' history. That is how I think of my own historical work on British broadcasting. The existence of Briggs's history made it possible to go back into the archives and begin a closer, more attentive study of the complex business of making programmes, across the major areas of broadcast output. How were the practices of gathering and broadcasting 'news' developed? How did broadcasters discover how to produce entertaining programmes for radio? How was music (what music? whose music?) developed as a major area of radio output? Such questions can only be addressed in detail if accounts of the institutional framework within which these activities were situated are already in place. It then becomes a complex business of gathering data, interpreting it and putting it into a coherent narrative frame.

It requires patience and persistence to sift through a holding as massive as the BBC Written Archives. Such work should ideally be done in a concentrated, continuous way. It is no use doing it occasionally over an extended period. You have to immerse yourself in an archive as I did, several days a week continuously for over a year, in order to feel your way around the holdings (so that you get a sense of where to look for a 'missing link'), but above all in order to begin, in time, to see how the bits and pieces fit together. It is like doing a gigantic jigsaw puzzle, except that a lot of the pieces are inevitably missing, and so you will have to fill in the blanks by circumstantial evidence where necessary. Archival work, then, shares several features with other qualitative research, including an extended stay in a locale as well as iterative procedures of sampling and analysis.◄

► qualitative empirical methodologies – Chapter 14

The most obviously 'lost' pieces in the puzzle, for historians of early radio, are the broadcast programmes themselves. The BBC began broadcasting in 1923, but there are no extant recordings of any programmes until the early 1930s, and only a tiny fraction of output before World War II was recorded and preserved. So how do you deal with this? There is, of course, a complete record of what was broadcast, day by day, in the programme schedules of the *Radio Times*, which started up only months after the BBC got going in 1923. Before the war, all programmes were scripted, and in many cases the transcripts of the programme as broadcast (with last-minute emendations and corrections pencilled in) were kept. For example, a very good picture of developments in radio documentary (or 'features' as they were called at the time in the BBC) can be built up from recordings and transcripts of programmes, and from a number of very useful production files which reveal (in the best cases) the whole process of the making of a particular programme from the initial idea through to transmission (Scannell 1986).

However, to take a notorious example, there are no transcripts of prewar news broadcasts (with the exception of the General Strike in 1926, and transmissions at the height of the Munich Crisis in 1938). The practice of keeping all bulletins began only with the outbreak of war. We simply do not know what news bulletins sounded like nor what, in detail, the structure and content of any bulletin was like before the war. Accounts of the beginnings of broadcast news are thus, in this strict sense, circumstantial. There is, nevertheless, a wealth of secondary source material about news from which a reasonably accurate account of its development may be built up. The files of the BBC's various management, policy-making and departmental committees were invariably useful. The magnificent press-cuttings collection was invaluable. Contemporary biographies by politicians and broadcasters were occasionally illuminating. *Hansard*, the verbatim record of the day-to-day proceedings of Parliament, was indispensable whenever there was a political row about news.

recordings of programmes

schedules and transcripts

organizational documents, press cuttings, and biographies

ANALYSIS BOX 12.1 HISTORICAL RESEARCH ON ARCHIVAL DATA

On top of questions concerning the availability of data, the nature of the topic and its status in previous research, one needs to be alert to connections between pieces of data one comes across in different contexts and on apparently different issues. In one of the many news files I examined (Scannell and Cardiff 1991), I came across an exchange of letters between the Home Office (the British ministry of interior affairs) and the BBC. The Home Office wrote to John Reith (Director General of the BBC) on 31 October 1932, querying the inclusion in the previous night's bulletin of a protest from the Metropolitan Police Federation about proposed cuts in police pay. Where had the BBC got this story, it wanted to know? Reith immediately replied that it came from the usual agency sources (the Press Association) and added that he had given instructions that 'no stuff from the agencies re cuts in pay, protest etc is to be broadcast . . . only HMG's [His Majesty's Government] official statements in future.' He further remarked that the same bulletin had included a message telephoned through to the News section from the Commissioner of Police, asking the public not to go out to watch demonstrations (Scannell and Cardiff 1991: 46–47).

It was difficult to make much sense of this at first, in the absence of any records of news bulletins, but I noticed the date and recalled that around this time unemployment had peaked at over 3 million. I then remembered accounts of the National Unemployed Workers' Movement which I had read as background to the BBC's handling of the issue of unemployment (Hannington 1977; Kingsford 1982). When I checked out Wal Hannington's book, all became clear. A massive protest march had arrived in London a day or so earlier and 'subversive' leaflets had been distributed in advance, addressed to the police force: 'Policemen! Defeat your own pay cuts by supporting Tuesday's demonstration against the economies!' (Kingsford 1982: 156). On the day of the demonstration – the day the Home Office queried the news item – there had been a huge gathering in Trafalgar Square and an impassioned speech from Hannington appealing to the police not to use their batons against the marchers and the large supporting crowd. But violence broke out, and two days later Hannington was arrested and charged with attempting to cause disaffection among members of the Metropolitan Police, contrary to the Public Order Act of 1919.

This example well illustrates the delicate hermeneutic◄ task that the historian faces when confronting primary data. As always, the date of the document, if available, is a crucial clue. But the text remains an enigma without detailed knowledge of what was happening in the country at precisely that time. Only when that has been discovered does the task of historical interpretation properly begin. What exactly does this nugget of information tell us? Does it show something of the subservience of the broadcasters (of Reith) to the government of the day? Perhaps. But how should that be understood? And here, the attitude of the historian comes into the equation. For it would be easy to construct some kind of conspiracy theory of hidden complicity between the broadcasters and their political masters in the management of news in ways that served the interests of those in power, thereby showing the role of the BBC in maintaining 'the dominant ideology' or something similar. Broadcasters themselves, however, were well aware of such dilemmas. I vividly remember the moment when I came across a memorandum, written days after the Munich Crisis, by the ex-Head of News, in which he declared that 'we [the BBC] have taken part in conspiracy of silence', and went on to say that the BBC had failed the British public by not giving it the necessary information as to the causes of the crisis or its implications – the inevitability of war (Scannell and Cardiff 1991: 88–89). A simple 'reading' of the developing relations between broadcasting and politics, starting with the General Strike of 1926 and going through to the outbreak of war, could plausibly develop a 'Bad News' thesis (Glasgow Media Group 1976) about the BBC's suppression and distortion of what was happening at the time. But this could be achieved

► hermeneutics – Chapter 2, p. 21

cont.

cont.

only by ignoring all the evidence of attempts by the broadcasters to resist the manipulations of government, most notably over two of the most sensitive political issues of the 1930s: unemployment and foreign affairs. We have documented in detail the resistances of programme- and policy-makers in both cases (see Scannell and Cardiff (1991: 64–68) on the 1934 Talks series on unemployment called *Time to Spare*; and pp. 74–78 on a 1935 series, *The Citizen and His Government*, which was suppressed by the government because it contained communist and fascist speakers).

The past must be understood in its own terms, in the first instance, before rushing to judgement with the wisdom of hindsight. In this regard, distant periods pose some of the same analytical challenges as other cultures.◀ Interpretations of the beginnings of broadcasting should be sensitive to the problems encountered by the broadcasters as they became involved in politics. It should be remembered that the formal conditions of full representative democracy were not established in the UK until 1919 by The Representation of the People Act. The *meaning* of democracy is something that gets worked out and discovered through the actual processes of history. This learning process has been at the heart of the relationship between broadcasting and politics from the beginning through to the present. A hermeneutics sensitive to this unending process would note, as we tried to, how the broadcasters gradually came to understand their own complicity with the political powers in the 'management' of news and information in the interwar period (Scannell and Cardiff 1991: 23–133). It would point to the basic problems for broadcasters of discovering how to 'do' informing, news-gathering and news-telling. There was no News Department in the BBC until 1934, and the practices of contemporary broadcast journalism with which we are all familiar today go back no further than the 1950s in the UK and the USA, and the 1960s and later in most other countries.

▶ cross-cultural and comparative research – Chapter 11, p. 179

The study of any aspect of broadcasting, and of other media, is impossible without knowledge of the wider political, social and cultural contexts within which they are situated. Again and again in our study of the production process within the BBC, David Cardiff and I had to reconstruct other histories: of entertainment in the prewar period, or of the state of musical culture at that time. There were no standard social or cultural histories to guide us on such matters, and so we had to reconstruct them ourselves from contemporary biographies, non-academic accounts and from magazines. It is essential to have a feel for the wider contexts within which broadcasting operates in order to write informed historical accounts of the activities of the broadcasters. I do not wish to be prescriptive as to how this is achieved. History is not a social science, and it tends to resist the impositions of rigid methodologies. The precise method of any particular historical investigation will be shaped and informed by the nature of the topic and the

available resources, but a willingness to read widely and to explore supplementary sources is vital. To this, I would add a sense of historical continuities and change over longer time spans than the actual period of study. The historian must look at what came before and after the topic which engages her or him. There is a tendency today still to write of the BBC and the meaning of public service broadcasting◀ as if it were set in place, once and for all, by its first Director-General, John Reith. But the meaning of public service has undergone significant and important changes in the past eighty years, and necessarily so, since it operates today in conditions very different from the 1920s when it began (see Scannell 1990, 1996b).

CONCLUSION

Histories of communication and of the media converge in the twentieth century, as is appar-

▶ public service broadcasting – Chapter 16, p. 277

ent in the works by Peters (1999) and Kittler (1999) already cited, and in Kern's (1983) fascinating study of 'the culture of time and space' at the turn of the last century, and Winston's (1998) synoptic history of media technology. The early 'mainframe' institutional histories of the press and broadcasting have been supplemented by all kinds of histories on particular aspects of the press and broadcasting in the past twenty-five years. The establishment of academic journals devoted to historical research◄ – *Media History* and *The Historical Journal of Film, Radio, and Television* – also indicates how well established this hybrid discipline, split across history and media and communication studies, has become.

What of the future? There is, first, a pressing need for historical work on all aspects of media and communication elsewhere in the world other than Europe and North America. If we take, for instance, the continent of Africa, only recently emerged from the epoch of white colonial domination, it is a difficult matter, in respect both of principle and method, to begin the necessary business of retrieving the history of a continent so long robbed of its own identity. In the postcolonial era,◄ along with everything else, there is the delicate question, forcefully posed by Ngugi Wa Thiong'o, concerning the decolonization of mind. For whom do African intellectuals write, in what language, and from what perspectives (Ngugi 1986)? The academic disciplines, whose normative status is largely taken for granted in the West, themselves pose tricky matters for African academics. 'History' as written and taught in the educational system of South Africa at every level in the apartheid era is, post 1994, in need of, and receiving, a thorough rethinking and rewriting. The press and broadcasting (radio is an important medium in many African countries) are a double-edged inheritance from the departed imperial powers. In Africa, they sit alongside oral traditions for both poetry and

song which may still be, for the majority of Africans, the dominant means through which stories circulate and opinions are formed. The interpretation of African culture in its own terms – without depending wholly on the intellectual and theoretical frames of the West – is a matter of concern in the emerging field of African media and cultural studies. There is currently a lively debate about the significance of *ubuntu* for the interpretation and understanding of African society and culture in general and the media in particular (Blankenberg 1999; Kamwangamulu 1999).

The profoundly ruptured history of communication in Africa – a history barely begun, because there was no time, before now, that it *could* be written – will be marked by these pressures and tensions. Meanwhile, what remains to be tackled in Europe and North America are synthetic media histories of one kind or another. A comparative review of national histories of the press and broadcasting would reveal, on the one hand, the cultural specificity and difference, country by country, in these developments, and, at the same time, their common patterns both in form and content. If it is a basic theoretical and methodological question for historians as to *whose* histories they are writing, one major concern is how to move beyond the histories of particular nation-states. Comparative media history does not yet exist, but it could begin to reveal the shared structural characteristics of national media systems and the unities and differences of media output in different countries and in different parts of the world. Such work might then confirm or disprove the claims of 'medium theorists' (mostly followers of McLuhan; see Meyrowitz 1994) as to the allegedly inherent, structural characteristics of written and electronic forms of communication, and thereby begin to reconcile those histories that privilege form with those that privilege content.

ubuntu: 'humanness' (literally: 'I only exist because of my ties to others'), emphasizing community life, collective responsibility, and communication

comparative media history

► journals and reference works – Chapter 1, p. 3

► postcolonial theory – Chapter 11, p. 179

III Practice

SCIENTIFIC APPROACHES AND SOCIAL IMPLICATIONS

Doing media research

Media and communication studies have developed a variety of analytical procedures and designs, drawing on the social sciences as well as the humanities. In overview, empirical studies have relied on six different prototypical methods, as laid out in Figure III.1.

In addition to the qualitative-quantitative distinction, these methods are characterized by their forms of data collection and the resulting types of evidence. Each basic method, as employed singly or in combination with other methods, raises a number of methodological, theoretical, epistemological, as well as political questions.

The following chapters present key concepts and criteria for the practice of empirical research. Two chapters describe and exemplify how various qualitative and quantitative methodologies may be applied to different types of research questions. One chapter explores and illustrates the complementarity of the two types of approaches:

- *Quantitative studies* are covered both in terms of their basic categories and operations, and with reference to the different relevances of surveys, experiments, and content analyses;
- *Qualitative studies* are presented, similarly, in terms of the systematics of interviewing, observation, and textual research, including issues of data collection and data analysis;
- *The complementarity* of qualitative and quantitative research is examined with reference both to concrete examples and to classic problems in the philosophy of science.

	Qualitative	Quantitative
Speech/ verbal language	interviewing	survey
Action/behavior	observation	experiment
Texts/documents	discourse analysis	content analysis

Figure III.1 Six prototypical empirical methods

cont.

cont.

Unification in the final instance

The chapters take as their premise that different methodological approaches can and should be combined so as to supplement each other. It is this premise, as borne out by a number of examples and arguments, which is summed up in the heading 'Unification in the final instance.' While much of this volume has already traced the convergence of previously distinct research traditions, the following chapters present and review a variety of practical resources available for present and future media studies.

Media research as social practice

Like mediated communication, media studies are themselves an integral part of the societies and cultures being studied. The final chapter returns to the social origins and contexts of research, and to the interests guiding different types of projects in different sectors of society. Many media students and researchers wish to make a difference through their work. One lesson from the field so far is that media studies *necessarily* make a difference. The question is how, in whose interest, and through which empirical and theoretical approaches?

13 The quantitative research process

Barrie Gunter

- an overview of *basic concepts* within quantitative research, including *hypothesis testing* and *sampling*
- reviews of *survey* research, quantitative *content analyses* and *experimental* studies of media, with analytical examples
- a *comparison of surveys and experiments*, their strengths and weaknesses
- a presentation of quantitative *data analysis*, including examples of *statistical procedures*.

INTRODUCTION

The field of media and communication research is characterised by quite a variety of different research perspectives. That fact stems from the hybrid nature of this field of empirical inquiry, in which investigative approaches have been derived from longer established academic disciplines in the social sciences.◄ Anthropology, economics, geography, history, linguistics, political science, psychology, sociology have all contributed theories and methodologies for studying the structure, organisation, content, uses and impact of media. While media scholars have, accordingly, debated the merits and shortcomings of different theories and methodologies within limited spheres of inquiry (Neuman 1994; Wimmer and Dominick 1994), perhaps the most significant debate within academic circles (though not the highest profile one in the public sphere) has centred on a dispute between different philosophies of social science about the research perspective that offers the most sensitive and meaningful insights into the

role and influence of the media in society. A 'positivist' or hypothetico-deductive school of thought has been lined up against critical and interpretive perspectives.◄ These different social-scientific perspectives vary in terms of the perceived objectives of research, the way social reality and human beings are conceived, the role of theory-driven empirical inquiry and the kind of evidence to which most weight is given (see Neuman 1994). Hypothetico-deductive approaches to media inquiry are concerned with the setting up, proving or disproving of hypotheses, and the eventual establishment of theoretical explanations of events or causal laws which explain relationships between individuals' activities in, and experiences of media, and their knowledge, beliefs, opinions and behaviour. These phenomena are usually operationally defined in quantitative terms to facilitate measurement of the strengths of causal links or degrees of association between them.

It is not the purpose of this chapter to elaborate upon the distinctions between these

---

► social-scientific sources of media studies – Chapter 3

► positivism and other philosophy of science – Chapter 15

philosophies of social science, nor to discuss their relative strengths and weaknesses. This chapter is concerned with the nature of quantitative research, examines the basic concepts of this kind of empirical inquiry, and discusses the principal forms it takes. The latter will be divided in terms of whether their main aim is to investigate associative links (surveys) or causal links (experiments) between variables. A further distinction will be made between methodologies concerned with the study of either media audiences or media content – the two foci of quantitative media studies. Since quantitative studies of media content largely involve a form of surveying of media output, this methodology will be discussed under the heading of survey research. It should perhaps be noted at this point, however, that the systematic analysis of media output may form part of an experimental investigation, too.

The chapter will also examine some of the basic principles of quantitative data analysis and presentation. In quantitative research, measurement is conducted through numbers. The quality of the research is crucially affected by the effectiveness of data processing, analysis and interpretation. The discussion of quantitative research methods inevitably examines not just their inherent strengths and weaknesses, but also when their application is appropriate and inappropriate. To be complete, this review also considers the evolution of quantitative research methodologies in relation to theoretical models of media analysis, and attempts to address any weaknesses of this link.

BASIC CONCEPTS IN QUANTITATIVE RESEARCH

The basic concepts that characterise quantitative research methodologies concern relevant modes of measurement and procedures to analyse the relationships between such measurements. A central notion is the *variable*, which is linked to additional fundamental elements of quantitative research such as concepts and constructs.

concepts   A *concept* represents an abstract idea that embodies the nature of observable phenomena, or an interpretation of why such phenomena

occur. For example, individuals may be differentiated in terms of their use of media – heavy users may be distinguished from light users. This media usage, in turn, may be linked to patterns of social behaviour, and may even be used to explain different behavioural patterns. In this context, media usage becomes an explanatory concept. In a different context, the concept of 'cultivation' may be used to describe distinctive patterns of perceptions or beliefs that individuals who are heavy media-users hold, and which distinguish them from the perceptions and beliefs held by light media-users (Gerbner *et al.* 1986; Wober and Gunter 1988).

A *construct* comprises a combination of   constructs concepts. This term is often used to describe a defining characteristic of individuals that is associated with their personality type. For example, the personality construct of 'sensation-seeking' is used to distinguish between people who seek varying levels of optimal stimulation from their environment (Zuckerman 1994). High sensation-seekers generally need higher levels of environmental stimulation than low sensation-seekers. High sensation-seekers, for instance, may be characterised by such concepts as sociability, tolerance for strong stimulation, risk-taking and a sense of adventure. Constructs have a dimensional quality, so that individuals may be classified as high or low on the personality dimension of sensation-seeking.

A *variable* is an empirical representation of a concept or construct. Whereas concepts and constructs have an abstract quality, variables provide operational measures that can be quantified and manipulated by researchers. For example, gender, age and socioeconomic class are variables. Personality characteristics such as aggressiveness, locus of control, extraversion and neuroticism can all be treated as variables. The amount of newspaper reading or television viewing also exemplify variables. Variables may   variables with be further defined and differentiated in terms   attributes of their constituent *attributes*. Attributes are values or categories into which variables can be divided. In the case of gender, there are two categories – male and female. In the case of age, individuals can be differentiated by age group or actual age. Television viewers can be differentiated by amount of viewing into values such as light, medium and heavy viewers on the basis of self-reported or independently observed viewing behaviour.

Types of variables

independent and dependent variables

Variables can be defined further in terms of their relationship with each other. A fundamental distinction is made between *independent* and *dependent* variables. The independent variable is a variable which can be manipulated by the researcher. It is also known as the 'causal' variable, in that it is a concept or construct that is believed to produce some measurable response or outcome. The independent variable is also referred to as the predictor variable in some studies. The dependent variable is the measure of the response or outcome. It is therefore also known as the 'effect' or 'criterion' variable. A principal objective of quantitative research is to establish the closeness of the relationship between independent and dependent variables (Neuman 1994; Wimmer and Dominick 1994). Ultimately, researchers wish to provide evidence that a particular independent variable has a causal relationship with a particular dependent variable (Bailey 1994).

To illustrate this idea, a media researcher may be interested in demonstrating that television news can improve the audience's knowledge of a political event or issue.◄ One theorist might argue that this outcome is dependent upon the way political news is presented in a news bulletin. Another might argue that it depends upon the frequency with which individuals are exposed to such stories (Gunter 1987b). In the first case, a study might be launched in which the position of a political news story in a bulletin is varied. For some viewers, the story is presented at the beginning of the bulletin, while for others it occurs at the end or in the middle. A serial-position hypothesis would lead one to predict that presentation in the middle of the bulletin would result in poorer post-viewing recall of the story by viewers (Gunter 1979; Tannenbaum 1954). In this case, the independent variable is the positioning of the story and the dependent variable

is the measurement of story content recall by viewers after the bulletin has been presented.

In the second case, a sample of viewers might be presented with a questionnaire that asks them to report how often they have watched television news over the past week or month (Gunter 1985b). Similar questions might be asked about exposure to radio news and newspapers. The same respondents would then be asked a series of knowledge questions about a political news story. A separate analysis might be carried out of the frequency with which that story was covered by the news media. The latter measure could be combined with the measure of self-reported news media exposure to define the independent variable of relevant political news exposure. Respondents with heavy and light news exposure could then be compared regarding their scores on the measures of political story knowledge, which would be the dependent variable here.

Hypothesis testing

Quantitative research is primarily concerned with demonstrating cause–effect relationships, and any research project begins by setting up a *hypothesis*. A hypothesis is a proposition to be tested, or a tentative statement of a relationship between two variables.◄ While hypothesis testing is not unique to quantitative research, it is one of its fundamental elements, and almost a required aspect of quantitative academic research. (Qualitative research, under a 'positivist' school of social science, may eschew hypothesis testing if its aim is purely exploratory, in which case it is concerned more with the discovery of potential hypotheses for future testing.)

Hypotheses make prognostications about the links between variables (Bailey 1994). They propose that under one set of conditions, if an independent variable is manipulated in a certain way (as in experimental studies) or is assumed to have a certain strength (as in survey research), it may be expected to exert a measurable impact on a designated dependent variable. The researcher then sets out to discover if

► recall studies – Chapter 9, p. 144

► hypothetico-deductive research – Chapter 15, p. 262

that prediction holds true. The essence of quantitative scientific enquiry is to prove or disprove hypotheses, and the outcome is seen as a contribution to the growth of knowledge. Scientists rarely restrict themselves to testing single hypotheses, however. Through repeated hypothesis testing and the development and verification of new hypotheses, a body of understanding is developed that essentially comprises a series of acceptable and accepted explanations for a range of dependent variables.

research as cumulation of knowledge

Reliability and validity

A core aim of social scientific inquiry, particularly within the 'positivist' tradition, is the establishment and demonstration of the reliability and validity of research findings. *Reliability* concerns the dependability and consistency of the relationship between two variables or in the score obtained on a single variable at more than one point in time. *Validity* indicates whether a measure properly captures the meaning of the concept or construct it represents. If heavy viewing of violent programmes on television is believed to cause aggressive behaviour in viewers, then for this belief to be accepted as true, two conditions must be met. First, repeated evidence must emerge that exposure to violence on television is followed by increased aggressiveness. Second, the measures of exposure to television violence and of aggressive behaviour must accurately represent those behaviours.

reliability through repetition of measurements and tests

Reliability can be established by carrying out repeated tests of phenomena and relationships between phenomena, by repeating such tests among different groups of people with the same results, and by having several researchers run the same test (Siegel and Hodge 1968). Where a particular concept or construct – for example, a personality dimension such as extraversion or sensation-seeking – is measured by a series of items, it should be possible to select at random any 50 per cent subset of the total set of items and find that they differentiate between individuals in the same way as any other 50 per cent subset of those items. This is known as split-half reliability testing. Alternatively, a researcher could construct two different questionnaires designed to measure the same

split-half reliability testing

concept and administer both to the same group of respondents. This is called multiple forms (Goode and Hatt 1952) or alternate forms (Sellitz *et al*. 1976) reliability.

multiple or alternate forms reliability

Validity can be much more difficult to establish with certainty. 'Measurement validity is the degree of fit between a construct and indicators of it' (Neuman 1994: 130). Partly because of this complexity, validity is assessed in several ways (Figure 13.1):

- *Face validity* offers a basic level of judgement that a measured variable really measures the phenomenon it represents. A test of proof-reading ability might ask individuals to read and correct errors in a passage of text. The test would provide a clear behavioural representation of the kind of ability being measured.

- *Predictive validity* assesses the ability of a measure to predict a future event that is logically connected to a concept or construct. If a test of extraversion distinguishes between how sociable and outgoing people are, then high scorers should be observed to initiate more conversations and speak to more people at a party full of strangers than would low scorers.

- *Concurrent validity* means that a measure is associated with another indicator that has already been shown to be valid. Thus, a new measure of sociability would be expected to exhibit a high and significant correlation with scores on an established extraversion scale.

- *Construct validity* is a more complex method of establishing a measure's validity. Since a construct usually comprises a collection of concepts and indicators, construct validity requires that a new measurement is shown to be related to a variety of other established and previously verified measures. In the development of a questionnaire measure of aggression, for example, researchers may ask whether it differentiates among individuals who might be expected to exhibit different aggression levels on the basis of other established aggression measures, or whether the new questionnaire measure distinguishes among individuals whom other judges (e.g., friends, peers, parents, teachers) have distinguished in the same way, or among whom one would expect such differ-

Judgement-based	Criterion-based	Theory-based
Face validity	Predictive validity Concurrent validity	Construct validity

Figure 13.1 Types of validity
Source: Wimmer and Dominick 1994: 99

ences to occur on theoretical grounds (e.g., gender differences in aggressiveness) (Milavsky *et al.* 1982).

A distinction may also be made between *internal validity* and *external validity*. Internal validity means that the design of a research project is free from theoretical or methodological error, and is a term mostly used in experimental studies. An experiment's results could be invalidated if it emerged that its measurements failed to capture the phenomena they purported to measure. External validity is also used primarily in the context of experiments. This concept addresses whether the results can be generalised to other situations or groups of people. Low external validity means that the results are unique to the specific experimental setting in which they were obtained, but are unlikely to occur anywhere else.

internal and external validity

Levels of measurement

There are four principal types of measurement in quantitative research. The type of measurement reflects the kind of concept or construct it represents. Some measurements make fairly superficial or crude distinctions between entities, while others operate at a higher or more refined level. An initial distinction may be made between *continuous* and *discrete* variables. Discrete variables can be measured at the *nominal* or *ordinal* levels, while continuous variables can be measured at the *interval* or *ratio* levels. Continuous variables have a number of measurable values which can be located along a mathematical continuum, and measurement is along a scale that rises in increments. Hence, the measurement of time can be made in terms of seconds or minutes; the measurement of dis-

continuous and discrete variables

tance can be made in terms of various units of length. Discrete variables, instead, make distinctions according to relatively fixed attributes. Objects fall into one category or another. Examples of this form of measurement include gender (male or female), marital status (single, married, divorced, widowed) and religion (Protestant, Catholic, Muslim, Hindu, etc.).

- The *nominal* level is the weakest form of measurement. Numbers can be used here only to signify categories of objects. For instance, voters can be classified in terms of the specific political party they voted for. Any 'object' which is thus placed within a particular category is deemed to be equivalent to any other, and there is no indication of the degree to which an object belongs to a category.

- At the next level of *ordinal* measurement, objects of analysis are ranked along a dimension, such as smaller to greater, or lower to higher. In the case of socioeconomic class, for example, people may be ranked as belonging to different classes, with some classes deemed to be higher than others. Middle class is therefore higher than working class, but there is no indication given of how much distance lies between one class and another.

- At the *interval* level, entities are measured along a dimension that has equal intervals. One commonly used example is temperature. The temperature scale rises in degrees with each degree mathematically equal to any other degree. The weakness of the interval scale is that it lacks a true zero or a condition of nothingness. An intelligence scale is another example of an interval scale. Lacking a true zero, however, it is not possible to say that a person with an IQ of 100 is twice as intelligent as one with an IQ of 50.

- The *ratio* scale is the most powerful form of measurement. This has all the properties of an interval scale and the existence of a true zero. Time, distance and speed are examples of ratio level scales. An object moving at ten miles an hour is moving exactly twice as fast as one moving at five miles an hour.

These basic concepts are applied in quantitative research, in particular, to measure media audiences, media content and cause–effect relationships between media and audiences. Quantitative methods have demonstrated either associations between media and audiences or direct, causal connections between them, and in the remaining sections of this chapter, these methods are examined in turn. In each case, the principal designs are reviewed first, before attention shifts to illustrations of how they have been applied by media researchers.

SEARCHING FOR MEDIA–EFFECT ASSOCIATIONS: SURVEY RESEARCH

Surveys are a major form of quantitative research that does not involve any manipulation of participants or their circumstances in advance. Surveys collect data after the fact. Because they obtain information from respondents about their knowledge, beliefs, attitudes, values and behaviours on a *post hoc* basis, surveys cannot test cause–effect relationships directly. Surveys instead explore relationships or degrees of association between variables. Thus, surveys are entirely dependent upon self-report information supplied by respondents, whereas experiments can complement questionnaire responses with direct observations by researchers. In the media and communication context, surveys have been conducted with both the general public (i.e., media audiences) and specialised groups (e.g., media producers). (For further information about best practice in conducting surveys, see Babbie 1990; Fink 1995a, 1995b; Oppenheim 1992.)

The original form of the modern survey, historically, was the census (Converse 1987; Moser and Kalton 1971). A census compiles information about the characteristics of an entire population. Early censuses were conducted to assess property ownership for taxation purposes, but they also provided a means to establish the availability of young men for military service and, in democratic societies, assisted in the division of populations and territories into constituencies electing their representatives in government. Surveys, in their turn, were developed to document poverty following industrialisation and urbanisation in the nineteenth century.

While censuses attempt to obtain data from everyone in a population, surveys use sampling techniques to select subsets of a population for analysis. With a population numbering many millions of people, it is usually not feasible to question everyone, so that smaller and more manageable numbers must be selected for data collection. The most important objective here is to ensure that the achieved population subset, or 'sample', represents the population as a whole. During the first half of the twentieth century, survey research benefited from advances in scientific sampling procedures and questionnaire design techniques.

A classic study illustrating the early adoption of survey research regarding media influences was made by Lazarsfeld *et al.* (1944). This study conducted a survey of American voters to try to understand, among other things, more about the role of the media (radio and newspapers) in election campaigns. Repeat interviewing of respondents was carried out across the duration of a presidential election campaign in order to assess their exposure to campaign material, as well as their opinions about candidates and awareness of policies. Respondents' social category memberships (sex, age, residence, economic status and education) emerged as important variables that influenced their degree of exposure to mass communication and their political candidate preferences. Further research by Katz and Lazarsfeld (1955) utilised survey methodology to establish the importance of informal social networks for public opinion formation. A specific communication process, labelled the 'two-step flow of communication', posited that the media have an indirect effect upon public opinion, which operates through 'opinion leaders'. ◀

▶ two-step flow – Chapter 10, p. 159

[margin notes: relations of association and after the fact; self-report information; the census; population and sample]

Surveys may be differentiated in terms of their purpose; their administration, including sampling; and their time span.

Purpose of a survey

Surveys may be broadly divided into descriptive and analytical exercises:

- A *descriptive* survey simply attempts to document current conditions or states of affairs. Public opinion polls, for instance, can provide information about people's present attitudes on a specified topic. Historically, descriptive surveys can be traced back to the censuses, whose purpose was to define general characteristics of entire populations.

- *Analytical* surveys also collect descriptive data, but attempt to go on to examine relationships among variables in order to test research hypotheses. Accordingly, a survey may assess the impact of an advertising campaign on public awareness of a brand and changes in the market share of a product. Such explanatory surveys have also played a prominent part in research into the social effects of the media (e.g., the impact of media violence).

Forms of administration

Surveys collect data through either questionnaires or interview schedules (see Figure 13.2). Respondents may complete questionnaires by themselves, or answer questions that are put to them by an interviewer. Self-completion questionnaires are often posted to respondents who complete this 'instrument' at home in their own time and then mail it back to the researcher. Such questionnaires must be self-explanatory, because respondents are not guided through the data collection procedure by a researcher in person. Questionnaires may also be administered to groups of multiple respondents simultaneously in a theatre or classroom situation. On such occasions, researchers can be on hand to assist respondents with questionnaire completion.

In addition, respondents may be interviewed orally, and here they are led through the questions by an interviewer. When this happens, respondents rarely see the complete questionnaire, whether the interviews are conducted by telephone or face-to-face. The latter form of administration may take place in respondents' own homes, in the researcher's office or in the street. Telephone interviews have the advantage that they can accomplish the data collection very quickly, and that they are relatively cheap. Interviews by telephone can also be conducted with respondents who, for geographical reasons, may be difficult to reach at home. However, such interviews must be kept fairly short, and cannot use questions where respondents need to be shown something visually. Personal, face-to-face interviews represent perhaps the most efficient form of survey administration. This is partly because longer interviews of up to an hour are possible in the home, although interviews in streets or shopping malls may be even shorter than telephone interviews. In addition to dealing with any meaning difficulties in questions, interviewers can use visual prompts, and with computer-assisted techniques, they can complete both data collection and analysis rapidly.

The issue of sampling

It is essential that the individuals in a survey should be representative of the total population from which they are drawn, if researchers wish to generalize their findings to the population as a whole. A key aspect of quantitative research, therefore, is sampling. Samples may be constructed either on a probability or non-probability basis. A probability sample is selected according to mathematical guidelines where-by the chance for the selection of each unit is known; a non-probability sample does not follow such guidelines. The advantage of probability sampling is that it allows researchers to calculate the amount of sampling error in a study. This means that researchers can determine the degree to which a sample is different from the population as a whole in terms of specific characteristics, when the distribution of those characteristics for the general population is already known.

Mail questionnaires	
Advantages	**Disadvantages**
Cheap to run Can reach wide geographical area Respondents complete questionnaire at own pace Offer anonymity Avoid interviewer bias	Questionnaires not always returned May suffer delays in responses Responses higher for some social categories than for others No control over how respondents complete questionnaires No one available to clarify questions if parts of questionnaire are not understood
Telephone interviews	
Advantages	**Disadvantages**
Relatively cheap to run Generate higher response rate than mail questionnaires Researcher can control order in which questions are answered Can provide rapid data collection and processing if computer-assisted techniques are used	Interviews must be kept short Can only reach respondents with telephones No visual prompts possible Open-ended questions are difficult to use
Face-to-face interviews	
Advantages	**Disadvantages**
Have the best response rate Permit the longest interviews Visual prompts can be used Interviewers control the way questions are answered Interviewers can probe for more detailed responses	Very expensive to run Interviewers may have problems reaching certain locations (e.g., remote areas, unsafe areas) Interviewer bias can be a problem

Figure 13.2 Advantages and disadvantages of different forms of survey administration

Non-probability sampling

This type of sampling is often used in media research. People are selected for study on the grounds that they are available, convenient to access and prepared to participate. Convenience samples may comprise college students enrolled in a researcher's own courses, or people intercepted in the street. Volunteer samples may be obtained by advertising for participants on notice-boards or in newspapers. In each of these cases, the researcher has little control over who comes forward to take part in the study. Consequently, such samples are likely to be biased in their demography and psychological characteristics as compared to the population in general.

convenience and volunteer samples

More systematic forms of non-probability sampling are, however, available. While these still do not meet the mathematical requirements of probability sampling, they may nevertheless deliver more robust samples:

• A *purposive* sample – often used in advertising research – is taken when respondents are selected according to a specific criterion, such as their purchase of a particular product.

• A *quota* sample is another selection procedure whereby participants are chosen to match a pre-determined percentage distribution for the general population. If, for example, the distribution of males and females is 49 per cent and 51 per cent in the total population, respondents are selected for a survey until this distribution is matched in the sample.

(A further technique is *haphazard* sampling, whereby participants are selected on the basis of appearance or mere practical convenience. This approach relies on subjective judgements by researchers, rather than any clearly devised system of selection. In some cases, researchers may attempt to recruit large numbers in order to compensate for the lack of a selection system, on the mistaken assumption that bigger means better. In representative sampling, it does not.)

Probability sampling

The techniques of probability sampling include random sampling, systematic random sampling, stratified random sampling and cluster sampling:

• *Random* sampling is the most basic form of probability sampling. Under this scheme, every individual or unit in a population has an equal chance of being selected. For this purpose, researchers may use a table of random numbers or a computer-based system that taps into electronic databases comprising census data or telephone numbers.

• With *systematic random* sampling, a criterion is fixed to select every nth person or unit from a population. To exemplify, a decision might be taken to select one in ten members of a population totalling 1000. A random starting point is then chosen, and from there, every tenth member is selected for a total sample of 100.

• With *stratified random* sampling, further restrictions are placed upon the selection procedure, although the fundamental element of randomness is retained. If, for example, the aim is to exactly match the sample's demographic distribution with that of the population as a whole in terms of gender, age and socio-economic levels, this aim can be built into the sampling frame. Hence, if 51 per cent of the population is female, random selection of females to the sample will cease once that target has been reached, namely 510 females of a target sample of 1000. Sampling may also be

stratified, or disproportionate, when studies select certain demographic groups in larger proportions than their population distributions because the end-users of the research have a special interest in particular population subgroups. This is typically the case with advertisers whose products are aimed at particular target markets.

• *Cluster sampling* involves a special case of stratification. A population may be divided in terms of its geographical distribution between different regions, districts and postal codes. The random sampling process is accordingly conducted in a progressive and hierarchical fashion. First, regions are randomly selected, next districts are randomly selected from within regions, then postal code districts are selected from within larger districts, and finally individuals are randomly selected from within postal codes. The weakness of this procedure lies in the fact that the postal code districts which are thus selected may represent particular kinds of neighbourhood, as defined by the age or class of their residents. Since other neighbourhoods that were not selected might represent different types of people, the final sample could be demographically distorted.

Time span

Surveys can be distinguished into cross-sectional or one-off studies that obtain, for instance, opinions at one point in time, and longitudinal or repeat studies which can be conducted with the same or different groups of people over time. With attitudes, beliefs and perceptions that are prone to change, repeat surveys are largely more informative than one-off surveys. It should be noted, however, that regardless of the survey schedule that is followed, all surveying involves the collection of self-report data from respondents in which they provide verbal accounts of their opinions or behaviour at specific times.

Cross-sectional surveys

This first type of survey attempts to establish an aspect of public opinion or behaviour at the time when the study is conducted. A sample of television viewers may be questioned about

synchronic studies

their current viewing patterns or their opinions about the standards of programmes. During political election campaigns, surveys are conducted to find out who respondents would vote for if the day of interview was polling day. A cross-sectional survey may also be used to investigate correlations between the extent and type of media use that is claimed by different segments of the public and their knowledge or opinions about issues.

Cross-sectional surveys have been used, among other things, to investigate the effects of mass media. In the context of the media violence debate, for example, respondents have been asked to identify or recall details about their television viewing and their aggressive dispositions. They may be given lists of programme titles, asked to report the programmes they like watching best of all, or complete viewing diaries to provide the researcher with some indication of how much they watch and what they watch (e.g., Greenberg 1975; Hartnagel *et al.* 1975; McCarthy *et al.* 1975; McLeod *et al.* 1972; Robinson and Bachman 1972). Within this approach, assumptions are made about the contents of named television programmes, but rarely are these assumptions tested by analysing the programmes themselves. Instead, it is taken as axiomatic that action-adventure or crime-drama programmes contain violence. Hence, if a respondent nominates such a programme among his or her favourites, that is taken as evidence of exposure to televised violence. In addition, respondents' personal aggression tendencies have been assessed through self-report measures and sometimes also through reports from other people (e.g., parents, teachers, friends, peers). However, such correlational surveys do not measure actual behaviour; they merely examine degrees of statistical association between verbally described behaviour.

Cross-sectional surveys have not been restricted to samples of the general public, even if these are by far the most frequent type. Surveys have been conducted among media professionals◀ to obtain data, for instance, on journalists' working practices, job satisfaction among people employed in media industries,

▶ surveys with media professionals – Chapter 5, p. 89

and their opinions concerning the impact of new communication technologies on the future of their businesses (Bergen and Weaver 1988; Demers and Wackman 1988; Ross, 1998).

Longitudinal research

Longitudinal surveys are an efficient procedure for examining long-term relationships between selected variables because they permit the collection of responses over time. One particular strength of longitudinal methodology is that it enables researchers to examine the plausibility of different types of causal hypotheses. First, researchers can begin to untangle the potential bidirectional causal relationships between media and audience attitudes or behaviour. In other words, exposure to media violence may increase the likelihood of aggressive behaviour, but an aggressive predisposition might also cause individuals to favour watching programmes containing violence (Huesmann *et al.* 1984; Lefkowitz *et al.* 1972; Milavsky *et al.* 1982). Second, research using longitudinal methodology can determine whether exposure to media is associated with long-term changes in audiences' attitudes and behaviour.

diachronic studies

Three types of longitudinal research may be differentiated:

1 *Trend studies*. A given population may be sampled and studied at different points in time, so that different respondents are questioned in each survey, but each sample is drawn from the same population. This type of study is often used during election campaigns (e.g., Gunter *et al.* 1986). Here, samples of respondents are surveyed about their voting intentions before, during and at the end of a political campaign. Furthermore, trend studies can be conducted using data from secondary sources. For instance, researchers have conducted historical analyses of the relationship over time between the penetration of television sets in a population and its crime rates, using existing statistical data (e.g., Centerwall 1989; Hennigan *et al.* 1982).

secondary analysis of statistical data

2 *Cohort studies*. A cohort study focuses on the same specific subset of a population each time data are collected, although the samples may be different. Normally the individuals

participating are linked in some way, perhaps by having the same birth date (a birth cohort), or because they have experienced the same significant life event. For example, a study might survey all children aged 5 to 6 in a community before the introduction of television. Then, two years later, after television transmission has begun, another survey may be conducted with those same children at age 7 to 8.

Cohort analysis is a technique that is especially suited to monitor changes in attitudes and behaviour which are associated with maturation. However, since exactly the same people may not be surveyed on each occasion (but different samples from the original cohort), any changes may be attributable to unidentified differences between the actual respondent groups, in addition to age and maturation differences.

To exemplify, Rentz *et al.* (1983) conducted a cohort analysis of consumers born in four time periods: 1931 to 1940, 1941 to 1950, 1951 to 1960 and 1961 to 1970. Soft drink consumption was measured in all the samples that were taken from these cohorts at intervals, and a range of potential predictors of this consumption assessed. The results indicated a large cohort effect, in the sense that the level of soft drink consumption which had been established early in life in each cohort tended to remain stable later in life, compared with the other cohorts. Rosengren and Windahl (1989) also used cohort analysis as part of their in-depth longitudinal study of television usage by Swedish youngsters. Among other things, they found a slight similar cohort effect, but concluded that age was the prime determinant of habitual television viewing.

3 *Panel studies.* Trend and cohort studies permit the analysis of process and change over time, which is rarely possible in a cross-sectional survey. Yet, a limitation of these two types of longitudinal study is that, on each occasion, different people are surveyed. As a result, it is not possible to track changes in attitudes or behaviour over time for specific individuals. In comparison, panel studies involve the collection of data over time from the same sample of respondents – this sample is called a 'panel.' For

example, in a study to test for the effects of televised violence on viewers' aggression, repeated surveys were carried out with the same individuals at intervals ranging from one to ten years in order to assess whether an earlier diet of violent programmes was associated not only with aggressiveness at that time, but with aggressive tendencies in later life (Milavsky *et al.* 1982).

Panel studies, however, also have their difficulties and limitations. For one thing, they need to be based on original data collection from the specific panel, whereas trend or cohort studies may be conducted through secondary analysis of previously collected data. For another, a special problem is the loss of panel members over time. People interviewed in the first survey wave may be unavailable for, or unwilling to participate in, the second or third waves. In other cases, people move house, die or become untraceable. Consequently, it is quite common that such 'attrition' causes the panel to gradually diminish in size as the study progresses.

Survey studies, whether cross-sectional or longitudinal, can only demonstrate correlational links between variables. Their reliance on self-report or other-report measures is fraught with potential inaccuracies. These may arise from the respondents' memory failure, ill judgement or inadequate knowledge, but as importantly from a form of questioning that provides non-valid verbalised representations of the aspects of everyday reality under study. Through experimental methodologies, quantitative researchers have examined relationships between media and audience variables more directly, as a later section explains in detail.

SURVEYING MEDIA OUTPUT

Survey principles may also be applied to the analysis of media content. This quantitative assessment of media output – content analysis◄ – may be traced back to the 1940s when wartime intelligence units monitored radio broadcasts for their music and news content as

► content analysis – example analysis, Chapter 7, p. 101

indicators of the morale and movements of the enemy (Wimmer and Dominick 1994). Content analysis was soon taken up by social scientists to monitor more general social and economic trends. As early as 1910, Max Weber had suggested launching a study to monitor press coverage of political and social issues alongside surveys of public opinion, thus anticipating agenda-setting research (see Beniger 1978).◄ In the second half of the twentieth century, the methodology was increasingly applied to a wide range of media issues. Prominent applications have examined patterns of news coverage in order to ascertain the agenda-setting role of media (McCombs and Shaw 1972) and patterns in the representation of social groups and events in order to assess cultivation effects of media upon public perceptions of social reality (Gerbner 1972).

An early definition of content analysis conceived it as 'a research technique for the objective, systematic, and quantitative description of the manifest content of communication' (Berelson 1952: 18). Krippendorf (1980) defined it as a research technique for making replicable and valid references from data to their context. Kerlinger (1986) suggested that content analysis is a method of studying and analysing communication in a systematic, objective and quantifiable manner for the purpose of measuring variables. This last definition particularly encapsulates the defining ingredients of any traditional form of quantitative analysis of media output. Content analysis is, first, systematic in that it utilises a principled form of media output sampling and content coding. Second, it is objective in that the researcher's own idiosyncrasies and biases should not affect the analysis. Operational definitions and rules for the classification of variables should be explicit, so that other researchers might repeat the procedure. Finally, content analysis is quantifiable in that its main focus is on counting occurrences of predefined entities in a media text. On this last point, purely quantitative forms of content analysis have been challenged for displaying a lack of sensitivity to hidden meanings that may be

conveyed by media texts (see Merten 1996). Thus, counting and quantifying may need to be supplemented by interpretive procedures which can clarify the weight and implications of singular media messages in terms of their potential impact upon the audience (Gunter 1985a; Hodge and Tripp 1986; Potter and Smith 1999).

Five main *purposes* of content analysis have been identified (Wimmer and Dominick 1994):

1 Describing patterns or trends in media portrayals
2 Testing hypotheses about the policies or aims of media producers
3 Comparing media content with real-world indicators
4 Assessing the representation of certain groups in society
5 Drawing inferences about media effects.

In each case, studies must return to and depart from the basics. A quantitative content analysis is designed to provide a descriptive account of what a media text (film, TV programme, advertisement, newspaper report, etc.) contains, and to do so in a form that can be repeated by others. In putting together a content analysis, then, the researcher must work through a number of stages of measuring and sampling.

Measuring media content

Having decided upon the general topic of investigation, it is necessary first to define the 'things' to be measured. Here, the basic concept is the 'unit of analysis' – the textual element that is to be counted. In addition to the unit of analysis as a whole, there may be features or attributes of that unit about which data are also collected. The data collection process as such proceeds by relying on a 'coding frame'. This is a form on which the occurrences of the different categories relating to the unit of analysis, its features and attributes, can be numerically catalogued.

To illustrate: a content analysis of gender representation in television advertising would focus on appearances by males and females. The unit of analysis in this context would be

unit of analysis

coding frame

► agenda-setting research – Chapter 9, p. 145

an appearance by a male or female character, either on screen or as a voice-over. Further analytical categories may then be deployed to describe in more detail the nature of these appearances. For instance, the researcher might be interested in establishing not only how often men and women appear at all in television advertisements, but also whether they appear with differing frequencies in different social roles or in connection with different product types (Furnham and Schofield 1986; Furnham and Skae 1997; Furnham *et al.* 1997).

Some studies have identified theoretically relevant patterns simply by analysing media content in terms of its major themes. In an investigation of the extent to which films released in Britain between 1945 and 1991 were characterised by crime themes, Allen *et al.* (1997) assigned films to one of ten genre categories (western, crime, war, romance, fantasy, sex, farce, adventure, drama, other) on the basis of details in the film synopses. The analysis had two parts. First, the presence of crime content in each synopsis was assessed by examining it for mentions of a crime, criminals, or the criminal justice system. Second, the film was classified according to the ten genre categories. In the case of crime films, this classification meant that the 'primary focus of the narrative is on the causes or consequences of illegal activities, central characters include criminals, victims and those who work in the criminal justice system (e.g., private eyes, amateurs, police, courts, gangsters)' (Allen *et al.* 1997: 92).

In the US National Television Violence Study, units of analysis were defined at more than one level (*National Television Violence Study* 1997; see also Potter and Smith 1999). Whereas previous television violence content analyses had emphasised counting violent acts as such, this study included more global measures of violence that would better represent the contextual features of violence. Three levels of measurement were devised: the 'PAT'; the scene; and the programme. A PAT represented an interaction between a perpetrator (P), an act (A) and a target (T). A sequence of PATs, either continuous or separated by brief cutaways or scene changes, might together make up a violent scene, and such sequences afforded an

opportunity to examine relationships between discrete acts of violence and their meanings within the scene. Finally, the researchers argued that larger meanings seemed to be conveyed by the pattern of violence as a whole within a programme, and that this meaningful pattern could be effectively interpreted only when analysed within the full context of the programme.

In addition to such incidents or actions, other units of analysis that are often coded include the agents in either fictional output or news. In the case of news, it is particularly an analysis of the sources of quotes, comments or other material that can yield insights (Lasorsa and Reese 1990). In fictional media content, an analysis of the attributes of actors or characters can yield evidence about the proportional representation of different social groups. Furthermore, studies of the presence of different types of sources in news or other factual output can provide evidence for assessing the balance, neutrality, thoroughness and impartiality of reporting. This form of analysis may examine the range of sources used; which groups, organisations or institutions they represent; and the context (interview, official meeting, press conference) in which they appear. Such analysis may also examine the kind of information sought and obtained from different sources, and any indications of the status of the source (Ericson *et al.* 1991).

Sampling media content

Once the body of content to be considered has been specified with reference to theoretical purpose, and the units of measurement have been selected, the researcher has to determine how much of that content to analyse. In some instances, the universe may be small enough to be analysed in its entirety. Generally, researchers must sample a subset of content from the total universe, since it is too large to be analysed in full. In contrast to mass publics, which will have been surveyed in their entirety in population censuses, thus enabling a construction of sampling frames based on known population parameters, such a point of comparison is not available for surveys of media output.

'population' of contents to be sampled

Partly for this reason, sampling in content analysis often takes place in more than one step. A first step may be to specify which content sources are to be sampled. For example, in a study of newspaper coverage of current events, the first step is to decide which particular national or local newspapers are to be analysed. Then a decision must be taken about how many editions of each newspaper to analyse, and over what period of time. A further step may be to decide how much, or which parts of the newspaper to analyse. At this level, one has to consider how many 'stories' to analyse and how these should be defined and delimited. Finally, the analyst will consider whether there are specific story ingredients that need to be measured.

Previous content studies have established some rough guidelines for sampling. Stempel (1952) drew separate samples of six, twelve, eighteen, twenty-four and forty-eight issues of a newspaper and compared the average content of each sample size in a single subject category against the corresponding total for the entire year. He found that each of the five sample sizes was adequate, and that increasing the sample beyond twelve issues did not significantly improve upon the accuracy of findings. In the longstanding content research into television violence, some studies have restricted programme samples to a single week (e.g., Gerbner *et al.* 1977), while others have opted for samples of up to four weeks. In some cases, chronological weeks are sampled, while others have compiled composite weeks by selecting one day from each of seven different weeks (Gunter and Harrison 1998; Gunter *et al.* 1996).

chronological and composite sample weeks

The issue of content sampling was examined very closely by the *National Television Violence Study* (1997). This study analysed a far larger sample of programme output from a larger number of television channels than any previous American content study, and the total project sample, unusually, covered programming broadcast throughout the day. What distinguished this research most of all, however, was its use of a random sampling frame to select programmes over a period of twenty weeks each year. The programmes were chosen with a modified version of random sampling, as described above. Two half-hour time slots (defined by hour of day and day of week) were randomly selected for each channel during each week that sampling occurred. Once a time slot had been selected, the *TV Guide* was consulted, and the programme corresponding to that time slot was entered into a scheduling grid several days before the actual broadcast in the target week, so that recording and coding could be prepared. This procedure was repeated until a full composite week of programmes for each channel had been compiled for analysis.

Limits to quantitative content analysis

Quantitative content analyses tend to be purely descriptive accounts of the characteristics of media output, and often make few inferences in advance about the potential significance of their findings for what they may reveal about production ideologies or impact on audiences. In order to support conclusions about media processes and effects, theoretically informed decisions have to be made about which aspects of media content to analyse and classify. The most informative content analyses, therefore, will be produced by analysts who choose their content categories with reference to an explicit theoretical framework. Purely descriptive, a-theoretical applications of this technique may yield reliable indicators of the manifest content of the media, but will contribute in only a limited way to a better understanding, either of the forces which lie behind that content, or of its eventual impact upon audiences.

TESTING CAUSALITY DIRECTLY: EXPERIMENTAL RESEARCH

Like surveys, experiments have been used in media research for more than fifty years. Experimental research usually involves a quantification of the effects of media upon their audiences, although experimental methods have also been used to investigate the way people use media. In the 1940s and 1950s, experimental methodologies were employed particularly to investigate the impact of media messages on opinions about the enemy in wartime (Hovland *et al.* 1953), and to study the effects of production techniques on learning from informational media (Belson 1967; Tannenbaum 1954; Tannenbaum and Kernick, 1954; Trenaman 1967). In the 1960s, experiments came to be used, not least, to study the effects of media violence (Bandura and Walters 1963; Berkowitz 1964; Feshbach 1961). Useful sources of information about experimental practice and designs are Bailey (1994) and Neuman (1994).

An experiment generally begins with a hypothesis about a likely outcome following an event, or set of events, that can be controlled or manipulated by the researcher. In media research, an experiment will typically create a set of conditions under which an individual, or group of individuals, are exposed to a media stimulus, and are then invited to respond in some way. The conditions are constructed in such a way that the media may be said to have caused a particular kind of audience response. For instance, if one wishes to test a hypothesis that a media depiction of violence may have an effect upon the behaviour of an audience, a minimum of two situations will be created in which different audience groups watch either a violent or a non-violent portrayal. Subsequently, both groups will be placed in another kind of situation in which there is an opportunity to behave aggressively. The research hypothesis might predict that those who have been exposed to media violence will behave more aggressively than those who have been shown non-violent material. Quantitative measurements would be taken to establish whether that prediction is borne out by the actual, observed behaviour of the two groups.

Experiments tend to investigate smaller numbers of respondents than surveys, because they operate on a different logic. Participants in an experiment are allocated to either experimental or control groups. The former are exposed to the manipulated independent variable(s), while the latter are not. However, participant samples may be non-representative. One reason for this is that much experimental research on media derives from psychological research traditions which have conceived of many of the psychological processes of interest as constants across individuals. Non-representa-

experimental and control groups

tative samples are compensated for, in part, by the 'random assignment' of participants to either experimental treatments or control conditions – a key concept in experimentation. Thus, even if the participants do not represent the wider population, within the confines of the experiment, the random assignment of participants to the two sets of conditions controls against biases in the findings. This procedure also aids replication. The conditions and steps of an experimental study are so minutely spelled out that another investigator could readily repeat the study to find out if the original results stand up.

random assignment of subjects to groups

The main advantage of experimental research is that it enables research to test for evidence of direct cause–effect relationships between variables. Hence, if one variable is presented at a particular point in time, there will be a measurable impact upon a second variable observed at a later point. In addition, experimental research allows the investigator to exercise control over some or all of these variables. In a study of the impact of media on an audience, the researcher can determine the content to which individuals are exposed, the context in which the exposure occurs, and the ways in which they are asked to respond subsequently.

relations of direct causality

One weakness of experiments is that they tend to be carried out in artificial conditions. A laboratory environment is quite different from the everyday, social environment. In media research, the need to control for the inherent complexities of media content when examining the effect of one of its aspects may result both in the respondents' consumption of media content under highly artificial conditions, and in a selection of media content extracts that fail to reproduce their normal media experience. An investigation of the impact of televised violence on viewers in which violent extracts of a few minutes' duration are shown to viewers thus removes the violence from its original programme context, which under ordinary viewing conditions might influence how viewers respond to violence.

A second weakness is that participants may 'second-guess' what the study is about, and what the experimenter expects to happen. By responding accordingly, they may give the experimenter what he or she wants. Such 'demand characteristics' can bias the results of an experiment, because participants no longer behave the way they might otherwise have done under the specified conditions. A related source of bias is 'experimenter bias'. In this case, the experimenter may unwittingly give away clues about the hypothesis by giving stronger encouragement to participants to behave in one way than in another. To counteract such problems of bias during the interaction, a double-blind technique may be used,◄ in which neither the person running the experimental session nor the participants know whether a given participant is in an experimental group or a control group.

Experimental designs

Experimental designs differ principally in terms of the number of stages and conditions they comprise. Some experiments employ tests before and after a manipulation of an independent variable; others use tests following the manipulation only. In some experiments, only one group of participants is studied, while in others, two or more groups may be studied.

Classic experimental design

pre-test–post-test with control group

This design is also known as a 'pre-test–post-test with control group' design. Such experiments use at least two groups, of which one is a control group. Participants are randomly allocated to these groups, and then tested prior to, and following, an experimental manipulation.

Pre-experimental designs

A classic experimental design is not always attainable if too few participants or resources generally are available. Researchers may then settle for lesser designs with fewer controls. A *one group, post-test only* design uses just one group and no pre-test. For example, a group of viewers may be shown a television news programme after which their knowledge of the news stories in question is tested. In this case, without a pre-test, it is impossible to determine how much knowledge they already held about

────────────

► double-blind techniques – Chapter 16, p. 290

these stories before seeing the programme, even if the findings of such a design may reflect on the processing of information from media or on their forms of presentation.

A slightly more advanced design is the *one-group, pre-test–post-test* design with only one group of participants, but including a pre-test as well as a post-test. Extending the example given above, participants would here be tested for their knowledge of relevant issues before the news programme, and then for any changes to that knowledge after viewing the programme. In the absence of a control group, who would be 'pre-tested' and 'post-tested' without seeing the news programme, it is again difficult to infer that any change in the experimental group's knowledge resulted from exposure to the programme. One alternative explanation might be that the pre-test itself encouraged participants to rehearse their knowledge of the news, so that by the second test they were able to perform better. An additional explanation of any knowledge change over time, if there is a gap of hours or days between the two tests, could be participants' exposure to other news media that also contained information about the stories in question.

A third version of a pre-experimental design is a *static group comparison*, in which a post-test only is employed, but applied to two groups. In this case, one group might be shown a news programme while another group would not. Any differences between the two groups in their post-test knowledge scores, however, might be due to pre-existing knowledge differences between them, and should not simply be explained in terms of exposure to a news programme.

Quasi-experimental designs

While quasi-experimental designs do not reach the control standards of the classical design, because they do not include a pre-test stage, unlike pre-experimental designs, they do at least employ a control group. With the *post-test only with control group* design, participants are randomly allocated to experimental and control groups, but are tested only after the experimental manipulation has been implemented. Although random assignment reduces the chances that the groups will differ before treatment, a researcher cannot be sure without a pre-test.

It should be added that, even with a pre-test, as in the classical design, measurement issues can arise. Thus, a pre-test may influence the way participants react during and after the experimental treatment because the initial test stage has given away clues as to the purpose of the experiment, or has given participants the opportunity to practise a relevant skill. The 'Solomon four-group design' offers a solution to this problem. Here, for some participants in both the experimental and control groups, pre-tests and post-tests are run, while for others, only post-tests are used. The aim is to control for possible effects of the pre-test as well as of the experimental manipulation on the post-test scores. If the groups who were pre-tested differ in their post-test performance from those who were not pre-tested, the researcher can conclude that the pre-test itself had an effect on post-test results, thus potentially biasing the findings concerning the effect of the central experimental manipulation.

Solomon four-group design (margin note)

Factorial designs

The experimental designs considered so far are all set up to investigate the effect of a single independent variable per group, regardless of whether control groups and a pre-test were used or not. In many studies, however, experimenters are interested in examining the effects of more than one independent variable upon a designated dependent variable among the same group of individuals. It is possible that two or more independent variables produce joint and distinctive effects upon a dependent variable. It is also possible that their effects are interdependent, so that one independent variable has an influence upon a dependent variable only in the presence of a second independent variable.

In factorial designs, accordingly, two or more independent variables or 'factors' are manipulated. Factors, in addition, may have two or more aspects to be considered in the analysis. For example, in an experimental study of the effects of various attributes of both television programmes and advertising on viewers' recall of the advertising, there may be three types of programming (holiday programme, car programme, cooking programme) and three types of advertisement (holidays, cars, cookery products). In a factorial design, these attributes, which amount to experimental treatments, would produce nine conditions, as each type of advertisement is embedded, in turn, in each type of programme. A full experimental study would thus require nine groups of participants.

Repeated measures designs

As suggested by the previous example, one of the main disadvantages of a factorial design is a practical one, since it requires different sets of participants for each experimental condition. Each time a new independent variable is introduced, the number of cells or groups that is generated within the design increases, requiring an increase also in numbers of participants. One way of resolving this problem is to obtain measures concerning more than one independent variable from the same group of participants. Such a repeated measures design, if applied to the factorial advertising experiment described above, could examine the same number of variables with just three groups. The groups would be defined by the type of programme they are exposed to, but each programme would be embedded with all three types of advertisement. This solution, of course, raises further questions of whether the presentation of the advertisements together, or their sequence, may affect the audience response.

Experimental contexts: the problem with laboratory research

To sum up, experiments may be equipped to test causal hypotheses, but are not without serious limitations. An important shortcoming of experiments testing for media effects on audience attitudes and behaviour stems from the conditions they create for examining such links (Cook *et al.* 1983; Stipp and Milavsky 1988). Laboratory conditions do enable researchers to exert control over the behaviour of their participants as well as over various environmental factors which might influence their behaviour in the real world. However, such research may lack external validity; its findings may not be generalisable beyond the laboratory.

issues of external validity (margin note)

In research on behavioural effects, for example, researchers have frequently created artificial measures of behaviour, especially when studying the effects of media violence on audience aggression (Berkowitz 1964; Berkowitz and Geen 1966; Donnerstein and Berkowitz 1981). While there are sound ethical reasons for this, the responses measured in experiments often fail to resemble what would be more commonly seen as 'aggressive behaviour.' The laboratory creates a social environment all of its own in which the usual sanctions against behaving in particular ways (e.g., aggressively) are suspended (Comstock 1998). At the same time, experimenters artificially constrain the responses participants might make. In aggression experiments, participants are normally given only one behavioural response option – one of aggression. Yet, in a laboratory experiment that was designed to test the effects of exposure to violent pornography on males' behavioural reactions towards a female target, the men under study showed little inclination to use aggression against this female if a non-aggressive response alternative was made available to them. Even when the female had earlier been insulting towards them, they still chose the non-aggressive alternative (Fisher and Grenier 1994).

Studies that utilise the repeated measures designs within a laboratory setting face special priming effects problems which arise from 'priming' or conditioning effects. An earlier exposure to similar stimulus materials may affect respondents' reactions to materials which are later presented by providing points of comparison or a frame of reference for judging those later materials. Again, participants may receive clues from the earlier materials as to the experimental hypothesis, which may lead them to behave in accordance with that hypothesis.

Research in naturalistic settings

To overcome problems of 'ecological' validity, experiments may be carried out in more naturalistic settings. Here, the participants in experiments are observed in surroundings where they may not be aware of the research going on. Two such categories of real-world experiment may be distinguished: those in which the

researcher manipulates a set of conditions in a naturalistic environment, and those in which the researcher takes advantage of some naturally occurring event or change of circumstances, the effects of which can be measured. The first type of study is commonly referred to as a field experiment, and the second type as a natural experiment (see MacBeth 1998):

1 In *field experiments*, researchers often study pre-existing groups, but they assign these groups to different conditions of media exposure. The groups may be observed, first, during a baseline period to establish their similarity, and again after the exposure period. An example would, again, be an experiment to study the effects of television programmes on viewers' aggressiveness. In a cable television environment in which the flow of programmes into people's homes could be controlled by the supplier, it would be possible to create two different groups: one that receives programmes containing violence, and another that receives violence-free entertainment. Over a number of days or weeks before, during and after this treatment, the viewers could be monitored by someone in their family for any changes of mood or behaviour that occurred as a result of this manipulation of their television diet (see Gorney *et al.* 1977).

2 In *natural experiments*, researchers take advantage of a naturally occurring change in the availability of media in order to assess the impact of this change on the people in that environment. For example, a community with access to television could be compared with another community that has less or no access to television. If the second community has television introduced to it for the first time, pre-TV and post-TV observations and tests may be conducted to assess the impact of television on that community – a type of research that has been ongoing since the early days of the medium (see Charlton 1997; Williams 1986).

The problems faced by field experiments are mainly ethical and practical. Some research issues would be unethical and socially irresponsible to investigate in the field.◄ For example,

---

▶ research ethics – Chapter 16, p. 289

studies of the effects of sexually violent pornography upon men's attitudes towards female sexuality, their propensity to commit rape themselves and their sympathy for rapists must be conducted under controlled conditions. The 'effects' measures cannot take the form of real behaviour (i.e. rape), but must rely on simulations in which changes of attitude or perception may be monitored, and then immediately countered through elaborate debriefing sessions with participants.

On the practical front, field experiments can be difficult to run because they occur in environments over which the experimenter's control is restricted. As a result, it may not be easy to create all the conditions that satisfy the requirements of a classic experimental design or of a sound factorial or repeated measures design. Participants may not always agree to make themselves available for observation in the same way they would in a laboratory experiment. Moreover, researchers may need to gain permission to make clandestine observations of participants, or to secretly manipulate aspects of their social environment in an attempt to instigate some change in their behaviour. This last consideration is especially important in research involving children.

SURVEYS OR EXPERIMENTS: HOW DO THEY COMPARE?

This chapter has focused on the two principal forms of quantitative research – surveys and experiments – which have been predominantly concerned with audiences, either by demonstrating cause–effect relationships or by establishing the possibility, through evidence of association, that such relationships might exist between media and audiences. The two approaches have, however, also been used to examine aspects of media production (see Wimmer and Dominick 1994). As general methodologies, surveys and experiments have their own inherent advantages and limitations, to be weighed in designing concrete empirical studies.

Experiments, in sum, are designed to examine cause–effect relationships between variables in a direct sense. For this purpose, researchers manipulate media and audiences under artifi-

cial conditions, or else take systematic measurements of phenomena that occur within natural environments where a specific event has taken place to bring about a radical change. There is nearly always an element of artificiality about experiments, because researchers must be able to relate measurable changes in one variable and measurable changes in another variable in such a way that a causal connection can confidently be inferred. The possibility that the 'criterion' or dependent variable was changed by some factor other than the independently manipulated causal variable must be reduced to a minimum.

The *weaknesses of experiments* are:

- their use of non-representative samples;
- the degree of artificial control over the environment being studied;
- the contrived nature of many of the media and audience measures that are deployed;
- the difficulty of controlling totally for extraneous factors that could have affected the criterion variables.

The results of experimental studies may therefore lack any validity, in the predictive or explanatory senses, in the real world beyond the controlled environment of the study.

Surveys, by comparison, enable researchers to study media and audiences in their natural environments. Relationships between media, communications and audiences are not manipulated in any artificial sense, but are observed as they occurred, unencumbered by experimental restrictions. Surveys also tend to involve much larger samples of people and media output than do experiments. Furthermore, whereas experiments tend to be dependent upon convenience or volunteer samples because they are usually more demanding of participants than other research methods, surveys are able to draw far larger samples that are representative of the general populations from which they are drawn in terms of important social and psychological characteristics. This means that their results can be more readily generalised to the wider populations from which samples were drawn.

The *weaknesses of surveys* are:

- their dependence on *post hoc*, self-reports of phenomena, which may suffer from inaccuracies of detail;
- their use of verbal measures of observable events that may similarly fail fully to represent what actually occurred;
- their reporting only of degrees of association, or correlation, between variables, which cannot on their own conclusively demonstrate causality.

To exemplify, survey respondents' verbal reports of how much time they normally spend watching television in hours per day may be characterised by a significant degree of error. Another means of surveying television viewing, used widely by broadcasting systems around the world, is the TV meter. A metering system usually has two components: one automatically registers when the TV set is switched on and which channel it is tuned to, and the other requires viewers to report their viewing, either in a paper diary or, more often these days, via a remote control handset. While technologically sophisticated, such measurement methods in fact merely indicate the presence of one or more persons in the room in which a TV set has been switched on (and only if the respondents remember to check in), and not whether they are actually watching the screen. Methodological tests have shown that when compared against direct observations, self-report measures are inaccurate to a degree which may render them useless for anything other than a very broad indication of whether someone is a relatively heavy or light viewer (Anderson and Burns 1991; Bechtel *et al.* 1972; Gunter *et al.* 1995).

In media effects studies, surveys are limited in the degree of detail with which they are able to measure a person's media consumption. Even if measures relying on respondents to recall, for instance, programmes they watched on television in the past week, or newspapers or magazines they read over the past month, are reasonably accurate *per se*, it may be necessary to know much more about the nature of the specific content of these media in order to assess its effects on audiences' knowledge, beliefs, attitudes or behaviours.

In one particular realm of research, where both surveys and experiments have been prominent, their appropriateness must be weighed with considerations other than the purity of measurement. Studies of children's fright reactions to films and television programmes have variously measured young viewers' responses to horror and other suspenseful content in laboratory settings; have questioned young respondents about their memories of scary movies; and have interviewed parents about their observations of their children's reactions to frightening films and television (Cantor 1994). Although survey interviews can yield interesting insights, they are, again, dependent upon children's or parents' recollections. Experimental methods can, with greater precision, explore whether specific kinds of portrayal cause children to become scared, and they can shed light on how such reactions change with maturity. Experimental studies have shown, for instance, that children under 8 years old are frightened by scary monsters seen on screen, whereas older children become more anxious about unseen dangers lurking off screen (Sparks and Cantor 1986). Whether an on-screen character is attractive or ugly, and whether it behaves cruelly or kindly, can have independent and interdependent effects upon how children react (Hoffner and Cantor 1985). These studies have only been able to demonstrate the significance of these mixtures of characteristics by experimentally manipulating a story to create different versions of the same character.

There are occasions, however, when researchers must temper their enthusiasm for using experiments and limit themselves to survey interviews, not least with children. Even though the evidence will be less powerful in an explanatory sense, the experimental manipulation of fear in children may be deemed unethical. The creation of genuinely adverse reactions among children, in response to a specially designed or selected horror scene, might add to the wealth of scientific knowledge, but could possibly cause undue harm that may not be easily undone. Accordingly, where there is a possibility that fright reactions may be detrimental to a child's development, such responses

TV meter systems

studies of children

ANALYSIS BOX 13.1 SURVEYS AND EXPERIMENTS COMPARED: THE CASE OF CULTIVATION RESEARCH

A prominent example of the difference between surveys and experiments is research into the cultivation effects of television. Through survey evidence, this research has found correlational links between the amount of viewing that is claimed by respondents and certain patterns in their social beliefs, perceptions and levels of anxiety (Gerbner et al. 1977, 1979, 1986). Such global measures of television viewing may lack the necessary sensitivity to the significant variations in the message content of television.

More detailed measures of viewing habits, using diaries, have indicated that certain social perceptions may be sensitive to influences from particular types of programmes, but not from others (Gunter 1987a; Wober and Gunter 1988). An analysis of British viewers found no link between their perception of personal victimisation in their local neighbourhood and any aspect of their television viewing, while a corresponding analysis of viewers in Los Angeles found the same perception to be associated with their reported viewing of US-produced crime drama shows (Gunter 1987a). This suggests, among other things, that if the information of certain programmes is seen by viewers to have a direct relevance to their immediate social context, it may affect their particular perceptions of that context. However, surveys can explore this link only in a very general fashion.

In comparison, the application of experimental methodology to cultivation research has made it possible to explore such links in greater detail. Just as certain general features of a television series, such as its cultural setting, may render its content especially pertinent to how some viewers form judgements about certain aspects of their own or other societies, such effects may also be influenced, at a more detailed level, by how, for instance, conflicts are resolved in the series. Experiments have shown that the same television drama can have different effects upon viewers' perceptions of crime and their associated anxiety reactions if the ending is manipulated, so that, in the version shown to one group, criminals are brought to justice, while in another version they are not (Bryant et al. 1981). Further, reality programmes that depict crime on television can have a more powerful impact on viewers' perceptions of crime than fictional depictions (Tamborini et al. 1984). While surveys may also reveal such differential degrees of association between social perceptions and the exposure to particular types of television content (Gunter and Wober 1982), they are less appropriate for establishing whether viewers were especially attentive to certain messages within programmes. If, instead, an experimental methodology is chosen, programmes can be edited to include or exclude specific ingredients, so that differential audience reactions may be systematically measured in post-viewing tests.

---

rightly tend to be studied after the fact through survey interviews.

Quantitative methodologies, like other research approaches, have strengths and weaknesses that must be taken into account by researchers, both before deciding upon their use and during their implementation. While there are those who would question the validity of any quantitative approach on epistemological grounds, such techniques have a useful contribution to make, particularly for the understanding of media output, its consumption and effects, provided that the interpretation of data never loses sight of their characteristic limitations. In this respect they are no different from the qualitative methodologies preferred by other epistemologies.

HANDLING QUANTITATIVE DATA

Quantitative research methodologies generate numerical data. Surveys (whether of audiences or content) and experiments are the basic 'methods' of the data collection, but they enter into theoretically informed 'methodologies' of analysis and interpretation.◄ Once numerical data have been collected, they need to be analysed through statistical techniques. These mathematical techniques are used to describe, organise, as well as explore relationships within the data. In epistemological terms, quantitative research is typically grounded in a hypothetico-deductive approach, in which investigators mount hypotheses (or predictions) about the expected associations or cause–effect relationships between variables. The aim of quantitative data collection and analysis, then, is to produce findings which lead to the acceptance or rejection of a specified hypothesis. Numerical data analysis through statistical procedures, as reviewed in this section, represents a systematic and objective way of determining whether significant patterns of relationships exist among those phenomena that have been measured in data collection.

Describing data

Data collected via either survey questionnaires, content coding frames or experimental instruments are coded numerically, extracted from (what are still mostly) paper formats, and entered into a computerised database, upon which various forms of statistical tests may then be performed. Both the accuracy with which this data transfer process takes place, and the application of statistical procedures that are appropriate for the particular type of data, are crucial to the entire quantitative research project – errors in these early stages can invalidate the final results.

Often, quantitative data analysis begins by adopting a simple descriptive approach in order to establish some initial patterns in the findings. A survey of public opinion about the competence of, for instance, national political leaders might first present the percentages of respondents who agreed, and respectively disagreed, that particular political figures were performing well. A further computation might produce the percentages who agreed with such sentiments, as broken down by the gender, age, social class

and political affiliations of respondents. Such results may be presented for visual display in a bar chart or summarised in a table.◄

A different type of study might ask a survey sample of 1000 respondents to state how many hours of television they watch each week. Here, descriptive statistics might be applied to show how many respondents viewed nothing, less than one hour a week, between one and two hours, two to four hours, or more than four hours. Next, a 'frequency distribution' could be generated, which shows how the respondents were distributed across these different volumes of viewing. Such data may be visually represented in a line graph or bar chart.

frequency distribution

Central tendency and variance

Data may be further analysed in terms of summary statistics, which render large amounts of data more manageable. Summary statistics measure two basic aspects of the distribution of 'scores' or measurements in a dataset: central tendency and dispersion, or variability. A *central tendency* measure indicates which out of a range of scores is the typical one. This typical score, in turn, may be defined in three different ways:

1 The *mode* is the most frequently occurring score in a range of scores. If, in a set of ten scores, five score '4', three score '2' and two score '1', the mode is '4'.

2 The *median* score is the mid-point in a range of scores. In the following set of scores, the median is '8': 2 4 5 6 (8) 10 12 15 16. The score '8' lies at the exact half-way point in this distribution of scores. In other cases, where there is an even number of scores and therefore no exact mid-point, the median must be calculated by averaging between the two centre scores: 3 3 5 8 (8.5) 9 10 13 14. Here, the median is 8.5, or the average of '8' and '9'.

3 The *mean* score is the average of the total range of scores. In the last example, the eight scores totalled 65, which, divided by 8, gives a mean score of 8.125.

─────────────────────

► methods and methodologies – Chapter 15, p. 258

► forms of representing research findings – Chapter 16, p. 275

Another fundamental descriptive measure is the degree of dispersion or variation in a set of scores. While central tendency measures indicate the typical score of a distribution, *dispersion* measures capture the extent to which the scores vary around that central point.

• *Range*, which is the simplest expression of dispersion, is the difference between the highest and lowest scores in a particular distribution.

• *Variance* provides a mathematical index of the degree to which scores deviate from the mean score, and tends to be expressed not in terms of the original scores, but as squared deviations from the mean. To compute the variance, one subtracts the mean of a distribution from each score, and then squares the result. These squared scores are then summed and divided by the number of original scores minus one. Variance is a powerful and widely applied measure, like the standard deviation, and both are illustrated below.

• The *standard deviation* is a third measure of dispersion that utilises the original units of measurement. The standard deviation is computed as the square root of the variance. If the variance of a distribution of scores is 100, the standard deviation (*SD*) for that distribution equals 10.

The normal distribution
The standard deviation and the mean can be used to further compute *standard scores* (*z* scores). Standard scores permit comparisons to be made between two or more distributions or groups of scores, because all the scores are standardised to the same metric, whereby the mean is zero and the standard deviation is one. Within a given group, the *z* score expresses the various scores on a frequency distribution in terms of a number of standard deviations from the mean. The point is that scores can thus be expressed in terms of their relative position within a distribution, and not as absolute values. To exemplify, suppose two groups of children, one of average age 10 years and another of average age 8 years, are found to display average reading ability scores of 85 and 68 respectively. While the older children clearly

have better reading scores than the younger children, the most relevant comparisons are not between the two groups, but internally between members of these groups, and between each group and a national average for that age. If, in fact, the average reading score for the 10-year-olds can be shown, relying on standard scores, to equal the average known reading score for their age group nationally (giving them a *z* score of zero), and the same is true of the 8-year-olds, then both groups may be considered average for their respective age groups.

Standard scores are also used in conjunction with another fundamental statistical concept – the normal distribution curve (Figure 13.3). If a distribution of scores is normally distributed, its graphical curve should be symmetrical and achieve its maximum height at its mean, which is also its median and its mode. One of the most important features of the normal curve is that a fixed proportion of the area below the curve – representing a known proportion of the population or other phenomena under investigation – lies between the mean and any unit of standard deviation. The normal distribution is an important analytical instrument because a number of natural as well as social phenomena are normally distributed, or nearly so. Not only the scores of mathematical tests, but phenomena such as the heights and weights of individuals, and their IQ scores, all have normal distributions. This means that if the average IQ score is 100 and the standard deviation is 15 points, the proportions of people with scores falling between 85 (*SD* = −1.0) and 100, and between 100 and 115 (*SD* = +1.0) should be the same. Likewise, the proportions of people with IQ scores between 70 (*SD* = −2.0) and 85, and between 130 (*SD* = +2.0) and 115 should also be the same. However, the proportions of people with IQ scores within one standard deviation of the mean will be much greater than the proportions with IQ scores between one and two standard deviations of the mean.

Testing hypotheses

Much quantitative research goes beyond the simple description of data and their distributions. In hypothesis testing, the researcher is

normal
distribution
curve

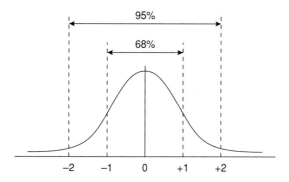

Figure 13.3 The normal distribution curve

interested in establishing whether two or more variables are associated, or whether the scores obtained in two or more groups are different – in both cases in an unambiguous or 'significant' way. When deciding whether to accept or reject a hypothesis, then, the researcher must examine the statistical significance of the results. The starting point is to set up a *null hypothesis*, or a hypothesis which asserts that any statistical differences or relationships that emerge within the dataset are due entirely to chance fluctuations or random error. The research hypothesis puts forward the alternative viewpoint: that the statistical relationships or differences are not due to chance, but represent real phenomena which can be explained theoretically in the research.

the null hypothesis

In determining whether a statistical test has upheld the research hypothesis, a probability level must be set, so that the null hypothesis can be tested against it. If the results indicate a probability level lower than this level, the null hypothesis may be rejected in favour of the research hypothesis. Conversely, if the probability level indicated by the statistical test is higher than the pre-set level, the null hypothesis must be accepted. The usual probability threshold is .05. This means that there is a 5 per cent chance that a relationship between two variables, or a difference between two groups, occurred randomly; but there is a 95 per cent probability that the result demonstrates a real relationship or difference.

probability levels

In testing hypotheses, it is important to select the appropriate statistical technique for the data type in question. A broad distinction is made between parametric and non-parametric tests. Non-parametric tests are appropriate only for nominal and ordinal data, while parametric tests are appropriate for interval and ratio data. Parametric results can be generalised to the population as a whole, while non-parametric results cannot. Parametric tests assume normally distributed data, while non-parametric statistics do not depend on assumptions about the precise distribution of the sampled population.

Using *non-parametric* statistics, researchers test whether frequencies of the phenomena observed match the frequencies that might be expected to occur by chance. A range of non-parametric tests are available for categorical or nominal (binomial test, Chi-square, Mcnemar test, Cochran Q test) and rank or ordinal data (Kolmogorov–Smirnov test, Sign test, Wilcoxon matched-pairs, signed-ranks test, Friedman two-way analysis of variance, Kruskal-Wallis one-way analysis of variance) (see Bryman and Cramer 1997; Siegel 1956). Probability tables for these tests may be found in Siegel (1956) and Hays (1973).

non-parametric statistics

Parametric statistics assume that the data are normally distributed, with means, variances and standard deviations readily calculable. As with nonparametric tests, distinctions may be made among different types of parametric statistics, depending on whether the comparisons are being made between groups or samples (t-test for groups in the sense of pairs, analysis of variance for three or more groups, or for samples of individuals). In addition, parametric analyses may explore whether correlations exist among scores on separate variables for one or more groups (using the Pearson correlation coefficient). While simple *correlation* measures a relationship of association between two variables, more complex *regression* analysis may be used to determine the degree to which one variable changes, given a change in another variable. An even more sophisticated form of analysis, *multiple regression*, enables the researcher to find out the extent to which one (criterion or dependent) variable changes as more than one other (predictor or independent) variable changes. In the latter case, each inde-

parametric statistics

(multiple) regression analysis

ANALYSIS BOX 13.2 TESTING FOR STATISTICAL SIGNIFICANCE: CHI-SQUARE

A popular technique for the analysis of nominal or categorical data, such as results from much content analysis, is Chi-square. In a study of the representation of violence on British television, Gunter and his colleagues examined the distribution of male and female aggressors (Gunter et al. 1999). Focusing on aggressors acting on their own (as distinct from in groups, gangs or crowds), a total of 1282 acts of male-perpetrated violence and 385 acts of female-perpetrated violence were found in drama programming. Together, these two categories comprised a total of 1667 violent acts. Is this difference in the gender distribution of aggressiveness on television statistically significant?

To find out, a Chi-square analysis was computed. If there is no inherent gender difference, it would be hypothesised that 50 per cent of acts would be male-perpetrated and 50 per cent female-perpetrated. Out of the current total, each gender would be responsible for 833.5 violent acts (the expected frequency). To compute a Chi-square, the expected frequency is subtracted from each observed frequency and squared. These squared results are then summed, and the total is divided by the expected frequency (e.g., $[1,282-833.5]^2 + [38-833.5]^2 / 833.5 = 482.7$).

With reference to this value of the coefficient, a goodness-of-fit test can be carried out. It is necessary, first, to determine the probability level (usually 5 per cent or .05) and, second, the number of *degrees of freedom*. The latter refers to the number of scores in a test that are free to vary in value. This is calculated as the number of groups of scores being compared, minus one (in the current example, the degrees of freedom would therefore equal one). The researcher next consults a probability table that indicates whether the calculated coefficient is significant. Such a table displays probability levels along the top and numbers of degrees of freedom down the side. If the Chi-square coefficient exceeds the number displayed in the appropriate cell (here, one degree of freedom by .05 level of probability), it is accepted as a significant result. If not, it is rejected as non-significant. A Chi-square with one degree of freedom must exceed 3.84 to be significant at the .05 level. The current result is, therefore, highly significant.

degrees of freedom

probability tables

---

pendent variable is examined in turn for its impact upon the dependent variable while, in each step of the analysis, statistical controls are introduced for all the other independent variables.

Pritchard and Hughes (1997) used multiple regression analysis in a content analysis of how nine characteristics of homicides might determine whether and how they were covered in newspapers. Newspaper stories were classified, and numerically coded, in terms of the presence or absence of specific attributes. There were four dependent variables: the average length of homicide stories; the number of news items about a homicide; the proportion of homicide items on the front page; and whether a homicide story was accompanied by a photograph.

The results are summarised in Table 13.1. It was the average story length and the number of items that were best predicted by the nine

independent variables. The scores displayed are so-called Beta weights, which indicate the individual predictive strength of each predictor variable. The scores with asterisks are the significant predictor variables. The R^2 score indicates the percentage of variance in each criterion variable (along the top of the table) which is accounted for by the combination of all the predictor variables (down the side of the table) that entered into that analysis.

In this analysis, the results show that homicides tend to get more newspaper coverage (number of items and average story length) when the event involves white participants, a female suspect, a female victim, or a child or elderly victim. The further likelihood of such a story appearing on the front page increases when the homicide involves whites, and when the victim is a child or elderly person. The likelihood of a photograph being published with

Table 13.1 Summary of a regression analysis for variables predicting four measures of homicide newsworthiness (Pritchard and Hughes 1997)

	Average story length	Number of news items published	Proportion of items on front page	Newspaper published photograph
White participants	.42**	.38***	.25*	.12
Female suspect	.33**	−.25*	−.18	−.19
Female victim	.26*	.30**	.15	.23
Victim child/senior	.33***	.33***	.31***	.31**
Census tract income	−.02	.13	.01	−.03
Suspect knew victim	−.11	−.02	−.12	−.10
Risky behaviour	−.06	−.02	.04	.01
Police information ban	−.15	−.16	−.15	−.25*
Race/gender interaction	−.25	−.25*	−.22	−.01
R^2	.29***	.31***	.18*	.17*

Notes:
N = 100
$*p < .05, **p < .01, ***p < .001$

the story increases when the victim is a child or elderly person, but decreases when there has been a police information ban on the details that could be released and included in the story.

CONCLUSION

This chapter has examined quantitative methodologies as they are applied in media and communication research. These methodologies have been used particularly to study media audiences and media content, and they do so by examining either associations between variables or cause–effect relationships. The guiding principle of quantitative research is the hypothetico-deductive approach – certain hypothetical expectations are proposed, and then accepted or rejected through the collection and analysis of scientific data.

The essential characteristic of quantitative research is that it reduces phenomena to numerical codes. Numerical measurement, however, can occur at more than one level, and an understanding of the different levels of measurement

is crucial, both to the correct use of statistical methods of data analysis and to the proper interpretation of data. At the simpler levels, data are used merely to categorise and rank phenomena. At more complex levels of analysis, data may be used to measure relationships among phenomena and to establish causal connections.

As a theoretical enterprise, much quantitative research aims to enhance knowledge by demonstrating both causal links between phenomena and the universality of such relations. In practice, research must frequently make a trade-off between an ideal research design that might effectively demonstrate the nature and causality of social phenomena, and a design that is feasible, given the available resources and the necessary ethical and other considerations. Also for this reason, quantitative studies – like other traditions of research – should be carefully scrutinised for their methodological limitations and the quality of their data before readers and users attach weight and credibility to their findings.

14 The qualitative research process

Klaus Bruhn Jensen

- an overview of *basic concepts* within qualitative media research, including *meaning* as produced in *everyday settings* and examined by researchers as *interpretive subjects*
- an argument for the importance of systematic *design* and *sampling* in qualitative research
- a review of *interviewing, observation*, and other *empirical approaches* to media and communication studies, with examples
- a discussion of *coding, discourse analysis*, and other forms of qualitative *data analysis* as special challenges for qualitative media research
- a presentation of *computer-supported* qualitative research.

INTRODUCTION

Into the 1980s, it was still common for humanistic and other qualitative researchers to refer to their own contributions to media studies as being 'non-scientific' (Farrell 1987: 123), perhaps to secure a relatively underdefined niche for something other than social 'science.' While the distinction between 'hard' science and 'soft' scholarship is still occasionally rehearsed in the new millennium (Rosengren 2000), the past two decades have witnessed a shift from passive tolerance to active dialogue between self-defined qualitative and quantitative researchers. Simultaneously, the field has witnessed a widespread effort to specify the requirements of qualitative research. This chapter reviews the current state of qualitative methodologies, as employed in media and communication research, emphasizing the systematics and operational stages of the qualitative research process.

First, the chapter identifies certain key concepts, originating from anthropology, sociology, as well as the humanities, which inform the conduct of contemporary qualitative studies. Second, the planning of empirical projects is described in terms of the several strategic, tactical, and technical choices that must be made during their conception and implementation. Third, these overviews lead into a review, with examples, of three prototypical methodologies in qualitative media studies, as defined by their means of data collection – in-depth interviewing, participating observation, and document or discourse analysis. In each case, data analysis presents a particular challenge for future qualitative research. The fourth section accordingly outlines procedures for the analysis and interpretation of qualitative data.

BASIC CONCEPTS IN QUALITATIVE RESEARCH

Compared to a prototypical quantitative research project, the 'basic' constituents of a qualitative project are best thought of as a 'middle range' of concepts (Merton 1968: 39). These concepts mediate between concrete research techniques and more grand theoretical frameworks. Compared to much humanistic-textual research, or to classic anthropological fieldwork, qualitative studies have gone a long way toward specifying the procedures of such a middle range of research. Qualitative researchers tend to conceive of their studies, most generally, as an iterative or repeated process, which allows for the flexible application of theoretical concepts and analytical procedures to a wide variety of empirical domains.

qualitative research as iterative process

Qualitative research is a heterogeneous area, as documented through a growing number of reference works (e.g., Bryman and Burgess 1999; Denzin and Lincoln 2000; Miles and Huberman 1994). Nevertheless, it is possible to identify at least three distinctive features that are shared by most current work. First, it is the concept of *meaning*, its embedding in and orientation of social action, which serves as a common denominator for different schools of thought. Human agents experience both their ordinary lives and extraordinary events as meaningful. Cultural artefacts and other vehicles of meaning provide people with a sense of identity, a position from which to exercise agency, and a means of orienting oneself in social interaction. The textual contents of the technological media, but also their materiality, scheduling, and social uses, are studied by qualitative research in order to explore empirically how the media generate meaning. It is the connection between meaning and action – as performed inside media organizations (e.g., Tuchman 1978) as well as by audiences (e.g., Scannell 1988) – which, in part, distinguishes recent qualitative work from earlier aesthetic and historical studies of mediated culture.

meaning

A second assumption of qualitative research is that meaningful actions should be studied, as far as possible, in their *naturalistic contexts*. In its strong form, this assumption calls for the classical variety of anthropological fieldwork, in which a researcher's lengthy immersion in a whole culture enables him or her to ultimately grasp in full 'the native's perspective' on reality (Malinowski 1922: 25). In a more modest form, qualitative studies involve a weighing of

naturalistic contexts

the native's perspective

theoretical aims with practical constraints. At issue are not just restrictions on time and money, but also epistemological questions (can a culture or context ever be known in full?) and ethical considerations (is it appropriate to impose oneself on the people that make up cultures and contexts?).

Qualitative researchers also perform sampling – of cultural settings, communities, informants, locales, periods, and activities. This happens as they transform theoretical concepts into empirical, researchable phenomena, for example, television viewers' definition of their citizenship as articulated in interviews (e.g., Monteiro and Jayasankar 1994), or their conception of the reality of melodrama as stated in solicited letters (e.g., Ang 1985). As elaborated below, there are several possible strategies besides probability sampling and the total description of all manifestations of a single case or community. The naturalistic ambition, rather, stipulates that the phenomena of interest should not be parsed prematurely, or isolated from the contexts which facilitate their interpretation.

A third common feature of qualitative research concerns the role of the researcher, who is defined emphatically as an *interpretive subject*. In one sense, all research depends on the human subject as a primary instrument. What distinguishes qualitative from quantitative projects in this regard is a global and continuous form of interpretation. In quantitative studies, interpretive agency tends to be exercised in a sequential and delegated form – segregating the phases of operationalization and analysis from interpretation and discussion, and delegating certain moments of a study to collaborators as well as machines, above all in computerized data analysis. The qualitative ambition, in comparison, has been for a single researcher to interpret 'meaning in action.'

researcher as human interpretive subject

In order to define the nature of such interpretation, much research has referred to a pair of concepts – *etic* and *emic* approaches to culture and society (Pike 1967). The idea derives from linguistics, but has been widely applied in anthropology and, to a degree, in other social sciences. A 'phonetic' approach to language assumes a continuum of sounds, as

emic and etic analysis

measured on acoustic scales. A 'phonemic' approach focuses on the distinctive set of sounds that constitute one particular language. By analogy, other cultural forms than language may be understood as either a sound engineer or a native speaker would, and they may be studied, accordingly, from either external or internal perspectives.

The analytical question, as debated since Pike (1967), is how the two aspects of interpretation and understanding relate to each other (see the contributions in Headland *et al.* 1990). For one thing, the emic, internal perspective is not simply found, but must be ascertained from some etic, external perspective. For another, this analytical perspective is itself emic, in that it represents both a historical period and an academic subculture. Much recent work has questioned the distinction, and has gone on, mostly from a postmodernist position, to redescribe research 'findings' as simply one more narrative about the culture in question (see Clifford and Marcus 1986; James *et al.* 1997; Marcus and Fischer 1999; Van Maanen 1988; also Chapter 16, this volume). Ultimately, this position would do away with distinctions between scientific and other forms of discourse, focusing on rhetorical and poetic aspects of research.◄

As part of empirical procedures, however, the distinction is clearly important for specifying different levels and stages of analysis throughout a research project. In qualitative media research, cross-cultural studies, for instance, have described distinctive local experiences (emic) of globally disseminated genres such as news and melodrama, as studied also by etic categories in content analysis and discourse studies (e.g., Jensen 1998; Liebes and Katz 1990). For both qualitative and quantitative studies, moreover, there is no way around the emic–etic consideration when devising codes and scales, as examined below, for the analysis of mediated meaning.

DESIGNING QUALITATIVE STUDIES

Formating the field

To design an empirical study is to identify and delimit a portion of reality – which is to be examined with reference to a theoretically informed purpose, or conceptualization, and according to a systematic procedure of data collection and analysis. Whether in qualitative or quantitative traditions, an operationalization of concepts and issues in this broad sense is required (S. L. Schensul *et al.* 1999: 50). Only an empirical 'microcosm' may be studied in any detail in order to substantiate theoretical, 'macrocosmic' inferences and conclusions (see further Alexander and Giesen 1987).◄ Planning, then, is a necessary part of that 'construction' of the field which most qualitative researchers recognize as their epistemological premise. An early reminder of the importance of planning comes from Malinowski (1922: 9), who concluded that while preconceived ideas can get in the way of research, the foreshadowing of problems in the field is an important preamble to empirical work.

In order to identify key features of qualitative designs, it is useful to distinguish three aspects of research design – strategy, tactics, and techniques (Gorden 1969). Notwithstanding any militaristic connotations, these aspects help to make explicit some of the premises and priorities that inform any empirical study:

- *Strategy*, first, refers to a general plan for entering a particular social setting, and for establishing means of communication and points of observation which may generate relevant evidence. Strategy builds a particular set of social relations between researchers and informants in a designated time and space – a temporary structure for preparing and reflecting upon new knowledge.

- *Tactics*, next, refers to attempts by the researcher to anticipate and prestructure, to varying degrees, the social interactions which will yield evidence. A case in point is the definition

conceptualization

operationalization

► rhetoric and poetics of research – Chapter 16, p. 287

► empirical microcosm and theoretical macrocosm – Chapter 15, p. 270

of people to be interviewed. They may be understood either as well-placed sources (informants, *informants* *and respond-* *ents* e.g., within a media organization) or representatives of a particular position in the social system in question (respondents, e.g., from an audience segment) (Lindlof 1995: 170–172).

• *Techniques*, finally, are the researcher's concrete means of interacting with and documenting the field. Verbal language is a main constituent of all the methodologies reviewed below, but other sign systems and artefacts equally serve as sources of qualitative data. Whereas it is the choice of techniques that most clearly distinguishes qualitative from quantitative designs, these instruments will be prefigured by strategy as well as tactics. These procedures, in turn, are anticipated by theoretical purpose and empirical substance of the given study. In sum, the 'why' and the 'what' of research come before the 'how' (Kvale 1987).

Sampling cases

The general formating, or operationalization, of the field is a first step in making a portion of reality accessible for empirical study. A necessary next step is the sampling of elements or constituents within that field. While media researchers may most commonly think of 'samples' as subgroups of 'populations' which consist of either people or texts, qualitative studies frequently sample other units of analysis, for instance, settings, activities, and events *units of* *analysis* (Lindlof 1995: 125). Furthermore, the sampling procedure differs from probability sampling,◀ which is most familiar from opinion polls, surveys, and other quantitative studies.

Qualitative studies often sample in two or *multi-step* *sampling: of* *and within* *contexts* more steps, first determining the relevant context of certain meaningful events, which, next, are singled out for detailed study. In an early qualitative classic of media research, Kurt and Gladys Lang (1953) examined the 1951 MacArthur Day parade by relying on thirty-one observers on-site in Chicago as well as two observers monitoring the television coverage. From each of these contexts, representations

▶ probability sampling – Chapter 13, p. 217

and accounts (including recorded observations, overheard remarks, and content elements) were compared. The findings indicated that on-site participants and television viewers would encounter two distinctively different perspectives on the same event. (As the authors have later emphasized, that particular and important finding was 'entirely serendipitous' (Lang and Lang 1991: 211). Interestingly, so was another classic finding, from a quantitative study, namely the two-step hypothesis concerning media impact (Lazarsfeld *et al.* 1944).)

Two-step and multi-step sampling is in keeping with the contextual orientation of qualitative research. This orientation implies, first, that statements and actions must always be interpreted with reference to their context(s). Contexts are of a variable nature and scope – from a long discursive sequence, to familial and community settings, and nation-states or entire cultures. Second, qualitative studies require, at least ideally, that such contexts remain accessible to the researcher in the process of analysis and interpretation. The qualitative research process amounts to a continuous operationalization and refinement of theoretical concepts with reference to empirical evidence generated through several analytical stages. As the Langs (1991) noted, some preliminary suggestions of how the media buildup to MacArthur Day had affected the public's expectations and demeanor in the streets could be tested against other evidence, including 'badges and behavioral cues' (p. 212).

Regarding sampling procedures, much re- *sampling* *procedures* cent qualitative work has offered descriptions of, and rationales for, distinctive approaches (e.g., Lindlof 1995: 126–131; Miles and Huberman 1994: 28). These contributions followed a long period when qualitative samples were mostly defined *en bloc*, and in negative terms, as 'non-random.' In this regard, qualitative sampling normally operates *within contexts* – which will have been preselected, like the 'populations' of quantitative studies, according to theoretical criteria. Three procedures are of particular importance:

1 *Maximum variation sampling* aims to capture as wide a range of 'qualities' or pheno-

mena as possible. This range is normally suggested by certain other, established characteristics, such as the popularity ratings of radio programs or the age of their listeners. In a study of how American viewers evaluated television and possible ways of reforming it, I compared two groups of viewers: below 35 and above 55 years of age. What distinguished the groups was that they had, and respectively had not, grown up with television as a cultural given (Jensen 1990). The study found, among other things, that the two groups relied on different types of metaphor to describe how more, and more diverse, programming could be made available. The older group referred to a 'library' of programs, whereas the younger group conceived of a continuous 'flow' of specialized channels.

2 *Theoretical sampling* can also be performed within contexts, for example, in studies of media organizations.◀ Here, the purpose often is, in a sense, to sample structures, i.e., different layers of the hierarchy which generates a given product. The strategic junctures may be hierarchical or spatial (in terms of the structure of the organization), or they may be temporal (in terms of the work process regarding that media product). Theoretical sampling can rely on what is sometimes called '(proto-)typical' and 'critical cases.' In order to explore a theoretical category, such as a movie or rock fandom (e.g., Lewis 1991), a project may focus on core members of an established organization, or it may examine borderline instances – a competing fan formation or devotees of a-tonal music – as limiting or test cases.

prototypical and critical cases

3 *Convenience sampling* is sometimes used as a derogatory term for studying those individuals most easily available to the researcher. However, a well-documented convenience sample can generate both valid and reliable insight into a social setting or event. An example is the early study by Cantril *et al.* (1940) which tried to explain a public panic in response to Orson Welles's 1938 radio production of *War of the Worlds*. The study relied on a variety of quanti-

▶ qualitative studies of media organizations – Chapter 4, p. 66

tative as well as qualitative approaches, and also employed convenience samples of respondents who were asked to recollect their experience of being frightened. Moreover, given the notorious difficulty of gaining entry to certain social arenas, convenience in the sense of physical and social accessibility is a legitimate consideration. (The alternative is to rule out research about such arenas – which may be motivated by ethical concerns.) A variant is 'snowball sampling,' in which initial contact with an informant generates further contacts. For each roll of the snowball, it is, in fact, possible to specify how a given choice relates to the overall purpose and design of a study, and, importantly, how earlier stages and insights enabled a more informed choice.

snowball sampling

The three types of qualitative sampling all generate and document a set of meaningful events, instances, or cases for further study. One type of (primarily) qualitative design – case study – particularly explores delimited entities, such as communities and organizations, but also singular individuals and events (see Gomm *et al.* 2000; Yin 1994). In addition to their inherent interest, a purpose of case studies is normally to arrive at descriptions and typologies which have implications for other, or larger, social systems. What case studies share with other qualitative research is the detailed attention given, first to phenomena within their everyday contexts, and second to their structural or thematic interrelations with other phenomena and contexts.

case study

Having formated the field of theoretical interest, and having sampled its empirical constituents, a qualitative project faces central choices concerning techniques or 'methods' – its concrete means of interacting with the field. These choices are normally posed in terms of the main instruments and procedures of data collection. (Again, such choices are anticipated by the domain and purpose of the study, and the choices have consequences for the subsequent analyses and for the potential social uses of the findings.) The following sections review the three main instruments of qualitative research: interviewing, observation, and document or discourse analysis. Chapter 15 returns to the combination of several methods and to the relations between 'methods' and 'methodology.'◀

INTERVIEWING

Interviewing is one of the most widely used data collection methods, also in media and communication research. A commonsensical justification for this fact is that 'the best way to find out what the people think about something is to ask them' (Bower 1973: vi). Particularly in-depth interviewing, with its affinities to conversation, may be well suited to tap social agents' perspective on the media, since spoken language remains a primary and familiar mode of social interaction, and one that people habitually relate to the technological media. The difficulty, of course, is that people do not always say what they think, or mean what they say. In research as in other social practice, communication has its purposes and contexts, which must be teased out by researchers, as by other communicators.

It is crucial, then, to realize that statements from focus groups or biographical interviews (or from surveys) are not simple representations, true of false, of what people think. All interview statements are actions, arising from an interaction between interviewer and interviewee. Interview statements are, in a strong sense of the word, 'data,' and they become sources of information only through analysis and interpretation. For one thing, interview studies ask people to 'discursify' things which commonly fall into the category of practical consciousness (Giddens 1984). For another, interviewers themselves have no perfect awareness either about their own performance or of the responses which they must process in a split second. The disambiguation of interview discourses (or the conclusion that an ambiguity is unresolvable) is the outcome of data analysis, and will remain an inference. This is in spite of the occasional suggestion in textbooks that a highly competent interview may stand fully interpreted when it ends (Kvale 1996: 189).

These points reiterate a classic insight of

rhetoric and of the 'hermeneutics of suspicion':◀ There is no way around language as a medium of access to social and cultural phenomena. Language is a permanent condition of research, not a removable obstacle. On the one hand, respondents' self-conceptions, opinions, and worldviews must be inferred from their language (and other systems of communication) and their argumentative structures, cultural themes, and narratives. On the other hand, linguistic categories offer means of quality control regarding the 'language work' of researchers, as explained below.

Figure 14.1 summarizes the key role of language in qualitative research, both as a tool of data collection and as an object of analysis. (The double notation concerning language as an object of analysis in observational studies indicates that language is often not documented or analyzed in systematic detail, as explained in the section on observation.)

In media research, qualitative studies have primarily employed three types of interviewing. The types reflect the basic options of interviewing one or more persons, with or without a pre-established relationship with each other:

1 *Respondent interviews*. In contrast to informant interviews (less common in media studies), the interviewee is here conceived as a representative of one or more social and cultural categories. The assumption is that these categories are inscribed in, and can be recovered from, the respondent's discourses with reference to the media. Respondent interviews have been prevalent not least in reception studies of the decoding of media.

2 *Naturalistic group interviews*. In order to explore, to the extent possible, what 'normally' goes on in a social setting, qualitative studies have examined naturally occurring groups in the case of both media production and reception. In production studies, interviews have commonly been an integral part of more inclusive observational methodologies, although specific (especially individual) interview methodologies

---

▶ methods and methodology – Chapter 15, p. 258

▶ interview analysis as hermeneutics of suspicion – Chapter 2, p. 22

Language

Methodology	Tool of data collection	Object of analysis
Interviewing	+	+
Observation	+	+/–
Documents/artefacts	–	+

Figure 14.1 The role of language in qualitative methodologies

have been employed (e.g., Newcomb and Alley 1983). For audience studies, household interviews may produce several conflicting perspectives (e.g., by children and parents) on what is a 'normal media day' in the home (e.g., Jensen *et al.* 1994). Interviews with fan groups (e.g., Spigel and Jenkins 1990) and with children and youth peer groups (e.g., Livingstone and Bovill 2001) can also supplement the observation of their distributed activities.

3 *Constituted group interviews.* Groups that are constituted specifically for the purpose of research represent a compromise between the respondent and naturalistic strategies. Group members remain bearers of particular demographics, while entering into an approximated natural group dynamic. An example is Liebes and Katz's (1990), which relied on households to invite acquaintances to their home in order to watch and discuss the *Dallas* television series. The classic inspiration for group interviews was the work by Robert K. Merton and his associates beginning in the early 1940s, which resulted in 'the focused interview' (Merton and Kendall 1955; see also Merton 1987). The general idea became especially influential in the shape of 'focus groups' in marketing and, later, in media research (for an overview see Morgan and Krueger 1998). Morrison (1998) is a key source to the development, and later abuses, of the method. In media studies, focused interviews with relatively homogeneous groups have proven useful for gaining access to their distinctive experiences of media content, sometimes in conjunction with other methods (e.g., Schlesinger *et al.* 1992).

focused interviews and focus groups

It should be added that a wide variety of communicative and other techniques are available for eliciting both mediated and lived experience (e.g., Bryman and Burgess 1999; Marshall and Rossman 1999; Punch 1998). The tradition of 'oral history' (Dunaway and Baum 1996), relying on the lengthy oral testimony not least from 'ordinary' people, who can tell history 'from below,' has made its mark also on media studies. In addition, while most qualitative as well as quantitative methodologies ask people to respond to society and culture as they now exist, some approaches invite groups to anticipate and evaluate forms of communication that are not yet in existence. Such studies could be said to stimulate the sociological imagination (Mills 1959). The study cited above about older and younger viewers' conception of television (Jensen 1990) relied on such a method, 'workshops on the future' (Jungk and Müllert 1981). In a critical reflection on focus groups, Barbour and Kitzinger (1999) note other action-oriented varieties of interviewing, such as Delphi and consensus groups.

oral history

workshops on the future

Across the different qualitative interview forms, three issues normally call for the researcher's attention: duration, structure, and depth:

1 *Duration.* Interviews range from brief dialogues that establish the meaning of a term at a production site, to repeated hour-long sessions with an individual or family, to even more comprehensive life-historical interviews (e.g., Bertaux 1981; Prue *et al.* 2000). Duration is determined largely by the overall purpose of a study, in addition to practical circumstances.

2 *Structure*. Probably the main challenge in planning and administering interviews is how to prestructure the interaction. Depending again on the theoretical purposes, the exchange may cover a predefined set of themes from several perspectives, but in no particular order, or it may follow a sequenced and subdivided interview guide (see, e.g., S. L. Schensul *et al.* 1999: 121–164). In all events, it is the responsibility of the researcher to justify choices in this regard, and to make explicit the procedures which led to particular inferences and conclusions.

3 *Depth*. The researcher's responsibility becomes even more acute when assessing the relevant 'depth' of a qualitative interview. Although the aim will be to elicit the respondent's terminology, or to probe a conceptual structure, the research interview process has similarities with the therapeutic interview, and may articulate tacit or repressed insights (Kvale 1996: 74–80). Depth, which is generally considered *the* strength of qualitative research, thus also poses serious issues for the ethics and politics of research.◀

OBSERVATION

'Observation' refers inclusively to a set of research activities that involve the continuous and long-term presence, normally of one researcher, and generally in one delimited locale. An observer is able to emphatically become the central instrument of research, relying on several sensory registers and on diverse media information. One difficulty of such immersion in the field – beyond the danger of 'going native' and conflating emic and etic perspectives – is documentation. This is important both for the ongoing collection and analysis of data, and for making transparent the steps from an initial observation to a later conclusion. Unless documentation is presented in an explicit, reflexive, and intersubjective manner, a fieldworker may become akin to an artist. Holistic interpretations of some possible world may be inspired and inspiring, but will often be non-negotiable and, hence, beyond

---

▶ research ethics and politics – Chapter 16

research. Within anthropology, debates about such issues have a long history. For example, it is only recently that the sharing of fieldnotes with other researchers has become a common practice (S. L. Schensul *et al.* 1999: 226).

One of the most influential metaphors, also in media studies (Deacon *et al.* 1999; Jensen and Jankowski 1991), for what observation accomplishes is Geertz's (1973) 'thick description.' (Geertz derived the concept from the philosopher, Gilbert Ryle (1971: 465–496).) The point is that a very detailed analysis of a setting is necessary in order to establish the implications of what people do or say, for example, when they use irony. Rather than spreading one's resources thinly across a large field, and predefining the phenomena of interest, efforts should be focused on a smaller field which is explored both for relevant phenomena and for descriptive categories. This approach is in keeping with the qualitative ambition of searching out one's analytical categories in the field itself – even though research questions and purposes inevitably orient a study. Some critiques have identified a rather vague notion of what thick description requires, leading in fact to 'thin' descriptions (Murdock 1997). Nevertheless, the open, inclusive approach is helpful especially in the early stages of a study, and is comparable, to a degree, to pilot studies in other research designs.

A common way of distinguishing varieties of fieldwork is to refer to its relative components of participation and observation, respectively. Summarizing earlier accounts of participating observation, Hammersley and Atkinson (1995: 104) indicate a scale from full observation to full participation, suggesting that there is normally a degree of each element in any fieldwork. Just as any interview question, in a sense, is leading in presuming a particular scope of relevant answers, so observers participate, and participants observe, as they try to interpret 'what is really going on.' In studies of media use in households and other private settings, for example, it is evidently difficult to maintain the observing role of a fly-on-the-wall. However, the study of media use in public places can also be said to involve a measure of participation (Lemish 1982).

thick description

participating observation

One advantage of the reference to degrees of observation and participation, and to interfaces with other data collection methods, is that it avoids the controversial, and questionable, terminology of 'ethnography,' which was imported into media and communication research particularly during the 1980s.◀ It is doubtful whether 'ethnographic' studies are different in kind from other multimethod media studies.

Compared to interview studies, which have been able to rely on affordable audiotape-recorders since around 1950 (Fielding and Lee 1998: 28), observational studies have continued to face special problems of documentation, relying on heterogeneous types of data, but with handwritten fieldnotes as the natural center-piece. Thus, while observers rely on several sensory registers, the resulting observations are only to a limited extent documented in several discursive registers, such as visual media and non-prose genres. In a summary volume on the subfield of visual anthropology, Margaret Mead concluded that anthropology had remained 'a discipline of words' (Hockings 1995: 3), a characterization that still rings true also in (visual) media studies (but see Bauer and Gaskell 2000; J. J. Schensul *et al.* 1999).

visual anthropology

Regarding fieldnotes, there have been few consensual, full-fledged procedures. This is in comparison to detailed conventions concerning interview transcript notations (for an overview see Potter 1996: 233–234) and content analysis. The presentation and analysis of verbatim notes in publications are still exceptions, certainly in observational media studies. This state of affairs has been exacerbated by the assumption that fieldnotes serve only as extensions of more essential 'head notes.' The further assumption – that interpretations could only be conducted adequately by the researcher who was present at the scene – has helped to perpetuate the view of the fieldworker as a creative loner, an artist. (When it emerged, Malinowski's (1967) 'secret' diary, which, among other things, revealed his contempt for the people being studied, undercut his descriptive monograph and questioned both the validity and the legitimacy of his accounts.)

▶ ethnography – Chapter 10, p. 164

In the past few decades, more attention has been given to systematic production of field records (e.g., Ellen 1984: 278–293; Lindlof 1995: 200–215; Spradley 1979: 69–77). A helpful typology distinguishes three purposes and genres:

1 *substantive* notes, which capture representations of the scene under study;
2 *logistical* notes, which add information about the circumstances under which these data were gathered;
3 *reflexive* notes, which initiate the process of analysis and theorizing on the basis of observations and other data (adapted from Burgess 1982).

An additional rule of thumb is to focus on substance (what) and logistics (how) in the field, and to reserve the main reflexive activity (why) for later stages of the research process. The researcher can only fulfill his/her role as the main instrument of research through a differentiated and staggered process of analysis, interpretation, and self-reflexivity.

The wider lesson for empirical studies is to approach fieldnotes not as self-contained representations, but as working documents from one stage or level of study. As elaborated in a later section, these documents, like interview recordings and transcripts as well as various other artefacts, feed into an equally differentiated analytical process.

field notes as working documents

DOCUMENTS, ARTEFACTS, AND UNOBTRUSIVE MEASURES

The third group of approaches to data collection is more heterogeneous than either observation or interviewing. What unites them is their relatively naturalistic or unobtrusive (Webb *et al.* 2000) nature – the data are 'found' rather than 'made' through the researcher's intervention in the field. On the one hand, data such as feature films and computer games, government reports and executive memos, are produced as part of the normal business of media, and thus are not 'biased' by the researcher. On the other hand, the data may therefore have a more limited or indirect explanatory value for the research question.

Overall, these approaches represent a potentially valuable, and somewhat neglected, source of evidence. In certain respects, they address issues which have fallen outside, or between, the most common social-scientific and humanistic methodologies. The humanistic tradition has remained largely text-centric, focusing on *pre-existing texts*; social-scientific studies have emphasized the production of *new data* regarding the *contexts* of media. In this last respect, it should be noted that media research has replicated a tendency in other social research to privilege new datasets, and to de-emphasize, for instance, written documents (Atkinson and Coffey 1997: 45; Hammersley and Atkinson 1995: 157–174). A case in point is biographies (but see Chamberlayne *et al.* 2000). This may be attributed, in part, to the original focus of anthropology on oral cultures, and of sociology on modernity as lived, perhaps reinforced by a certain romanticism for 'authentic' data.

As suggested by the headline of this section, the approaches are characterized each by their central object of analysis, rather than any unifying method. First of all, the textual output of media has naturally been a central object of analysis in qualitative media studies, being the vehicles of cultural forms and historical worldviews.◀ Moreover, qualitative research has been instrumental in extending the notion of 'text' to processes of intertextuality and of meaningful social interaction. The texts include advertising, publicity, as well as audience exchanges with and about media.◀

production and reception documents   A second type of text or document relates to production and reception. Like other modern organizations, the media are highly prolific generators of documents that prepare and feed into the media texts proper. Like other cultural institutions, they attract written responses such as audience letters (e.g., Collins 1997), but also diaries, autobiographies, and fan fiction reflect on the social role of media (see Hammersley and Atkinson 1995: 159). Film studies, for instance, have relied on diverse data sources regarding early movie audiences (e.g., Stokes and Maltby 1999a).

Figure 14.2 suggests a further distinction between evidence that is associated with, and primarily originates from, sources in the private (intimate) or public domain. In each case, it is necessary to keep in mind that, like observational records, interview transcripts, as well as audience measurements, the documents thus 'inherited' are not ready-made representations of social facts. They are the outcome of previous social interactions, whose circumstances must be part of the object of analysis and interpretation.

Third, artefacts and various physical arrangements pertaining to media are also relevant sources of evidence. Media are most commonly thought of as means of representation, or vehicles of meaning, but media are also physical objects and constitutive elements of other social action. One example is the use of a newspaper or other reading material as a resource for warding off unwanted contact, typically in a public context such as mass transit, but also in the home as a means of insisting on one's personal time or space (Radway 1984: 61).◀ Another example is the design of media hardware such as early television sets and their embedding in the home setting, as studied by Spigel (1992) with reference to their depiction in magazines. Media hardware also constitutes objects-to-think-with.◀ Similarly, cinema architecture establishes an experiential setting, not only for movie viewing, but for the collective activity of 'going to the movies' (e.g., Gomery 1992).

It should be added that computer media and networked communication pose new difficulties as well as opportunities, with the research strategies still in the making.◀ For data collection, digital technologies offer increasingly miniaturized equipment, for example, digital cameras, for use on-site or on-line. (The relevance of computers for qualitative data analysis is taken up below.) In general, computer-mediated communication has problematized the dis-

---

▶ media texts – Chapters 7–8

▶ intertextuality – Chapter 11, p. 186

▶ physical arrangements – Chapter 10, p. 169

▶ media artefacts as objects-to-think-with – Chapter 1, p. 6

▶ methodologies of computer media studies – Chapter 11, p. 183

	Production	Reception
Private	Autobiographies by film stars, journalists, or other media practitioners	Clippings and other memorabilia concerning a media personality or genre
Public	Organizational archives, from policy papers to rewrites and worksheets	Letters to the editor, fan magazines, or computer-mediated news groups

Figure 14.2 Examples of documents relating to media production and reception

tinction between media and their embedding social context. The dispersed, customizable, and interactive features of computer media all contribute to their integration into social contexts of action (and into interpersonal communication), the study of which requires several forms of evidence.

To sum up, this third group of approaches holds untapped opportunities for media and communication research. One of the relatively few sustained efforts has addressed children's experience of their media use, which often lends itself better to, for instance, drawings than verbal evidence (e.g., Rydin 1996). In the classic on unobtrusive measures (Webb *et al.* 2000), the references to media are many, including infra-red recordings of audiences in darkened cinemas (p. 154), and fingerprints used to determine which advertisements have been seen or read (p. 44) – the ethical concerns here become acute. Beyond the growing, but still limited attention to images and artefacts as research evidence, some work has gone on to study 'the seen' (Emmison and Smith 2000: ix) – the observable two- and three-dimensional contexts of social and cultural life, including public space and material culture, shopping malls and graffiti. The growth of 'virtual' worlds in computer-mediated communication is likely to draw renewed attention also to the spatial, architectural aspects of media in society.

children's drawings

public space and material culture

DATA ANALYSIS

Coding and analysis

The question of what constitutes 'analysis' has been a central area of controversy between qualitative and quantitative traditions of media studies. From one perspective, a textual analysis or case study might be said to perform, not an 'analysis' (e.g., an explicit segmentation and subsequent categorization of component parts to anticipate later inferences and conclusions), but a new 'synthesis,' a general reinterpretation of the object of analysis. Qualitative data analysis has, indeed, suffered from an insufficient specification and documentation of its procedures and stages. As of the present, however, a whole range of approaches and techniques are being applied. Studies rarely employ standardized logical or mathematical models, but certainly rely on systematic procedures. In fact, recent qualitative research has helped to reopen the dialogue with quantitative research concerning the definition and status of 'description' and 'interpretation,' 'findings' and 'discussion,' 'analysis' and 'synthesis.'

analysis and synthesis

Like any scientific enterprise, a qualitative study is committed to carrying out an analysis whose elements, procedures, and stages are explicit, documented, and can be argued about. A hallmark of any competent research report is that it delivers a qualified basis for disagreement – for resolving, or specifying, differences regarding methodology, theory, or epistemology.

What distinguishes qualitative research, in particular, is that key concepts and other minimal constituents are defined and redefined as part of the research process itself. Moreover, the contexts in which such constituents are to be interpreted equally remain open to redefinition throughout the study. Accordingly, synthesis is not a single concluding act, but a continuous activity of assessing data and articulating concepts. Far from justifying unspecified references to 'patterns' that 'emerge' through a 'spiral of insight,' the qualitative research process requires systematic and distinctive formats of presentation and argument.

Several practical issues can be laid out with reference to the notion of 'coding.' Some traditions treat coding as a necessary and self-evident ingredient of, even a synonym for, 'analysis.' Importantly, the term covers two different understandings of how words, numbers, and mental categories can be matched to phenomena in reality. In slightly different inflections, the two conceptions have recently been described as heuristic and factual codes (Silverman 2000: 170), and as indexing and representational devices (Fielding and Lee 1998: 176).

heuristic and factual codes

On the one hand, a code may be taken as an account or *representation* of a portion of the field of study, capturing and fixating certain qualities of a person, event, text, or other unit of analysis for the purpose of later comparison. The aim is to arrive at exhaustive and mutually exclusive categories. Coding in this sense, moreover, aims to establish a standard by which such qualities may be conferred across contexts and, in the end, quantified.

On the other hand, a code may be understood as a *resource* or instrument for identifying and retrieving a given portion of the field. In a next step, this unit of analysis may be examined either for its immanent structure and specific qualities, or with reference to some additional portion of its context. Here, the ambition of research in each case is to examine a wider setting, which is said to always circumscribe and embed the central object of analysis and its meaning.

The two conceptions of coding are clearly the legacy of quantitative and qualitative research traditions, respectively. At the same time, coding offers an interface between the two traditions, since an index may be developed into a representation, and vice versa. Typically, a qualitative study will identify subsets and sequences of data which are related thematically or structurally, and which can be singled out for detailed and perhaps comparative analysis. In this connection, it bears repeating that the movement from fieldnotes, tapes, and transcripts to final research reports comprises several steps – memoing, modeling, drafting, recontextualizing – each of which lends itself to documentation, if not necessarily standardization. Referring to financial audits of firms and organizations, Lincoln and Guba (1985: ch. 11) developed the term '<u>U</u>' to refer also to ways of keeping the research process transparent to the researcher in question, and accountable to colleagues and readers (see also Atkinson and Coffey 1997).

audit trail

Variants of data analysis

The history of qualitative data analysis spans rhetoric, hermeneutics, and semiotics, as well as several strands of social science (for an overview, see Fielding and Lee 1998: 21–55; Chapter 2, this volume). Much early social science was based not on codes, but on the study of cases. This was, in part, a response to the search for general categories and theoretical frameworks within emerging disciplines. One approach was outlined by Znaniecki (1934), who, under the heading of analytic induction, wanted to replace enumerative induction and probabilistic statements with the intensive study of single cases in a stepwise attempt to arrive at general, even universal categories of social phenomena. Despite examples of the approach also in media studies (Lang and Lang 1953), it has not gained wide acceptance, partly because of its time-consuming procedures and limited practical applications, partly because of epistemological doubts concerning the universality of its categories.

Occasionally, proposals have been made for formalizing qualitative analysis into matrices or truth tables. For example, there have been attempts at accounting for cases (social events, processes, or units) with reference to the combination of historical and cultural conditions under which particular cases occur (e.g., Ragin 1987, 1994). A second, more broadly defined approach to studying cases was prevalent from the 1920s onward in the Chicago School studies particularly of urban life, but also of media as in the Payne Fund studies.◄ Third, grounded theory, below, took part of its inspiration from analytic induction.

By the 1950s, a noticeable shift had

► Payne Fund case studies – Chapter 10, p. 158

occurred in social science that could be summed up as a 'transition from case-based to code-based analysis' (Fielding and Lee 1998: 27).◄ The growing professionalization of research as well as the increasing availability of technologies such as tape-recorders, typewriters, and, subsequently, computers are among the explanations for this shift. The question was, and remains, what exactly this entails – for example, where on a continuum from heuristic to factual coding does an analysis situate itself? In qualitative studies, three attempted responses are of particular interest.

Thematic coding

A widespread approach in media research has been a loosely inductive categorization of interview or observational extracts with reference to various concepts, headings, or themes. The process comprises, to varying degrees, the comparing, contrasting, and abstracting of the constitutive elements of meaning. It is the very occurrence of a particular theme or frame in a context of communication which is of primary interest to qualitative research. Such categorizations of data, in turn, can support inferences concerning, for example, the selective reception and reconstruction of news items by different audience groups (e.g., Morley 1980).

consensual coding   Some qualitative research has relied on consensual or group coding of themes in order to substantiate their conclusions (e.g., Neuman *et al.* 1992: 32–33). In addition, some studies have emphasized the development of models and nonverbal tools as integral elements of a stepwise analytical procedure. A main contribution has come from Miles and Huberman

data display   (1994), who place special emphasis on 'data display' in the form of figures and graphics as aids in interpretation. Perhaps surprisingly in a field which otherwise tends to work through models of communication and representation, such approaches are rarely encountered in qualitative media studies.

To a degree, this inclusive understanding of categorical analysis is compatible with coding

---

► from case-based to code-based research – Chapter 15, p. 256

as performed in content and survey studies. In an important early contribution to qualitative research, Lazarsfeld and Barton (1951) explored ways of transforming classifications of empirical units into typologies, indices, and models. Even though their inclination, in keeping with the period, was toward formalization, the article highlighted the many possible varieties and stages of data analysis. The authors also acknowledged the necessary interpretive labor of the researcher throughout the analytical process.

Grounded theory

The second main variety of qualitative data analysis is 'grounded theory' (Glaser and Strauss 1967). It became influential in the social sciences from the 1960s as a framework that would name and legitimate an alternative, particularly to survey research. As suggested by the name, the approach is a methodology which tends to assume that theory can be 'found' in the field, if the research activity is sufficiently 'grounded' in the categories of that field.

constant comparative method   Relying on a 'constant comparative method,' researchers in this tradition have developed a detailed set of procedures for collecting and analyzing empirical data. A characteristic feature is the several, and often repeated, stages of sampling, analyzing, memoing, and interpreting materials; another feature is a stepwise process of coding data at different levels of abstraction. Most important, perhaps, is the assumption that this sequence may ultimately produce theoretical 'saturation' – an equilibrium between

theoretical saturation   empirical evidence and explanatory concepts. Compared to other qualitative traditions which will often rely on theoretical sampling, grounded theory has emphasized an iterative, inductive variety of both sampling and theory development.

As part of the more recent return to qualitative methodologies, the approach has been disseminated widely through textbooks (Strauss 1987; Strauss and Corbin 1990) and included in reference works (e.g., Denzin and Lincoln 2000). It should be mentioned, however, that the terminology appears to be more widespread than the practice, and is 'sometimes invoked

... to legitimize an inductive approach' (Fielding and Lee 1998: 178). This description applies to media studies, despite occasional references to a more elaborate use of the approach (Lindlof 1995: 223).

Part of the explanation for this state of affairs may be problems inherent in the foundations of grounded theory. In particular, other researchers have questioned the apparent premise of grounded theory that a researcher may enter the field without theoretical presuppositions (for an overview see Alvesson and Sköldberg 2000: 12–36). Not only is that position epistemologically dubious, but it may encourage and justify researchers in not reflecting on the scientific as well as social conditions shaping their work. Instead, later textbooks within the tradition have suggested increasingly cumbersome procedures, designed to ensure the grounding of categories in the field itself. In fact, the origins of the procedures are often not clear, nor is it evident how they differ from other available qualitative methods. A further concern is that, at least in Strauss's version (Strauss and Corbin 1990), the analytical procedures cut off social events from their context of other events, as each event is analyzed, reanalyzed, and condensed within increasingly abstract categories.

The uncertain status of the theoretical categories of grounded theory and the question of how to relate them to empirical phenomena has been part of the backdrop to an unusually vehement confrontation between the two founders of the tradition. Glaser (1992) attacked his co-author for an 'immoral undermining' (p. 121) of their original joint contribution and demanded the withdrawal of a volume co-authored by Strauss (Strauss and Corbin 1990). In the end, it remains unclear what distinguishes grounded theory beyond a rather commonsensical notion of sampling, comparing, and reflecting in a reiterated sequence, as conducted by most (qualitative) researchers. The frequent referencing of the tradition may testify to the general weakness of some earlier qualitative data analysis, and to the need to further develop such approaches as thematic coding and discourse analysis.

Discourse analysis

A third approach to data analysis draws its inspiration from discourse studies.◄ Special attention is given to it here because of its potential for further qualitative research. On the one hand, discourse analysis offers a systematic and operational approach to different kinds of coding, including consensual and thematic procedures. On the other hand, it avoids the condensation and decontextualization of meaning which is implicit in grounded theory as well as most quantitative versions of coding.

A way of tapping the advantages of both coding and close analysis is to distinguish between two moments of data analysis:

1 *Heuristic coding* – a preliminary and iterative assignment of verbal and other codes to different portions and levels of a dataset. Examples range from metaphors, expressed in a single word or image, to complex narratives about particular issues.

2 *Discourse analysis* – a more definitive and detailed categorization of a data extract and its constituents. As exemplified in Box 14.1, aspects of form as well as of thematic content offer relevant units of analysis, from a respondent's use of pronouns in an interview, to the narratives constructed jointly by a circle of viewers as observed around a television set.

Heuristic coding allows researchers to produce a working document, or summary, of elements and structures occurring in a dataset. This first analytical step does not preclude, but rather supports a later detailed analysis of discursive segments in context. One purpose of this later stage of analysis may be to test hypotheses that have emerged, including the identification of possible counterexamples. An advantage of this two-pronged approach is that it promotes multiple forms and levels of analysis. A related advantage is that both heuristic codes and linguistic categories are compatible with content analysis and survey techniques. This is exemplified by studies of so-called keywords-in-context research (KWIC) (Fielding and Lee 1998: 53), a **keywords in context**

► discourse studies – Chapter 7, p. 104

ANALYSIS BOX 14.1 DISCOURSE ANALYSIS OF QUALITATIVE INTERVIEW DATA

In a study of the reception of television news by American men at different educational levels, a combination of heuristic coding and discourse analysis was employed to explore the experiential qualities and social uses of the news genre (Jensen 1986). The data analysis was structured according to a set of themes which had been operationalized in the interview guide. The heuristic coding identified references to these themes, both in response to the dedicated questions, and elsewhere in each interview. Next, the relevant textual sequences were examined in further detail through discourse analysis. The following illustration pays special attention to the level of continuous discourse (argument), but also considers the levels of speech acts and interaction. Of special interest at the discourse level are:

- *generalizations* – summary statements, often signaled by adverbials, conjunctions, and verbal or 'do'-emphasis, and by initial or final placement in the speaker's turn;
- *substantiations* – the supporting reasons or examples given for a generalization;
- *implicit premises* – the unquestioned point of departure for an argument, either a logical presupposition or a natural assumption in context;
- *implications* – what follows from a statement with varying degrees of certainty, depending on the speech community, the immediate context, as well as the wider social and cultural setting.

At issue in the following quotation is the theme of flow – whether the respondent carries over from another television program to the news. Asked by the interviewer (I) whether he does that, this respondent, a junior university professor, says:

> 'No. (I: No?). I don't think so, because I have a real thing, when I was living at home my sister is one who just always has some appliance on (I: H-hm), and I really, something deep in me, I really dislike that (I: H-hm), so that, no, if I get up and if the first story didn't catch me, or maybe even if I was done with that program I'd turn it off (I: H-hm) and not keep it on just because it had been on the hour before' (p. 177).

The generalization – a denial of this possibility – is expressed both in the initial emphatic 'no' and in the summarizing 'so that, no.' However, two quite different substantiations are offered. The first reference is to a situation where the first news story does not catch him; the implied premise of the uncompleted sentence is that if that story did catch him, he would or might keep watching. The second substantiation, perhaps on second thought, asserts that if the previous program had ended, he would turn off the TV.

The disjuncture between the two substantiations served as one occasion to reconsider other responses by this and other respondents. One conclusion of the study, as suggested also by other research, was that the respondents aimed to project an image – to offer an 'implication' – of themselves as rational citizens, not least in relation to a 'serious' genre such as news. Presumably, they 'ought to' select news specifically as part of their media diet. In the study, the theme of watching news as a way of participating in political democracy tied in with other themes, particularly the feeling of being a legitimated member of an imagined political community (Anderson 1991). This generalized use of news was opposed, in different ways, to any concrete, instrumental value of news as a political resource.

At the level of *discourse*, this brief quotation also contains the rudiments of a narrative regarding family life, specifically the respondent's sister, with implications for gender-specific media use. The narrative is constituted, in part, at the level of the *speech acts*:

cont.

cont.

- *Personal pronouns* – a characteristic feature is the consistent and insistent use of 'I,' apparently a self-assured and self-aware position, which the respondent applies equally to living at home and to his current living conditions.
- *Impersonal grammar* – in reference to his sister, the respondent seems to suggest that she does not actively use the media, but merely 'has on' a semi-autonomous technology, what is derogatorily termed 'some appliance.' (It is worth adding, however, that, also in his own case, the first news story is something that must 'catch him,' not vice versa.)
- *Metaphor* – is not a strong feature in the example. Still, metaphors serve to emphasize the respondent's distanciating evaluations ('deep in me,' 'have a real thing'), and the reference to media as 'appliance' (and to a program 'catching' a person) similarly helps to establish the distance between the speaker and particular uses of the medium.

At the level of *interaction*, the respondent re-emphasizes his personal position:

- *Turn-taking* – the specific design gave respondents the opportunity to elaborate at length, which this respondent did; this was a short reply. Here, he responded to the verbatim question, 'If you were watching the program right before the news program, would that make you more inclined to watch the news?' It is worth noticing that the relativity of 'inclined to watch' is canceled by the respondent, who instead frames a clear-cut choice as signaled initially by 'no.'
- *Semantic networks* – a longer sequence, preferably a full interview or other interaction, is needed to assess the interrelations between concepts. Still, the lexical choices, including various emphatic formulations ('a real thing,' 'just always,' 'really,' 'something deep in me'), are in line with the respondent's profiling of himself as a rational citizen.

technique which facilitates enumeration as well as contextual interpretation.

It is a characteristic feature of discourse and other language studies since the 1970s that they have emphasized the understanding of communication as social action. A case in point is the communication or 'language work' of research. In his influential functional linguistics, Halliday (1973, 1978) identified three aspects of the social uses of language:◄

Speech acts

Utterances serve as means of representing, and of interacting with, social reality. All utterances may be categorized as a type of speech act – a performance in a particular context for a particular purpose.◄ *Orders* will be negotiated within a media production team; journalistic sources may be offered a *promise* of anonymity in return for a statement. In addition to such

types of speech acts, three elements in particular lend themselves to discourse analysis as indicators of how people (including a researcher in the empirical field) interact:

1 *personal pronouns* (I, you, one, they, etc.) – especially in reference to themselves, people use pronouns to signal different degrees of distance from a topic or opinion, and of solidarity with others;

2 *impersonal grammar* – through the use of passive sentences and other linguistic forms, both media and people are often less than precise regarding 'who does what,' and sometimes these structures imply a worldview where things just happen;◄

3 *metaphors* – alone, in pairs, or in several varieties, metaphors can serve as an organizing principle behind a description or argument and, hence, as a key to a respondent's conception of particular phenomena.

▶ functional linguistics – Chapter 7, p. 105

▶ speech acts – Chapter 2, p. 38

▶ statements without an agent – Chapter 7, p. 105

Interaction

The interaction between two or more people which makes up most empirical media research is important for two different purposes. First, the gradual development of viewpoints in, for instance, focus groups lends itself to close analysis, which may trace important conceptual distinctions and continuities. Second, the researcher's own role in the interaction calls for quality control – what is also considered under the intersubjectivity or reliability of research.◄ In qualitative research, such analyses can assess whether studies, in fact, explore the respondents' perspective. For both purposes, two aspects of discourse provide indicators:

1 *turn-taking* – a description of the structure, order, and length of interventions by respondents and researcher(s) (Sacks *et al.* 1974);

2 *semantic networks* – an examination of central terms and concepts, as introduced and redeveloped by both researcher and respondent(s) (e.g., Corley and Kaufer 1993).

Discourses

Defined as meaningful wholes with argumentative, narrative, and other purposes, discourses represent the largest unit of qualitative data analysis. In addition to the rhetorical and literary traditions, a source of inspiration for discourse analysis in this regard has been the study of informal argument (Toulmin 1958). To exemplify, the actant model,◄ which was developed from folktales, has proven applicable to how people narrate and argue about themselves – the 'Story of Me' (Jensen 1995: 137).

The analysis in Box 14.1 illustrates the principles of all three levels of discourse analysis with reference to an argumentative interview discourse. To clarify, the purpose is not to conduct a comprehensive formal analysis of interviews and other data *as language* – the analysis of language (and other signs) here is an auxiliary operation to better understand research evidence as it arises *from communication*. It is

► reliability and other quality control – Chapter 15, p. 266

► the actant model – Chapter 8, p. 127

important, then, to distinguish between discourse as 'structure' and as 'evidence' (Gee *et al.* 1992: 229–230).

discourse as structure and as evidence

Nevertheless, language and its components are main vehicles of evidence in qualitative research, and require the attention of qualitative researchers. Language is comparable, in quantitative research, to mathematical symbols and procedures. Numbers have a different relevance for quantitative media researchers than they do for mathematicians, but still require their attention.

In response to a final concern – that discourse analysis requires specific linguistic training in order for media researchers to transfer it to a qualitative project – this may be said to raise a rather more general issue for much interdisciplinary research. Interdisciplinary approaches are premised on the assumption that the transfer and integration of methods or, alternatively, collaboration and the use of expert consultants, is feasible. Quantitative projects routinely consult with statisticians; it is likely that qualitative projects will increasingly involve discourse-analytical consultants, or include their competences in interdisciplinary groups. Discourse analysis presents itself as a candidate for a 'statistics' or systematics of qualitative research.

a 'statistics' of qualitative research

To sum up, the three variants of qualitative data analysis are displayed and compared in Figure 14.3:

1 *Thematic coding* represents an attempt to identify, compare, and contrast meaning elements, as they emerge from and recur in several different contexts. What distinguishes thematic coding from much quantitative content analysis is the emphasis on defining each of these elements in relation to their context.

2 *Grounded theory* seeks to condense or compress its central categories of meaning through the research process, partly through iterative sampling, partly through repeated analyses.

3 *Discourse analysis* proposes a combination of coding, primarily for heuristic purposes, with in-depth linguistic analysis of selected meaning elements.

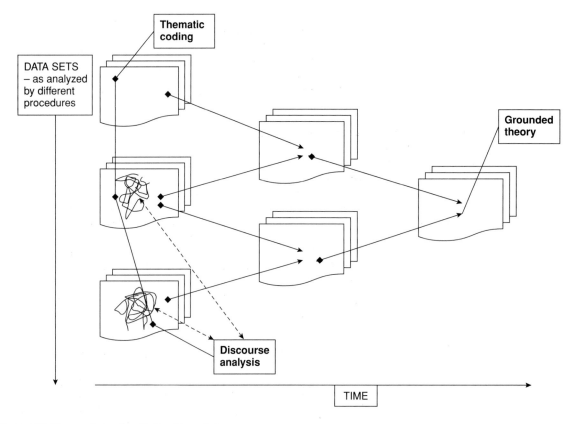

Figure 14.3 Three variants of qualitative data analysis

Computer interfaces

Over the past decade, the ambition of developing more systematic approaches to qualitative research has been evident also in an increased reliance on computers. Dedicated software for data analysis and for the administration of the research process has become available (Weitzman 2000; Weitzman and Miles 1995), and its potentials (and problems) in research design and theory development are being explored (Fielding and Lee 1998). The main practical value so far has been more efficient means of heuristic coding, in addition to facilities for retrieving evidence in different configurations, including tabular and graphic formats. Increasingly, qualitative software also supports the analysis of sound, still, and moving images. Such resources are likely to encourage a greater use of nonverbal data forms.

One prospect is that 'hypertext' systems, in various forms, will support the research process as a whole – from theoretical exploration, literature search, and networking, through data collection, annotation, and analysis, to publication, debate, and revision. Not least, the computer allows for extensive data sharing and collaborative qualitative projects, which have been comparatively rare in the past. The sharing of evidence may involve not only colleagues but respondents, and, in time, segments of the public. For one thing, a computerized research process facilitates 'member checks' (Lindlof 1995: 168) – conferring with respondents about the interpretation of data (although conclusions remain the researcher's right and responsibility). For another, computer-mediated communication, at least in principle, provides a link between qualitative research and public

data sharing

member checks

debate, which has been more of an arena for quantitative research traditions in the past.

Concretely, the bulk of many qualitative reports, including close analyses of transcripts, has sometimes served as an argument against their publication in the major journals which, for better or worse, define a field. More differentiated publication formats can assign full digital documentation to (what is now known as) an Internet site or to another medium. At the same time, computer-mediated publication may provide one more interface between qualitative and quantitative research traditions. It

seems likely that the meta-medium (Kay and Goldberg 1999 [1977]), which both mainstreams increasingly rely on, could support the development also of more common analytical terms and concepts.

Fifty years ago, Lazarsfeld and Barton (1951: 155) provided a reassuring argument, and an agenda of complementarity, which is pursued in the next chapter: 'There is a direct line of logical continuity from qualitative classification to the most rigorous form of measurement.'

15 The complementarity of qualitative and quantitative methodologies in media and communication research

Klaus Bruhn Jensen

- an overview of the *two main paradigms* which inform media and communication research
- a presentation of *six levels of analysis* that are shared across different research traditions
- a comparison and exemplification of *three forms of inference* from the philosophy of science
- a reassessment of *reliability*, *validity*, *generalization*, and *probability* in empirical media studies
- a discussion of *realism* as a framework for convergence.

INTRODUCTION

The legacy for media and communication research from a century of sometimes intense conflict within the general theory of science has been a set of conceptual dichotomies that used to divide the field into two main camps with some additional internal fronts and alliances. Even while studies of scientific practice have shown that the reality of laboratories and libraries may rarely conform to textbook models (e.g., Hacking 1983; Latour 1987), these conceptions have had real and largely counterproductive consequences for how different research traditions have understood both themselves and their 'others.' The perception of fundamental difference has generated various kinds of response – from 'imperialism,' seeking to subordinate or delegitimate other approaches, to 'apartheid,' protecting one's own worldview through insulation from those of others (see Jensen 1995: 141–145). This chapter presents an overview of the current, ongoing convergence in the practice of research, and provides examples of the

neither 'imperialism' nor 'apartheid'

complementarity of different types of empirical media studies.

Departing from the received conceptual dichotomies regarding qualitative and quantitative research, the chapter first takes the modest position that the two mainstreams have different strengths, and might proceed in parallel. To begin a more detailed comparison, the chapter distinguishes several forms and levels of 'analysis,' which also involve different notions of 'method' and 'methodology.' Next, the different types of analysis are related to the two classic forms of inference – induction and deduction – to which is added a third – abduction. The presence of each in qualitative as well as quantitative media studies is exemplified, and their respective requirements lead into a reconsideration of criteria of validity, reliability, and other key concepts in empirical work. These various comparisons suggest the promise of a realist model of science, which may accommodate diverse research traditions. Finally, the chapter presents three concrete ways of combining qualitative and quantitative methodologies with a view to further research.

FROM CONFLICT TO COMPLEMENTARITY

Two paradigms

Figure 15.1 displays a list of interrelated conceptual dichotomies, as still received in much
media research (see further Jensen 1995: ch. 9).
paradigms The two columns qualify as 'paradigms' (Kuhn
1970), defined as particular configurations
of ontological, epistemological, and methodological assumptions about reality and how to
study it (Guba and Lincoln 1994: 108). In the
present context, it is their methodological
assumptions, and their background in the
theory of science, that are the focus of interest.
(For an overview on paradigms, see Conant and
Haugeland 2000.)

methodology the level of methodology. It is commonly recognized that quantitative research instruments are

particularly suited to establish the *recurrence* of
events or objects (e.g., the expression of a particular opinion, or a specific content feature).
Qualitative approaches, in their turn, explore
the singular *occurrence* of meaningful phenomena, but with reference to their full context
(e.g., a film narrative or everyday media uses in
a household). Defined thus as an indivisible
whole, human *experience* calls for an *exegesis* –
a reiterated and continuous interpretation of
meaningful elements whose context may be
redefined as the interpretation proceeds. In contrast, the whole of human experience may also
be defined as the sum of its parts, divisible at
least in operational terms and, hence, manipu-
lable in an *experiment*, whose findings are
expressed in *measurements*. It is in this latter
regard that the quantitative conception of
meaning is sometimes referred to as a *product* –

Methodology	
Recurrence	Occurrence
Experiment	Experience
Measurement	Exegesis
Product	Process
Theory of science	
Gesetzeswissenschaften	*Ereigniswissenschaften*
Naturwissenschaften	*Geisteswissenschaften*
Nomothetic	Idiographic
Erklären	*Verstehen*
External	Internal
Information	Meaning
Epistemology	
Nature	History
Causes	Intentions
Objects	Subjects

Figure 15.1 Two paradigms of social and cultural research

a delimited vehicle that may be conferred without ambiguity to other meaning products in other contexts. Qualitative methodologies, in comparison, tend to approach meaning as a *process* which is tied to its shifting contexts.

The historical background to these methodological variants was attempts within the philosophy or theory of science to stipulate procedures for the study of society and culture. Such procedures took on renewed importance following the development of social sciences from the late 1800s. One famous statement of purpose was Weber's (1964: 88) definition of sociology as 'a science which attempts the interpretive understanding of social action in order thereby to arrive at causal explanation of its course and effects,' referring specifically to *both* interpretations *and* causes. Many contemporary debates were anticipated in the *Methodenstreit* (struggle over methods) of the period, centered in German thought, which confronted historicist and naturalist notions of the 'facts' of social life (for an overview see Hammersley 1995).

On the one hand, one may search for one or more laws (*Gesetz*), as previously established in sciences of nature (*Naturwissenschaften*). One thus takes a generalizing or *nomothetic* attitude and tries to explain (*erklären*) society. On the other hand, one may study one or more singular events (*Ereignis*), as associated with philosophy, aesthetics, and other disciplines of the 'human spirit' (*Geist*). Here, one takes an individualizing or *idiographic* attitude with the aim of understanding (*verstehen*) society. With the advent of information and communication theory (which has restated classic issues of philosophy), several related distinctions emerged. Media and communication studies have tended to take either an *external* perspective on *information* as a technical, neutral carrier, or an *internal* perspective on *meaning* as an always interpreted and interested construct.

These ingredients of the theory of science have mediated between the specific answers suggested by empirical research, and those epistemological questions which appear 'eternal,' in the sense that they have refused to go away for millennia of documented research. As such, they have returned, sometimes with a vengeance, in new scientific fields.

the philosophy or theory of science (margin)

Methodenstreit (margin)

epistemology (margin)

The media field has faced general questions of whether technologies and other aspects of matter or *nature* may determine particular forms of communication within society and *history*. A recurring issue has been whether explanatory models from the natural sciences might be transferred, more or less directly, to the study of society and culture. Media practitioners, legislators, as well as publics all bring *intentions* into mediated communication. Hence, it becomes necessary to ask specifically how – through which social structures and cultural processes – their motivated actions are coordinated, and become *causes*.

In the end, media and communication research is faced with the fundamental dichotomy of *subject* and *object*. This relationship is both a substantial feature of communication and a condition of research. In communicative interaction, the key 'object' of interest is normally another subject or social group, as suggested by Mead's (1934) concept of the significant other. In empirical studies, the purpose is to describe, interpret, and explain such interaction, as seen inevitably from the researcher's perspective, but through reference to the categories of understanding that make up the participating subjects' perspective.

the significant other (margin)

Code-based and case-based analysis

A first step in bridging the apparent abyss between the two paradigms is to ask whether some division of labor can be sustained. At least in principle, most contemporary research would recognize that its choice of methods must depend on what aspect of mediated communication is being examined, and on the purpose of study – the 'how' of research depends on its 'what' and 'why' (Kvale 1987). Few researchers would want to argue (or admit) that their conceptualizations and designs are driven by certain methods that are preferred as such. Certainly, different approaches would seem to be required to account for editorial decision-making processes or for the employment patterns of women and men in news media; for the structure of metaphor in newspaper headlines as opposed to the coverage of a particular event in different newspapers; and for audience decodings of, versus their exposure to, particular items of information. More generally, particular stages, for example, of media reception and impact, are natural candidates for study by particular methodologies.

A justification for matching particular research questions with particular methodologies is found at the level of concrete analytical procedures. The two paradigms may be distinguished, in broad terms, by their reliance on either case-based or code-based operations (Fielding and Lee 1998: 27). On the one hand, *code-based* analysis assumes that, for instance, a survey response may be assigned unequivocally to one category for analytical purposes. A classic example is the opinion polls leading up to a general election. The polls owe much of their predictive value to being clearly defined, not only because the options are mutually exclusive (one designated party, abstention, or undecided), but also because the act of voting (and of responding to a poll) is a familiar practice and a cultural convention.

On the other hand, *case-based* analysis seeks, at least initially, to avoid reduction of the complexity of data, for instance, from a depth interview. Instead, the process of interaction with respondents may be seen to carry over into the process of analysis. The categories of understanding and meaning may be identified, redefined, and clarified throughout the research process as a whole. To exemplify, a case-based analysis might explore conceptions of what is a 'political' issue in the media and how, according to respondents, it relates to institutionalized political activities.

In procedural terms, then, a code-based analysis relies on predefined categories which both decontextualize and disambiguate the units of meaning. A case-based analysis allows its categories to be informed and modified by the context in an iterative fashion. It also remains open to ambiguities in the delimitation and interrelation of the units of meaning throughout the analytical process.

One particular issue which has continued to divide the paradigms is whether code-based analysis could, and should, gradually replace case-based analysis. This might be the ideal within single studies, but also, more controversially, for entire disciplines as they mature. The qualitative, case-oriented emphasis of early social science has been explained, in part, by its preliminary search for 'global, overall perspectives' (Jankowski and Wester 1991: 46), over and above its roots in philosophy and other humanities.

In the post-1945 period, code-based analysis became established as the scientific norm. By the same token, qualitative research was largely assigned the role of performing 'pilot studies' pilot studies that would pre-test codes and, to a degree, develop theory. One question which has remained controversial, then, is whether case-based, qualitative analysis may be said to have an independent explanatory value. To clarify the concrete disagreements, and to assess the prospects for convergence, it is necessary, next, to differentiate the several stages and levels of analysis which qualitative and quantitative studies share.

SIX LEVELS OF ANALYSIS

Figure 15.2 distinguishes six levels of research, as associated with different stages of planning, conducting, documenting, and interpreting an empirical project. Here, the levels are described in terms of their 'discourses' or symbolic instruments – the varied social uses of language, mathematical symbols, graphical representations, and other instruments which enter into the practice of research:

1   The empirical *object of analysis* will typically be everyday and institutional discourses arising from some media-related social interaction. The particular materials range widely, from organizational memoranda and media texts to test responses in an experimental setting. While some materials are 'found' (e.g., radio programs from a sound archive), and others 'made' (e.g., observation of a production site), each constitutes a possible source of evidence regarding a particular purpose of inquiry.

2   Also in the case of evidence that is 'found,' the second level of *data collection methods* – from content sampling frames to interview guides – serves to demarcate and document a

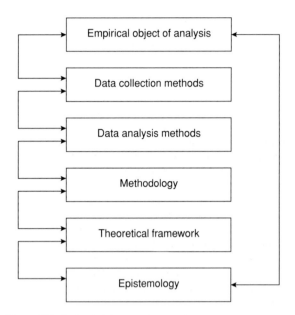

Figure 15.2 Six levels of empirical research

particular portion of reality. The evidence gathered will next be examined from a particular theoretical perspective, again according to the purpose of inquiry.

3 *Data analysis methods* entail diverse operations of categorizing, segmenting, and interpreting the evidence or dataset. This level of analysis typically involves comparisons. In a basic sense, all analysis is comparison of units; in a wider sense, comparative analysis, for instance, of contents and audience responses, is a main ingredient of many media studies. In addition, empirical studies commonly include a 'meta-analytical' component in the form of statistical tests or an 'audit trail' of the steps of a qualitative analysis.◄

4 It is at the level of *methodology*, defined as a theoretically informed plan of action in relation to an empirical field, that the distinction between qualitative and quantitative research becomes most apparent. Even though, for example, a quantitative and a qualitative inter-

───────────────

► meta-analysis as quality control, including statistical tests and audit trails – Chapter 14, p. 246

view study share certain techniques, in each case the full set of techniques amounts to a distinctive mapping of theoretical concepts onto empirical phenomena. As elaborated below, it is the specific linking of a necessarily selective empirical 'microcosm' with a theoretical 'macrocosm' which, above all, distinguishes quantitative and qualitative research as traditions and paradigms.

5 A *theoretical framework* of interrelated concepts lends relevance and meaning to the configuration of empirical data, or findings. Theory may be thought of as a 'frame,' as referred to in several traditions (Eysenck and Keane 1995; Goffman 1974), which focuses attention and allows for certain interpretations, while discouraging others. Crucially, quantitative and qualitative approaches may be subsumed under the same theoretical framework. It is methodology, not theory, that distinguishes qualitative and quantitative research.

methodology, not theory, distinguishes qualitative and quantitative research

6 Theoretical frameworks are 'substantive,' in the sense that they account for a particular domain of reality, here communication and culture. Theoretical choices, further, are supported by meta-theoretical or *epistemological* arguments and assumptions. The epistemological level of analysis provides preliminary definitions of the 'object' of study, as well as justifications concerning the nature of the 'analysis.'

Debates across the qualitative–quantitative divide have generally focused on these individual levels. In particular, the levels of data collection and analysis is where the two mainstreams have parted company. In fact, the relationship between the paradigms is better understood if one notes in detail how each paradigm joins – and separates – these levels of analysis.

On the one hand, quantitative research tends to assume that a separation of the moments of conceptualization, design, data collection, data analysis, and interpretation is both possible and desirable. This practice derives from a distinction between 'the context of discovery' and 'the context of justification,' as originally associated with logical positivism (for an overview see Passmore 1972). The underlying argument is that scientific research is characterized, above

contexts of discovery and justification

all, by its procedures for testing and justifying beliefs, and that the process of discovering and hypothesizing beliefs is not part of the scientific method proper. The resulting emphasis on formalization and operationalization is reflected, for example, in the structure of the standard research article with its sections on 'previous research,' 'hypotheses,' 'method,' 'analysis,' and 'discussion.'◄

On the other hand, qualitative research holds that at least certain phenomena call for a research process that moves liberally between all the analytical levels in order to articulate and elaborate analytical categories. This general procedure of 'in-depth' analysis is evident both in data collection and analysis. Certain steps of analysis are repeated, for example, through 'snowball sampling' or in developing thematic categories for the textual analysis of an interview. Here, the minimal act of analysis is a constitutive part of a sequence. As a whole, the sequence reconfigures empirical data, and develops theory to account for them, rather than matching predefined categories with data elements. It is these characteristics which make for the sort of flexible data collection and analysis that is associated with qualitative research, and it is this same absence of hard-and-fast techniques that has motivated recent developments toward more systematic and transparent forms of qualitative analysis.◄

Apart from the very early stages and instruments of research, an additional focus of the debates between qualitative and quantitative positions has been the very final stages of the research process – its epistemology and overall logic. Reference is traditionally made to two forms of logical inference – induction and deduction. Recent theory of science, however, has recovered a third type, which helps to spell out some differences as well as similarities between qualitative and quantitative methodologies.

► conventions of publication – Chapter 16, p. 274

► systematic qualitative data analysis – Chapter 14, p. 245

THREE FORMS OF INFERENCE

Induction, deduction, and abduction

Standard accounts of the theory of science still assume that research infers either from a general principle or law to individual instances (deduction), or from the examination of several instances to a law (induction). The requirements of each type have been at the core of the development of natural sciences, and of modern theory of science, since the eighteenth century. Their relevance for the humanities, the social sciences, as well as interdisciplinary fields has been debated particularly since the late nineteenth century (for an overview see Pitt 1988). In comparison, the third form of inference – abduction – has rarely been considered explicitly as a model of scientific reasoning. First of all, then, each of the types should be described.

While Aristotle had identified abduction as a type of inference (Blaikie 1993; Hanson 1958), it was reintroduced into modern philosophy by Charles Sanders Peirce in an 1878 article and related to the other two main types. The basic idea is that there are three components to an inference – a rule which, when applied to a single case, produces a conclusion or result. These components yield three possible combinations:

DEDUCTION
Rule. All the beans from this bag are white.
Case. These beans are from this bag.
Result. These beans are white.

INDUCTION
Case. These beans are from this bag.
Result. These beans are white.
Rule. All the beans from this bag are white.

[ABDUCTION
Result. These beans are white.
Rule. All the beans from this bag are white.]
Case. These beans are from this bag.
(Peirce 1986: 325–326)

Formally, only the deduction is a valid inference. Here, given the meaning of the constituent terms, the rule can be applied without any uncertainty to the case, so that the result follows as a matter of course. In the induction, the implication is that, if one examines a sufficient number of beans (cases), one may be willing to conclude that they are all white. This way of reasoning appears commonsensical, and enters into both everyday life and sciences. The point of the abduction, finally, is that it introduces a rule which may explain why one encounters particular (surprising) facts in a particular context.

The bean example is, of course, trivial. In other cases, the newly devised rule may represent an exceptionally bright idea, as in Sherlock Holmes's solution of crime mysteries (Sebeok and Umiker-Sebeok 1983). Scientific discovery can also be seen to rely on abduction.

The three forms of inference are rarely found in a pure form in any given empirical study. More often, different combinations will serve the purpose of inquiry, and it may be argued that an aspect of each type is required to produce new insight. An example is the prototypical form of social-scientific study. Such a study departs from a relatively specific hypothesis that has been derived from a more general premise (deduction), and which is then tested against a large number of concrete instances (induction). The outcome of the data analysis may be a pattern of findings that is only partly in accordance with the hypothesis, and which gives rise to the formulation of a new rule (abduction) to be investigated in further research. (The original premise of the study might in itself have been the outcome of a bright idea or bold conjecture – abduction.)

One advantage of such a combinatorial understanding of scientific inference is that it leaves open the question of whether research projects actually conform to the models of either logic or methods textbooks. A closer examination of how researchers, in fact, interpret and infer from their data can serve to make explicit some hidden premises. It can also help to identify more options for the design of future research.

An inductive heritage

Induction has a long heritage, both in the history of science and in human evolution. In the latter respect, one may assume that the human capacity for generalizing and abstracting from single events has been a key factor in natural evolution, being an instrument of adaptation and, ultimately, survival (Megarry 1995). (Indeed, the many cultural forms of expression of humans may be described, functionally, in terms of induction that serves to accumulate, externalize, and communicate experience for a range of practical purposes.) In addition the common-sense or lay theories (Furnham 1988) which guide people through a day of practical activities have important ingredients of induction. ◄

induction in culture and evolution

Historically, induction has been a central problem for philosophers and empirical researchers alike. While David Hume had noted, in the mid-1700s, that an induction from 'some' to 'all' can never, strictly speaking, be logically valid, an inductive ideal of science remained attractive throughout the nineteenth century, as associated, for example, with John Stuart Mill's *A System of Logic* (1843). This work sought to detail how inferences could be accumulated in various scientific fields, depending on their specific subject matter (Mill 1973–1974). In the twentieth century, an inductive ideal of science rose to new prominence, and then fell definitively, in the shape of logical positivism. Nevertheless, references to 'positivism' (especially critical ones) still abound also in media research, suggesting the need to clarify the basic issues and positions.

Taking its general cue from Mill's contemporary, Auguste Comte, and his call for a 'positive philosophy' that would be non-speculative and applicable to real human concerns, logical positivism developed into an influential school of thought during the interwar years. Much of the specific, technical inspiration came from the linguistic and formal turn of philosophy at the time. The linguistic turn started from the assumption that the structure of sentences corresponds to the structure of facts in

logical positivism

► lay theories – Chapter 16, p. 275

reality.◄ Moreover, logical positivism upheld an absolute distinction not only between facts and values, but between empirical observations and theoretical conceptions of reality. Accordingly, any meaningful statement about the world is either elementary in itself (reducible to sense impressions in a given space and time), or may be decomposed into such elementary propositions which are either true or false. It is from this base of atomistic facts that more complex regularities or laws may be inferred by verifying that a larger set of propositions corresponds to the way the world is.

Within such a reductionist understanding of knowledge, most of the topics of both social-scientific and humanistic research fall outside the realm of science. One response to positivism – the 'apartheid' option – has been to contrast this (assertedly) natural-scientific understanding of research with an interpretive counterpart (Figure 15.1.) The resulting dichotomies have affected the social sciences throughout their history, and have reappeared in media studies, as noted above.

A second, 'imperialistic' response has been an (often implicit) attempt to transfer some of the ideals of logical positivism to research on culture and society. Hammersley (1989: 17) identified three features of such an unacknowledged positivism, as it continues to operate in much social science:

1 the view of science as the identification of *universal laws*, or at least context-independent regularities;
2 the grounding of science in *elementary sensations*;
3 the requirement that all scientific research proceed according to the *same methodological principles*.

This last requirement in particular still tends to divide research into different 'camps,' such as the two paradigms of media studies, and to produce allegations of (quasi-)positivism. In fact, both positivism and inductivism, if understood as epistemological programs, may be treated as positions of the past. This is not

to deny that the two positions, to a degree, still inform particular features of research practice.

The following sections describe the two main epistemological positions which can be seen to have replaced positivism and inductivism in current media and communication research. First, however, two varieties of contemporary research should be noted for their more or less explicit commitment to induction. First, grounded theory◄ became influential especially among qualitative researchers for its insistence on generating explanatory categories from the field itself and its informants – inducing theory from empirical data. Whereas this position may blind researchers to the theoretical frameworks which they inevitably bring with them into the field, it has served an important purpose by attracting renewed attention to the practical, lived categories of understanding with which people engage media and other social interaction.

The second example of an inductive orientation is descriptive studies, often with an applied or administrative purpose.◄ Among the main examples are marketing studies of media audiences and evaluation research which supports government policy decisions. Although the aim here is normally not to state or test particular theories, nevertheless the findings are commonly seen as offering a general account, for example, of media infrastructures and their impact on society. At least, companies and state agencies are willing to base investments and legislation on the descriptions. In this connection, Wober (1981) has called for a distinction between audience 'research' with some explanatory or interpretive ambition, and audience 'measurement,' which provides baseline figures. An implication for readers of descriptive research reports is that *their* findings are also theory-loaded (Hanson 1958), so that the claims of such research must be weighed equally – or more – carefully against its more or less implicit theory. This is all the more important, since the majority of all media studies are

research vs. measurement

▶ the linguistic turn – Chapter 2, p. 26

▶ grounded theory – Chapter 14, p. 247

▶ descriptive and administrative research – Chapter 16, p. 281

probably of the administrative and ambiguously inductive variety.

A deductive mainstream

hypothetico-deductive research

The quantitative mainstream of international media and communication research is normally described as 'hypothetico-deductive.' It proposes to test hypotheses which have been deduced from some general 'law.' In a first step, it is deduction which ensures that a hypothesis is neither logically inconsistent nor tautological – which would make it irrelevant for empirical research. If, next, a relevant hypothesis may be seen to contradict or perhaps specify an accepted law, it calls for further study. Again, it is deduction (from 'all' to 'some') which serves to predict what the researcher will find under certain specified empirical circumstances. If, finally, the findings correspond to the prediction, the hypothesis is confirmed, and can be admitted into the body of accepted and cumulated theories of the field.

falsification and verification

Importantly, however, confirmation does not equal 'verification' in the stronger sense associated, not least, with logical positivism. The hypothetico-deductive position, as elaborated especially by Popper (Popper 1972 [1934]; see also Hempel and Oppenheim 1988 [1948]), instead assumes that scientists must seek to *falsify* their hypotheses. Only if falsification fails is one justified in still holding the hypothesis, and only preliminarily. Further studies, by oneself or by others, may end up falsifying it after all (which, in effect, admits inductivism through the back door in a multistep research process).

What might appear to be a 'philosophical' nuance nevertheless has important consequences, both for what is accepted as knowledge in a field, and for the procedures of science – also regarding society and culture. Because societies and cultures are 'open' systems compared to the more closed and, hence, predictable systems studied by the natural sciences, most social and cultural research of the hypothetico-deductive variety cannot unequivocally falsify or verify a hypothesis. Instead, studies are backed by measures of statistical probability – which accounts for their 'quantitative' nature.

In formal terms, then, a prototypical quantitative study will pose a 'null hypothesis,' which suggests that any relations between the variables, as anticipated by the theory and documented by the data, are due to chance fluctuations or random error.◄ If this is the case, as defined by a conventionally agreed level of probability, a falsification of the original hypothesis has occurred. Thus, the quantitative research process operates on a principle of deduction, even if the 'laws' in questions are ascertained in a stochastic rather than a determinist sense (Hempel and Oppenheim 1988 [1948]: 13–18).◄

The agenda-setting hypothesis

A classic contribution to media studies – agenda-setting research – exemplifies the general deductive logic. McCombs and Shaw (1972) departed from previous findings regarding political communication, suggesting that, 'although the evidence that mass media deeply change attitudes in a campaign is far from conclusive, the evidence is much stronger that voters learn from the immense quantity of information available during each campaign' (p. 176). While thus recognizing previously established regularities in the audience response, the authors went on, first, to deduce a conceptual distinction between 'attitudes' and 'agendas,' and, second, to operationalize this distinction in an empirical comparison of news content and voter statements. Their hypothesis stated that 'the mass media set the agenda for each political campaign, influencing the salience of attitudes toward the political issues' (p. 177).

The study, accordingly, matched 'what … voters *said* were key issues of the campaign with the *actual content* of the mass media used by them during the campaign' (p. 177). The authors further deduced two particular conditions under which the hypothesis might be examined empirically: only voters who were undecided on who to vote for, and hence might be more open to campaign information, entered into the sample interviewed, and the respon-

---

► null hypothesis – Chapter 13, p. 232

► stochastic and other models of meaning, Chapter 2, p. 30

dents were sampled randomly from lists of registered voters in a particular community in order to limit other sources of variation, for example, regional differences in media coverage. (Yet, following a pre-test, major national sources such as television network news, *The New York Times*, *Time*, and *Newsweek* were included in the content sample.)

The resulting datasets consisted in respondents' answers regarding 'major problems as they saw them' (p. 178), and in news as well as editorial comments during a specified period overlapping with the interview period. Each of these datasets was coded into predefined categories concerning both political issues and other aspects of a campaign. As is commonly the case in content studies, the intercoder reliability◄ of the procedure was tested, and lay above .90, which bears witness to well-defined and operational categories. In sum, the application of these various analytical categories amounted to a mapping of conceptually deduced distinctions onto instances of political information in a particular empirical field, as offered by media and taken by voters.

Two findings, in particular, illustrate the logic. First, the design aimed to establish causality, and found that the media had 'exerted a considerable impact' (p. 180) on the respondents' perceptions of the political issues. The coding of content had distinguished between 'major' and 'minor' coverage of topics (referring to their prominence in terms of position and time or space allowed). In both instances, the analysis found very strong correlations between media emphasis and voters' judgments (+.967 and +.979).

Second, in order to determine whether voters might be attending to, and reproducing, the agenda that their preferred candidates presented in the media, a further analysis was made of those respondents who had a preference for one candidate (without being finally committed). Here, a comparison was made between these respondents' references to the issues associated with a particular party or candidate, and their references to issues in all the news. Both for major and minor issues, the

findings suggested that 'the voters attend reasonably well to *all* the news, *regardless* of which candidate or party issue is stressed' (p. 182). The fact that 'the judgments of voters seem to reflect the *composite* of the mass media coverage' (p. 181) again lends support to the agenda-setting hypothesis.

In their discussion of the findings overall, McCombs and Shaw (1972) were careful to qualify their conclusions regarding the original hypothesis. Most importantly, they acknowledged that the correlations reported in their study do not *prove* the hypothesis. However, 'the evidence is in line with the conditions that must exist if agenda-setting by the mass media does occur' (p. 184). Put differently, the carefully deduced design failed to falsify the hypothesis. In addition, the agenda-setting hypothesis presents itself as a more justified alternative than, for example, a theory concerning selective perception, which would have been supported if voters had been found to attend particularly to their preferred candidates. The authors also described the study as 'a first test . . . at a broad societal level' (p. 184), and called, among other things, for further research on a social-psychological level regarding individual attitudes and uses of media.

An additional lesson from the discussion in McCombs and Shaw (1972) is that the weighing of competing hypotheses and interpretations ultimately takes place at a theoretical level, not at the level of measurements or other analytical procedures (Figure 15.2). The discussion of 'probability,' below, reconsiders the textbook maxim (often violated) that correlation does not equal causation. In this example, the correlations between media coverage and voter judgments are indicative of causality, but the nature of the causation must be accounted for in terms of a conceptual framework or theory. The theory itself may be falsified in future empirical studies, in addition to being challenged by alternative theories.

An abductive substream

Abduction is the third form of inference, and has been afforded much less attention than either deduction or induction in the theory of

---

◄ intercoder reliability – Chapter 13, p. 212

science as well as in empirical research. This section describes abduction as the (unacknowledged) logic of much qualitative research, and goes on to consider the place of abduction in relation to other methodologies as well.

Since inductivism has come to appear untenable as an epistemological program, the interpretive paradigm has been hard pressed, either to defer to the hypothetico-deductive model, or to specify an alternative. In direct opposition to what he termed Hempel and Oppenheim's (1988 [1948]) 'covering-law model,' Dray (1957) specified how historical events cannot be examined as a variant of natural events (which may all be 'covered' by one law), but require a different type of 'rational explanation.' In another influential contribution, Danto (1965) suggested that narratives provide a model for understanding, and for empirically studying, historical events and human actions (see also Bruner 1986). Further, Ginzburg (1989) identified an 'evidential paradigm,' within which, for example, Sigmund Freud and Sherlock Holmes were both able to uncover an underlying structure, respectively in dreams and crimes.

covering-law model

narrative as research model

evidential paradigm

While no consensus comparable to the hypothetico-deductive model has yet emerged, one advantage of abduction is that it lends itself to comparison and combination with the traditional types of inference. Since Peirce's early formulation, its relevance has occasionally been considered in both philosophy and other disciplines, including mainstream sociology (Merton 1968: 158). It was reasserted by, among others, Hanson (1958) as part of the post-1945 questioning of both inductive and hypothetico-deductive prototypes of research. Recently, abduction has been reintroduced into social and cultural research as an alternative to the inductivist self-understanding of grounded theory (Alvesson and Sköldberg 2000), as a strategy of interpretive social science (Blaikie 1993), and as a characteristic of qualitative media research (Jensen 1995). In fact, qualitative empirical studies that tend to refer to themselves as interpretive and broadly inductive often rely on an abductive procedure.

To illustrate, Radway's (1984) study of romance reading was an exemplary contribution to early empirical reception studies (for later work see Radway 1997). One quality was its combination of a history of the genre with an account of its system of production and distribution, as well as in-depth research into its female readers' decodings and social uses of the texts. The field study of readers comprised interviewing and observation in an 'interpretive community'◄ which had formed around a particular bookstore. This case-based analytical strategy entailed a stepwise and highly contextualized articulation of meaningful categories, which this study shares with much other qualitative work.◄ The researcher went through several stages of establishing the meaning of romance reading for these women, relying on both face-to-face interviews and questionnaires. By probing motivations such as 'education' and 'escape,' and by taking cues from some especially articulate informants and presenting their responses to others in later interviews, the analysis came to differentiate a blanket term such as 'escape' into additional categories of relaxation and time for self-indulgence.

Radway (1984) summed up the attraction of romance reading in concluding that 'it creates a time or space within which a woman can be entirely on her own, preoccupied with her personal needs, desires, and pleasure' (p. 61). A central implication is a shift of emphasis, away from romances as texts that offer a more or less escapist universe for the reader's identification and gratification, and toward an understanding of the very activity of reading as a social practice which enables these women to position themselves in, and apart from, the rest of everyday life. Media discourses are not only *representations of* the world, but also *resources in* the world.

An inductivist interpretation might take these categories to emerge from the field itself. It is more appropriate, however, to describe them as the outcome of abduction by the researcher, as she repeatedly engaged the informants' worldviews. In trying to grasp their perspective 'from within,' in 'emic' terms,◄ Radway can be

---

► interpretive communities – Chapter 10, p. 167

► case-based and code-based analysis – p. 256

► emic and etic analytical categories – Chapter 14, p. 236

said to have performed a sequence of abductive inferences. Her purpose was to account for these women's experiences of their reading, and of their lives, by introducing concepts or rules that would made the informants' statements meaningful and relevant in the context where they were made.

As noted by Peirce, the essence of abductive reasoning may be expressed in the form of a syllogism. Here, first, is Radway's recapitulation of one of her main findings, namely that romance reading is a specific kind of social act:

> In summary, when the act of romance reading is viewed as it is by the readers themselves, from within a belief system that accepts as given the institutions of heterosexuality and monogamous marriage, it can be conceived as an activity of mild protest and longing for reform necessitated by those institutions' failure to satisfy the emotional needs of women. Reading therefore functions for them as an act of recognition and contestation whereby that failure is first admitted and then partially reversed. Hence, the Smithton readers' claim that romance reading is a 'declaration of independence' and a way to say to others, 'This is my time, my space. Now leave me alone.'
>
> (Radway 1984: 213)

Next, the central and somewhat surprising notion, that romance reading is a 'declaration of independence,' can be explicated in the form of an abduction:

> Romance reading is a declaration of independence.
>
> All uses of texts by readers to claim their own time are declarations of independence.
>
> Conclusion: Romance reading is a use of texts by readers for claiming their own time.

Whereas the first premise registers a puzzling fact from the empirical universe of romance readers (puzzling to the extent that the romance genre tends to represent women in dependent roles), the second premise introduces the conception or rule that texts are resources in every-

day life. At the same time, the second premise may be seen to sum up the research process which served to gradually articulate various conceptions of the romance genre and of the act of reading. In this regard, the singular statement arguably builds on several previous abductions from an iterative process.

One quality of formalization is that it facilitates a systematic comparison of the several different kinds of reasoning that enter into the practice of empirical research. In the case of qualitative research projects, the category of abductive inference can help to explicate their various contextual and empathetic forms of interpretation. For the further development of qualitative research this is an important challenge, both in the field and in the several later stages of analysis.

Abduction is at the core of that interchange between researcher and informants which serves to establish – infer – relevant categories and concepts for the specific purpose of inquiry. By reconsidering and reformulating their perspectives on romance reading, Radway's (1984) informants produced new insights, not only for research, but presumably for themselves, as they verbalized their conceptions, perhaps for the first time. Abduction (like induction) is a common aspect of everyday reasoning as well. By formalizing or systematizing the components of their analysis and interpretation, qualitative studies gain a resource, first, for structuring key moments of the analytical process and, second, for deciding who (informants, researchers, both) originates which abductions. Third, the category of abduction can help to document the steps of the research process, and to make them transparent to others in the name of intersubjectivity and interdisciplinarity.

Several kinds of abduction occur in scientific as well as everyday reasoning. Eco (1984) has outlined a preliminary typology:

- *Overcoded* abduction is a basic form of comprehension that works semi-automatically. 'When someone utters /man/, I must first assume that this utterance is the token of a type of English word' (Eco 1984: 41). No complex inference is needed to first establish the fact that people may speak different languages, and next that English is the appropriate choice in context.

• In performing an *undercoded* abduction, however, one must choose between several possible interpretations of a word or statement. In Eco's words, 'when one utters /this is a man/, we have to decide whether one says that this is a rational animal, a mortal creature, or a good example of virility, and so on' (p. 42).

• *Creative* abduction, finally, occurs when the very rule of interpretation has to be invented for the specific purpose, for example, in the case of poetic language, as it enters into both poetry and advertising. In science, Darwin's interpretation of humans as the latest animal to enter the evolutionary chain was an (unusually) creative abduction.

abductive aspects of hypotheses

By thus treating abduction as a specifically innovative element – a creative potential that may be administered in research in several different ways – it becomes possible to relate it back to deduction and induction, and to consider their combination in various forms of research. In this perspective, the hypotheses of quantitative projects arguably are not merely deduced. They are, in part, the outcome of undercoded abductions which articulate new conceptual relations or configurations with reference to earlier research. Qualitative projects,

qualitative research as iterative abduction

in their turn, perform a sequence of (iterative) undercoded abductions, which ideally accumulate at the end as a robust idea or theory. In a sense, the abductive labor of hypothetico-deductive research is focused in the early phases, while in qualitative studies the sequence of abductions is distributed along and across the entire research process.

Overcoded abduction, moreover, arguably enters into the administration of (already familiar) analytical categories and procedures. This is the case for both qualitative and quantitative methodologies. Creative abductions, finally, are the kind of unusual event and scarce resource which both mainstreams can only hope to produce once in a while. They emerge in the operationalization of innovative hypotheses, and through the exploration of new meanings in the field.

In conclusion, the three types of inference point to several different types of relationship between empirical analysis and theory development in media and communication research. While many, perhaps most, actual research projects may be said to include aspects of abduction, deduction, as well as induction, two main varieties have been identified – hypothetico-deductive reasoning in combination with quantitative types of data analysis, and iterative abductive reasoning employing qualitative discourse and other data analysis. The reviews in this chapter indicate that a unification of these traditions in the first instance – in their concrete means of empirical analysis – has not occurred, and is unlikely to occur in the future. However, in addition to sometimes joining their empirical forces within a shared theoretical framework, qualitative and quantitative traditions hold a further potential for unification as components of interdisciplinary fields of research, such as media studies. Exactly how this potential may be tapped is one of the most important and difficult questions for future research, and is outlined in the next section.

UNIFICATION IN THE FINAL INSTANCE

Validity and reliability reconsidered

A final aspect of most research projects – supporting their primary analytical operations and inferences – is to perform various types of 'quality control.' The purpose is to assess analyses and conclusions according to the standards invoked by the study itself and, in a next step, to make both the standards and the findings accessible for collegial, public scrutiny.

Through categories of validity and reliability,◄ quantitative research has provided the most elaborate set of measures and procedures for evaluating empirical findings and procedures (see also Black 1999). At the same time, the specific techniques have been perceived as less relevant to the concerns of qualitative research (Kirk and Miller 1986). In some cases, this perception arguably has led to a neglect of

► quantitative concepts of reliability and validity – Chapter 13, p. 212

the issues involved, as noted by, among others, Höijer (1990). In other cases, qualitative researchers have proposed new terminologies which would recognize the processual and contextual nature of qualitative research, for instance, trustworthiness, credibility, dependability, transferability, and confirmability (Lincoln and Guba 1985). So far, however, such alternative terminologies have not taken hold, certainly in media research. Instead, the conceptual and operational definitions of 'validity' and 'reliability' may be extended.

In brief, reliability addresses the consistency of descriptions and interpretations over time, typically in the form of repeated measurements. In the example from agenda-setting research given above (McCombs and Shaw 1972), the intersubjective agreement of coders was expressed in a measure of intercoder reliability. Validity, in turn, addresses the extent to which a research 'instrument' measures what it was intended or is claimed to measure – all research aims for truth in some such sense. An additional distinction is made between *internal* validity (evaluating the consistency of the concepts and procedures that are applied to the empirical context) and *external* validity (assessing whether the findings from this context may be generalized to other situations or populations). In the agenda-setting example, both the conception of 'agenda,' and the relationship between the community studied and the larger electorate were considered.

Validity as well as reliability have traditionally been expressed in measures that serve as summary assessments of the research. It is this summary feature, in particular, which has led qualitative researchers to call for more continuous and contextual assessments of both the research process and its findings. Some have, validation for example, advocated 'validation' as a continuous activity throughout the research process (e.g., Kvale 1996).

Figure 15.3 presents a schematic overview of validity and reliability, as they relate to each other and to other components of the research process. In both qualitative and quantitative studies, *reliability* concerns the intersubjective component of research in a general sense. Being an inherently interactional, social phenomenon,

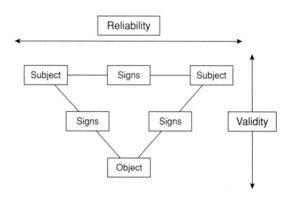

Figure 15.3 Dimensions of validity and reliability

intersubjectivity is established not only by comparing minimal measurements in the early stages of a study, but by addressing emerging findings, forms of documentation, and issues of interpretation. For instance, while the use of two independent coders for categorizing the same dataset is standard procedure in several quantitative traditions, intercoder reliability can also be ensured by consensual coding and other collective approaches to analysis and interpretation (e.g., Neuman *et al.* 1992). Similarly, informants may be involved in some stages of analysis, through several waves of interviewing, and by 'member checks,' as in Radway's (1984) study of romance reading.

reliability as inter-subjectivity

Most generally, reliability remains an issue after the conclusion of the research process proper – in reanalyses of data and discussions of findings, both among researchers and in other social contexts. The category of reliability, then, leads into questions concerning the social organization and uses of research and its knowledge interests. 'Reliable' findings amount to knowledge which individuals and institutions are prepared to act on.◄

The category of *validity*, equally, opens onto a wider scientific as well as social terrain. Compared to various specific, quantitative measures of validity, a qualitative study typically attends to the internal validity of its categories by exploring and comparing, for instance,

---

▶ reliability as social relevance – Chapter 16, p. 274

informants' conceptual repertoires, while its external validity must normally be left undecided, until other cases or larger samples have been examined. In addition, 'triangulation,' which combines several analytical perspectives on the same empirical context, has beeen given special attention by qualitative researchers.◀ These different conceptions of validity arise, in part, from two distinctive concepts of 'generalization' within quantitative and qualitative research, respectively (e.g., Yin 1994: 30).

validity:
empirical vs.
theoretical
generalization

Empirical or statistical generalization refers to the capacity of quantitative research to apply predefined (hypothetically deduced) categories to a representative set of empirical instances, thus supporting external validity. *Theoretical* or analytical generalization refers to the articulation (abduction) of new concepts or interrelations which conceive empirical instances in a more consistent or insightful manner, hence prioritizing internal validity.

The general topic of quality control in empirical research thus represents a fertile area for theory development and interchange between paradigms. For instance, aspects of validity and reliability have been brought together in notions

pragmatic
validity

of pragmatic or communicative validity, emphasizing the process of validation (see Flick 1998: 221–240; Kvale 1996: 244–251). Before introducing a framework which may satisfy several criteria of generalization, reliability, and validity, it remains to consider the other constituents of Figure 15.3.

The figure acknowledges that different research traditions rely on different 'signs' – research instruments, analytical procedures, means of documentation – which enable researchers as 'subjects' to engage their 'objects' of analysis. In social and cultural research, these signs or discourses take on a special significance as communications, because here the 'objects' of analysis are more commonly subjects who provide interpretations of themselves and their circumstances – of which research performs a second-order interpretation. Communication theory faces and rearticulates many issues from the theory of science: How is knowledge of other minds, and of reality as such, possible?

▶ triangulation – p. 272

An important task for the theory of science is to devise meta-discourses which allow for comparison of, and reflection on, the different kinds of knowledge that the signs of different theoretical and epistemological traditions are able to communicate. Signs make reality researchable, communicable, and disputable. In Mead's (1934) terms, researchers and their informants, at least for a moment, become significant others for each other through communicative interaction. Researchers equally conduct a specific kind of social interaction among themselves, and the research institution as such ultimately engages the rest of society in a double hermeneutic concerning the meaning of social life (Giddens 1984).

Realism reasserted

Realism has become an influential position in recent theory of science. Pavitt (1999), for one, has suggested that this is now the dominant position; indeed, that it already informs the practice of much current media and communication research. The positions of 'logical empiricism' (from logical positivism through Popper) and constructivist 'perspectivism' (from Kuhn to poststructuralism and beyond) have sometimes been perceived as absolute opposites, or as the two legs of an unresolvable dilemma. Realism presents itself as a likely candidate for a framework within which convergence may proceed.

While several varieties of a contemporary realist position may be singled out under headings of scientific, transcendental, and critical realism (see further Archer *et al.* 1998), its main implications for empirical media studies can be laid out with particular reference to the early work of Bhaskar (1979) (who later turned to more metaphysical as well as political concerns). At its most general level, Bhaskar's (critical) realism has three premises:

1 *Ontological realism.* Rejecting skepticist and nominalist positions which variously have held that no knowledge of the empirical world is possible, or that reality is nothing but the sum of our descriptions of it, realism reverses the burden of proof, in a sense. A realist would

argue that we must assume the existence of reality as a limit condition or regulatory ideal in order to account for the sorts of natural and cultural phenomena one encounters in science as well as in everyday life.

2 *Epistemological relativism*. From a moderate constructivist position, realism assumes that knowledge of both nature and other minds depends on a reiterated sequence of perceptions, cognitions, and inferences, all of which may be questioned, rejected, and revised.

3 *Judgmental rationality*. Like other human practice, science must depend on the exercise of rationality which, at some point, must end in (fallible) judgments about what to do next – as an individual researcher, a scientific field, or a society. Up to that point, the business of science is to continuously compare and contrast alternative accounts of the same reality with reference to a wide range of means and criteria for representing and interpreting reality.

In moving from such general premises toward specific research procedures, Bhaskar and other realists have questioned a certain presumptuous 'anthropocentrism' in the theory of science: 'Copernicus argued that the universe does not revolve around man. And yet in philosophy we still represent things as if it did' (cited in Archer *et al.* 1998: 45). Concretely, logical positivism, for one, proposed to reduce reality, as legitimately studied by science, to what is immediately accessible to the human senses. By contrast, the mechanisms of reality must be said to operate prior to their discovery by humans. Reality is 'intransitive' (in grammatical terms), but it is made 'transitive' as an object of discovery in a variety of forms.

transitivity, transfactuality, and stratification

The argument concerning transitivity leads into a related argument concerning transfactuality, namely that facts of several kinds exist. These facts are not reducible to each other, and they call for different forms of inquiry. Both of these arguments may be taken to support a further point regarding the stratification of reality. On the one hand, aesthetic experience or microsociological order are real phenomena, as established by interpretive traditions of research. On the other hand, they do not represent a separate mode of reality. A relationship of emergence obtains between these and other aspects of reality, such as the biological capacities of humans and the structural conditions of social life.

emergence

In methodological terms, this line of argument implies a distinction between three domains of reality, as addressed at different levels of research (Figure 15.4).

1 The *empirical* domain is the source of concrete evidence – *experience* of the world. By experiencing and documenting, for example, how journalists collect information, and how readers respond to it as news, researchers procure a necessary, though not sufficient condition of empirical research.

2 The *actual* status of this documentation is a matter of inference. It is by characterizing and conceptualizing the empirical materials as evidence of *events* (e.g., reporter-source interactions or decodings) that one can infer their actuality and their association with mediated communication.

3 The domain of the *real* is more inclusive than both the empirical and actual. Research seeks to establish the *mechanisms* which may account for events (e.g., a system of political communication which operates according to economic prerogatives, professional routines, as well as ideals of citizenship). In this manner, research is able not only to perceive, document, and categorize, but to explain a portion of reality.

In sum, experiences, events, and mechanisms are all real. Experiences may seem to 'push' themselves upon researchers as evidence of events. However, the task of research is to mount a countervailing 'pull' – to infer the underlying mechanisms by a great deal of methodological and theoretical labor.

The realist framework is of special interest in a convergence perspective. It indicates that while different empirical procedures (e.g., experiments or depth interviews) document and, in a sense, privilege particular kinds of events (the recall or decoding of media content), they may nevertheless bear witness to related

	The real	The actual	The empirical
Experiences	x	x	x
Events	x	x	
Mechanisms	x		

Figure 15.4 Three domains of reality, incorporating three types of phenomena

mechanisms. Instead of engaging in conflict over a singular definition of the empirical domain, a realist strategy thus proposes to take advantage of several methodologies in order to document various aspects of mediated communication. It is the overriding task of research to inquire into the actuality of the phenomena as documented, and to explore whether they may be subsumed under similar explanatory mechanisms.

Probabilities

An important example of a concept which lends itself to such meta-theoretical development and dialogue across the qualitative–quantitative divide is 'probability.' As shown by Hacking's (1975) historical analysis, the concept gradually acquired an ambiguous meaning in modern philosophy and empirical sciences. Indeed, much thinking about probability has conflated two distinct meanings, with problematic consequences for research practice:

1 *Stochastic* probability has to do with stable relative frequencies, as established by statistical procedures. Here, the purpose is to rule out, beyond reasonable doubt, that the particular configuration of (*empirical*) findings could have occurred by chance (the null hypothesis).◄

2 *Epistemological* probability concerns 'the degree of belief warranted by evidence' (p. 1). Here, the concept of probability applies to the (*actual*) events and (*real*) mechanisms to which the empirical evidence is said to bear witness.

► null hypothesis and stochastic probability – Chapter 13, p. 232

The implication of the distinction is sometimes summed up in the dictum that 'correlation does not equal causation.' In other words, statistical measurements and other formalisms do not in themselves warrant conclusions about causality and other types of association. Theoretical and substantive arguments are always required to assign explanatory value to the empirical measures.

Relating Hacking's (1975) analysis to the media field, Ritchie (1999) has suggested that much current empirical media research fails on this crucial point. The slippage occurs when 'the statistical probabilities associated with the null hypothesis are ... used to support inferences about the epistemological probabilities of a preferred interpretation' (p. 7). Put differently, the fact that the null hypothesis, which assumes random findings, is sufficiently improbable (statistically), is mistaken for evidence that a specific alternative hypothesis, namely the one deduced at the outset of a study, is more probable (epistemologically). The logic of hypothesis testing may thus contribute to a conflation and confounding of two distinct levels of scientific analysis and argument. Like validity and reliability, the category of probability lends itself to refinement in a convergence perspective.

All empirical research necessarily examines an empirical 'microcosm' with reference to a theoretical 'macrocosm' (for a history of the concepts in social research see Alexander and Giesen 1987). Qualitative and quantitative methodologies may be defined, in part, with reference to their conception of and approach to the empirical microcosm. Figure 15.5 indicates (top right-hand corner) how the populations and samples of quantitative projects make

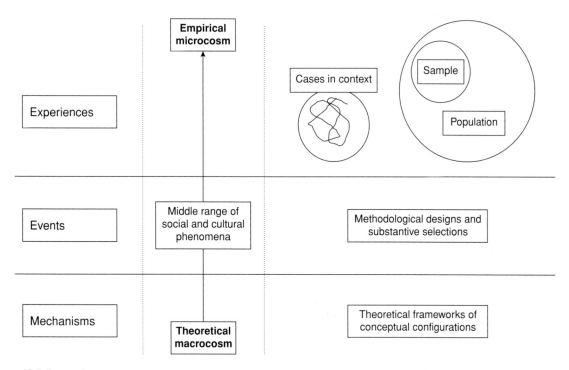

Figure 15.5 Empirical microcosms, theoretical macrocosms

up two levels of an empirical universe, in which each level represents a set of relatively self-contained units. In qualitative projects, contexts, cases, and informants are made into objects of analysis according to different principles of sampling.◄ It is the reciprocal conditioning and constitution of such units within networks which motivate both their selection and the qualitative research questions.

The various modes of data collection and analysis that are associated with qualitative and quantitative research traditions represent different means of gaining *experience* of particular aspects of the media field – and not others. The chapters in this volume may be taken to conclude that both quantitative and qualitative methodologies are best suited for studying particular kinds of social and cultural *events* – and not others. The matching of research questions and methodologies will depend not least on the degree to which the relevant theoretical

► sampling in qualitative research – Chapter 14, p. 238

categories and issues are already well established and familiar – both to respondents and researchers – in public discourse. What unites the two main forms of empirical research on media production, texts, reception, and contexts is that they address a middle range of social and cultural phenomena which call for both detailed documentation (empirical experience) and grand theorizing (theoretical mechanisms). Ultimately, it is the *mechanisms* of modern culture and mediated communication, as defined and related in a theoretical macrocosmos, that both main traditions will be working, and cooperating, to uncover in further research.

CONVERGENCE IN PRACTICE: THREE APPROACHES

Whereas convergence is in evidence in several of the media-related literatures summarized in this volume, much work is required to integrate and consolidate elements from the theory of science and communication theory, as well as from diverse methodologies. Methodologies represent a strategic area of dialogue and cooperation, because they join theoretical concerns with the practical requirements of empirical work. In fact, over the past decade, a growing number of publications have outlined ways of combining or 'mixing' qualitative and quantitative methodologies (e.g., Bernard 1995; Brannen 1992; Creswell 1994; Miles and Huberman 1994; Tashakkori and Teddlie 1998). Several of these approaches have transfer value for media and communication research.

In conclusion, it is possible to single out three principal forms of combining qualitative and quantitative methodologies (Hammersley 1996: 167–168):

1 *Facilitation.* The common practice traditionally has been to treat qualitative and quantitative components as relatively separate stages of a sequence. The norm in survey research and other quantitative studies of, for example, media consumption is to conduct a qualitative 'pilot' study. The aim is to arrive at categories and formulations that are both understandable and meaningful to respondents. Less frequently, a quantitative phase, for instance, a mapping of a social and lifestyle segment, can facilitate subsequent in-depth analyses of the interpretive categories that make up the lifestyle.◄

2 *Triangulation.* As developed especially by Denzin (1970, 1989), triangulation is a general strategy for gaining several perspectives on the same phenomenon. In attempting to verify and validate findings, the strategy addresses aspects of both reliability and validity. Triangulation may be performed through several datasets, several investigators, and several methodologies, in the latter case combining, for instance, experimental and observational approaches to human–computer interaction.◄ (Denzin's (1989: 239) additional suggestion that theories might also be triangulated seems more problematic, since theoretical interpretation normally involves closure around a single perspective, however preliminary. Methodological triangulation also leads up to a weighing and interpreting of the several sets of evidence from one position.)

3 *Complementarity.* The most challenging, and so far the least common, option is complementarity. Different methodologies may be best suited to examine different aspects of a research question, and not necessarily in the same concrete empirical domain. In the final instance, methodologies and findings can be joined with reference to a common theoretical framework. The existence of scientific 'camps' has often worked against exploring even the potential of complementarity. Neverthless, both classic studies such as Cantril *et al.* (1940) and recent developments in media studies (for an overview see Potter 1996) suggest that complementarity can and should be a significant feature of research practice in the future.

► lifestyle research – Chapter 9, p. 153

► human-computer interaction – Chapter 11, p. 184

16 The social origins and uses of media and communication research

Klaus Bruhn Jensen

- a presentation of the several *types of 'theory'* which connect research with social practice
- a review of the *normative theories* of media
- a description of media and communication *research as a social institution*
- a comparison of the main applications of media research in *policy* and *politics*
- a discussion of both *ethics* and *logistics* as aspects of the relations between researchers, the *academic community*, *respondents*, and wider *social communities*.

THEORIES INTO PRACTICE

Making public

This final chapter returns to a number of the issues which motivate media students and researchers in the first place. Indeed, why study the media? (Silverstone 1999). Individual researchers are prompted, in part, by the same concerns which bring major economic and political agents to focus on the area. The modern media are sources of power as well as of meaning – mediated meanings can have powerful social consequences. Accordingly, this chapter examines the three-way relationship between the media, research, and the rest of the social system. Media studies, like their object of analysis, originate from a particular social and historical setting. Part of the relevance of media studies is that they may contribute to the social conditions under which communication will take place in the future.

Like the media themselves, then, university departments and other research organizations may be understood theoretically as institutions-to-think-with, enabling (second-order)

reflexivity about the role of media in society.◄ In offering their perspectives, researchers participate in a double hermeneutic (Giddens 1984): they reinterpret the 'lay theories' (Furnham 1988) of 'ordinary' social agents, and feed those reinterpretations back into society. For example, citizens' lay theories of the category of 'public opinion' vary widely (Herbst 1993), may differ from those of political and media theorists, but are, nevertheless, informed over time by scientific theory, in part, through media. In addition, programming decisions by television executives have been centrally shaped by new research on the 'active' audience (Eastman 1998).

Alvesson and Sköldberg (2000: 248) have gone on to suggest several additional types of hermeneutics. For instance, a 'triple' hermeneutics would be performed by critical theory with the specific aim of exposing and ending relations of social dominance. The general point of hermeneutics in this regard is that all social

double and triple hermen-eutics

► media research as second-order institution-to-think-with – Chapter 1, p. 6

practice is informed by 'theories,' defined as generalized conceptions of what the world is like, and how things can be done. As concluded by one early founder of the media field, Kurt Lewin, 'Nothing is as practical as a good theory' (Greenwood and Levin 1998: 19). It is particularly through an interchange with other types of theory – as held by media professionals, legislators, and the general public – that communication theory and research may make a difference in practice.

Having thought matters through within their institutions, media researchers publish their findings. Publication in academic settings, however, is only one way of making public the knowledge which is generated by research projects. To make public is to make findings available for social practice. The interested constituencies may be large or small, specialized or general, representing dominant or oppositional interests, and may operate in either the short or the long historical term. One central constituency is media businesses that are willing to pay not only to have studies conducted, but to have the results kept away from any significant public for competitive reasons.

publication: knowledge into social practice

An extended category of 'publication' clears the ground for an examination of how different forms of research relate to other social institutions, as allies as well as adversaries. In order to assess the present and future relevance of media research, it is important to consider both its scientific methodologies and its social practices. While publication in journals, conference proceedings, books, as well as more popular formats remains a necessary infrastructure and a procedure legitimating the scientific institution, researchers and students are well advised to consider other channels and contexts of impact – including the unanticipated consequences of their research activity.

Following a definition of several forms of 'theory,' this chapter elaborates on the so-called normative theories, which fueled the early rise and subsequent transformations of the modern media, and which still motivate much contemporary research. An overview of current media and communication research as an institution, next, notes its main academic and commercial varieties and the intellectual cultures driving

them. A distinction between 'politics' and 'policy' further helps to specify different kinds of interchange between research and media – from an instrumental alliance to an adversarial relation challenging the media as they now exist. While both quantitative and qualitative methodologies enter into studies from policy as well as political perspectives, the methodological boundaries, to a degree, dissolve in the social uses of media research. In conclusion, the chapter reviews a number of practical, ethical, and professional issues in planning student projects as well as research programs.

Four types of theory

Applying an extended understanding of theory as plans of action to the media field, McQuail (2000: 7–9) has made a useful distinction between four types of 'theory':

1 *Scientific theory*. The most common understanding of the term is that theory consists in 'general statements about the nature, working and effects of mass communication, based on systematic and objective observation of media and other relevant factors' (p. 7). In this sense, both qualitative and quantitative studies provide explanatory concepts and models that apply to a range of empirical instances.

2 *Normative theory*. While scientific theories have also normally been underpinned, in one way or another, by ideals of how the media ought to operate in society, the normative theories represent a separate area of inquiry into the ways and means of organizing and financing mediated communication. Dating from the seventeenth century, normative theory has remained central through to current debates about public service broadcasting and the Internet.

3 *Operational theory*. Media professionals command a repertoire of procedures that amount to operational theory, from practical rules-of-thumb to ingrained ethical and ideological positions regarding the purpose and status of their work. Reflecting its interested and practical nature, professional knowledge overlaps with both normative and everyday theory.

ANALYSIS BOX 16.1 THE SIGNS OF SCIENCE

Media and communication researchers rely on varied means of representation and expression in order to arrive at an understanding of the empirical field themselves, to share findings and issues with colleagues, and to present their studies to an interested public. While other sections of this chapter consider both different ways of 'making public' and the relevant audiences, the purpose of this brief element is to reflect on the signs of science – the concrete means of communicating research. This can be an important way of keeping research self-reflexive, scientifically as well as socially. As noted, for instance, in the discussion of rhetoric in Chapter 2, signs and numbers are never innocent, but carry implicit premises (see further Barrow 1992).

Models and other means of display have been integral to the development of media studies (for additional references on scientific illustration, see Lee and Mandelbaum 1999; McQuail and Windahl 1993; Shore 1998). Whereas tables and figures may be associated specifically with quantitative traditions of research, Chapter 14 noted how visual display, coding, and modeling are also an important part of qualitative analysis.

Throughout this volume, a number of verbal, mathematical, and graphic forms have been used to communicate different points. In review, some of the main types may be described as follows:

- literature reviews and theoretical arguments in all chapters in *verbal discourse*;
- conceptual models of a portion of the field, as represented in either *graphic displays* (e.g., Figure 5.2) or in multiple-field *matrices* (e.g., Figure 7.2);
- analytical examples (e.g., the analysis boxes, such as Box 14.1), employing prose, graphic displays, and *images* to represent the object of analysis and aspects of the analytical process (e.g., Chapter 8 on *The Big Sleep*);
- tables summarizing findings in terms of a *numerical distribution* (e.g., Table 13.1);
- *scattergram*, indicating correlations between data elements concerning, for instance, opinions and media preferences (Figure 9.4);
- *time line*, locating shifting technologies and institutions of communication in relation to each other (Figure 2.1).

(Other common formats of presentation include bar charts, histograms, line graphs, and pie charts. (See further Deacon *et al.* 1999: 93–98.))

---

4 *Everyday theory.* Finally, the public's interaction with media as consumers, citizens, and, occasionally, sources of information is guided by a number of everyday or common-sense notions of what media are, how they operate, and in whose interests.

Other chapters in this volume have emphasized the scientific theories which constitute the academic media field. The professional and everyday theories that enter into media production and reception have also, in part, been addressed. This chapter shifts the emphasis toward normative theory, examining, as well, its interrelations particularly with scientific theory.

Being a strategic cultural resource, a major

economic sector, and a political institution in their own right, the technological media have generated a large proportion of commercially motivated as well as socially concerned research. From its initiation, the field was part and parcel of the emergence by the 1930s of what Beniger (1986) termed 'the control society' – characterized by a greatly intensified surveillance of society, both by individuals through the media, and by private as well as public agencies through, for example, market research and opinion polling. Several of the early 'milestones' of media research◄ were produced in response to perceived social problems (e.g., violence,

the control society

► milestones of media research – Chapter 10, p. 158

propaganda) which were associated with the media as well as with the new urban and international realities embedding them – a different culture of time and space (Kern 1983).

The *mediatization* of (Western) societies is perhaps best understood as one element of the processes of *bureaucratization* and *rationalization* that were then taking place as aspects of modernization in politics and economy.◄ A key role of media became that of facilitating the overall stability and integration of increasingly complex social systems. *Cui bono?* The normative theories provided a framework of ideas and ideals for addressing issues of social power, personal identity, and political and cultural rights in relation to mediated communication.

NORMATIVE THEORIES

The entire set of normative theories illustrates how ideas with a long history are sometimes mobilized for particular historical purposes. Certain of their constituents date from Renaissance and Enlightenment ideals and, indeed, from the Socratic dialogue as a means of true insight, and of doing what is morally good. However, the normative theories were articulated specifically to the media field in the context of the Cold War. Also in this emerging academic field, the period pitted different models of society against each other. The classic publication identified four theories, with special reference to the printed press (Siebert *et al.* 1956):

1 *Authoritarian theory*. A traditional model of publicity took for granted a social and religious cosmology which may be described as a pyramid or chain of being.◄ Here, everything had its righful place, and 'information' flowed top–down from the monarch, being the representative of divine authority on earth. Far from being a means of oppression, the pyramid could be understood as a framework that enabled individuals to flourish on the road to their destiny. Only especially reliable persons were

allowed to disseminate information on any social scale, being subject, as well, to censorship, and their audiences were just that – recipients of messages from political and religious authorities who knew better. While rarely advocated as such, being the unspoken doxa of the medieval, feudal order, the authoritarian theory provided the contrast against which most later theories defined themselves.

2 *Libertarian theory*. It was liberal theory which, in the areas of both politics and communication, challenged authoritarian models. Liberalism informed the larger shift from traditional to modern social structures, as epitomized in the public sphere.◄ Not only were humans defined as ends in themselves, with certain inalienable political, economic, and cultural rights; they were also conceived as rational animals with the ability collectively to define and administer such rights. One unifying metaphor became the 'marketplace of ideas,' suggesting that the market for goods and services would also empower individuals to promote their political interests and cultural ideals through the press (or to establish one themselves). The resulting competition of ideas, presumably, would benefit society as such.

3 *Totalitarian theory*. The occasion for formulating the normative theories, as noted above, was the Cold War, specifically the implementation of a totalitarian or communist theory of the press in a number of countries following World War II. The distinction between totalitarian and authoritarian theory (and their relation to fascism during the 1930s) can be, and has been, debated. Still, it was characteristic that the central control of communist regimes over media was officially conceived as a means of fundamentally restructuring society, rather than preserving any social pyramid. Centralized control, moreover, equaled state or government control over all means of production, whether it was meaning or material goods being produced. Following the breakup of communist systems in Europe from 1989, in the People's Republic of China the development of new journalistic practices still takes place within a

► modernization – Chapter 11, p. 143
► the great chain of being – Chapter 2, p. 21

► the public sphere – Chapter 1, p. 7

relatively fixed political-economic system (e.g., Pan 2000).

4 *Social responsibility theory*. A shift in emphasis, from liberal ideals toward an understanding of the press and other media as trustees or representatives of the public, has taken place in the Western world particularly since 1945. For one thing, the growing concentration and conglomeration of the media sector increasingly undercut any simple notion of a 'free press.' For another, some new media forms, especially radio and television, at least for a period were limited in number for technological reasons. Furthermore, all technological media require economic resources and professional skills on a scale which promotes large organizations and concentration generally. Whereas references to social responsibility accordingly have been witnessed in several media types, European public service broadcasting represents a particularly elaborate and institutionalized expression of social responsibility theory.◄

Apart from the inherently controversial status of normative theories, later commentators have noted that the four types fail to capture several developments in media over the past four decades. In particular, media systems in the developing world and the growth of media forms with increased public participation – from local radio to the Internet – have led to the formulation of two further positions (see also McQuail 1983):

5 *Development theory*. In the context of decolonization, the 1960s witnessed intensifying debates about media in relation to the 'Third World' (while the other two 'worlds' were confronting each other in the Cold War). The issues included an imbalance in the flow of news in the world and the possible international as well as national, local means of redressing it. Attempts at developing a comprehensive theory in this regard had to weigh conflicting interests – a generally desirable 'free' flow of information in the world versus the right of individual cultures

to gain a hearing in world media, and to determine the shape of their own media systems. Debate was further complicated by the fact that references to ideals such as 'free flow' and 'self-determination' could serve as fronts, either for economic expansionism or for governments promoting themselves abroad and repressing their citizens at home. As suggested by the work of the MacBride (1980) Commission, the issues have proven difficult to formulate in any comprehensive normative theory, but continue to generate international debate as well as research. For example, Husband (1996) has introduced the notion of a 'right to be understood' in the multi-ethnic public sphere.

the right to be understood

6 *Democratic-participant theory*. Particularly in the Western world, the 1960s witnessed a second type of upheaval around media, associated with the political mobilization and cultural critique by anti-authoritarian movements.◄ On the one hand, the social responsibility of the mainstream media, their political and cultural diversity in practice, was challenged. On the other hand, information and communication technologies appeared to offer the means of a novel form of political as well as cultural democracy. Moving beyond the liberal and responsibility theories, democratic-participant theory proposed steps toward ensuring public involvement, by structural means and not merely by individual initiative (Enzensberger 1972 [1970]). It is this participatory ambition which, in part, has fueled 'grass-roots' media (e.g., Downing 2000; Glessing 1970), and it continues to inform ideals regarding Internet communication (e.g., Rheingold 1994).

In continuing debate and research, several additional varieties of normative theory have been outlined (see Nerone 1995; Nordenstreng 1997), some of which are outgrowths or close allies of scientific media theories, for example, on intercultural or postcolonial issues.◄ Broadly speaking, however, most normative (and many scientific) theories today emphasize

---

► public service broadcasting – p. 283

► anti-authoritarian movements – Chapter 3, p. 56

► intercultural and North–South communication – Chapter 11, p. 177

either critical-reformist or pluralist-functionalist criteria – a conflictual or consensual model of society – in evaluating media performance. A related opposition between 'state' and 'market' is commonly referred to in policy discussions of how to ensure the 'freedom' of media.

Part of the difficulty of debating the real conflicts and high stakes in the area beyond simple oppositions has been the ambiguity of the concept of freedom in sociopolitical and, later, communication theory. Different accounts tend to assume either a negative definition (freedom *from* state interference in communication) or a positive definition (freedom *to* demand certain media provisions as a civic right). Habermas (1989 [1962]) traced this ambiguity to shifting notions of how state or government agencies should interact with various sectors of economic and other social life. The modern period was inaugurated by the negative definition of freedom, as the new middle classes asserted their political and economic rights *vis-à-vis* the state. However, a positive redefinition of rights, involving economic regulation and social services along Keynesian principles, followed from world crises in the late nineteenth century and especially the 1930s. It was this reorganization of the society–state nexus which presumably preserved the larger system of industrial capitalism and representative government.

One should constantly keep in mind that current debates about normative media theory take place in the context of highly regulated political economies – at least in the Western world, and despite measures of deregulation particularly since the 1980s. Any reference to a negative definition of media freedom ('less state interference, more freedom of expression') is likely to serve rhetorical, not analytical purposes. The substantial point of contention is the particular forms in which the regulation of technologically mediated communication will take place – from national laws affecting film production to the international assignment of Internet domain names. Also in the future, the questions that media researchers will be asked to study and comment on involve conflicts and compromises regarding who will benefit most from the *de facto* positive definition of social freedom.

Against this historical background, the 'four-plus-two' normative theories remain relevant points of reference by articulating political, economic, and cultural ideals which still enter into contemporary public and policy debates. (On issues of justice, with largely unexamined implications for media, see Rawls 1999.)

The normative 'theories' have been supported primarily by abstract reasoning and principled argument. Nevertheless, they amount to strongly held beliefs on which whole societies have been prepared to act, to use pragmatist terminology (Joas 1993), and, indeed, to plan their entire system of communication. A central role of media research, approximately since the 1956 statement of the normative theories, has been to differentiate and strengthen the social bases of reasoning, argument, and action in relation to the media. Media and communication research has developed at the crossroads of several social sectors and intellectual currents.

MEDIA RESEARCH AS A SOCIAL INSTITUTION

Intellectual cultures

A modern *locus classicus* regarding the relationship between theory and practice (Lobkowicz 1967) – between knowing that something is the case and knowing how to act accordingly – was the statement by Karl Marx in his *Theses on Feuerbach* (1845), that 'The philosophers have only interpreted the world, in various ways; the point, however, is to change it.' Whether or not individual scholars have drawn either revolutionary or reformist consequences from such a view, it is undeniable that, at the institutional level, research participates in actively shaping and maintaining modern societies in countless ways. This has been evident not least within science and technology during the twentieth century (for an overview see Biagioli 1999). In a structural sense, then, basic research also eventually comes to be <u>applied</u>. Compared, however, to a widespread nineteenth-century notion of sciences as means of both material and cultural progress, much twentieth-century research found itself struggling to come to terms with its sense of a mission. The complic-

[margin note:] from negative to positive definitions of freedom

[margin note:] basic and applied research

ity of research in world wars, colonialism, and questionable forms of social and cultural engineering meant that its legitimacy was not a given.

Media and communication research emerged within the university after 1945 at the juncture between several intellectual cultures (see the historical overviews in Resource box 16.1). The history of the modern university (Rudy 1984) is, in one sense, a history of reality being partitioned into researchable and manageable domains, to be studied through increasingly specialized theory and methods, and to be managed in practical life by specialists graduating in each of these specialties. Following the founding of the research university in the early 1800s,◄ the late nineteenth century had witnessed the establishment of the social sciences as a separate 'faculty' alongside the humanities.◄ A recognizable specialty of (mass) media studies emerged from the 1930s, as witnessed by the 'milestones' of Figure 10.1. (Resource box 11.1 provides references regarding national variations of this development.)

It was not until the 1950s, however, that an actual institutionalization occurred, notably in American social science (for an overview see Schramm 1997), which began to accumulate a separate body of theory and methodology, and to consolidate its social contexts of influence. During these same decades, humanities departments, including film, literature, linguistics, and history, similarly prepared important contributions to media research by expanding the subject matters of the established disciplines far beyond high arts and official history and, in the process, by reinvigorating and revising their analytical procedures and theoretical frameworks. Following the political as well as epistemological upheaval and stock-taking between the 1960 and 1970s, a process of convergence between social-scientific and humanistic traditions gained momentum during the 1980s, as reviewed in this volume.

One of the continuing debates is whether media studies constitute an established or **field or** emerging discipline, or an interdisciplinary field **discipline?** (for an overview see Levy and Gurevitch 1994).

► the modern research university – Chapter 2, p. 15

► social sciences as separate faculty – Chapter 3

There is no doubt that media research has a permanent presence as a social institution. The indicators are university departments, journals, conferences, consultancies, and continuous interventions in public debate. Nevertheless, it should be emphasized that the area remains heterogeneous. First, bibliometric research suggests that 'communication study' still consists of two relatively separate subspecialties of research, focusing on interpersonal and mass communi- **interpersonal** cation respectively (Rogers 1999). Second, also **vs. mass** within mass communication research, analyses **communi-** of journal publications suggest the existence of **cation** three relatively self-contained literatures, representing social science, interpretive studies, and critical analysis (Fink and Gantz 1996). With the growth of computer-mediated communication, which, in certain respects, rejoins the two types, however, a move toward integration seems likely in coming decades. Indeed, it does not appear too far-fetched to imagine that faculties of communication and culture which comprise social-scientific, humanistic, and technological components will be the structural response of universities, once again, to a changing social context (Jensen 2000b).

In his often cited account of divisions within academia, Snow (1964) identified two intellectual cultures, as represented by 'the literary intellectuals' and 'the physical scientists' (p. 4). Perhaps surprisingly in view of its enabling technologies and engineering aspects, the media field so far has had a negligible natural-scientific element. Instead, it is the humanities and social sciences that have provided the theoretical building blocks, compatible or not. Still, 'the scientific method,' as associated above all with the natural sciences, has figured prominently within methodology and theory of science, and perhaps even more so in debates over the politics of doing research. These latter debates have frequently centered on the question of whether particular social interests are served by particular kinds of scientific knowledge.

Knowledge interests

The concept of knowledge interests implies that an ulterior purpose is ingrained in the very principles and procedures of scientific inquiry.

RESOURCE BOX 16.1 HISTORIES OF MEDIA AND COMMUNICATION RESEARCH AS A FIELD

Over the past decade, more historical accounts of the development of media studies have begun to appear. Presumably, this follows, in part, from the fact that media and communication research is now an established institution in society and a relatively mature field of inquiry. The second generation of researchers, now occupying university chairs, may also perceive a need to revisit and reassess their roots, partly in response to convergence.

At one level, the development of the field is the outcome of interventions from the social sciences and the humanities, as traced in Chapters 2 and 3, in response to the central role of media in modem societies. At a more specific level, different national cultures – in universities, in politics, and in the media themselves – have produced a range of forms in which research and teaching are organized. The references in Box 11.1 cover some of these aspects.

Given its longer history as well as its centrality and resources generally, the North American research community has produced some of the more elaborate historical accounts (e.g., Delia 1987). At the same time, different accounts of the U.S. experience bear witness to quite different conceptions of both historiography and politics. As such, they are instructive, not only regarding controversial issues within U.S. research, but also for the writing of histories of the field elsewhere. The following references are indicative, both of relatively more administrative or critical perspectives, and of their different sources in the history of ideas:

- Hardt 1992 – a monograph with review and discussion, emphasizing critical and interpretive aspects of U.S. communication studies, and linking these to pragmatism and the wider intellectual history of the U.S.A.
- Dennis and Wartella 1996 – an edited collection with contributions from several of the central figures of U.S. research, including accounts of its roots in Europe and in Chicago School sociology. In a review, Hardt (1999) found that this 'remembered history' by key individuals served more as a professional position statement than as an analytical historiography, implying that it may be a Whig history written from the still largely functionalist perspective of the victors.
- Schramm 1997 – a retrospective account by the researcher who is normally considered to be the central figure in institutionalizing communication studies in the U.S.A., supplemented with perspectives supporting this conclusion, by Steven M. Chaffee and Everett M. Rogers. Hardt (1999), in his turn, argued that 'Wilbur Schramm had failed to forge a discipline,' and that instead 'mass communication research was legitimated intellectually by the centrality of communication in social theory and cultural studies' (p. 239).

Importantly, these interests are different in kind from, albeit related to, researchers' personal convictions and questions of how research is funded or situated institutionally. The category of knowledge interests provides a framework for examining the relationship between social ends and scientific means in a more nuanced fashion than is often the case, for example, in accounts simply contrasting commercial and academic research. Knowledge interests begin to address the relative autonomy of different

kinds of media research, and to clarify issues of knowledge and power which have come to the fore in recent decades.

The concept was formulated as such by Habermas (1971 [1968]), who distinguished three types of knowledge interest. Each is associated with the characteristic subject matters and social functions of three faculties of study:

1 *Control through prediction.* In the case of natural sciences, a central purpose of inquiry is

to be able to plan future activities in the material world, in detail and with confidence. Predictions and hypotheses make for human intervention into nature under controlled circumstances. By developing and accumulating criteria for anticipating physical, chemical, and biological phenomena and processes, the modern sciences have mastered the natural environment to an unprecedented degree. This has facilitated the human management of resources, time, and space as well as extensive social planning, notably in agriculture and industrial production. (*Media example*: Quantitative surveys predicting the preferences of audiences.)

2 *Contemplative understanding.* In the humanities, scholarship has revolved around cultural forms of expression which are subjected to contemplation – interpretation through introspection. Aesthetic works, for one, could be understood as ends in themselves that should be analyzed for their inherent meaning and value. Historical events, for another, might bear witness to universal, even eternal aspects of the human condition, even if the religious overtones of contemplation have gradually been downplayed. By disseminating their (re)interpretations of culture and history to a wider public, humanistic scholars came to serve, not least, as the professional keepers of cultural tradition. (*Media example*: Qualitative textual studies exploring media representations of social reality.)

3 *Emancipation through critique.* If the natural sciences procured the material and collective bases of modern society, whereas the humanities addressed the individual's life experiences, the social sciences were called upon to examine material as well as experiential, collective as well as individual conditions of social life. While this ambiguous status is in evidence in the two paradigms of media research,◄ Habermas suggested that social-scientific inquiry does have a distinctive knowledge interest, at least potentially, namely emancipation. By performing a critique of the prevailing forms of social organization, and by clarifying alternatives, the social sciences can promote the emancipation of humans from

living conditions that are not of their own making. (*Media example*: Participatory models of communication.)

These three forms of knowledge interest must be understood as ideal types that are subject to variation and combination in scientific practice. However, Habermas (1971 [1968]) further argued that the different methodological and theoretical requirements do not transfer well from one domain of research to another. In particular, he concluded that the emancipatory potential of social sciences tends to be lost if one imports, and gives priority to, the 'technical' knowledge interest of the natural sciences. The argument is familiar from some media research which has depicted audience surveys and television meters as (quantitative) means of cultural control (e.g., Ang 1991).

It is important to emphasize that the element of critique does not follow from the political-ideological attitude of the individual researcher. While a commitment to the emancipation of specific socioeconomic groups will be the typical personal motivation, the distinctive features of critical research are found in its practices, its epistemologies, and in the institutions ensuring its relevance to the rest of society. A competent critical study, thus, adheres systematically to particular methodological and theoretical approaches that are likely to have an emancipatory potential. Critical research is also concerned with researchable, rather than merely debatable or normative issues.

Sectors of research

The different intellectual currents which may be summed up, for convenience, as knowledge interests are found to varying degrees in the social institutions and sectors that perform or rely on media research. From the early beginnings of the field, an awareness of the different purposes of research has been reflected in its terminology. The classic distinction was introduced by Lazarsfeld (1941):

- *Administrative research* refers to the kind of goal-oriented and instrumental studies which resolve specific issues, typically for the purpose

► two paradigms of media research – Chapter 15, p. 255

of planning some media production or activity. Studies in this vein 'solve little problems, generally of a business character' (p. 8).

• *Critical research* addresses the wider societal, cultural, and historical issues of mediated communication, often in a reception perspective, from which 'the public interest' may be assessed. Here, studies take up 'the general role of our media of communication in the present social system' (p. 9).

When Lazarsfeld (1941) described the critical variety of research, he did so, in part, under the influence of the 'first generation' of Frankfurt School scholars who had fled Nazi Germany for the U.S.A. While highly suspicious of the 'culture industry' (Adorno and Horkheimer 1977 [1944]) they encountered there, their response went beyond a normative rejection. One of the points that they introduced to media studies was an analytical, Kantian notion of critique that seeks to explicate the conditions of belief, which are themselves one of the conditions of the social status quo (Hammersley 1995: 30). By reflecting on the media as they now exist, and by uncovering alternatives, critical studies outline *what might be*. In this regard, Lazarsfeld recognized the creative, theoretical potential of critical research. Habermas, who is normally seen as the main representative of a 'second generation' of the Frankfurt School, in his turn specified critique as one of several knowledge interests.

When making the distinction between critical and administrative research, Lazarsfeld (1941) found that the two types, largely synonymous in his description with basic and applied research, could and should cross-fertilize. His own accomplishments, centered in the Bureau of Applied Social Research at Columbia University, seemed to suggest as much. In addition to early 'milestones' in media research, he and his collaborators pioneered several general approaches, from the panel method to focused interviewing. Many critical researchers, however, including European expatriates who, like Theodor Adorno, found a temporary home in Bureau projects, were highly unsympathetic to the implications of administrative research (Delia 1987: 52). Commercial and other instru-

the Frankfurt School

mental interests might narrow the theoretical scope of projects, curtail their later uses, and, in the long term, undermine the intellectual freedom of researchers to choose their research questions and methods. Readers of the last sentence of Lazarsfeld's article may have felt confirmed that critical research was being assigned the role of generating bright ideas to be exploited (financially and ideologically) in the administrative mainstream of research: 'there is here a type of approach which, if it were included in the general stream of communications research, could contribute much in terms of challenging problems and new concepts useful in the interpretation of known, and in the search for new, data' (Lazarsfeld 1941: 16).

On closer examination, the two varieties exhibit similarities as well as differences, and have combined in various research traditions and organizations. Both rely on qualitative as well as quantitative methodologies. (The marginalizing of qualitative studies as preliminary pilots, perhaps surprisingly, seems more prevalent in academic contexts.) In both cases, moreover, projects may be reactive or proactive, evaluating what already is, or shaping what is not yet. Critical projects can be the most instrumental of all, since they design research questions and methods, for example, to expose inequalities in the availability of communication resources, or to develop such resources. Recently, researchers within cultural studies have advocated more focused social uses of this tradition in policy contexts (Bennett 1992), and a greater reliance on quantitative evidence as well (Lewis 1997).

reactive and proactive research

In all cases, research projects and their findings should be assessed with some reference to their social infrastructure – their funding, organization, time frames, and anticipated uses – over and above their theoretical models and methodological approaches. This infrastructure conditions the reflexivity which researchers may exercise on behalf of themselves, their colleagues or clients, particular sociopolitical constituencies, or the public at large. Despite national and cultural variations, it is possible to identify certain main types of media research institutions, as displayed in Figure 16.1.

A central divide separates private enterprise

	Commercial company	**University department**	**Independent research institute**	**Documentation center**
Funding	Income from clients	Public funding	Commercial income and/or public funding	Commercial income and/or public funding
Organization of research activity	Management hierarchy	Autonomous researchers within collegial government	Board of trustees and management hierarchy	Board of trustees and management hierarchy
Time frames	Days to years	Years to decades	Days to decades	Years to centuries
Anticipated uses of results	Strategic planning and product development	Description and critique of past and present media forms	Descriptive as well as proactive analyses	Description and documentation of media contents and uses
Examples	Marketing sections; Advertising agencies; Consultancies	Media studies departments; Schools of communication	Research bureaus and *ad hoc* centers; Thinktanks	Archives with proprietary and/or public (museum) access

Figure 16.1 Types of media research organization

and public service, also in the world of research. This is suggested by the first two types – university departments and commercial companies. Although reliable measures of the relative size of each of these main sectors are difficult to calculate, it is safe to say that commercial projects outdistance academic ones in terms of both financial resources and the number of single studies. Any simple divide between public and private research, however, is complicated by the fact that university departments, in many countries, increasingly depend on commercial sponsorship to fund their research. Furthermore, commercial research is frequently subcontracted outside the media organization in question, sometimes to academic institutions. The research entities of public service media occupy an additional middle ground.

The third type – independent research institutes – has been a staple feature of media research since Lazarsfeld's Bureau, avoiding some of the negative connotations of both 'state' and 'market' and attracting clients from both sides of the divide. The fourth type – documentation centers – has more commonly been associated with historical, arts, and other humanistic archives than with empirical research on contemporary culture and society (although some film institutes have filled this role). At present, such entities are gaining importance, both as a strategic resource in media production and planning, and as support for the affiliated research activities.◄

(It is worth adding that public service broadcasting and public domain research represent comparable conceptions of the social organization and dissemination of knowledge. In both cases, knowledge is understood as a 'public good' (Samuelson 1954), in relative autonomy from market forces. In the case of broadcasting, it is this understanding that has been challenged

► museums and archives for media research – p. 285

under the heading of deregulation (see, e.g., Blumler and Gurevitch 1995; Garnham and Locksley 1991).)

In the end, it is the different time frames which, most of all, distinguish the social roles of each type of research organization. Whereas commercial projects typically are scheduled for short-term instrumental purposes, academic studies may suggest a course of action in the (very) long term. If research is defined summarily as the representation of reality for a purpose, the practical question becomes when, where, and how this purpose is enacted. Short- and long-term purposes may also be expressed in terms of either policy or political uses of research.

POLITICS VERSUS POLICY

Policy contexts

Policies are codified plans of action. The importance of policy in both public administration and commercial companies is one structural consequence of increased complexity, internally in modern organizations as well as in the larger social context. Collective and coordinated action requires deliberation and planning, and, because of their scale and cost, the resulting policies further call for evaluation and adjustment. Both the nature of the deliberations and the criteria of evaluation follow largely from predefined organizational goals. Accordingly, policy research is focused within existing institutions, and on agendas set by those institutions. The area has been growing since 1945, one key figure being the communication scholar, Harold D. Lasswell (e.g., Lerner and Lasswell 1951). The expanding sector of evaluation research may be understood as one subvariety of policy studies in this broad sense (e.g., Patton 1990).

evaluation research

From its inception, media research has contributed to planning and evaluating the media's performance. Because these uses are relatively familiar, they can be described more briefly than the following types. At least three policy contexts can be identified:

1 *Business administration*. Within private enterprise, practically all media employ in-house as well as commissioned research to support their business. Studies address not only audiences, but also the internal development of content and the strategic placement of the organization in relation to competitors, regulators, and the general public (e.g., Grunig 1992).

organizational communication

2 *Public planning*. Compared to the specific policies of media businesses, public policy delineates the general framework in which media operate. A typical arena of influence for media researchers has been commission work leading into decisions within the political system, as sometimes supported by specially funded studies. To exemplify, most European countries during the 1980s and 1990s witnessed a great deal of commission work and research regarding satellite and cable technologies and their implications for public service broadcasting.

state commissions

3 *Non-governmental organizations*. Beyond and between the business and state contexts, citizens' groups, thinktanks, and other organizations regularly develop or advocate particular media policies. They do so with a view not only to legislative frameworks, but also to the role of media, for example, in the educational system. In addition to commissioning research, these organizations serve as audiences for politically motivated and socially concerned media studies.

It is not by coincidence that the three policy contexts correspond to elements in the dominant model of contemporary society, as laid out in Figure 1.3 – the spheres of private businesses, state agencies, and civil society. It is by engaging these institutions that research can address the structural conditions of meaning production. It is in these main contexts, for better or worse, that the future of mediated communication is being shaped most concretely.

Political processes

A second set of approaches to applying media research socially bracket present institutional agendas and look to the future. Compared to the delimited *contexts* of policy, these approaches shift the emphasis toward less well-defined, but potentially more far-reaching *processes* of change. (As in the case of policy contexts, both qualitative and quantitative methodologies are of relevance for such political processes.)

By insisting on the autonomy of the research institution, and by resisting a hegemony of other institutional logics, much academic work may be said to adopt a long-term strategy of interchange with other social institutions. In some cases, the strategy entails the countering of specific policies with alternative political viewpoints. For example, media studies may expose the hidden or unacknowledged interests of either commercial or government policies. In this regard, academic media and communication researchers carry on aspects of the classic, **critical role** critical role of the intelligentsia (Mannheim **of the** 1976 [1922]: 136–146).
intelligentsia

Corner (1991) has identified two intellectual projects in recent media research, originally within reception analysis, but with equal relevance for other areas of study. On the one hand, the field as such has been committed to Enlightenment ideals concerning the democratic accessibility of *public knowledge* through **public** various factual genres. From propaganda re- **knowledge** search to decoding studies of news, an import- **project** ant research question has been how well audiences are able to process mediated information, and to employ it in the political process. On the other hand, the last couple of decades in particular have witnessed both textual and audience research rehabilitating the value and **popular** relevance of *popular culture*, especially fiction **culture** genres.
project

Compared to the policy contexts of research, its wider political arenas of influence are centered around the public sphere as a forum of social reflexivity and intervention. In addition, the interventions of media research address related institutions within, for instance, education and politics:

- *Public debate.* Most generally and uncontroversially, media research contributes to (and occasionally initiates) debates in the public sphere, its political as well as cultural components (Figure 1.3). The contributions range from popular publications at the conclusion of a project to syndicated commentaries. In the process, researchers may promote the general

self-reflexivity of media, as they address issues such as political 'spin doctors' or lifestyle advertising. In a case such as the public jour- **public** nalism movement in the U.S.A., a more ambi- **journalism** tious aim has been for research to support a reinvigoration of both the press and political participation (for an overview and references see Haas 1999).

- *Media education.* Beyond their own graduate and undergraduate students, media and communication researchers have contributed to the democratization (or relativization) of the cultural standards and 'texts' of curricula at most educational levels. In addition, the field has been successful, in a number of countries, in arguing the need for a component of 'media **media literacy** literacy' in general education (Masterman 1985; Messaris 1994; Potter 1998). This is in spite of the fact that the exact purpose and placement of media education (as a separate subject or within other subjects) remain debated. With the introduction of computer-supported learning, a redefinition of (media) literacy is again likely to occur.

- *Museums and archives.* As suggested in Figure 16.1, documentation centers constitute an increasingly strategic resource for media production as well as research. Also from political and public perspectives, the preservation and documentation of contemporary media pose important issues (Jensen 1993b). The point is not only to enable future scholars to (re)write media history, or to assess contemporary research models and findings. Only if the breadth and depth of media, including their everyday uses and audience experiences, remain available and documented – alongside the high cultural forms that still reign supreme in museums and archives (and among employed archivists) – will coming generations have the possibility of assessing and learning from their past, our present. The Payne Fund (Jowett *et al.* 1996) and Mass Observation (Richards and Sheridan 1987) studies of the 1930s provided indications of the kinds of evidence needed. The challenge has been taken up in at least some recent work (e.g., Day-Lewis 1989; Gauntlett and Hill 1999).

Standpoint interventions

A third, heterogeneous group of research strategies – beyond policy and politics – are united by an explicit commitment to social and cultural change, perhaps on a revolutionary scale. This is in comparison to the more reformist orientation of the political processes reviewed in the last section. (Because they tend to explore political and epistemological alternatives, studies here rely largely on qualitative approaches.)

The orientation of these strategies might be defined as being *versus institutions* – they not only bracket social agendas, but actively oppose major social institutions and, occasionally, the very institutionalization of society. Furthermore, their analyses sometimes call for a radical break with the methodological and epistemological premises of other research. A frequent implication is that alternative social arrangements must be outlined through alternative epistemologies. As theorized most influentially by Foucault (1972), this implication sometimes leads on to a stronger position of questioning the legitimacy of any and all forms of knowledge.

Within media research, it is especially the cultural studies tradition◀ which has advanced these issues and generated debate with other research traditions (e.g., Ferguson and Golding 1997). Since the 1970s, much work has taken previous social and cultural research to task for articulating and promoting interests associated with the Western world, the economic middle class, the political mainstream, and with a pervasive patriarchal mode of social interaction. One counter-strategy has been to treat knowledge in the plural, also terminologically, exploring alternative 'knowledges' in the interest of the disempowered.

Some of these debates have crystallized in **political correctness** the notion of 'political correctness.' The implication is that research questions, findings, and explanatory frameworks are perhaps not being assessed by their scientific or professional merits, but by their immediate relevance and legitimacy, for instance, in making up for past and current silences and injustices in the wider

▶ cultural studies – Chapter 2, p. 39

social system (for an overview see Levy 1992). Against such more traditionalist concerns, critical researchers have reiterated that neither 'professionalism' nor 'science' are innocent categories. Asante (1992: 141), for one, has countered that the charge of 'political correctness' represents 'a peculiar mixture of notions about freedom of speech, affirmative action, sexism, and the decline of white male privilege in a pluralistic society.'

At least three types of interventions involve a concerted commitment to social change through research.

Feminist methodology

The term 'standpoint' has been related to **standpoint epistemology** methodology and theory of science by feminist research, as elaborated especially by Harding (1986). The point of departure is that all knowledge is produced from a socially situated standpoint, and that the life experiences of women – arguably silenced in much of the history of ideas – provide a necessary corrective to other science. Thus, feminism might enable a 'strong objectivity' by allowing both women and men to transcend classic canons of objectivism and to take a (more) reflexive position in the research process (see also Alcoff and Potter 1993; Harding 1987).

Compared to the biological essentialism of Irigaray (1997 [1977]) and others, standpoint feminism represents an attempt to historicize the nexus between knowledge and power. In practice, however, the pendulum swings easily to another extreme of 'sociological essentialism.' Some writings seem to suggest that feminism and other cognate traditions, standing on the shoulders of the disempowered, necesssarily offer more insightful theories as well as better empirical bases of change. In media research, this tendency is found in work asserting that, compared to certain recognized classics, studies of women's culture, of ethnic minorities, and of marginalized youth subcultures not only have a contribution to make, but are unrecognized origins of key ideas regarding the place of media in everyday life (Drotner 1996: 41).

The orientation of feminist methodology and epistemology is toward the very long term.

By reshaping the research institution, feminist studies may, in turn, help to reshape those other social institutions that are affected by research. In doing so, feminist research links up with the wider feminist movement and its struggle for equal rights.◀

Textual deconstructionism

This second position for change shares with much feminism the ambition of challenging a unified concept of knowledge. Deconstructionism, however, is almost entirely focused on texts as the locus of both dominance and change. Departing from poststructuralist theories of discourse and postmodernist conceptions of culture,◀ many textual media studies of, for instance, film and television seek to expose either misrepresentations or reified representations of reality.

Neither empirical audiences, however, nor the concrete social contexts in which texts take effect, have much of a place in these studies. Instead, deconstructionist works may be seen to perform an interpretive reworking of media texts, and to offer their reinterpretations to no constituency or context in particular. At least some key publications leave readers with the impression of an inverse relationship between quite revolutionary ambitions and less than concrete political strategies (e.g., Kristeva 1984). (For a critique of the associated terminology concerning the 'social construction' of reality, see Hacking 1999.)

Deconstructionism dissolves boundaries, not only between text and reality, but between the text being studied and the study itself. Like some art criticism, media criticism in this vein might be understood as another artwork in its own right. The work of Richard Rorty has been influential by promoting a definition of science as story-telling (e.g., Rorty 1979, 1998). Research may be taken as one of many contributions to 'the conversation of humankind.' Some recent qualitative work has also proposed to expand the range of genres in which science tells stories (e.g., Denzin and Lincoln 2000).

Given its disregard for other social practices, textual deconstructionism is most likely to make an impact within the educational system, which may trickle down or disseminate the ideas. A second area of impact is the media themselves, where notions of postmodernism have been widespread, and where program developers have taken specific inspirations from deconstructionism (e.g., Caldwell 1995).

Action research

A third type of intervention may be described briefly as action research, although the tradition recognizes several participatory and applied variants (for overviews see Greenwood and Levin 1998; Reason and Bradbury 2001). Like the two positions above, action studies challenge established institutions, normally in cooperation with, or initiated by, interest groups within the institution. Unlike the other types, action research presents an operational strategy for social change, for example, within industrial democracy or community development. Ideally, studies become 'co-generative' (Greenwood and Levin 1998: 109) by having 'everyday theorists'◀ as partners in the formulation of research questions as well as empirical strategies.

In media and communication studies, action research has apparently been less widespread than in some other fields. However, 'development communication' programs included some involvement of the communities and cultures that were end-users of the technologies being diffused.◀ More recently, some community media work (e.g., Jankowski 1991) and studies of computer-mediated communication (e.g., Preece 1994) have relied on participatory strategies.

Like other political and policy strategies, these various 'standpoint' interventions leave a number of political and epistemological questions to be addressed in future research practice and debate. To conclude, the final section presents some of the additional practical as well as ethical considerations which arise in

---

▶ feminism – Chapter 2, p. 34

▶ poststructuralism and postmodernism – Chapter 2, p. 33

▶ everyday theory – p. 275

▶ development communication – Chapter 11, p. 179

RESOURCE BOX 16.2 KEY STUDIES AND REFERENCE WORKS FOR INDIVIDUAL MEDIA

Books
*   Vincent 2000 – a comprehensive overview of the development of literacy in modern Europe, with reference to books and other media of communication, and to their social uses;
*   Radway 1997 – a recent study of books as a medium that continues to serve as a central ingredient of popular culture.

Newspapers
*   Habermas 1989 [1962] – still an essential resource regarding the historical development and current functions of the press;
*   Schudson 1978 – a classic social history of the U.S. press, in this respect complementing the European focus of Habermas;
*   Curran and Seaton 1997 – a historical analysis of the British press, with many references.

Film
*   Andrew 1976 – a solid introduction to the main classic film theories;
*   Mast et al. 1990 – an anthology of classical texts in film studies, covering the range of traditions;
*   Bordwell and Carroll 1996 – an important intervention contrasting cognitive and other film theory.

Radio
*   Crisell 1994 – one of the first comprehensive introductions to an under-researched medium;
*   Hendy 2000 – another broad overview of the medium, including its changing technologies and its place in, for instance, African and Latin American cultures;
*   Scannell and Cardiff 1991 – an exemplary social history of radio, with implications for current studies of broadcasting.

Television
*   Williams 1974 – the classic study which defined television (and radio) in terms of their characteristics of 'flow';
*   Ellis 1982 – a redevelopment of the understanding of television flow, and a comparison of television with film, also in terms of the audience experience;
*   Newcomb 1997 – a three-volume encyclopedia and study resource on most aspects of television.

Computer media
*   Mayer 1999 – a collection of key texts contributing to the definition and study of the computer as a medium;
*   Castells 1996 – a comprehensive analysis of the relations between information and communication technologies and the social and cultural practices which they enable.

planning both student projects and research programs.

THE SOCIAL TRIAD OF RESEARCH PRACTICE

Research practice may be understood as a particular kind of rule-governed social interaction. It involves, minimally:

- the *researcher*
- his/her *respondents* (or other sources of evidence)
- the community of *colleagues* who, sooner or later, will assess the quality of findings and of professional conduct.

This triad operates across all the different sectors and intellectual cultures of media studies. It cumulates a body of theory and evidence, and it enacts the institution of research on a daily basis.

Most of this volume has, in the nature of the matter, emphasized the researcher's perspective as a professional and social subject. The encounter with 'ordinary' people, and with colleagues, presents additional and concrete challenges and choices. Such encounters acutely involve the perspectives and rights of others.

A common denominator for researchers' relations with respondents and colleagues is research ethics (for an overview see Resnik 1998). The category of ethics blends into *politics*: politics formulates rules of collective conduct in society, whereas ethics addresses standards of individual conduct. The ethics that apply to a given domain of social activity, further, overlap with the more general standards of *morality* that are prevalent in a historical period and cultural setting.

research ethics, politics, morality

Some aspects of research ethics are codified in legislation (as is politics and morality), and are subject to enforcement by legal as well as executive authorities. Whereas the ethical and legal frameworks of media and communication research vary between countries, the main issues may be laid out, as they relate to research subjects and the research community (see also Deacon *et al.* 1999: 365–387; Priest 1996: 207–230).

Research subjects

To begin with a seemingly trivial premise, research subjects are just that – subjects. Unlike rocks or books, subjects may be harmed a great deal, both socially and emotionally, by empirical media studies. And, while self-determination is the prerogative of any (research) subject, it is the responsibility of the researcher to anticipate and prevent harm. Research competence thus requires an awareness of ethical pitfalls, as established in previous research, as well as empathy and respect. (Perhaps surprisingly, organizations such as the International Association for Media and Communication Research and the International Communication Association have not developed codes of research ethics.)

In preliminary terms, the requirements may be stated as practical rules of thumb: 'Do as you would be done by' and 'Leave things as you find them' (Deacon *et al.* 1999: 385). The first principle is a variation on the Kantian categorical imperative, which accepts a standard of conduct only if it amounts to a reversible or general rule. The second principle specifies the right of research subjects to self-determination. Researchers should not intervene proactively unless this has been part of an explicit agreement as in, for instance, action research.

the categorical imperative

Depending on the research question and the concrete field of analysis, empirical researchers face several dilemmas. First, 'harm' may be of different types, and may only manifest itself in the longer term. Although empirical media studies rarely become life-threatening, compared to, for instance, medical research, the disclosure of, for instance, documents concerning product development from within a media organization may produce significant losses, financially or in terms of legitimacy. Similarly, the publication of politically charged debates within focus groups without sufficient anonymization may result in participants losing social status or 'face' in their community.

Second, these two examples suggest how research subjects have different potential levels of vulnerability, and should normally be treated accordingly. In their reception study of women viewing mediated violence, Schlesinger *et al.* (1992) exercised special care in screening and debriefing their respondents, some of whom had been physically abused in their own lives. By comparison, in production and other organizational studies, informants are normally approached as representatives of an organization or profession, who are aware of this role and, to a degree, of the nature of research. Nevertheless, ethical dilemmas also arise regarding what information should be provided or withheld in the attempt to complete a study. A case in point is the Glasgow University Media Group's undercover work within British television (1976, 1980).

informed consent

A standard procedure in professional codes of ethics is 'informed consent' (Resnik 1998: 133). Its purpose is to enable subjects to agree or decline to participate in a study. Their decision should be based on information about the components of the study, its potential consequences for themselves, and its likely social uses. Informed consent is one key element of the Nuremberg Code (1949), a set of protocols for research on human subjects which was established during the Nuremberg Trials on Nazi war crimes that also included scientific experimentation. While debated as to its sufficiency and practical implementation, informed consent represents an important and applicable principle concerning what (not) to do with research subjects. Compared to the procedure

double-blind and double-insight procedures

of 'double-blind' experiments in, for instance, medical science (neither patient nor therapist knows who gets the active drug being tested, and who gets the placebo), informed consent may be said to aim for a procedure of 'double insight' involving, ideally, both sides.

confidentiality and anonymity

In next reporting their studies, researchers face issues of confidentiality in general, and anonymity in particular. These issues may be stated in terms of information and communication theory. Most important, it is the ethical obligation of empirical researchers to preserve respondents' anonymity by *withholding* information. In quantitative studies, a potential abuse is the recycling and recombination of several datasets, so that individuals may be targeted in subsequent marketing campaigns. In qualitative research, harm is more likely to

result because readers of a report are able to identify a particular individual through a rich, contextual description. In both of these cases, the problem is not so much that the information is publicized. (Such problems arise when information is proprietary, typically for commercial reasons, and hence confidential.) The problem is that the information can be linked to its original source. In fact, neither qualitative nor quantitative methodologies depend for their explanatory value on such a link being made. From the researcher's perspective, the source is of interest not as a unique entity with biographical (and biological) characteristics, but as a social and cultural prototype, or as a representative specimen of a social segment.

From the sources' perspective, they have a right *not* to be associated with the information they offered in the context of research. Their right may be understood as a 'reverse copyright': the social contract of most media studies implies that research subjects speak as types, not tokens – as anybody, not somebody. The principles of reverse copyright, and of double insight, can be understood as responses to the ambivalent status of media and other social and cultural research between nomothetic and idiographic research – between laws and cases.◀

reverse copyright

Analysis box 16.2 outlines a set of guidelines for empirical student projects, which also have relevance for the planning of larger research programs.

The research community

Another set of issues is located along the second leg of the research triad, which connects researchers with their professional peers. As an abstract ideal, science calls for the complete dissemination of all potentially relevant information among the international community of scholars. As an interested social practice, research requires that individual scholars weigh this ideal against, for instance, anonymity requirements, but also against more material considerations, such as intellectual property

---

▶ idiographic and nomothetic research – Chapter 15, p. 255

ANALYSIS BOX 16.2 TEN RULES FOR EMPIRICAL STUDENT PROJECTS

1   First make sure to ascertain the rules and procedures in your social and cultural context and academic institution regarding *review* of research involving human subjects.

2   Always treat the people under study as *people*. They are neither things nor texts. A standard procedure for ensuring their rights and preventing harm is 'informed consent.'

3   Exercise *caution* and *concretion*. Be prepared to give up a question (or an entire study) if, in context, it violates the ethical, cultural, or personal limits of the people involved. Be prepared to explain concretely the relevance of any question to informants and others.

4   Practice *reflexivity*. The analysis of (cautiously collected and concrete) data begins in the empirical field. In qualitative as well as quantitative projects, supplementary evidence and notes will support both the respectful use of respondents' contributions and the explanatory value of later interpretations.

5   Safeguard the *anonymity* of people and the *confidentiality* of information throughout the research process.

6   Be honest about the *sources of ideas* informing a study and the *contributions of peers* in developing and conducting it.

7   A research report includes accounts both of *process and outcome,* and of *successes and failures* in each respect.

8   Two key requirements of a research report are a systematic *documentation* of evidence and an explication of the bases of theoretical *inference*.

9   Explore several different *publication formats*, including a means of *feedback* to the people contributing to a study.

10 Consider *what's next* – further research, the social relevance of findings, and the possible unanticipated consequences of the research.

---

rights and the protection of their own careers or their clients. The research community is itself a social system of checks and balances, privileges and sanctions. The chief issues in this area can be reviewed with reference to the different stages of the research process.

Especially in academic research, an early and decisive juncture is the approval of an empirical project by a national or institutional review board (IRB). In some countries, such approval is required before any study can be undertaken with human subjects, and officially on behalf of a university. While debated along the same lines as the informed consent procedure, an initial review process provides some assurance that gross ethical misconduct will

institutional review boards

not occur. Next, the basic criteria of ethical research include intellectual honesty in the presentation of the sources of ideas, a complete accounting of successes and failures in data collection and analysis, and a systematic documentation of evidence and the bases of theoretical inference (see Resnik 1998: 53–95). An overriding concern is the link between the contexts of discovery and justification, ◄ explicating and substantiating the relationship between research as process and as product.

At their conclusion, most research projects face a second review, typically in the form of a

---

► contexts of discovery and justification – Chapter 15, p. 258

peer review peer review – an anonymous (double-blind) evaluation by experienced researchers. This has been standard procedure in many fields since the mid-twentieth century, and determines whether a study will be published in major journals. Once again, peer review has been the object of criticism, for example, for favoring entrenched traditions. Still, the procedure presents itself as one of the least worst alternatives in the inevitably controversial enterprise of evaluating the standards of research projects. In a next step, access to the empirical datasets of other researchers is a way of keeping the research community critically reflective and in dialogue. An example of debates arising from such a secondary data analysis was Hirsch's (1980, 1981) questioning of Gerbner and colleagues' cultivation hypothesis.◄

Despite such specific conflicts, and despite stand-offs between qualitative and quantitative traditions, it may be concluded that media studies have entered the new millennium as a field in communication with itself. Certainly, *culture wars* what is sometimes denoted 'the culture wars' over the aesthetic ideals of traditional Western high art has continued to occupy and occasionally divide media studies. Moreover, 'the *science wars* science wars,' which flared up following Alan Sokal's hoax in a 1996 paper (reprinted in Sokal and Bricmont 1998) – the publication of a deliberately nonsensical article in a major journal in order to expose the lack of scientific rigor in postmodern cultural studies and related traditions – have been in evidence in some of the political and epistemological debates outlined in this chapter. In both types of 'wars,' however, some of the most vehement interventions have originated within the traditions in question. Morris (1990), for one, put cultural studies on trial for its banality, its solemn textual paraphrasing of the fact that cultures and societies are complex and contradictory phenomena. Ritchie (1999), for another, questioned the validity of much survey and other quantitative research because of its ambiguous concepts of 'probability.'

Intellectual conflict with social implications is part of the ongoing business of media and communication research. A recent international example centered on the work of Noelle-Neumann (1984) on 'the spiral of silence.' The point is that if people perceive their views to be in the minority, as represented, for instance, in the media, they are less likely to state these views. As a result, they participate in a circle or spiral that is potentially vicious for democracy. One of Noelle-Neumann's specific arguments has been that a predominance of left-wing views among German journalists and media has helped to silence right-wing political views in that country.

Noelle-Neumann herself has been quite explicit regarding her right-wing political position and her work as a strategy adviser for the German Christian Democratic Party. An acrimonious debate, however, began when Simpson (1996) drew attention to her apparent sympathies with the Nazi party during World War II. Most centrally, Simpson linked her conclusions in the present with a set of theoretical assumptions and methodologies which were originally developed for her research during the war. In a similarly fierce response, Kepplinger (1997) suggested, in essence, that the critique was *ad hominem*. His counter-argument was that the quality of methodologies as well as findings can be judged independently of their historical origins and contemporary applications.

This particular debate may be especially controversial and painful against the background of world war atrocities. However, the underlying questions are of a general nature. They concern the relations between knowledge, interest, and power. They have no simple answers, and will require continuous engagement in media studies.

THE END OF COMMUNICATION

The political and epistemological issues of 'doing research' may be summed up in a fantasy involving two key figures in American sociology: C. Wright Mills and Paul F. Lazarsfeld (cited in Gitlin 1978: 223). The first sentence of Mills's *The Sociological Imagination* (1959) reads, 'Nowadays men often feel that their private lives are a series of traps.' The fantasy imagines Lazarsfeld as replying: 'How many

► cultivation research – Chapter 9, p. 15

men, which men, how long have they felt this way, which aspects of their private lives bother them, do their public lives bother them, when do they feel free rather than trapped, what kinds of traps do they experience, etc., etc., etc.'

What these two different scientific and political temperaments arguably share, nevertheless, is a realization that research responds to contemporary concerns and realities. Mills's sweeping statements and Lazarsfeld's more mundane operationalizations both assumed that, by describing and interpreting social and cultural conditions, research can make a difference in social practice.

The orientation toward social action is something that research shares with communication. Both media research and mediated communication have ends, whether explicitly or implicitly. This realization is an important corrective to one of the most influential contemporary theorists of communication, Jürgen Habermas. Following his early historical work, Habermas's (1984 [1981]; 1987 [1981]) later theory of communication came to insist on an abstracted 'ideal speech situation' as the source of genuine human interaction and insight.

What Habermas came to neglect is the fact that all communication inevitably comes to an end (see further Jensen 1995: 185–191).

Political democracy is a case in point. As suggested by Schudson (1997), it is necessary to distinguish between 'sociable' and 'problem-solving' communication in modern societies. 'As far as democracy is concerned, the response to the familiar rhetorical question, "Can't we just talk about it?", should be: No' (Jensen 2001: 94). It is the conclusion of mediated communication and its regulated transformation into concerted social action that is the hallmark of democracy, not an interminable process of communication. The end of communication serves the ends of democracy.

A similar argument may be made for research about mediated communication. Research inevitably comes to an end. The end of the research process is the beginning of other social practices. By keeping itself aware of its origins, its uses, and its potential unanticipated consequences, media and communication research can finally claim the status of a scientifically mature and socially relevant field of study.

References

Aarseth, E. J. (1997) *Cybertext: Perspectives on Ergodic Literature*, Baltimore, MD: The Johns Hopkins University Press.

Abercrombie, N. and Longhurst, B. (1998) *Audiences: A Sociological Theory of Performance and Imagination,* London: Sage.

Abrams, M. H. *et al.* (1962) *The Norton Anthology of English Literature* (Vol. 2), New York: Norton.

Adams, W. C. (ed.) (1982) *Television Coverage of International Affairs*, Norwood, NJ: Ablex.

Adorno, T. and Horkheimer, M. (1977) 'The Culture Industry: Enlightenment as Mass Deception,' in J. Curran, M. Gurevitch, and J. Woollacott (eds), *Mass Communication and Society*, London: Edward Arnold [orig. publ. 1944].

Ahern, T. J. (1984) 'Determinants of Foreign Coverage in U.S. newspapers,' in R. Stevenson and D. L. Shaw (eds) *Foreign News and the New World Information Order*, Ames, IA: Iowa State University Press.

Alasuutari, P. (ed.) (1999) *Rethinking the Media Audience: The New Agenda*, London: Sage.

Alcoff, L. and Potter, E. (eds) (1993) *Feminist Epistemologies*, New York: Routledge.

Alexander, A., Owers, J., and Carveth, R. (eds) (1998) *Media Economics: Theory and Practice*, Mahwah, NJ: Lawrence Erlbaum Associates.

Alexander, J. and Giesen, B. (1987) 'From Reduction to Linkage: The Long View of the Micro–Macro Link,' in J. Alexander, B. Giesen, R. Münch, and N. Smelser (eds) *The Micro–Macro Link*, Berkeley: University of California Press.

Alexander, J., Boudon, R., and Cherkaoui, M. (eds) (1997) *The Classical Tradition in Sociology: The American Tradition*, London: Sage.

Allen, J., Livingstone, S., and Reiner, R. (1997) 'The Changing Generic Locations of Crime in Film: A Content Analysis of Film Synopses, 1945–1991,' *Journal of Communication*, 47 (4): 89–101.

Altenloh, E. (1913) *Zur Soziologie des Kino* [The Sociology of the Cinema], Leipzig: Spamersche Buchdruckerei.

Altheide, D. L. (1976) *Creating Reality*, Beverly Hills, CA: Sage.

Altheide, D. L. and Snow, R. P. (1979) *Media Logic*, Beverly Hills, CA: Sage.

Althusser, L. (1977) *For Marx*, London: Verso [orig. publ. 1965].

Altman, R. (1986) 'Television/Sound,' in Tania Modleski (ed.) *Studies in Entertainment*, Bloomington, IN: Indiana University Press.

Altman, R. (ed.) (1980) *Cinema/Sound, Yale French Studies*, 60.

Altman, R. (ed.) (1992) *Sound Theory/Sound Practice*, New York: Routledge.

Altman, R. (1999) *Film/Genre*, London: British Film Institute.

Alvarado, M. and Buscombe, E. (1978) *Hazell: The Making of a TV Series*, London: British Film Institute/Latimer New Dimensions.

Alvesson, M. and Sköldberg, K. (2000) *Reflexive Methodology: New Vistas for Qualitative Research*, London: Sage.

Anderson, B. (1991) *Imagined Communities: Reflections on the Origin and Spread of Nationalism* (2nd edn), London: Verso [orig. publ. 1983].

Anderson, D. R. and Burns, J. (1991) 'Paying Attention to Television,' in J. Bryant and D. Zillmann (eds) *Responding to the Screen: Reception and Reaction Processes*, Hillsdale, NJ: Lawrence Erlbaum Associates.

Anderson, J. (1996) *Communication Theory: Epistemological Foundations*, New York: The Guilford Press.

Andrén, G., Ericsson, L. O., Ohlsson, R., and Tännsjö, T. (1978) *Rhetoric and Ideology in Advertising*, Stockholm: Liber Förlag.

Andrew, J. D. (1976) *The Major Film Theories: An Introduction*, New York: Oxford University Press.

Ang, I. (1985) *Watching Dallas*, London: Methuen.

Ang, I. (1991) *Desperately Seeking the Audience*, London: Routledge.

Anon (1935–1958) *The History of the Times* (Vols 1–5), London.

Appadurai, A. (1996) *Modernity at Large: Cultural Dimensions of Globalization*, Minneapolis: University of Minnesota Press.

Archer, M., Bhaskar, R., Collier, A., Lawson, T., and Norrie, A. (eds) (1998) *Critical Realism: Essential Readings*, London: Routledge.

Aristotle (1994) *Categories and De Interpretatione* (trans. J. L. Ackrill), Oxford: Clarendon Press.

Arnheim, R. (1974) *Art and Visual Perception*, Berkeley: University of California Press.

Aron, D. (1998) 'Towards a Link Between Production and Reception in Television Documentary,' Paper presented at the 48th Annual Conference of the International Communication Association, Jerusalem.

Asante, M. K. (1992) 'The Escape into Hyperbole: Communication and Political Correctness,' *Journal of Communication*, 42(2): 141–147.

Asante, M. K. and Gudykunst, W. B. (eds) (1989) *Handbook of International and Intercultural Communication*, Newbury Park, CA: Sage.

Ashcroft, B., Griffiths, G., and Tiffin, H. (eds) (1995) *The Post-Colonial Studies Reader*, London: Routledge.

Atkinson, P. and Coffey, A. (1997) 'Analysing Documentary Realities,' in D. Silverman (ed.) *Qualitative Research: Theory, Method, and Practice*, London: Sage.

Austin, J. L. (1962) *How to Do Things with Words*, Oxford: Oxford University Press.

Babbie, E. (1990) *Survey Research Methods* (2nd edn), Belmont, CA: Wadsworth Publishing Company.

Bailey, K. D. (1994) *Methods of Social Research* (4th edn), New York: The Free Press.

Bakhtin, M. M. (1981) *The Dialogic Imagination*, Austin: University of Texas Press.

Bal, M. (1985). *Narratology: Introduction to the Theory of Narrative*, Toronto: University of Toronto Press [orig. publ. 1977].

Ball-Rokeach, S. (1985) 'The Origins of Individual Media–System Dependency,' *Communication Research*, 12(4): 485–510.

Bambach, C. R. (1995) *Heidegger, Dilthey and the Crisis of Historicism*, Ithaca, NY, and London: Cornell University Press.

Bandura, A. and Walters, R. (1963) *Social Learning and Personality Development*, New York: Holt, Rinehart & Winston.

Barbour, R. S. and Kitzinger, J. (eds) (1999) *Developing Focus Group Research: Politics, Theory, and Practice*, London: Sage.

Barker, M. and Brooks, K. (1998) *Knowing Audiences: Judge Dredd, Its Friends, Fans, and Foes*, Luton, Beds: University of Luton Press.

Barnhurst, K. G. and Wartella, E. (1998) 'Young Citizens, American TV Newscasts, and the Collective Memory,' *Critical Studies in Mass Communication*, 15(3): 279–305.

Barnouw, E. (1966–1970) *A History of Broadcasting in the United States* (Vols 1–3), New York: Oxford University Press.

Barnouw, E. (ed.) (1989) *International Encyclopedia of Communications*, New York: Oxford University Press.

Barrow, J. D. (1992) *Pi in the Sky: Counting, Thinking, and Being*, London: Penguin.

Barthes, R. (1964a) *Elements of Semiology*, New York: Hill & Wang, 1967 [English trans.]

Barthes, R. (1964b) 'Rhetoric of the Image,' in R. Barthes, *Image, Music, Text*, London: Fontana Press, 1984 [English trans.].

Barthes, R. (1966) 'Introduction to the Structural Analysis of Narratives,' in S. Sontag (ed.) *A Barthes Reader*, London: Jonathan Cape, 1982. [English trans.]

Barthes, R. (1970) *S/Z*, Paris: Seuil.

Barthes, R. (1973) *Mythologies*, London: Paladin [orig. publ. 1957].

Barthes, R. (1980) *Camera Lucida: Reflections on Photography*, New York: Hill & Wang [repr. in 1981].

Batscha, R. M. (1975) *Foreign Affairs News and the Broadcast Journalist*, New York: Praeger.

Baudrillard, J. (1988) *Selected Writings*, Cambridge: Polity Press.

Bauer, M. W. and Gaskell, G. (eds) (2000) *Qualitative Researching with Text, Image, and Sound: A Practical Handbook*, London: Sage.

Baym, N. K. (2000) *Tune In, Log On: Soaps, Fandom, and Online Community*, Thousand Oaks, CA: Sage.

Bazin, A. (1967–1971) *What Is Cinema?*, Berkeley: University of California Press.

Bechtel, R. B., Achelpohl, C., and Akers, R. (1972) 'Correlates between Observed Behaviours and Questionnaire Responses on Television Viewing,' in E. A. Rubinstein, G. A. Comstock, and J. P. Murray (eds) *Television and Social Behavior, Vol.4. Television in Day-to-Day Life: Patterns of Use*, Washington, DC: U.S. Government Printing Office.

Beck, U. (1999) *World Risk Society*, Cambridge: Polity Press.

Beck. U. (1994) 'The Reinvention of Politics: Towards a Theory of Reflexive Modernization,' in

Beck, U. *et al.* (1994) *Reflexive Modernization: Politics, Tradition and Aesthetics in the Modern Social Order*, Cambridge: Polity Press.

Beck, U., Giddens A., and Lash, S. (1994) *Reflexive Modernization. Politics, Tradition and Aesthetics in the Modern Social Order*, Cambridge: Polity Press.

Becker, H. (1982) *Art Worlds*, Berkeley: University of California Press.

Behlmer, R. (ed.) (1981) *Memo From David O. Selznick*, New York: Viking Press [reprint. orig. publ. 1972].

Bell, A. and Garrett, P. (eds) (1998) *Approaches to Media Discourse*, Oxford: Blackwell.

Bell, M. M. and Gardiner, M. (eds) (1998) *Bakhtin and the Human Sciences: No Last Words*, London: Sage.

Bellour, R. (1973) 'The Obvious and the Code,' in P. Rosen (ed.) *Narrative, Apparatus, Ideology: A Film Theory Reader*, New York: Columbia University Press, 1986.

Bellour, R. (1979) *L'analyse du film* [Film Analysis], Paris: Albatros.

Belson, W. A. (1967) *The Impact of Television*, London: Crosby Lockwood & Son.

Benedikt, M. (ed.) (1991) *Cyberspace: First Steps*, Cambridge, MA: MIT Press.

Benhurst, K. and Mutz, D. (1997) 'American Journalism and the Decline of Event-Centered Reporting,' *Journal of Communication*, 47(4): 27–53.

Beniger, J. R. (1986) *The Control Revolution*, Cambridge, MA: Harvard University Press.

Beniger, J. R. (1978) 'Media Content as Social Indicators: The Greenfield Index on Agenda-setting,' *Communication Research*, 5: 437–453.

Benjamin, W. (1977) 'The Work of Art in the Age of Mechanical Reproduction,' in J. Curran, M. Gurevitch, and J. Woollacott (eds) *Mass Communication and Society*, London: Edward Arnold [orig. publ. 1936].

Bennett, T. (1992) 'Putting Policy into Cultural Studies,' in L. Grossberg, C. Nelson, and P. Treichler (eds) *Cultural Studies*, New York: Routledge.

Bennett, T. (1995) *The Birth of the Museum*, London: Routledge.

Bennett, T. and Woollacott, J. (1987) *Bond and Beyond*, London: Methuen.

Berelson, B. (1949) 'What "Missing the Newspaper" Means,' in P. F. Lazarsfeld and F. M. Stanton (eds) *Communications Research 1948–9*, New York: Duell, Sloan, and Pearce.

Berelson, B. (1952) *Content Analysis in Communication Research*, Glencoe, IL: The Free Press.

Bergen, L. A. and Weaver, D. (1988) 'Job Satisfaction of Daily Newspaper Journalists and Organization Size,' *Newspaper Research Journal*, 9(2): 1–14.

Berger, C. R. and Chaffee, S. H. (eds) (1987) *Handbook of Communication Science*, Beverly Hills, CA: Sage.

Berger, J. (1972) *Ways of Seeing*, Harmondsworth: Penguin.

Berger, P. L. and Luckmann, T. (1966) *The Social Construction of Reality*, London: Allen Lane.

Berkowitz, L. (1964) 'The Effects of Observing Violence,' *Scientific American* 21: 35–41.

Berkowitz, L. and Geen, R. G. (1966) 'Film Violence and the Cue Properties of Available Targets,' *Journal of Personality and Social Psychology*, 3: 525–530.

Berman, M. (1982) *All That Is Solid Melts into Air: The Experience of Modernity*, London: Verso.

Bernard, H. R. (1995) *Research Methods in Anthropology: Qualitative and Quantitative Approaches*, Walnut Creek, CA: Alta Mira Press.

Bertaux, D. (ed.) (1981) *Biography and Society*, Beverly Hills, CA: Sage.

Bhabha, H. K. (1994) *The Location of Culture*, London: Routledge.

Bhaskar, R. (1979) *The Possibility of Naturalism*, Brighton: Harvester Press.

Biagioli, M. (ed.) (1999) *The Science Studies Reader*, New York: Routledge.

Billig, M. (1995) *Banal Nationalism*, London: Sage.

Biltereyst, D. (1991) 'Resisting American Hegemony: A Comparative Analysis of the Reception of Domestic and US Fiction,' *European Journal of Communication*, 6(4): 469–497.

Biltereyst, D. (2001) 'Global News Research and Complex Citizenship: Towards an Agenda for Research on Foreign/International News and Audiences,' in S. Hjarvard (ed.) *News in a Globalized Society*, Gothenburg: Nordicom.

Black, T. R. (1999) *Doing Quantitative Research in the Social Sciences*, London: Sage.

Blaikie, N. (1993) *Approaches to Social Enquiry*, Cambridge: Polity Press.

Blankenberg, N. (1999) 'In Search of a Real Freedom: *Ubuntu* and the Media,' *Critical Arts* 13(2): 42–65. Durban: University of Natal (www.und.ac.za/und/ccms).

Blumer, H. and Hauser, P. H. (1933) *Movies, Delinquency, and Crime*, New York: The Macmillan Company.

Blumler, J. G. (ed.) (1992) *Television and the Public Interest: Vulnerable Values in Western European Broadcasting*, London, and Newbury Park, CA: Sage.

Blumler, J. G. (1979) 'The Role of Theory in Uses and Gratifications Studies,' *Communication Research*, 6(1): 9–36.

Blumler, J. G. and Gurevitch, M. (1995) *The Crisis of Public Communication*, London: Routledge.

Blumler, J. G., McLeod, J. and Rosengren, K. E. (eds) (1992) *Comparatively Speaking: Communication and Culture across Space and Time*, Newbury Park, CA: Sage.

Boddy, W. (1990) *Fifties Television: The Industry and Its Critics*, Urbana, IL: University of Illinois Press.

Bogdanovich, P. (1967) *John Ford*, Berkeley: University of California Press.

Bolter, J. D. (1991) *Writing Space: The Computer, Hypertext, and the History of Writing*, Hillsdale, NJ: Lawrence Erlbaum.

Bolter, J. D. and Grusin, R. (1999) *Remediation: Understanding New Media*, Cambridge, MA: MIT Press.

Boorstin, D. (1961) *The Image: A Guide to Pseudo-Events in America*, New York: Atheneum.

Booth, W. (1961) *The Rhetoric of Fiction*, Chicago, IL: University of Chicago Press.

Borde, R. and Chaumeton, E. (1955) *Panorame du film noir americain* [Outline of the American 'Black' Film], Paris: Les Éditions de Minuit.

Borden, D. L. and Harvey, K. (eds) (1998) *The Electronic Grapevine: Rumor, Reputation, and Reporting in the New Online Environment*, Mahwah, NJ: Lawrence Erlbaum.

Bordewijk, J. and Kaam, B. (1986) 'Towards a New Classification of Tele-information Services,' *Intermedia*, 14(1): 16–21.

Bordwell, D. (1985a) *Narration in the Fiction Film*, London: Methuen.

Bordwell, D. (1985b) 'The Classical Hollywood Style, 1917–60,' in D. Bordwell *et al. The Classical Hollywood Cinema: Film Style and Mode of Production to 1960*, New York: Columbia University Press.

Bordwell, D. (1989) 'Historical Poetics of Cinema,' in R. Barton Palmer (ed.) *The Cinematic Text: Methods and Approaches*, New York: AMS Press.

Bordwell, D. and Carroll, N. (eds) (1996) *Post-Theory: Reconstructing Film Studies*, Madison, WI: University of Wisconsin Press.

Bordwell, D. and Thompson, K. (1997) *Film Art: An Introduction*, New York: McGraw-Hill.

Bordwell, D., Staiger, J., and Thompson, K. (1985) *The Classical Hollywood Cinema: Film Style and Mode of Production to 1960*, New York: Columbia University Press.

Borzekowski, D. L. G. and Robinson, T. N. (1999) 'Viewing the Viewers: Ten Video Cases of Children's Television Viewing Behaviors,' *Journal of Broadcasting and Electronic Media*, 43(4): 506–528.

Boudon, R., Cherkaoui, M., and Alexander, J. (eds) (1997) *The Classical Tradition in Sociology: The European Tradition*, London: Sage.

Bourdieu, P. (1977) *Outline of a Theory of Practice*, Cambridge: Cambridge University Press.

Bourdieu, P. (1984) *Distinction*, Cambridge, MA: Harvard University Press [orig. publ. 1979].

Bourdieu, P. (1988) *Homo Academicus*, Cambridge: Polity Press.

Bower, G. H. and Cirilo, R. K. (1985) 'Cognitive Psychology and Text Processing,' in T. A. van Dijk (ed.) *Handbook of Discourse Analysis* (Vol. 1), New York: Academic Press.

Bower, R. T. (1973) *Television and the Public*, New York: Holt, Rinehart & Winston.

Boyd-Barrett, O. (1980) *The International News Agencies*, London: Constable.

Boyd-Barrett, O. and Rantanen, T. (eds) (1999) *The Globalization of News*, London: Sage.

Boyd-Barrett, O. and Thussu, D. (1992) *Contra-flow in Global News. International and Regional News Exchange Mechanisms*, London: John Libbey.

Branigan, E. (1992) *Narrative Comprehension and Film*, London: Routledge.

Brannen, J. (ed.) (1992) *Mixing Methods: Qualitative and Quantitative Research*, Aldershot: Avebury.

Braudel, F. (1972, 1974) *The Mediterranean and Mediterranean World in the Age of Philip II* (Vols 1–2), New York: Harper & Row.

Braudel, F. (1980) *On History*, London: Weidenfeld & Nicolson.

Breed, W. (1955) 'Social Control in the Newsroom,' *Social Forces*, 33: 326–335.

Bremond, C. (1979) [1966] 'The Logic of Narrative Possibilities,' *New Literary History*, 11: 387–411.

Briggs, A. (1961–1995) *The History of Broadcasting in the United Kingdom* (Vols 1–5), Oxford: Oxford University Press.

Briggs, A. (1980) 'Problems and Possibilities in the Writing of Broadcasting History,' *Media, Culture and Society* 2(1): 5–13.

Brodkey, L. (1987) *Academic Writing as Social Practice*, Philadelphia, PA: Temple University Press.

Brooker, P. and Brooker, W. (eds) (1997) *Postmodern After-Images: A Reader in Film, Television, and Video*, London: Edward Arnold.

Brown, M. E. (1994) *Soap Opera and Women's Talk: The Pleasure of Resistance*, Thousand Oaks, CA: Sage.

Bruner, J. (1986) *Actual Minds, Possible Worlds*, Cambridge, MA: Harvard University Press.

Bruner, J. (1994) 'The Narrative Construction of "Reality,"' in M. Ammaniti and D. N. Stern (eds) *Psychoanalysis and Development*, New York: New York University Press.

Brunsdon, C. (1989) 'Text and Audience,' in E. Seiter, H. Borchers, G. Kreutzner, and E.-M. Warth (eds) *Remote Control: Television, Audiences, and Cultural Power*, London: Routledge.

Bryant, C. and Jary, D. (eds) (1991) *Giddens' Theory of Structuration: A Critical Appreciation*, London: Routledge.

Bryant, J., Carveth, R. A., and Brown, D. (1981) 'Television Viewing and Anxiety: An Experimental Examination,' *Journal of Communication*, 31: 106–119.

Bryce, J. (1966) 'The Nature of Public Opinion,' in B. Berelson and M. Janovitz (eds) *Reader in Public Opinion and Communication*, New York: The Free Press [orig. publ. 1900].

Bryman, A. and Burgess, R. G. (eds) (1999) *Qualitative Research*, London: Sage.

Bryman, A. and Cramer, D. (1997) *Quantitative Data Analysis with SPSS for Windows*, London: Routledge.

Bryson, N. (1991) 'Semiology and Visual Interpretation,' in N. Bryson *et al.* (eds) *Visual Theory: Painting and Interpretation*, Cambridge: Polity Press.

Buckingham, D. (ed.) (1993) *Reading Audiences: Young People and the Media*, Manchester: Manchester University Press.

Buckland, W. (2000) *The Cognitive Semiotics of Film*, Cambridge: Cambridge University Press.

Burgess, R. G. (1982) 'Keeping Field Notes,' in R. G. Burgess (ed.) *Field Research: A Sourcebook and Field Manual*, London: Unwin Hyman.

Burke, K. (1950) *A Rhetoric of Motives*, New York: Prentice-Hall.

Burke, K. (1957) *The Philosophy of Literary Form*, New York: Vintage.

Burke, P. (ed.) (1991) *New Perspectives on Historical Writing*, Cambridge: Polity Press.

Burke, P. (1992) *History and Social Theory*, Cambridge: Polity Press.

Burns, R. (ed.) (1995) *German Cultural Studies: An Introduction*, Oxford: Oxford University Press.

Butsch, R. (2000) *The Making of American Audiences: From Stage to Television, 1750–1990*, Cambridge: Cambridge University Press.

Butterworth, H. (1965) *The Whig Interpretation of History*, New York and London: W. W. Norton & Co.

Caldwell, J. T. (1995) *Televisuality: Style, Crisis, and Authority in American Television*, New Brunswick, NJ: Rutgers University Press.

Calhoun, C. (ed.) (1992) *Habermas and the Public Sphere*, Cambridge, MA: MIT Press.

Cantor, J. (1994) 'Fright Reactions to Mass Media,' in J. Bryant and D. Zillmann (eds) *Media Effects: Advances in Theory and Research*, Hillsdale, NJ: Lawrence Erlbaum Associates.

Cantor, M. (1971) *The Hollywood Television Producer: His Work and His Audience*, New York: The Free Press. Revised version 1988, New Brunswick, NJ: Transaction Books.

Cantril, H., Gaudet, H., and Herzog, H. (1940) *The Invasion From Mars*, Princeton, NJ: Princeton University Press.

Capella, J. N. (1996) 'Symposium: Biology and Communication,' *Journal of Communication*, 46(3): 4–84.

Carey, J. W. (1989) *Communication as Culture*, Boston, MA: Unwin Hyman.

Carey, J. W. and Kreiling, A. W. (1974) 'Popular Culture and Uses and Gratifications: Notes Toward an Accommodation,' in J. G. Blumler and E. Katz (eds) *The Uses of Mass Communications*, Beverly Hills, CA: Sage.

Carringer, R. (1996) *The Making of Citizen Kane*, Berkeley: University of California Press.

Castells, M. (1996) *The Rise of the Network Society*, Oxford: Blackwell.

Cater, D. (1959) *The Fourth Branch of Government*, Boston, MA: Houghton-Mifflin.

Cayrol, R. and Mercier, A. (1998) 'Political Communication Scholarship in France,' *Political Communication*, 15: 383–421.

Centerwall, B. S. (1989) 'Exposure to Television as a Cause of Violence,' *Public Communication and Behaviour*, 2: 1–58.

Chaffee, S. H. and Hochheimer, J. (1985) 'The Beginnings of Political Communication Research in the United States: Origins of the "Limited Effects" Model,' in E. M. Rogers and F. Balle (eds) *The Media Revolution in America and Western Europe*, Norwood, NJ: Ablex.

Chamberlayne, P., Bornat, J. and Wengraf, T. (eds) (2000) *The Turn to Biographical Methods in Social Science*, London: Routledge.

Charlton, T. (1997) 'The Inception of Broadcast Television: A Naturalistic Study of Television's Effects,' in T. Charlton and K. David (eds) *Elusive Links: Television, Video Games and Children's Behaviour*, Tewkesbury: Park Published Papers.

Chatman, S. (1989) *Story and Discourse: Narrative Structure in Fiction and Film*, Ithaca, NY: Cornell University Press (5th paperback edn) [orig. publ. 1978].

Chatman, S. (1990) *Coming to Terms: The Rhetoric of Narrative in Fiction and Film*, Ithaca, NY: Cornell University Press.

Chion, M. (1985) *Le son au cinéma* [Sound in Cinema], Paris: Éditions de l'Étoile.

Chion, M. (1988) *La toile trouée* [The Perforated Screen], Paris: Seuil.

Chion, M. (1994) *Audio-vision. Sound on Screen*, New York: Columbia University Press [orig. publ. 1990].

Chion, M. (1995) *La musique au cinéma* [Music in Cinema], Paris: Fayard.

Chion, M. (1998) *Le son* [Sound], Paris: Nathan.

Chion, M. (1999) *The Voice in Cinema*, New York: Columbia University Press [orig. publ. 1982].

Chomsky, D. (1999) 'The Mechanisms of Management Control at the *New York Times*,' *Media, Culture and Society*, 21(5): 579–599.

Chomsky, N. (1965) *Aspects of the Theory of Syntax*, Cambridge, MA: MIT Press.

Christians, C. and Traber, M. (eds) (1997) *Communication Ethics and Universal Values*, Thousand Oaks, CA: Sage.

Clark, A. (1983) *Raymond Chandler in Hollywood*, New York: Proteus.

Clarke, D. S. (1990) *Sources of Semiotic*, Carbondale: Southern Illinois University Press.

Clifford, J. and Marcus, C. E. (eds) (1986) *Writing Culture: The Poetics and Politics of Ethnography*, Berkeley: University of California Press.

Coakley, J. (ed.) (2000) *Handbook of Sports Studies*, London: Sage.

Cohen, A., Levy, M., Roeh, I., and Gurevitch, M. (1996) *Global Newsrooms, Local Audiences. A Study of the Eurovision News Exchange*, London: John Libbey.

Cohen, B. (1963) *The Press and Foreign Policy*, Princeton, NJ: Princeton University Press.

Collins, C. (1997) 'Viewer Letters as Audience Research: The Case of Murphy Brown,' *Journal of Broadcasting and Electronic Media*, 41(1): 109–131.

Comstock, G. A. (1978) *Television and Human Behavior*, New York: Columbia University Press.

Comstock, G. A. (1998) 'Television Research: Past Problems and Present Issues,' in J. K. Asamen and G. L. Berry (eds) *Research Paradigms, Television, and Social Behavior*, Thousand Oaks, CA: Sage.

Comstock, G. A., Murray, J. P., and Rubinstein, E. A. (eds) (1971) *Television and Social Behavior*, Washington, DC: Government Printing Office.

Conant, J. and Haugeland, J. (eds) (2000) *Thomas S. Kuhn: The Road Since Structure*, New York: Basic Books.

Converse, J. M. (1987) *Survey Research in the United States: Roots and Emergence, 1890–1960*, Berkeley: University of California Press.

Conway, J. C. and Rubin, A. M. (1991) 'Psychological Predictors of Television Viewing Motivation,' *Communication Research*, 18(4): 443–463.

Cook, N. (1998) *Analysing Musical Multimedia*, Oxford: Oxford University Press.

Cook, P. (1999) *The Cinema Book*, London: British Film Institute.

Cook, T. D., Kendziersky, D. A., and Thomas, S. A. (1983) 'The Implicit Assumptions of Television Research: An Analysis of the 1982 NIMH Report on Television and Behaviour,' *Public Opinion Quarterly*, 47: 161–201.

Cooley, C. H. (1894) 'The Theory of Transportation,' *Publications of the American Economic Association*, 9(3): 221–370.

Cooper, B. (1999) 'The Relevancy and Gender Identity in Spectators' Interpretations of *Thelma and Louise*,' *Critical Studies in Mass Communication*, 16(1): 20–41.

Corley, K. M. and Kaufer, D. S. (1993) 'Semantic Connectivity: An Approach for Analyzing Symbols in Semantic Networks,' *Communication Theory*, 3(3): 183–213.

Corner, J. (1991) 'Meaning, Genre, and Context: The Problematics of "Public Knowledge" in the New Audience Studies,' in J. Curran and M. Gurevitch (eds) *Mass Media and Society*, London: Edward Arnold.

Cottle, S. (2000) 'New(s) Times: Towards a "Second Wave" of News Ethnography,' *Communications: The European Journal of Communication Research*, 25(1): 19–41.

Coulthard, M. (1985) *An Introduction of Discourse Analysis* (2nd edn), London: Longman.

Cowan, G. (1979) *See No Evil: The Backstage Battle Over Sex and Violence on Television*, New York: Simon & Schuster.

Coward, R. and Ellis, J. (1977) *Language and Materialism*, London: Routledge & Kegan Paul.

Creswell, J. W. (1994) *Research Design: Qualitative and Quantitative Approaches*, Thousand Oaks, CA: Sage.

Crisell, A. (1994) *Understanding Radio* (2nd edn), London: Routledge.

Croteau, D. and Hoynes, W. (2001) *The Business of Media: Corporate Media and the Public Interest*, Thousand Oaks, CA: Pine Forge Press.

Crouse, T. (1973) *The Boys on the Bus*, New York: Random House.

Crow, B. K. (1986) 'Conversational Pragmatics in Television Talk: The Discourse of "Good Sex,"' *Media, Culture and Society*, 8: 457–444.

Cunningham, S. (1988) 'Kennedy-Miller: "House Style" in Australian Television,' in S. Dermody and E. Jacka (eds) *The Imaginary Industry: Australian Film in the late '80s*, North Ryde, Australia: Australian Film, Television and Radio School.

Curran, J. (ed.) (2000) *Media Organizations in Society*, London: Edward Arnold.

Curran, J. and Seaton, J. (1997) *Power Without Responsibility: The Press and Broadcasting in Britain* (5th edn), London: Routledge.

Curtin, M. (1996) 'On Edge: Culture Industries in the Neo-network Era,' in R. Ohmann, G. Averill, M. Curtin, D. Shumway, and E. Traube (eds) *Making and Selling Culture*, Hanover, NH: Wesleyan University Press.

Curtin, M. (1999) 'Feminine Desire in the Age of Satellite Television,' *Journal of Communication*, 49(2): 55–70.

D'Acci, J. (1994) *Defining Women: The Case of Cagney and Lacey*, Chapel Hill: University of North Carolina Press.

Dahl, H. F. (1976) 'The Art of Writing Broadcasting History,' *Gazette. International Journal for Mass Communication Studies*, 3: 130–137.

Dahl. H. F. (1994) 'The Pursuit of Media History,' *Media Culture & Society*, 16(4): 551–564.

Danto, A. C. (1965) *Analytical Philosophy of History*, Cambridge: Cambridge University Press.

Dayan, D. and Katz, E. (1992) *Media Events*, Cambridge, MA: Harvard University Press.

Day-Lewis, S. (1989) *One Day in the Life of Television*, London: Grafton.

Deacon, D., Fenton, N., and Bryman, A. (1999) 'From Inception to Reception: The Natural History of a News Item,' *Media, Culture & Society*, 21: 5–31.

Deacon, D., Pickering, M., Golding, P., and Murdock, G. (1999) *Researching Communications: A Practical Guide to Methods in Media and Cultural Analysis*, London: Edward Arnold.

Dearing, J. and Rogers, E. M. (1996) *Agenda-Setting*, Thousand Oaks, CA: Sage.

DeFleur, M. L. (1964) 'Occupational Roles as Portrayed on Television,' *Public Opinion Quarterly*, 28: 57–74.

DeFleur, M. L. (1975) *Theories of Mass Communication*, New York: David McKay.

DeFleur, M. L. and Larsen, O. N. (1987) *The Flow of Information*, New Brunswick, NJ: Transaction Press [orig. publ. 1958].

Delia, J. (1987) 'Communication Research: A History,' in C. R. Berger and S. H. Chaffee (eds) *Handbook of Communication Science*, Newbury Park, CA: Sage.

Demers, D. P. and Wackman, D. B. (1988) 'Effect of Chain Ownership on Newspaper Management Goals,' *Newspaper Research Journal*, 9(2): 59–68.

Dennis, E. E. and Wartella, E. (eds) (1996) *American Communication Research: The Remembered History*, Mahwah, NJ: Lawrence Erlbaum.

Denton, R. E. (ed.) (1993) *The Media and the Persian Gulf War*, Westport, CT: Praeger.

Denzin, N. (1970) *The Research Act: A Theoretical Introduction to Sociological Methods*, Englewood Cliffs, NJ: Prentice-Hall.

Denzin, N. (1989) *The Research Act: A Theoretical Introduction to Sociological Methods* (3rd edn), Englewood Cliffs, NJ: Prentice-Hall.

Denzin, N. and Lincoln, Y. S. (eds) (2000) *Handbook of Qualitative Research* (2nd edn), Thousand Oaks, CA: Sage.

Derrida, J. (1976) *Of Grammatology*, Baltimore, MD: Johns Hopkins University Press [orig. publ. 1967].

Dewey, J. (1926) *The Public and its Problems*, London: George Allen & Unwin.

Dichter, E. (1947) 'Psychology in Market Research,' *Harvard Business Review*, 25(4): 432–443.

Dickey, S. (1993) *Cinema and the Urban Poor in South India*, Cambridge: Cambridge University Press.

Dissanayake, W. (1988a) 'The Need for Asian Approaches to Communication,' in W. Dissanayake (ed.) *Communication Theory: The Asian Perspective*, Singapore: Asian Mass Communication Research and Information Center.

Dissanayake, W. (ed.) (1988b) *Communication Theory: The Asian Perspective*, Singapore: Asian Mass Communication Research and Information Center.

Doherty, T. (1999) *Pre-code Hollywood: Sex, Immorality, and Insurrection in American Cinema*, New York: Columbia University Press.

Donnerstein, E. and Berkowitz, L. (1981) 'Victim Reactions in Aggressive Erotic Films as a Factor in Violence against Women,' *Journal of Personality and Social Psychology*, 36: 180–188.

Donohue, G., Olien, C., and Tichenor, P. (1987) 'Media Access and Knowledge Gaps,' *Critical Studies in Mass Communication*, 4(1): 87–92.

Donohue, G., Tichenor, P., and Olien, C. (1975) 'Mass Media and the Knowledge Gap,' *Communication Research*, 2: 3–23.

Dorfman, A. and Mattelart, A. (1975) *How to Read Donald Duck: Imperialist Ideology in the Disney Comic*, New York: International General [orig. publ. 1971].

Douglas, M. (1987) *How Institutions Think*, London: Routledge & Kegan Paul.

Douglas, M. (1996) *Thought Styles: Critical Essays on Good Taste*, London: Sage.

Douglas, M. (1997) 'The Depoliticization of Risk,' in R. Ellis and M. Thompson (eds) *Culture Matters: Essays in Honour of Aaron Wildavsky*, Boulder, CO: Westview Press.

Downey, G. L. (1998) *The Machine in Me: An Anthropologist Sits Among Computer Engineers*, New York: Routledge.

Downing, J. D. H. (2000) *Radical Media: Rebellious Communication and Social Movements*, Thousand Oaks, CA: Sage.

Doyle, B. (1989) *English and Englishness*, London: Routledge.

Dray, W. (1957) *Laws and Explanation in History*, London: Oxford University Press.

Drew, P. and Heritage, J. (1992) 'Analyzing Talk at Work: An Introduction,' in P. Drew and J. Heritage (eds) *Talk at Work: Interaction in Institutional Settings*, Cambridge: Cambridge University Press.

Drotner, K. (1988) *English Children and their Magazines 1751–1945*, Yale, CT: Yale University Press.

Drotner, K. (1994) 'Ethnographic Enigmas: "The Everyday" in Recent Media Studies,' *Cultural Studies*, 8(2): 341–357.

Drotner, K. (1996) 'Less Is More: Media Ethnography and Its Limits,' in P. I. Crawford and S. B. Hafsteinsson (eds) *The Construction of the Viewer*, Højbjerg, Denmark: Intervention Press.

Drotner, K., Jensen, K. B., Poulsen, I. and Schrøder, K. C. (1996) *Medier og kultur* [Media and culture], Copenhagen, Denmark: Borgen.

Duke, L. (2000) 'Black in a Blonde World: Race and Girls' Interpretations of the Feminine Ideal in Teen Magazines,' *Journalism and Mass Communication Quarterly*, 77(2): 367–392.

Dunaway, D. K. and Baum, W. K. (eds) (1996) *Oral History: An Interdisciplinary Anthology* (2nd edn), Walnut Creek, CA: Alta Mira Press.

Duncan, H. D. (1968) *Symbols in Society*, New York: Oxford University Press.

During, S. (ed.) (1999) *The Cultural Studies Reader* (2nd edn), London: Routledge.

Eagleton, T. (1983) *Literary Theory: An Introduction*, Minneapolis: Minnesota University Press.

Eastman, S. T. (1998) 'Programming Theory under Stress: The Active Industry and the Active Audience,' in M. Roloff (ed.) *Communication Yearbook* (Vol. 21), Thousand Oaks, CA: Sage.

Eco, U. (1968) *La struttura assente. Introduzione alla ricerca semiologica* [The Absent Structure. Introduction to Semiological Research], Milan: Bompiani.

Eco, U. (1976) *A Theory of Semiotics*, Bloomington: Indiana University Press [orig. publ. 1968, revised 1975].

Eco, U. (1984) *Semiotics and the Philosophy of Language*, London: Macmillan.

Eco, U. (1987) 'Narrative Structures in Fleming,' in U. Eco (ed.) *The Role of the Reader*, London: Hutchinson [orig. publ. 1965].

Edelman, M. (1971) *Politics as Symbolic Action*, Chicago, IL: Markham.

Edwards, D. and Potter, J. (1992) *Discursive Psychology*, London: Sage.

Eisenstein, E. L. (1979) *The Printing Press as an Agent of Change: Communication and Cultural Transformation in Early Modern Europe* (Vols 1–2), Cambridge: Cambridge University Press.

Eisler, H. and Adorno, T. W. (1947) *Composing for the Films*, London: Dobson.

Ellen, R. F. (ed.) (1984) *Ethnographic Research: A Guide to General Conduct*, London: Academic Press.

Elliott, P. (1972) *The Making of a Television Series*, London: Constable.

Elliott, P. (1974) 'Uses and Gratifications Research: A Critique and a Sociological Alternative,' in J. G. Blumler and E. Katz (eds) *The Uses of Mass Communications*, Beverly Hills, CA: Sage.

Ellis, J. (1975) 'Made at Ealing,' *Screen*, 16(1): 78–127.

Ellis, J. (1982) *Visible Fictions*, London: Routledge & Kegan Paul.

Emery, M. and Emery, E. (1988) *The Press in America*, Englewood Cliffs, NJ: Prentice-Hall.

Emmison, M. and Smith, P. (2000) *Researching the Visual: Images, Objects, Contexts, and Interactions in Social and Cultural Inquiry*, London: Sage.

Enzensberger, H. M. (1972) 'Constituents of a Theory of the Media,' in D. McQuail (ed.) *Sociology of Mass Communications*, Harmondsworth: Penguin [orig. publ. 1970].

Epstein, E. J. (1973) *News from Nowhere*, New York: Random House.

Ericson, R. V., Baranak, P. M., and Chan, J. B. L. (1987) *Visualizing Deviance: A Study of News Organization*, Toronto: University of Toronto Press.

Ericson, R. V., Baranek, P. M., and Chan, J. B. L. (1991) *Representing Order. Crime, Law and Justice in the News Media*, Milton Keynes: Open University Press.

Erlich, V. (1955) *Russian Formalism: History, Doctrine*, The Hague, Mouton.

Ettema, J. S. and Whitney, D. C. (eds) (1994) *Audiencemaking: How the Media Create the Audience*, Thousand Oaks, CA: Sage.

Evans, J. and Hall, S. (eds) (1999) *Visual Culture: The Reader*, London: Sage.

Eysenck, M. W. and Keane, M. T. (1995) *Cognitive Psychology: A Student's Handbook* (3rd edn), Hove, Sussex: Psychology Press.

Fairclough, N. (1992) *Discourse and Social Change*, Cambridge: Polity Press.

Fairclough, N. (1993) 'Critical Discourse Analysis and the Marketization of Public Discourse: the Universities,' *Discourse & Society*, 4(2): 133–168.

Fairclough, N. (1995) *Media Discourse*, London: Edward Arnold.

Fairclough, N. (1998) 'Political Discourse in the Media: An Analytical Framework,' in A. Bell and P. Garrett (eds) *Approaches to Media Discourse*, Oxford: Blackwell.

Fallon, D. (1980) *The German University: A Heroic Ideal in Conflict with the Modern World*, Boulder: Colorado Associated University Press.

Farrell, T. B. (1987) 'Beyond Science: Humanistic Contributions to Communication Theory,' in C. R. Berger and S. H. Chaffee (eds) *Handbook of Communication Science*, Newbury Park, CA: Sage.

Fenby, J. (1986) *The International News Services*, New York: Schocken Books.

Ferguson, M. and Golding, P. (eds) (1997) *Cultural Studies in Question*, London: Sage.

Feshbach, S. (1961) 'The Stimulating vs Cathartic Effects of a Vicarious Aggressive Experience,' *Journal of Abnormal and Social Psychology*, 63: 381–385.

Feuer, J., Kerr, P. and Vahamagi, T. (eds) (1984) *MTM: 'Quality Television*,' London: British Film Institute.

Fielding, N. G. and Lee, R. M. (1998) *Computer Analysis and Qualitative Research*, London: Sage.

Filmer P., Philipson, M., Silverman, D. and Walsh, D. (1972) *New Directions in Sociological Theory*, London: Collier-Macmillan.

Findahl, O. (1985) 'Some Characteristics of News Memory and Comprehension,' *Journal of Broadcasting and Electronic Media*, 29(4): 379–396.

Fink, A. (1995a) *The Survey Handbook*, Thousand Oaks, CA: Sage.

Fink, A. (1995b) *How To Ask Survey Questions*, Thousand Oaks, CA: Sage.

Fink, E. J. and Gantz, W. (1996) 'A Content Analysis of Three Mass Communication Research Traditions: Social Science, Interpretive Studies, and Critical Analysis,' *Journalism and Mass Communication Quarterly*, 73(1): 114–134.

Finnemann, N. O. (1999) *Thought, Sign, and Machine: The Computer Reconsidered*. Available: http://www.hum.au.dk/ckulturf/DOCS/PUB/nof/TSM [accessed December 15, 1999].

Fish, S. (1979) *Is There a Text in This Class? The Authority of Interpretive Communities*, Cambridge, MA: Harvard University Press.

Fisher, W. A. and Grenier, G. (1994) 'Violent Pornography, Antiwomen Thoughts, and Antiwomen Acts: In Search of Reliable Effects,' *Journal of Sex Research* 31(1): 23–38.

Fishman, M. (1980) *Manufacturing the News*, Austin: University of Texas Press.

Fiske, J. (1987) *Television Culture*, London: Methuen.

Fiske, J. (1990) *Introduction to Communication Studies*, London: Routledge.

Fiske, J. and Hartley, J. (1978) *Reading Television*, London: Methuen.

Flick, U. (1998) *An Introduction to Qualitative Research*, London: Sage.

Flitterman-Lewis, S. (1983) 'The Real Soap Operas,' in E. A. Kaplan (ed.) *Regarding Television: Critical Approaches – An Anthology*, Frederick, MD: University Publications of America.

Flourney, D. M. and Stewart, R. K. (1997) *CNN. Making News in the Global Market*, Luton, Beds: University of Luton Press.

Forbes, J. and Kelly, M. (eds) (1995) *French Cultural Studies: An Introduction*, Oxford: Oxford University Press.

Foster, H. (1985) *Postmodern Culture*, London: Pluto Press.

Foucault, M. (1972) *The Archaeology of Knowledge*, London: Tavistock.

Fowler, R. (1985) 'Power,' in T. van Dijk (ed.) *Handbook of Discourse Analysis* (Vol. 4), London: Academic Press.

Fowler, R., Hodge, B., Kress, G., and Trew, T. (eds) (1979) *Language and Control*, London: Routledge & Kegan Paul.

Fredin, E. S., Monnett, T. H., and Kosicki, G. M. (1994) 'Knowledge Gaps, Social Locators, and Media Schemata: Gaps, Reverse Gaps, and Gaps of Disaffection,' *Journalism and Mass Communication Quarterly*, 71(1): 176–190.

Furnham, A. (1988) *Lay Theories: Everyday Understanding of Problems in the Social Sciences*, Oxford: Pergamon Press.

Furnham, A. and Schofield, I. (1986) 'Sex-role Stereotyping in British Radio Advertisements,' *British Journal of Social Psychology*, 25: 165–171.

Furnham, A. and Skae, E. (1997) 'Changes in the Stereotypical Portrayal of Men and Women in British Television Advertisements,' *European Psychologist*, 2: 44–51.

Furnham, A., Abramsky, S., and Gunter, B. (1997) 'A Cross-cultural Content Analysis of Children's Television Advertisements,' *Sex Roles*, 37(l/2): 91–99.

Gadamer, H.-G. (1975) *Truth and Method*, New York: The Seabury Press [(orig. publ. 1960].

Galtung J. (1971) 'A structural theory of imperialism,' *Journal of Peace Research*, 8: 81–147.

Galtung, J. (1973) 'Galtung-Ruge Revisited' (with a transcription of the subsequent debate at the conference 'Nordisk konferens om konflikt – och massmediaforskning' [Nordic conference on conflict and mass media research]), Department of History, Lund University, Sweden, 6–7 April, unpublished.

Galtung, J. and Ruge, M. H. (1962) *Presentasjonen af utenriksnyheter. En undersøkelse av nyhetsmeldingene fra Cuba og Kongo juli 1960* [The Presentation of Foreign News. An Analysis of News Reports from Cuba and Congo, July 1960], Report no. 14–1, Avdeling for Konflikt- og Fredsforskning, Oslo, Norway.

Galtung, J. and Ruge, M. H. (1965) 'The structure of foreign news,' *Journal of Peace Research*, 2: 64–91.

Gamson, W. A. (1992) *Talking Politics*, New York: Cambridge University Press.

Gans, H. J. (1957) 'The Creator–Audience Relationship in the Mass Media: An Analysis of Movie Making,' in B. Rosenberg and D. White (eds) *Mass Culture: The Popular Arts in America*, New York: Free Press.

Gans, H. J. (1979) *Deciding What's News*, New York: Vintage.

Gardner, G. (1987) *The Censorship Papers: Movie Censorship Letters From the Hays Office: 1934–1968*, New York: Dodd Mead.

Gardner, H. (1985) *The Mind's New Science: A History of the Cognitive Revolution*, New York: Basic Books.

Garfinkel, H. (1967) *Studies in Ethnomethodology*, Englewood Cliffs, NJ: Prentice-Hall.

Garnham, N. and Locksley, G. (1991) 'The Economics of Broadcasting,' in J. G. Blumler and T. J. Nossiter (eds) *Broadcasting Finance in Transition: A Comparative Handbook*, New York: Oxford University Press.

Garrison, B. (2000) 'Journalists' Perceptions of On-line Information-Gathering Problems,' *Journalism and Mass Communication Quarterly*, 77(3): 500–514.

Gauntlett, D. and Hill, A. (1999) *TV Living: Television, Culture, and Everyday Life*, London: Routledge.

Gay, P. du, Hall, S., Janes, L., Mackay, H., and Negus, K. (1997) *Doing Cultural Studies: The Story of the Sony Walkman*, London: Sage.

Gaziano, C. (1997) 'Forecast 2000: Widening Knowledge Gaps,' *Journalism and Mass Communication Quarterly*, 74(2): 237–264.

Gee, J. P., Michaels, S. and O'Connor, M. C. (1992) 'Discourse Analysis,' in M. D. LeCompte, W. L. Millroy, and J. Preissle (eds) *The Handbook of Qualitative Research in Education*, San Diego, CA: Academic Press.

Geertz, C. (1973) 'Thick Description,' in *The Interpretation of Cultures*, New York: Basic Books.

Gelder, K. and Thornton, S. (eds) (1997) *The Subcultures Reader*, London: Routledge.

Genette, G. (1980) *Narrative Discourse*, Oxford: Basil Blackwell [orig. publ. 1972].

Genette, G. (1997) *Palimpsests: Literature in the Second Degree*, Lincoln: University of Nebraska Press [orig. publ. 1982].

Genova, B. K. L. and Greenberg, B. S. (1979) 'Interests in News and the Knowledge Gap,' *Public Opinion Quarterly*, 43(1): 79–91.

Gerbner, G. (1972) 'Violence in Television Drama: Trends and Symbolic Functions,' in G. A. Comstock and E. A. Rubinstein (eds) *Television and Social Behaviour, Vol. 1: Media Content and Control*, Washington, DC: U.S. Government Printing Office.

Gerbner, G. and Gross, L. (1976) 'Living with Television: The Violence Profile,' *Journal of Communication*, 26(3): 173–199.

Gerbner, G., Gross, L., Morgan, M., and Signorielli, N. (1986) 'Living with Television: The Dynamics of the Cultivation Process,' in J. Bryant and D. Zillmann (eds) *Perspectives on Media Effects*, Hillsdale, NJ: Lawrence Erlbaum.

Gerbner, G., Gross, L., Morgan, M., Signorielli, N., and Jackson-Beeck, M. (1979) 'The Demonstration of Power: Violence Profile No. 10,' *Journal of Communication*, 29: 177–196.

Gerbner, G., Gross, L., Eleey, M. F., Jackson-Beeck, M., Jeffries-Fox, S., and Signorielli, N. (1977) 'Television Violence Profile No. 8: The Highlights,' *Journal of Communication*, 27: 171–180.

Gerth, H. and Mills, C. W. (1954) *Character and Social Structure: The Psychology of Social Institutions*, London: Routledge & Kegan Paul.

Giddens, A. (1984) *The Constitution of Society*, Berkeley: University of California Press.

Giddens, A. (1990) *The Consequences of Modernity*, Cambridge: Polity Press.

Giddens, A. (1991) *Modernity and Self-Identity*, Cambridge: Polity Press.

Giddens, A. (1994) 'Living in a Post-traditional Society,' in U. Beck *et al.* (eds) *Reflexive Modernization: Politics, Tradition, and Aesthetics in the Modern Social Order*, Cambridge: Polity Press.

Gilbert, G. N. and Mulkay, M. (1984) *Opening Pandora's Box: A Sociological Analysis of Scientists' Discourse*, Cambridge: Cambridge University Press.

Gillespie, M. (1995) *Television, Ethnicity, and Cultural Change*, London: Routledge.

Ginneken, J. van (1998) *Understanding Global News: A Critical Introduction,* London: Sage.

Ginzburg, C. (1989) 'Clues: Roots for an Evidential Paradigm,' in C. Ginzburg (ed.) *Clues, Myths, and the Historical Method*, Baltimore, MD: Johns Hopkins University Press.

Gitlin, T. (1978) 'Media Sociology: The Dominant Paradigm,' *Theory and Society*, 6: 205–253.

Gitlin, T. (1979) 'Prime Time Ideology,' *Social Problems*, 26: 251–266.

Gitlin, T. (1980) *The Whole World Is Watching*, Berkeley: University of California Press.

Gitlin, T. (1983) *Inside Prime Time*, New York: Pantheon.

Gitlin, T. (1997) 'The Anti-political Populism of Cultural Studies,' in M. Ferguson and P. Golding (eds) *Cultural Studies in Question*, London: Sage.

Glaser, B. G. (1992) *Basics of Grounded Theory Analysis: Emergence vs. Forcing*, Mill Valley, CA: Sociology Press.

Glaser, B. G. and Strauss, A. L. (1967) *The Discovery of Grounded Theory: Strategies for Qualitative Research*, Chicago: Aldine.

Glasgow University Media Group (1976) *Bad News*, London: Routledge & Kegan Paul.

Glasgow University Media Group (1980) *More Bad News*, London: Routledge.

Glenn, T. C., Sallot, L. M. and Curtin, P. A. (1997) 'Public Relations and the Production of News,' *Communication Yearbook*, 20: 111–115.

Glessing, R. J. (1970) *The Underground Press in America*, Bloomington: Indiana University Press.

Goffman, E. (1974) *Frame Analysis*, Cambridge, MA: Harvard University Press.

Goffman, E. (1979) *Gender Advertisements*, London: Macmillan [orig. publ. 1976].

Goldhaber, G. M. and Barnett, G. A. (eds) (1988) *Handbook of Organizational Communication*, Norwood, NJ: Ablex.

Golding, P. and Elliott, P. (1979) *Making the News*, London: Longman.

Golding, P. and Harris, P. (eds) (1997) *Beyond Cultural Imperialism*, London: Sage.

Golding, P. and Middleton, S. (1982) *Images of Welfare*, Oxford: Martin Robertson.

Golding, P. and Murdock, G. (1991) 'Culture, Communication, and Political Economy,' in J. Curran and M. Gurevitch (eds) *Mass Media and Society*, London: Edward Arnold.

Gombrich, E. H. (1960) *Art and Illusion*, Princeton, NJ: Princeton University Press.

Gomery, D. (1992) *Shared Pleasures: A History of Movie Presentation in the United States*, Madison: University of Wisconsin Press.

Gomm, R., Hammersley, M. and Foster, P. (eds) (2000) *Case Study Method: Key Issues, Key Texts*, London: Sage.

Goode, W. J. and Hatt, P. K. (1952) *Methods in Social Research*, New York: McGraw-Hill.

Goody, J. (ed.) (1968) *Literacy in Traditional Societies*, Cambridge: Cambridge University Press.

Goody, J. (1987) *The Interface between the Written and the Oral*, Cambridge: Cambridge University Press.

Goody, J. (2000) *The Power of the Written Tradition*, Washington, DC: Smithsonian Institution Press.

Goody, J. and Watt, I. (1963) 'The Consequences of Literacy,' *Comparative Studies in Society and History*, 5: 304–345.

Gorbman, C. (1987) *Unheard Melodies. Narrative Film Music*, Bloomington and Indianapolis: Indiana University Press.

Gorden, R. L. (1969) *Interviewing: Strategy, Techniques, and Tactics*, Homewood: The Dorsey Press.

Gorney, R., Loye, D., and Steele, G. (1977) 'Impact of Dramatised Television Entertainment on Adult Males,' *American Journal of Psychiatry*, 134(2): 170–174.

Gottlieb, S. (ed.) (1995) *Hitchcock on Hitchcock: Selected Writings and Interviews*, Berkeley: University of California Press.

Grabe, M. E., Lang, A., Zhou, S. and Bolls, P. D. (2000) 'Cognitive Access to Negatively Arousing News: An Experimental Investigation of the Knowledge Gap,' *Communication Research*, 27(1): 3–26.

Graber, D. (1984) *Processing the News: How People Tame the Information Tide*, New York: Longman.

Graham, H. and Labanyi, J. (eds) (1995) *Spanish Cultural Studies: An Introduction – The Struggle for Modernity*, Oxford: Oxford University Press.

Gramsci, A. (1971) *Selections from the Prison Notebooks*, New York: International Publishers.

Grant, B. K. (1986) *Film Genre Reader*, Austin: University of Texas Press.

Grant, B. K. (1995) *Film Genre Reader II*, Austin: University of Texas Press.

Gray, A. (1992) *Video Playtime: The Gendering of a Leisure Technology*, London: Routledge.

Greatbatch, D. (1998) 'Conversation Analysis: Neutralism in British News Interviews,' in A. Bell and P. Garrett (eds) *Approaches to Media Discourse*, Oxford: Blackwell.

Greenacre, M. J. (1993) *Correspondence Analysis in Practice*, London: Academic Press.

Greenberg, B. S. (1964) 'Person-to-Person Communication in the Diffusion of a News Event,' *Journalism Quarterly*, 41: 489–494.

Greenberg, B. S. (1975) 'British Children and Televised Violence,' *Public Opinion Quarterly*, 38: 531–547.

Greenwood, D. J. and Levin, M. (1998) *Introduction to Action Research: Social Research for Social Change*, Thousand Oaks, CA: Sage.

Greimas, A. J. (1966) *Structural Semantics. An Attempt at a Method*, Lincoln, NE: University of Nebraska Press [English trans. 1983].

Gripsrud, J. (1995) *The Dynasty Years: Hollywood Television and Critical Media Studies*, London: Routledge.

Grodal, T. K. (1997) *Moving Pictures: A New Theory of Film Genres, Feelings, and Cognition*, New York: Oxford University Press.

Gross, A. G. (1990) *The Rhetoric of Science*, Cambridge, MA: Harvard University Press.

Grossberg, L., Nelson, C., and Treichler, P. (eds) (1992) *Cultural Studies*, London: Routledge.

Grunig, J. E. (ed.) (1992) *Excellence in Public Relations and Communication Management*, Hillsdale, NJ: Lawrence Erlbaum.

Guba, E. G. and Lincoln, Y. S. (1994) 'Competing Paradigms in Qualitative Research,' in N. Denzin and Y. S. Lincoln (eds), *Handbook of Qualitative Research*, Thousand Oaks, CA: Sage.

Gudykunst, W. B. and Kim, Y. Y. (1992) *Communicating with Strangers: An Approach to Intercultural Communication* (2nd edn), New York: McGraw-Hill.

Gudykunst, W. B. and Kim, Y. Y. (1997) *Communicating with Strangers: An Approach to Intercultural Communication* (3rd edn), New York: McGraw-Hill.

Gulich, E. and Quasthoff, U. M. (1985) 'Narrative Analysis,' in T. A. van Dijk (ed.) *Handbook of Discourse Analysis* (Vol. 2), New York: Academic Press.

Gumpert, G. and Cathcart, R. (eds) (1986) *Inter/Media: Interpersonal Communication in a Media World*, New York: Oxford University Press.

Gunter, B. (1979) 'Recall of Television News Items: Effects of Presentation Mode, Picture Content and Serial Position,' *Journal of Educational Television*, 5: 57–61.

Gunter, B. (1985a) *Dimensions of Television Violence*, Aldershot, Hants: Gower.

Gunter, B. (1985b) 'News Sources and News Awareness: A British Survey,' *Journal of Broadcasting*, 29: 397–406.

Gunter, B. (1987a) *Television and the Fear of Crime*, London: John Libbey.

Gunter, B. (1987b) *Poor Reception: Misunderstanding and Forgetting Broadcast News*, Hillsdale, NJ: Lawrence Erlbaum.

Gunter, B. (2000) *Media Research Methods: Measuring Audiences, Reactions, and Impact*, London: Sage.

Gunter, B. and Harrison, J. (1998) *Violence on Television: An Analysis of Amount, Nature, Location and Origin of Violence in British Programmes*, London: Routledge.

Gunter, B. and Wober, J. (1982) 'Television Viewing and Public Trust,' *British Journal of Social Psychology*, 22: 174–176.

Gunter, B., Furnham, A., and Lineton, Z. (1995) 'Watching People Watching Television: What Goes on in Front of the TV Set?,' *Journal of Educational Television*, 21(3): 165–191.

Gunter, B., Svennevig, M., and Wober, M. (1986) *Television Coverage of the 1983 General Election*, Aldershot, Hants: Gower.

Gunter, B., Harrison, J., Arundel, J., and Osborn, R. (1999) 'Female Victimisation on Television: Extent, Nature and Context of On-screen Portrayals,' *Communication*, 24(4): 387–405.

Gunter, B., Harrison, J., Arundel, J., Osborn, R., and Crawford, M. (1996) *Violence on Television in Britain: A Content Analysis*, Report to the BBC, BSC, BSkyB, Channel 4, ITC, and ITV, Sheffield: University of Sheffield, Department of Journalism Studies.

Gurevitch, M. (1992) 'The Globalization of Electronic Journalism,' in J. Curran and M. Gurevitch (eds) *Mass Media and Society*, London: Edward Arnold.

Haas, T. (1999) 'What's "Public" About Public Journalism? Public Journalism and the Lack of a Coherent Public Philosophy,' *Communication Theory*, 9(3): 346–364.

Habermas, J. (1971) *Knowledge and Human Interests*, Boston, MA: Beacon Press [orig. publ. 1968].

Habermas, J. (1984) *The Theory of Communicative Action* (Vol. 1), Boston, MA: Beacon Press [orig. publ. 1981].

Habermas, J. (1987) *The Theory of Communicative Action* (Vol. 2), Cambridge: Polity Press [orig. publ. 1981].

Habermas, J. (1989) *The Structural Transformation of the Public Sphere*, Cambridge, MA: MIT Press [orig. publ. 1962].

Hacker, K. L., Coste, T. G., Kamm, D. F., and Bybee, C. R. (1991) 'Oppositional Readings of Network Television News: Viewer Deconstruction,' *Discourse and Society*, 2(2): 183–202.

Hacking, I. (1975) *The Emergence of Probability*, London: Cambridge University Press.

Hacking, I. (1983) *Representing and Intervening: Introductory Topics in the Philosophy of Natural Science*, Cambridge: Cambridge University Press.

Hacking, I. (1999) *The Social Construction of What?*, Cambridge, MA: Harvard University Press.

Hall, S. (1973a) 'The Determination of News Photographs,' in S. Cohen and J. Young (eds) *The Manufacture of News*, London: Constable.

Hall, S. (1973b) *Encoding and Decoding in the Television Discourse* (Stencilled Occasional Paper 7), Birmingham: Centre for Contemporary Cultural Studies.

Hall, S. (1983) 'The Problem of Ideology – Marxism without Guarantees,' in B. Matthews (ed.) *Marx: A Hundred Years On*, London: Lawrence & Wishart.

Hall, S. (1986) 'Cultural Studies: Two Paradigms,' in R. Collins, J. Curran, N. Garnham, P. Scannell, P. Schlesinger, and C. Sparks (eds) *Media, Culture, and Society: A Critical Reader*, London: Sage [orig. publ. 1980].

Hall, S. and Jefferson, T. (eds) (1975) *Resistance Through Rituals*, London: Hutchinson.

Hall, S., Connell, I., and Curti, L. (1976) 'The "Unity" of Current Affairs Television,' *Working Papers in Cultural Studies*, No. 9: 51–94, Centre for Contemporary Cultural Studies, University of Birmingham.

Hall, S., Hobson, D., Lowe, A., and Willis, P. (eds) (1980) *Culture, Media, Language*, London: Hutchinson.

Halliday, M. A. K. (1973) *Explorations in the Functions of Language*, London: Edward Arnold.

Halliday, M. A. K. (1978) *Language as Social Semiotic: The Social Interpretation of Language and Meaning*, London: Edward Arnold.

Hallin, D. C. (1986) *The 'Uncensored War': The Media and Vietnam*, New York: Oxford University Press.

Hallin, D. C. (1992) 'Sound Bite News: TV Coverage of Elections 1968–1988,' *Journal of Communication*, 42(2): 5–24.

Halliwell, L. (1999) *Halliwell's Film & Video Guide 2000*, New York: Harper-Perennial.

Halloran, J. (1970) *The Effects of Television*, London: Panther.

Halloran, J., Elliott, P., and Murdock, G. (1970) *Communications and Demonstrations: A Case Study*, Harmondsworth: Penguin.

Hammersley, M. (1989) *The Dilemma of Qualitative Method: Herbert Blumer and the Chicago Tradition*, London: Routledge.

Hammersley, M. (1995) *The Politics of Social Research*, London: Sage.

Hammersley, M. (1996) 'The Relationship Between Qualitative and Quantitative Research: Paradigm Loyalty Versus Methodological Eclecticism,' in J. T. E. Richardson (ed.) *Handbook of Qualitative Research Methods for Psychology and the Social Sciences*, Leicester: British Psychological Society.

Hammersley, M. and Atkinson, P. (1995) *Ethnography: Principles in Practice* (2nd edn), London and New York: Routledge.

Hannerz, U. (1996) *Transnational Connections: Culture, People, Places*, London: Routledge.

Hannington, W. (1977) *Unemployed Struggles, 1919–1936*, London: Lawrence & Wishart.

Hansen, A., Cottle, S., Negrine, R., and Newbold, C. (1998) *Mass Communication Research Methods*, London: Macmillan.

Hansen, M. (1990) 'Early Cinema – Whose Public Sphere?,' in T. Elsaesser (ed.) *Early Cinema: Space, Frame, Narrative*, London: British Film Institute.

Hanson, N. R. (1958) *Patterns of Discovery: An Inquiry into the Conceptual Foundations of Science*, Cambridge: Cambridge University Press.

Haraway, D. J. (1997) *Modest-Witness@Second-Millennium.FemalemanMeets_Oncomouse: Feminism and Technoscience*, New York: Routledge.

Harding, S. (1986) *The Science Question in Feminism*, Ithaca, NY: Cornell University Press.

Harding, S. (ed.) (1987) *Feminism and Methodology: Social Science Issues*, Bloomington: Indiana University Press.

Hardt, H. (1979) *Social Theories of the Press: Early German and American Perspectives*, London: Sage.

Hardt, H. (1992) *Critical Communication Studies: Communication, History, and Theory*, London: Routledge.

Hardt, H. (1999) 'Review of Dennis and Wartella,' *Communications: The European Journal of Communication Research*, 24(2): 239–240.

Harrison, C. and Wood, P. (eds) (1992) *Art in Theory – 1900–1990: An Anthology of Changing Ideas*, Oxford: Blackwell.

Hartley, J. and Pearson, R. (eds) (2000) *American Cultural Studies: A Reader*, Oxford: Oxford University Press.

Hartnagel, T. F., Teevan, J. J. Jr., and McIntyre, J. J. (1975) 'Television Violence and Violent Behaviour,' *Social Forces*, 54: 341–351.

Harvey, D. (1989) *The Condition of Postmodernity*, Oxford: Blackwell.

Hauben, M. and Hauben, R. (1997) *Netizens: On the History and Impact of Usenet and the Internet*, Los Alamitos, CA: IEEE Computer Society Press.

Hauser, A. (1951) *The Social History of Art* (Vols 1–4), New York: Vintage.

Have, P. Ten (1999) *Doing Conversation Analysis: A Practical Guide*, London: Sage.

Havelock, E. A. (1963) *Preface to Plato*, Oxford: Blackwell.

Hays, W. L. (1973) *Statistics for the Social Sciences*, New York: Holt, Rinehart & Winston.

Headland, T., Pike, K., and Harris, M. (eds) (1990) *Emics and Etics: The Insider/Outsider Debate*, Newbury Park, CA: Sage.

Heath, S. (1975) 'Films and System: Terms of Analysis, Part I,' *Screen*, 16(1): 7–77; 'Part II,' *Screen* 16(2): 91–113.

Heath, S. B. (1980) 'The Functions and Uses of Literacy,' *Journal of Communication*, 30(1): 123–133.

Heider, F. (1958) *The Psychology of Interpersonal Relations*, New York: Wiley.

Heim, M. (1987) *Electric Language*, New Haven, CT: Yale University Press.

Held, D. and Thompson, J. B. (eds) (1989) *Social Theory of Modern Societies: Anthony Giddens and His Critics*, Cambridge: Cambridge University Press.

Held, D., McGrew, A., Goldblatt, D. and Perraton, J. (2000) *Global Transformations: Politics, Economics, and Culture*, Cambridge: Polity Press.

Hempel, C. G. and Oppenheim, P. (1988) 'Studies in the Logic of Explanation,' in J. Pitt (ed.) *Theories of Explanation*, New York: Oxford University Press [orig. publ. 1948].

Hendy, D. (2000) *Radio in the Global Age*, Cambridge: Polity Press.

Hennigan, K. M., Del Rosario, M. L., Heath, L., Cook, T. D., Wharton, J. D., and Calder, B. J. (1982) 'Impact of the Introduction of Television on Crime in the United States: Empirical Findings and Theoretical Implications,' *Journal of Personality and Social Psychology*, 42: 461–477.

Herbst, S. (1993) 'The Meaning of Public Opinion: Citizens' Constructions of Social Reality,' *Media, Culture & Society*, 15(3): 437–454.

Heritage, J. (1985) 'Analyzing News Interviews: Aspects of the Production of Talk for an Overhearing Audience,' in T. van Dijk (ed.) *Handbook of Discourse Analysis* (Vol. 3), London: Academic Press.

Heritage, J. and Greatbatch, D. L. (1991) 'On the Institutional Character of Institutional Talk: The Case of News Interviews,' in D. Boden and D. H. Zimmerman (eds) *Talk and Social Structure: Studies in Ethnomethodology and Conversation Analysis*, Oxford: Polity Press.

Herman, E. S. and Chomsky, N. (1988) *Manufacturing Consent: The Political Economy of the Mass Media*, New York: Pantheon Books.

Hermes, J. (1995) *Reading Women's Magazines: An Analysis of Everyday Media Use*, Oxford: Polity Press.

Herzog, H. (1941) 'On Borrowed Experience: An Analysis of Listening to Daytime Sketches,' *Studies in Philosophy and Social Science*, 9: 65–95.

Herzog, H. (1944) 'What Do We Really Know about Daytime Serial Listeners?,' in P. F. Lazarsfeld (ed.) *Radio Research 1942–3*, New York: Duell, Sloan, & Pearce.

Hilmes, M. (1997) *Radio Voices: American Broadcasting, 1922–1952*, Minneapolis: The University of Minnesota Press.

Himmelweit, H. T., Vince, P., and Oppenheim, A. N. (1958) *Television and the Child*, London: Oxford University Press.

Hine, C. (2000) *Virtual Ethnography*, London: Sage.

Hirsch, P. (1980) 'The "Scary World" of the Non-Viewer and Other Anomalies – A Reanalysis of Gerbner et al.'s Findings in Cultivation Analysis,' *Communication Research*, 7(4): 403–456.

Hirsch, P. (1981) 'On Not Learning from One's Mistakes, Part II,' *Communication Research*, 8(1): 3–38.

Hjarvard, S. (1993) 'Pan-European Television News: Towards a European Political Public Sphere?,' in P. Drummond, R. Paterson, and J. Willis (eds) *National Identity and Europe*, London: British Film Institute.

Hjarvard, S. (1995) *Internationale TV-nyheder. En historisk analyse af det europæiske system for udveksling af internationale TV-nyheder* [International TV News], Copenhagen, Denmark: Akademisk Forlag.

Hjarvard, S. (1999) 'TV News Exchange,' in O. Boyd-Barrett and T. Rantanen (eds) *The Globalization of News*, London: Sage.

Hjarvard, S. (ed.) (2001) *News in a Globalized Society*, Gothenburg, Sweden: Nordicom.

Hjelmslev, L. (1963) *Prolegomena to a Theory of Language*, Madison: University of Wisconsin Press [orig. publ. 1943].

Hobson, D. (1980) 'Housewives and the Mass Media,' in S. Hall, D. Hobson, A. Lowe, and P. Willis (eds) *Culture, Media, Language*, London: Hutchinson.

Hobson, D. (1982) *Crossroads: The Drama of a Soap Opera*, London: Methuen.

Hockings, P. (ed.) (1995) *Principles of Visual Anthropology* (2nd edn), Berlin: Mouton de Gruyter.

Hodge, B. and Kress, G. (1988) *Social Semiotics*, Cambridge: Polity Press.

Hodge, B. and Tripp, D. (1986) *Children and Television*, Cambridge: Polity Press.

Hoffner, C. and Cantor, J. (1985) 'Developmental Differences in Responses to a Television Character's Appearance and Behaviour,' *Developmental Psychology* 21: 1065–1074.

Hoggart, R. (1957) *The Uses of Literacy*, Harmondsworth: Penguin.

Höhne, H. (1984) *Report überNachrichten-Agenturen* [Report on News Agencies] (2nd edn), Baden-Baden, Germany: Nomos Verlagsgesellschaft.

Höijer, B. (1990) 'Studying Viewers' Reception of Television Programmes: Theoretical and Methodological Considerations,' *European Journal of Communication*, 5(1): 29–56.

Holsti, O. R. (1969) *Content Analysis for the Social Sciences and Humanities*, Reading, MA: Addison-Wesley.

Holub, R. C. (1984) *Reception Theory: A Critical Introduction*, London: Methuen.

Hoskins, C., McFadyen, S., and Finn, A. (1997) *Global Television and Film: An Introduction to the Economics of the Business*, Oxford: Clarendon, and New York: Oxford University Press.

Hovland, C. I., Janis, I. L., and Kelley, H. H. (1953) *Communication and Persuasion*, New Haven, CT: Yale University Press.

Hovland, C. I., Lumsdaine, A. A., and Sheffield, F. D. (1949) *Experiments on Mass Communication*, Princeton, NJ: Princeton University Press.

Høyer, S., Lauk, E., and Vihalemm, P. (eds) (1993) *Towards a Civic Society: The Baltic Media's Long Road to Freedom*, Tartu: Nota Baltica.

Huesmann, L. R., Eron, L. D., Lefkowitz, M. M., and Walder, L. O. (1984) 'Stability of Aggression over Time and Generations,' *Developmental Psychology*, 20(6): 1120–1134.

Hughes, H. M. (1937) 'Human Interest Stories and Democracy,' *The Public Opinion Quarterly*, April: 73–87.

Hughes, H. M. (1940) *News and the Human Interest Story*, Chicago, IL: University of Chicago Press.

Hughes, R. (1991) *The Shock of the New: Art and the Century of Change* (updated and enlarged edn), London: Thames & Hudson.

Hur, K. K. (1984) 'A Critical Analysis of International News Flow Research,' *Critical Studies in Mass Communication*, 1: 365–378.

Husband, C. (1996) 'The Right to be Understood: Conceiving the Multi-Ethnic Public Sphere,' *Innovation*, 9(2): 205–215.

Huyssen, A. (1986) *After the Great Divide: Modernism, Mass Culture, and Postmodernism*, London: Macmillan.

Hyuhn, S. B. (2000) 'Product Differentiation in National Television Newscasts,' *Journal of Broadcasting and Electronic Media*, 44(1): 62–77.

Inglehart, R. (1990) *Culture Shift in Advanced Industrial Society*, Princeton, NJ: Princeton University Press.

Inglehart, R., Nevitte, N., and Basanez, M. (1996) *The North American Trajectory: Cultural, Economic, and Political Ties Among the United States, Canada, and Mexico*, New York: Aldine de Gruyter.

Innis, H. A. (1956) *The Fur Trade in Canada: An Introduction to Canadian Economic History* (2nd edn), Toronto: Toronto University Press [orig. publ. 1930].

Innis, H. A. (1972) *Empire and Communications*, Toronto: University of Toronto Press [orig. publ. 1950].

Innis, H. A. (1964) *The Bias of Communication*, Toronto: University of Toronto Press [orig. publ. 1951].

International Motion Picture Almanac, New York: Quigley Publishing.

International Television and Video Almanac, New York: Quigley Publishing.

Irigaray, L. (1997) 'This Sex Which Is Not One,' in L. Nicholson (ed.) *The Second Wave: A Reader in Feminist Theory*, London: Routledge [orig. publ. 1977].

Irwin, W. (1969) 'The American Newspaper: A Study of Journalism in its Relation to the Public,' *Collier's* January–June, reprinted with comments by Clifford F. Weigle and David G. Clark, Ames, Iowa: The Iowa State University Press [orig. publ. 1911].

Iser, W. (1974) *The Implied Reader. Patterns of Communication in Prose Fiction from Bunyan to Beckett*, Baltimore, MD: Johns Hopkins University Press [orig. publ. 1972].

Iser, W. (1978) *The Act of Reading. A Theory of Aesthetic Response*, London: Routledge & Kegan Paul [orig. publ. 1976].

Iser, W. (1989) *Prospecting: From Reader Response to Literary Anthropology*, Baltimore, MD: Johns Hopkins University Press.

Ito, Y. and Tanaka, N. (1992) 'Education, Research Institutes, and Academic Associations in Journalism and Mass Communications in Japan,' *KEIO Communication Review*, 14: 15–35.

Iyengar, S. and Kinder, D. R. (1987) *News that Matters*, Chicago, IL: University of Chicago Press.

Jakobson, R. (1960) 'Closing Statement: Linguistics and Poetics,' in T. A. Sebeok (ed.) *Style in Language*, Cambridge, MA: MIT Press.

James, A., Hackey, J. and Dawson, A. (eds) (1997) *After Writing Culture: Epistemology and Praxis in Contemporary Anthropology*, London: Routledge.

Jameson, F. (1991) *Postmodernism, Or, The Cultural Logic of Late Capitalism*, London: Verso.

Jandt, F. E. (2001) *Intercultural Communication: An Introduction* (3rd edn), Newbury Park, CA: Sage.

Jankowski, N. W. (1991) 'Qualitative Research and Community Media,' in K. B. Jensen and N. W. Jankowski (eds) *A Handbook of Qualitative Methodologies for Mass Communication Research*, London: Routledge.

Jankowski, N. W. and van Selm, M. (in press) *Researching New Media*, London: Sage.

Jankowski, N. W. and Wester, F. (1991) 'The Qualitative Tradition in Social Science Inquiry: Contributions to Mass Communication Research,' in K. B. Jensen and N. W. Jankowski (eds) *A Handbook of Qualitative Methodologies for Mass Communication Research*, London: Routledge.

Jankowski, N. W., Prehn, O. and Stappers, J. (eds) (1992) *The People's Voice*, London: John Libbey.

Janowitz, M. (ed) (1966) *W. I. Thomas on Social Organisation and Social Personality: Selected Papers*, Chicago, IL: The University of Chicago Press.

Janowitz, M. (1967) *The Community Press in an Urban Setting* (2nd revised edn), Chicago, IL: University of Chicago Press [orig. publ. 1952].

Janson, H. W. (1991) *History of Art* (4th edn), Englewood Cliffs, NJ: Prentice-Hall.

Jauss, H. R. (1982) *Toward an Aesthetic of Reception*, Brighton, Sussex: Harvester Press.

Jenkins, H. (1992) *Textual Poachers: Television Fans and Participatory Culture*, New York: Routledge.

Jensen, E., Braxton, G., and Calvo, D. (2000) 'NBC, NAACP In Pact to Boost Minorities in TV,' *Los Angeles Times*, 6 January, A-1.

Jensen, J. F. (1999) 'Interactivity: Tracking a New Concept in Media and Communication Studies,' in P. A. Mayer (ed.) *Computer Media and Communication: A Reader*, Oxford: Oxford University Press.

Jensen, K. B. (1986) *Making Sense of the News: Towards a Theory and an Empirical Model of Reception for the Study of Mass Communication*, Aarhus, Denmark: University of Aarhus Press.

Jensen, K. B. (1988) 'News as Social Resource,' *European Journal of Communication*, 3(3): 275–301.

Jensen, K. B. (1990) 'Television Futures: A Social Action Methodology for Studying Interpretive Communities,' *Critical Studies in Mass Communication*, 7(2): 129–146.

Jensen, K. B. (1993a) 'One Person, One Computer: The Social Construction of the Personal Computer,' in P. B. Andersen, B. Holmqvist, and J. F. Jensen (eds) *The Computer as Medium*, Cambridge: Cambridge University Press.

Jensen, K. B. (1993b) 'The Past in the Future: Problems and Potentials of Historical Reception Studies,' *Journal of Communication*, 43(4): 20–28.

Jensen, K. B. (1994) 'Reception as Flow: The "New Television Viewer" Revisited,' *Cultural Studies*, 8(2): 293–305.

Jensen, K. B. (1995) *The Social Semiotics of Mass Communication*, London: Sage.

Jensen, K. B. (ed.) (1998) *News of the World. World Cultures Look at Television News*, London and New York: Routledge.

Jensen, K. B. (1999) 'Local Empiricism, Global Theory: Problems and Potentials of Comparative Research on News Reception,' *Communications: The European Journal of Communication Research*, 23(4): 427–445.

Jensen, K. B. (2000a) 'Interactivities: Constituents of a Model of Computer Media and Communication,' in I. Bondebjerg (ed.) *Moving Images, Culture, and the Mind*, Luton, Beds: University of Luton Press.

Jensen, K. B. (2000b) 'On the Edge: A Meta-Analysis of the State of Media and Communication Research,' *Nordicom Review*, 21(2): 23–30.

Jensen, K. B. (2001) 'Why Virtuality Can Be Good for Democracy,' in S. Hjarvard (ed.) *News in a Globalized Society*, Gothenburg, Sweden: Nordicom.

Jensen, K. B. and Jankowski, N. W. (eds) (1991) *A Handbook of Qualitative Methodologies for Mass Communication Research*, London: Routledge.

Jensen, K. B., Schrøder, K. C., Stampe, T., Søndergaard, H., and Topsøe-Jensen, J. (1994) 'Super Flow, Channel Flows, and Audience Flows: A Study of Viewers' Reception of Television as Flow,' *Nordicom Review*, 2: 1–13.

Joas, H. (1993) *Pragmatism and Social Theory*, Chicago, IL: University of Chicago Press.

Johansen, J. D. (1993) *Dialogic Semiosis*, Bloomington: Indiana University Press.

Johnson, L. (1988) *The Unseen Voice: A Cultural History of Early Australian Radio*, London: Routledge.

Johnson, M. (1987) *The Body in the Mind*, Chicago, IL: University of Chicago Press.

Jones, S. G. (ed.) (1998) *Cybersociety 2.0*, Thousand Oaks, CA: Sage.

Jones, S. G. (ed.) (1999) *Doing Internet Research*, Thousand Oaks, CA: Sage.

Jordan, A. (1992) 'Social Class, Temporal Orientation, and Mass Media Use within the Family System,' *Critical Studies in Mass Communication*, 9(4): 374–386.

Jowett, G. S., Jarvie, I. C., and Fuller, K. H. (1996) *Children and the Movies: Media Influence and the Payne Fund Controversy*, Cambridge: Cambridge University Press.

Jungk, R. and Müllert, N. (1981) *Zukunftswerkstätten* [Workshops on the Future], Hamburg, Germany: Hoffmann & Campe.

Kalinak, K. (1992) *Settling the Score: Music and the Classical Hollywood Film*, Madison: University of Wisconsin Press.

Kaminsky, S. M. and Mahan, J. H. (1985) *American Television Genres*, Chicago, IL: Nelson-Hall.

Kamwangamulu, N. M. (1999) 'Ubuntu in South Africa: a Sociolinguistic Perspective to a Pan-African Concept,' *Critical Arts* 3 (2): 24–41, Durban: University of Natal (www.und.ac.za/und/ccms).

Kaniss, P. (1991) *Making Local News*, Chicago, IL: University of Chicago Press.

Kaplan, E. A. (1988) *Rocking Around the Clock: Music Television, Postmodernism, and Consumer Culture*, New York: Routledge.

Katz, E. and Lazarsfeld, P. F. (1955) *Personal Influence*, Glencoe, IL: Free Press.

Katz, E. and Wedell, G. (1977) *Broadcasting in the Third World: Promise and Performance*, Cambridge, MA: Harvard University Press.

Katz, E., Blumler, J., and Gurevitch, M. (1974) 'Utilization of Mass Communication by the Individual,' in J. G. Blumler and E. Katz (eds) *The Uses of Mass Communications*, Beverly Hills, CA: Sage.

Katz, E., Gurevitch, M., and Haas, H. (1973) 'On the Use of Mass Media for Important Things,' *American Sociological Review*, 38(2): 164–181.

Kay, A. and Goldberg, A. (1999) 'Personal Dynamic Media,' in P. A. Mayer (ed.) *Computer Media and Communication: A Reader*, Oxford: Oxford University Press [orig. publ. 1977].

Kaye, B. K. and Sapolsky, B. S. (1997) 'Electronic Monitoring of In-Home Television RCD Usage,' *Journal of Broadcasting and Electronic Media*, 41: 214–228.

Kelly, C. and Shepherd, D. (eds) (1998) *Russian Cultural Studies: An Introduction*, Oxford: Oxford University Press.

Kennedy, G. A. (1980) *Classical Rhetoric and Its Christian and Secular Tradition from Ancient to Modern Times*, Chapel Hill: University of North Carolina Press.

Kepplinger, H.-M. (1997) 'Political Correctness and Academic Principles: A Reply to Simpson,' *Journal of Communication*, 47(4): 102–117.

Kerlinger, F. N. (1986) *Foundations of Behavioural Research* (3rd edn), New York: Holt, Rinehart & Winston.

Kern, S. (1983) *The Culture of Time and Space, 1880–1918*, Cambridge, MA: Harvard University Press.

Kincaid, D. L. (ed.) (1987) *Communication Theory: Eastern and Western Perspectives*, San Diego, CA: Academic Press.

Kinder, M. (1 984) 'Music Video and the Spectator: Television, Ideology, and Dream,' *Film Quarterly*, 38: 2–15.

Kingsford, P. (1982) *The Hunger Marchers in Britain, 1920–1940*, London: Lawrence & Wishart.

Kirk, J. and Miller, M. (1986) *Reliability and Validity in Qualitative Research*, Beverly Hills, CA: Sage.

Kittler, F. A. (1999) *Gramophone, Film, Typewriter*, Stanford, CA: Stanford University Press.

Kjørup, S. (1996) *Menneskevidenskabeme: Problemer og traditioner i humanioras videnskabsteori* [The Human Sciences: Problems and Traditions in the Theory of Science of the Humanities], Roskilde, Denmark: Roskilde Universitetsforlag.

Klapper, J. (1960) *The Effects of Mass Communication*, Glencoe, IL: Free Press.

Klingender, F. D. and Legg, S. (1937) *Money Behind the Screen*, London: Lawrence & Wishart.

Knapp, M. L. and Miller, G. R. (eds) (1994) *Handbook of Interpersonal Communication* (2nd edn), Thousand Oaks, CA: Sage.

Koss, S. (1981, 1984) *The Rise and Fall of the Political Press in Britain* (Vols 1 and 2), London: Hamish Hamilton.

Kozloff, S. (1988) *Invisible Storytellers: Voice-over Narration in American Fiction Film*, Berkeley, CA: University of California Press.

Kozloff, S. (2000) *Overhearing Film Dialogue*, Berkeley, CA: University of California Press.

Kracauer, S. (1953) 'The Challenge of Qualitative Content Analysis,' *Public Opinion Quarterly*, 16(2): 631–642.

Kracauer, S. (1960) *Theory of Film: The Redemption of Physical Reality*, London: Oxford University Press.

Kracauer, S. (1995) *The Mass Ornament: Weimar Essays*, Cambridge, MA: Harvard University Press [orig. publ. 1963].

Kraus, S. and Davis, D. (1976) *The Effects of Mass Communication on Political Behavior*, University Park, PA: Pennsylvania State University Press.

Kress, G. and van Leeuwen, T. (1996) *Reading Images: The Grammar of Visual Design*, London: Routledge.

Kress, G., Leite-García, R. and van Leeuwen, T. (1997) 'Discourse semiotics,' in T. van Dijk (ed.) *Discourse as Structure and Process*, London: Sage.

Krippendorf, K. (1980) *Content Analysis: An Introduction to its Methodology*, Beverly Hills, CA: Sage.

Kristeller, P. O. (1961) *Renaissance Thought: The Classic, Scholastic, and Humanist Strains*, New York: Harper.

Kristeva, J. (1984) *Revolution in Poetic Language*, New York: Columbia University Press [orig. publ. 1974].

Kroeber, A. L. and Kluckhohn, C. (1952) *Culture: A Critical Review of Concepts and Definitions*, Cambridge, MA: Peabody Museum of American Archaeology and Ethnology.

Kubey, R. and Csikszentmihalyi, M. (1990) *Television and the Quality of Life: How Viewing Shapes Everyday Experience*, Hillsdale, NJ: Lawrence Erlbaum.

Kuhn, T. S. (1970) *The Structure of Scientific Revolutions* (revised edn), Chicago, IL: University of Chicago Press [orig. publ. 1962].

Kuiper, K. (1996) *Smooth Talkers: The Linguistic Performance of Auctioneers and Sportscasters*, Mahwah, NJ: Erlbaum.

Kvale, S. (1987) 'Validity in the Qualitative Research Interview,' *Methods*, 1: 37–72.

Kvale, S. (1996) *InterViews: An Introduction to Qualitative Research Interviewing*, Thousand Oaks, CA: Sage.

Labov, W. and Waletzky, J. (1967) 'Narrative Analysis,' in J. Helm (ed.) *Essays on the Verbal and Visual Arts*, Seattle: University of Washington Press.

Lacan, J. (1977) *The Four Fundamental Concepts of Psychoanalysis*, Harmondsworth: Penguin.

Lacey, K. (1994) 'From *Plauderei* to Propaganda: On Women's Radio in Germany, 1924–35,' *Media Culture & Society*, 16(4): 589–608.

Lakoff, G. and Johnson, M. (1999) *Philosophy in the Flesh: The Embodied Mind and Its Challenge to Western Thought*, New York: Basic Books.

Landow, G. P. (1997) *Hypertext 2.0: The Convergence of Contemporary Critical Theory and Technology* (2nd edn), Baltimore, MD: Johns Hopkins University Press.

Lang, G. E. and Lang, K. (1981) 'Watergate: An Exploration of the Agenda-Building Process,' in G. C. Wilhoit and H. D. Bock (eds) *Mass Communication Review Yearbook* (Vol. 2), Beverly Hills, CA: Sage.

Lang, K. and Lang, G. E. (1953) 'The Unique Perspective of Television and Its Effects: A Pilot Study,' *American Sociological Review*, 18: 3–12.

Lang, K. and Lang, G. E. (1991) 'Studying Events in Their Natural Settings,' in K. B. Jensen and N. W. Jankowski (eds) *A Handbook of Qualitative Methodologies for Mass Communication Research*, London: Routledge.

Lange, D. L., Baker, R. K., and Ball, S. J. (1969) *Mass Media and Violence*, Washington, DC: U.S. Government Printing Office.

Langer, J. (1998) *Tabloid Television: Popular Journalism and the 'Other' News*, London: Routledge

Larsen, P. (1974) 'Analyse af TV-avisen' [Analysis of Television News], in M. B. Andersen and J. Poulsen (eds) *Mediesociologi. Introduktion til massekommunikationsforskning* [Media Sociology: Introduction to Mass Communication Research], Copenhagen, Denmark: Rhodos.

Larsen, P. (1989) 'Beyond the Narrative. Rock Videos and Modern Visual Fictions: Readings, Experiences,' in M. Skovmand (ed.) *Media Fictions*, Aarhus, Denmark: Aarhus University Press.

Larsen, P. (2000) 'The Sound of Images: Classical Hollywood and Music,' in I. Bondebjerg (ed.) *Moving Image, Culture and The Mind*, Luton, Beds: University of Luton Press.

Lashley, K. S. and Watson, J. B. (1922) *A Psychological Study of Motion Pictures in Relation to Venereal Disease Campaigns*, Washington, DC: Interdepartmental Social Hygiene Board.

Lasorsa, D. and Reese, S. (1990) 'News Source Use in the Crash of 1987: A Study of Four National Media,' *Journalism Quarterly*, 167: 60–71.

Lasswell, H. D. (1938) *Propaganda Technique in the World War*, New York: Alfred A. Knopf [orig. publ. 1927].

Lasswell, H. D. (1966) 'The Structure and Function of Communication in Society,' in B. Berelson and M. Janowitz (eds) *Reader in Public Opinion and Communication*, Glencoe, IL: The Free Press [orig. publ. 1948].

Latour, B. (1987) *Science in Action*, Milton Keynes: Open University Press.

Lazarsfeld, P. F. (1934) 'The Psychological Aspect of Market Research,' *Harvard Business Review*, 13(1): 54–71.

Lazarsfeld, P. F. (1941) 'Remarks on Administrative and Critical Communications Research,' *Studies in Philosophy and Social Science*, 9: 2–16.

Lazarsfeld, P. F. and Barton, A. H. (1951) 'Qualitative Measurement in the Social Sciences: Classification, Typologies, and Indices,' in D. Lerner and H. D. Lasswell (eds) *The Policy Sciences: Recent Developments in Scope and Method*, Stanford, CA: Stanford University Press.

Lazarsfeld, P. F. and Merton, R. K. (1960) 'Mass Communication, Popular Taste, and Organised Social Action,' in W. Schramm (ed.) *Mass Communications*, Urbana: University of Illinois Press [orig. publ. 1948].

Lazarsfeld, P. F., Berelson, B., and Gaudet, H. (1944) *The People's Choice*, New York: Duell, Sloan & Pearce.

Lee, J. B. and Mandelbaum, M. (1999) *Seeing is Believing: 700 Years of Scientific and Medical Illustration*, New York: New York Public Library.

Lefkowitz, M., Eron, L. D., Walder, L. O., and Huesmann, L. R. (1972) 'Television Violence and Child Aggression,' in E. Rubinstein, G. Comstock and J. Murray (eds) *Television and Adolescent Aggressiveness*, Washington, DC: U.S. Government Printing Office.

Leiss, W., Kline, S., and Jhally, S. (1986) *Social Communication in Advertising: Persons, Products and Images of Well-Being*, London: Methuen.

Lembo, R. (2000) *Thinking Through Television*, Cambridge: Cambridge University Press.

Lemert, C. (1993) *Social Theory*, San Francisco, CA: Westview Press.

Lemish, D. (1982) 'The Rules of Viewing Television in Public Places,' *Journal of Broadcasting and Electronic Media*, 26: 757–791.

Lerner, D. (1958) *The Passing of Traditional Society*, New York: Free Press.

Lerner, D. and Lasswell, H. D. (eds) (1951) *The Policy Sciences: Recent Developments in Scope and Method*, Stanford, CA: Stanford University Press.

Lévi-Strauss, C. (1958) *Structural Anthropology*, New York: Penguin.

Lévi-Strauss, C. (1991) *Totemism*, London: Merlin Press [orig. publ. 1962].

Levine, L. W. (1988) *Highbrow/Lowbrow: The Emergence of Cultural Hierarchy in America*, Cambridge, MA: Harvard University Press.

Levy, M. (ed.) (1992) 'Symposium: Communication Scholarship and Political Correctness,' *Journal of Communication*, 42(2): 56–149.

Levy, M. and Gurevitch, M. (eds) (1994) *Defining Media Studies: Reflections on the Future of the Field*, Oxford: Oxford University Press.

Levy, M. and Windahl, S. (1985) 'The Concept of Audience Activity,' in K. E. Rosengren, P. Palmgreen, and L. Wenner (eds) *Media Gratifications Research: Current Perspectives*, Beverly Hills, CA: Sage.

Lewis, J. (1983) 'The Encoding/Decoding Model: Criticisms and Redevelopments for Research on Decoding,' *Media, Culture & Society*, 5(2): 179–197.

Lewis, J. (1985) 'Decoding Television News,' in P. Drummond and R. Paterson (eds) *Television in Transition*, London: British Film Institute.

Lewis, J. (1991) *The Ideological Octopus: An Exploration of Television and Its Audience*, New York: Routledge.

Lewis, J. (1997) 'What Counts in Cultural Studies,' *Media, Culture & Society*, 19(1): 83–97.

Lewis, L. (ed.) (1991) *The Adoring Audience*, London: Routledge.

Lichtenstein, A. and Rosenfeld, L. B. (1983) 'Uses and Misuses of Gratifications,' *Communication Research*, 10(1): 97–109.

Licklider, J. C. R. and Taylor, R. W. (1999) 'The Computer as a Communication Device,' in P. A. Mayer (ed.) *Computer Media and Communication: A Reader*, Oxford: Oxford University Press [orig. publ. 1968].

Liebes, T. and Katz, E. (1990) *The Export of Meaning*, New York: Oxford University Press.

Lievrouw, L. and Livingstone, S. (eds) (2002) *Handbook of New Media: Social Shaping and Social Consequences*, London: Sage.

Lincoln, Y. S. and Guba, E. G. (1985) *Naturalistic Inquiry*, London: Sage.

Lindlof, T. R. (1987) 'Ideology and Pragmatics of Media Access in Prison,' in T. R. Lindlof (ed.) *Natural Audiences: Qualitative Research of Media Uses and Effects*, Norwood, NJ: Ablex.

Lindlof, T. R. (1995) *Qualitative Communication Research Methods*, Thousand Oaks, CA: Sage.

Lippmann, W. and Merz, C. (1920) 'A Test of the News: An Examination of the News Reports in the *New York Times* on Aspects of the Russian Revolution of Special Importance to Americans March 1917–March 1920,' *The New Republic [Special Supplement]*, Vol XXIII, Part II, No 296, 4 August.

Livingstone, S. (1990) *Making Sense of Television: The Psychology of Audience Appreciation*, Oxford: Pergamon Press.

Livingstone, S. (1998) *Making Sense of Television: The Psychology of Audience Interpretation* (2nd edn), London: Routledge.

Livingstone, S. and Bovill, M. (eds) (2001) *Children and their Changing Media Environment: A European Comparative Study*, Hillsdale, NJ: Lawrence Erlbaum.

Livingstone, S. and Lunt, P. (1994) *Talk on Television*, London: Routledge.

Lobkowicz, N. (1967) *Theory and Practice: History of a Concept from Aristotle to Marx*, Notre Dame: University of Notre Dame Press.

Lothe, J. (2000) *Narrative in Fiction and Film: An Introduction*, Oxford: Oxford University Press.

Lovejoy, A. O. (1936) *The Great Chain of Being*, Cambridge, MA: Harvard University Press.

Lowenthal, L. (1961) 'The Triumph of Mass Idols,' in L. Lowenthal, *Literature, Popular Culture, and Society*, Englewood Cliffs, NJ: Prentice-Hall [orig. publ. 1941].

Lowery, S. A. and DeFleur, M. L. (1983) *Milestones in Mass Communication Research: Media Effects,* (2nd edn), New York: Longman.

Lowery, S. A. and DeFleur, M. L. (1995) *Milestones in Mass Communication Research: Media Effects* (3rd edn), New York: Longman.

Lukács, G. (1989) *The Historical Novel,* London: Merlin Press [orig. publ. 1916].

Lull, J. (1980) 'The Social Uses of Television,' *Human Communication Research,* 6: 197–209.

Lull, J. (1988a) 'Critical Response: The Audience as Nuisance,' *Critical Studies in Mass Communication,* 5: 239–243.

Lull, J. (ed.) (1988b) *World Families Watch Television,* Newbury Park, CA: Sage.

Lull, J. (1991) *China Turned On: Television, Reform, and Resistance,* London: Routledge.

Lutz, C. A. and Collins, J. L. (1993) *Reading National Geographic,* Chicago, IL: University of Chicago Press.

Lynd, R. S. and Lynd, H. M. (1929) *Middletown: A Study in American Culture,* London: Constable.

Lyotard, J.-F. (1984) *The Postmodern Condition,* Minneapolis: University of Minnesota Press [orig. publ. 1979].

MacBeth, T. M. (1998) 'Quasi-experimental Research on Television and Behavior: Natural and Field Experiments,' in J. K. Asamen and G. L. Berry (eds) *Research Paradigms, Television and Social Behavior,* Thousand Oaks, CA: Sage.

MacBride, S. (ed.) (1980) *Many Voices, One World,* Paris: UNESCO.

MacCabe, C. (ed.) (1986) *High Theory/Low Culture: Analysing Popular Television and Film,* Manchester: Manchester University Press.

MacDonald, M. R. (ed.) (1998) *Traditional Storytelling Today: An International Sourcebook,* Chicago, IL: Fitzroy Dearborn.

McAdams, D. (1999) 'Opportunity of a Lifetime,' *Broadcasting and Cable,* 18 October: 23–28.

McAvoy, K. (2000) 'TV Economics,' *Broadcasting and Cable,* 27 November: 54–66.

McCarthy, E. D., Langner, T. S., Gerstein, J. C., Eisenberg, V. G., and Orzeck, L. (1975) 'Violence and Behaviour Disorders,' *Journal of Communication,* 25(4): 71–85.

McChesney, R. (1999) *Rich Media, Poor Democracy: Communication Politics in Dubious Times,* Urbana: University of Illinois Press.

McCloud, S. (1994) *Understanding Comics,* New York: HarperCollins.

McCombs, M. E. and Shaw, D. L. (1972) 'The Agenda-Setting Function of the Press,' *Public Opinion Quarterly,* 36: 176–187.

McCombs, M. E., Lopez-Escobar, E. and Llamas, J. P. (2000) 'Setting the Agenda of Attributes in the 1996 Spanish General Election,' *Journal of Communication,* 50(2): 77–92.

McGuire, W. J. (1973) 'Persuasion, Resistance, and Attitude Change,' in I. D. S. Pool (ed.) *Handbook of Communication,* Chicago, IL: Rand McNally.

McLeod, J. M., Atkin, C. K., and Chaffee, S. H. (1972) 'Adolescents, Parents and Television Use: Adolescent Self-report Measures from Maryland and Wisconsin Samples,' in G. A. Comstock and E. A. Rubinstein (eds) *Television and Social Behaviour, Vol. 3, Television and Adolescent Aggressiveness,* Washington, DC: U.S. Government Printing Office.

McLuhan, M. (1962) *The Gutenberg Galaxy,* Toronto: Toronto University Press.

McLuhan, M. (1964) *Understanding Media,* New York: McGraw-Hill.

McNelly, J. T. (1959) 'Intermediary Communicators in the International Flow of News,' *Journalism Quarterly,* 36: 23–26.

McQuail, D. (1976) *Toward a Sociology of Mass Communications,* London: Collier-Macmillan.

McQuail, D. (1983) *Mass Communication Theory: An Introduction,* London: Sage.

McQuail, D. (2000) *McQuail's Mass Communication Theory* (4th edn), London: Sage.

McQuail, D. and Windahl, S. (1993) *Communication Models for the Study of Mass Communication* (2nd edn), London: Longman.

McQuail, D., Blumler, J. G., and Brown, J. R. (1972) 'The Television Audience: A Revised Perspective,' in D. McQuail (ed.) *Sociology of Mass Communications,* Harmondsworth: Penguin.

McRobbie, A. (1991) *Feminism and Youth Culture: From 'Jackie' to 'Just Seventeen',* Basingstoke, Hants: Macmillan.

Malinowski, B. (1922) *Argonauts of the Western Pacific,* London: Routledge.

Malinowski, B. (1967) *A Diary in the Strict Sense of the Term,* London: Routledge & Kegan Paul.

Manheim, J. B. (1998) 'The News Shapers: Strategic Communication as Third Force in Newsmaking,' in D. Graber, D. McQuail, and P. Norris (eds) *The Politics of News: the News of Politics,* Washington, DC: Congressional Quarterly Press.

Mann, C. and Stewart, F. (2000) *Internet Communication and Qualitative Research: A Handbook for Researching Online,* London: Sage.

Mannheim, K. (1976) *Ideology and Utopia,* London: Routledge & Kegan Paul [orig. publ. 1922].

Manzella, J. C. (1997) *Mediating Newspeople: Cultures of Writing and the Mechanisms of*

Change at Three Daily Newspapers, unpublished Ph.D. dissertation, University of Connecticut.

Marcus, G. E. and Fischer, M. M. J. (1999) *Anthropology as Cultural Critique* (2nd edn), Chicago: University of Chicago Press.

Marks, E. and de Courtivron, I. (eds) (1981) *New French Feminisms*, Brighton: Harvester Press.

Marshall, C. and Rossman, G. B. (1999) *Designing Qualitative Research* (3rd edn), Thousand Oaks, CA: Sage.

Martin, J. K. and Nakayama, T. K. (1999) 'Thinking Dialectically About Culture and Communication,' *Communication Theory*, 9(1): 1–25.

Martin-Barbero, J. (1993) *Communication, Culture, and Hegemony*, London: Sage.

Martinet, A. (1964) *Elements of General Linguistics*, London: Faber and Faber [orig. publ. 1960].

Mast, G., Cohen, M., and Braudy, L. (eds) (1999) *Film Theory and Criticism: Introductory Readings* (5th edn), New York: Oxford University Press.

Masterman, L. (1985) *Teaching the Media*, London: Comedia.

Mathieson, M. (1975) *The Preachers of Culture: A Study of English and its Teachers*, London: George Allen & Unwin.

Mayer, J. P. (1948) *British Cinemas and Their Audiences: Sociological Studies*, London: Denis Dobson.

Mayer, P. A. (ed.) (1999) *Computer Media and Communication: A Reader*, Oxford: Oxford University Press.

Mead, G. H. (1934) *Mind, Self, and Society*, Chicago, IL: University of Chicago Press.

Meadel, C. (1994) *Histoire de la radio dans les années trente* [History of Radio During the 1930s], Paris: Anthropos/INA.

Megarry, T. (1995) *Society in Prehistory: The Origins of Human Culture*, London: Macmillan.

Meinhof, U. H. and Richardson, K. (eds) (1999) *Worlds in Common?*, London: Routledge.

Melnik, S. R. (1981) *Eurovision News and the International Flow of Information*, Bochum: Studienverlag Dr. N. Brockmeyer.

Merleau-Ponty, M. (1962) *Phenomenology of Perception*, London: Routledge & Kegan Paul [orig. publ. 1945].

Merten, K. (1996) 'Reactivity in Content Analysis,' *Communications*, 21(1): 65–76.

Merton, R. K. (1949) 'Patterns of Influence: A Study of Interpersonal Influence and Communications Behaviour in a Local Community,' in P. F. Lazarsfeld and F. Stanton (eds) *Communications Research, 1948–49*, New York: Harper Brothers.

Merton, R. K. (1968) *Social Theory and Social Structure* (enlarged edn), New York: Free Press.

Merton, R. K. (1987) 'The Focussed Interview and Focus Groups: Continuities and Discontinuities,' *Public Opinion Quarterly*, 51(4): 550–566.

Merton, R. K. and Kendall, P. L. (1946) 'The Focused Interview,' *American Journal of Sociology*, 51: 541–557

Merton, R. K. and Kendall, P. L. (1955) 'The Focused Interview,' in P. F. Lazarsfeld and B. Rosenberg (eds) *The Language of Social Research*, Glencoe, IL: Free Press [orig. publ. 1946].

Merz, C. (1926) 'When American Movies Go Abroad,' *Harpers*, January: 159–165.

Messaris, P. (1994) *Visual 'Literacy': Image, Mind, and Reality*, Boulder, CO: Westview Press.

Messaris, P. (1997) *Visual Persuasion*, Thousand Oaks, CA: Sage.

Metz, C. (1974) [1968] *Film Language: A Semiotics of the Cinema*, New York: Oxford University Press.

Metz, C. (1982) *The Imaginary Signifier: Psychoanalysis and the Cinema*, Bloomington: Indiana University Press.

Meyrowitz, J. (1985) *No Sense of Place: The Impact of Electronic Media on Social Behavior*, New York: Oxford University Press.

Meyrowitz, J. (1993) 'Images of Media: Hidden Ferment – and Harmony – in the Field,' *Journal of Communication*, 43(3): 55–66.

Meyrowitz, J. (1994) 'Medium Theory,' in D. Crowley and D. Mitchell (eds) *Communication Theory Today*, Cambridge: Polity Press.

Mick, D. G. and Buhl, C. (1992) 'A Meaning-Based Model of Advertising Experience,' *Journal of Consumer Research*, 19: 317–338.

Middleton, R. (1990) *Studying Popular Music*, Milton Keynes: Open University Press.

Milavsky, J. R., Kessler, R., Stipp, H., and Rubens, W. S. (1982) *Television and Aggression: Results of a Panel Study*, New York: Academic Press.

Miles, M. B. and Huberman, A. M. (1994) *Qualitative Data Analysis: An Expanded Sourcebook* (2nd edn), Thousand Oaks, CA: Sage.

Mill, J. S. (1973–1974) *Collected Works of John Stuart Mill* (Vols 7 and 8), Toronto: University of Toronto Press.

Miller, D. and Slater, D. (2000) *The Internet: An Ethnographic Approach*, Oxford: Berg.

Mills, C. W. (1959) *The Power Elite*, Oxford: Oxford University Press.

Mills, C. W. (1970) *The Sociological Imagination*, Harmondsworth: Penguin [orig. publ. 1959].

Millum, T. (1975) *Images of Woman: Advertising in Women's Magazines*, London: Chatto & Windus.

Moi, T. (1985) *Sexual/Textual Politics: Feminist Literary Theory*, London: Methuen.

Molotch, H. and Lester, M. (1974) 'News as Purposive Behavior,' *American Sociological Review*, 39: 101–112.

Monteiro, A. and Jayasankar, J. P. (1994) 'The Spectator-Indian: An Exploratory Study on the Reception of News,' *Cultural Studies*, 8(1): 162–182.

Montgomery, K. (1989) *Target: Prime Time: Advocacy Groups and the Struggle Over Entertainment Television*, New York: Oxford University Press.

Montgomery, M. (1986) 'DJ Talk,' *Media, Culture and Society*, 8: 421–440.

Moores, S. (1988) '"The Box on the Dresser": Memories of Radio and Everyday Life,' *Media Culture & Society*, 10(1): 23–40.

Moores, S. (1993) *Interpreting Audiences: The Ethnography of Media Consumption*, London: Sage.

Moran, A. (ed.) (1996) *Film Policy: International, National, and Regional Perspectives*, London and New York: Routledge.

Morgan, D. L. and Krueger, R. A. (1998) *The Focus Group Kit*, Thousand Oaks, CA: Sage.

Morley, D. (1980) *The 'Nationwide' Audience*, London: British Film Institute.

Morley, D. (1981) '"The Nationwide Audience": A Critical Postscript,' *Screen Education*, 39: 3–14.

Morley, D. (1986) *Family Television*, London: Comedia.

Morley, D. (2000) *Home Territories: Media, Mobility, and Identity*, London: Routledge.

Morley, D. and Chen, K.-H. (eds) (1996) *Stuart Hall: Critical Dialogues in Cultural Studies*, London: Routledge.

Morley, D. and Robins, K. (1995) *Spaces of Identity: Global Media, Electronic Landscapes, and Cultural Boundaries*, London and New York: Routledge.

Morris, M. (1990) 'Banality in Cultural Studies,' in P. Mellencamp (ed.) *Logics of Television*, Bloomington: Indiana University Press.

Morrison, D. (1992) *Television and the Gulf War*, London: John Libbey.

Morrison, D. (1998) *The Search for a Method: Focus Groups and the Development of Mass Communication Research*, Luton, Beds: University of Luton Press.

Morrison, D. and Tumber, H. (1988) *Journalists at War*, London: Sage.

Morse, M. (1998) *Virtualities: Television, Media Art, and Cyberculture*, Bloomington: Indiana University Press.

Mortensen, F. (1977) 'The Bourgeois Public Sphere: A Danish Mass Communications Research Project,' in M. Berg, P. Hemanus, and J. Ekecrantz (eds) *Current Theories in Scandinavian Mass Communication*, Grenaa, Denmark: GMT.

Mosco, V. (1996) *The Political Economy of Communication*, London: Sage.

Moser, C. A. and Kalton, G. (1971) *Survey Methods in Social Investigation*, Aldershot, Hants: Gower.

Mowlana, H. (1993) 'The New Global Order and Cultural Ecology,' *Media, Culture & Society*, 15(1): 9–27.

Mowlana, H. (1997) *Global Information and World Communication* (2nd edn), London: Sage.

Mowlana, H. and Wilson, L. J. (1990) *The Passing of Modernity*, New York: Longman.

Mulvey, L. (1992) 'Visual Pleasure and Narrative Cinema,' in G. Mast, M. Cohen, and L. Braudy (eds) *Film Theory and Criticism: Introductory Readings* (4th edn), New York: Oxford University Press [orig. publ. 1975].

Münsterberg, H. (1970) *The Film: A Psychological Study*, New York: Dover Publications [orig. publ. 1916].

Murdock, G. (1982) 'Large Corporations and the Control of Communications Industries,' in M. Gurevitch, T. Bennett, J. Curran, and J. Woollacott (eds) *Culture, Society, and the Media*, London: Methuen.

Murdock, G. (1997) 'Thin Descriptions: Questions of Method in Cultural Analysis,' in J. McGuigan (ed.) *Cultural Methodologies*, London: Sage.

Murdock, G. (2000) 'Talk Shows: Democratic Debates and Tabloid Tales,' in J. Wieten, G. Murdock, and P. Dahlgren (eds) *Television Across Europe: A Comparative Introduction*, London: Sage.

Murdock, G. and Golding, P. (1977) 'Capitalism, Communication, and Class Relations,' in J. Curran, M. Gurevitch, and J. Woollacott (eds) *Mass Communication and Society*, London: Edward Arnold.

Murdock, G. and Pickering, M. (eds) (forthcoming) *Machineries of Experience: Media and The Making of Modernity*, Oxford: Blackwell.

Murray, J. H. (1997) *Hamlet on the Holodeck*, New York: Free Press.

Myers, G. (1994) *Words in Ads*, London: Edward Arnold.

Nagel, T. (1986) *The View from Nowhere*, Oxford: Oxford University Press.

Naremore, J. (ed.) (2000) *Film Adaptation*, London: Athlone Press.

National Television Violence Study (Vol.1) (1997) Thousand Oaks, CA: Sage.

Neale, S. (1980) *Genre*, London: British Film Institute.

Neale, S. (2000) *Genre and Hollywood*, New York: Routledge.

Negroponte, N. (1995) *Being Digital*, London: Hodder & Stoughton.

Negt, O. and Kluge, A. (1993) *Public Sphere and Experience*, Minneapolis: University of Minnesota Press [orig. publ. 1972].

Nelson, J. S., Megill, A., and McCloskey, D. M. (eds) (1987) *The Rhetoric of the Human Sciences*, Madison: University of Wisconsin Press.

Nerone, J. C. (ed.) (1995) *Last Rights: Revisiting Four Theories of the Press*, Urbana: University of Illinois Press.

Neuman, W. L. (1994) *Social Research Methods: Qualitative and Quantitative Approaches* (2nd edn), Boston, MA: Allyn & Bacon.

Neuman, W. R. (1976) 'Patterns of Recall among Television News Viewers,' *Public Opinion Quarterly*, 40(1): 115–123.

Neuman, W. R. (1989) 'Parallel Content Analysis: Old Paradigms and New Proposals,' in G. A. Comstock (ed.) *Public Communication and Behavior* (Vol. 2), Orlando, FL: Academic Press.

Neuman, W. R., Just, M., and Crigler, A. N. (1992) *Common Knowledge: News and the Construction of Political Meaning*, Chicago, IL: University of Chicago Press.

Newcomb, H. (1974) *Television. The Most Popular Art*, Garden City, NY: Anchor Press.

Newcomb, H. (1978) 'Assessing the Violence Profile Studies of Gerbner and Gross: A Humanistic Critique and Suggestion,' *Communication Research*, 5(3): 264–282.

Newcomb, H. (ed.) (1997) *Encyclopedia of Television*, London: Fitzroy Dearborn.

Newcomb, H. and Alley, R. (1983) *The Producer's Medium: Conversations with Creators of American TV*, New York: Oxford University Press.

Newcomb, H. and Hirsch, P. (1984) 'Television as a Cultural Forum: Implications for Research,' in W. D. Rowland and B. Watkins (eds), *Interpreting Television*, Beverly Hills, CA: Sage.

Ngugi, W. (1986) *Decolonizing the Mind*, London: James Currie and Heinemann.

Nicholson, L. (ed.) (1997) *The Second Wave: A Reader in Feminist Theory*, London: Routledge.

Nnaemeka, T. and Richstad, J. (1980) 'Structured Relations and Foreign Newsflow in the Pacific Region,' *Gazette*, 26(4): 235–257.

Noelle-Neumann, E. (1984) *The Spiral of Silence*, Chicago, IL: University of Chicago Press.

Nofsinger, R. E. (1991) *Everyday Conversation*, Newbury Park, CA: Sage.

Nohrstedt, S. A. and Ottosen, R. (eds) (2000) *Journalism and the New World Order: Gulf War,*

National News Discourses, and Globalization, (Vol. 1), Gothenburg, Sweden: Nordicom.

Nora, S. and Minc, A. (1980) *The Computerization of Society*, Cambridge, MA: MIT Press.

Nordenstreng, K. (1972) 'Policy for News Transmission,' in D. McQuail (ed.) *Sociology of Mass Communications*, Harmondsworth: Penguin.

Nordenstreng, K. (1984) 'Defining the New International Information Order,' in G. Gerbner and M. Siefert (eds) *World Communication: A Handbook*, New York: Longman.

Nordenstreng, K. (1997) 'Beyond Four Theories of the Press,' in J. Servaes and R. Lie (eds) *Media and Politics in Transition*, Leuven, Belgium: Acco.

Nordenstreng, K. and Schiller, H. I. (eds) (1979) *National Sovereignty and International Communication*, Norwood, NJ: Ablex.

Nordenstreng, K. and Varis, T. (1974) *Television Traffic – A One-way Street? A Survey and Analysis of the International Flow of Television Programme Material*, Reports and Papers on Mass Communication, no. 70, Paris: UNESCO.

O'Donnell, H. (1999) *Good Times, Bad Times: Soap Operas and Society in Western Europe*, London: Leicester University Press.

O'Sullivan, T. (1991) 'Television, Memories and the Culture of Viewing,' in J. Corner (ed.) *Popular Television in Britain*, London: British Film Institute.

Ong, W. (1982) *Orality and Literacy: The Technologizing of the Word*, New York: Cornell University Press.

Oppenheim, A. N. (1992) *Questionnaire Design, Interviewing and Attitude Measurement*, London: Pinter.

Outhwaite, W. (1975) *Understanding Social Life: The Method Called Verstehen*, London: George Allen & Unwin.

Palmgreen, P. and Rayburn, J. D. (1985) 'An Expectancy–Value Approach to Media Gratifications,' in K. E. Rosengren, L. Wenner, and P. Palmgreen (eds) *Media Gratifications Research: Current Perspectives*, Beverly Hills, CA: Sage.

Palmgreen, P., Wenner, L. and Rayburn, J. D. (1980) 'Relations Between Gratifications Sought and Obtained: A Study of Television News,' *Communication Research*, 7(2): 161–192.

Pan, Z. (2000) 'Spatial Configuration in Institutional Change: A Case of China's Journalism Reforms,' *Journalism*, 1(3): 253–281.

Parameswaran, R. (1999) 'Western Romance Fiction as English-Language Media in Postcolonial India,' *Journal of Communication*, 49(3): 84–105.

Park, H.-W. (1998) 'A Gramscian Approach to Interpreting International Communication,' *Journal of Communication*, 48(4): 79–99.

Park, R. E. (1922) *The Immigrant Press and Its Control*, New York: Harper.

Parkin, F. (1971) *Class Inequality and Political Order*, London: MacGibbon & Kee.

Parsons, T. (1951) *The Social System*, Glencoe, IL: Free Press.

Passmore, J. (1972) 'Logical Positivism,' in P. Edwards (ed.) *The Encyclopedia of Philosophy* (Vol. 5), New York: Macmillan.

Paterson, C. (2001) 'Media Imperialism Revisited: The Global Public Sphere and the News Agency Agenda,' in S. Hjarvard (ed.) *News in a Globalized Society*, Gothenburg, Sweden: Nordicom.

Patterson, T. (1998) 'Political Roles of the Journalist,' in D. Graber, D. McQuail, and P. Norris (eds) *The Politics of News: the News of Politics*, Washington, DC: Congressional Quarterly Press.

Patton, M. Q. (1990) *Qualitative Evaluation and Research Methods* (2nd edn), Newbury Park, CA: Sage.

Pavitt, C. (1999) 'The Third Way: Scientific Realism and Communication Theory,' *Communication Theory*, 9(2): 162–188.

Pearl, D., Bouthilet, L., and Lazar, J. (eds) (1982) *Television and Behavior: Ten Years of Scientific Progress and Implications for the Eighties*, Washington, DC: U.S. Government Printing Office.

Pearson, R. and Uricchio, W. (eds) (1990) *The Many Lives of the Batman*, New York: Routledge.

Peirce, C. S. (1931–1958) *Collected Papers*, Cambridge, MA: Harvard University Press.

Peirce, C. S. (1985) 'Logic as Semiotic: The Theory of Signs,' in R. Innis (ed.) *Semiotics: An Introductory Anthology*, London: Hutchinson.

Peirce, C. S. (1986) *Writings of Charles S. Peirce* (Vol. 3), Bloomington: Indiana University Press.

Peirce, C. S. (1992) *The Essential Peirce* (Vol. 1), Bloomington: Indiana University Press.

Peirce, C. S. (1998) *The Essential Peirce* (Vol. 2), Bloomington: Indiana University Press.

Pelfrey, R. (1985) *Art and Mass Media*, New York: Harper & Row.

Perelman, C. (1979) *The New Rhetoric and the Humanities*, Dordrecht, The Netherlands: Reidel.

Peters, J. D. (1999) *Speaking into the Air: A History of the Idea of Communication,* Chicago, IL: University of Chicago Press.

Philo, G. (1990) *Seeing and Believing: The Influence of Television*, London: Routledge.

Pike, K. L. (1967) *Language in Relation to a Unified Theory of the Structure of Human Behavior* (2nd edn), The Hague, The Netherlands: Mouton.

Pitt, J. (ed.) (1988) *Theories of Explanation*, New York: Oxford University Press.

Pollock, J. C. and Guidette, C. L. (1980) 'Mass Media, Crisis, and Political Change: A Cross-National Approach,' in D. Nimmo (ed.) *Communication Yearbook* (Vol. 4), New Brunswick, NJ: Transaction Books.

Popper, K. R. (1972) *The Logic of Scientific Discovery*, London: Hutchinson [orig. publ. 1934].

Porat, M. (1977) *The Information Economy: Definition and Measurement*, Washington, DC: U.S. Government Printing Office.

Porter, D. (ed.) (1997) *Internet Culture*, London: Routledge.

Porter, R. (1991) 'The History of the Body,' in P. Burke (ed.) *New Perspectives on Historical Writing*, Cambridge: Polity Press.

Posner, R., Robering, K. and Sebeok, T. A. (eds) (1997–1998) *Semiotics: A Handbook of the Sign-Theoretic Foundations of Nature and Culture*, Berlin: Walter de Gruyter.

Postman, N. (1985) *Amusing Ourselves to Death*, New York: Viking Press.

Potter, J. (1996) *Representing Reality. Discourse, Rhetoric and Social Construction*, London: Sage.

Potter, J. and Wetherell, M. (1987) *Discourse and Social Psychology: Beyond Attitudes and Behaviour*, London: Sage.

Potter, J. and Wetherell, M. (1996) 'Discourse Analysis,' in J. A. Smith, R. Harré, and L. Van Langenhove (eds) *Rethinking Methods in Psychology*, London: Sage.

Potter, W. J. (1996) *An Analysis of Thinking and Research about Qualitative Methods*, Mahwah, NJ: Lawrence Erlbaum.

Potter, W. J. (1998) *Media Literacy*, Thousand Oaks, CA: Sage.

Potter, W. J. and Smith, S. (1999) 'Consistency of Contextual Cues about Violence across Narrative Levels,' *Journal of Communication*, 49(4): 121–133.

Pound, R. and Frankfurter, F. (eds) (1922) *Criminal Justice in Cleveland*, Cleveland, OH: The Cleveland Foundation.

Preece, J. (1994) *Human–Computer Interaction*, Wokingham: Addison-Wesley.

Press, A. (1991) *Women Watching Television: Gender, Class, and Generation in the American Television Experience*, Philadelphia: University of Pennsylvania Press.

Press, A. (2000) 'Recent Developments in Feminist Communication Theory: Difference, Public Sphere, Body, and Technology,' in J. Curran and M. Gurevitch (eds) *Mass Media and Society* (3rd edn), London: Edward Arnold.

Priest, S. H. (1996) *Doing Media Research: An Introduction*, Thousand Oaks, CA: Sage.

Pritchard, D. and Hughes, K. D. (1997) 'Patterns of Deviance in Crime News,' *Journal of Communication*, 47(3): 49–67.

Project (1996) *The Media History Project*, Available: www.mediahistory.com (accessed 2001, March 9).

Propp, V. (1958) *Morphology of the Folktale*, Bloomington: Research Center, Indiana University [orig. publ. 1928].

Prue, C., Bornat, J., and Wengraf, T. (eds) (2000) *The Turn to Biographical Methods in Social Science*, London: Routledge.

Punch, K. F. (1998) *Introduction to Social Research: Quantitative and Qualitative Approaches*, London: Sage.

Radway, J. (1984) *Reading the Romance: Women, Patriarchy, and Popular Literature*, Chapel Hill: University of North Carolina Press.

Radway, J. (1988) 'Reception Study: Ethnography and the Problem of Dispersed Audiences and Nomadic Subjects,' *Cultural Studies*, 2(3): 359–376.

Radway, J. (1997) *A Feeling for Books: The Book-of-the-Month Club, Literary Taste, and Middle-Class Desire*, Chapel Hill: University of North Carolina Press.

Ragin, C. R. (1987) *The Comparative Method: Moving Beyond Qualitative and Quantitative Strategies*, Berkeley: University of California Press.

Ragin, C. R. (1994) *Constructing Social Research: The Unity and Diversity of Method*, Thousand Oaks, CA: Pine Forge Press.

Rawls, J. (1999) *Collected Papers*, Cambridge, MA: Harvard University Press.

Ray, L. and Sayer, A. (eds) (1999) *Culture and Economy after the Cultural Turn*, London: Sage.

Reason, P. and Bradbury, H. (eds) (2001) *Handbook of Action Research: Participative Inquiry and Practice*, London: Sage.

Reeves, B. and Nass, C. (1996) *The Media Equation: How People Treat Computers, Television, and New Media Like Real People and Places*, New York: Cambridge University Press.

Reinharz, S. (1992) *Feminist Methods in Social Research*, New York: Oxford University Press.

Remnick, D. (1998) 'Bad News: How Broadcast Journalism Is Downsizing the World,' *The New Yorker*, 74: 4–5.

Renn, O. (1991) 'Risk Communication and the Social Amplification of Risk,' in R. Kasperson and P. Stallen (eds) *Communicating Risks to the Public: International Perspectives*, Dordrecht: Kluwer Academic.

Rentz, J., Reynolds, F., and Stout, R. (1983) 'Analysing Changing Consumption Patterns with Cohort Analysis,' *Journal of Marketing Research*, 20: 12–20.

Resnik, D. B. (1998) *The Ethics of Science: An Introduction*, London: Routledge.

Rheingold, H. (1994) *The Virtual Community*, London: Minerva.

Richards, J. and Sheridan, D. (eds) (1987) *Mass Observation at the Movies*, London: Routledge & Kegan Paul.

Richardson, K. and Meinhof, U. H. (1999) *Worlds in Common? Television Discourse in a Changing Europe*, London: Routledge.

Ricoeur, P. (1981) *Hermeneutics and the Human Sciences: Essays on Language, Action and Interpretation*, Cambridge: Cambridge University Press.

Ricouer, P. (1983) *Time and Narrative* (Vol. 1), Chicago and London: University of Chicago Press.

Riley, J. W. and Riley, M. W. (1965) 'Mass Communication and the Social System,' in R. K. Merton, L. Broom, and L. S. Cottrell (eds) *Sociology Today*, New York: Harper & Row.

Rimmon-Kenan, S. (1983) *Narrative Fiction: Contemporary Poetics*, London: Methuen.

Ritchie, D. (1999) 'Probably, Probably Not: Rhetoric and Interpretation in Communication Research', Paper presented at the International Communication Association Conference, San Francisco, CA.

Roach, C. (1997) 'The Western World and the NWICO: United They Stand?,' in P. Golding and P. Harris (eds) *Beyond Cultural Imperialism: Globalization, Communication, and the New International Order*, London: Sage.

Robertson, R. (1992) *Globalization: Social Theory and Global Culture*, London: Sage.

Robertson, R. (1995) 'Glocalization: Time–Space and Homogeneity–Heterogeneity,' in M. Featherstone, S. Lash, and R. Robertson (eds) *Global Modernities*, London: Sage.

Robinson, A. (1995) *The Story of Writing*, London, Thames & Hudson.

Robinson, J. P. and Bachman, J. (1972) 'Television Viewing Habits and Aggression,' in G. A. Comstock and E. A. Rubinstein (eds) *Television and Social Behaviour* (Vol. 3), *Television and Adolescent Aggressiveness*, Washington, DC: U.S. Government Printing Office.

Robinson, J. P. and Converse, P. (1972) 'The Impact of Television on Mass Media Usage,' in A. Szalai (ed.) *The Use of Time*, The Hague, The Netherlands: Mouton.

Robinson, J. P. and Levy, M. (1986) *The Main Source*, Beverly Hills, CA: Sage.

Roe, K. and De Meyer, G. (2000) 'Music Television: MTV-Europe,' in J. Wieten, G. Murdock, and P. Dahlgren (eds) *Television Across Europe: A Comparative Introduction*, London: Sage.

Rogers, E. M. (1962) *The Diffusion of Innovations*, Glencoe, IL: Free Press.

Rogers, E. M. (1986) *Communication Technology*, New York: Free Press.

Rogers, E. M. (1999) 'Anatomy of Two Sub-disciplines of Communication Study,' *Human Communication Research*, 25(4): 618–631.

Rogers, E. M. (2000) 'Reflections on News Event Diffusion Research,' *Journalism and Mass Communication Quarterly*, 77(3): 561–576.

Rogers, E. M. and Storey, J. D. (1987) 'Communication Campaigns,' in C. R. Berger and S. H. Chaffee (eds) *Handbook of Communication Science*, Newbury Park, CA: Sage.

Rorty, R. (ed.) (1967) *The Linguistic Turn*, Chicago, IL: University of Chicago Press.

Rorty, R. (1979) *Philosophy and the Mirror of Nature*, Princeton, NJ: Princeton University Press.

Rorty, R. (1991) *Objectivity, Relativism, and Truth*, Cambridge: Cambridge University Press.

Rorty, R. (1998) *Truth and Progress*, Cambridge: Cambridge University Press.

Rose, B. G. (1985) *TV Genres: A Handbook and Reference Guide*, Westport, CT: Greenwood Press.

Rosengren, K. E. (1970) 'International News: Intra and Extra Media Data,' *Acta Sociologica*, 13(1): 96–109.

Rosengren, K. E. (1974) 'International News: Methods, Data and Theory,' *Journal of Peace Research*, 11: 145–156.

Rosengren, K. E. (2000) *Communication: An Introduction*, London: Sage.

Rosengren, K. E. and Windahl, S. (1989) *Media Matter: TV Use in Childhood and Adolescence*, Norwood, NJ: Ablex.

Rosengren, K. E., Arvidson, P., and Sturesson, D. (1978) 'The Barsebäck Panic,' in C. Winick (ed.) *Deviance and Mass Media*, Beverly Hills, CA: Sage.

Rosengren, K. E., Wenner, L., and Palmgreen, P. (eds) (1985) *Media Gratifications Research: Current Perspectives*, Beverly Hills, CA: Sage.

Ross, A. (1910) 'The Suppression of Important News,' *Atlantic Monthly*, CV: 303–311.

Ross, S. S. (1998) 'Journalists' Use of On-line Technology and Sources,' in D. L. Borden and K. Harvey (eds) *The Electronic Grapevine: Rumor, Reputation, and Reporting in the New On-Line Environment*, Mahwah, NJ: Lawrence Erlbaum.

Rowbottom, S. (1974) *Hidden From History*, Harmondsworth: Pelican Books.

Ruby, J. E. (1965) *The Daily News Exchange Scheme of the European Broadcasting Union*, unpublished Master's thesis, Indiana University.

Rudy, W. (1984) *The Universities of Europe 1100–1914: A History*, London: Associated University Presses.

Rush, M. (1999) *New Media in Late Twentieth-Century Art*, London: Thames & Hudson.

Rydin, I. (1996) *Making Sense of TV Narratives: Children's Readings of a Fairy Tale*, Linköping, Sweden: Linköping University.

Ryle, G. (1971) *Collected Papers* (Vol. 2), London: Hutchinson.

Sabin, R. (1993) *Adult Comics: An Introduction*, London: Routledge.

Sacks, H., Schegloff, E. A., and Jefferson, G. (1974) 'A Simplest Systematics for the Organisation of Turn-Taking in Conversation,' *Language*, 50: 696–735.

Sahlins, M. (1985) *Islands of History*, Chicago, IL: University of Chicago Press.

Saïd, E. (1978) *Orientalism*, New York: Random House.

Sallach, D. (1974) 'Class Domination and Ideological Hegemony,' in G. Tuchman (ed.) *The TV Establishment*, Englewood Cliffs, NJ: Prentice-Hall.

Samuelson, P. A. (1954) 'The Pure Theory of Public Expenditure,' *The Review of Economics and Statistics*, 36(4): 387–389.

Sarris, A. (1968) *The American Cinema: Directors and Directions, 1929–1968*, New York: Dutton.

Saussure, F. de (1959) *Course in General Linguistics*, London: Peter Owen [orig. publ. 1916].

Sayer, A. (2000) *Realism and Social Science*, London: Sage.

Scannell, P. (1986) '"The Stuff of Radio": Developments in Radio Features and Documentaries before the War,' in J. Corner (ed.) *Documentary and the Mass Media*, London: Edward Arnold.

Scannell, P. (1988) '*Radio Times*. The Temporal Arrangements of Broadcasting in the Modern World,' in P. Drummond and R. Paterson (eds) *Television and its Audiences*, London: British Film Institute.

Scannell, P. (1990) 'Public Service Broadcasting: The History of a Concept,' in A. Goodwin and G. Whannel (eds) *Understanding Television*, London: Routledge.

Scannell, P. (ed.) (1991) *Broadcast Talk*, London: Sage.

Scannell, P. (1996a) *Radio, Television, and Modern Life*, Oxford: Blackwell.

Scannell, P. (1996b) 'Public Service Broadcasting: From National Culture to Multiculturalism 1923–1995,' in M. Raboy (ed.) *Public Broadcasting for the Twenty-First Century*, London: John Libbey.

Scannell, P. (2000) 'For-anyone-as-someone Structures,' *Media Culture & Society*, 22(1): 5–24.

Scannell, P. and Cardiff, D. (1991) *A Social History of British Broadcasting: 1922–1939: Serving the Nation* (Vol. 1), Oxford: Blackwell.

Schatz, T. (1988) *The Genius of the System*, New York: Pantheon.

Schensul, J. J. and LeCompte, M. D. (eds) (1999) *The Ethnographer's Toolkit*, Walnut Creek, CA: Alta Mira Press.

Schensul, J. J., LeCompte, M. D., Nasasti, B. K., and Borgatti, S. P. (1999) *Enhanced Ethnographic Methods: Audiovisual Techniques, Focused Group Interviews, and Elicitation Techniques* (Vol. 3), Walnut Creek, CA: Alta Mira Press.

Schensul, S. L., Schensul, J. J., and LeCompte, M. D. (1999) *Essential Ethnographic Methods: Observations, Interviews, and Questionnaires* (Vol. 2), Walnut Creek, CA: Alta Mira Press.

Scheufele, D. (1999) 'Agenda-Setting, Priming, and Framing Revisited: Another Look at Cognitive Effects of Political Communication,' Paper presented at the International Communication Association Conference, San Francisco, CA.

Schiller, D. (1981) *Objectivity and the News*, Philadelphia: University of Pennsylvania Press.

Schiller, H. I. (1969) *Mass Communications and American Empire*, New York: Kelley.

Schiller, H. I. (1976) *Communication and Cultural Domination*, White Plains, NY: International Arts and Science Press.

Schlesinger, P. (1978) *Putting 'Reality' Together: BBC News*, London: Constable.

Schlesinger, P., Dobash, R. E., Dobash, R. P., and Weaver, C. (1992) *Women Viewing Violence*, London: British Film Institute.

Schmitt, R. (1972) 'Phenomenology,' in P. Edwards (ed.) *The Encyclopedia of Philosophy* (Vol. 6), New York: Macmillan [orig. publ. 1967].

Schramm, W. (1964) *Mass Media and National Development*, Stanford, CA: Stanford University Press.

Schramm, W. (1997) *The Beginnings of Communication Study in America: A Personal Memoir*, Thousand Oaks, CA: Sage.

Schramm, W. and Lerner, D. (eds) (1976) *Communication and Change: The Last Ten Years – and the Next*, Honolulu: University Press of Hawaii.

Schramm, W., Lyle, J., and Parker, E. (1961) *Television in the Lives of Our Children*, Palo Alto, CA: Stanford University Press.

Schrøder, K. C. (1997) 'Cynicism and Ambiguity: British Corporate Responsibility Advertisements and their Readers in the 1990s,' in M. Nava, A. Blake, I. MacRury, and B. Richards (eds) *Buy This Book: Studies in Advertising and Consumption*, London: Routledge.

Schrøder, K. C. (1999) 'The Best of Both Worlds? Media Audience Research Between Rival Paradigms,' in P. Alasuutari (ed.) *Rethinking the Media Audience: The New Agenda*, London: Sage.

Schudson, M. (1978) *Discovering the News*, New York: Basic Books.

Schudson, M. (1984) *Advertising, the Uneasy Persuasion*, New York: Basic Books.

Schudson, M. (1991) 'News Production Revisited,' in J. Curran and M. Gurevitch (eds) *Mass Media and Society* (2nd edn), London: Edward Arnold.

Schudson, M. (1997) 'Why Conversation Is Not the Soul of Democracy,' *Critical Studies in Mass Communication*, 14(4): 297–309.

Schulz, W. (1976) *Die Konstruktion von Realität in Nachrichtenmedien* [The Construction of Reality in News Media], Freiburg and Munich: Karl Alber.

Schulz, W. (1997) 'Political Communication Scholarship in Germany,' *Political Communication*, 14: 113–145.

Schütz, A. (1956) *The Phenomenology of the Social World*, London: Heinemann [orig. publ. 1932].

Schwartz, S. H. and Bilsky, W. (1990) 'Toward a Theory of the Universal Content and Structure of Values: Extensions and Cross-cultural Replications,' *Journal of Personality and Social Psychology*, 58(5): 878–891.

Scott, J. (1991) 'Women's History,' in P. Burke (ed.) *New Perspectives on Historical Writing*, Cambridge: Polity Press.

Scribner, S. and Cole, M. (1981) *The Psychology of Literacy*, Cambridge, MA: Harvard University Press.

Searle, J. R. (1969) *Speech Acts*, London: Cambridge University Press.

Sebeok, T. A. (ed.) (1986) *Encyclopedic Dictionary of Semiotics* (2nd edn), Berlin: Mouton de Gruyter.

Sebeok, T. A. and Umiker-Sebeok, J. (1983) '"You Know My Method": A Juxtaposition of Charles S. Peirce and Sherlock Holmes,' in U. Eco and T. A. Sebeok (eds) *The Sign of Three*, Bloomington: Indiana University Press.

Seiter, E., Borchers, H., Kreutzner, G., and Warth, E.-M. (eds) (1989) *Remote Control: Television, Audiences, and Cultural Power*, London: Routledge.

Sellitz, C., Jahoda, M., Deutsch, M., and Cook, S. (1976) *Research Methods in Social Relations*, New York: Holt, Rinehart & Winston.

Sennett, R. (1974) *The Fall of Public Man*, Cambridge: Cambridge University Press.

Sepstrup, P. (1989) 'Research into International TV Flows,' *European Journal of Communication*, 4(4): 393–408.

Seymour-Ure, C. (1989) 'Prime Ministers' Reaction to Television: Britain, Australia, and Canada,' *Media, Culture & Society*, 11(3): 307–325.

Shanahan, J. and Morgan, M. (1999) *Television and Its Viewers: Cultivation Theory and Research*, Cambridge: Cambridge University Press.

Shannon, C. and Weaver, W. (1949) *The Mathematical Theory of Communication*, Urbana, IL: University of Illinois Press.

Sharpe, J. (1991) 'History from Below,' in P. Burke (ed.) *New Perspectives on Historical Writing*, Cambridge: Polity Press.

Sharrock, W. and Anderson, B. (1986) *The Ethnomethodologists*, London: Tavistock.

Shimp, T. A. and Gresham, L. G. (1983) 'An Information Processing Perspective on Recent Advertising Literature,' *Current Issues and Research in Advertising*, 5: 39–75.

Shoemaker, P.J. and Reese, S. D. (1991) *Mediating the Message*, New York: Longman.

Shoemaker, P. J. (1991) *Gatekeeping*, Newbury Park, CA: Sage.

Shore, B. (1998) 'Models Theory as a Framework for Media Studies,' in B. Höijer and A. Werner (eds) *Cultural Cognition: New Perspectives in Audience Theory*, Gothenburg, Sweden: Nordicom.

Shrum, L. J. (1996) 'Psychological Processes Underlying Cultivation Effects: Further Tests of Construct Accessibility,' *Human Communication Research*, 22(4): 482–509.

Siebert, F., Peterson, T., and Schramm, W. (1956) *Four Theories of the Press*, Urbana, IL: University of Illinois Press.

Siegel, P. M. and Hodge, R. W. (1968) 'A Causal Approach to the Study of Measurement Error,' in H. M. Blalock, Jr. and A. B. Blalock (eds) *Methodology in Social Research*, New York: McGraw-Hill.

Siegel, S. (1956) *Nonparametric Statistics for the Behavioural Sciences*, Tokyo: McGraw-Hill.

Sigman, S. J. and Fry, D. L. (1985) 'Differential Ideology and Language Use: Readers' Reconstructions and Descriptions of News Events,' *Critical Studies in Mass Communication* 2: 307–322.

Silj, A. (1988) *East of Dallas: The European Challenge to American Television*, London: British Film Institute.

Silverman, D. (2000) *Doing Qualitative Research: A Practical Handbook*, London: Sage.

Silverstone, R. (1994) *Television and Everyday Life*, London: Routledge.

Silverstone, R. (1999) *Why Study the Media?*, London: Sage.

Simon, H. W. (ed.) (1989) *Rhetoric in the Human Sciences*, London: Sage.

Simpson, C. (1996) 'Elisabeth Noelle-Neumann's "Spiral of Silence" and the Historical Context of Communication Theory,' *Journal of Communication*, 46(3): 149–173.

Sinclair, J., Jacka, E., and Cunningham, S. (1996) *New Patterns in Global Television: Peripheral Vision*, New York: Oxford University Press.

Sinclair, U. (1920) *The Brass Check: A Study of American Journalism*, Long Beach, CA: Published by the author.

Slaatta, T. (1999) *Europeanisation and the Norwegian News Media: Political Discourse and News Production in the Transnational Field*, Department of Media and Communication, Report No. 36, Oslo, Norway: University of Oslo.

Slemon, S. (1995) 'The Scramble for Post-Colonialism,' in B. Ashcroft, G. Griffiths, and H. Tiffin (eds) *The Post-Colonial Studies Reader*, London: Routledge.

Slevin, J. (2000) *The Internet and Society*, Cambridge: Polity Press.

Smith, D. (1974) 'Theorizing as Ideology,' in R. Turner (ed.) *Ethnomethodology*, Baltimore, MD: Penguin.

Smulyan, S. (1994) *Selling Radio: The Commercialization of American Broadcasting, 1920–1934*, Washington, DC: Smithsonian Institute Press.

Smythe, D. W. (1977) 'Communications: Blindspot of Western Marxism,' *Canadian Journal of Political and Social Theory*, 1(3): 1–27.

Snow, C. P. (1964) *The Two Cultures and a Second Look*, Cambridge: Cambridge University Press.

Sokal, A. and Bricmont, J. (1998) *Fashionable Nonsense: Postmodern Intellectuals' Abuse of Science*, New York: Picador.

Solso, R. L. (1994) *Cognition and the Visual Arts*, Cambridge, MA: MIT Press.

Sonesson, G. (1989) *Pictorial Concepts: Inquiries into the Semiotic Heritage and its Relevance to the Interpretation of the Visual World*, Lund, Sweden: Lund University Press.

Sparks, C. (1997) 'Post-Communist Media in Transition,' in J. Corner, P. Schlesinger, and R. Silverstone (eds) *International Media Research: A Critical Survey*, London: Routledge.

Sparks, C. and Tulloch, J. (2000) *Tabloid Tales: Global Debates over Media Standards*, Boulder, CO: Rowman & Littlefield.

Sparks, G. G. and Cantor, J. (1986) 'Developmental Differences in Fright Responses to a Television Programme Depicting a Character Transformation,' *Journal of Broadcasting and Electronic Media*, 30: 309–323.

Spigel, L. (1992) *Make Room for TV: Television and the Family Ideal in Postwar America*, Chicago, IL: University of Chicago Press.

Spigel, L. and Jenkins, H. (1990) 'Same Bat Channel, Different Bat Times: Mass Culture and Popular Memory,' in R. Pearson and W. Uricchio (eds) *The Many Lives of the Batman: Critical Approaches to a Superhero and His Media*, London: British Film Institute.

Spivak, G. C. (1988) 'Can the Subaltern Speak?,' in C. Nelson and L. Grossberg (eds) *Marxism and the Interpretation of Culture*, London: Macmillan.

Spradley, J. P. (1979) *The Ethnographic Interview*, Fort Worth, TX: Harcourt Brace Jovanovich.

Sreberny, A. (2000) 'The Global and the Local in International Communications,' in J. Curran and M. Gurevitch (eds) *Mass Media and Society* (3rd edn), London: Edward Arnold.

Sreberny, A. and Stevenson, R. L. (eds) (in preparation) 'Rethinking International News: Theory and Research at the end of the Millennium,' Creskill, NJ: Hampton Press.

Sreberny, A., Nordenstreng, K., Stevenson, R., and Ugboajah, F. (eds) (1985) *Foreign News in the Media: International Reporting in 29 Countries*, Paris: UNESCO.

Stacey, J. (1994) *Star Gazing: Hollywood Cinema and Female Spectatorship*, London: Routledge.

Stam, R., Burgoyne, R., and Flitterman-Lewis, S. (1992) *New Vocabularies in Film Semiotics: Structuralism, Post-structuralism and Beyond*, London: Routledge.

Standage, T. (1998) *The Victorian Internet*, London: Weidenfeld & Nicolson.

Stempel, G. H. (1952) 'Sample Size for Classifying Subject Matter in Dailies,' *Journalism Quarterly*, 29: 333–334.

Stevenson, R. L. and Shaw, D. L. (eds) (1984) *Foreign News and the New World Information Order*, Ames, IA: Iowa State University.

Stipp, H. and Milavsky, R. (1988) 'US Television Programming Effects on Aggressive Behaviour of Children and Adolescents,' *Current Psychology: Research and Review*, 7: 76–92.

Stokes, M. and Maltby, R. (eds) (1999a) *American Movie Audiences: From the Turn of the Century to the Early Sound Era*, London: British Film Institute.

Stokes, M. and Maltby, R. (eds) (1999b) *Identifying Hollywood's Audiences: Cultural Identity and the Movies*, London: British Film Institute.

Stone, A. R. (1991) 'Will the Real Body Please Stand Up? Boundary Stories about Virtual Cultures,' in M. Benedikt (ed.) *Cyberspace: First Steps*, London: MIT Press.

Stone, L. (1979) *The Family, Sex and Marriage, 1500–1800*, Harmondsworth: Penguin.

Stone, L. (1987) *The Past and the Present Revisited*, London and New York: Routledge & Kegan Paul.

Strauss, A. L. (1987) *Qualitative Analysis for Social Scientists*, Cambridge: Cambridge University Press.

Strauss, A. L. and Corbin, J. (1990) *Basics of Qualitative Research*, Newbury Park, CA: Sage.

Street, A. T. (1909) 'The Truth about Newspapers,' *Chicago Tribune*, 25 July.

Striphas, T. (ed.) (1998) *The Institutionalization of Cultural Studies*, London: Routledge.

Sumpter, R. S. (2000) 'Daily Newspaper Editors' Audience Construction Routines: A Case Study,' *Critical Studies in Mass Communication*, 17(3): 334–346.

Surgeon-General's Scientific Advisory Committee on Television and Social Behavior (1972) *Volumes I–VI*, Washington, DC: U.S. Government Printing Office.

Swales, J. M. and Rogers, P. (1995) 'Discourse and the Projection of Corporate Culture: The Mission Statement,' *Discourse and Society*, 6(2): 223–242.

Tamborini, R., Zillmann, D., and Bryant, J. (1984) 'Fear and Victimisation: Exposure to Television and Perceptions of Crime and Fear,' in R. N. Bostrum (ed.) *Communication Yearbook* (Vol. 8), Beverly Hills, CA: Sage.

Tannenbaum, P. H. (1954) 'Effect of Serial Position on Recall of Radio News Stories,' *Journalism Quarterly*, 31: 319–323.

Tannenbaum, P. H. and Kemick, J. (1954) 'Effects of Newscast Item Leads upon Listener Interpretation,' *Journalism Quarterly*, 31: 33–37.

Tashakkori, A. and Teddlie, C. (1998) *Mixed Methodology: Combining Qualitative and Quantitative Approaches*, Thousand Oaks, CA: Sage.

Thomas, W. I. and Znaniecki, F. (1927) *The Polish Peasant in Europe and America*, New York: Knopf.

Thompson, E. P. (1968) *The Making of the English Working Class*, London: Gollancz [orig. publ. 1963].

Thompson, J. B. (1995) *The Media and Modernity*, Cambridge: Polity Press.

Thompson, K. (1998) *Moral Panics*, London: Routledge.

Thompson, M. (1999) *Forging: War. The Media in Serbia, Bosnia and Hercegovina* (2nd edn), Luton, Beds: University of Luton Press.

Thorson, E. (1990) 'Consumer Processing of Advertising,' *Current Issues and Research in Advertising*, 12: 197–230.

Thorson, E. (1994) 'Using Eyes on Screen as a Measure of Attention to Television,' in A. Lang (ed.) *Measuring Psychological Response to Media*, Hillsdale, NJ: Lawrence Erlbaum.

Thrasher, F. M. (1927) *The Gang*, Chicago, IL: University of Chicago Press.

Tichenor, P., Olien, C., and Donohue, G. (1970) 'Mass Media Flow and Differential Growth in Knowledge,' *Public Opinion Quarterly*, 34(2): 159–170.

Todorov, T. (1971) 'The Two Principles of Narrative,' *Diacritics*, 1: 37–44.

Todorov, T. (1990) *Genres in Discourse*, Cambridge: Cambridge University Press [orig. publ. 1978].

Tomlinson, J. (1999) *Globalization and Culture*, Cambridge: Polity Press.

Tönnies, F. (1974) *Community and Association*, London: Routledge & Kegan Paul [orig. publ. 1887].

Toulmin, S. (1958) *The Uses of Argument*, Cambridge: Cambridge University Press.

Trenaman, J. S. M. (1967) *Communication and Comprehension*, London: Longman.

Trenaman, J. S. M. and McQuail, D. (1961) *Television and the Political Image*, London: Methuen.

Trew, T. (1979) 'Theory and Ideology at Work,' in R. Fowler, Hodge, B., Kress, G. and Trew, T. (eds) *Language and Control*, London: Routledge & Kegan Paul.

Tuchman, G. (1978) *Making News: A Study in the Construction of Reality*, New York: Free Press.

Tuchman, G., Daniels, A. K., and Benet, J. (eds) (1978) *Hearth and Home: Images Of Women in Mass Media*, New York: Oxford University Press.

Tulloch, J. (1989) 'Approaching the Audience: The Elderly,' in E. Seiter, H. Borchers, G. Kreutzner, and E.-M. Warth (eds) *Remote Control: Television, Audiences, and Cultural Power*, London: Routledge.

Tunstall, J. (1977) *The Media are American: Anglo-American Media in the World*, London: Constable.

Tunstall, J. and Machin, D. (1999) *The Anglo-American Media Connection*, Oxford: Oxford University Press.

Turkistani, A. S. (1988) *News Exchange via Arabsat and News Values of Arab Television News People*, Indiana University, unpublished Ph.D. thesis.

Turkle, S. (1995) *Life on the Screen: Identity in the Age of the Internet*, New York: Simon & Schuster.

Umiker-Sebeok, J. (ed.) (1987) *Marketing Signs*, Berlin: Mouton de Gruyter.

Underwood, D. (1993) *When MBAs Rule the Newsroom*, New York: Columbia University Press.

UNESCO (1953) *The Flow of News*, Paris: UNESCO.

UNESCO (1985) *Foreign News in the Media: International Reporting in 29 Countries*, Reports and Papers on Mass Communication No. 93, Paris: UNESCO.

UNESCO (1989) *World Communication Report*, Paris: UNESCO.

Urry, J. (2000) *Sociology Beyond Societies: Mobilities for the Twenty-First Century*, London: Routledge.

van Dijk, J. (1999) *The Network Society*, London: Sage.

van Dijk, T. (ed.) (1997) *Discourse Studies: A Multidisciplinary Introduction* (Vols 1–2), London: Sage.

van Dijk, T. A. and Kintsch, W. (1983) *Strategies of Discourse Comprehension*, New York: Academic Press.

van Maanen, J. (1988) *Tales of the Field*, Chicago: University of Chicago Press.

van Zoonen, L. (1992) *Feminist Media Studies*, London: Sage.

van Zoonen, L., and Wieten, J. (1994) '"It Wasn't Exactly a Miracle": The Arrival of Television in Dutch Family Life,' *Media Culture & Society*, 16(4): 641–660.

Varis, T. and Jokelin, R. (1976) *Television News in Europe: A Survey of the News-Film Flow in Europe*, Tampere, Finland: Institute of Journalism and Mass Communication.

Venturi, R., Brown, D. S., and Izenour, S. (1972) *Learning from Las Vegas*, Cambridge, MA: MIT Press.

Vestergaard, T. and Schrøder, K. (1985) *The Language of Advertising*, Oxford: Basil Blackwell.

Vincent, D. (2000) *The Rise of Mass Literacy: Reading and Writing in Modern Europe*, Cambridge: Polity Press.

Viswanath, K. and Finnegan, J. R. (1996) 'The Knowledge Gap Hypothesis 25 Years Later,' *Communication Yearbook*, 19: 187–227.

Volkmer, I. (1999) *CNN – News in the Global Sphere: A Study of CNN and Its Impact on Global Communication*, Luton, Beds: University of Luton Press.

Volosinov, V. N. (1973) *Marxism and the Philosophy of Language*, New York: Seminar Press [orig. publ. 1929].

Volosinov, V. N. (1985) 'Verbal Interaction,' in H. A. Innis (ed.) *Semiotics: An Introductory Anthology*, Bloomington: Indiana University Press.

Walker, J. A. (1994) *Art in the Age of Mass Media*, London: Pluto Press.

Wallerstein, I. (1974) *The Modern World-System* (Vol. 1), New York: Academic Press.

Wallerstein, I. (1980) *The Modern World-System* (Vol. 2), London: Academic Press.

Wallerstein, I. (1989) *The Modern World-System* (Vol. 3), London: Academic Press.

Watson, J. B. (1924) *Psychology from the Standpoint of a Behaviorist*, Philadelphia, PA: J. B. Lippincott.

Watson, J. B. (1930) *Behaviorism*, Chicago, IL: University of Chicago Press.

Watson, J. and Hill, A. (1999) *Dictionary of Media and Communication Studies* (5th edn), London: Edward Arnold.

Weaver, D. and Wilhoit, G. C. (1996) *The American Journalist in the 1990s*, Mahwah, NJ: Lawrence Erlbaum.

Webb, E. J., Campbell, D. T., Schwartz, R. D., and Sechrest, L. (2000) *Unobtrusive Measures* (revised edn), Thousand Oaks, CA: Sage.

Weber, M. (1958a) 'Politics as a Vocation,' in H. H. Gerth and C. W. Mills (eds) *From Max Weber*, New York: Oxford University Press [orig. publ. 1918].

Weber, M. (1958b) *The Protestant Ethic and the Spirit of Capitalism*, New York: Charles Scribner's Sons [orig. publ. 1930].

Weber, M. (1964) *The Theory of Social and Economic Organization*, New York: The Free Press.

Webster, D. (1988) *Looka Yonder! The Imaginary America of Populist Culture*, London: Routledge.

Webster, J. G. and Phalen, P. F. (1997) *The Mass Audience: Rediscovering the Dominant Model*, Mahwah, NJ: Lawrence Erlbaum.

Weitzman, E. (2000) 'Software and Qualitative Research,' in N. Denzin and Y. S. Lincoln (eds) *Handbook of Qualitative Research* (2nd edn), Thousand Oaks, CA: Sage.

Weitzman, E. and Miles, M. B. (1995) *Computer Programs for Qualitative Data Analysis*, Thousand Oaks, CA: Sage.

Wetherell, M. and Potter, J. (1992) *Mapping the Language of Racism: Discourse and the Legiti-mation of Exploitation*, London: Harvester Wheatsheaf.

Wetherell, M., Taylor, S., and Yates, S. (eds) (2001) *Discourse Theory and Practice: A Reader*, London: Sage.

Whannel, G. (1992) *Fields in Vision: Television Sport and Cultural Transformation*, London: Routledge.

White, D. M. (1950) 'The "Gate Keeper": A Case Study in the Selection of News,' *Journalism Quarterly*, 27: 383–390.

Wieten, J., Murdock, G., and Dahlgren, P. (eds) (2000) *Television Across Europe: A Comparative Introduction*, London: Sage.

Wilcox, D. F. (1900) 'The American Newspaper: A Study in Social Psychology', *Annals of the American Academy of Political and Social Science*, 16: 56–92.

Wilke, J. (1984) *Nachrichtenauswahl und Medienrealität in vier Jahrhunderten* [News Selection and Media Reality in Four Centuries], Berlin: Walter de Gruyter.

Williams, R. (1962) *Communications*, Harmondsworth: Penguin.

Williams, R. (1974) *Television: Technology and Cultural Form*, London: Fontana.

Williams, R. (1975) *Culture and Society 1780–1950*, Harmondsworth: Penguin [orig. publ. 1958].

Williams, R. (1977) *Marxism and Literature*, London: Oxford University Press.

Williams, R. (1983) *Keywords*, London: Fontana.

Williams, T. M. (ed.) (1986) *The Impact of Television: A Natural Experiment in Three Communities*, New York: Academic Press.

Williamson, J. (1978) *Decoding Advertisements. Ideology and Meaning in Advertising*, London: Marion Boyars.

Wimmer, R. D. and Dominick, J. R. (1994) *Mass Media Research: An Introduction* (4th edn), Belmont, CA: Wadsworth.

Wimsatt, W. (ed.) (1954) *The Verbal Icon*, London: Methuen.

Wimsatt, W. and Brooks, C. (1957) *Literary Criticism: A Short History*, New York: Alfred A. Knopf.

Winch, P. (1963) *The Idea of a Social Science*, London: Routledge.

Windahl, S., Signitzer, B., and Olson, J. (1992) *Using Communication Theory*, Newbury Park, CA: Sage.

Winston, B. (1998) *Media, Technology, and Society – A History: From the Telegraph to the Internet*, London: Routledge.

Winthrop-Young, W. and Wutz, M. (1999) 'Translators' Introduction,' in F. A. Kittler *Gramophone, Film, Typewriter*, Stanford, CA: Stanford University Press.

Witmer, D. F., Colman, R. W., and Katzman, S. L. (1999) 'From Paper-and-Pencil to Screen-and-Keyboard: Toward a Methodology for Survey Research on the Internet' in S. G. Jones (ed.) *Doing Internet Research: Critical Issues and Methods for Examining the Net*, Thousand Oaks, CA: Sage.

Wittgenstein, L. (1953) *Philosophical Investigations*, London: Macmillan.

Wittgenstein, L. (1972) [1921] *Tractatus Logico-Philosophicus*, London: Routledge & Kegan Paul.

Wober, J. M. (1981) 'Psychology in the Future of Broadcasting Research,' *Bulletin of the British Psychological Society*, 34: 409–412.

Wober, M. and Gunter, B. (1988) *Television and Social Control*, Aldershot, Hants: Avebury.

Wolfe, T. (ed.) (1973) *The New Journalism*, New York: Harper & Row.

Wood, R. (1965) *Hitchcock's Films*, London: Zwemmer.

Wood, R. (1968) *Howard Hawks*, London: Secker & Warburg.

Wright, C. R. (1959) *Mass Communication: A Sociological Perspective*, New York: Random House.

Wu, W., Weaver, D., Owen, D., and Johnstone, J. W. L. (1996) 'Professional Rules of Russian and US Journalists: A Comparative Study,' *Journalism and Mass Communication Quarterly*, 73(3): 534–548.

Yin, R. K. (1994) *Case Study Research: Design and Methods* (2nd edn), Thousand Oaks, CA: Sage.

Zillmann, D. and Bryant, J. (1994) 'Entertainment as Media Effect,' in D. Zillmann and J. Bryant (eds) *Media Effects: Advances in Theory and Research*, Hillsdale, NJ: Lawrence Erlbaum.

Zillmann, D. and Vorderer, P. (eds) (2000) *Media Entertainment: The Psychology of its Appeal*, Mahwah, NJ: Lawrence Erlbaum.

Znaniecki, F. (1934) *The Method of Sociology*, New York: Farrar and Rinehart.

Zuckerman, M. (1994) *Behavioural Expressions and Biosocial Bases of Sensation Seeking*, Cambridge: Cambridge University Press.

Index